SURGERY

AND ITS

ADAPTATION

HOMŒOPATHIC PRACTICE.

BY

WILLIAM T. HELMUTH, M. D.

Illustrated with Numerous Engravings on Wood.

PHILADELPHIA:
MOSS & BROTHER.
1855.

PREFACE.

THE author of this volume has a satisfactory reason for its publication at the present time, in the desire so urgently and generally expressed for a surgical work in connection with Homœopathy. A perusal of its contents will satisfy the reader that the materials have been collected from a tolerably wide field of research. That much important matter has been overlooked is unhesitatingly admitted; the chief labor, however, has been accomplished, and should the work be favorably received, in a future edition more practical matter will be embodied, omissions supplied, and its defects as a whole remedied.

The descriptions by Homœopathic practitioners of some of the unusual varieties of disease, are deficient in that accuracy and precision of detail, which are essential to certainty of practice. These imperfections may be attributed often to the obscure nature of the disorders themselves; in many instances to their complicated conditions arising from the fact of not having been submitted to Homœopathic treatment in the earlier periods of their existence; to their comparative infrequency of occurrence, as well as the limited means yet discovered for their removal.

From the volume there is purposely excluded many surgical details, together with a large amount of matter connected with surgery, but not with its practice; the chief object of the publication having been the collection and arrangement of those materials which are considered as constituting the medical treatment of surgical diseases. Little as may have been, and much as remains yet to be accomplished, an impartial scrutiny cannot fail to discover, that Homœopathy has already contributed considerably to alleviate and cure a vast amount of disease previously beyond the reach of medical treatment. If so much progress has been made in so short a period of time, it may be confidently expected that future physiological provings will substitute medicinal for surgical instruments, by which many diseases now so formidable and fearful will be successfully combated.

Time, however, and the united efforts of numbers of properly educated practitioners, will be necessary before there can be accumulated that amount of rigid and intelligent experiment, close description and truthful testimony, all confirmed by practical experience, by which for several of the specific and malignant forms of disease a reliable or certain treatment will be ascertained.

It would be foreign to the occasion as well as derogatory, to notice in a work devoted to a branch of medicine so essentially exalted in its nature as surgery, the very illogical objections so often repeated against everything connected with Homœopathy. Its absurdity and impotency in the estimation of some are proven even in the fact, that Homœopathic practitioners have recourse to mechanical means for the treatment of accidents, or the removal of mutilated or diseased parts; in other words, because medicines have not physical power to supply the place of cutting instruments, bandages, fracture boxes and pulleys, it is unworthy the attention of an intelligent mind. As this objection, however, applies equally to alloeopathy, the two conflicting doctrines are thereby placed in the same position, and there the Homoeopathic physician may be quite satisfied in allowing them to remain.

An outward abuse, however, of Homœopathy, with a clandestine use of several of its medicines, and often in minute doses—for example of *arnica, ipecacuanha, aconite, pulsatilla, bryonia, belladonna* and others, certainly does not comport with that moral dignity, which should be one of the attributes of the physician; nor is it in accordance with those rules of ethics by which the medical profession profess to be governed. A posterity, however, and that not very remote, will render the tribute to whom it justly belongs.

In a few instances only, throughout the work, have the strength and frequency of repetition of dose been mentioned; to have done so frequently would have increased unnecessarily the bulk of the volume; the presumption being entertained, that such knowledge is already possessed by those who venture upon surgical practice. Full instructions as to the mode of preparation of the medicines, the potency usually employed, and the circumstances regulating repetition, are contained in the Homœopathic Pharmacopœia and numerous practical works. As a general rule it may be observed that most success will be obtained from dynamizations not lower than the third, and in a large proportion of cases, especially in those of a chronic or sub-acute character, as likewise in those of a specific nature, the twelfth, eighteenth and thirtieth dilutions will be found to be possessed of most curative action, and that more certain and positive effect will be obtained from their exhibition at long rather than at short intervals.

It will be observed during the perusal of this work, that portions of it, and more particularly those that relate to the mechanical treatment of injuries and surgical diseases, have been selected from standard authorities. The chapter on "the Means and Instruments for arresting Hemorrhage" is taken from "the Practical Surgery" of Mr. Fergusson;* that upon Amputation from the modern work of Mr. Druitt;† and with the necessary substitution and addition of Homœopathic treatment, those upon Fractures and Dislocations from Dr. Hastings' "Practice of Surgery."‡ The various other authors who have been consulted, and the medical periodicals that have contributed to the formation of the present publication, are mentioned in the foot notes throughout the volume.

PHILADELPHIA, July 11, 1855.

---

* Pp. 34—37. † Druitt's Modern Surgery, pp. 534—546.
‡ Pp. 164—238.

CONTENTS.

SURGERY,

AND ITS ADAPTATION TO

HOMŒOPATHIC PRACTICE.

CHAPTER I.

INFLAMMATION.

Perhaps there is no subject, to which the attention of those interested in the investigation of medical questions has been directed, that has caused such diversity of opinion; and to account satisfactorily for which, more hypotheses have been advanced, than that of Inflammation.

However, after much laborious and patient investigation, and many protracted discussions, the majority of the profession of the present day, coincide in the opinion that Inflammation—properly so called, or when fully established—consists in an engorgement of the capillary vessels, dependent on their* *diminished* action, and the relaxed condition of their coats, together with more or less accelerated motion of the heart and arteries; and that from such an abnormal condition arise the well known characteristic symptoms—pain, heat, swelling and redness. (*Dolor, calor, tumor, rubor.*)

In all organic textures, the transmission of the blood from the minute branches of the arteries to the minute veins is effected through a net-work of microscopic vessels (the capil-

* Dr. Fletcher's Elements of General Pathology, p. 161. Miller's Principles of Surgery, p. 108.

laries), in the meshes of which the proper substance of the tissue lies. The diameter of these vessels varies somewhat in the different textures of the body, the most common size, however, being about $\frac{1}{3000}$ of an inch.* It must be obvious, therefore, that if the action of these radicles be diminished, by any cause whatsoever, that the blood will not pass with sufficient acceleration through them; and that in a short period, the heart still continuing its action, they would become enlarged by the unusual accumulation of blood.

This engorgement, this agglomeration of blood disks in the capillary tubes; dependent on their diminished action and increased power of the heart and arteries, is Inflammation. The whole process may be clearly demonstrated by a common surgical example, frequently encountered in routine practice—the application of some corrosive substance to the skin. The period of incubation might be designated, as the time that elapses between the application of the irritant and the establishment of the inflammatory process.

In the first stage there is not only an increased flow of blood to the affected part, but the circulation is carried on with increased velocity, which may result from the contraction of the capillaries, which, as has been before stated, are the essential seat of the disease.

As the coats of these tubes appear to be analogous to the involuntary muscular tissue of the human body, this contraction has been termed by some physiologists "spasm," while the subsequent relaxation and distention that occurs when Inflammation is fairly established has been designated "paralysis." As this dilatation proceeds, those radicles, that in the normal condition were only capable of transmitting the liquor sanguinis, now, by their extension, admit of the introduction of the red globules; and those that previously circulated but a single file of the colored corpuscles, are now filled with them in agglomerated masses, and the augmentation of such a condition necessarily tends more and more to retard the circulation.

---

* Kirkes and Paget, Manual of Physiology, p. 105.

The capillaries being overburdened with blood, there is consequently more transudation than in a non-affected part, and this consists generally of serum, which may be found in the interstitial spaces or upon open surfaces. The natural function of the part is exalted, if the normal action be secretion, the product is in increased quantity; nutrition is enhanced, and the surrounding tissues somewhat increased in bulk.

This stage is not wholly inconsistent with health, and has been termed by recent physiologists "vital turgescence;" indeed it may be reasonable to suppose, that at certain periods of existence such a condition, when caused by a vital stimulus, is necessary to certain organs, in order that they may perform their destined functions, and thus fulfilling the office assigned them by the Creator, complete in perfectness the wonderful mechanism of the human economy. The blush upon the maiden's cheek, and the increased vascular action that takes place during the secretion of milk in the mammæ, are not diseases; but it is probable that nature, when she has performed the duty incumbent upon her, checks the normal stimulus she has brought to her aid, and this being withdrawn, the part having accomplished its mission, returns to the quiescent condition from which it has been aroused.

As the inflammatory process progresses, the arterial trunks partake in the excitement, and in endeavoring to overcome the resistance, enlarge, pulsate, and throw an increased quantity of blood to the part; the already distended capillaries become more enlarged, the little contractility they possess becomes weaker, and the blood disks within them more agglomerated; exudation is increased in quantity and deviates from the healthy standard; the tissues around become enlarged and softened, because the exuded plastic material is too great for the normal appropriation of the textures, and if still the unhealthy action continues, the attenuated walls of the capillaries, unable to withstand greater distention, give way, and extravasation results; the surrounding tissues become filled with liquor sanguinis, pus commences to be formed, and the destroyed tissue of the part is mingled with the contents of the vessels.

Such are the pathological changes that are manifested from the commencement to the completion of the inflammatory process; and if these occur with rapidity, and decline in the same ratio, the inflammation may be termed *acute;* if, on the contrary, the action be sluggish, and weeks and months elapse before the climax is established, the decline be of long duration, and the termination imperfect, the disease becomes *chronic* in its character; and it is such a condition that frequently baffles and disheartens the practitioner with unsatisfactory results, and unlooked-for complications.

The acute form may assume a chronic character, from improper treatment, the habits of the patient, the condition of the affected part, &c., &c., &c.

The most prominent symptoms that denote the presence of inflammation, are, as has been above stated, the pain, heat, swelling, and redness.

Pain is the most characteristic symptom of inflammation, and is caused by the compression of nervous filaments, from the encroachment of the swelling upon them, which acts as a mechanical force; consequently, the pain increases as the tumefaction advances, particularly if the surrounding textures are firm and unyielding. The function also of the sentient nerves is perverted, and they become, themselves, one of the seats of inflammatory action. Moreover, at each throbbing impulse of the heart and arteries, the *nervi vasorum* of the distended and elongated vessels add something to the general amount of pain. But such causes, as well as their results, are liable to vary. The pain present in inflammation is not uniform. It is, as has been before mentioned, in a great measure influenced by the elasticity of the textures in which inflammation occurs. Thus, when a bone is affected with the disease, it is more painful than when the skin is attacked. The intensity of the inflammatory action, and the sensitiveness of the affected part, also, to a great extent, influence the amount of pain.

Heat.—"The symptoms and consequences of inflammation,"

writes Mr. Liston,*—"and amongst others, heat—are modified by the distance of the affected part from the centre of the circulation. All actions, healthy as well as morbid, proceed with more vigor in the superior extremities—the head, the neck, and the trunk—than in the more remote parts of the body; for in the former the blood is transmitted more speedily, if not in greater quantity, and is not so liable to be impeded in its return." This is evidently true, as ascertained by the thermometer. The normal temperature of the body, at the heart and upper parts of the trunk, varies from 98° to 100°, at the extremities about 92°,† but there is very little rise of the mercury from the heat of an inflamed part, and though the patient complains of extreme heat, burning and throbbings, the thermometer only indicates a rise of four or five degrees.‡ This, however, can be readily accounted for. During the inflammatory process the nerves of sensation, partaking in the general abnormal action, become perverted, indeed, increased sensibility is one of the signs of inflammatory action; this accounts for the *sensation* of heat so frequently noticed and complained of by the patient; and if we also remember that a very fruitful source of animal heat is referred to the changes that take place in the blood circulating in the capillaries; and as these changes are carried on with great rapidity in inflammation, we can readily imagine that the heat of the part which is the seat of the abnormal action, may be somewhat elevated.

Heat must also be connected with other symptoms, to assist in the diagnosis of inflammation, for we all know, and are every day told of burnings in different portions of the body, when there is not the faintest trace of any inflammatory action.

Swelling.—This effect arises from several causes; first, the effusion of coagulable lymph and serum; secondly, the increased quantity of blood in the vessels; thirdly, the depo-

* Liston's Elements of Surgery.

† Cyclopedia of Practical Medicine, p. 738.

‡ Loc. cit.

sition of new matter; fourthly, the interruption of absorption, particularly noticed by Soemmering.

The swelling is, for the most part, confined to the cellular texture, and is commonly the greatest where the inflammation commences; but this symptom, when viewed alone, cannot by any means indicate the disease, others must be conjoined with it. In the simplest form of œdema, is there inflammation present?

The *redness* is evidently caused by the increased quantity of blood contained in the capillaries, and of the introduction of the red globules into those radicles, which previously would not permit their admission. The color of the blood, also, in inflammation assumes a deeper tint, but there are some instances in which the inflammatory process may have been present to a certain extent, and the parts be paler.* This, however, is not generally the case. The enlargement and engorgement of the capillaries, was made plainly distinguishable by Mr. Hunter: he says, "I froze the ear of a rabbit and thawed it again; this occasioned considerable inflammation, an increased heat and thickening of the part. This rabbit was killed when the ear was in the height of inflammation, and the head being injected the two ears were removed and dried. The uninflamed ear dried clear and transparent, the vessels were distinctly seen ramifying through its substance, but the inflamed ear dried thicker and more opaque, and its arteries were considerably larger.

It may not be uninteresting to insert here a few remarks concerning the analogy between fever and inflammation. The theory appears to be very plausible, and supported with well founded arguments; however, the object of referring to the subject, is merely to give the student an insight into the matter, hoping that the inquiring mind, anxious for further elucidation, will be led to other investigations, that may prove conclusive, either *for* or *against* the theory. "It must be

---

* Liston's Elements of Surgery.

abundantly obvious," writes the late John Fletcher,* "that it is the first stage of fever which is (as in inflammation) that of increased action, at least with regard to the extreme vessels of the surface of the body (the essential seat of the morbid change), and the second that of diminished action with respect to these vessels; and this, whether the exciting cause be stimulant or sedative. It is true—the increased excitement of these vessels being always attended by a diminished excitement of the rest of the body, and the diminished excitement of these vessels by an increased excitement of the rest of the body—it is difficult to divest one's self of the notion, that the cold stage of fever is one of deficiency of action, and the hot stage of increase of it; and it was this which gave occasion to Dr. Armstrong to call the three stages of continued fever (corresponding to the cold, the hot, and the sweating stage of an intermittent) by the names of the stage of oppression, that of excitement, and that of collapse—names which, it must be remembered, apply *only to the state of the body in general,* and not of the capillary vessels of the surface, which, during the stage of oppression, are in a state of preternatural excitement; during that of excitement, in a state of corresponding collapse; and during that of collapse, in a state of reaction. 'Whenever,' says Dr. W. Phillip, 'increased temperature, swelling and redness appear, the capillary vessels are debilitated, and preternaturally distended.' Now, in the hot stage, the whole surface is affected with increased temperature, redness, and swelling. The deduction is obvious, and the analogy of fever, in every respect, with inflammation, is too manifest to require further comment. In fact, inflammation and fever differ only in their seat and in their degree: the seat of inflammation being anywhere, and more or less circumscribed, and its degree commonly considerable; whereas, the seat of fever is in the whole surface of the body, and its degree commonly slight. It is here, however, meant, that the degree of inflammation, in any

* Elements of General Pathology, p. 176.—ed. J. J. Drysdale, M. D., and J. R. Russell, M. D. Edinburgh, 1842.

given number of capillary vessels, is commonly slight in fever, compared to that of inflammation, properly so called; but the number of them much more than compensates for the slightness of the inflammation of each, and the constitutional affection is, of course, great in proportion."

The symptoms as above stated—pain, heat, swelling, and redness—are those that are most frequently manifested in inflammation, and are in themselves, generally, sufficient to the allopathic practitioner, not only to designate the disease, but also to suggest the *system** of treatment that must be employed; but, to the homœopathic physician, though the pain, heat, swelling, and redness proclaim the pathological action that is being established, they are of but little utility with regard to the treatment. The medicines exhibited according to the law of *simile* are not to be prescribed for the *name* inflammation, but for the *character* and *kind* of the *symptoms* that present themselves in such an unhealthy condition; the study becomes more arduous, the investigation more thorough, and the examination more minute; the character of the pain must be ascertained, whether it be boring, sticking, tearing, lancinating, &c.; the conditions that aggravate or relieve the sufferings must be investigated; the time of occurrence, and the causes that produced the disease, must be understood; the temperament, age, sex, and habits of the patient must be noticed, and the supervening constitutional symptoms also receive their due share of attention, before the appropriate medicines may be selected and administered.

There are many instances, however, when some of the local

---

* Concerning the theories of inflammation adopted by allopathic writers and the fallacy of their treatment, we may refer the reader to a number of articles, entitled "Phenomena and Theory of Inflammation connected with Homœopathic Statistics," written by Dr. Ozanne, and which appeared in the Homœopathic Times (London), during the year 1852; and also to a paper, "On the usual Antiphlogostic Treatment of the Old School," by Dr. J. W. Arnold, of Heidelberg. The latter essay was reprinted in this country, in the Quarterly Homœopathic Journal. Boston, 1849, pp. 24–35,

manifestations of inflammation cannot be appreciated, but the constitutional symptoms—quick, full pulse, dry, furred tongue, high-colored urine, thirst, &c.—may, perhaps, lead to the detec-tection of the disease; "but," says Mr. Fergusson,* "some of these, even, are not entirely to be depended on, seeing that they may be present without the existence of inflammation; whilst, again, that disease may be in full vigor, and yet the symptoms may be such, that *the most experienced may be deceived.*" Again, he says, referring to the same subject, "exceptions to these observations must be familiar to every one who has seen even a *little* practice."

Here, then, in the treatment of this disease, the homœopathic practitioner has a most decided advantage, and one that may be instrumental in rescuing his patient from the grave.

Let us suppose that one of the "most experienced" physicians of the old school be summoned to attend a case, where "the disease may be in full vigor," and the presenting symptoms not such as would indicate to his mind, the high state of inflammatory action that is taking place in the system. What would be the course pursued? Either to treat the *name* of some other affection, that the symptoms may somewhat resemble, and which may be entirely at variance with the true state of the disease; or, perhaps, to prescribe for the invalid some "neutral mixture," without the most remote idea of the dangerous condition of the patient, who, under such treatment, in a short period may terminate his sufferings in death. But, on the other hand, the Homœopathic physician—although to his mind the pathological condition of the part may be equally obscure—has the light of a law of nature, universal, and coëxtensive with disease, to guide him in the selection of his remedy.

That there must be some presenting symptoms is obvious, for, says Hahnemann, "There is no curable malady, nor any *invisible morbid change* in the interior of man, which admits of cure, that is not made known by symptoms, or morbid

* Practical Surgery, p. 70.

indications, to the physician of accurate observation." Therefore, if the medicine be selected and administered in strict accordance to the law *similia similibus*, those symptoms will be removed, at least if the disease be curable; and if removed, the affection, with its internal change, whether structural or functional, will have disappeared also. Hahnemann again says, "The cure which is effected by the annihilation of the symptoms of a disease, *removes at the same time the internal change* upon which the disease is founded, that is to say, destroys it in its totality. It is accordingly clear that the physician has nothing more to do than to destroy the totality of the symptoms, in order to effect a simultaneous removal of the *internal change*, that is to say, annihilate the disease itself." He says further, "It is not possible to conceive or prove by any experience after the cure of the whole of the symptoms of a disease, together with all its perceptible changes, that there remains, or possibly can remain, any other than a healthy state, or that the *morbid alteration* which had taken place in the interior of the economy has not been annihilated."

But let it not here be understood, that a knowledge of pathology is of no practical avail to the student of Homœopathy; on the contrary, by understanding the pathological changes that occur in any organ of the body, a class of medicines is suggested to the mind of the practitioner, and from this genus, the remedy must be selected, in accordance to the presenting symptoms.

But when such a case, as the one alluded to, occurs, when the pathological changes are obscure, the physician who prescribes in accordance to *one* certain law, is, to say the least, far more liable to effect a cure, than he who, led astray by a thousand flickering lights of conjecture and empyricism, knows not whether to stimulate or deplete, and therefore frames in his mind an hypothesis, draws a conclusion, whether false or true, and prescribes accordingly.

In alluding to the subject of inflammation, an eminent Homœopathic physician of this city writes: "Inflammation of the cellular, osseous, nervous, and muscular tissues, is circumscribed and the pain throbbing. In morbid growths and in tubercle the objective symptoms are different, nor is there much pain nor increase of heat. In other varieties of abnormal growth the appearances again are dissimilar, and the pains are acute and lancinating. Inflammation of the lining membrane of the larynx is admitted to be quite different from inflammation of the lining membrane of the trachea. Inflammation, seated in the same tissue of the same organ, assumes at different times different characters, as is observed in cutaneous affections. How are these differences to be understood and encountered? Can they all be grouped together and treated as that pathological condition termed inflammation? If *systems* of medicine and not the law of *simile* be true, they ought to be so understood and treated, and the successful result of such practice would confirm the truth of the systems. But they are not treated upon any general principle. In diseases of the dermoid system, the chief reliance is reposed upon what are termed specifics. An impartial mind can entertain no other idea, than that the different subjective symptoms as exhibited, for example, in different varieties of pain, such as tearing, burning, darting, lancinating, pressive, piercing, boring, are the result of essentially different morbid actions; each one, therefore, of necessity requiring its appropriate remedy. To these differences a critical attention must be given for the most successful application of means. It is unpardonable ignorance at the present time, when the bright rays of true medicine are illuminating our pathway with floods of light, to have an imperfect knowledge only of symptoms, and to confound all distinctions."

The consequences of inflammation are often more conspicuous than the disease itself; as, for example, suppuration, ulceration, granulation, and gangrene, in all of which the symptoms of inflammation are thrown into the shade, as it were, by the remarkable features peculiar to each, and therefore the treatment of the disease, in all its phases, can only be rightly understood by one who is well acquainted with the nature of these different conditions. As it is, in general, a most desirable object, however, to prevent any of these consequences occurring, the chief aim at the commencement of the treatment is to endeavor to do so, and to bring about what is usually called the resolution of the disease—that is, to cause the subsidence of all the symptoms, and to leave the part as if no disease had ever been present. But inasmuch as it can only be hoped for, while the action is yet beneath the inflammatory acme, the treatment must be commenced early, and the remedy nicely adapted to the disease, for if the abnormal action has reached its height, true resolution—that is, complete restoration of the part, as regards both structure and function, to its original and normal state—is impossible.

"Resolution may be gradual or sudden, spontaneous or artificial, imperfect or complete; the more early and slight the action, the more likely is the resolution to be rapid, spontaneous and perfect. When sudden, the term *delitescence* is commonly employed; denoting an occurrence favorable in itself, but invariably associated in the mind of the experienced practitioner, with a suspicious prognosis. Were the delitescence effected simply, and there an end, the immediate benefit derived would be without alloy. But experience tells us, that the abrupt and sudden disappearance of advancing vascular action in one part, is often, if not usually, followed by the appearance of similar disorder elsewhere. And, as we have no guarantee that the change may be to an equally harmless locality, such change must at all times be a matter of suspicion, and often of danger. The process which effects subsidence of the original action and the establishment of the new, is termed *metastasis*.

Resolution being about to occur, increased deposit probably takes place, of serum, liquor sanguinis, or both. By this means, among others, the burdened vessels are more or less relieved; they recover their wonted tone and calibre, and the red corpuscles resume their individual distinctness; the agglomerate mass, also, of both red and colorless corpuscles, first oscillate and then move steadily on. Absorption, which has been embarrassed hitherto, or altogether held in abeyance, comes actively into play; and the extra-vascular deposit is more or less rapidly removed. Ultimately, an equality of action is arrived at, between the depositing blood vessels and removal by absorption; the balance of healthy nutrition in the part is restored, and normal function is resumed.

Although this, as a result, cannot always be expected, still it frequently does occur, and when this is the case it is the most desirable termination of the inflammatory process—at all events, the first treatment should be directed to the establishment of resolution, which, if it does not prove sufficient for this end, may mitigate some of the after consequences of inflammation. It frequently happens, however, that by the appropriate Homœopathic treatment, the *tendency* of parts to take on inflammatory action may be removed, and thus the patient may be relieved of a considerable amount of suffering, and the probable tedium of a long and debilitating confinement, and the physician from the harassing and perplexing complications that so frequently present themselves as the sequelæ of inflammation.

The following are the medicines that appear best adapted to accomplish such a desirable end:

(1.) *Cham.*, *Graph.*, *Hepar*, *Petrol.*, *Silic.*, *Staphys.*, *Sulph.* (2.) Baryta-carb., Calc.-c., Lye, Nit.-ac., Rhus., Sepia.

Should these not be sufficient, and the inflammatory action appears to be progressing, the medicines to be relied on, are,

(1.) *Acon.*, *Ars.*, *Bell.*, *Bry.*, *Hepar*, *Merc.*, *Phosph.*, *Silic.*, *Sulph.* (2.) Asa., Arn., Calc.-c., China, Graph., Mang., Nati.-m., Petrol., Puls., Rhus.

These, perhaps, it will be sufficient to name, although there are many others of minor importance, that are serviceable in treating the concomitant symptoms of inflammation.

Aconite is peculiarly adapted to inflammations occurrring either in the internal or external parts, when the pains are lancinating, or when there is much synochal fever. Also, for acute local congestions with erethysm of the nerves, it appears to be, according to Noack and Trenks, best adapted to individuals of a plethoric habit, lively character, bilioso-nervous or sanguineous constitution, with dark hair and light complexion. This medicine is certainly one of the greatest so termed antiphlogistic remedies, and is highly recommended by some practitioners of the old school. In one of the best surgical works of the present day, we read, "Aconite is a powerful antiphlogistic. It tends to relieve by cutaneous and other secretions, but its most important effect is, to lower the heart's action and general circulation. In this respect, indeed, it is the most simple and yet the most powerful of sedatives. Small doses, such as a *drop* or *half a drop* of the strong tincture in *aqueous* solution, repeated every hour, every half hour, or every two hours, are quite safe and truly antiphlogistic; often under their use, the pulse will be found to come down *even* rapidly, the other febrile symptoms at the same time giving way." Again, from another modern surgery, we quote the following: "*Aconite* and *Belladonna* are useful antiphlogistics in certain cases, as in the inflammatory stage of erysipelas, inflammation, rheumatism, &c. They should be employed with care, however, and given in small doses." Aconite is, indeed, serviceable in the *first* stage of almost every variety of inflammation where the pains appear particularly aggravated at night. In active congestion also, this powerful medicine displays a remarkable degree of action, particularly in persons with bright redness of the cheeks, especially in young girls of a plethoric habit, disposed to congestions, nervous or irritable, and leading sedentary lives.

Arnica.—We find it recorded that this *panacea lapsorum* is suitable for those stages of inflammation, where the vital powers begin to become extinct, and where there is a tendency to low grades of fever. Under such circumstances, it is the contrary of Aconite, which, as has been before mentioned, corresponds to the more acute variety; but the effects of Arnica are most fully developed in those inflammations that are consequent upon blows and injuries of all kinds, but particularly in those that are contused, when there is hot, hard, and shining swelling of the affected part; when there is dry heat over the whole body, with general sinking of strength. The use of

Arnica, and other medicines adapted to the treatment of wounds, will be mentioned in a subsequent portion of this work.

Arsenicum is suitable to inflammatory conditions, involving to a very high degree the sensitive sphere; threatening gangrene, or paralysis of the nerves of the parts. It is peculiarly suitable to individuals of impoverished, exhausted, and nervous constitutions; also, to the leucophlegmatic temperament, and to both acute and chronic inflammation.

Belladonna is especially adapted to persons of a plethoric habit of body, with tendency to congestion of blood to the head. As indicated by its pathogenesis, the various symptoms attending upon vertigo, with the heaviness of the head, glowing redness of the face, dilated pupils, dimness of vision, &c. It is also suitable to scrofulous, irritable individuals. What *Acon.* is to inflammatory fevers, *Bell.* is to the inflammation itself, or the inflammatory action of the capillaries. If, after the inflammatory action has been subdued by *Acon.*, other symptoms remain, (chiefly nervous,) *Bell.* is of infinite value; the more delicate the inflamed organ or tissue, the more suitable is this medicine; it is also very useful in alternation with *Merc.* for inflammations of the lymphatics and glands. Under this medicine we also find erysipelatous inflammations, with swelling, or even mortification of the parts—redness, inflammation, and swelling of the whole skin—red, not swelling, of the affected parts.

Bryonia.—This is a medicine of great value in inflammations of many organs and tissues of the body, when there are flying, darting pains, with chilliness, or when the inflammatory swellings are tense, hot, and rather pale, with stinging during motion. In the dermoid tissues also, its action is powerfully displayed, and it is suitable to very many inflammations that occur in those structures. The temperament indicating *Bry.* is the choleric or bilious—persons with brown complexions, brown or black hair, and irritable disposition. The pains are aggravated at night and by movement or contact.

Graphites is also useful in many varieties of inflammation of the skin, particularly *chronic* inflammations.

Camphora is useful in general or local asthenic inflammations, especially when of a rheumatic and erysipelatous character, with a weak, soft pulse, and shrivelled, flaccid skin.

China.—As this medicine is particularly adapted to a state of asthenia or exhaustion of the vital powers of the organism, with relaxation of the solids, and deficiency of animal heat; it is said to be extremely useful in asthenic, passive inflammation.

Hepar is especially suitable in the second stage of inflammation; it has a powerful influence over the suppurative process, and hastens it when advancing, and also tends to heal the part after the evacuation of the pus. *Mercunus*, however, forwards the formation of matter more rapidly under certain circumstances, particularly in inflammation of the glands. *Sulph.* and *Silic.* are also important medicines, and particularly in chronic inflammations. *Rhus Tox.*—Inflammatory swelling and redness, with increased burning and stinging.

Of course, it would be highly improper to administer any of the above mentioned medicines merely for the few indications that have been mentioned, the *totality of symptoms* must be considered; but it would certainly be a work of supererogation; indeed, it would be impossible to mention in this chapter the medicines that are to be exhibited in every case of inflammation, for the disease, as is well known, occupies not only the attention of the surgeon, but constitutes a large proportion of those affections that are encountered by the ordinary practitioner in the daily performance of his duty.

The following medicines may, however, be mentioned:

Inflammation of the *Glands.*

(1.) *Bell.*, *Merc.*, *Phosph.* (2.) Acon., Baryta-e., Camph., Nux Vom., Puls., Sil., Sulph. (3.) Ars., Bry., Canth., Carb-a., Cham., Hep., Lyc., Nitr.-Acid, Rhus., Staph.

Inflammation of the *Bones.*

(1.) *Merc.*, *Puls.*, *Sil.*, *Staph.* (2.) Acon., Asaf., Bell., Calc., Lyc., Nit.-Ac., Phosph., Sulph. (3.) Ars., Bry., Clem., Con., Hep., Mang., Mezer., Rhus., Sep.

Inflammation of the *Periosteum.*

(1.) *Asaf., Merc., Mez., Ph.-ac., Sil.* (2.) Bell., Chin., Puls., Staph.

Inflammation of *External parts.*

(1.) *Acon., Ars., Bell., Puls., Sil., Staph., Sulph.* (2.) Bry., Calc.-c., Cham., Euphr., Hepar, Lyc., Merc., Nitr., Nitr.-ac., Phosph., Rhus., Spig. (3.) Ant.-c., Am., Asaf., Bary.-c., Bor., Cann., Creos., Cupr., Dig., Hyos., Ignat., Led., Natr., N.-vom., Petrol., Plumb., Ran.-bulb., Sassap., Sep.

Inflammation of *Internal parts.*

(1.) *Acon., Bell., Bry., Canth., Merc., N.-Vom., Phosph., Puls.* (2.) Ars., Cann., Cham., Chin., Hyosc., Kali, Lyc., Nitr., Scill., Sulph., Veratr. (3.) Calad., Calc., Camph., Colch., Coloc., Con., Dros., Euphorb., Hepar, Iod., Ipecac., Mang., Mez., Natr.-m., Nitr.-ac., Par., Ph.-ac., Rhus., Sec.-cor., Sep., Spong., Stram.

Inflammation of *Mucous Membrane.*

(1.) *Acon., Ars., Bell., Merc., N.-vom., Sulph.* (2.) Agar., Bor., Bry., Calc., Canth., Cham., Dros., Ignat., Natr.-mur., Par., Phosph., Puls., Scill., Sep., Sil. (3.) Amm.-mur., Ant.-crud., Arg., Bar., Carbo-a., Cocc., Con., Euphra., Graph., Jod., Lyc., Natr., Nitr.-acid, Ph.-ac., Sab., Spongia, Verat.

Inflammation of the *Skin.*

(1.) *Hep., Merc., Sil.* (2.) Acon., Ars., Asaf., Cham., Nit.-ac., Rhus., Staph., Sulph. (3.) Bell., Borax, Bry., Calc., Camph., Mezer., Natr.

LOCAL TREATMENT.

In all cases, the first circumstance that must receive attention, is the removal of such exciting causes as may happen to be present. Of course, we could not expect to treat successfully, any case of disease while the exciting cause is still operating. A slight inflammation arising from a small splinter, cannot be cured until the extraneous body is removed.

In wounds it is often found that foreign substances excite an unnecessary degree of inflammation; these should be taken away as speedily as possible: splintered pieces of bone often give rise to the abnormal action, and require removal. The head of a bone being out of its place may cause inflammation in the part in which it lies; it therefore must be placed in its natural position before inflammatory action can be subdued. There are very many other exciting causes that may soon be detected, and the sooner they are remedied the better.

Rest of the inflamed locality, if possible, should be absolute; when the muscles are affected, they should be placed in such a position that they may be entirely relaxed.

Position is all-important in the management of local inflammation; the part should be placed in such posture, that gravitation will act as a sanguineous drain, and at the same time oppose further injection of the inflamed part.

The efficacy of a poultice in the treatment of inflammation is a disputed point in our school; some practitioners (and these generally the most skillful) discard the use of such adjuvants entirely, while others have recourse to them frequently, and speak loudly in favor of such means. As a general rule they should *not* be used, but in *some instances*, in *certain stages* of inflammation, a poultice may be of service if *applied* and *removed* at the *proper time*. If the inflammatory process is slow, and the patient is afflicted with some other affection, (a cough for instance,) that demands attention, or the suppuration is imperfect, an *unmedicated* warm poultice *may* be applied; but the practitioner must be positive that inflammation has undoubtedly set in, otherwise such treatment would produce aggravation instead of amelioration of the symptoms. When this question is settled in the mind of the surgeon, and the inflammatory process has *passed the first stage*, the power of heat and moisture cause a relaxation and distension of the parenchyma and the engorged vascular trunks causing more copious effusion, which relieves the overburdened vessels, and the circulation can be more readily resumed.

But the very moment this end is attained, the poultice must be removed, or of course, the same agents continuing to act, inflammation would be set up anew, and fresh trouble, and increased pain be the consequence. The poultice must then be withdrawn at the proper time, and the part be kept at perfect rest, and protected from external injury.

CHAPTER II.

SUPPURATION.

If resolution has not been accomplished by those means already referred to, before the acme of the inflammation, suppuration is inevitable. It has been noticed that the walls of the capillaries were already distended to the utmost, that the circulation had almost approached a state of stagnation; if the abnormal action still continues, the walls of the vessels give way, the entire function of the part is either perverted or destroyed, the textures are broken up, and pus is generated; however, though the formation of matter is generally connected with inflammatory action, the student must be prepared in some instances, under peculiar circümstances and in certain constitutions, to witness suppuration, when there has been no previous solution of continuity, and without those symptoms that have been alluded to as indicative of a high state of inflammatory action; for, says Mr. Liston,* "pus is frequently contained in the serous and mucous cavities, when no breach of continuity can be discovered, at least we find a fluid not distinguishable from purulent matter; it *may* be a vitiated secretion, but still it presents the usual characters of pus. But it occurs, generally, when there has been a previous lesion of structure, and in this case its progress is most distinctly marked. In exposed cellular texture, for example, particles of blood are effused; the serum is afterward absorbed, and the lymph remains; this latter gives transmission to minute vessels, which deposit the purulent matter, whilst others secrete particles of organized matter to form granulations in order to repair the loss of substance. This process is often unattended with any great degree of constitutional disturbance."

The pus globule, according to Gluge,† "consists of a whitish

---

* Elements of Surgery, p. 28.

† See Fletcher's Elements of General Pathology.

gray mass, not very resistent and somewhat elastic. In this mass four or five dark points, seldom more, are observable, which do not lie only on the surface but penetrate the interior of the globule. They are easily separated from the white mass, whose surface, which was in contact with the dark kernel, is quite smooth. Neither the tissue, the organ, nor the degree of inflammation, has any effect in changing the character of the pus globules, which are the same as found in bone, sinew, muscle, lung and brain, and as taken from gangrenous, syphilitic, or other sores. This last observation is supported by Valentin." (vol. ii. p. 259, 1837.) The corpuscles are generally spherical, but vary considerably in size, but most frequently they are about $\frac{1}{2500}$ of an inch in diameter; they resemble in appearance the white corpuscles of the blood; they are soluble to a great extent in dilute acids, and when macerated several nuclei are found.

To the eye, pus is a yellowish-white creamy liquid, sometimes of a slight greenish tinge, with scarcely any peculiarity of odor, and heavier than water according to chemical examination. The pus globule is said to be a protein-compound, consisting of the binoxide and tritoxide of proteine,* but these bodies are included in regularly organized cellules, and they float in a clear liquid called the *liquor puris*. This secretion is closely analagous with the serum of blood, and differs from it chemically only in the fact that its protein compounds are oxydized.†

---

* Gardner's Medical Chemistry, p. 305.

† An analysis of pus gives the following elements,—

Water, - - - - - -	86.1
Fat soluble in hot alcohol, - - -	1.6
Matter soluble in cold alcohol, (fat and ozmazome,)	4.3
Matter soluble in hot and cold alcohol, (pyina,) albumen, globules, and grains of pus, - -	7.4
Loss, - - - - - -	.6
	100

The above is quoted by the Editors of Fletcher's Pathology. Note, p. 271.

Pus, as has already been described, is what has been termed by many writers *laudable* or healthy pus, and as such, resists putrefaction for a length of time; but there are very many circumstances that may cause the matter to assume different characters; these are thus described by Mr. Miller: "A chemical action—perhaps the result of atmospheric contact—may be superadded to the vital action, producing by decomposition of the albumen of the serum, hydro-sulphate of ammonia, whose presence is indicated by an offensive odor, and by the blackening of silver probes brought in contact with the pus. Putrescence may be thus begun in the fluid, while it is yet in contact with the living part."

"Disintegration of the surrounding textures by ulceration, is often coëxistent with the formation of pus. It is then mixed with the fluid *debris* of the part, and in consequence, becomes more prone to chemical change.

"Or it may be mixed with blood either fluid or solid. It is reddened thereby, and found to contain blood discs or masses of coagula. It is then termed *sanious* or *grumous*.

"In those of weak systems, it is often deficient in solid matter, consisting chiefly of a thin serum; it is then termed *serous*.

"In the scrofulous and cachectic, besides being serous, it often contains flakes or masses of a curdy appearance; and to such pus the term *scrofulous* is usually applied.

"Sometimes it is impregnated with a subtle virus, as the venereal or vaccine; it is then said to be *specific*.

"Or it may be variously mixed with secretions from mucous and serous membranes, and termed in consequence, *sero-purulent* and *muco-purulent*."

Such are the changes that may be noticed in suppuration, and by understanding them the student and young practitioner will often be able to trace more minutely the origin of the disease and render a more perfect diagnosis.

Pus is rarely absorbed, and in the generality of instances if not assisted in its discharge by the surgeon, finds for itself an opening, leaving a scar, that ever after denotes that disease has once been present in the system.

When suppuration is fairly established, the more acute sufferings of the patient subside, the throbbing which was before frequent, disappears, and the sharp piercing pains become more dull and constant. Generally about the centre of the tumor a small conical eminence appears, that is most commonly of a paler hue than the surrounding textures; when such appearances present themselves the abscess is said to be *pointing*.

The fluctuation of a fluid can often be perceived beneath the integuments by careful examination with the fingers, but in some cases it so happens that the presence of matter may be so deep seated, that this sensation cannot be appreciated by the practitioner. The attendant occurrences and the presenting symptoms cannot be too carefully studied, when such a condition is suspected, for the discovery of the existence of deep seated matter, is a circumstance of the highest importance, and one which involves the practitioner's reputation, and frequently the life of the patient.

Mr. Cooper says, "In no part of the surgeon's employment is experience in former similar cases of greater use to him, than in the present; and however simple it may appear, yet nothing, it is certain, more readily distinguishes a man of observation and extensive practice, than his being able easily to detect collections of deep seated matter. On the contrary, nothing so materially injures the character and professional credit of a surgeon, as his having in such cases given an inaccurate or unjust prognosis; for, in diseases of this kind, the nature and event of the case are generally at last clearly demonstrated to all concerned."

The only characteristic constitutional symptom, that is said to denote the formation of matter, is that of shivering. On this subject, however, as there is some difference of opinion among the profession, concerning its usefulness as an indication of formation of pus, Mr. Fergusson is quoted. "It is," says he, "in my opinion, less worthy of estimation than some seem to imagine:—it frequently happens in instances of disease where suppuration never ensues; it often occurs even in a state of health, and equally often when it does happen, it may be overlooked. Shivering is a symptom which the surgeon is often deeply interested in, not so much, however, from the dread of suppuration, as that it denotes some peculiar condition of the system fraught with much danger to life,—as, for example, if within the first ten days after a capital amputation, or after lithotomy, a patient is seized with shivering, there is much reason to anticipate a fatal result; and although this may not occur in all such instances, every practical surgeon must bear me out in the formidable estimation I have made of this symptom. But whether it has preceded suppuration or not, the surgeon will seldom be thus satisfied that matter has formed."

Though the treatment of suppuration will be more minutely enlarged upon, under those diseases in which it occurs, the following medicines will, in the generality of cases, be serviceable.*

The principal remedies for suppuration are:

(1.) *Asa., Hep., Lach., Merc., Puls., Sil., Sulph.* (2.) Ars., Bell., Calc., Canth., Carb.-v., Caust., Cist., Dulc., Kreos., Lyc,. Mang., Nitr.-ac., Phos., Rhus., Staph., Sulph.-ac.

For *Bloody Pus*:—(1.) *Asa.. Hep., Merc.* (2.) Ars., Carb.-v., Caust., Nitr.-ac., Puls., Sil.

For *Jelly-like*:—*Cham., Merc., Sil.*

Ichorous:—(1.) *Ars., Asa., Carb.-v., Chin., Merc., Nitr.-ac., Rhus., Sil.* (2.) Calc., Caust., Kreos., Phos., Sulph.

Watery, thin:—(1.) *Asa., Caust., Merc., Sil., Sulph.* (2.) Ars. Calc., Carb.-v., Lyc., Nitr.-ac., Ran., Rhus., Staph.

Fetid, cadaverous:—(1.) *Asa., Carb.-v., Chin., Hep., Sil., Sulph.* (2.) Ars., Calc., Graph., Kreos., Lyc., N.-vom., Phos.-ac., Sep.

Viscid:—*Asa., Con., Merc., Phos., Sep.*

Brown, brownish:—*Ars., Bry., Carb.-v., Rhus., Sil.*

Yellow:—(1.) *Hep., Merc., Puls., Sil., Sulph.* (2.) Ars., Calc., Carb.-v., Caust., Phos., Rhus., Sep., Staph.

---

* See Chapter VII., Sections 1, 2, 3, 4.

Greenish:—*Asa.*, *Aur.*, *Caust.*, *Merc.*, *Puls.*, *Rhus.*, *Sep.*, *Sil.*

Gray:—*Ars.*, *Caust.*, *Merc.*, *Sil.*

Leaving a *black stain*:—*Chin.*

Sour Smelling, or causing an acid taste:—*Calc.*, *Hep.*, *Merc.*, *Kal.*, *Sulph.*

Salt:—*Amb.*, *Ars.*, *Calc.*, *Graph.*, *Lyc.*, *Puls.*, *Sep.*, *Staph.*, *Sulph.*

Acrid, corrosive:—(1.) *Ars.*, *Caust.*, *Merc.*, *Nitr.-ac.*, *Ran.*, *Rhus.*, *Sep.*, *Sil.* (2.) Carb.-v., Cham., Clem., Lyc., Natr., Petr., Staph., Sulph., Sulph.-ac.

Laudable pus:—(1.) *Hep.*, *Lach.*, *Merc.*, *Puls.*, *Sil.*, *Sulph.* (2.) Bell., Calc., Mang., Phos., Rhus., Staph.

Malignant:—(1.) *Asa.*, *Chin.*, *Hep.*, *Merc.*, *Phos.*, *Sil.* (2.) Ars., Calc., Carb.-v., Caust., Kreos., Nitr.-ac., Rhus., Sulph., Sulph.-ac.

Too profuse:—(1.) *Hep.*, *Merc.*, *Phos.*, *Puls.*, *Sep.*, *Sulph.* (2.) Ars., Calc., Chin., Lyc., Rhus., Sil.

Suppressed, or prematurely stopping:—*Calc.*, *Hep.*, *Lach.*, *Merc.*, *Sil.*

CHAPTER III.

ULCERATION AND SLOUGHING.

Ulceration is that process by which a solution of continuity is effected in a living solid; it is of much more frequent occurrence in the cellular and adipose tissue, than in muscles, tendons, ligaments, nerves or blood vessels.

Until lately, the Hunterian theory was generally received, that such breach of continuity was effected by what was termed ulcerative absorption, or in other words, that the absorbent vessels were chiefly concerned in the establishment of the process; modern pathologists, however, appear to regard ulceration as the molecular death of a part; a gradual softening and disintegration of tissue, molecule by molecule; the effete matter being mixed with purulent and other secretions, and thus carried out of the system. This process is generally one of true inflammation, or connected in some degree with inflammatory action.

If the inflammatory process continues, suppuration, softening, disintegration, and detachment of the tissues in minute portions, follow in succession the abnormal action; the separated molecules become mixed with the pus and are removed with the discharge of the matter; it would appear therefore, that with such a process, absorption would be but little connected.

The more important arguments in support of this doctrine, are the following:—

1*st.*—"Ulceration is an immediate result of inflammation, or is coëxistent with it; and, during inflammation, absorption in a part inflamed is very much diminished, if not altogether arrested. Inflammatory action simply subsiding, on having just touched its true acme, or barely so, is followed almost immediately by very actively renewed absorption, by which the inflammatory deposits are speedily cleared away. But when the action does not so subside, and advances to suppuration with ulceration, the result is otherwise; absorption is not renewed, with any energy, if at all, until the action has abated. During the persistence of such action, inflammatory deposits may, to a certain extent, disappear; but only by disintegration along with the original tissues, and admixture with the extruded purulent discharge.

2*d.*—"If ulceration consists in mere absorption, why is it invariably accompanied by discharge?

3*d.*—"Certain structures resist all excitants of absorption, long and successfully, yet are remarkably prone to ulceration; and the inference appears plain, that the two actions—one opposed, the other embraced by the same part at the same time—must be dissimilar.

4*th.*—"In the case of virulent inoculations, whence the system is to be contaminated by absorption of virus from the part inoculated, as, for instance, in the primary venereal ulcer—it is considered that the system is safe during the formation of that ulcer. The part inflames and ulcerates; in no long time after the first blush of inflammation, the ulcer is fully established;

and during the first few days, according to the Hunterian theory, there should have been great and constant activity of the absorbents pouring virus into the circulation, together with the *debris* of texture. But the experience of the practitioner tells an opposite tale; there seems to be little or no absorption during that period, for if the ulcer be cured in this its earliest stage, the disease is arrested, and there is no absorption of virus into the system.

5th.—" Ulceration is most rapid, when absorption is generally supposed to be least active; that is, during the persistence of acute inflammation.

6th.—" Absorption is proved to be feeble during acute inflammation."*

There are several other circumstances, which are opposed to the theory of ulcerative absorption, and indeed form conclusive evidence that the absorbents do not perform that action in ulceration, that was attributed to them by Mr. Hunter.

Ulceration is a step beyond suppuration. The inflammatory process having reached its climax, in infiltration, and partial softening of the textures, if ulceration supervenes, the molecules become further softened, and carried away with the discharge from the part; this is effected easily from open surfaces, but when ulceration is progressing in an unbroken part, a small abscess or pustule is formed, and after their contents is evacuated the ulcerated surface is revealed.

The terms *acute, inflamed, chronic,* phagedenic, sloughing ulcer, &c., are all modifications of the process of ulceration; the severity of which is in proportion to the grade of the inflammation, and the vitality of the part.

If the inflammatory process is moderate, and the ulceration is established steadily, it may be termed *acute*; if, however, the degree of abnormal action is greater, the ulcer is said to be *inflamed,* on account of the unusual amount of pain, heat, swelling and redness, that surround the part; if the inflammation is of a still higher grade, the destruction of the tissues is

* See Miller's Principles of Surgery.

still more rapid, and a *phagedenic* sore is produced; and if still the inflammatory action progresses, partial death of the part is effected, and a *sloughing* ulcer is the result.

However, after ulceration has been established by inflammation, the latter may subside, and the ulcerated surface be repaired in a short period; but if the inflammation is sluggish, the ulceration proceeds slowly and becomes chronic in character.

The process by which an ulcerated surface is repaired is termed *granulation*, and the covering of these granulations with cuticular formation, or the absolute healing of the part, is designated cicatrization; these two actions, when united, constitute healing by the second intention.

Healing by the first intention, or *adhesion*, cannot occur after inflammation has reached its acme, on account of the breaking up of the textures, &c., that are consequent upon that unhealthy action; indeed, when healing by adhesion does take place, there must be a sufficiency of normal circulation through the part, which, as has been before mentioned, cannot be the case in true inflammation. The process is simply this: the cut surfaces being nicely adapted, liquor sanguinis exudes, the serum is carried off, and the fibrin remains; this in time becomes fully organized, adheres to the surfaces of the wound, and continuity is restored.

Healing by the second intention (granulation and cicatrization,) is the process by which ulcerated surfaces are repaired, and is also the usual mode by which wounds, in which there is much loss of substance, are healed.

The granulations are formed in layers, and by liquor sanguinis, that, while the ulceration is progressing, mingles with the abnormal secretions and is carried away; but as the inflammatory action ceases, a portion of the fibrin remains, and becomes incorporated with the original tissue, forming *granulations*—small, red, irregularly raised points, vascular and fleshy.

The liquor sanguinis continues to be secreted, and new layers of granulations are formed upon the old, while the pus that is still poured out to a certain extent, serves as a covering to protect the whole. As the new layers are forming, the old ones become organized,* and as the process continues, the cavity becomes filled.

The means by which the new integument is, as it were, engrafted upon the granulations, from the thin outspreading of cuticle to the formation of true skin, is *cicatrization.*

When the healthy action appears to be arrested the granulations become larger and paler, and become flabby and gelatinous; when such appearances are present, the granulations are termed *unhealthy.*

The same causes that create inflammation are productive of ulceration. These actions are portions of the same process, commencing with vital turgescence, and terminating in gangrene.

Ulceration is the medium between suppuration and gangrene; in the former the action does not proceed far enough to disintegrate the textures; and in the latter the death of the part is effected in mass, and not molecule by molecule.

Sloughing.—Death of a part, an undoubted termination of inflammation, as well as of all other vital change, may be reached at once, from intensity of action, deficiency of power, or a combination of both.

The broken up texture caused by ulceration, softened, and infiltrated by liquor sanguinis, pus, and extravasated blood, has its circulation wholly arrested and it dies; not slowly and imperceptibly by particles, but plainly, at once, and in mass. Vital action has ceased, and chemical change advances unopposed, and the part is decomposed by putrescence."†

The term *slough* is used to denote the death of the soft parts, and *exfoliation* or *sequestrum* is applied to a dead piece of bone.

The medicine for different forms of ulceration, will be found in the chapter upon ulcers.‡

---

* For a very interesting account of the formation of the different tissues of the animal body, from the development of the nucleolus to the perfection of a part, see Quekett's Lectures on Histology, London, 1852.

† Miller's Principles of Surgery.

‡ See Chapter VIII., Sections 1, 2, 3, 4.

CHAPTER IV.

MORTIFICATION.

"The word Gangrene," says Mr. Guthrie,* "is often used synonymously with mortification. By the public it is presumed to mean the same thing. Technically, it is more correctly confined to the inflammatory state in which mortification commences, and with which it proceeds unto the destruction of the life of the part or sphacelus." Mortification includes the whole process of dying, from its commencement to its completion.

The symptoms that are present in inflammation become modified when *gangrene* is about to commence.† The redness passes into a dark and livid hue; for circulation has ceased, and the blood is becoming decomposed. Circulation having been arrested, so is exudation, and the swelling is less tense. On the surface, however, effusions may take place, and that profusely. All vital action decaying, pain and heat remarkably abate, and often cease suddenly. Sensation gradually leaves the part. Just before, even a moderate degree of pressure aggravated the pain, now, even rude handling is borne with impunity. Nutrition, the source of animal heat, having ceased, temperature necessarily decreases, and usually with rapidity; rapid putrescence takes place; and, as the result of chemical change, an offensive odor is more or less freely exhaled. The surface is frequently studded with *phlyctena;* that is, elevations of the scarf-skin by putrid serum; readily distinguished from the dark vesicles filled with bloody serum, which not unfrequently attend on simple bruise; by observing that the *epidermis is detached from the cutis, not only at the elevated spot, but all around,* and that, consequently, the

---

* Lectures on the more Important Points in Surgery.—London Lancet, Sept., 1850, p. 251.

† See Miller's Principles of Surgery, p. 267.

phlyctena may be made to slide from place to place, by slight pressure. Besides the phlyctena is not attended with heat, pain and swelling, as in the mere vesicle, but is associated with all the other symptoms of advancing gangrene. When this is limited to the part originally inflamed, the discoloration is circumscribed, and may have its border even abrupt; but when the action and injury which led to it have both been severe—when the power of both part and system have been brought low—and when, in consequence, gangrene is to spread—discoloration is gradually lost in the surrounding skin, and dark streaks are seen shooting diffusedly upwards in the limb.

Sphacelus, or completion of the gangrene, is indicated by the part having become completely cold and insensible. It is shrunk in its dimensions, soft and flaccid, almost pulpy to the touch; and it *crepitates* distinctly, containing not only liquid, but gaseous contents—the result of putrescence. All vital action has ceased, and the chemical reigns paramount. The color is usually dark, when the part is exposed to atmospheric influence; but when removed from this, as in sloughing of the areolar tissue, or of the fascia, or in necrosis—the integuments remaining yet entire—the dead portions retain their normal hue but little changed.

When a part dies to a limited extent—as a portion of skin, areolar tissue, artery or tendon—the sphacelated part is termed a *slough;* and the process of death *sloughing*.

Sphacelus being complete, and gangrene not extending, nature instantly adopts means whereby she may free herself from a part which is of no further use, and whose continued presence may prove seriously injurious. Its recovery is impossible; and if it be allowed to remain in close contact with the living textures, these cannot fail to absorb more or less of the noxious results of putrescence, both gaseous and fluid; whereby a poisonous effect will be produced on the system, already brought low by constitutional disorder attendant on the gangrene. The living part in immediate contact with the dead, inflames; and, in consequence, the abrupt livid line is bordered by a diffuse, red and painful swelling—*the line of demarcation.*

This vesicates; the vesicle bursts; puriform matter is discharged; and an inflamed and ulcerating surface is disclosed—*the line of separation.* The furrow, so begun, gradually deepens; at first advancing with considerable rapidity, through the skin, and areolar tissue, which are prone to ulcerate; but receiving a check, when fascia, tendon, and other fibrous tissue is reached. The advance is seldom perpendicular, but in a sloping direction; and the inclination is usually toward, and as it were, beneath the dead part; gangrene being generally most extensive superficially. In time, even the most resisting of the soft textures are got through by ulceration, nothing but bone remaining undivided. No hemorrhage occurs during this gradual division of parts; for the inflammatory process has passed leisurely through its ordinary grades; exudation and organization of fibrin precede the suppuration and ulceration, protecting the otherwise loose tissues from purulent infiltration, and sealing up the otherwise open orifices of arteries and veins.

Nature's amputation, so conducted, is unfortunately a reverse of the ordinary operation, producing a stump which is conical, and otherwise but ill-fashioned for useful purposes. The surgeon is, therefore, called upon to interfere in most cases; modifying the arrangement, and securing division of the bone at a higher point.

When gangrene does not involve the whole thickness of a limb, the line of demarcation is formed around the sphacelated portion, and the part sloughs away, leaving an ulcerated surface beneath, in which the process still continues until the unhealthy structure is cast off.

The constitutional symptoms in mortification generally assume the typhoid character. The pulse is quick and tremulous, the skin hot, tongue dry and of a brownish tinge, and the patient restless and uneasy. Delirium, subsultus tendinum, nausea and hiccup are frequently present. With regard to the causes of mortification Dr. Gibson writes,* "In general

* Late Professor of Surgery in the University of Pennsylvania.

the disease results from inflammation. Gun-shot wounds, fractures, dislocations, simple punctures, concentrated acids, poisons, stimulating applications, infiltration of acrid fluids into the cellular membrane, lightning, burns, long-continued pressure, intense cold, *must all operate, more or less, through the medium of inflammation, in producing their several effects.*"

There are also some *specific* causes of gangrene, which will afterwards be noticed.

Mortification has been divided into acute and chronic, the former comprising the humid inflammatory or traumatic, the latter the dry and idiopathic. Generally speaking, the acute is humid and the chronic dry—the fluids being retained in the former, and gradually parted with in the latter—however, this is not invariably the case.

For the purpose of illustrating the *acute* form of gangrene, the following, may serve as an example.—When there exists a compound fracture of the lower ends of the bones of the leg, with great contusion and laceration, a high degree of inflammation is the certain result, in consequence of the severity of the injury; here all the symptoms of the disease will be well marked; pain, heat, swelling and redness, will all be conspicuous. If gangrene threatens, the swelling will probably attract most attention; perhaps the pain and feeling of heat may then be less, and instead of a bright red, the part may assume a bluish tinge; it may also appear colder, and the cuticle will be elevated by the phlyctena, or vesicles. At such a time, if the part is touched by the fingers, it will feel tense and crepitating, for there will be air in the *soft textures.* In such a case the constitutional symptoms are probably of less moment than the local, as denoting the extent of the mischief. At first there will be the usual constitutional indications of severe local inflammation, latterly the pulse will sink and become irregular; the skin will be pale, cold and clammy; the countenance will assume an anxious, haggard appearance, and there may be vomiting, hiccup, and delirium. Under these circumstances there need scarcely be a doubt that gangrene is present, and to such a case the terms—*acute, humid* and *traumatic gangrene* are applied.*

Of course there may be acute, humid gangrene, without the traumatic. The example above cited was selected because it represented the three characteristics.†

Dry gangrene—or as it has been termed, senile gangrene—is generally seen in advanced years, and in many cases is the result of deficient circulation.

This variety of gangrene may commence with a burning sensation, which continues for a time, and ceases suddenly; or without any well marked symptoms of inflammation, the toes and feet may become cold, discolored and shriveled, and finally converted into a hard, dry mass, insensible and of a purple hue. Frequently there is no sloughing, and each part retains its original form, the skin remains entire, the nails adhere to the toes, and the part becomes hard and cold, and is perfectly free from fetor. Sometimes, however, the fetid odor and sloughing are considerable, and attended by severe constitutional symptoms, although these are of rather rare occurrence.

It is frequently very difficult to assign any cause to this variety of the disease. In some instances, however, it can be traced to the diseased rye. During very moist seasons, *secale-cornutum, ergot, cockspur,* (a medicine whose excellent qualities, in many diseases, is fully appreciated by the Homœopathic practitioner,) is generated in considerable quantities, constituting a disease, in which the grains of rye become larger, firmer,

---

* Fergusson's System of Practical Surg., p. 100.

† Mr. Guthrie, also, makes another division, and one which he considers more important than any other, viz:—*constitutional* and *local.* He says, "Surgeons have, I am aware, spoken and written of chronic and idiopathic mortification, or certain states depending on internal causes, which have occupied a considerable time before they gave rise to any great development of evil; whereas the difference between local and constitutional mortification may depend on a few hours—a time so short, and yet so precious, that it becomes a matter of life and death in many instances."

and of a much darker color than natural; the diseased being mixed with the sound grain, is often eaten by whole families, and for a time without producing any detrimental effect, but finally the dry gangrene make its appearance, and the population of whole districts become afflicted with the disease.

But such aggravated form of gangrene, arising from the continued use of *secale cornutum*, is of much more frequent occurrence in European countries, particularly France, than in North America.

"The patients who have suffered from it, have experienced pain and heat with swelling, generally in the lower limbs, though occasionally in the upper. These symptoms abating, the parts became cold, insensible and discolored, and were gradually separated from the body. The disease attacked patients of both sexes and every age, did not appear to be infectious, and was frequently fatal."*

Canstatt, however, gives a much fuller description of gangrene caused by the internal use of secale; for this we may refer the student to Hartmann's Chronic Diseases, volume ii., pp. 152–153.

Treatment.—The medicines that are best adapted to the treatment of gangrene are—*Ars.*, *Chin.*, *Crot.*, *Lach.*, *Sec.-cor.*, *Silic.*, Acon., Bell., Carbo.-veg., Euphorb., Hell., Hyos., Sabina, Squill., Sulph.

Arsenicum has very many symptoms that belong to gangrene, and under its use in alternation with *carbo.-veg.*, we have seen senile gangrene subdued. This medicine corresponds to very many of the constitutional symptoms, and has the following local manifestations.

Numbness, stiffness and insensibility of the feet, with swelling and pain.

Coldness of the feet, with contracted pulse.

Swelling of the feet, with hot shining and burning red spots, and bluish blisters.

Hard—red—blue painful swelling, itching swelling, colorless

---

* Liston's Elements of Surgery, p. 40.

swelling of the malleoli, with tearing pains, which are relieved by external warmth.

The skin of the bottom of the feet is insensible, thick as leather, with rhagades.

The toes are stiff and do not allow him to tread.

Titillation and creeping, itching of the great toe.

Ulcerated and spreading blisters on the tips of the feet.

Parchment-like dryness, coldness and blueness of the skin.

Black blisters, with burning pain.

Discoloration of the nails.

Crotalus.—

Swelling of the feet with coldness.

Painful numbness of the toes, as after a cramp.

Swelling of the bitten leg, burning like fire.

Heat and intolerable gnawing of the feet.

Livid spots with frequent fainting fits and imperceptible pulse.

The swollen part is cold and painful to pressure.

Hot swellings, with cold skin and sickly appearance.

Insensibility of the swollen part.

Gangrene over the whole body.

The spot where the bite was inflicted looks black, with red dark circle, blackish redness of the sub-adjacent muscles and cellular tissue, and inflammation extending from the place of the bite to the pectoral muscle, where gangrenous spots are exhibited.

The skin where the bite has been inflicted becomes gangrenous and is separated from the muscles by a fetid fluid.

Lachesis.—

Gangrenous blisters.

Black-blue blisters, vesicles the size of a hazle nut, with violent itching and burning, as if the flesh would be torn from the bones.

Swelling and inflammation of the bitten limb, with violent pains, dry mouth, constant fever, dry skin, and constant thirst.

The lightly brown areola becomes bluish-black.

Gangrene of the bitten part, and gangrenous blisters.

Tingling in the toes, with heat and numbness.

Cracked skin between the toes, also deep rhagades.

Blue-red, large swelling of the leg and foot; prickings around the malleoli and calf, and aggravation of the swelling in the warmth.

Coldness of the feet also, as from ice.

Itching places on the tibia, with pain as if burnt, changing to painful spots after rubbing, with blue-red dark borders, and dry scurfs.

Tingling in the right tibia, from the knee to the dorsum of the foot and into the toes, with cold feet, and icy cold malleoli.

Secale-cor.—

The skin is dry and brittle, withering dry.

The skin all over the body looks lead-colored, the parts becoming shriveled and insensible, and not emitting a drop of blood on being cut into.

Burning in the skin as if a spark of fire had fallen on it.

Bloody blisters on the extremities, becoming gangrenous.

Black suppurating blisters.

Formication of the hands and feet.

Numbness, insensibility and coldness of the limbs.

The limbs become cold, pale and shriveled, as if they had been lying in warm water for a long time.

Gangrene of the limbs, the limbs becoming suddenly cold and lead-colored, and losing all their sensibility.

Gangrene, deadness and falling off of the limbs.

Pain, accompanied with slight swelling without inflammation, followed by coldness, blue color, gangrene and deadness of the limbs.

Numbness of the fingers and tips of the fingers.

Tingling sensation in the anterior portion of the thighs and calves, as if gone to sleep.

Gangrene of the feet up to the knees.

Gangrene of the lower limb, and spontaneous dropping off of the same.

In threatened traumatic gangrene, when there is violent synochal fever, of course *aconite* should be prescribed, and *calendula* in solution may be applied to the wounded part, or *arnica* diluted may be employed locally if there be but little solution of continuity. The former medicine has been highly recommended as a vulnerary, and it has been used with great success in Europe in all kinds of lacerated wounds; it has a powerful action over suppuration and its consequences, indeed its beneficial influence in wounds of all descriptions is remarkable. This subject, however, will be again alluded to, when treating of wounds.

Belladonna is also a very important remedy, and must be exhibited when the constitutional symptoms demand its exhibition, particularly when the patient complains of burning heat and unquenchable thirst, and especially if there be that characteristic trembling of the extremities, clouds and spots before the eyes, with dilated pupils. This medicine is useful in dry and humid gangrene.

China must be used when there has been profuse hemorrhage, which has greatly debilitated the patient. When there is coldness of the whole body, particularly of the extremities, with pale and clammy face, the parts around the wound becoming blue, swollen and soft. If there be gangrenous spots, with inability to swallow, hiccup, vomiting, *hyos.* may be administered; if typhoid symptoms present excessive prostration, *rhus-tox.* or *phosph.* should be exhibited.

Carbo.-veg. is indicated in some cases of humid gangrene, but from the general sphere of its action, it is especially serviceable in *gangrena senilis.* It has in its pathogenesis several symptoms that present themselves in the disease, and has been of much service practically in the treatment. *Euphorbium* is also useful in the gangrene of old persons.

Silic. and *Sulph.* are also important medicines in both forms of gangrene, and perhaps with *Arsen.*, *Crotalus*, *Lachesis*, *Secale-cor.*, and also *Carbo.-veg.*, and *Solanam nigrum*, are the most useful medicines for the treatment of gangrene as occurring in old persons.

It may be useful also, in this affection, to wrap the feet or other parts affected in *carded wool.* This practice is recommended by Sir B. Brodie in his Lectures on Mortification, and is mentioned by Mr. S. Cooper in his "First Lines." There have been several cases treated successfully by this method,* and no doubt these means may assist in maintaining the warmth of the part, while by the proper administration of medicine the cause upon which the disease depends may be removed.

The following medicines have also been recommended—*Chinin., Merc., Mur.-ac., Plumb., Sabin, Scill., Sulph.-ac., Tart.*

CHAPTER V.

VARIETIES OF INFLAMMATION.

Section 1.—Erysipelas.

Erysipelas is an inflammatory affection, accompanied with fever, which, together with drowsiness, is generally present a few days before the attack; the latter symptom disappearing when the disease is fully established.

The inflammation is generally confined to the epidermis, which becomes hot, red and swollen, and sometimes covered with blisters, (erysipelas bullosum,) but in very violent cases, the deeper seated tissues are affected, and the disease is termed phlegmonous erysipelas. Every part of the body is liable to be attacked, although the face, legs and feet are most frequently affected.

Erysipelas does not often attack persons before the age of puberty; it is a disease of advanced life, and is more frequently encountered among females than males, particularly those of a sanguine, irritable temperament.

* See a paper "On the Treatment of Gangrena Senilis," by Henry S. Taylor, Esq., Surgeon, Guildford.—London Lancet, Nov. 1845, p. 443.

In some individuals, there appears to exist a predisposition to the disease. In other instances it returns periodically, attacking the patient once or twice a year, and sometimes oftener, thereby greatly exhausting strength.

Erysipelas is occasioned by the several causes that are liable to excite inflammation; such as injuries of all kinds, the external application of acrid substances to the skin, exposure to cold, obstructed perspiration, suppressed evacuations, &c., &c. The disease also appears to be under certain circumstances epidemic, caused by a peculiar state of the atmosphere, and this is frequently the case in crowded ships or in hospitals.

In slight cases, when the extremities are attacked, this disease makes its appearance with roughness, pain, heat and redness of the skin, which becomes pale when the finger is pressed upon it, but immediately returns to its former color when the pressure is removed. There also prevails a slight febrile disposition, and the patient is rather hot and thirsty. If the attack is mild, these symptoms will continue for a day or two, when the surface of the affected part assumes a yellowish tinge, the cuticle may separate in small scales, and the patient experience no further inconvenience; but if the attack is severe, and the symptoms of high inflammation are present, there will be intense throbbing pain in the head, pain in the back, great heat, thirst and restlessness; the affected part will swell, the pulse become frequent, and either hard and tense, or it may be small and rebounding; and about the fourth day, a number of small vesicles make their appearance, containing a limpid, or in some cases a yellowish fluid. In unfavorable cases, these blisters have sometimes degenerated into obstinate ulcers, which have assumed a gangrenous character. This, however, does not happen frequently, for though the surface of the skin and the bullæ may assume a bluish, or even a blackish tinge, yet such appearances generally disappear, together with the other symptoms of the complaint.

The appearance of these vesicles is not always present in an attack of erysipelas, and when they do show themselves, the period of their eruption is very uncertain.

The trunk is also attacked with erysipelas, but less frequently than the extremities; but infants a few days after birth, may be affected in this manner, the genital organs being generally involved.

When erysipelas attacks the face, the premonitory manifestations are chilliness, succeeded by heat, thirst, restlessness, glistening eyes, coated tongue, redness of the cheeks and other febrile symptoms; and when the disease attacks this portion of the body, there is drowsiness, or a tendency to coma or delirium, and the pulse is very frequent and full. At the end of two or three days a scarlet redness appears on some parts of the face, which may extend to the scalp, and then gradually down the neck, leaving tumefaction in every part occupied by the redness. When the swelling and redness have continued for a time, blisters varying in size, and containing a thin, colorless and sometimes acrid liquor, arise on the face, which becomes turgid and swollen, and the eyelids are sometimes swelled to such a degree, that the patient for the time is deprived of sight. The fever sometimes becomes less when the inflammation is established, but in the majority of cases it increases as the latter extends, and unless checked by the appropriate means, may continue for the space of eight or ten days. If such is the case, the coma and delirium increase greatly, and the patient may be destroyed between the seventh and eleventh day. If the attack be mild the inflammatory symptoms subside gradually, and the disease terminates in a few days.

Erysipelas of the face is more dangerous than when other portions of the body are attacked, because there is a tendency of the inflammation to attack the brain. The prognosis is unfavorable if the fever assume a malignant type, or when there is theatenened metastasis to internal noble organs.

Treatment.—The medicines that are most serviceable in erysipelas, are *Acon., Bell., Bry., Euphorb., Puls., Rhus-t., Sulph.*

Acon.—In simple erysipelas, with the ordinary fever and other accompanying symptoms, this remedy will frequently be sufficient to arrest the disease, without the administration of any other medicine; it is also of great service when in violent cases there is intense synochal fever, but *belladonna* is more preferable in many cases, where there is coma, delirium, flushed cheeks, throbbing carotids, where the swelling is tense, and there is present a stinging or shooting pain, increased by contact or at night, when the erysipelas extends in rays, and there appears to be a disposition of the inflammation to attack the deeper seated tissues, (*erysipelas phlegmonodes.*) In a majority of cases, *acon.* in the commencement of the disease, and *bella.* exhibited when the affection has fairly set in, will be sufficient to complete the cure.

Bryonia may be employed, in cases in which the affection attacks the joints, when there are drawing, tearing pains, increased by motion.

Euphorb.—This is suited to erysipelas of the head and face, with digging, boring and gnawing pains, followed when ameliorated by creeping and itching of the part. When there is considerable swelling and the vesicles are small, the fluid rather yellowish than white, and a considerable amount of heat, this medicine is also indicated.

Pulsatilla is indicated when the erysipelas shifts from one place to another, (*erysipelas erraticum,*) and when the hue of the skin is less intense, and there are shooting pains. This medicine should also be recollected when the disease affects the ear. Hartmann remarks, "pulsatilla is never indicated in pure erysipelas of the face, except when accompanied with stitches, in which case the disease is apt to go to the brain; this can be more effectually prevented by *belladonna* than by pulsatilla."

Rhus-tox.—This is the principal medicine for vesicular erysipelas, it is also indicated in erysipelas where there is extensive œdema, or where there is a tendency to metastasis of the disease to the brain; *rhus radicans* has been very highly extolled for facial erysipelas, as has been also *graphites* and *hepar*, but of course there must be corresponding symptoms to indicate their use.

According to *Reissig*, *nux vom.* is well adapted to this disease when it attacks the knees or feet, when there is intense pain and bright red swelling.*

If there be a tendency to metastasis to the brain, *cuprum acet.* is an extremely valuable medicine, as the author has had opportunity of witnessing. Dr. Schmid of Vienna, also corroborates this statement.

Belladonna and *rhus-tox.* are adapted to that form of this disease which is found in hospitals. The erysipelas partakes of the phlegmonous character, and therefore the former remedy would perhaps be the preferable. If the disease assume a gangrenous form, the vesicles become dark and blackish, with prostration, dry skin, frequent but easily quenchable thirst, *arsen.* should be administered, or perhaps *carbo-veg.* may also be indicated in *erysipelas gangrenosa,* particularly if there be night and morning sweats, excessive prostration and disposition to typhoid symptoms.

Rhus should also be remembered, and administered if suitable for such a condition. If there be a disposition to ulceration, *sulph., hepar, graph., silic.,* are important medicines.†

Section 2.—Boil—Furunculus.

A boil is a prominent, hard, red and circumscribed tumor, very often extremely painful, and though terminating in suppu-

* "I had a case of Erysipelas where the disease re-appeared frequently, always on one side of the face only, and where every attack was preceded for several days by a violent cardialgia. A single dose of *nux vom.* 15, effected a permanent cure, showing that accompanying symptoms often indicate a different remedy, from what are generally considered specifics for Erysipelas. In such cases *Sulphur* might likewise be resorted to, particularly when a throbbing, stinging pain is experienced in the swelling." *Hartmann's Acute Diseases,* vol. ii., p. 39.

† There have been many interesting cases of erysipelas reported in the Homœopathic Periodicals of the day. One of the best can be found in the British Journal of Homœopathy, vol. vi., p 532.

ration, the process by which the pus is formed is frequently of long duration. The inflammation is of the sthenic type, affecting the skin and areolar tissue ; the latter becoming disorganized, constitutes what is termed the *core* of a boil.

A common furuncle differs from a carbuncle, because the latter is asthenic, not only constitutionally but locally, the life of the patient being often endangered by the disease, while a boil is sthenic in itself, is generally indicated by a robust and plethoric temperament, and is in most instances free from fever or any constitutional disturbance. The cases in which fever, &c., may be expected, are those in which the tumor is large and situated on a sensitive part, or when a number of these swellings appear at the same time in different places. A carbuncle contains no core, and has several openings for the exit of sloughs.

As suppuration progresses in the tumor, the apex of the cone becomes yellowish, and surrounding this, the hardness of the swelling disappears, though still the base is firm and unyielding. The pus is superficial, the slough or core being at the base.

According to Richerand, the origin of boils depends upon a disordered state of the gastric organs ; this is frequently the predisposing, while the exciting cause may be a prick, a scratch, or some other slight irritation. Constitutional irregularity, however, is, in very many instances, sufficient in itself to produce this variety of inflammation.

Boils may appear in any part of the cellular tissue, and are mostly found among young plethoric individuals, or in those persons who are given to high living and suffer from dyspepsia. Some individuals appear to be particularly liable to the formation of furuncle, and the hips and buttocks are frequently the seat of the disease; it is in this locality that they are extremely vexatious, as the afflicted mortal can neither sit with comfort, or walk without pain, which is occassioned when the muscles are rendered tense, and, moreover, the individual is constantly kept in a ferment of anxiety and suffering, consequent upon the frequent blows that are invariably, unaccountably and inadvertently inflicted upon the tender and painful tumor.

A boil, after suppuration is complete, bursts at its apex, and the purulent secretion is discharged, after which, the pain, heat and swelling subside, but unless the slough is also extracted, the part may remain in a sub-acute inflammatory condition, the disorganized tissue acting as any other mechanical irritation.

Treatment.—The Homœopathic treatment of boils is very efficacious; indeed the careful practitioner can frequently administer prophylactic medicines to those in whom there is a tendency to this variety of inflammation, thereby saving the patient from great inconvenience and a considerable amount of pain.

In the treatment of furuncle a poultice is never required; well selected and properly administered medicines, being sufficient to accomplish the cure. There is naturally existing in the minds of the older portion of the community, whether physicians or laymen, a favorable predisposition in regard to the application of a poultice. Those who have been born, bred and habituated to the application of such means for almost every variety of local inflammation, cannot without some hesitation resign the adjuvants; but experience teaches, that patients *are* cured as speedily, and in most instances more radically, of such inflammation, by Homœopathic medicines, than by purging the patient with drastics, "touching the liver" by means of mercury, and enveloping the tumor with a poultice of mush, oatmeal, flaxseed or slippery elm.

The medicines that are mostly applicable in the treatment of boils, are *Arn.*, *Bell.*, *Calc.*, *Hep.*, *Lyc.*, *Phos.*, *Sulph.*, or *Alum*, *Ant.-c.*, *Led.*, *Merc.*, *Mur.-ac.*, *Nit.-ac.*, *Nux-vom.*, *Sep.*, *Thuj.*

To eradicate the disposition to boils, the medicines are *Calc.*, *Lyc.*, *Nux-vom.*, *Phos.* and *Sulph.*

If the boils are large, *Hepar*, *Lyc.*, *Nit-ac.*, *Sil.* or *Hyos.*, *Phosph.*, *Tart.-e.*

If small, *Arn.*, *Bell.*, *Sulph.*, *Zinc.*

If suppuration progress slowly, *Merc.* will hasten the formation of matter.

When there are *stinging* pains in the boil the medicine is *Nux-vom.*

When there is troublesome itching, *Carb-veg.* or *Thuja*, the latter particularly when the redness extends to some distance around.

If the pain is *lancinating*, *Calc.-carb.* If the pain is stinging, when the boil is touched, *Lyc.* If this be present during motion, *Mur.-ac.*

If *burning*, *Colocynth.*

If there is *burning* pain extending to some distance around, *Antim.-crud.*

There are also many other remedies mentioned for boils, appearing on the different parts of the body, but it is probable that if the above symptoms are present, the medicines will relieve, without regard to locality. However, the student is referred to the symptomen codex, to ascertain the particular situation of the boil, if the treatment above recommended has been unsuccessful.

Section 3.—*Anthrax—Carbuncle.*

A carbuncle is, in some respects, analagous to a furuncle, though the former is much more dangerous, the inflammation being more extensive and gangrenous in character.

The tumor is deep seated, hard and circumscribed, and rapidly advances, becoming livid and attended with severe burning or lancinating pain. The inflammation, as has been before stated, is of the asthenic type, and attacks the skin and sub-adjacent areolar tissue.

As the inflammatory process progresses, the tumor becomes soft, of a purple hue, and spongy; suppuration, ulceration and sloughing of the cellular tissue supervenes, and numerous small apertures form in the skin, through which a thin saneous pus is discharged, together with the disintegrated areolar tissue. This condition is one of the most important diagnostic signs between anthrax and common boil, for in the latter, however large, there is but a single opening.

The usual situation of carbuncle is the back, from the nape of the neck to the pelvis, though any portion of the body may be attacked. The size varies from that of a chestnut to that of the palm of the hand, the constitutional symptoms, when the tumor is large, being dangerous in the extreme.

The fever, primarily, is simple, or may be bilious in its character; but as the disease progresses, typhoid symptoms make their appearance and increase, and as the occult gangrene extends, prostration becomes more extreme, and hiccup, delirium, coma, and even death may ensue.

The swelling is generally flat, bluish and spongy, only slightly elevated above the surrounding skin, and in most instances circular, and circumscribed by a distinct line of demarcation, which, as in other sloughs, indicates the separation of the dead from the living tissues.

Carbuncles are most common in advanced life, although they may be seen in young persons, especially among those who have been accustomed to hardships or severe privations. It is also encountered in adults who indulge in the excesses of the table, or who have debilitated their constitutions by a life of debauchery.

The medicines for carbuncle are, *Arsen.*, *Bell.*, *Chin.*, *Hyos.*, *Acid.-mur.*, *Acid.-nit.*, *Rhus*, *Secal.-cor.*, *Silic.*

Arsenicum is indicated, when the burning in the seat of the carbuncle is intense, and when this symptom is present for some distance around the tumor, or when there is a sensation in the swelling as though boiling water was running beneath the integument, when the pulse is small, irregular and frequent, and there is cold perspirations. It is also adapted to individuals of a nervous, choleric temperament, who have been reduced by long sufferings; when there is emaciation, vomiting of fluids, burning thirst, or bilious diarrhœa.

Belladonna.—When the cerebral symptoms are well developed, red face, shining eyes, severe heat—when the parts around the carbuncle have a tendency to erysipelatous inflammation. Dr. Pardo thinks *bell.* is best adapted in the transition from gangrene to sphacelus.

China is recommended by Dr. Pardo, "when the asthenic character of the disease is particularly well marked, with symptoms of a febris putrida, the more so when the patient is leucophlegmatic and much reduced by loss of blood, or if the carbuncle develop itself under the influence of swamp miasms."

Hyos. is particularly serviceable when the disease is present in nervous or hysterical individuals; when there is coma-vigil or great restlessness, caused by excessive nervous excitement, shaking of the head in all directions, optical illusions, constriction of pharynx, when there is itching around the part.

Mur.-ac. is said to be the main remedy, when the carbuncle appears in scorbutic individuals, with ulcers on the gums, and if in addition to the local symptoms, there be a feeling of emptiness in the stomach and abdomen; frequent desire to urinate with profuse emission of clear urine.

Rhus-tox.—When there is burning itching around the carbuncle, with vertigo as if one were about to fall, stupor, pale face, disfigured and convulsed; pointed nose, sanguineous or serous frothy diarrhœa.

Lachesis or *Kreosote* may also prove serviceable in this disease.

Calcarea Muriatica has also been employed by Rademacher with great success.

Dr. Pardo * and Dr. Victor de Iturralde † mention several cases of carbuncle, that were cured by Homœopathic treatment; the medicines employed were *ars.*, *bell.* and *silic.* The latter named gentleman used chiefly *bell.*, and after relating his success, he remarks: "The irritability under the usual treatment was great; by Homœopathic treatment, however, nine-tenths less."

Incisions are requisite, and must be employed in those cases of carbuncle, in which ulceration has advanced and sloughs have formed. In many instances, however, by the proper administration of the Homœopathic medicines, the inflammation is dispersed, and suppuration and ulceration either limited or prevented. But when there are many openings and large sloughs, the bis-

---

* Bulletin Official de la Soc. Hahnemann, vol. ii., No. 12, 1848.

† Loc. cit., vol. ii., No. 1, 1847.

toury must be freely used. The apertures should all be made to connect by the requisite division of the parts, or the whole tumor may be opened by a crucial incision. Such means must be resorted to, together with the exhibition of the proper Homœpathic remedy, if we wish to succeed in the treatment of disease. The use of incision is obvious; it evacuates purulent formation, affords exit to the tenacious slough, and prevents infiltration, from which the most serious results have ensued.

Section 4.—Pernio—Chilblain.

Pernio is an inflammatory affection, usually the secondary effect of cold, caused by heat and circulation being prematurely restored. It is commonly met with in the extreme parts of the body, as the fingers, toes, heels, ears and nose; as these are not only habitually exposed to cold, but also are of comparatively weak circulation, and consequently of low power.

The skin is at first pale and presents a somewhat shriveled appearance, but this is in a short time succeeded by tumefaction and dark redness, with a sensation of heat and intense itching. The swelling also, sometimes cracks, and bleeds, and there is a tendency to ulceration.

These are usually the presenting symptoms in ordinary chilblain; however, if the disease advances, the skin assumes a purplish cast, the tingling, burning and itching become intolerable, and vesicles form, which contain a serous fluid; these do not desquamate in the ordinary manner, but burst, and disclose beneath a painful and ill-conditioned sore, that discharges a thin watery fluid; this ulcer is often slow to heal, and may assume the character of an irritable or indolent sore, which is generally superficial, but may become gangrenous, or may penetrate to a considerable depth, involving tendons or bone.

The milder form of the complaint—that unattended with ulceration—is of frequent occurrence in this climate during the winter season. It particularly appears on the feet of those who have been compelled to stand or labor in the snow, which melting, penetrates through the leather of the shoe or boot, thus wetting the feet, which are often imprudently held near a warm fire, and allowed to dry; this premature restoration of heat engenders the affection.

Chilblains often disappear spontaneously in the summer, but return again in the winter season, generally attacking those parts that have previously suffered.

This affection is also very liable to occur in those individuals afflicted with dyspepsia or other disease which renders extreme circulation imperfect.

The medicines for chilblains are—*agar.*, *arn.*, *ars.*, *bry.*, *bell.*, *carbo-a.*, *kali-c.*, *lyc.*, *nit.-ac*, *nux-vom.*, *petr.*, *phosph.*, *puls.*, *sulph.*, *zinc.-met.*

Agaricus is of great service, when the itching is *very intense*, and accompanied with burning. This medicine is frequently sufficient to cure the affection, and allays the *itching* in a short time.

Arnica "is a certain remedy when the inflammation of the chilblain is caused by pressure, friction," &c.*

Arsen. should be used if the vesicles appear or become blackish, and there is tendency to gangrene, or *china* may be prescribed under such circumstances if other symptoms correspond; it is particularly indicated if humid gangrene should have set in; *opium* also, may sometimes be indicated.

Kali-carb, for inflamed chilblains with aching, or with cutting pains.

Nit.-ac. when there is much itching with swelling and pain. *Petrol.* and *phosph.* are also very serviceable when the suffering is intense.

Nux-vom. is indicated when the inflammation is superficial, with bright red swelling, with burning itching, or when the tumefied part cracks and bleeds readily.

Puls. must be administered if the swelling is bluish, hot and attended with throbbing pains, particularly if the patient is of a gentle or phlegmatic disposition. *Bell.* may also be indi-

* See Hartman's Acute Diseases, vol. ii., p. 41.

cated in this form of chilblain, if the disposition of the individual is sad and indifferent, though at times vehement.

Rhus-tox., "when there is burning itching in the afternoon and evening; when not scratching there is a pricking in the chilblain, obliging him to scratch; blotches after scratching."

Sulph. is suitable when there is redness and swelling with a tendency to suppuration, and also "for thick red chilblain on the finger, itching during warmth, also painful."

Zinc.-met.—"Chilblains on the hand, itching and swelling violently."*

Nit.-acid and *petroleum* have been recommended when the inflammation sets in with very cold weather.

For "chilblains on the feet, with pain and redness during the summer season," *antim. crud.*

Section 5.—Burns and Scalds.

The practitioner is frequently called upon to treat injuries that have resulted from the application of heated solids or fluids to the skin. Sometimes the danger to the system is slight, but at others, when the heated matter has come in contact with a large surface, the prognosis is very unfavorable. By the term scald is understood the effect of heated fluids, when applied to any portion of the body, while the consequences of hot solids or ignited combustibles, are termed burns. The latter class is in the generality of instances the most serious, although the former, though not injuring the skin deeply, gives rise to very alarming symptoms, when a large extent of surface is involved.

A slight degree of heat, is only productive of a sharp hot pain, with redness of the surface, and these may both subside without any other unpleasant symptoms, but in very many instances effusion of serum immediately takes place beneath the cuticle. In other cases the cutis may be destroyed by the

---

* See Mat. Med., vol. ii., pp. 690, 924, 1033. Ibid. vol. i., p. 121.

intensity of the heat. Parts also that at first do not present appearances of any very serious injury, may afterwards be involved, perish, and be cast off as a slough. The surrounding textures also have their vitality diminished, and when they come to be the seat of the inflammatory process, are unable to sustain the increased action, and from the want of corresponding power sloughing very often ensues.

Burns on the trunk and genital organs are very serious and productive of the most disastrous results, and extensive injuries of this kind, no matter in what portion of the body, are much to be dreaded. The constitutional symptoms are often well marked; they are, great sinking of the vital powers, (which generally is present immediately after the reception of the injury,) shivering, weakness, cold extremities, anxiety, vomiting. And these may be readily accounted for, when it is remembered what an important office is fulfilled by the texture that is in almost every instance the first to be implicated.

The classification of burns has been differently proposed by various authors Dr. Thompson* arranges them,

1st. Into such as produce an inflammation of the cutaneous texture; but an inflammation, which, if it be not improperly treated, almost always manifests a tendency to resolution.

2d. Into burns, which injure the vital powers of the cutis, occasion the separation of the cuticle, and produce suppuration on the surface of the cutaneous texture.

3d. Into burns, in which the vitality and organization of a greater or less portion of the cutis, is either immediately or subsequently destroyed, and a soft slough or hard eschar produced.

Pearson also names three varieties, and his arrangement is approved and followed by Dr. Gibson, viz:

1st, *superficial;* 2d, *ulcerated;* 3d, *carbunculous.*

The best classification, however, is that of Dupuytren, which is recommended by Dr. Henriques.† He divides burns into six degrees.

---

* Lectures on Inflammation.

† See British Journal, vol. xi., p. 97.

The first occurs when a small quantity of caloric has been applied for a short space of time, which determines simply a greater or less degree of inflammation of the skin, and resembling much, simple erysipelas.

In the second degree, there is not only cutaneous irritation or augmented organic action, but there is also vesication or the formation of bladders more or less considerable, which resemble strikingly the blisters of very acute vesicular erysipelas.

The third degree is characterized by disorganization of the dermoid tissue, and its conversion into a hard, black and dry slough.

In the fourth degree, both the dermoid and sub-cutaneous tissues are completely disorganized.

The fifth degree comprises those only in which there is disorganization of the skin and all the subjacent tissues, except the osseous; and in the sixth, there is carbonization of the osseous tissue, as well as of the surrounding soft parts.

From the fact, says Dr. Henriques,* that caloric does not act with the same degreee of intensity upon the whole burnt surface, it will readily be understood that only the first degree can occur alone, and that two or more degrees will be found in all other cases of burns. This is admirably illustrated in the application of the moxa; where it will be found, at the part where the heat is immediately applied, the skin diseased and gangrenous; whilst simple inflammation will be present around the edges of the slough, which gradually diminishes, the inflammation assuming the figures of concentric circles.

The dangers of this form of injury are various, says Mr. Miller, even to a greater extent than wounds, they are not mere causalities happening to a part. 1. The system receives a shock, which, when the injury is extensive and severe, or when it involves an important part, may terminate the patient's life by syncopé. 2. Imperfect or nervous reaction may result to an excessive and uncontrollable degree, the patient sinking exhausted under febrile tumult of the asthenic kind at an early

---

* Loc. cit.

period. Sometimes a deceptive lull precedes this form of reaction. An elderly patient, badly burned, may walk to the hospital, and yet die in forty-eight hours afterward. 3. Or reaction of the sthenic type proves excessive, and under the violence of inflammatory fever, life may be endangered. 4. During the progress of inflammatory fever, the internal organs, more especially the lungs, are apt to suffer, seriously complicating the case. At a more advanced period, fatal diseases of the intestinal mucous coat, may occur. 5. More remotely tedious cicatrization, confinement, and discharge are prone to peril the system by hectic. Death escaped, life may be rendered miserable, by the deformity and impairment of function often inseparable from the healing of the burn.

It will be clearly evident from the above, that an extensive burn is an extremely dangerous accident, and one, from which, though the patient may ultimately recover, may leave deformity, perhaps remaining for life, or only capable of removal by painful and extensive operation.

The indications for the treatment of burns are—

1st. To allay the intensity of the pain.

2d. To arrest the internal reactionary effects.

3d. To prevent deformity.

The above indications are fulfilled in Homœopathic Therapeutics, by external appliances, and internal remedial agents. The most appropriate external applications are, *arnica*, *canth.*, *urtica-urens*. The injured parts should be washed, first, with a lotion of ten drops of the mother tincture of either of the above mentioned remedies, and half a pint of French pale brandy;* after which the whole affected surface must be enveloped by thick layers of carded cotton, which not only totally protect the part from atmospheric air, but also appear to possess a specific action on injuries of this class. The value of this application was discovered accidentally by a lady living in

* This treatment is taken from a paper by Dr. Henriques, on the "Homœopathic Treatment of Burns." British Journal of Homœopathy, vol. xi., p. 100.

Harford County, Maryland, whose child was scalded by boiling water, over nearly its whole body. The mother was carding cotton in an adjoining room at the time of the accident, and having no medical assistance within reach, undressed the child as quickly as possible, and covered the whole burnt surface with masses of cotton. The effect was wonderful; for the child soon became perfectly quiet, fell asleep, and upon removing the cotton a few hours afterwards, no inflammation whatever could be perceived.*

When the epidermis is destroyed, as in burns of the third degree, the best mode of preventing suppuration, and of promoting the reproduction of the cutis, is by penciling the injured parts with arnicated collodion; and protecting the parts from the external air with thick layers of carded cotton, as in former instances. In burns of the fourth, fifth and sixth degree, when there is considerable loss of substance, a solution of *calendula* or *crocus* is the best application.

In order to remedy constitutional disturbances, which always occur with more or less intensity and gravity, the best remedies are, in the first instances, *opium*, *arnica*, *coffea*, *carbo-veg*.

Opium is indicated principally in children, who frequently show a disposition to convulsions and other spasmodic affections from the feelings of fright, which this accident produces in the extreme nervous susceptibility natural to this age.

Arnica is useful in all cases and ages to allay the extreme sensibility of the whole body, the general restlessness and intense pain in the seat of injury.

Coffea is necessary to promote sleep and allay nervous excitement.

Carbo-veg. is peculiarly adapted to those extreme cases formerly alluded to, in which the pain is so excessive as to threaten the complete extinction of life.

When excessive reaction takes place, and there is dry, burning heat of the skin, with thirst, head hot and painful, face red, pulse hard, frequent and contracted, *aconite* is the medicine

* See Gibson's Institutes and Practice of Surgery, vol. i., p. 72.

indicated. Should suppuration take place, and the discharge be so great as to impair the constitution, it will be necessary to administer *hepar sulphuris*, and *china*, to combat its morbid effects. *Causticum* and *calcerea carbonica* may sometimes be indicated in such cases.

To favor the sloughing of eschars, and to promote healthy granulation and cicatrization in the most severe cases of burns, either *arsenicum*, *nit.-ac.*, *lachesis*, *rhus-tox.* or *secale cor.*, may be required, according to the totality of symptoms present in any given case.

In explaining the variety of lesions which caloric produces, it has been stated, that the second degree was characterized by the separation of the epidermis and the formation of blisters. It is important to bear in mind that, in removing the clothes from the injured parts, we must be careful not to tear away the epidermis, because it would greatly increase the sufferings of the patient, from the exposure of the raw surface to the irritating influence of the atmospheric air; if the blisters are intact, it will be advisable to prick them with a fine needle, and allow the serum to escape; after which recourse must be had to the remedies.

The third and last indication of which it is necessary to speak, relates to the formation of abnormal adherences, which burns frequently produce; this is a most important point in the treatment of these injuries, because they not only produce deformity, but also impede the free motion of parts where they occur; and sometimes prevent the exercise of an important function.

In some instances, no matter how judicious the treatment, this most disagreeable and unfortunate result cannot be prevented. It is a natural consequence of the contractive force of the inodulary or cicatrizing tissue. In order to avoid it, however, the process of cicatrization must be carefully and constantly watched, and so regulated that the *cicatrix may have the same extent of surface as the original skin that has been destroyed;* and in preventing it from being formed by the drawing together of the edges of the surrounding skin; this can be effected, first, by the administration of appropriate medicines, when the granulations are unhealthy; second, by the proper position of the injured part; third, by the method of dressing the wound; fourth, by the use of fitting mechanical apparatus; fifth, by specific dynamic agents internally administered. Notwithstanding all these means, should we fail in preventing deformity, there is still a resource in operative surgery, which will certainly relieve the patient.

When the process of cicatrization is accompanied by excessive inflammatory action of the surrounding edges, either *ars.*, *hepar*, *merc.*, *nit.-ac.*, *phosph.*, *ruta.* or *silicea* will be found useful, according to the particular indications of the special case. When the granulations appear luxuriant or excessive, *alum*, *sep.*, *thuja*, are indicated. When cicatrization is interrupted by excessive suppuration, the most appropriate remedies are *asaf.*, *caust.*, *hepar*, *merc.*, *puls.*, *rhus.*, *silic.* or *sepia.* When the ulcerated surface bleeds, the remedies most indicated are *arn.*, *ars.*, *creos.*, *crocus*, *phos.-ac.* or *secale-cor.*

The external application of soap (not the Emplastrum Saponis of the Allopathic Pharmacopœia) is recommended by Homœopathic physicians. A thick lather should be made of Castile soap with water, several coatings of which should be applied, the first being allowed to dry before others are laid on. The application of cotton, however, is preferable.

CHAPTER VI.

WOUNDS.

Wounds are solutions of continuity in any texture of the body, occasioned by violence. This definition includes not only the most extensive laceration or incision, but also the slightest contusion or abrasion.

Surgeons have arranged these injuries under the following heads: *Incised*, *punctured*, *contused*, *lacerated*, *poisoned* and *gun-shot*, and these have been subdivided into *wounds* of the *head*, *face*, *neck*, *thorax*, *abdomen* and *extremities*.

There are certain wounds that are not confined to the soft parts, but affect even the bones ; sabre-wounds are of this variety, as they frequently separate at once, both a part of the scalp and the subjacent portion of the skull. Many wounds of the head, thorax and abdomen, injure the organs contained in those cavities ; in short, the degree of danger and variety of wounds depend on the extent of the injury, the kind of instrument inflicting the wound, the size and importance of the blood vessels that have been injured, the situation and texture of the affected part, and the age and constitution of the patient.

Injuries of this kind involving large joints, blood vessels and nerves, are considered as the most dangerous, although a very slight wound, under unfavorable circumstances, may be productive of the most violent symptoms, and even death.

The constitutional effects of a wound are in proportion to its magnitude, but this will also depend greatly upon the nature of the parts injured. In severe wounds, it generally happens that the whole system for a time is excessively prostrated, there is more or less insensibility, sickness or vomiting, quick, small pulse, cold, clammy skin, slow respiration, and if the patient has any command of speech, the voice is very feeble. This condition is termed by surgeons the *stage of collapse*, and supervenes not only upon injuries, but also upon many operations which the surgeon is called upon to perform.

" The treatment of wounds (writes Croserio) depends on the *nature of the tissue injured, the part wounded, the nature and form of the lesion, the circumstances which accompanied it, and the condition and constitution of the patient.*

" In studying the pathogenetic effects of *arnica montana*, we find nearly all the general and local symptoms of sensation, and even the physical symptoms, such as ecchymosis, etc., which result from mechanical violence to the living body ; such as *vertigo*, so that one is like to fall ; *heaviness of the head ; loss of memory ; varied pains in the head ; ringing in the ears ; dilated pupils ; swelling of the nose ; epistaxis ; the head is so heavy he cannot support it ; coagula of blood from the vagina ; pains like those of a luxation ; sundering pains ;*

shocks and blows in the body like electricity ; breaking pains in all the limbs, etc. It is not surprising, therefore, that Hahnemann regarded it as the special specific in wounds, and restored it to the honored and merited title, entirely forgotten by modern physicians, of *panacea lapsorum*, which Fehr had given it two hundred years before, although the symptoms which are manifested in the wounds of certain tissues and organs, in certain circumstances, are better represented in the pathogeny of other remedies, such as *rhus toxicodendron, aconite, symphytum officinale, sulphuric acid, causticum*, etc., which, consequently, are more appropriate in such cases. I will review briefly the different conditions of wounds, in order to point out the most appropriate medicines, and the method of their administration.

"Wounds of parts, the base of which is the cellular membrane, the skin, the mucous membranes, the muscles, and the serous membranes, require *arnica*. If the wound is small and superficial, requiring but a day or two for its recovery, external application of the remedy is sufficient ; but in more grave cases, it must be given internally at the same time. If there be a solution of continuity of the skin, the wound should be covered with a pledget of lint, dipped in the pure tincture of *arnica*, which should be renewed morning and evening, for five or six days, and then be replaced by a large compress, dipped in a solution of a single drop of the tincture in an ounce of fresh water ; which has the double advantage of keeping the skin of the wounded part cool, and maintaining the specific action of the remedy. The compress should be dipped in the solution as often as it becomes dry. If the skin remains undivided, the pledget may give place to simple frictions of the part, with the same tincture. It is necessary to give careful attention to subjects with a fine, sensitive skin ; that the external application be not continued too long ; for it may produce irritations or eruptions on the part, which are removed with difficulty. The Count de V., an old man, of nervous temperament, fair complexion, and fine skin, after a fall by which he received a severe blow on the patella, followed by an extremely painful swelling, made application of the pure tincture of *arnica* to the parts, and the desire of a rapid recovery induced him to renew the dressing several times a day, with an excessive quantity of the tincture. After the fifth day of its use, red and painful pimples, like the eruption of *variola*, appeared on the knee, and the hand employed in the friction; and although the remedy was discontinued, the eruption soon covered the whole hand, and extended to all the parts which had been touched with the tincture. In a few days, the pimples overran the whole lower extremities, even to the soles of the feet, and then extended to the abdomen, back, arms, scalp, in a word, the whole surface of the body was covered with a copious eruption like distinct small-pox. It was not accompanied by fever, or any symptoms which would warrant the suspicion of eruptive fever; although the patient was of a gouty diathesis, and had many chronic symptoms, which revealed a psoric taint, still the order of its appearance left no room for doubt as to the origin of this phenomenon, viz., the dynamic action of *arnica*. His cure was long and difficult. Antidotes to *arnica* were of no avail. *Sulphur* and other antipsorics were alone of service. This case has made me cautious in the application of the tincture of *arnica*. After four or five days, I dilute it with a quantity of water; more or less, according to the sensibility of the skin. If the wound be deep or extensive, or if there be reason to suspect a dynamic action on the tissue of the part wounded, or on other parts, *arnica* should be immediately administered internally, and repeated as often as may be necessary, for an interval of two or three days. If the injury has been attended with circumstances calculated to excite terror, as a fall, and if it be recent, it will be well to administer first a dose of *aconite*, and an hour after, *arnica*.

"Wounds in tissues of great sensibility, as of the nerves, or in tissues very susceptible of inflammation, require *aconite*, and when they are very painful, and accompanied with inflammation, even without fever; and especially, if there be fever, they should always be combated with *aconite* before the use of *arnica*, if indeed this last be at all necessary.

"Wounds which are not kept open by accidental causes, such as the movement of the parts, foreign bodies, or a great alteration of tissue, and which are not healed in the time which their extent would seem to require, suggest the presence of psoric taint in the constitution. In such cases, if, after one or two doses of *arnica*, there is no amendment, I give *sulphur* 30, every five days, till I perceive some effect from it; I then leave it to exhaust its action, and ordinarily the cure is effected without any other remedy, or *arnica* may then prove efficacious.

"Fibrous tissues, as the tendons and ligaments, require *rhus toxicodendron*, 30, internally administered, especially if the wounded parts have suffered violent tension, as in sprains, luxations, or muscular efforts; and at the same time, the remedy may be externally employed. *Rhus* vi., 9th, in three ounces of water. This remedy is often of surprising efficacy in injuries of ancient date. The lady of a superior officer of the 66th regiment of the line, in garrison at Metz, was confined to her pallet by a sprain received three months ago. All allopathic means employed for her relief had proved fruitless. I sent her *rhus* 30, to be dissolved in eight tablespoonfuls of water, a spoonful to be taken every morning. She immediately experienced the best results; was able to walk about her room the first day, and the fifth, through the city.

"Glandular tissues, cellular in their texture, when recently wounded, require *arnica;* but if the injury has been neglected, and indurations have formed in the organ, *conium* 30, in eight spoonfuls of water, a spoonful every morning, is to be prescribed. Injuries of the bones are healed most promptly by *symphytum officinale* 30, internally, once a day. This remedy accelerates the consolidation of fractures surprisingly. I have seen a transverse fracture of the femur so united in three weeks, as to dispense with the bandage, and permit all necessary freedom of movement of the limb, though, as a precaution, the patient was kept in bed two weeks longer. A fractured radius, near its carpal extremity, of an aged lady, was perfectly healed in three weeks, without deformity of the wrist-joint. In these cases I used *arnica* internally and externally, the first five days, to prevent local inflammation and traumatic fever, afterwards the *symphytum*, as above described.

"Of the parts wounded, I have little to add to what has just been said of the tissues. I will only remark that the pathogenetic effects of *arnica* on the head are so numerous and characteristic, that it is not surprising its curative effects on this part of the body have been so frequent and important. The observation of Dr. Crepu, of Grenoble, in the *Bibliothèque Homœopathique*, is remarkable for the numerous cures of these lesions. In all cases of wounds of the head, *arnica*, both internally and externally, is to be employed, but with the exercise of caution as to the dose, because of the great affinity of this remedy with the head, that we may avoid dangerous medicinal symptoms. If not called to the patient till the injury has developed violent inflammatory fever, with redness of the face, *aconite* should be first administered, and if this be not sufficient, *belladonna*, especially if there is delirium, before having recourse to *arnica* internally, although this complication need not hinder the immediate local application of this remedy, as already directed.

"The eye is so sensitive, vascular, and ready to take on inflammation, that, when wounded, we must immediately have recourse to *aconite*, 30, in three tablespoonfuls of water, a teaspoonful every two hours, and even every hour, if the inflammation is severe. Hahnemann recommended this remedy in cases of foreign bodies lodged in the eye, and experience has many times confirmed the utility of the prescription. In wounds of the organ, it is indispensable. In severe cases, I apply, locally, a solution of *aconite* 6, in a glass of water. This remedy suffices for the whole cure. It is to be continued in all cases till the inflammation and pain are entirely dissipated. The wounds of the lids class with those of the skin, and if the globe is not affected, *arnica* will suffice for their cure.

"Wounds of the chest, whether penetrating or otherwise, as well as severe contusions of this cavity, require *arnica*, whether there be hemorrhage or not. If the heart or its pericardium be involved, perhaps *aconite* may be serviceable in the first instance.

"Wounds of the mammary glands fall under the observations already presented in relation to glands; but their sensibility renders *aconite* necessary when acute inflammation is developed, and *phosphorus* 30, when there are indications of suppuration. A young lady received a blow on the breast. She had neither pain nor indurations in it before the third day. On the fifth, an allopath ordered fifteen leeches. The pain and inflammation increased from this time. I was called the eighth day. The breast was a deep red, with shooting pains extending to the axilla. Fluctuation was perceived in the centre of the tumor. I gave *phosphorus* 30, in four tablespoonfuls of water, to take a spoonful immediately, and evening and morning, with the removal of all topical applications. The next morning, she reported a better night. The breast had nearly regained its natural size and color; the abscess appeared reduced to a fourth of its previous extent; and the third day the cure was complete.

"Penetrating wounds of the abdomen, with lesions of the peritoneum, or contained organs—as the liver, intestines, or bladder—also involve organs very susceptible of inflammation, and of that, too, which is exceedingly dangerous. The old school are accustomed to exhaust or destroy their patients to prevent this inflammation, (as happened to Canel, late editor of the French *National*,) by abstractions of blood, which is ever insufficient for the attainment of the object. Hahnemann has given to the art of healing more efficacious and more rational means, with which to meet these serious injuries. *Aconite*, administered immediately as directed for wounds of the eyes, at once calms the nervous excitement and anxiety of the patient, and at the same time prevents the vascular excitement, which ends in the inflammation of the parts. If visceral inflammation be already developed, with symptoms of peritonitis, after a dose of *aconite*, recourse must be had to *belladonna* 30, repeated till the inflammation be resolved. *Arnica* will complete the cure.

"The treatment of wounds is modified somewhat by the nature and form of the lesions. Those produced by a direct percussion, whether simple contusions or solutions of continuity, or by a cutting or pointed instrument, require *arnica* ; thus, gun-shot and bayonet wounds, falls, &c., demand this remedy. Superficial contusions, and those of long duration and those from riding on horseback, yield most speedily to a local application of *sulph.-ac.* Mechanical lesions, produced by a simple distention of tissue, such as sprains and luxations, often yield only to *rhus-tox.*, administered as above directed. *Arnica* is often followed by prompt success in injuries of this description.

"The treatment of burns should be varied according to the extent and depth of the organic lesion, and the attending circumstances. Burns which do not penetrate beyond the epidermis, are resolved with great promptness by the application of *arnica*, but I have had no experience with it in more profound injuries of this sort. *Carb.-veg.* 30, internally, has been recommended, by which great advantage is said to have been obtained. It soothes the frightful pain with great promptness. In deep burns, in which it is to be feared the viscera have been involved, as the danger consists in consecutive inflammation, *aconite* should be of great value. When inflammation has been prevented or subdued by *aconite*, the sloughing of the eschars will be promoted by *arsenic* 30, repeated according to the necessity of the case. If the suppuration be very abundant, *china* 12, may be preferred. If the acute pains of the burn do not yield to *carbo-veg.*, recourse should be had to *coffea* 3.

Dr. Goullon, of Weimar, has employed *causticum* for a long time with great success, given internally, every three or four hours, and externally, in solution, especially when the injury has been of long continuance, and has been buried in ointments. The pathogenetic symptoms which attend the phlyctnoidal eruptions of this antipsoric led him to the choice of the remedy.

"The accompanying circumstances which may present especial indications of treatment are terror, and other moral emotions, which the cause of the injury may have produced. If the patient has been affected with terror, the remedy is *aconite*; if he has had anger or rage, *chamomilla* or *bryonia;* if he is addicted to excesses of alcoholic drinks, or if intoxicated at the time of the injury, he should immediately have a dose of *nux-vom.*, and afterwards, the remedy specific for the injury received. If he has lost much blood, he should have *china* 12, and *arnica* seven or eight hours after.

"Of course, the dynamic treatment which homœopathy brings to the cure of wounds should be aided by the mechanical appliances of surgery, when they are required. Parts should be retained in the most complete repose; wounds should be cleansed, and the junction of divided tissues maintained by appropriate means. Parts displaced are to be restored. Divided vessels are to be tied or compressed; and foreign bodies removed by the necessary operations.

"The regimen to be observed is that appropriate to convalescents, and neither the severe diet nor the sanguineous depletions resorted to by the old school, to prevent inflammation. The proper administration of homœopathic remedies, internally and externally, attains this object much more successfully, and by sustaining the vital forces by appropriate nutrition, they repair with greater facility the losses occasioned by the wound.

"When inflammation supervenes in a wounded part, after removing its cause, give *aconite* as directed; and if the part be threatened with or attacked by erysipelas, *belladonna.* When profuse suppuration is produced by the presence of a foreign body in the wound, or by lesion of the bones, as in the case of gun-shot wounds, with considerable comminution of the fragments, *china* 12, every day, is indicated. It is also serviceable in the diarrhœa produced by the absorption of pus, and in colliquative sweats. If these symptoms are obstinate, recourse must be had to *sulphur. Silicea, mercury* and *phosphorus* may be useful in some such cases.

"The gangrene which occurs in wounds should be treated according to the supposed causes. I have, however, found *china* 12, morning and evening, very serviceable. If it be extensive, with ichorus suppuration, *arsenic* 30, in three tablespoonfuls of water, a teaspoonful every three hours, and lotions of the same attenuation, are preferable.

"In surgical operations, homœopathy possesses many precious resources with which to ensure success. It is well known that, of the operations the best performed, death often follows after a longer or shorter period, in consequence of traumatic or suppurative fever, secondary abscess, of absorption or excessive secretion of pus; so that the operation the most plainly indicated, and best performed, is often the cause of the more sudden destruction of the patient. Surgery is painfully impotent to prevent or cure these accidents. Bleeding, and only bleeding and diet, with opiates, its sole resources, ought to be, and are, followed by unfavorable results, for the debility consequent on blood-letting increases greatly the moral and physical sensibility of the patient to the pains and emotions of operations, and consequently can never prevent the evils developed by these causes. Just as a feeble valetudinarian or convalescent will be more readily made ill by external causes of disease, than the strong and robust, as is proved by daily observation. For the same reason, an individual enfeebled by blood-letting or severe diet is less likely to sustain a severe operation than in his natural state. This truth, so simple in itself, is the reason why so great care is taken to avoid exposures to cold and other causes of disease, while fasting in the morning. It required the flippancy of the schools to set at naught observations of so long standing, and so oft repeated. Homœopathy, having removed these prejudices, provides means more in accordance with natural laws, the superior efficacy of which, experience has ever confirmed. The late Dr. Gueyrard employed them in a case of amputation of the thigh, by Professor Berard, with the greatest success: cicatrization followed, without either traumatic fever or suppuration. September 20th, 1841, I assisted the same professor in the excision of *cervix uteri*, invaded by a cancerous fungus. The patient, forty-five years of age, of a nervous temperament, had for two years been subject to considerable uterine discharges, which she supposed indicated that the catamenia were about to cease, and gave them no particular attention, till at last she was seized with severe pains in the loins, abdomen and thighs, when I apprized her of the necessity of ascertaining the cause of her distress. MM. Marjolin and Lisfranc confirmed the diagnosis of disorganization of the cervix, and declared its immediate removal indispensable. Professor Berard would only undertake the operation on the condition that I should continue my attendance on the patient. I forbade the potions he directed to calm her nervous excitement, arising from the necessity of submitting to such an operation. In order to attain this object, she was only directed to inhale *ignatia* the day preceding that of the operation, and *aconite* an hour before its commencement, and at the moment of her being placed on the table. The operation was performed with the greatest exactness, and lasted twenty minutes; yet this female, so nervous and timid, had no fainting. After the operation she had an injection of the solution of the tincture of *arnica*, in water, and inhaled very lightly, *aconite*; and as soon as the patient was removed to her bed, I dissolved *arnica* 12, in a glass of water, of which she took a teaspoonful every four hours, while the local application of the remedy was continued. The excised portion was of the size of a hen's egg, and embraced the whole cervix. The division was through the healthy tissue of the uterus. The hemorrhage during and immediately after the operation was trifling; but two hours after it became frightful. It was arrested by the two assistants who had been left with the patient, in anticipation of this accident, by compression of the abdominal aorta. After this there was not the slightest unfavorable occurrence; the patient had positively no fever, and the wound cicatrized the twelfth day. The symptoms of abdominal irritation or congestion, which sometimes exhibited themselves, were combated with *belladonna* and *nux vomica*. The catamenia have never returned, and her health has been good during the year which has elapsed since the operation. Will it continue? Time will show.

"In the meantime it must be acknowledged, that homœopathy was here of great service, since the operator has declared, that it was the only case in which he had known a similar result.

"The report of this case shows the manner of employing homœopathic medicaments, in grave operations, where large wounds are inflicted, as in amputations, extirpation of tumors, etc. Pledgets of charpie, and compresses dipped in solution of tincture of *arnica*, and the dressings to be wet several times a day with this solution, till the cure is effected, as directed in the case of wounds.

"Dr. Wurtzler, of Bernbourg, in a memoir presented to the Central Homœopathic Society, in 1841, recommends *aconite* immediately after the operation, and says its effects are astonishing. The pains were entirely dissipated at the end of three hours, at the latest, and the patients slept immediately after the operation very quietly, as in some instances they had not done for years. Sometimes the terror produced by the shock of the operation required *opium*. One patient also slept very calmly under the influence of *arnica*. The pathogenetic symptom of jerkings of the limbs renders it immensely valuable in amputations and fractures, where patients are so tormented by jerking of the muscles of the affected limb during sleep.

"Operations on the eyes require the same management as has been directed for wounds of these organs. Dr. Wurtzler, in the memoir just cited, makes some very interesting observations on these operations.

"The chief remedy of the operations on the eyes," says he, "appears to be *aconite*. Before I ascertained this application of the remedy, I had tried several medicaments without success, and particularly *arnica* proved powerless. In many cases, *aconite* alone is sufficient for the entire cure; at times, as exceptions, I have been compelled to have recourse to some other remedy.

"In patients of very gentle disposition, *aconite* is not always appropriate. Then the violent lancinating pains in the temples and eyes are removed by *ignatia*.

"If there follow violent pains, with vomiting, *bryonia* will be useful.

"If the pains were by shocks, with vomiting and lientery, *asarum* relieved.

"If the pains were burning, with diarrhœa, *arsenic* gave relief.

"*Crocus* removed pulsation and beating pains in the eyes. If there be lancinating pains through the temples, with complete loss of appetite, *thuja* is the appropriate remedy.

"After depression of a cataract, when the crystalline lens was broken in small fragments, *senega* produced their absorption.

"When, after the cure, vision was affected by various colors, particularly when objects appeared covered with blood, *strontiana* gave perfect relief.

"In operations in the cavity of the abdomen, and on the organs of generation, the same treatment should be had recourse to as in wounds of these parts. *Aconite*, and sometimes *belladonna*, should be continued after the operation, so long as inflammation threatens, before passing to the use of *arnica*, after which, the wounds belong to the class of ordinary injuries, and should have the same treatment. I have not spoken of the preparatory treatment to which surgeons have thought proper to subject their patients previous to their operations, and which always has an effect contrary to that desired, because this belongs to the medical treatment of the disease requiring the operation, when this has proved insufficient for its cure. This treatment is of the greatest value if it has been properly directed, for it will have destroyed, in a great degree, the psoric taint of the constitution, which so frequently reproduces the disease where this precaution has been neglected.

"The subjects of operations are in a pathological condition which renders them extremely susceptible of impressions from external objects, and surgery rightly recommends the greatest caution in preserving them from such influences; but if accidents from this source have already occurred, the resources of homœopathy are powerful to arrest and remove them, by administering, the soonest possible, the specific against the presumed cause, and the symptoms it has developed. Care must be exercised to arrest these complications in their outset, for they soon attain a gravity which compromise the success of the operation.

"The prompt and salutary effects of homœopathic remedies, so often experienced, as I have already shown, in all sorts of wounds and surgical operations, are so easily proved, that it is shameful, and even criminal, on the part of the Army Board of Health, (*Conseil de Salubrité des Armées,*) that they have not taken the necessary measures to prove the reality of these advantages. What a difference in the fate of the unhappy man struck by a shot on the field of battle, if there were a small supply of *arnica* to mingle with a little water, with which the surgeons could bathe his wound. Those acute pains which so torment him during the first few days, the traumatic and suppurative fevers, the copious suppurations, which so often exhaust and carry down to the grave, and the more terrible gangrene and tetanus, so frequent in warm climates—all these sufferings and dangers can be avoided by it, and the wounded will only endure the sufferings inseparable from the destruction of the tissues affected by the wounding body; their recovery will be more prompt, and never followed by those protracted and painful convalesences so expensive to government, by the wounded being left the subjects of interminable pains through all their subsequent lives. We hope, when these facts come to the knowledge of that great mind who has the direction of the department of war, his love for the soldier will induce him to order the necessary measures for the investigation of a truth so important to the welfare of the troops and the economy of public treasure."

Section 1.—*Incised Wounds.*

Incised wounds are inflicted with a sharp, cutting instrument, and are generally considered the simplest of all the varieties previously mentioned, but the latter feature must depend to a certain extent on the parts that are injured. The most troublesome symptom is hemorrhage, and this aside, there is but slight danger connected with them—fibres have been simply divided, they have suffered no contusion or laceration, and consequently they are less likely to inflame severely, or to suppurate or slough.

Simple incised wounds pour out more blood than the contused or lacerated, although in the latter much more important blood vessels may be injured, but their coats not being divided entirely or fairly, they recede, owing to the size of the instrument by which the wound is produced, or to their inherent elasticity or contractility.

If the hemorrhage be arterial, the blood has a florid, bright red color, and if vessels of any magnitude are severed it spouts in jets; if the blood be venous, it is a dark red or purplish, and flows gradually.

Treatment.—In the treatment of incised wounds, the surgeon should endeavor to accomplish three objects, viz: 1st. Arrest the hemorrhage. 2d. Remove all extraneous matter from the wound. 3d. Coaptate the edges in the manner most favorable for their union.

Arterial hemorrhage is most effectually checked by the application of a ligature to the ends of the vessels, (it is frequently necessary in the treatment of incised wounds to ligate both extremities,) when the bleeding is slight, it may be arrested either by compression or twisting the divided ends of the artery.*

After the first and most important object has been effected, attention must be directed to the second consideration—" removal of all extraneous matter." The wound should be carefully examined, and all such substances, which, by their presence would prove a source of irritation, (glass, dirt, clots, &c., &c.,) should be gently removed, as it is impossible for the wound to heal by the first intention, if such be allowed to remain.

Hemorrhage having been staunched, and the wound cleansed, the third consideration, *coaptation*, is to be thought of. In former days it was deemed advisable to effect the union immediately

---

* See chap. on arresting hemorrhage.

and completely, but the experience of modern surgery teaches the expediency of *moderate delay* and *incompleteness.*

If the external wound be put together while oozing blood continues, even though slightly, especially if the part be covered with lint, bandages, &c., adhesion is necessarily thwarted, on account of the oozing blood, which, being unable to escape, accumulating, forms a coagulum between the lips of the wound, and this, acting as any other extraneous body, prevents the union.

All attempts at closure should, therefore, be delayed for a time, in wounds of moderate extent; and in those of large dimensions, the approximation of the edges should be incomplete. In cases where the wound is not extensive, a few moment's delay suffices, and when the cut surfaces present a glazed appearance, they should be nicely adapted and retained, either by straps or sutures.

If the oozing from the lips of the wound continue for some time, and if a considerable amount of blood is thus discharged, the internal administration of *arnica, crocus, diadema, creosote* or *phosphorus,* should be internally administered. If the patient's strength appears to be failing very rapidly, the countenance becomes deadly pale, or assumes a livid appearance, *china-off.,* should be prescribed, and the dose repeated every ten or fifteen minutes, until the symptoms commence to disappear.

After the bleeding has entirely ceased, adhesive plaster and position are frequently sufficient to complete the cure; this method, if practicable, is much preferable to any other for promoting union; but there are cases in which the wound is so situated, or so extensive, as not to admit of the application of adhesive straps, and when such is the case, recourse must be had to sutures. Those most commonly employed are the interrupted or twisted.

In wounds that are slight, a French surgeon, M. Vidal, employs small spring forceps, which at their extremities are provided with hooks, sufficiently sharp to hold the integument, without transfixing or laceration: when they have been allowed to remain, from ten to fourteen hours, the wound may have sufficiently healed to permit their removal, after which all other means required for retention, are said to be unnecessary.

When strapping is deemed sufficient to produce adhesion, the part should be placed in the position that relaxes the fibres of those muscles, which if remaining tense, would tend to retard union. The surrounding skin should then be perfectly freed from moisture, and if there be any hair upon the part, it should be carefully shaved. The plaster that is now most in vogue, and is regarded by experienced surgeons as preferable to any other, is that composed of a strong solution of isinglass, in spirit, spread evenly upon oiled silk, fine animal membrane, or upon silk gauze; the latter is recommended by Mr. Miller, as the best, when prepared in the following manner: The gauze should first be rendered water-proof by a coating of boiled oil, and then laid over with layers of the dissolved isinglass. The advantages of this plaster are, that though it adheres with much tenacity, it does not encourage inflammation, that its frequent removal is not necessary, and that, being translucent, the whole track of the wound may be examined, as though no dressings were present. The straps should be long, and extend some distance from the wound, in order that they may supply the place of the bandage, in supporting the surrounding parts. Interstices should be left between the straps, to allow the escape of the serous discharge, that passes off during the process of adhesion.

If sutures have been employed together with the plaster, they should be allowed to remain uncovered, in order that they may be easily removed, when their aid is no longer essential. The sooner they can be dispensed with, the more rapid will be the adhesion.

After the wound has been dressed, the patient should be placed in bed, all stimulating diet should be prohibited, and all causes of excitation be, if possible, removed; *arnica* should then be administered *internally*. If the patient be robust, and there is a tendency to fever, delirium, &c., *acon.* or *bell.* may be employed. *Staphys* has been recommended for *incised wounds*.

After surgical operations, &c., *acon.* has been very highly recommended. Dr. Wurtzler writes, "After amputations, extirpations and other surgical operations, I have invariably derived the most important service from the employment of *aconitum.* In most instances a complete cessation of pain took place, three hours after its administration; traumatic fever never supervened, and the patients almost always fell into a placid and refreshing slumber; but rarely was it found necessary to have recourse to *opium*, and that only when startings from sleep took place from local or general convulsive jerkings or twitchings."

Section 2.—Punctured Wounds.

Punctured wounds are inflicted by sharp and narrow instruments, as needles, pins, thorns, nails, splinters, &c., which bruise and tear as well as cut. They are, when slight, attended with little danger, but when of any considerable extent, the injury is always serious. Much also depends upon the constitution of the patient, and the situation of the wounded part. A superficial wound along the integument, and not involving the textures beneath, is of trivial importance; but when the direction is from the surface internally, there is always some danger to be apprehended, either from the injury inflicted upon some internal organ, or from inflammation occurring in the deep part of the wound, inducing the formation of matter, which being confined, infiltration of the surrounding textures is likely to supervene, giving rise to much constitutional and local disturbance. Large collections of matter have formed beneath the fasciæ, giving rise to excessive pain, and even permanent contraction or extension of the limbs, by uniting the muscles or their cellular texture together.

Dr. Gibson mentions a case of a young man, whose forearm was covered with sinuses, from which matter could be pressed in every direction. The fingers were permanently contracted, and consequently useless. The disease arose from a very trivial wound inflicted by a needle, fixed in the end of an arrow.

The lymphatics often swell from punctured wounds. A wound in the foot may produce a sympathetic bubo, or a wound in the hand may give rise to inflammation and swelling of the axillary glands.

Treatment.—It was formerly the custom among surgeons to endeavor, by immediately dilating punctured wounds, to convert them into incised, and treat them as that variety of injury; but this cruel practice is fast becoming exploded, although dilatation may be necessary under peculiar circumstances—viz: If a portion of the weapon that inflicted the wound be imbedded in the injured textures, its removal requires that incisions be made to permit the introduction of instruments used in extraction. If an artery be punctured, it must be ligated; and this requires a certain degree of dilatation. Or, again, when by the formation of matter, infiltration of the surrounding tissues is threatened, free incisions must be employed.

But in many cases of punctured wounds, after ascertaining that there is no extraneous substance present, by the use of the isinglass plaster, and by placing the part at rest and in the proper position, union by the first intention takes place, and the wound in a short time heals. If, however, inflammation appear and suppuration threaten, *hepar, mercurius,* or *silicea,* should be administered. If the local inflammation is excessive, *cham., bell.,* or *rhus,* will prove serviceable; but by the judicious and early exhibition of *arnica* or *aconite,* the above symptoms may be prevented. *Nit.-acid* and *cicuta-vir.* have been recommended in the treatment of this variety of wounds.

Ledum is said to be one of the most serviceable medicines in punctured wounds and affections attendant upon them. The characteristic symptom for its exhibition is *coldness* during the fever. M. Teste remarks—"*Ledum* is for wounds inflicted with sharp instruments, what *arnica* is for contusions."

The above writer mentions instances in which this medicine was productive of most beneficial results.

"1st. In several whitlows, caused by the pricks of a needle.

"2d. Violent bite of a water rat.

"3d. In a serious wound inflicted upon a young lady, who fell, with an embroidery needle in her hand, which pierced through and through. No hemorrhage occurred, but I observed the *intense cold,* which *accompanies* and *characterizes ledum fever.*"*

If there be any laceration present, *calendula officinalis* should be used internally, and also as an external application. Indeed, this remedy has been highly extolled by Dr. Thorer, as exercising great control over the processes of granulation and cicatrization. The directions for preparing the *aqua calendula officinalis,* are as follows:—

"Fill one-third of a clean bottle with petals, or leaves of the flowers; the remaining two-thirds with fresh pure spring water. Cork the vial well, and expose it for two or three days to the rays of the sun. The water is by this process rendered slightly aromatic; it is then poured off from the leaves into a bottle, which must be sealed and placed in a lower temperature. While the liquid is being exposed to the rays of the sun, it must be narrowly watched, and as soon as there are signs of incipient fermentation, measures must be taken to arrest it."

If, as a consequence of punctured wounds, tetanus supervene, *acon., arn., angust., cicuta,* may be employed.†

Section 3.—*Contused Wounds.*

In every contusion there must be a certain degree of injury inflicted upon the parts beneath, though the integument from its elasticity may remain unbroken.

Ecchymosis in the generality of instances, occurs from the

---

* Teste—Mat. Med., p. 77.

† See chapter on Tetanus.

rupture of smaller blood-vessels, their contents being poured into the surrounding cellular tissue. If larger vessels have been torn, danger is to be apprehended from the extensive infiltration of blood, giving rise to inflammation, suppuration and gangrene.

If, together with the contusion, the intergument is broken, the injury is then termed a *lacerated wound.* Such wounds, when first inflicted, give rise to little pain, because the nerves of the part have suffered from the concussion; but after a time, when the part has to a certain extent recovered its nervous power, the pain increases in proportion to the inflammation that is established.

The degree of violence of contused wounds, is in proportion to the velocity with which the contusing weapon is carried against the parts, and the resistance of the textures to which it is applied. If the parts yield, the shock is diminished, and consequently the injury is less considerable.

Treatment.—In simple bruises, or in the most violent contusions, provided there is no abrasion of the integument, the remedy is *arnica,* administered internally, applied as a lotion externally, or both.

The extraordinary virtues of this "panacea lapsorum," is not only appreciated by the whole medical profession, but as a domestic medicine its excellent qualities are fully understood, and the frequency with which it is employed with success, bears testimony to its usefulness in all manner of *bruises.*

As an external application, the tincture should be diluted, according to the sensitiveness of the skin of the patient, but in the generality of cases, one part of the pure tincture to ten or twelve parts of water will be sufficient. If ecchymosis be present to any extent, the internal administration of *arnica* or *sulph-ac.*, will generally suffice.

If, however, by the use of the diluted *arnica,* there be any aggravation of pain, or if any of the pathogenetic effects of the drug are manifested, *calendula-officinalis* must be employed. *Helianthus* and *symphytum* have also been recommended.

If contused wounds be slight, and the vitality of the affected part not much impaired, union by the first intention should, at least, be attempted, inasmuch as partial agglutination may prevent deformity and other ill consequences; but if the injury be of any considerable extent, adhesion is impossible, for the bruising is such, that the texture is immediately deprived of life, or its vitality is so much diminished that death is inevitable.

In all cases, sutures should be dispensed with, and isinglass adhesive straps employed, to retain the edges of the wound as nearly in situ as possible. Rest and perfect relaxation of the muscles of the part are indispensable.

When ligaments or tendons are implicated, *rhus tox.*, as adapted particularly to extension of such tissues, is preferable to *arnica* as an external application, and should also be administered internally.

If gangrene threaten, *china-off.* should be immediately prescribed; but if the wounded part assume a bluish tinge, and the patient's strength sink rapidly, *arsen.*, or *carb.-veg.*, must be administered.

When there has been considerable loss of substance from contused wounds, the parts can only heal by granulation, and if there be present any dead or dying tissue, it must first slough away. When such is the case, the patient must be kept at rest and *hepar* or *mercurius-sol.*, be administered to aid nature in her efforts to cast off the slough, and when this has been effected, *calendula, silicea* or *sulphur* may be administered to forward the granulations, and complete the cure. If the bones or periosteum has been affected by the injury, *mez.*, *phos.-ac.* and *ruta.*, should be employed; the latter is especially serviceable, when the wound has involved the tarsal or metacarpal joints.

In all injuries when there is great contusion, *arnica* should be immediately administered internally, and if high fever delirium supervenes, it may be alternated with *acon.*, *bell.*, *hyos.* or *stram.*, according to the indications for each medicine. If the fever assume a lower grade and typhoid symptoms are present, *rhus, ars.* or *carb.-veg.*, must be employed agreeably to the presenting symptoms.

Section 4.—Lacerated Wounds.

A wound is said to be *lacerated*, when its edges present a torn and ragged appearance.

In this variety of injury, there is generally but little hemorrhage, and it is this circumstance that frequently leads inexperienced practitioners to establish a false prognosis regarding the termination of the case, but the experienced surgeon does not allow himself to be deceived by the absence of hemorrhage; on the contrary, in proportion as there is little bleeding, the violence that the fibres and vessels have received is estimated. Whole limbs have frequently been torn from the body, without the occurrence of profuse hemorrhage.

In La Motte's *Traitê des Accouchemens*, can be found an interesting account of an injury of this kind, that happened to a lad, who, while playing near the wheel of a mill, entangled his arm and forearm in the machinery. The limb was violently torn away from the shoulder joint, but the hemorrhage was so trivial that it was stopped with a little lint, and the boy very soon recovered.

The indisposition to hemorrhage manifested by lacerated wounds is owing to the following circumstances. The orifices of the bleeding vessels, from the laceration, become drawn together or as it were puckered, consequently, the stream of blood is diminished in volume; they also retract to a greater degree than when they have been evenly divided; the sheathes of the vessels are drawn, at the lacerated extremity, to a point, which also tends to retard the flow of blood, and the arterial coats being divided at different times contract separately, the internal and middle being the first that are separated. These circumstances, as will be perceived, tend greatly to arrest the hemorrhage, which otherwise would necessarily occur.

Any irregular body, driven with violence, may produce a lacerated wound. They may also be caused by falling from a height upon uneven surfaces; but machinery, when in full motion, produces, perhaps, the most fearful and disastrous lacerations.

There are cases of this description recorded by Carmichael, Morand, Chesselden, and also in many of the medical and surgical journals, that are highly interesting, as denoting from what frightful laceration the system may ultimately recover.

Complete union by the first intention is impossible in lacerated wounds; inflammation and suppuration are certain, and the dead tissues must be thrown off in the form of a slough, and if this be large, severe constitutional symptoms are likely to supervene; but this is not the only difficulty which has to be encountered, gangrene often spreads rapidly in the surrounding textures, thus increasing the danger to both life and limb; or tetanus may threaten with its alarming symptoms.

Treatment.—The first attention of the surgeon when called upon to treat a lacerated wound, must be directed to the removal of all extraneous bodies, and if it be present, arresting hemorrhage. It sometimes happens that dirt, sand, &c., are begrimed in the wound, and this is particularly the case when the injury has been occasioned by the patient falling from a height upon uneven ground and loose stones. After all such foreign matter has been extracted, and the wound cleansed carefully, the most important blood-vessels that have been implicated must be searched for and ligated, and a dose of *arnica* administered internally.

It is advisable never immediately to cut away any of the lacerated soft parts, because it frequently happens that some portion of them may heal by adhesion, thus leaving a less amount of surface to be repaired by the reproductive process, (granulation and cicatrization.)

Adhesive straps should then be loosely applied, and in such a manner that a free exit be allowed for the matter to escape. *Calendula officinalis*, prepared as before directed, should be applied to the part, and also administered internally in the usual form, as it is known to prevent, in many instances, that prolonged suppuration that so frequently occurs in extensive lacerations, and also exercises a powerful influence over granulation and cicatrization. If, however, the expectation of the practitioner be disappointed, and suppuration is excessive, *hepar*, *silic.*, or *sulph.*, should be substituted.

If the patient is restless, uneasy, and excited by the least emotion, and the local pain severe, *cham.* will prove serviceable; or if, together with the pain, there is high fever and delirium, *acon.* or *bell.* should be resorted to, the latter particularly if the patient is of a robust habit of body. Either of the above may be alternated with *arnica* or *calendula.*

If the patient becomes extremely weak, with thirst, &c., hot dry skin, and gangrene threaten, *ars.* must be substituted; or if the symptoms correspond, *carbo-veg.*, *china*, or *lach.*, are to be employed.

While the ulceration and sloughing are progressing, the wound must be narrowly watched, as there is danger of hemorrhage ensuing. Tetanus may also be present, the proper medicines for which will be found in another portion of this work. (See Tetanus.)

In some cases, however, notwithstanding the best directed efforts in both constitutional and local treatment, gangrene appears to be spreading rapidly; in such the question of amputation must be seriously considered. (See Question of Amputation.)

Section 5.—Poisoned Wounds.

A poisoned wound is characterized by the presence of some poisonous material, which is itself the principal source of danger, the wound being generally a mere puncture or scratch. The prognosis in such injuries must depend upon the extent of the wound and the virulence of the poison introduced into the system.

The virus* pervades the body through the blood, and thence reacting deleteriously on the nervous system, interferes to a greater or less extent with all the animal functions. The effects are never instantaneous. A certain number of seconds,

* Miller's Principles.

(not less than nine,) are requisite for absorption, even of the most deadly poisons. Some of the more intense, as that of the most venomous serpents, would seem to have a direct influence on the nervous centres; probably by contact of the poison with the nerves of the part injured. Certain it is, that the nearer the wounded part is to the brain, the more speedily are the untoward symptoms developed. But even admitting that this direct nervous implication be true, it can only obtain to a comparatively slight extent; and we are still forced to hold that the main agent of diffusion through the system is the circulating blood. For it seems established, at least in the majority of cases, that the contact of poison with the surface of the body is not sufficient to give rise to general symptoms, so long as its diffusion throughout the body, by the circulation, is prevented.

When virus has been introduced into the system, and is not speedily thereafter extruded by elimination, it is supposed that a process takes place in the blood, somewhat analogous to fermentation, and hence the term *Zymosis;* whereby the whole circulating fluid is deteriorated, and the poison at the same time multiplied, perhaps to a great extent; and, according to the poison, this process varies much as to the time which is requisite for its completion.

Some poisons, of much virulence, produce their deleterious and perhaps fatal effects very speedily—so soon as introduced by the blood into the system; as happens in the bites of the most venomous snakes. Others, again, do not exhibit their results until the process of *zymosis* has been tardily completed, as in hydrophobia. A third class appear to have a doubly zymotic character. At first, the part is inoculated; and there the poison accumulates by *zymosis,* forming the characteristic pustule and sore. Thence the system becomes contaminated through absorption; and in the blood a second or general zymotic process is effected, whence the secondary symptoms are produced.

Among insects, the bee, wasp, hornet, and yellow jacket, inflict a slight wound, and infuse into it poison contained in a bladder situated at the base of the sting. The virus flows from the vesicle through the sting at the instant this passes into the flesh. Such wounds are, in this country,* generally trivial, and their effects pass off in a short time; but sometimes they are productive of intense pain and violent inflammation. The virus of the hornet, or of the yellow jacket, is more highly acrimonious than that of the common bee, and there are instances on record in which both human beings and inferior animals have lost their lives from wounds inflicted by these insects. Dr. Gibson records a case of a female, who died in fifteen minutes after having been stung by a yellow wasp. Another case is also mentioned by the same author, of a young woman who lost her life from swallowing a bee inclosed in a piece of honeycomb.

The mosquito, certain varieties of spider, and some species of fly, inflict severe and oftentimes dangerous wounds. In unhealthy constitutions, or in individuals whose skin is very susceptible to inflammation, the sting of the mosquito will degenerate into a troublesome sore. Dr. Dorsey (Elements of

---

* Insects are the curse of tropical climates. The *bête rouge* lays the foundation of a tremendous ulcer. In a moment you are covered with ticks. Chigoes bury themselves in your flesh, and hatch a large colony of young chigoes in a few hours.—(p. 404.) They will not live together, but every chigo sets up a separate ulcer, and has his own private portion of pus. Flies get entry into your mouth, into your eyes, into your nose; you eat flies, drink flies, and breathe flies, Lizards, cockroaches, and snakes, get into the bed; ants eat up the books; scorpions sting you on the foot. Everything bites, stings, or bruises. Every second of your existence you are wounded by some piece of animal life that nobody has ever seen before, except Swammerdam and Meriam. An insect, with eleven legs, is swimming in your tea-cup; a nondescript, with nine wings, is struggling in the small beer; or a caterpillar, with several dozen eyes in his belly, is hastening over bread and butter! All nature is alive, and seems to be getting all her entomological hosts to eat you up as you are standing, out of your coat, waistcoat, and breeches. Such are the tropics! All this reconciles us to our dews, fogs, vapors, and drizzle; to our apothecaries rushing about with gargles and tinctures; to our old British constitutional coughs and swelled faces.—*Sid. Smith's Works*, vol, ii., p. 147.

Surgery, vol. i., p. 68) mentions a case where gangrene and death supervened from a bite of this insect. The patient was previously enjoying good health. There is also recorded—by Dr. Mease, in the Domestic Encyclopædia—an instance in which the sting inflicted by a spider was productive of fatal results.

The tarantula—a species of spider, that is found in South America, Mexico, and in Europe, particularly in the neighborhood of Naples—whose bite has been pronounced by some authors to be exceedingly severe, while others deny that ill consequences of any severity result from the virus injected into the system.

The scorpion is an insect whose sting in warm climates is so severe that death frequently ensues. It attains its largest growth in Persia, India, and Africa, where it is termed the *scorpio afer*. The reservoir that contains the poison is situated near its tail, and is ejected from two small orifices on each side of the tip of the sting. The symptoms produced in animals after they had been bitten, were—swelling, convulsions, retching, vomiting, and death soon supervened.

The appearances presented when individuals have been bitten by the scorpion, are related by Mr. Allan to be similar to those produced by the stings of bees, but much more aggravated.*

The two species of American serpents that are the most venomous, are the copperhead and the rattlesnake. Of the latter there are ten species. The older naturalists mention but eight; but the two others—*crotalus cumanesis* and the *crotalus laeflingii*—were discovered by Humboldt and Bonpland. All are poisonous; but those whose virus is most malignant are the *crotalus horridus*, *miliarius*, and *durissus*. The poison of the rattlesnake is of a yellow color, tinged slightly with green; during the extreme heat, particularly in the procreating season, it becomes of a much darker hue.†

---

* Allan's System of Pathological and Operative Surgery, vol. i., p. 370.
† Gibson's Practice of Surgery, vol. i., p. 108.

Mr. Catesby* informs us that the Indians, who, in their constant wanderings in the woods are liable to be bitten by snakes, know immediately if the wound will prove fatal. If it be on any part at a distance from the large blood vessels, or where circulation is not vigorous, they at once apply their remedies; but if any artery or vein of considerable magnitude is involved, they quietly resign themselves to their fate.

Sir Everard Home, in some observations on the poisons of the black spotted snake of St. Lucia, the *cobra di capella*, and the rattlesnake, remarks:—

"The effects of the bite of a snake vary according to the intensity of the poison. When the poison is very active, the local irritation is so sudden and so violent, and its effects on the general system are so great, that death soon takes place. When the body is afterward inspected, the only alteration of structure met with, is in the parts close to the bite, where the cellular membrane is completely destroyed, and the neighboring muscles very considerably inflamed. When the poison is less intense, the shock to the general system does not prove fatal. It brings on a slight degree of delirium, and the pain in the part bitten is very severe. In about half an hour, swelling takes place from an effusion of serum in the cellular membrane, which continues to increase, with greater or less rapidity, for about twelve hours, extending, during that period, into the neighborhood of the bite. The blood ceases to flow in the small vessels of the swollen parts; the skin over them becomes quite cold; the action of the heart is so weak that the pulse is scarcely perceptible, and the stomach is so irritable that nothing is retained by it. In about sixty hours these symptoms go off; inflammation and suppuration take place in the injured parts; and when the abscess formed is very great, it proves fatal. When the bite has been in the finger, that part has immediately mortified. When death has taken place, under such circumstances, the absorbent vessels and their glands have undergone no change similar to the effects of morbid poisons,

* Preface to Natural History of Carolina.

nor has any part lost its natural appearance, except those immediately connected with the abscess. In those patients who recover with difficulty from the bite, the symptoms produced by it go off more readily and more completely than those produced by a morbid poison, which has been received into the system."*

The viper is a serpent, whose bite is exceedingly venomous. It is the virus of the lance-headed viper, (*trigonocephalus lachesis*,) with which the members of our school are so familiar, by the labor of research and the self-sacrificing investigations of Dr. Hering.

This poison has somewhat the appearance of saliva, but it is less tenacious. It readily forms into drops, and falls without threading. It is slightly greenish in color, and when exposed to the air, concretes into a dry yellow mass.†

The bite of rabid animals produces, in many instances, that disease termed *rabies canina*, or *hydrophobia*, although this affection does not necessarily follow; for it has certainly been ascertained, that, out of numerous persons bitten by dogs undoubtedly mad, few have sustained material injury.

The first symptoms of hydrophobia generally manifest themselves between the seventh and fortieth day; but there are cases recorded of the virus remaining latent in the system for months and years. The wound is often slight, and heals readily until the precursory symptoms of the disease begin to manifest themselves—when it inflames, becomes painful, breaks open afresh, assuming a livid and spongy appearance, and secreting an ichorous humor. The patient complains of pain, extending from the wound, or cicatrix, along the nerves. The part bitten feels numb, becomes stiff and immovable, or it may be convulsively moved.

The patient is troubled with excessive apprehension, the countenance indicates great anxiety, or the features may assume a melancholy expression. The sleep is restless and

* Case of a man who died in consequence of the bite of a rattlesnake.

† Jahr's Pharmacopœia and Posology, p. 221.

uneasy, interrupted by frequent startings, or there is complete sleeplessness. There are also present drawing pains in the nape of the neck, burning in the fauces and stomach, sensitiveness to draughts of air, with vertigo, nausea, and vomiting of green bile. Constant urging to urinate, the urine passing in drops, or an irresistible desire for copulation, are symptoms that are not unfrequently encountered.

When the convulsive stage sets in, there is that frightful aversion to liquids which characterized this disease, and from which it derives its name.* Although the patient is tormented with violent thirst, even the thought of fluid at once excites most painful and distressing symptoms. If the attempt be made to swallow a few drops of water, the throat and chest become constricted, and the most violent, suffocative convulsions of the facial, thoracic, and abdominal muscles ensue. The convulsions are excited by the most trivial incidents. The movement of a curtain, contact, &c., give rise to spasm. There is also often present another very distressing symptom—the collection of thick, ropy, viscid phlegm, adhering with such tenacity to the throat that it is extremely difficult, and often impossible to eject. Dr. Marcet, in the Medico-Chirurgical Transactions, records a case of this disease in which the phlegm was thrown off with such extreme torture that the patient exclaimed—"O! do something for me! I would suffer myself to be cut to pieces! I cannot raise the phlegm; it sticks to me like bird-lime!"

Finally, tetanic or epileptic convulsions take place, and the appearance presented by the sufferer during these spasms is most horrible and appalling. The face expresses intense

---

* In a letter published in the Lancet, of September, 1829, the following remarks occur:—"*Drinking* water is now no criterion by which we can judge of the existence or not of rabies. The name of hydrophobia is now universally allowed to be incorrect, there being no dread of water itself, but of the horrible spasms which the attempt to swallow liquids induces. Even this is not so constant an attendant on the disease as it was formerly supposed to be. There are many well marked cases of rabies *without either a horror of fluids or difficulty of swallowing*."

anguish and despair; the eyes are protruded, bloodshot, and roll wildly in their sockets; the delirium is furious, during which muscular strength increases to such a degree that the patient is with difficulty controlled. He howls, bites, and spits, or endeavors to tear himself to pieces. This attack continues about fifteen minutes, and subsides for a short period, leaving a state of complete exhaustion. It is during such intervals that consciousness is sometimes present, and often it happens when a slight gleam of reason returns, that the patient warns his attendants to what danger his rage may expose them, or prays them in earnest tones to terminate his sufferings.

Sometimes vomiting occurs. Men may be attacked with priapism, and women with furor uterinus. The beats of the pulse are small, irregular, and very frequent—about 130 to 150 per minute.

As the disease progresses, the paroxysms increase in frequency and violence, and death ensues in two to eight days, generally from exhaustion, (*apoplexia nervosa,*) or the patient may die, suffocated, in convulsions. These are the symptoms that occur in most cases of Hydrophobia; but there are modifications in this, as well as in other diseases. In some instances, the patient may be able to swallow some liquids, and not water; or the symptoms may only appear during a paroxysm; or they may be purely nervous.

This disease is said to originate and develop itself spontaneously among the canine or feline race. The virus can be transmitted to men and to all warm-blooded animals.

Rabies, in the dog, is said to be of two varieties. "The first is characterized by augmented activity of the sensorial and locomotive functions, continued and peculiar barking, and a strong disposition to bite. The affection commences with some alteration in the peculiar habits and disposition of the animal, who, as the case may be, is more irritable, more tractable, more lively, or more sluggish than usual; or these several conditions may alternate in one and the same animal. An early symptom consists in an inclination to lick, or carry in the mouth, various inedible substances, especially such as are cold. The animal after a time gets restless; snaps in the air, as if at flies; frequently leaves the house, but soon returns; and is obedient and seems attached to its master. According to Blainé, constipation constantly exists. There is usually complete loss of appetite; but the animal seems to suffer from thirst, drinking eagerly, until, as indeed usually occurs, the mouth and tongue become swollen. The eyes are red, and become dull, haggard, and half-closed, the skin of the forehead being also wrinkled, which gives the animal a peculiar aspect. The nose, tongue, and throat now usually become swollen, and the coat becomes rough and staring. According to Hertwig, the mouth is generally very dry; but Blaine has constantly observed a flow of thin saliva. After some time, the gait becomes unsteady and staggering, and finally the extremities are paralyzed. The tail, in this form of the disease, is not drawn between the legs; and the head is carried erect, the nose being pointed upwards. A disposition to bite, sooner or later, invariably occurs. It is not, however, permanent, but recurs periodically. It is directed against both inanimate and animate objects—most especially against the cat—less so towards other animals, and least of all towards man. When the animal bites, he does not previously bark, or fly at the object of his attack, but approaches in a quiet or even friendly manner, and makes a sudden snap.

"The second form of the disease is distinguished by inactivity and depression. There is no disposition to bite—probably from the lower jaw being paralyzed—nor is there any indication for change of place manifested. The first symptoms are unusual quietness, and apparent depression of spirits. The voice is peculiarly altered, as it is in the foregoing variety; but there is much less disposition to bark. The mouth is open, the lower jaw hangs as if paralyzed, and is raised only under the influence of strong excitement. There is a constant flow of slaver from the mouth. The animal either does not drink at all, or does so with difficulty; but manifests no fear of water; and, on the contrary, willingly immerses the nose in that fluid. The tongue is almost constantly protruded from the mouth."*

The anatomical changes that are noticed in the bodies of those persons who have died from hydrophobia, are as follows: The subject decays rapidly; the blood is dark fluid, and quickly imbibed by the system. The veins are engorged, air is frequently found in the larger vessels, and emphysema develops itself rapidly. The whole surface of the body is blue-red; the epidermis is very dry; all the muscles are dark red, and, like the tendons, they are rigid and tight.

The introduction of morbific matter into the system is sometimes productive of the worst results. One of the most deleterious poisons seems to be engendered in the body during the puerperal disease, and when by any accident there has been inoculation with this virus, results the most fatal have followed. Anatomists, or those engaged in macerating, or making preparations, have suffered severely from accidental wounds inflicted by the instruments they are using. Violent inflammation frequently follows such causalities; the axillary glands inflame and suppurate; the whole limb is painful; abscesses form, and gangrene and death may result. Many examples of such cases are on record.

Treatment of Poisoned Wounds.—The bites of the mosquito and other insects, which are common in our climate, are often quite painful, and cause considerable annoyance. However, a lotion composed of a weak solution of *arnica* tincture, if applied to the bitten part, eases almost immediately the pain and itching. *Camphora* and lemon-juice,† as external applications, are also highly recommended for this purpose. Dr. Gibson writes‡—"The *aqua ammoniæ* applied to a part stung by bees, I have known to act like a charm." The internal administration of *ledum* is also recommended by M. Teste.§ He says—"Against mosquito bites, a single teaspoonful of a

* British and Foreign Medical Review, No. XXV., p. 50.

† Laurie's Homœopathic Practice of Physic, p. 541.

‡ Institutes and Practice of Surgery, p. 119.

§ Mat. Med., p. 77.

tumblerful of water, in which a few globules of the 15th dilution of *ledum* had been dissolved, quieted completely, in a few minutes—I might even say a few seconds—the itching caused by the bite, without any application being necessary. Also, the stings of bees and wasps have been treated with *ledum* in a most satisfactory manner."

If, after the sting of any insect, the part becomes swollen, tense, hot, with erysipelatous blush, *bella.* should be administered, and if fever supervene, *acon.* may be used in alternation. *Arnica* is also an important remedy, and should be used, both internally and as an outward application, when the swelling assumes a bluish cast, and there is a bruised sensation around the part. If the pain is stinging, and there is itching, and a thin discharge from the wound, *creos.* should be administered. This medicine has also been recommended as a lotion, of about ten drops of the tincture to a pint of water.

The following medicines have also been found very serviceable; the indications for their use will generally be found in the constitutional symptoms that present themselves: *Ant.-crud., calad., lach., merc., seneg., sep.*

In Morocco, where the scorpion is very common, most families keep a bottle of olive oil, in which the bodies of several of these reptiles have been infused, and when bitten, apply it to the wound, and with reputed success. A ligature is also generally placed above the wounded part, to interrupt the progress of the poison, and the wound is afterward scarified. "In Tunis, when any person is stung by a scorpion," says Mr. Jackson,* "or bit by any venomous reptile, they immediately scarify the part with a knife, and rub in olive oil as quick as possible, which arrests the progress of the venom. If oil is not applied in a few minutes, death is inevitable, particularly from the sting of a scorpion. Those in the kingdom of Tunis are the most venomous in the world." According to the same author, the *coolies*, or porters, who work in the oil stores, have their bodies constantly saturated with oil, and on

* Jackson's Reflections on the Commerce of the Mediterranean.

this account, not only never suffer in the slightest degree from the bites of scorpions, and other reptiles which creep over them at night, as they sleep on the ground, but there is not a single instance known of one of these people ever having taken the plague, although the disease frequently rages in Tunis in the most frightful manner.

The use of olive oil has been highly extolled by many writers, as a remedy for the bites of poisonous serpents. Dr. Miller,* of South Carolina, relates the case of a man who was bitten in the sole of the foot by a very large rattlesnake. Although very little time elapsed before he reached the patient, his head and face were prodigiously swelled, and the latter black. "His tongue was enlarged and out of his mouth; his eyes as if starting from their sockets; his senses gone, and every appearance of immediate suffocation." Two table-spoonfuls of olive oil were immediately got down, but with great difficulty. The effect was almost instantaneous; in thirty minutes it operated freely by the mouth and bowels, and in two hours the patient could articulate, and soon after recovered. The quantity of oil taken internally and applied to the wound, did not exceed eight spoonfuls. In the course of twelve years Dr. Miller has met with several similar cases, in which the oil has proved equally successful.†

The application of dry heat has also been highly lauded for the neutralization of the virus inflicted by serpents, &c.

In the western parts of our country, where rattlesnakes abound, and persons frequently are bitten, the treatment consists in forcing the patient to swallow from a pint to a quart of some alcoholic stimulant—generally common whisky. Although this method of treatment may appear novel and strange, still the effects produced are recorded as most wonderful. In the iron regions of Missouri, among the mountains, the rattlesnake is frequently found, and the inhabitants although they fear the reptile, are destitute of that *dread* which generally connects itself to our minds regarding the crotalus; this proba-

* New York Medical Repository, vol. ii., p. 242.

† The above is taken from Gibson's Surgery.

bly arises from the belief that their remedy is infallible. A year or two since, a boy was chasing a squirrel in the locality above mentioned, when the animal, as the child supposed, ran into a hollow tree. The boy immediately thrust his arm into the opening, and was bitten by a large rattlesnake. The hand and arm soon after commenced swelling, and the glands in the axilla had become somewhat enlarged, when medical assistance was procured. Common whisky was immediately administered by the half-tumblerful, until the child must have swallowed nearly a pint and a half. The stimulus did not appear to produce any exhilirating effect, but drowsiness came on and the patient slept for some time; on awaking, though the arm was still considerably swollen and painful, it was more natural in color. From this time improvement continued, and the patient ultimately recovered.*

The best method of practice, however, if the surgeon is present when the bite is inflicted, or is called immediately after, is the free excision of the part. The indications for treatment are to prevent absorption of the virus, and obtain its expulsion from the part. Therefore a ligature must be thrown immediately around the limb, in order to obstruct return of venous blood, and if the part be favorably situated, free excision be instantly practised—if the latter is impracticable, incision should be made, and the flow of blood encouraged by every means. Suction by the mouth is also exceedingly beneficial after either operation, and should never be neglected. The suction must be continued long and repeated often. It is of the greatest importance to ascertain whether the *snake* that has inflicted the wound is venomous or not. Dr. Hering writes, "All *venomous* snakes have in the upper jaw but *two teeth*, very long and large. All snakes that have two rows of teeth above and below are not venomous. After the bite of a venomous snake, a cutting and sometimes a burning pain is experienced. Immediately after sucking the wound, rub into it fine kitchen salt until the part is saturated with it; or, if that cannot be

* The above was told to the author, during a short stay in the regions referred to. The authority is undoubtable.

obtained, gunpowder, ashes of tobacco, or wood ashes may be used as a substitute. The patient should be kept as quiet as possible; the greater the motion or the anxiety, the worse will be the consequences."

If there is vomiting, giddiness or fainting, and blue spots make their appearance, *ars.* or *carbo-veg.* should be administered. The former of these medicines has been used with considerable success by the old school physicians. Dr. Gibson* writes, "As an internal medicine, *arsenic* has been lately found more decidedly beneficial than any other."

Mr. Ireland† has recorded five cases, in all of which the most violent symptoms produced by the bite of the *coluber carinatus*, a poisonous serpent very common at the island of St. Lucia, were speedily arrested, and cures finally effected, by the use of this medicine. The supposed efficacy of the Tanjore pill, a medicine very commonly employed in India against the bites of serpents, the chief ingredient of which is arsenic, first led Mr. Ireland to employ Fowler's mineral solution. He gave it to the extent of two drachms every half hour, and repeated for four hours, with the best effects. Severe vomiting and purging followed the exhibition of the medicine, and the patients were soon after relieved.

The administration of the above mentioned medicine, in smaller doses, would prove more serviceable, and save the patient an immense amount of additional suffering.

A person bitten by a dog, under suspicious circumstances, writes Mr. Miller, is usually much alarmed, and applies for relief without delay. The first business of the surgeon is to inquire into the history of the accident; the disposition of the dog; its apparent condition at the time; whether loose or chained; whether provoked or not. For it may happen that the animal was not to blame, having either been provoked to assault, or having inflicted the bite with the idea of discharging a supposed duty on an aggressor. Such a wound is not supposed to contain any virus.

---

* Loc. cit., vol. i., p 123.

† Medico-Chirurgical Transactions, vol. ii., p. 394.

If there be any reasonable grounds for doubt concerning the state of the animal at the time when the bite was inflicted, the treatment should be conducted as though the person had been inoculated by the virus. The best method is immediate and free excision of the parts, and at the same time if there be any presenting symptoms, those medicines best adapted to them should be administered. If there was unquestionable and undeniable authority concerning the efficacy of homœopathic treatment of hydrophobia, it would undoubtedly be wrong to subject the patient to an operation, and although the cases recorded, particularly those by Mr. Leadam and Mr. Ramsbotham, have the appearance of *genuine* hydrophobia, and are evidences of the powerful action of homœopathic drugs in this affection; still the disease is so terrible in its nature, that the surgeon has indeed necessity for being doubly armed against it, for if excision fail, he has medicines at his command, the symptoms of which are very nearly allied to those manifested by hydrophobic patients, as will be hereafter shown. Moreover, the poison is an extraneous matter introduced into the system, and surely the homœopathic surgeon may be justified in using mechanical means for its removal. But let it be remembered, that if some time has elapsed between the infliction of the bite, and the application of the patient for relief, this method of treatment will prove of no avail, and immediate recourse must be had to medicines, the chief of which are *belladonna, hyoscyamus, lachesis, stramonium, cantharides.*

The following indications for the first three of these medicines are quoted from Mr. Leadam, M. R. C. S. L.,* whose valuable paper on a "Case of supposed Hydrophobia," every student should peruse.

"*Belladonna.*—Hydrophobic symptoms, Hahnemann, 65 to 105. The symptoms are descriptive of various forms of headache.

---

* British Journal of Homœopathy, vol. vii., p. 145. This paper was also reprinted in this country in the Quarterly Homœopathic Journal, vol. i., p. 308, Boston 1849. See also Mr. Ramsbotham's Case of Hydrophobia, B. J. H., vol. viii.

105. Violent throbbing in the brain, from before, backward and towards both sides; externally this throbbing terminates in the shape of painful stitches.

107. Stitching ache in the temples from within outwards.

108. Cutting ache in the temples, from within outwards; this pain becomes more and more violent, and spreads through the brain, where it is felt as a violent throbbing.

121. The whole of the head is affected with a stitching ache, especially the forehead.

124. Sharp stitches through both frontal eminences, from within outwards.

125. Excessive headache; dull stitches dart through the brain in all directions.

129–30. Stabbings in the brain.

131. A few lancinations traverse the occiput, immediately behind the ear, as fast as lightning; they almost made him scream; in the evening.

152. Pain externally over the whole head, such as is felt in the integuments, after violently pulling the hair.

170. Distracted features.

172. Paleness of face with thirst.

175. An extreme paleness of the face, is instantaneously changed to redness of the face, with cold cheeks and hot forehead.

185. Sweat only in the face.

339. Increased sensitiveness of the meatus auditorius.

379. Spasmodic movements of the lips; the right corner of the mouth drawn outwards.

380. Risus sardonicus; spasmodic distortion of the mouth.

382. Bloody foam at the mouth; vacillation and gnashing of the teeth.

404. The head is drawn backwards; burying of the head into the pillow.

415. Grinding of the teeth, with copious saliva running from the mouth.

509. Impeded deglutition.

510. Painless inability to swallow.

511. Short-lasting, but frequently-recurring contraction of

the œsophagus, the more during than between the acts of deglutition.

516. Painful contraction of the fauces; when preparing the parts for the act of deglutition, a tension and stretching is experienced by them, although deglutition is not accomplished.

521. He has the greatest trouble in swallowing water, and can only get down very little of it.

522. Aversion to every kind of liquid; she demeans herself frightfully when seeing it.

523. Pouring drinks down her throat makes her mad.

524. Inability to swallow.

570. Desire for drinks without caring about drinking; he approached the cup to his lips, and then set it down again immediately.

830. Difficult respiration.

831. Violent, small, frequent, anxious respirations.

832. Pressure in the præcordeal region; this arrests the breathing and causes a feeling of anguish.

920. Convulsive concussion of the upper limbs, as if caused by an excess of shuddering.

1067. Convulsive movements of the limbs.

1069. Twitching of the limbs.

1070. The most violent spasm after a slight vexation.

1072. Lassitude and anxiousness accompany the spasms of the limbs.

1073. Convulsions.

1074. Convulsive momentary extension of the limbs when waking from sleep.

1089. Spasmodic extension of the limbs, with distortion of the eyes.

1094. Trembling, with convulsive concussions of the body.

1134. Frightful dreams, which one recollects very vividly.

1142. Anguish prevents one from falling asleep.

1144. Starting in a dream; this wakes him up, his forehead and the scrobiculus cordis being covered with sweat.

1189. He is tormented by a burning thirst and by heat, and desires to drink from time to time; but when offered a drink he repels it.

1212. Extreme sensibility to the cold air.

1219. A convulsive shuddering lifts him up in his bed; in two hours heat and general sweat come on, without thirst either during the shuddering or heat.

1314. Great anguish about the heart.

1315. Anxious and fearful.

1325. Complains about an intolerable anguish in the moments which are free from rage; this makes her feel desirous of dying.

1339. He talks about wolves; full pulse.

1340. Delirious prattle about dogs that swarm about him.

1341. He is beside himself; rages; talks much about dogs.

1345. Paroxysms of delirium.

1374. Violent shaking of the head, foam at the mouth, and loss of consciousness.

1377. Horrible contortions of the muscles of the face.

1400. Great irritability and sensibility of the senses; taste, smell, tact, sight and hearing are more refined and keener than usual; his feelings are more easily stirred up.

1403. He becomes angry easily, even at trifles.

1410. Rage; the boy did not know his parents.

1412. He tosses about in his bed in a perfect rage.

1413. He tears his shirt and clothes.

1415. Frenzy, with attempts at violence.

1417. Instead of eating that which he had called for, he bit the wooden spoon in two, gnawed at the dish, and grumbled and barked like a dog.

1418. Rage, the patient being sometimes very cunning, and alternately singing and screaming or spitting and biting.

1421. He wants to bite those around him.

1425. He bites everything in his way.

1426–27. Inclination to bite and tear everything around him.

1428. Bites and spits.

1429. Attempts to jump out of bed.

1430. Apprehends death.

1433. Is afraid of an imaginary black dog, &c.

Lachesis offers the following symptoms. Jahr.

1. Dartings in the head.

2. Deep stinging throughout the whole head.

3. Sticking with pressure in the right side of the head.

4. Tearing lancinations in the forehead, above the eyebrows.

5. Distortion of the face.

6. Distortion of the mouth to the left side during a fit.

7. Hurried talking, with headache and redness of the face, or with mental derangement and constrictive sensation in the throat.

8. Difficulty of swallowing food, or drink, or saliva.

9. Dryness of the pharynx and œsophagus, preventing deglutition.

10. Jerking and twitching of the hands.

11. Twitching of the left lower limb while sitting.

12. Tingling in the toes, also with heat and numbness or prickling.

13. Constant sopor after cessation of pains.

14. Convulsions and other spasms, with violent shrieks, &c.

15. Sensation of internal trembling, as from anguish.

16. Violent convulsions of the limbs and face, with rigid stretching of the body.

Hahnemann gives among the symptoms of *hyoscyamus:*

113. Impeded deglutition.

114. The posterior part of the throat is affected.

115. Frequent hawking up of mucus.

116. Burning heat in the throat.

117. Dryness and subsequent fine stinging in the region of the larynx.

118. Parching dryness of the fauces.

119. Great dryness in the throat and thirst.

122. Dryness in the throat.

123. Thirst and dryness in the throat.

124. Thirst occasioned by stinging dryness in the throat.

125. His throat feels so dry and constricted, that a little tea came near choking him.

128. Constriction of the throat.

129. Inability to swallow.

131. He twice spat out a liquid, which had been introduced into his mouth.

132. Hydrophobia.

133. Intolerable thirst.

134. Unquenchable thirst.

135. Dread of drinks.

136. Violent sweat after thirst.

137. After drinking he was now attacked with convulsions, now he did not recognize those present.

138. He asks for drink, and is, nevertheless, unable to swallow.

139. Frequent spitting of saliva.

414. Mental derangement with occasional muttering.

451. Alternations of ease and rage.

452. Mania, he can scarce be governed.

453. He is extremely strong in his rage.

465. Peevish, sad.

467–72. Went from place to place. Anguish. Fits of anxiety. Horrid anguish.

473. Concussive startings, alternating with trembling and convulsions.

475. Strange fear that he will be bit by animals.

585. Excessive sweat.

Stramonium.—The following symptoms are recorded in Jahr's new manual.

1. Endeavors to escape, imagines he is all alone all the time and is afraid.

2. He endeavors to beat those around him, with a terrible cry and rage.

3. He bites a person's hand.

4. Great desire to bite and to tear himself with his teeth, even his own limbs.

5. Alternations of convulsions and rage.

6. Hydrophobia.

7. Delirious, he had no memory or consciousness.

8. With his eyes staring and his pupils dilated, he saw noth-

ing, did not recognize any of his family, carried his hands about as if he would grasp at something, and stamped with his feet.

9. Frightful fancies; his features show fright and terror.

10. Convulsions of the head.

11. Swollen face, turgid with blood.

12. Dilation of pupils; staring eyes.

13. His tongue is paralyzed, it trembles when he attempts to put it out.

14. Bloody froth at the mouth.

15. Hydrophobia; restlessness, violent convulsions, the patient being so violent that he had to be tied; he rolled about in his bed sleepless, and uttering crowing screams; he was delirious, without memory or consciousness; his pupils were extremely dilated; violent desire to bite and to tear everything with his teeth; extreme dryness of the inner mouth and fauces; the sight of a light, a mirror, or water, excited horrible convulsions, irresistible aversion to water, with constrictions and convulsions of the œsophagus; froth at the mouth and frequent spitting.

16. Dread of, or aversion to water or any other liquid, with spasmodic motion.

17. Aversion to watery liquids; he became enraged when his lips were moistened.

18. Frequent spitting; slaver hanging out of the mouth.

19. Tenacious mucus in the mouth.

20. Stiffness of the whole body.

The following symptoms of Hydrophobia are taken from the proving of the virus, by J. Redman Coxe, Jr.,* M. D., assisted by other members of the profession.

1. Slight dizziness and nausea.

2. Violent pressing outward in the forehead, the patient put the head to the wall.

3. A very intolerable, snappish, irritable headache, with stiffness of the jaws and numb hands.

(Nearly all the symptoms relating to the head, are such as might be present in the incipient stage of hydrophobia.)

---

* See Philadelphia Journal of Homœopathy, vol. iii., p. 262.

4. Twitchings of the face and hands.
5. Rending and tearing pain in the malar bones.
6. Face pale, yellow, nearly brown.
7. Both jaws feel stiff, with tingling in the cheek bones.
8. Jaws stiff and sore.
9. Jaws feel stiff and a disposition to gape.
10. Rending pain in right upper jaw, towards the ear.
11. Mouth full of saliva and total disinclination to drink.
12. Saliva more viscid, constant spitting; feeling of general malaise all over, without pain.
13. Increase of saliva.
14. A large quantity of viscid saliva in the mouth.
15. Saliva more plentiful, but thin and of a yellow color.
16. A desire to swallow, and spittle more viscid than usual.
17. Difficulty in swallowing liquids.
18. Sensation as of inability to swallow, but can do so when trying.
19. Difficulty in swallowing liquids; epiglottis appeared partially paralyzed.
20. Burning down the œsophagus.
21. Constant desire to swallow.
22. Violent spasm of the throat with sense of suffocation.
22. Strange constrictive sensation, with inability to swallow without great pain.
23. Constrictive sensation in the throat, much worse when swallowing liquids.

Drs. Hartlaub and Trinks recommend *cantharides* as a preventive of hydrophobia. It should be prescribed for the following symptoms:* Alternate paroxysms of rage and convulsions, which may be excited by touching the larynx, by making pressure on the abdomen, and by the sight of water; the eyes look fiery and roll about in their sockets in the wildest manner. The patient is scarcely able to swallow, especially liquids, on account of a burning and dryness of the mouth. There is an excessive desire for sexual intercourse, with constant painful erections, and continual itching and burning of

* Hartmann's Chronic Diseases, vol. ii., p. 164.

the internal sexual parts. The oppression of breathing and anguish are less striking, than in cases for which *bella.* and *hyos.* are indicated; the convulsions, however, sometimes being frightful. In general, *cantharides* appears to be more indicated when the inflammatory symptoms are the most prominent, and when the impeded deglutition does not proceed from a spasmodic constriction of the fauces, but from the inflammation of those parts, or from pains caused by swallowing.

There is a species of hydrophobia, not arising from the inoculation of virus, but proceeding from some violent mental emotion; the disease is termed symptomatic hydrophobia. Fear and imagination, after a bite from a perfectly healthy animal, may give rise to symptoms that very nearly resemble those of the genuine affection. Sometimes very serious trouble is occasioned by large doses of *bella.*, *canth.* or *mercury*, the drug disease assuming as it were the form of a medicinal hydrophobia. The treatment of these affections is generally simple, when their cause is correctly ascertained.

When putrid animal matter has been received into the system by means of wounds, as in dissection, there should be a ligature worn for a time, and suction by the mouth be immediately resorted to, after which, collodion should be applied over the wounded surface; if the wound after a time present rather a bluish appearance with swelling, *china-off.* or *arsenicum* should be given; if mortification or abscess ensue, the treatment has already been mentioned.

Section 6.—*Gunshot Wounds.*

Gunshot wounds receive their name from the manner in which they are produced. They are generally occasioned by fire-arms, by the explosion of rockets and shells, and also comprise many wounds, that, during battle, are inflicted by splinters of wood on board ship, or by stones from ramparts.

This variety of injury partakes more or less of the nature

of contused and lacerated wounds, and is often accompanied with extreme danger, the patient being either immediately or remotely destroyed; or there may exist extensive mutilations, giving rise to abscesses, sinuses, or diseased bones, which are frequently extremely tedious and difficult to heal. Indeed, the after life of the patient may be fraught with such intense suffering, that the approach of death is hailed with joy as the only relief. The kind and extent of the injury must depend upon the form and size of the instrument inflicting the wound, upon the velocity with which it is carried, and a variety of other circumstances.

A ball moving with great rapidity, and striking the body, enters readily, and pursues its course generally in a straight line, either passing through the part or lodging at a greater or less depth. On the contrary, a ball which moves slowly, enters with difficulty, and instead of following a direct line, is diverted by the slightest obstacle, always taking an angular course. Owing to this circumstance, it often happens that a bullet strikes some part of the body, and apparently passes through, but upon examination, it will be found that it has taken a circuitous route, or traversed the head between the bone and the scalp, or passed entirely around the abdomen or neck. When such is the case, the superficial track is marked by a discolored line, sometimes slightly emphysematous. Other instances there are, in which the ball strikes an extremity, runs beneath the integument, or among the muscles, and is lodged many inches—or even two or three feet—beyond the point at which it entered.*

The aperture made by the bullet's entrance is small, and with margins inverted; often it appears of much less dimen-

---

* In one instance, which occurred in a soldier, with his arm extended, in the act of endeavoring to climb up a scaling ladder, a ball, which entered about the centre of the humerus, passed along the limb, and over the posterior part of the thorax, coursed among the abdominal muscles, dipped deep through the glutei, and presented in the fore part of the opposite thigh, about midway down.—*Hennen's Principles of Military Surgery*, p. 34.

sions than the foreign body which has passed through it, and sometimes it may even simulate the incised character. In such cases, the ball has come from some distance, and has struck with considerable force and velocity; the aperture, consequently, is made with comparatively little bruising or tearing, and the elastic textures close upon its track.

The aperture of exit, on the contrary, has its margins ragged and everted; and is of larger dimensions than that which marks the entrance.* When the injury has been inflicted at a short distance, the aperture of entrance is comparatively large, has no smoothness in its edges, and is obviously of a lacerated character; then, too, portions of the wadding are usually impacted in some part of the track, and the surface may be marked by the grains of powder.† There are many instances in which there are not two openings. In such cases, the ball, after having entered, lodges under the integument, in the muscles, or in a bone.

Extraneous substances may be carried before a bullet—such as buttons, coins, keys, &c. These always produce irritation in proportion to the irregular shape of the foreign matter.

In other cases, portions of clothing may be driven before the ball, and be imbedded deeply in the wound. When such is the case, it frequently happens that when the cloth is removed, the bullet is discharged with it.

Balls have been buried, and never been found. They become, in such instances, enclosed in a cyst, or surrounded by bony formation, the patient experiencing little or no inconvenience from them; or they may change their position, and traverse the body, giving rise to pain, long suppuration, hemorrhage, or convulsions. Again, balls by striking forcibly the edge of a

* There has lately been some discussion concerning the size of the wound of entrance and that of exit. The French surgeons, and particularly M. Roux, of Paris, (who has had large experience in such wounds, behind the barricades in that city,) contend, that, in gunshot wounds, it frequently happens that the aperture of entrance is larger than the opening made by the ball as it passes from the body.—*London Lancet*, 1855.

† See Miller's Principles of Surgery.

sharp bone, may be divided, each portion of the bullet taking for itself a separate route.

"It is no uncommon thing," writes Mr. Thompson,* "for a ball in striking against the sharp edge of a bone, to be split into two pieces, each of which takes a separate direction. Sometimes it happens that one of the pieces remains in the place which it struck, while the other continues its course through the body. Of a ball split by the edge of the patella, I have known one-half pass through at the moment of the injury, and the other remain in the joint for months, without its presence there being suspected. In the same manner, I have known a ball divided by striking against the spine of the scapula, and one portion of it pass directly through the chest, from the point of impulse, while the other moved along the integuments till it reached the elbow-joint. But the most frequent examples of the division of bullets, which we had occasion to see, were those which were produced by balls striking against the spherical surface of the cranium. It sometimes happens that one portion of the ball enters the cranium, while the other either remains without, or passes over its external surface. Not unfrequently, in injuries of the cranium, the balls are lodged between its two tables, in some instances much flattened and altered in their shape, and in other instances, without their form being changed."

The course which bullets take is at all times uncertain, "for very slight obstacles cause a retroversion from the rectilinear direction." A shot may rebound from the water, and a button or a handkerchief has been the means of preserving life. "Although," says Mr. Chevalier, "in many cases, a mathematical explication of the course of a ball cannot be given, this arises entirely from the want of data, the laws of matter being fixed and immutable. But when the data are known, as, for instance, the velocity and direction of the shot, the position of the patient, or of the wounded part at the time of the accident, and the structure of the parts penetrated, a much

---

* See Thompson's Reports of Obs. in Military Hospitals in Belgium.

more probable conjecture of the course of the ball may generally be formed than if these circumstances had not been regarded."

The opening by which the ball has made its exit is frequently very near the aperture of its entrance. Indeed, there are cases on record, in which the aperture of exit and that of entrance were the same. Dr. Hennen mentions an instance, in which a ball entered the *pomum Adami*, and, after running completely around the neck, was found in the very orifice at which it entered.

Gunshot wounds partaking of the nature of contused and lacerated wounds, seldom bleed profusely externally, and for the same reason; but often, though the bleeding is not manifest, a fatal hemorrhage may be taking place internally. Secondary hemorrhage is also of frequent occurrence in this variety of wound, from the detachment of the slough, &c. But it must also be remembered, that though immediately after the injury the bleeding may be but slight, in a short time the hemorrhage may become profuse, and particularly if the wound be inflicted in vascular parts, like the face and neck; and this may occur even though the larger branches of the artery may not be opened.

When a large artery is only partially divided, the bleeding is more profuse and dangerous than when the vessel is completely severed; and in such cases, the hemorrhage often continues until the patient expires.

Mr. Guthrie* mentions three cases in which life was lost from wounds of carotid, femoral, and humeral arteries, no means having been adopted to arrest the hemorrhage.

There is a peculiar shock which attends upon gunshot wounds—an extraordinary perturbation, or agitation, which the bravest are not able to resist. This, however, is not invariably present; for, says Dr. Hennen,† "the effects of a gunshot wound differ so materially in different men, and the

---

* On Gunshot Wounds, p. 8.

† Principles of Military Surgery, p. 33.

appearances are so various, according to the nature of the part wounded, and the greater or lesser force with which it has been struck, that no invariable train of symptoms can be laid down as its *necessary* concomitants. If a musket or pistol ball has struck a fleshy part, without injuring any material blood vessel, we see a hole about the size of, or smaller, than the bullet itself, with a more or less discolored lip, forced inwards; and if it has passed through the parts, we find an everted edge and a more ragged and larger orifice at the point of its exit. The hemorrhage is in this case very slight and the pain inconsiderable, insomuch that, in many instances, the wounded man is not aware of his having received any injury. If, however, the ball has torn a large vessel, or nerve, the hemorrhage will generally be profuse, or the pain of the wound severe, and the power of the part lost. Some men will have a limb carried off, or shattered to pieces by a cannon ball, without exhibiting the slightest symptoms of mental or corporeal agitation; nay, even without being conscious of the occurrence; and when they are, they will coolly argue on the probable result of the injury; while a deadly paleness, instant vomiting, profuse perspiration, and universal tremor, will seize another on the receipt of a slight flesh wound. This tremor, which has been so much talked of, and which, to an inexperienced eye, is really terrifying, is soon relieved by a mouthful of wine, or spirits; but, above all, by the tenderness and sympathizing manner of the surgeon, and his assurance of the patient's safety."

Surgeons at the present day, deny the existence of the so termed *wind contusion*, or the effects produced by the wind of a ball; and explain the injuries heretofore attributed to them as produced by spent balls, which have really struck, yet with so little quickness of force as to merely bruise, without inflicting an open wound.

The nerves also suffer, to a great extent, in gunshot wounds, especially those of the extremities. Even after the wound has healed, there may be very distressing sensations around and in the cicatrix, which pains are generally aggravated in damp, cloudy weather, or from cool, moist easterly winds.

The progress of cure in gunshot wounds is often extremely tedious, from the numerous accidents that are likely to ensue. Excess of inflammation, erysipelas, abscess after abscess, excessive suppuration, sloughing, gangrene, non-union of fracture, caries, necrosis, hectic, and tetanus, are some of the untoward events that may occur to prevent the healing of a gunshot wound.

Treatment.—Gunshot wounds, are, to a certain extent, amenable to the rules of treatment that have been mentioned as applicable to contused and lacerated wounds.

The suppression of hemorrhage and the removal of the foreign body, should be attended to immediately. If blood be poured out copiously, the vessel must be ligated, even though incisions be necessary. As soon as the hemorrhage has ceased, it is of much importance to ascertain if foreign substances have lodged in the wound. If the opening be large enough to admit the finger, it may be inserted; or if the wound be small, or if the finger be too short to reach the bottom, a probe must be used. The best of the kind is the long gunshot probe, which, from its length, is preferable to the ordinary instrument carried in the pocket case. It is well, however, before commencing any operation, to administer to the patient *acon.* and *arnica* in alternation; or if there is excessive prostration, *china* may be employed, as such treatment may tend to expedite the disappearance of the shock, and relieve pain.

The patient should then be placed as nearly as possible in the position that he occupied at the time the wound was received, and the probe passed along the wound, gently, but with determination. If from any circumstances the surgeon has reason to believe that extraneous matter is imbedded anywhere in the track of the ball, probing should be instituted as soon as practicable after the infliction of the injury. If this operation be delayed for a time, the lips of the wound close, the whole track becomes so swollen and painful, that it is not only frequently impossible to ascertain the direction the foreign body has taken, but the operation, slight as it may appear, causes intense suffering. But immediately after the wound has been inflicted, the probe carried through the recently made passage, glides along with comparative ease to the bottom of the wound, where it may encounter the foreign body, which may, if practicable, be withdrawn by the forceps, or removed by a counter-opening made just over it. In every case, however, in which the ball is not easily discoverable, all examinations should be abandoned, and the extraneous body allowed to remain in its situation until its locality is better known. Mr. Hunter disapproved of making counter openings, excepting when the integuments under which the ball was lodged were so contused, that sloughing was inevitable; in such cases, the parts might be considered as already dead, and an opening might be made for extraction, but it is the more modern practice to cut down upon the foreign body and extract it, if it is not too deeply imbedded.

Guthrie mentions, that he has cut out a number of bullets that were more than an inch below the surface. However, the surgeon should always be guided by the locality and texture of the wounded part; if the ball be deep and firmly impacted, it is preferable to wait for the relaxation of the textures that occurs during suppuration, before attempting its removal, as at this time the foreign body itself, in obedience to the general law, has begun to seek the surface. It should always be remembered, as has been before stated, that a ball may be enclosed in a cyst, or surrounded by bony formation, and remain for years in such a condition, that the patient experiences little or no uneasiness from its presence.

The forceps that are the most preferable for extracting balls, "should be very narrow, longer and more slender than those contained in the pocket case, with small and very sharp teeth;" these are recommended by Dr. Gibson, who remarks, "I have used them for several years past, and found them very greatly superior to any others I have tried, particularly in those cases where the ball has not been lodged beyond three or four inches in depth; and where it has been deeper seated, advantage has seldom been gained from attempts to remove it by other means."

There have been various instruments recommended for the extraction of balls; perhaps "Percy's Bullet Forceps" have attained the greatest celebrity.

When a bone has been struck, or even grazed, very careful examination is necessary—assisted by incision, if need be—in order to ascertain if splintering has occurred or not. For recent experience in Paris seems to have shown, that unless all bruised and splintered fragments are thoroughly removed at the time, these portions become necrosed, and serious consequences by inflammation and suppuration are likely to ensue.*

The remainder of the treatment should be conducted on the same plan as that noticed under contused and lacerated wounds.

If the wound has been inflicted in a vascular part, and there is considerable oozing of blood from the smaller vessels, the medicines that will frequently subdue such hemorrhage, if *arnica* has not proved efficacious, are *crocus*, *phosphorus* or *diadema*. The latter being recommended "for hemorrhage from every orifice of the body, *for violent bleeding from wounds;*" or perhaps *sabina* may prove useful, provided the remaining symptoms correspond.

If there is merely a contusion caused by a spent ball, *arnica* is the specific. After the extraction of the foreign matter, not only to mitigate suffering, but also to prevent exhausting suppuration, *calendula* must be prescribed. Or if the patient complain during the suppurative process, of boring pain in the head, particularly in the forehead, whizzing and throbbing in the ears, chilliness, particularly of the extremities, *hepar* will be the better medicine.

If the fever be high, with delirium, &c., *acon.* and *bell.* in alternation; or one of the above with some other medicine, may be employed.

If the fever exacerbate at night, and also the other symptoms, and if suppuration proceed slowly, *mercurius*.

---

* Miller's Principles of Surgery, p. 677.

Creos. may be employed if the discharge from the wound is thin and sanious, or consists of decomposed blood, and the patient is debilitated. *Nit.-acid* should also be administered in somewhat similar cases.

Silicea is also another predominant medicine, and should be exhibited, if the wound is very difficult to heal, and the suppuration very profuse; if the inflammation has a tendency to spread, and there is drawing pains in the limbs; also, when the patient is constantly chilly, with insufferable thirst and frequent flushes of heat in the head.

Sulph. must be employed when the patient complains of frequent internal chilliness, or there may be spasmodic jerkings through the limb; when the pains in the wound are aggravated by change of weather, and the patient sleepless and very restless; also for profuse suppuration and unhealthy pus. This medicine is also very well adapted to promote granulation and cicatrization, as is also *silicea,* or according to Thorer, *calendula-off.*

There are also other medicines that may be valuable in the treatment of gunshot wounds, but the practitioner must in all cases select the medicine, whose symptoms correspond to the most of those that are experienced by the patient, always, however, bearing in mind the pathological condition of the part, as it is an index, as it were, to the genus of the remedies, from which the appropriate medicine must be selected.

If gangrene threaten, or to prevent the spreading of such disease, the best medicines are *ars.*, *carb.-veg.* or *china-off.*

Very frequently, the first care of the surgeon is to determine whether to amputate the limb, or to endeavor to save the part. Of course, whenever there is a reasonable hope that the wound may be healed, without the performance of a painful operation, it is the duty of the surgeon to endeavor to produce such favorable results. There are cases, however, when amputation is absolutely necessary. "The question of amputation must therefore be settled by the probability of gangrene, by regard to the power of the system, in the prospect of a tedious and suppurative cure, as influenced by age, habits and previous condition;

by the probability of the limb proving useful or otherwise, if retained; and by the disposable means of conducting the treatment. If it be determined to remove the limb, a second question arises as to the proper time for doing so; whether the amputation shall be *primary*, performed before inflammatory accession; or *secondary*, after the suppurative stage has been established, with decadence of the constitutional inflammatory symptoms. In military practice, there is now little diversity of opinion on this subject—decided preference, for very obvious reasons, being given to the primary operation. The shock having passed off—as usually happens within a few hours—the part is taken away during the interval of systemic repose, between depression and excessive reaction; a period whose average range is from six to eighteen hours. The mangled limb is converted into a simple flesh wound; and the dangers of gangrene, high inflammatory fever and hectic, are removed by anticipation.

"Certain circumstances are usually understood to render the performance of amputation either essential or expedient. 1st. When the limb has been carried away, leaving a shattered and unseemly stump. To refrain from amputation in such a case, were willingly to encounter immediate risk by gangrene, subsequent danger by hectic, under a wasting and long protracted suppuration; and certainty of the stump, even when healed, proving unserviceable. 2. When a limb has been struck by shot, and shattered, although not carried away; when bones are broken, blood-vessels and nerves torn, and muscles bruised to disorganization, gangrene is inevitable and operation imperative. 3. When a mass of the soft parts has been carried away, involving the principal vessels, yet without injury to the bone; or when the main vessels remaining entire the rest of the limb is hopelessly shattered and bruised, still gangrene is certain and amputation demanded. 4. When the part is crushed to disorganization, without wound of the integument; as by a spent ball; a state evidenced by the pulpy, loose feel, coldness and impaired sensibility of the part. 5. When joints are opened, and the bones composing them broken. This applies almost without reservation to the hip, knee and ankle joints. But the joints of the upper extremity are in many cases exempt, and seldom afford unqualified indication for immediate removal; there being in this part of the body a much greater tolerance of injury, as well as power of repair. 6. Compound fractures of the thigh, more especially at its upper part, are usually found to proceed untowardly; and therefore, the majority of such cases are held to demand primary amputation.

"However plainly the local injury may indicate amputation, the operation should not be performed, unless there exist a reasonable hope of recovery.

"Secondary amputation becomes imperative, when gangrene occurs and spreads rapidly, uncontrolled by medicine, or when the constitution appears to sink from unmanageable hectic.

"Sloughing, ulceration, or exfoliation of bone, may, under certain circumstances, require secondary amputation."*

Section 7.—*Tetanus.*

This disease is a well known, and but too frequent result of injuries, and so intractable is the affection under any method of treatment, that its occurrence is always regarded by the practitioner as unfortunate in the extreme; and although the influence that homœopathy possesses over this, as well as over many dangerous surgical diseases, modifies in some degree the danger of the affection, still, until the light of further investigation be brought to bear upon it, the surgeon cannot otherwise than regard it with a suspicious prognosis.

Tetanus is characterized by a permanent spasm of the muscles of a portion, or nearly the whole of the body, rendering it stiff and straight. When the spasm presents itself in the muscles of the neck, throat and jaws, the term *trismus* or *lock-jaw* designates such a condition. When the muscles of the back are

* Miller's Principles of Surgery, p. 677. Edinburgh, 1850.

affected, the word *opisthotonos* expresses the affection, while *emprosthotonos* denotes an exactly opposite condition, the body being bent forwards. *Pleurosthotonos* is the term used when the muscles of the side of the body are affected with tetanic spasm.

The disease may be either traumatic or idiopathic, the latter often arises without any assignable cause, and is usually chronic; the former, being acute, follows upon a wound, or other injury, is much more dangerous and of more frequent occurrence. The spinal system is the seat of the disease; there is an "excitable state of the spinal cord, and medulla oblongata, not involving the ganglia of special sense. This may be the result of causes altogether internal, as in the idiopathic form of the disease; in which the condition exactly resembles that which may be artificially induced by the administration of strychnine, or by its application to the cord. Or it may be first occasioned by some local irritation, as that of a lacerated wound; the irritation of the injured nerve being propagated to the nervous centres, and establishing the excitable state in them. When the complaint has once established itself, the removal of the original cause of irritation, (as by the amputation of the injured limb,) is seldom of any avail; since the slightest impressions upon almost any part of the body are sufficient to excite the tetanic spasm."*

The brain only becomes affected in the last stage of the disease, when the delirium and stupor supervene that are present before death.

Dr. Cullen † writes, "In this disease the head is seldom affected with delirium or even confusion of thought, till the last stage of it; when, by the repeated shocks of a violent distemper, every function of the system is greatly disordered."

The spasm in the generality of instances approaches in the most insidious manner; if trismus is about to commence, there is slight difficulty in swallowing, and the patient cannot open

---

* Carpenter's Physiology, p. 517.

† First Lines of the Practice of Physic, vol. iii.

his mouth to the usual width, there is also hardness of the muscles about the neck and throat; the spasm increases, the mouth becomes distorted, the pulse quick and irregular, the teeth clenched, and the temporal and masseter muscles become hard and bulging; the face is distorted by the spasmodic action; the corrugator supercilii act upon the eyebrows and draw them into angles; the forehead is wrinkled, the nostrils dilate, and the angles of the mouth are drawn backward. The orbicularis oris binds the lips firmly on the teeth, which, however, are now always more or less seen, and sometimes wholly disclosed. The expression is indicative of much suffering, and is quite peculiar to the disease; it may indeed be said to be pathognomonic.

Hitherto the only muscles that have been affected are the voluntary, but at this stage of the disease, the involuntary become attacked; the first affected is the diaphragm, and consequently breathing is performed with difficulty; the other muscles of the system soon participate, until the whole body becomes fixed and rigid. The arms are the last affected, and the fingers may retain their motive power to the last. The bowels are constipated, and there is difficulty in passing urine, occasioned by the spasm of the muscles of the perineum and neck of the bladder.

The disease is more common in hot, than in temperate climates, and children and adults are more liable to be attacked, than youth or aged individuals. It arises most frequently from wounds, etc., inflicted in tendinous parts, that are well supplied with nerves, but it has been occasioned by mere bruises or blows. It also has followed an injury done to the nerves, as when torn in wounds, or ligated together with an artery.

The size of the wound is of no consequence, in regard to its influence upon tetanus, as severe incised, lacerated or contused wounds may heal without its accession, while the disease may appear from a slight puncture or mere scratch.

The duration of time between the infliction of a wound and the accession of tetanus varies. The case which illustrates the shortest period on record, between infliction and invasion, is that related by Prof. Robison, of Edinburgh, in which a negro expired in fifteen minutes after having torn his thumb with a broken china plate.*

If three weeks elapse, the patient may be considered safe.

Treatment.—The remedies that are adapted, and those that have been most successfully used in tetanus, are *acon.*, *ang.*, *arn.*, *ars.*, *bella.*, *camph.*, *cham.*, *cic.-vir.*, *cupr.-mett.*, *hyos.*, *ipecac.*, *ignat.*, *lauro.*, *nux-vom.*, *opium*, *rhus-tox.*, *secal.-cor.*, *stram.*, *verat.*

Aconite is useful, and has been successfully employed in "trismus, with frequent alternation of redness and paleness of the face and distortion of the eyes." It is also to be administered for opisthotonos, the upper and lower limbs drawn in; the hand and thumb being clenched; also, when the lower limbs are constantly drawn close to each other, the eyes turned upwards and the face covered with a cold sweat.

Arnica may be employed in cases of tetanus arising from wounds; although the cases in which it has proved most efficacious, are those in which it was employed after the use of some other medicine. In a case of trismus, with opisthotonos, arising from a wound in the leg, after the violence of the disease had been abated by *mercurius*, the cure was completed by two doses of *arnica* 12. *Arnica* should also be applied to the wounded surface, in water, as well as administered internally, or the treatment may be commenced from the first with this medicine, if the symptoms correspond; short panting breathing; jerks and shocks, as if produced by electricity, tremor of the limbs, &c.

Angustura. Trismus with convulsions of the muscles of the back, twitchings in the top of the shoulder; oppression and spasms of the chest.

Arsenicum must be used when the tetanic spasms are accompanied with frightful concussion of the limbs, when the patient lies as a dead person, extremely pale, but warm, with hands clenched, which are turned to and fro; when the arms are slowly drawn up and down, mouth much distorted and breathing

* Rees' Cyclopedia—article Tetanus.

imperceptible; also when there is stiffness of the limbs, particularly of the knees and feet.

Belladonna is adapted to many of the symptoms of tonic spasms; to these belong partial spasms; shivering and trembling of limbs; spasmodic, constrictive sensations in the epigastrium, which are accompanied by shortness of breath, and an anxious, distressing feeling in the breast; drawing and stiffness in the neck and spine; spasmodic contractions in the tongue; yawning and vertigo; painful stiffness of the muscles of mastication, accompanied with convulsions in all the limbs and chilliness; contortion of the eyes, extension of the extremities, violent distortion of all the muscles, opisthotonos; pleurosthotonos, especially to the left side; paroxysms of stiffness and immobility of all the limbs, or of single limbs only, aggravated by the least contact. Trismus, with painful constriction and narrowing of the fauces, oppression of the chest, labored irregular breathing, delirium and stupor. When *belladonna* is adapted to trismus, especially in the cases of infants, the following symptoms must be present: sudden starting and drawing together of the body and limbs; slight, twitching motions; strabismus; inability to swallow, and finally severe spasms; anxious, spasmodic respiration; dilated pupils; motionless staring eyes; involuntary discharges of fæces.

Camphora. For tetanic spasms, loss of consciousness; limbs extended and fixed, head bent sideways, lower jaw rigid and wide open, lips drawn inwards, unceasing distortion of the muscles of the face, coldness all over the body, oppressed, anxious, panting breathing—Trismus. *Cicuta virosa* is a valuable remedy in tetanus, particularly when the disease presents itself in the form of *trismus,* at the same time there being general tetanic rigidity. The cases that are on record in which this medicine has proved serviceable, have all originated in immediate irritation of the brain and spinal marrow, from injuries inflicted upon the head or along the spinal column. *Cicuta* is indicated when there is deadly paleness of the face, with coldness, grinding of the teeth, foam at the mouth, and inability to swallow; opisthotonos. Tonic spasms of the cervical muscles, cramps, stiffness of the whole body, with coldness, or with curvature of the limbs, which cannot be straightened; paleness and yellowness of the face.

Cuprum-met.—Under this medicine, we find the following symptoms: Paleness of the face, spasmodic contractions of the jaw, foam at the mouth, vomiting, jerking of the limbs, with distortion; opisthotonos, with the limbs spread out to the sides, and the mouth open; rigidity of the limbs and trunk; jaws closed, with loss of consciousness, redness of the eyes, ptyalism, and frequent micturition.

Cham. should be used if there are twitchings of the eyes and eyelids; convulsive jerkings of the facial muscles, the lips being drawn downward; foam at the mouth, and concussion of the limbs.

Ignatia, when there is trismus or opisthotonos, occasioned by fright or chagrin. In a case of opisthotonos, in which the head was drawn powerfully back by tonic spasms, the countenance livid, pupils dilated, respiration and deglutition of fluids difficult; *ignatia* effected a cure.

Ipecac. must be employed when there is a contractive sensation in the throat and chest, either in opisthotonos or emprosthotonos, when there are convulsive twitchings of the lower limbs and feet, together with chilliness and stiffness of the body, with spasmodic jerkings of the arms towards each other; nausea, vomiting, and distorted muscles of the face.

Hyos. is indicated by staring, distorted eyes, spasmodic closure of the lids, bluish face, clenching of the teeth. In trismus, when the patient is conscious. Foam at the mouth, constriction of the throat, twisting of the neck to one side, with rigidity of the hands, contortions, and spasmodic curvings of the body.

Lauroceracus has the following symptoms, which indicate its use in tetanus: Hippocratic countenance, disposition to clench the jaws, spasmodic constriction of the larynx, staring eyes, foam at mouth, stiffness of the neck, and twitchings about the head.

Nux-vomica is indicated when there are continued tetanic

convulsions, alternating with violent concussion of the whole body; violent convulsions of the whole body, with extreme rigidity of the limbs; when the muscles of the chest are affected, occasioning dyspnœa; frightful spasms of the whole body every three or six minutes, with opisthotonos, drawing in of the muscles of the chest, distorted eyes, and redness of the face; spasmodic attacks, merely from touching the hand; alternate opisthotonos and trismus; frightful convulsions, particularly opisthotonos, returning and abating several times in one minute, with full consciousness; violent convulsions, lasting from one to two minutes; all the muscles becoming suddenly stiff, jaws clenched, frequent and irregular pulse and profuse sweat; tetanic spasms excited by the least contact.

Opium may be used when there are jerkings of the facial muscles, distortion of the mouth; trismus, with irregular, difficult respiration, spasmodic trembling of the limbs, with foam at the mouth; tetanic spasms, with opisthotonos and rigidity of the whole body, the trunk being curved in the form of an arch.

Rhus-tox. must be exhibited when there is rigidity, as from contraction of the tendons; tingling and twitching of the limbs; opisthotonos, with great languor; contraction of the fingers, oppression of the chest; pale, sickly countenance. It is also very suitable when the disease arises from injuries inflicted in ligamentous parts.

Secale-cor.—This medicine is adapted to the following symptoms: Humming and roaring in the ears; Hippocratic countenance; trismus, the mouth being spasmodically distorted; trembling and rigidity of the limbs, which cannot be overcome; opisthotonos and emprosthotonos, with cold sweat during the paroxysms, subsultus tendinum, rapid sinking of strength; the thumbs are clenched, with violent contraction of the fingers; grinding of the teeth, vomiting, oppresssion of chest, &c.

Stramonium should be thought of when, during the interval between the paroxysms, the eyes of the patient glisten and sparkle, or when the convulsions appear, there is grinding of the teeth, muttering; oppression at chest; violent motion of the limbs, with stretching and trembling of the hands, clenching of the thumbs.

Veratrum.—Pale, Hippocratic countenance; trismus, grinding of the teeth, spasmodic constriction of the œsophagus, with contracted pupils. There is also spasmodic constriction of the palms of the hands and soles of the feet; twitching of the eyes; the paroxysms are preceded by anguish or despair, the patient being beside himself.

CHAPTER VII.

HEMORRHAGE.

Means and Instruments for Suppressing Hemorrhage.

The term hemorrhage implies the escape of blood from a vessel or vessels in any part of the body; but the following observations apply more particularly to those bleedings that occur in the practice of surgery. The loss of blood may be so trifling that it may continue for years without producing any marked effect on the constitution, as is often witnessed in the case of bleeding hemorrhoids; or it may be such as to threaten immediate dissolution, as happens in surgical operations, and accidental wounds involving vessels of magnitude; the escape may be from a single vessel or from many at the same time; an artery or a vein singly may be the source of hemorrhage, or both may pour out their blood; the occurrence may be the result of spontaneous rupture; the vessels may be torn, cut, or bruised; they may be partially wounded, or completely divided. The bleeding may be the immediate result of an injury, in which case it is termed "primary," or it may happen as the result of sloughing or ulceration succeeding a wound, when it is said to be "secondary." When all primary bleeding has ceased, or been arrested by the surgeon, in the course of a few hours a copious flow may again take place, to which the term "intermediate" has been appropriately applied.

Hemorrhage, under each of the circumstances here alluded to, is of frequent occurrence, and there is no single department of the surgeon's duties, which requires more skill, decision and promptitude than that in question.

Fig. 1.

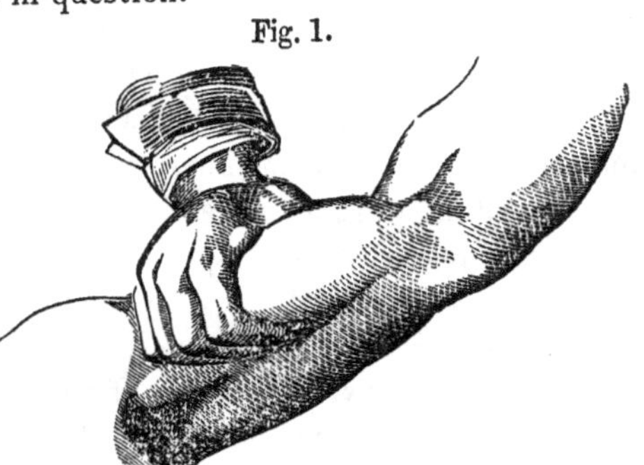

The means and instruments for temporary suppression of bleeding from wounded arteries, (the most troublesome and also the most formidable occurrence in all cutting operations in the living body,) are few and simple in the hands of the experienced surgeon. In amputations of large portions of the extremities, a slight degree of pressure with the fingers or thumbs will, if judiciously applied over the main artery, be sufficient.

Fig. 2.

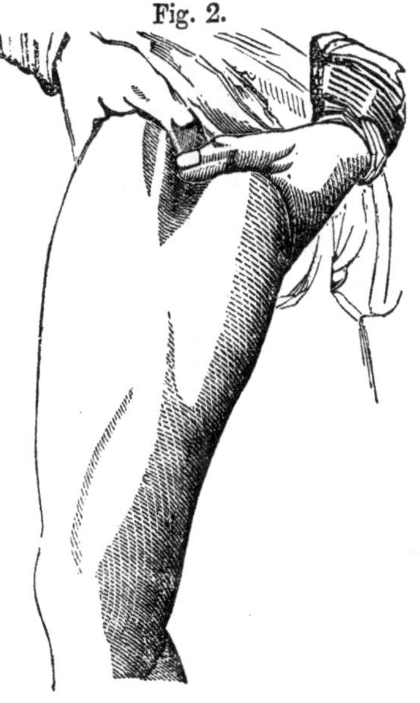

On the upper extremity the circulation may be readily arrested with the fingers, (Fig. 1.) If their points are properly placed over the artery, a very slight force suffices, and any part of the arm may be selected. In all amputations of the lower extremity, when such pressure is required, it had better be made on the brim of the pelvis, (Fig. 2;) if exerted lower down, much additional force is necessary; and even then, especially if the thigh be fat and muscular, it is not always effectual. Occasionally the circulation is stopped in the leg by thrusting the fingers into the ham; but unless the patient be much emaciated, and considerable force be used, the plan is far from being a certain one. Some consider it advantageous to compress as near the place of operation as possible, because in the generality of instances less blood will escape. The principle is a good one, when judiciously acted on; but, in attempting to put it into effect, care must be taken that no impediment is cast on the due performance of the operation—as by preventing a proper retraction of the soft parts—and, also, that the pressure is not applied in a situation where it will be of little or no avail.

In the generality of instances, it is preferable that the pressure be applied over the brim of the pelvis, considering that the ease and efficiency with which this method is accomplished, are fully equivalent to the loss of the small additional quantity of blood intended to be saved by applying it lower down.

Fig.3.

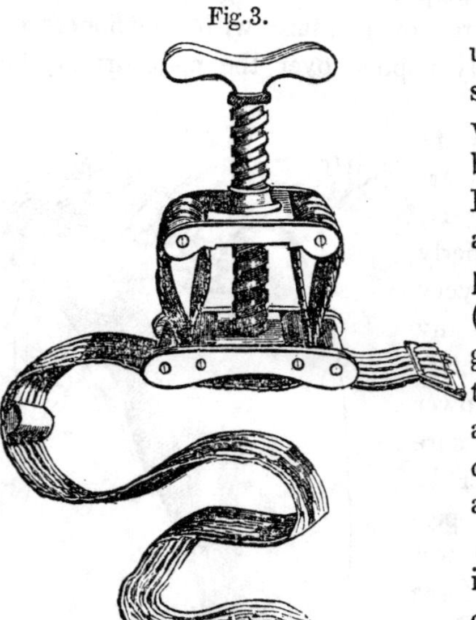

In either the lower or upper extremity, compression may be applied in a variety of places, as will be afterwards explained. For the purposes above alluded to, most surgeons prefer the tourniquet, (Fig. 3,) as being in general more trustworthy than the fingers of assistants, which in protracted operations become fatigued and benumbed.

On the upper extremity, the tourniquet is generally applied about the situation indicated in figure 4; but any other part between the arm-pit and elbow may, according to circumstances, answer equally as well.

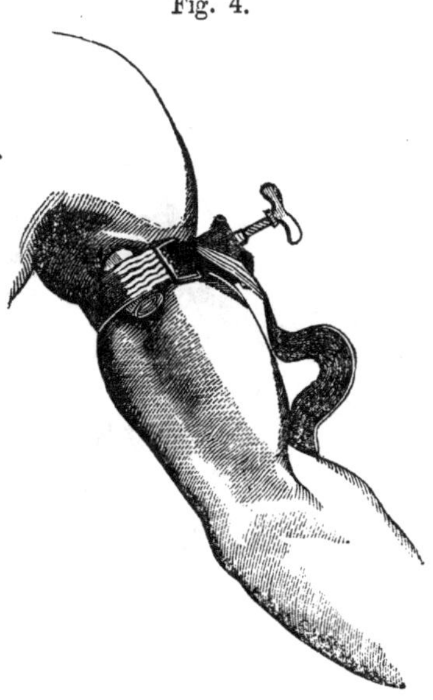
Fig. 4.

On the lower limb, the place usually selected for the application of this instrument is the upper third of the thigh, as represented in sketch 5. If amputation in the thigh is to be performed, the tourniquet should be placed as high as possible; and it should always be remembered that its presence impedes the retraction of the soft parts. In amputations of the leg, some surgeons place the compress on the lower third of the thigh; a large pad, proportioned to the depth of the popliteal space being used on the occasion. This method has received the preference by experienced surgeons.

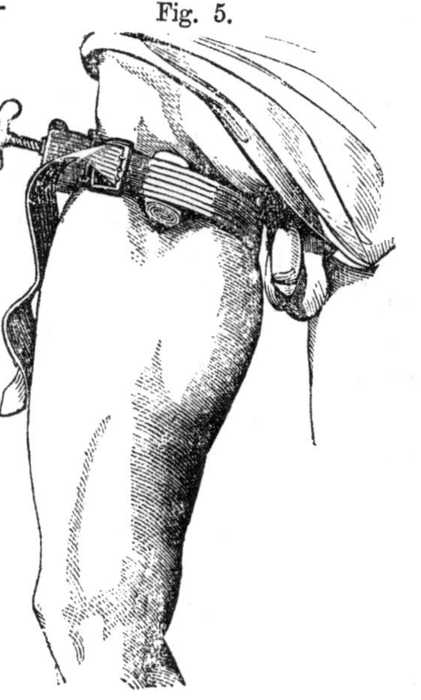
Fig. 5.

If the operation is to be performed on the foot, and a tourniquet be thought requisite, it may be applied with proper effect, immediately above the ankle, one roller being placed over the anterior tibial artery, and another over the posterior.

If the instrument is properly applied at the knee, in the position represented in figure 6, amputatiom may be performed anywhere between the knee and ankle, without, in many instances, the loss of a single ounce of blood.

Fig.6.

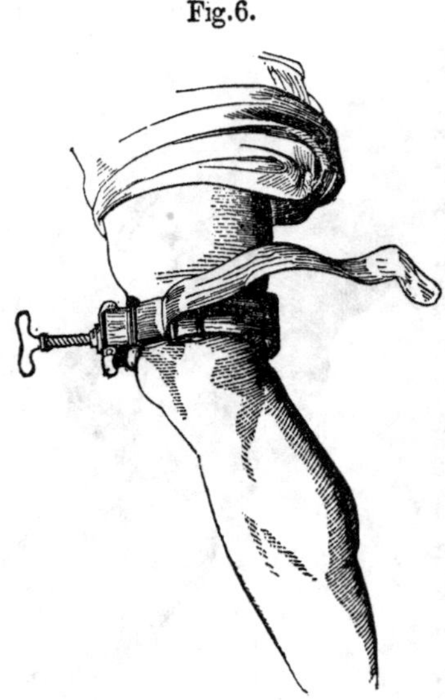

The tourniquet may be applied to either extremity in the following manner: a pad, such as is seen in fig. 3, or what is better a hard roller, (such as exhibited in the other cuts,) about two inches in length and one in thickness, is to be applied to the integument, over and parallel with the course of the main artery, and secured there by one or two turns of its free end; the strap of the instrument is then to be carried round the limb, and fastened by means of the buckle, when the requisite amount of pressure can be applied by turning the screw. The latter movement effects the separation of the two plates with which the strap is connected, and thus diminishes the circumference of that part which is round the limb, and at the same time forces the roller against the artery. If care be not taken in its application, there may be as much danger in trusting to this instrument, as to the fingers; the strap must be sufficiently strong to resist the application of any reasonable degree of force. It appears to be of little consequence on which side of the limb the screw is placed; some surgeons prefer it over the main artery, others directly on the opposite surface of the extremity; but in every instance the roller or pad must be placed directly over the vessel, and the buckle be a sufficient distance from the plates, to allow the screw to be turned freely without any interference.

After vessels are cut in an operation, it is sometimes found necessary to apply additional pressure, which could not possibly be effected if the buckle and plates were in close proximity. It should also be remembered, that when the strap is fastened to the buckle, the screw should be immediately turned, for a very slight pressure round the limb, even that occasioned by the weight of the tourniquet, will retard the circulation through the veins, especially in those which are superficial; and thus whilst the blood still passes with its usual power into the lower part of the limb, a considerable accumulation occurs in the veins below the instrument, and a larger quantity is lost during the operation, than can be deemed in accordance with good surgery.

There are other pieces of apparatus which may be used for the same purposes as the tourniquet, but the above, since its invention by Petit, has generally been considered the most perfect, and it is an instrument which every surgeon should have in his possession. Though he may dispense with its use when surrounded by able assistants, and is himself possessed of great self-confidence, he may, on some occasions, have reason to regret that such means have not been at hand; or even should this not be the case, he will, at best, only display a degree of foolish vanity in his own resources and good fortune, if, in vaunting his temerity, he attempts to bring into desuetude an instrument which has the sanction of the highest authorities, and which has so long been considered indispensable in the practice of surgery.

Various pieces of mechanism have been used and recommended to arrest hemorrhage, but there are none that appear to supersede the tourniquet.

A very ingenious and simple contrivance, invented by Dr. Signoroni, of Padua, and improved and patented in this country, has been successfully used, not only for the suppression of hemorrhage, but also to produce prolonged compression on arteries. It consists of two elliptical bars, united by a hinge at one extremity; the free ends being supplied with pads; by means of a screw working at the joint these bars may be opened or closed at pleasure. The amount of pressure may be regulated by the screw, which being in the form of a key may be removed, the patient being prevented thereby from altering the degree of compression, which, although productive of pain, is often deemed necessary by the surgeon. This contrivance, although exhibiting considerable ingenuity, is not equal to the tourniquet in preventing profuse bleeding during operations.

This instrument (figure 3,) embraces tightly the whole limb, and prevents all circulation in the part beyond the point of application; on that account its prolonged use might be dangerous or destructive to the member, and it therefore can only be employed as a temporary means for suppressing hemorrhage. It may be desirable, in some instances, to impede the flow of blood through the principal vessels of a limb, at the same time leaving all other parts so devoid of pressure, that free collateral circulation may continue; the fingers or hand may be employed to produce this effect, but it is evident that uniform pressure cannot be long maintained by this method. In such cases the instrument of Dr. Signoroni, before alluded to, may be used; it is perhaps one of the best that can be employed when compression of a single artery is required; by its continued application external aneurisms are said to have been cured.

For the permanent suppression of hemorrhage, the open extremities of divided vessels must be secured by some local mechanical means, of which the most common is the ligature. It should be applied in the following manner: An artery that pours forth a considerable quantity of blood, the flow of which is not arrested by ordinary means, should be seized with the "artery forceps," held in the right or left hand of the surgeon, and the vessel drawn a short distance out of its sheath, and after having been carefully separated from the textures with which it may be in contact, a thread should be cast around it, a little beyond the point of the instrument; the ligature should then be drawn together and tied sufficiently tight to prevent its slipping. Thus each vessel may be closed until nature effects its permanent obliteration.

The thread for a ligature should be a small round cord of hemp or silk, about twelve inches long, possessed of sufficient strength to allow moderate force to be applied in forming the knot, which should be tied in such a manner that it will not loosen.

The surgeon's knot, as it is called, which is made by passing one end of the thread twice over the other, before turning each end back again to form the second noose, may be applied, but it seems little used by surgeons of the present day, perhaps in consequence of statements made by Boyer, viz: that Chopart, in the presence of some of the most distinguished professors in Paris, in operating for popliteal aneurism, could not completely restrain the flow of blood by tying the surgeon's knot; a second ligature was applied, and then a third, without success; when, after some deliberation, it was thought advisable to amputate, as it was supposed that the artery was so ossified, that it would not close with a ligature. On examination of the vessel after the operation, it was found in the natural state, and that the knots had not completely closed the canal.

The sailor's or reef-knot, as exhibited in figure 7, when the noose and loops are well made and tightly drawn together, is sufficient in the generality of cases to secure the bleeding vessels; but there can be no harm, indeed it would be proper to form a third knot with the ends of the ligature, when there is the slightest apprehension of its slipping. One end of the thread should then be cut off, and the other allowed to remain hanging from the wound.

Fig. 7.

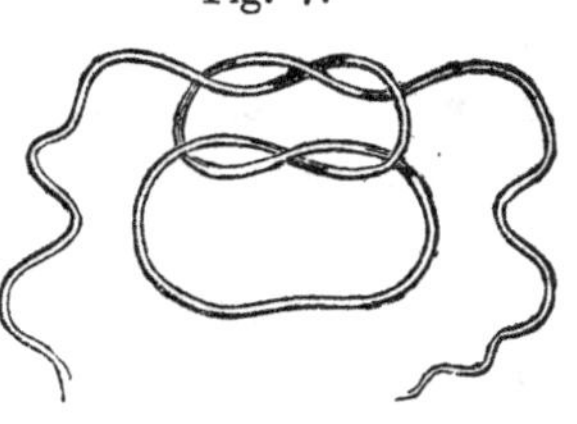

In all instances in which a wound is dressed with a view to union by the first intention, this plan is preferable to that advised by Dr. Hennen and others, who recommend the division of both ends of the ligature; indeed it is even better to permit both portions to remain, than to leave the noose to find its own way to the surface, a process which is sometimes both tedious and troublesome, as well as a source of much anxiety and pain to the patient. Taking into consideration the injury inflicted, and the extent of a wound when a ligature is required, the presence of one or both ends of the thread is a matter of little additional consequence; but if a wound be expected to heal by granulation, both extremities of the ligature should be removed, but even in such cases, much annoyance may be caused by the noose remaining imbedded in the granulations.

The ligature that is most highly recommended consists of small, smooth, and well-spun twine, which, as it comes from the manufacturer, is sufficiently stiff to permit a noose being cast without the aid of beeswax. Silk may be used; but it should not be supposed that a material of more excellent quality will be productive of less irritation in the wound.

Whatever the substance employed, it should be of sufficient bulk to enable the individual who ligates the vessels, to readily feel in the bustle of an operation, that there is something between his fingers.

Very fine silk ligatures are also objectionable, not only for the reasons above mentioned, but also because they may entirely divide all the coats of the vessel instead of the internal tunics.

Mr. Lawrence, in some instances, has recommended fine silk to be employed in deligating arteries, in order that both extremities of the thread may be cut away, thus allowing the smallest possible foreign substance (the noose and the knot,) to remain in the wound; but although the objections stated above regarding thin silken thread as a ligating substance, may be set aside by great care and careful manipulation, there appears to be no particular advantage in the plan, particularly when the portions of ligatures usually allowed to remain, may not weigh more than one-twentieth of a grain.

Sometimes the thread remains in the cicatrix, but much more frequently it is carried away in the discharge, either during the primary healing of the wound, or by subsequent suppuration.

It may happen that a wound will at once close over a thread left in this condition; but in the course of a few weeks or months inflammation and swelling appear, suppuration supervenes, and when the abscess is opened, or bursts of its own accord, the noose will make its appearance. This result forms the principal objection to the practice; if, for example, a patient who has undergone an operation for scirrhous mamma, be dismissed after the lapse of three weeks or a month, with the wound healed, and some time after a painful swelling and suppuration occur in the cicatrix, she naturally supposes that there is a return of the original malady, and will not be convinced to the contrary, until the abscess has closed; and as it may even then be uncertain that all the knots are carried away, for they cannot always be seen, or may be overlooked in the discharges,) she may, during the lapse of a considerable period, still dread a return of her sufferings in the same mamma.

Instead of the ordinary forceps, an instrument with a slide or catch upon it will be of service, when no competent assistant is near. When the artery is seized, the blades will remain shut, and the instrument may be allowed to hang until a ligature can be applied. The catch may be so adjusted, that it may be slipped out of the way or turned aside, to allow the instrument to be used, as the common forceps, at the will of the surgeon. Various ingenious contrivances have been invented to render these forceps efficient and of general utility; all of them, however, are modifications of the instruments used by Amussat in torsion of the arteries, a method of arresting hemorrhage, which, though it has been much practiced on the continent, has never yet received the entire sanction of the profession, and which appears to possess such trifling advantages over the ligature, as to still render the latter preferable. The points of the forceps may be finished with hooks, which are admirably adapted to seize and hold firm any object, such as an artery; indeed the instrument, either with or without the catch, is of invaluable service in removing small tumors from the neck, axilla, and such other parts, where it is desirable to draw the swelling well out before using the knife to divide the textures behind. In hemorrhage from smaller vessels, these forceps may also be applied with advantage, and by twisting the artery on itself, the bleeding may be arrested.

It sometimes happens, that the vessels cannot be readily seized with the forceps, or cannot be drawn out of their sheaths, to allow a thread to be applied. A pointed hook, or tenaculum, will then be of advantage; some even prefer it to the forceps on all occasions. The sharp point is thrust through the bleeding vessel, and some of the surrounding parts, (for we can scarcely avoid including some of the neighboring tissues, where all are thickened and matted together,) and then raised, so that the thread may be tied beyond the convexity.

In arresting the flow of blood to particular parts, as in secondary hemorrhage, after amputations, or in the operation for the cure of aneurism, when the main artery is cut down upon at a distance from the disease, the common aneurism needle, (fig. 8,) is used. Various sorts and shapes are recommended

Fig. 8.

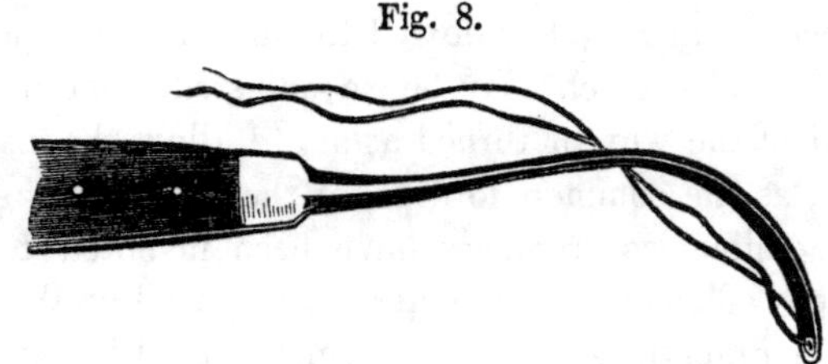

by different surgeons; but one like the sketch will be found most convenient for general purposes. The metal should not bend nor break with moderate force, and the eye should be near the point, which should not be so sharp as to endanger either artery or vein. The handle should resemble that of a common scalpel.

When a ligature is applied to an artery, the nearer it is placed to the neighboring textures, so much the better; care should be taken, however, that none of these are included, particularly the veins and nerves; and in operation for aneurism, the less an artery is disturbed in passing the needle and thread under it, so much the more favorable opportunity is supposed to be given for its permanent closure.

In some rare and troublesome cases of bleeding, when the vessel or vessels cannot without much difficulty be seized with the forceps, it is necessary, in order to arrest the flow of blood, to pass a needle and thread through the textures on each side, in order to include some of the surrounding parts within the noose. Common surgical needles are represented in fig. 9, or one as seen at fig. 10, set in a handle like that of the aneurism needle.

Fig. 9. Fig. 10.

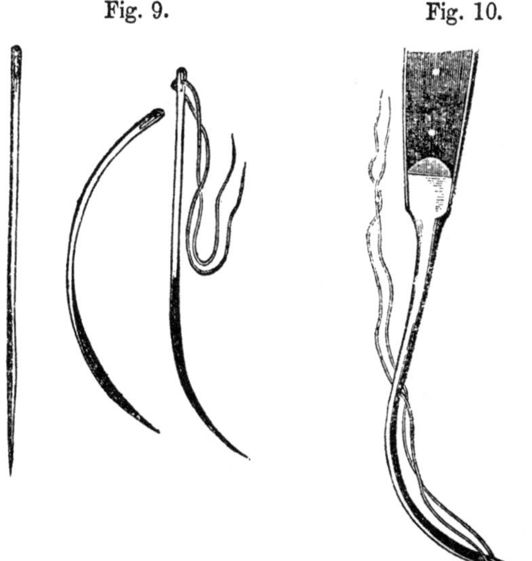

If the parts be deep-seated and difficult to reach, the latter instrument will be most convenient, more particularly if some force is required to push the needle through the resisting textures. For passing threads through small tumors, this instrument will also be found exceedingly convenient.

When these means are resorted to, a little more than the bleeding vessel must necessarily be included in the ligature; and though this circumstance is of no great moment, the rule in surgery, of including the bleeding vessel only, when such a proceeding is practicable, ought never to be forgotten. The end of each thread should be cut with scissors, for when a knife, however keen, is used for the purpose, it will drag out the parts, causing additional pain, and in some instances may actually separate the ligature. The common dissecting scissors will answer; but there may be danger in some cases from the sharp point, therefore, such as those here exhibited, (fig. 11,) are preferable; which, for the sake of distinction, may be called the surgical scissors. Their length should be between four and five inches, and the curve near the hinge will be found of advantage on many occasions.

Fig. 11.

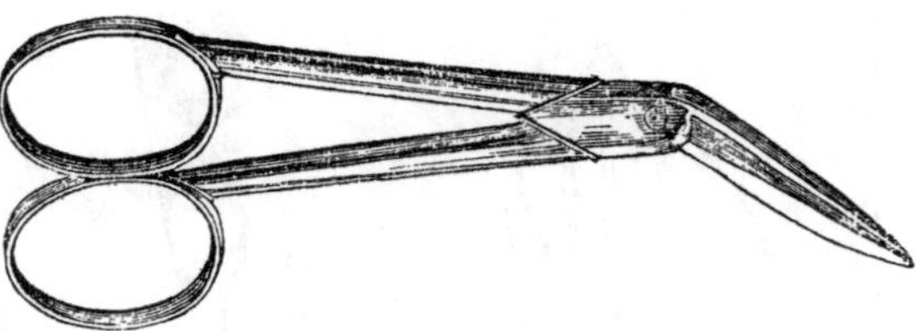

The foregoing observations have reference chiefly to arterial hemorrhage, and that, too, occurring during operations, or immediately after the infliction of wounds; but the surgeon has other kinds of bleeding to deal with, and his assistance is required at other and equally important occasions. Although hemorrhage from arteries is that which is most to be dreaded, it cannot be doubted that the wound or rupture of a large vein, may be equally prejudicial, and therefore the surgeon, in all cutting operations, should endeavor to avoid such vessels. In operations for aneurism, or for the removal of tumors, the larger veins should be carefully protected, for the purpose of preventing hemorrhage, and other unfortunate results which may follow their injury; but such vessels must often be wounded or cut across; as, for example, in operations about the neck, and in amputation. It rarely happens that bleeding from veins is at all troublesome to arrest, unless it be from vessels of the first magnitude.

Perhaps the most to be dreaded of all venous hemorrhages, is that which occurs during operations at the root of the neck, (as on the principal arteries,) and in amputations near the trunk. In the former case, unless some very large vessel is wounded, the blood ceases to flow from the aperture as soon as the struggles of the patient subside, and the respirations become more natural. A slight degree of pressure with the finger is all that in the generality of instances is required, but if this cannot be readily accomplished, a curved copper spatula may suffice, forceps with a catch may be used, or an instrument such as represented in figure 12, has been devised for the purpose of temporary compression.

The blades shut of their own accord, and after being opened and placed upon the bleeding vessel, they retain their hold on the parts with sufficient tightness.

Fig. 12.

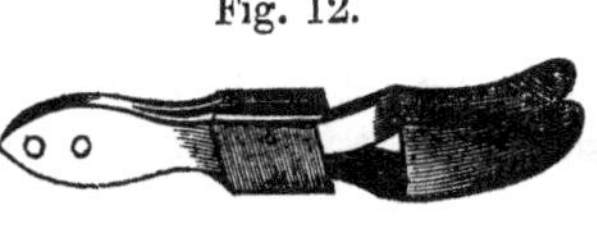

Even ligatures may in some cases be applied. In arresting the bleeding from veins, the threads may be drawn with a tightness sufficient to prevent the blood from flowing; it is deemed by some the best plan to remove them, as soon as the chief part of the operation has been accomplished. In some cases, the surgeon finds it necessary to allow the ligatures to remain, or to replace them, in the event of the hemorrhage continuing; but this measure should not be resorted to, unless the bleeding cannot be restrained otherwise. It must be remembered that, in the neck, hemorrhage may be equally troublesome, from either end of the vein; and on the external jugular, for example, a ligature may be required both on the upper and lower side of the wound.

Venous hemorrhage during amputation, is commonly most conspicuous when the fingers are used instead of the tourniquet, to arrest the circulation; as the main vessels are then alone compressed, the smaller arteries, given off above, convey a large quantity of blood to the part of the limb below the pressure, and it is apt to run from the corresponding veins into the lower part of the larger tubes, and so escape through their divided extremities. The valves in the veins in a great measure prevent this: it often happens, however, but usually ceases as soon as the fingers are removed. Sometimes it is not desirable to raise the fingers until the large arteries have been secured with ligatures; and in such a case, whilst they are being applied, the best manner of proceeding is, for an assistant to place the point of his finger over the bleeding orifice; or such an instrument as that represented above may be applied. At the shoulder, in the leg immediately below the knee, and above the middle of the thigh, the large veins are apt to be troublesome, during the taking up of the arteries, but the bleeding generally ceases when pressure is removed from above, the flaps approximated, and the stump placed in a proper position. In some instances, as in removing the great toe with its metatarsal bone, it is difficult to secure the bleeding arteries in the usual manner; and in consequence of the hemorrhage appearing partly venous, the wound may be stuffed with lint, and a bandage applied over all with good effect; but this course prevents union by the first intention, and should not, therefore, be resorted to unless the necessity be urgent.

In amputations, and in all other operations involving the division of veins, it is seldom requisite to apply more than moderate pressure to arrest the flow of blood from the divided ends. Formerly it was the custom to secure the vein and artery in the same ligature, but such a plan is now obsolete, excepting in rare cases, when the surgeon can scarcely do otherwise.

In securing the main artery of a limb, especial care must be taken to exclude the accompanying vein and nerve. This method is a great improvement upon the plan formerly adopted by surgeons, who in the generality of instances embraced within the ligature all the textures that surround the vessel, thus causing increased suffering to the patient and unnecessary trouble to the operator. Recent experience proves, that notwithstanding the fatal results of ligating the internal saphena, (as practiced by Home and others,) the danger of interfering with veins is comparatively of slight import; and as it is rarely necessary to apply a ligature to arrest venous hemorrhage, there is no occasion to inflict that additional wound upon the vessels, which a thread would inevitably produce.

When there is oozing of blood from veins or arteries, it can frequently be arrested by the application of dry lint, or of that substance immersed in cold water; if this, however, fails to produce the desired effect, the compress should be moistened with a solution of *arnica* or *calendula*, which medicines at the same time may be internally administered. If considerable laceration of the soft parts has given rise to the necessity of operation, the latter will be preferable; if contusion, the former should be exhibited.

Sometimes a pad, composed of patent lint, applied and retained by a roller upon the affected part, will by its presence form coagula and arrest the hemorrhage.

If these means also fail, the internal administration of *diadema-aranea*, together with the external application of a solution of the same medicine—composed of one part of the tincture to ten of water—will probably produce the desired effect. *China* may also arrest this form of hemorrhage; as may also *crocus* and *sabina;* provided the symptoms of the patient correspond to those of the medicine. *Agaricus* may in obstinate cases prove of great value. This medicine was the chief ingredient in the famous styptic of Broussard, whose preparation for arresting all manner of bleedings was regarded with wonder and even superstition.

In all cases, the part from which hemorrhage occurs should, if possible, be placed in a position rather above the level of the heart, as this may in some degree lessen the discharge of blood.

Secondary hemorrhage is often more alarming and more uncontrollable than that which occurs during the performance of operations, or as the immediate effect of injuries. This "secondary" bleeding usually happens after amputations and operations for aneurism, about the period when the ligature separates from the principal artery, and it is a well-known result of gun-shot injuries which involve one or more of the principal vessels of a part. It may ensue in consequence of the adhesive process not having taken place at the seat of ligature or in the other wounded vessel, or it may be the result of unhealthy inflammation, or of ulceration in the wound, causing the vessels to open after having been closed by the proper effusion of lymph. The bleeding which occurs in ulceration and sloughing, such as occasionally happens at the ham, groin, and neck, (although it may be for the first time, i. e. primary,) is somewhat analogous, as there is a similar unhealthy action—a similar deficiency of adhesion.

When the artery is small, the medicines before mentioned may relieve, or if these means do not prove successful, the vessels may be seized with the forceps, and twisted upon themselves (torsion). This method of arresting hemorrhage from trivial wounds is very successful, and is generally employed with success by the surgeons of the present day. However, even here the ligature is undoubtedly the safer preventive.

The pressure should be made directly on the bleeding point, by graduated compresses and bandages; and it will be of advantage, too, if the force be applied to the main artery, or arteries leading to the aperture, as on the humeral, radial, and ulnar, in wounds deep in the hand. In some parts of the body, as at the root of the neck, the surgeon cannot do otherwise than trust to pressure, which method must always be considered as hazardous in the extreme. When, however, this cannot be avoided, medicines may be administered internally. When the stream is profuse, on certain occasions—as when the blood flows from a stump—those means already explained may be resorted to.

There may in some instances a question arise in the mind of the surgeon concerning the portion of the vessel to which the ligature should be applied. When this is the case, this circumstance must be remembered—that the very occurrence of secondary hemorrhage may be regarded as sufficient proof that the parts have rather repelled the adhesive process, and that at all events ulceration and other unhealthy action have been progressing at the seat of hemorrhage. In such cases it will be advisable to ligate the principal vessel of the limb at a considerable distance from the divided end of the artery; for example—in a stump after amputation of the leg, the femoral artery should be tied in the middle or upper third of the thigh. The impetuosity of the current is thus stemmed—indeed the hemorrhage generally arrested—but if not, a slight degree of pressure will accomplish the desideratum. In some cases, even after the reproductive process has advanced to a considerable extent, the ligature may slough away, and thus cause another alarming hemorrhage.

CHAPTER VIII.

LIGATION OF ARTERIES.

Section 1.—*Topography of the neck.**

The median line in front, and the two sterno-cleido mastoidei muscles, divide the neck into two *anterior lateral triangles*, whilst the spaces between the sterno-cleido mastoidei muscles and the two trapezei muscles form the two *posterior lateral triangles.* The omo-hyoid muscles divide each of these triangles, into two, forming, 1st, the *posterior inferior* ; 2d, the *posterior superior ;* 3d, the *anterior inferior ;* and 4th, the *anterior superior* triangles. The posterior inferior triangle contains the subclavian artery and vein, the brachial plexus of nerves, and the transverse cervical artery. This is the space for the ligation of the subclavian artery above the clavicle. The posterior superior triangle contains the cervical plexus of nerves and lymphatic glands. The anterior inferior triangle contains the carotid artery, internal jugular vein, the par vagum, and sympathetic nerves. The anterior superior triangle is bounded above by the digastric muscle and lingual nerve ; it contains the carotid artery, internal jugular vein, descendens noni, par vagum, and sympathetic nerves. In this space the carotid artery is quite superficial, and consequently may be tied with greater facility than in any other. The *digastric space* is formed by the digastric muscle below, and the inferior maxillary bone above : it is divided by the stylo-maxillary ligament into an anterior and posterior part. The anterior digastric space contains the submaxillary gland, the lingual and facial arteries, the lingual and gustatory nerves, and the sublingual gland. The posterior digastric space contains the parotid gland, external carotid artery, one branch of the seventh pair of nerves, and the portio dura ; still more deeply, the styloid process, internal carotid artery, jugular vein, the eighth and ninth pairs, and the sympathetic nerve.

* See Hastings' Practice of Surgery, pp. 132 to 142.

Section 2.—Ligature of the Radial Artery.

A line drawn from the middle of the elbow joint to the styloid process of the radius, marks the course of the artery, which is quite superficial. Its upper half lies between the supinator radii longus at the outer, the pronator radii teres at the inner side: it is between its two venæ comites; the radial nerve, which only touches it about its middle, lies at its outer side, leaving it at its lower third to pass to the back of the fore-arm and hand. In the lower part of its course it is in front of the bone, having the tendon of the flexor carpi radialis within, and the supinator radii longus without: just as the artery is about to pass under the tendons of the extensors of the thumb, it gives off the superficialis volæ, which supplies the muscles of the thumb and anastomoses with the arcus sublimis: the radial artery, getting to the back of the hand, dips down between the metacarpal bones of the first finger and thumb, gets to the palm of the hand, and forms the arcus profunda.

Operation.—The radial artery can be taken up with ease in any part of its course from the wrist to its origin, by pinching up a fold of the skin over its course, and passing a scalpel through, cutting outward, making an incision in the integuments about an inch in length; the fascia must be carefully divided, by pinching up a portion of it at one angle of the external incision and nicking it with the knife, then pass the grooved director underneath and divide it by running the knife along the groove of the director: this is a general rule for getting down upon arteries. Another is, not to separate an artery from the surrounding parts more than is sufficient to pass a ligature around it. The vessel being exposed, an armed needle or the director is passed under it, being careful to separate it from veins and nerves; the ligature is to be tied and one end cut off, the other left hanging from the wound, which should be brought together by adhesive plaster.

Section 3.—Ligature of the Ulnar Artery.

A line drawn from the external border of the tendon of the biceps flexor cubiti muscle, to the radial edge of the middle of the ulna, and then carried to the palmar edge of the pisiforme bone, will mark the course of the artery, which is much more deeply situated than the radial: it has the flexor carpi ulnaris at its inner, and the flexor sublimis digitorum on the outer side: it lies on the flexor profundus digitorum, beneath the superficial layer of muscles and the aponeurosis that separates them. At the inferior third of the fore-arm it is superficial, and bounded by the tendons of the above muscles; it passes at the side of the pisiforme bone, over the annular ligament, and, reaching the palm of the hand, forms the arcus sublimis; it is attended by two venæ comites. The ulnar nerve, coming from behind the elbow, joins the artery above the middle of the fore-arm, passing along its ulnar side.

Operation.—The artery can be ligated at any part of its course, by making an incision over it, and proceeding in the same way as in the former case: in taking up the ulnar in its upper third, the incision in the integuments must be at least two inches in length.

Section 4.—Ligature of the Brachial Artery.

This artery lies in the groove between the coraco-brachialis and biceps flexor cubiti in front, and the triceps extensor and insertions of the latissimus dorsi, and teres major behind. In the lower part of the arm it lies in front of the brachialis anticus: the brachial vein is at the inner side; where there are two venæ comites; the artery is between them: the internal cutaneous nerve runs somewhat in front and to its inner side. The ulnar nerve is a little within, and behind the artery. The median nerve, in the upper two-thirds of the arm, lies rather in front of the artery at its external margin, and about two inches and a half above the elbow it crosses in front of the artery and gets to its inner side. The brachial vessels are surrounded rather by a loose cellular tissue than a complete sheath.

Operation.—The artery is quite superficial, and may be tied at any part of its course, by pinching up a fold of the integuments over the artery, and dividing them by an incision about two inches in length, and then proceeding with the knife and grooved director as before directed for the division of fascia; place the director under the vessel, looking carefully that nothing but the artery is included within the ligature.

Section 5.—Ligature of the Subclavian Artery.

The subclavian artery emerges from the thorax between the scalenus anticus and medius muscles, and passes under the middle third of the clavicle: it is bounded internally by the tubercle on the first rib and the edge of the scalenus anticus, which muscle separates the artery from the subclavian vein. Externally is the scalenus medius muscle and the brachial plexus of nerves, the nearest nerve of this plexus lying about a quarter of an inch to its outer side and rather behind: this nerve is about the size of the artery, and should not be mistaken for it. Below and anterior to the artery lies the subclavian vein, which receives at the external edge of the scalenus anticus and in contact with the artery, the external jugular, supra-scapular, and sometimes the anterior jugular and acromial veins. The posterior cervical artery arises mostly from the subclavian, and crosses the root of the neck above the subclavian, on the outer face of the scaleni muscles to get to the trapezius, and is often directly in the course of the incision in cutting down upon the subclavian artery.

Operation.—The operation is usually performed in the posterior inferior triangle of the neck. Depress the shoulder and clavicle as much as possible, pinch up a fold of the integuments and make an incision three inches long, parallel with and about half an inch above the clavicle; divide the platysma myoides, and push the omo-hyoideus muscle and external jugular vein out of the way; divide the fascia upon the director, if it cannot be sufficiently broken away with the finger and the handle of the scalpel. If the posterior cervical artery or any other be cut, it must be tied at once; find the tubercle on the first rib with the index finger, and in a groove to its outer side will be felt the artery pulsating; pass an aneurismal needle from below upwards, and from within outwards, guided under the artery by the finger, at the same time pushing the nerves upon its outer side out of the way; assured that nothing but the artery is within the loop of the ligature, tie it, and bring the wound together as in other cases.

Section 6.—*Ligature of the Common Carotid.*

About the level of the superior margin of the thyroid cartilage the common carotid divides into the external and internal carotids. The common carotid may be tied at any part of its course, but the place of election is the anterior superior triangle; here the artery is covered merely by the platysma myoides and superficial fascia. The descendens noni passes down in front on the outside of the sheath of the vessels; the vein lies external to the artery; the pneumogastric nerve in the sulcus between and posterior to the vein and artery; these three parts are contained within the sheath; immediately behind it lies the sympathetic nerve. The artery runs beneath the anterior edge of the sterno-cleido mastoideus muscle.

Operation.—Gather up a fold of the integuments, and make an incision about an inch in extent along the edge of this muscle; divide the platysma, fascia, and sheath of the vessels, upon the grooved director, taking care in the division of this last to avoid the descendens noni as much as possible; the sheath being open, pass the director or needle under the artery from without inwards, guarding particularly against including the par vagum in the ligature; it requires but little care to guard against this accident, as the vein, artery, and nerve are separated one from another in a great measure by thin layers of fasciæ: the vessel having been tied, the wound is brought together as in former cases.

Section 7.—*Ligature of the Lingual Artery.*

The lingual artery arises from the external carotid, above the cornu of the thyroid cartilage; it ascends above the os hyoides to the base of the tongue, passing between the hyoglossus and genio-hyoglossus muscles. The artery is unattended by nerve or vein, but is deeply situated.

Operation.—Throw the head back; make an incision two inches long just above the cornu of the os hyoides; the submaxillary gland is exposed and pushed out of the way; the digastric muscle is pushed upwards, and immediately under it lies the hypoglossal or ninth pair of nerves, which must be pushed up also; about one line below the nerve the pulsations of the lingual artery can be felt through the hyoglossus muscle; this having been divided with great care, an armed aneurismal needle should be passed around the artery, which should be tied, and the wound brought together as in other cases.

Section 8.—*Ligature of the Facial Artery.*

The facial generally comes off from the external carotid, but sometimes arises in common with the lingual artery. It mounts over the inferior maxillary bone in a groove at the anterior border of the masseter muscle. The best place to tie it is at the edge of this muscle, after it has turned over the jaw. The facial vein is at its temporal side; it is crossed by branches of the facial nerve: over this spot the integument is to be raised, and opened to the extent of half an inch or less; the needle carrying the ligature is passed from without inwards, to exclude the vein. Dress the wound as usual.

Section 9.—*Ligature of the Anterior Tibial Artery.*

On the dorsum of the foot the artery passes under the annular ligament, attended by two venæ comites and a nerve. A line drawn from the ankle joint, midway between the malleoli to the interosseous space between the first and second metatarsal bones, will mark out the course of the artery. It rests upon the tarsal bones between the tendon of the extensor pollicis pedis on the inside, and the first tendon of the extensor digitorum brevis on the outside.

Operation.—Raise a fold of the skin on the dorsum of the foot over the course of the artery; divide it by passing a pointed scalpel through the fold, making an incision about an inch in length; divide the fascia with the aid of the handle of the knife and the grooved director, until the artery is laid bare; pass the ligature under it, avoiding the veins and nerve, tie with the surgeon's knot, and bring the parts together with adhesive straps.

Ligature of the Artery at its Lower Third.—Here it lies between the tibialis anticus internally, and the extensor pollicis proprius externally; it is flanked by its venæ comites. The anterior tibial nerve is nearer the surface, lying external to the artery.

Operation.—Feel for the space between the above-named muscles, and divide the skin over it about two inches in length; divide or break through the fascia; separate the muscles with the finger, which may be passed down upon the artery, which lies moderately deep: its pulsations can be felt; pass the director or aneurismal needle under it from without inwards, avoiding the anterior tibial nerve and the veins; tie the vessel and dress the wound as in previous instances.

Ligature of the Artery at its Middle and Upper Third.—Here the artery lies between the tibialis anticus internally, and the extensor communis digitorum externally, preserving the same relations with the veins and anterior tibial nerve as in the former position.

Operation.—Feel for the space between the above-named muscles, which is easily found by putting the muscles in action; it is generally about an inch from the spine of the tibia; raise a fold of the skin, making an incision three inches long; separate the muscles with the finger, which, when passed down pretty deeply, will feel the pulsations of the artery; pass the needle from without inwards; tie and dress as in former cases.

Section 10.—*Ligature of the Posterior Tibial Artery.*

The posterior tibial artery, behind the malleolus internus, lies midway between the edge of the tendo-achillis and the malleolus internus. It is attended by two veins and the posterior tibial nerve, which lies a little distance behind it.

Operation.—Divide the integuments over the course of the artery, which is quite superficial; divide the fascia carefully, and the artery will be found rather behind the malleolus; pass the ligature from behind forwards, including nothing but the artery within its loop; tie, and close the wound as in former instances.

Ligature of the Artery at its Upper Third.—At this part of its course it is rather difficult to ligate; it is situated beneath the soleus muscle and deep-seated aponeurosis of the leg, resting upon the tibialis posticus and flexor longus digitorum, about the middle of the leg. It is attended by two venæ comites and the posterior tibial nerve, which is at its outer side. The artery is about the middle of the diameter of the leg, and very deeply situated.

Operation.—Divide the integuments about an inch behind the inner edge of the tibia, making an incision about four inches long; place the leg in a position to relax the muscles, raise the soleus from the tibia, and divide the deep aponeurosis on the director; then feel the artery with the finger, and direct the aneurismal needle under it, taking care to exclude everything but the artery within the ligature; tie the vessel, and bring the wound together with adhesive straps.

Section 11.—*Ligature of the Femoral Artery.*

This artery is quite superficial, lying in the sulcus between the vastus internus and the adductor muscles. About the middle of the thigh it is covered by the sartorius. The femoral vein, in the upper part of its course, is at its inner side; lower down it gets posterior to it. The crural nerve is about half an inch outside of the artery, two or three of its branches being very near it, one crossing it. The saphena major descends within the sheath of the vessels, passing along the outer and fore part of the artery, down the middle third of the thigh. A line drawn from the middle of Poupart's ligament to the internal condyle of the femur traces the route of the artery.

Operation.—Feel for the depression between the vastus internus and the adductors of the thigh; divide the integuments for about three inches, avoiding the vena saphena; draw the sartorius muscle to the outside; raise and divide the sheath of the vessels on the director; pass the ligature from within outwards, being careful to exclude the saphenous nerve; tie the vessel, and close the wound as in other cases.

Ligature of the Femoral above the Profunda.—The arteria profunda is given off about two inches below the crural arch.

Operation.—Make an incision about three inches long, over the course of the artery, commencing at Poupart's ligament; clear away the lymphatic glands and fascia; divide the sheath of the vessels on the director, and pass the ligature between the vein and artery from within outwards; tie the ligature, and bring the wound together as before directed.

Section 12.—*Ligature of the Iliac Arteries.*

The primitive iliacs divide opposite the sacro-iliac symphysis into internal and external iliacs. The primitive iliacs are about two inches and a half long: near their bifurcation they are crossed by the ureters, spermatic vessels, and nerves. They lie at the inner side of the psoas muscles. The left iliac, in addition, is crossed by the branches of the inferior mesenteric artery. The internal iliac, about an inch and a half long, is directed downwards and inwards to the sacro-sciatic notch, where it divides into its various branches: the vein lies at its outer side. The external is a continuation of the primitive iliac. A line drawn from the umbilicus to a point half an inch inside of the centre of Poupart's ligament marks the course of the artery, which is at the inner side of the psoas muscle, with the vein upon its inner, and two or three small nerves from the lumbar plexus at its outer side. The anterior crural nerve lies at the outer side of the psoas muscle. Near Poupart's ligament the external iliac artery gets in front of the psoas muscle: about this point it is crossed by the circumflex ilii vein, spermatic vessels, and vas deferens, which, on turning down into the pelvis, touch its inner side. Just above Poupart's ligament it gives off the epigastric and circumflex ilii arteries.

Operation.—Place the patient on his back, with the thighs and trunk slightly flexed; make an incision through the integuments, half an inch from the external abdominal ring, passing in the direction of the anterior superior spinous process of the ilium, about an inch above Poupart's ligament; cut through the tendon of the external oblique, and get under the edges of the internal oblique and transversalis muscles; raise the fascia transversalis on the director with great care, and divide it; then strip off the peritoneum from the loose cellular tissue with the fingers, and feel for the artery, which can be readily reached; pass the aneurismal needle, guided by the finger, from within outwards, avoiding the vein and other vessels; the ligature being passed, tie it, and bring the wound together, dressing as in former instances.

The only difference between tying the external iliac and the primitive iliac, is the necessity of carrying the incision higher up towards the crest of the ilium.

It may sometimes be necessary to tie the arteria ad cutem abdominis, as well as some branches of the epigastric and circumflex ilii arteries, in this operation.

CHAPTER IX.

ABSCESS.

When pus is fully formed, and collected into the parenchyma of a part, the condition is termed abscess, which, on account of the frequency of its occurrence and its numerous complications, is of great interest to the surgeon.

Lining the cavity that contains the pus, especially if the abnormal condition have continued for any length of time, is found a tissue, having a membranous appearance and a membranous function, and possessing a power of maintaining the formation of pus; hence it is termed the *pyogenic membrane*. This tissue is endowed with very considerable capability of secretion, but as an absorbent surface it is comparatively feeble. In regard to this latter point, however, it may be useful to remember that the pus globule, when extra-vascular and complete, is of comparatively large size, not soluble in its own serum, and therefore but little amenable to ordinary absorption; the serous portion of pus may be taken up readily enough, but the solid part probably remains but little affected. And thus the feebleness of absorbent power may depend, not so much on defect of either structure or function in the pyogenic membrane, as on the nature of the fluid on which it has to operate.

Sudden suppression of purulent formation, is always to be regarded as an untoward event. It is more liable to occur in the case of free and open suppuration, than in an unopened abscess. It may be the result of some accidental occurrence, the nature of which we may be unable at the time to ascertain, or it may be caused by injudicious stimulation, designedly applied to the part; but the suppression, no matter how it may be induced, is always likely to be followed by disastrous consequences.

The process of *pointing*, and the great necessity of observing *fluctuation*, have been alluded to in the chapter upon suppuration; but there remains to be mentioned, one of the most important circumstances connected with abscess, which if neglected may be attended with fatal results, or at least with great danger and trouble.

It sometimes happens that an abscess is situated directly in the course of an artery, and when such is the case, the greatest care and discrimination should be exhibited in the diagnosis, between the collection of pus and aneurism; the most experienced have been misled by circumstances, and deceived by appearances. Dupuytren himself, whose ability and surgical skill have always been regarded by the profession with the greatest esteem, failed in his diagnosis, and once plunged a lancet into an aneurism, mistaking it for an abscess.

The diagnostic signs are:

From the earliest stage of abscess the tumor is hot, throbbing, hard and incompressible; in aneurism the tumor is of natural temperature, and is soft and fluctuating.

The skin covering an abscess is inflamed and discolored, that which covers an aneurism is of natural color or perhaps paler.

In abscess the formation of the tumor is much more rapid than in aneurism.

In aneurism the tumor is pulsating; in abscess it is fluctuating, but has no pulsation.

The enlargement in abscess cannot be diminished by pressure, in aneurism the contrary is the case. When, however, the diagnosis is sufficiently established, it may become a question to the surgeon, whether the pus shall be evacuated by the lancet, or whether it would be proper to endeavor to produce absorption.

It is stated on the best authority, that large abscesses have been in a *few* instances absorbed. Small quantities of pus frequently disappear, therefore, the practitioner, if the case permit, should endeavor, by administering the proper medicines, to bring about such a result; if this, however, cannot be effected, it is preferable to employ the lancet, rather than wait till nature accomplishes the discharge. On this subject Mr. Fergusson writes, "It is, I imagine, too much the custom to allow matter to be discharged naturally. In most parts of the body, if the suppuration be deep-seated, the matter may extend widely, and do much harm by the separation of textures, ere it can reach the surface; and even when it does so, and is discharged through some small opening, it rarely happens that the interior of the abscess closes entirely; a discharge continues long afterwards, and ultimately the interference of the surgeon is required. From this it may be seen, that I am averse to leaving such cases entirely to nature; occasionally the surgeon cannot do otherwise, and sometimes, even with all his care, matter will burst forth when he does not expect it. If an abscess in the perineum, for example, be left for a day or two, under the supposition that the delay will be advantageous, even though it may be intended to use the knife to open it, the practitioner is often amazed to find that the matter has, in the lapse of four-and-twenty hours, made an exit through the skin or mucous membrane in the vicinity of the anus; yet it seldom happens, in such instances, that the knife is not ultimately required.

"However, except under pressing circumstances, I must

declare myself an advocate for delay in opening abscesses. I am of opinion, that in ordinary abscess, a bubo, for instance, if an opening is not made until the matter has approached near to the surface, the subsequent progress of the case is much more rapid and satisfactory, provided that a proper opening be made. I have seen a good deal of the practice of making early openings, and have invariably observed, that more pain was thereby induced, and I have often fancied, an additional amount of suppuration, whilst the after treatment has been remarkably tedious."

When it is deemed necessary to open an abscess, the incision should always be made where the integument is thinnest, or in other words, where the abscess points, at which place, often a discoloration is manifest.

In most cases the opening should be made freely, and the matter liberated at one operation; but when the abscess is large, and the constitution of the patient feeble, the exposure of so large a surface and the speedy evacuation of a quantity of matter, might be dangerous in the extreme; it is then recommended to ascertain to what degree the sac may be diminished, by lessening gradually the quantity of fluid, after the manner recommended by Abernethy. That is, by making a small oblique opening, and allowing as much of the contents of the cyst to flow out, as the natural elasticity of the walls will permit; the wound will, perhaps, afterwards heal by the first intention, the aperture may close perfectly, the patient not be injured by the operation, and there will be much less fluid in the abscess; this procedure may be continued, until the sac becomes sufficiently diminished in size, to allow it to be laid open in the same manner as smaller abscesses. When a lancet is used, it should be held in the position represented in fig. 13.

Fig. 13.

Fig. 14.

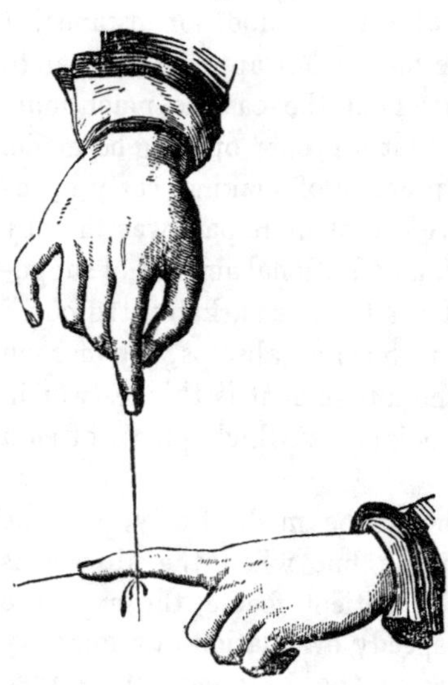

When the pus is deep-seated, the fore finger of the left hand, and perhaps the middle also, being placed over the abscess with gentle pressure, the back of the knife should be caused to rest against the side of the fore finger, (as seen in fig. 14,) the point should then be thrust through the skin; and the coverings of the matter divided as far as may be deemed expedient; the blade may then be turned slightly on its long axis, when probably the pus will spring up along its surface. These methods are recommended by Mr. Fergusson, who remarks, "In opening abscesses, whatever be the instrument used, I invariably prefer puncturing first and then cutting from within outward, to the method pursued by some, of making a sort of dissection, by successive incisions, through the skin and other textures."*

But the Homœopathic surgeon, may be able, in many instances, to overcome the necessity of operating, by the administration of appropriate medicines; by the action of which, the suppurative process may be hastened, and the abscess allowed to open spontaneously; this should always be effected if practicable, and the medicines that have been most efficacious in producing such a result, are *hepar*, *merc.* and *silic.*

When there is much constitutional disturbance on account of the violence of the inflammatory action, *acon.* and *bell.* are to be used, either separately, or in complicated cases in alternation; the doses to be repeated *pro re nata;* the proper antiphlogistic regimen also being observed.

* Practical Surgery, p. 88.

Lachesis is pronounced an excellent remedy, when there has been much distension of the skin, which has a bluish tinge, or where the structure has been destroyed by the magnitude of the abscess.

The medicines for abscesses, are, (1.) *bell., hep., merc., sil., sulph.* (2.) *Calc., lyc., phos., puls., sep.*

For *acute abscesses: ars., asa., bell., bry., cham. hep., led., mezer., phosph., puls., sulph.*

For *chronic abscesses: asa., aurum., calc., carb.-veg., con., hep., iod., laur., lycop., mang., merc., merc.-corr., nitr.-ac., phos., sep., sil., sulph.*

ARSENICUM: Intolerable burning pains, during the fever; or when the abscess threatens to become gangrenous, or is accompanied with great debility. *Chills, fever, and consecutive sweat;* secretion of offensive matter during the second period; muscular prostration.

ASAFŒTIDA: Abscesses discharging a *colorless, serous pus;* violent pains on contact, and great sensitiveness of the adjoining parts; also when there is intermittent pulsations in the tumor, with darting, tearing pains, which are somewhat relieved by pressure.

BELLADONNA: Pressure, burning and stinging in the abscess; *cheesy* and *flocculent pus.* It is especially suitable for hepatic abscesses, and also covers very many of the constitutional symptoms that present themselves during the suppurative stage.

BRYONIA: The tumor is *either very red* or *very pale,* with tensive pain, with sharp sticking and lancinating pains, throbbings in the part, symptoms being worse towards evening and at night.

HEPAR: When abscess occurs in lymphatic, phlegmatic individuals, with white delicate skin, blonde hair; especially when the pains are *pressive,* aggravated at night, and by exposure to cold; when maturation is imperfect, although for this symptom, Dr. Kaspar prefers *mercurius.** *Baryta-*

* Dr. Rummel is opposed to opening an abscess, until the whole tumefaction is matured, and he prefers cold-water fomentations, and upon them

carb. and *carbo-an.*, are also powerful medicines for promoting suppuration, when the tumor appears very hard; the former, by some authors, is regarded almost a *specific.*

MEZER: For abscesses of *fibrous parts,* and of *tendons,* or for abscesses arising from abuse of mercury, attended by stinging and throbbing pains.

PULSATILLA: When the abscess *bleeds readily,* with stinging or cutting pains; or when an *itching,* burning and stinging are experienced in the surrounding parts; especially if varices be present, or, likewise, if the abscesses arise *after violent and long-enduring inflammations.*

RHUS: Especially for abscesses of the *axillary* or *parotid* glands, when the swelling is painful to the touch, or discharges a *bloody-serous* pus, with stinging and gnawing pains.

MERCURIUS: *Slowly suppurating abscesses.* Continual thirst, coldness of the hands and feet, with internal chilliness during the febrile stage, with drawing pains in the abscess, and *all the symptoms excessively aggravated at night.*

SILICEA: Abscesses with stitching and throbbing pains. This remedy hastens suppuration, or restores it when it has become arrested in consequence of the suppression of nervous influence. The pus may be laudable or ichorous. It is also serviceable after matter has been discharged, to promote granulation and cicatrization. *Calendula officinalis* is highly recommended by Dr. Thorer, when the suppuration is profuse and exhausting, especially in traumatic abscesses.

SULPHUR is especially suited for chronic abscess, and for a tendency to suppuration, dependent upon a psoric or scrofulous diathesis. When the pains are throbbing or stinging; or when, after the evacuation of pus, there is a tendency to ulceration. This remedy is frequently indicated to complete the cure of the disease.

---

a thick warm covering, (we should prefer oiled-silk to warm poultices.) *Hepar-sulph.* 30 has proved very useful, especially in suppuration of the glands, also in the syphilitic and gonorrhœal bubo. Sometimes under its use, the suppurative process is rapidly followed by absorption, and the abscess disappears without being opened. Quarterly Homœ. Journal, vol. i., p. 139.

The importance of applying pressure in the treatment of extensive abscesses is strongly recommended by Mr. Solly,* who writes, "I am not aware how far the plan, which it is my object in this paper to advocate, is in general use or not, but I am so convinced of its value, that I shall venture to bring it forward. I refer to the careful application of pressure over the surface of extensive abscesses, after their contents have been discharged, and the *early disuse of the poultice and its congener, warm water dressing*. I always prefer cotton wool to any other kind of pad, as it fits better with all irregularities of surface; and I find that a greater amount of deep pressure can be kept up by strips of plaster than by a roller. By these means the surfaces of the abscess are kept well in contact, they adhere together and the discharge soon ceases."

Section 1.—*Abscess of the Antrum Highmorianum.*

Abscesses of the antrum highmorianum, fortunately for mankind, are not of very frequent occurrence, as they are in the majority of instances tedious in their cure, and productive of much pain. The disease may arise from blows on the face, chronic inflammation of the pituitary membrane lining the nostrils, exposure to a cold and damp atmosphere, but more frequently from decayed teeth, which by the irritation they occasion in the membrane lining the cavity, produce the inflammatory process which terminates in the formation of pus.

This affection in its first stages is very difficult to diagnose, and the first intimation that the patient receives of the disease is pain, which is most generally referred to a carious tooth, and laboring under such a mistake, several teeth are often extracted; this, however, does not relieve the suffering, unless one of the fangs has penetrated through the floor of the antrum, and being removed allows free exit to the matter that has been secreted and accumulated in the cavity. If this is not the case the pain continues extending farther up, and more

---

* London Lancet, April, 1855.

in the direction of the nose and orbit, than is the case in ordinary toothache; but even this circumstance does not lead the patient or the practitioner to suspect, the true nature of the affection; in fact, such pain may often be present in facial neuralgia, without any disease of the antrum whatsoever. The sufferings of the patient continue for a length of time, increasing in violence, until finally a tumor becomes perceptible below the malar bone; this enlargement may extend over the whole cheek, but there is a circumscribed hardness situated above the back molars. The pus may be evacuated through the cheek, or the matter may move towards the palate, forming a swelling there, and rendering the bone in the vicinity carious, unless the patient be relieved; or a portion of it may be discharged through the nose, when the patient is lying with his head low, and on the side opposite to that which is affected; or, as in many instances is the case, the matter may trickle down between the fang and the socket of the tooth. The pus that is thus discharged is often so extremely fetid that no one can enter the room occupied by the patient without being disgusted by the odor, and the patient is rendered disagreeable to himself on account of the matter flowing into the mouth and throat when lying down. The pain is severe and generally throbbing; sometimes it remits, but for a short period, returning again with increased violence.

The formation of pus in the antrum is often attended with disease of the superior maxillary bone, and is in all instances tedious, and in many difficult to cure.

The first step in the treatment must be to evacuate the pus, after which the surgeon can more readily ascertain the condition of the cavity—whether there be caries, or if any morbid growth be present within; the selection of remedial measures consequently being rendered more certain.

All the grinding teeth of the superior maxillary bone, excepting the first molar, correspond with the floor of the antrum. These teeth sometimes extend into it, and the fangs are only covered by the membrane lining the cavity; therefore the simplest method of evacuating the pus is by drawing one of the teeth. A caries, or a continued toothache in one of the molar, should decide the practitioner which tooth to extract; but if all appear to be sound, the direction is, to strike gently each one of them, and that which appears most tender, or gives rise to most pain, should be selected.

The third or fourth molar most generally is extracted, after which operation, if the pus is discharged, no further operation is required; if the matter does not follow the removal of the tooth, a stilet or small trocar must be pushed into the cavity to produce the desired effect. After the evacuation of the pus, a probe may be gently pushed into the antrum, and the condition of the bone, &c., ascertained. After the contents of the cavity have been discharged, it should be cleansed by means of an injection, thrown into the part from a small syringe, with a somewhat curved pipe. A piece of bougie must also be worn, to allow the matter that collects to be evacuated, and *hepar, ars.*, *lyc.* or *silic.* be administered, or other medicines (mentioned in the chapter upon abscesses,) employed, according to the presenting symptoms.

"Dr. Gullen, of Weimar, from experience in several cases, strongly recommends *ars.* and *lyc.* in this complaint. *Arsenic* generally removes the dreadful throbbing, divulsive pain, which assumes the quotidian type for the most part; and *lyc.* is useful in arresting the thick yellow discharge, which frequently continues after the pain has ceased. Dr. Gullen recommends the higher dilutions of both these remedies, and the use of *silic.* after the discharge has abated."*

To obviate the necessity of extracting teeth, *La Morier*, of Montpelier, proposed to perforate the antrum above the alveolar processes, immediately over the third grinder; but, says Dr. Gibson, "the disease, however, so seldom occurs without being accompanied or caused by carious teeth, that such an operation, though practicable, can scarcely ever be rendered necessary.

* British Journal of Homœopathy, vol. i., p. 407.

After the evacuation of the pus, the cavity must be carefully examined by means of gentle probing. If the internal lining membrane be diseased, *calc.-c.*, *mez.*, *phosh.-ac.* may prove serviceable, if other symptoms correspond; should, however, the affection have been produced by the decayed tooth, its extraction and the discharge of the matter will afford great relief, and the exciting cause being removed, the medicines will doubtless exert their beneficial actions. But too frequently the disease has extended itself, not only to the membrane lining the cavity, but also to the bone itself; in such instances, the treatment, of course, must be directed to the carious bone.

The medicines that have proved most serviceable for disease of the osseous structure, are, *calc.*, *lyc.*, *merc.*, *phosph.-ac.*, *silic.*, *staphys*, *sulph.*—or, *ars.*, *asaf.*, *aur.*, *hepar*, *nit.-ac.*

From clinical cases that have been recorded, we learn, that *phosph.* is an excellent medicinal agent for diseases of the bones, particularly caries or necrosis. In the British Journal of Homœopathy,* there is an interesting account of a child that became affected with diseased bones from the vapor of *phosph.* Such testimony as this should at once lead the practitioners of our school, to investigate more thoroughly the action of our medicines, as in these instances especially, the power of drugs over diseases is distinctly perceptible.

Aurum. and *nit.-acid* are excellent medicines when the patient has previously been affected with syphilis; *mez.* will be found efficacious in mitigating, and often arresting the intolerable *burning* pains which are present, particularly at *night.*

This medicine, perhaps, is better adapted to the disease when the bone itself has not been implicated, but when the whole lining membrane of the cavity is in an abnormal condition. *Mezereon* acts more particularly on periosteum than on *bone.* It is adapted to dull, crampy pain, and tearing in the malar bone, with anguish, paleness of the face, continued chilliness, sometimes cold sweat, constant thirst, tongue coated white, want of appetite, pale urine, and frequent, small pulse.

* Vol. vi., p. 284.

Kali-hydrioticum is a medicine that has been frequently overlooked in the treatment of this disease; it is suitable not only to those cases that have originated from the syphilitic poison, but is likewise serviceable when there is a violent darting pain extending to the ears, or when there is a constant *grumbling* sensation in the tooth and face, when there is excessive accumulation of saliva, with importunate thirst night and day.

As palliatives for the pain that is often so severe as to be almost unbearable, *spigelia, nux-vom., china* or *phosph.*, will be found of much service. *Spigelia* must be administered when there is a pressure experienced in the region of the antrum, with darting and tearing pains, accompanied with burning.

Nux-vom. is indicated when there are tearing pains in the malar bones, with continual painful soreness of the teeth, together with *boring* and gnawing pains.

China will relieve the pains when they are cutting and burning, or when there is drawing pressure in the molars, with sensation of numbness in the side, or when there is a beating or throbbing in the malar bone, with fine stitches through it.

Phosph., when there is burning and throbbing in the region of the antrum, when there is a continual, dull, aching pain (grumbling) in the molars, with jerking and tearings.

Mercurius is an important medicine, and is well suited to the disease after the pus has been evacuated, and when there is caries of the bone; when the pain extends to the ears, is darting and tearing, and particularly unbearable at night.

Teucrium is warmly commended for diseases of the antrum. *Staphysagria* will also prove serviceable, not only for the darting pains in the antrum, but also for any unnatural bony formation. In addition to the medicines already mentioned, *Sulph., carbo-v., antimonium-crud.*, may be indicated in this affection.

Section 2.—Mammary Abscess, Mastodynia Apostematosa.

Abscesses of the mammæ, although most frequently occurring in females who are nursing, may also be present in women who have never been pregnant; indeed, by some writers, we are informed that men have been affected with the disease.

A patient about to suffer from this variety of abscess, experiences for a day or two before the local inflammation manifests itself, general lassitude, restlessness, and uneasiness, together with slight soreness of the gland. Afterwards, there may be coldness of the body and shiverings; the mamma becomes enlarged, heavy, painful, and may assume a redness all over its surface, or the tint may be deeper in some parts than in others. If the glandular portion be most affected, the breast appears, when handled, to be lobulated and hard; but if the skin and cellular tissue are the seat of the disease, the tenseness is uniform throughout. As inflammatory action proceeds, the pain becomes throbbing, extends to the axilla, and is often intense, and the patient is unable to bear the slightest pressure upon the part, even the contact of clothing aggravating the suffering. The disease is most common about two or three months after delivery, or during the weaning period, when a large quantity of milk, by distending the breasts, gives rise to the inflammatory process which terminates in the formation of pus. It is said that when the inflammation is confined to the integument, suppuration follows more speedily than when the true glandular substance is affected. After the symptoms have continued for four or five days, unless the progress of the inflammation has been arrested, suppuration may be expected; but there are cases in which the inflammatory process proceeds so slowly that pus is not formed for a much longer period, during which time the patient becomes much exhausted by loss of rest, excessive pain, and the accompanying fever.

The most common causes of this variety of abscess are, suppression of milk from various causes, a current of air upon the breasts, an accumulation of milk through some fault in suckling the child or from weaning, external injuries, or stimulants which are too frequently allowed to nurses or mothers suckling their children.

There is also a somewhat peculiar abscess of the mammary gland, noticed particularly by Mr. Hey. The inflammation is very deep-seated, the process tedious, and when suppuration has supervened and the matter has extended towards the surface, it is discharged through several openings, which become fistulous, and when these sinuses are opened, a soft, purple fungus is discovered beneath them; the surrounding parts of the gland are hard and lobulated.

This form of mammary abscess is difficult to heal; the discharge continues for a length of time, hectic is superinduced, and the patient may be placed in a very precarious position.

Treatment.—The homœopathic treatment of this disease is very efficacious, and if the medicines are employed in the early stages of the affection, resolution can be accomplished. Warm applications, poultices, &c., should never be employed in abscess of the mammæ, as they not only tend to increase the afflux of fluids, and create more extensive suppuration, but they interfere with the action of the remedial agents administered internally,* and are prone to induce indurations. The only local treatment that should be used should be a light suspensory bandage, to support the tumor in order to prevent its weight from causing additional pain, and frequent bathing with tepid water after the abscess has been opened, that the part may be kept perfectly clean.

If, after the chilliness, the patient experience a tensive, burning, or darting pain in the breasts, if they are somewhat swollen and red, *bryonia* should be prescribed; or if before the symptoms above mentioned appear, and there is only slight swelling, *aconite.* These two medicines are often sufficient to produce resolution; the child, however, should be allowed to suck, even though pain is produced. In some instances the breast pump is serviceable, when the female is desirous of weaning the infant, but often its use may be dispensed with, the homœopathic treatment being sufficient to cure the affection. If the milk continues to be secreted in too great quantity, and *bryonia* does not relieve, *puls.* will be found of great service.

---

* Croserio's Obstetrics.

Calc. carb. has also been used with success, and *lycop.* proved effectual in an obstinate case of the kind.*

Belladonna must be used when there is, together with the throbbing pain, a shining erysipelatous redness. And also, when the inflammation is caused by the suppression of the milk by violent emotions, if the patient be robust, with tendency to congestions, &c. If this medicine does not relieve, and the patient complains of chilliness and shuddering, which at this stage of disease generally indicate the formation of pus, *mercurius* should be administered, or if the symptoms require, *hepar* may be prescribed. If these are not sufficient and suppuration is progressing, *phosph.* has been highly recommended by Dr. Croserio. He says, " Since I have seen the marvellous effects of *phosph.* in abscess of the breasts, I have employed no other medicine, when there have been evident signs of suppuration. This medicine, administered upon these circumstances, at the thirtieth dynamization, one globule in water, a teaspoonful every six hours, promptly calms the pain, procures the opening of the abscess and its cure, without leaving any visible trace of the cicatrix upon the breast.

" I could cite many cases of these prodigious cures.

" The efficacy of *phosph.* in abscesses, shows itself quite as remarkably in the cure of the rebellious fistulæ of these organs, resulting from allopathic treatment, as also in the induration of the mammary glands, remaining after the opening of the abscess by the knife. The homœopathic physician ought not to open these abscesses with a cutting instrument, because occupying a part where there is nothing to fear from the effusion of pus, he can wait its spontaneous opening from the specific administered, which has the advantage of avoiding the pain, the emotion, and a disagreeable consecutive cicatrice; and facilitating the complete resolution of the obstruction of the mammary gland, and also prevents the serious degenerations which sometimes follow these accidents."

There are some abscesses, however, that are so deep-seated,

---

* Dr. I. Lembke's General Homœo. Gaz., Vol. XXVII.

that although the pus may be fully formed, the time that it takes in making a passage for itself to the surface, is considerable. In such cases as these there can be no objection to the physician using the lancet, and evacuating the pus, as the operation is trivial and the pain slight, compared to what the patient must suffer during the time that is occupied, while the matter is making its way to the surface.

After the pus has been evacuated, *silic.*, in most instances, is sufficient to complete the cure. This medicine is also serviceable when the discharge is serous, and has continued for a length of time.

If indurations remain, *conium, merc., phosph.-ac., silic.* or *sulph.* must be administered, each according to the symptoms.

If the inflammation be consequent upon bruises, *arnica* may be applied externally, in a weak solution, and internally in the form of globules; and should much pain, fever, &c., be present, in alternation with it, *aconite* may be prescribed.

Section 3.—Hepatic Abscess.

The frequency of occurrence of hepatic abscess is less under homœopathic than allopathic treatment, because by the administration of homœopathic medicines, the inflammation existing in the liver is generally subdued before suppuration ensues.

There are, however, cases that, notwithstanding the best directed efforts to procure resolution, terminate in suppuration, and among these may be classed those inflammations that are occasioned by wounds, or other injuries; or when the disease is present in individuals who are weakened by some constitutional affection, biliary concretions, or the presence of worms in the biliary ducts.

Kirkland* relates a remarkable instance of the latter; and also Dr. Thomas Bond,† and Dr. Gibson,‡ of this city. The

* Inquiry into the Present State of Medical Surgery, vol. ii., p. 186.
† Medical Observations and Inquiries, vol. i., p. 68.
‡ Gibson's Institutes and Practice of Surgery, vol. i., p. 209.

latter gentleman writes, "a very beautiful preparation made by the late Dr. Wesenhall, of Maryland, of a liver, the substance and ducts of which are filled and perforated in every direction, by numerous and very large lumbrici, which destroyed the child by irritation and suppuration, is contained in my surgical cabinet deposited in the University."

In abscess of the liver, or rather before suppuration has been established, the patient experiences a stinging, burning pain in the right hypochondrium, below and around the false ribs, frequently extending to the epigastric region or sternum, and in some instances, even to the thorax. This pain may be very severe, or it may be a continual, dull aching pain, aggravated by lying on the affected side, or by any external pressure; there is also more or less pain experienced in the right shoulder.

There are also present gastric symptoms, such as hiccough, loathing eructations, attended with anguish, or there may be nausea, vomiting, bitter taste, yellow tongue, &c. Rigors generally precede the immediate formation of pus, and swelling may appear in the right side, and as the disease progresses, fluctuation may be perceived. The pus may burrow in various directions, in accordance with the situation of the abscess; it may proceed to the region of the hip, along the dorsal vertebræ, or it may be discharged into the transverse colon, stomach, duodenum, or into the lung; the latter is a very unfavorable situation, as the patient frequently dies of hectic.*

After the abscess has opened, the pus that is discharged changes its character; at first it is thick and creamy, but after a short time it becomes greenish, fetid, or of a dark brown color. Large cavities are formed in the liver, and in some instances the whole structure of the organ may be destroyed, and there are cases on record, where this has been the case, as has been revealed by post mortem examinations.

Treatment.—The desideratum in treating an inflammation of the liver, no matter by what cause it is occasioned, is to pro-

---

* Sometimes the abscess has discharged itself into the pericardium. See London Lancet, Aug. 1845, p. 154.

cure resolution. The medicines that are most serviceable in producing such a result are, chiefly, *acon.*, *bell.*, *bry.*, *cham.*, *merc.*, *nux-vom.*, *sulph.* The indications for their use, will be found in any work upon the homœopathic practice of medicine.

The medicines that are best adapted to hepatic *abscess* are, *ars.*, *bell.*, *hepar*, *merc.*, *silic.*, *sulph.* If the matter has made its way towards the surface of the body, the prognosis is more favorable, than when it is discharged into any of the surrounding tissues or organs. If the pus has commenced to form, *hepar* should be administered, or if the process of formation be slow, *merc.* and *silic.* may hasten the suppuration, and allay the pain; the latter is the best medicine, particularly when there is hardness of the surrounding parts, with distention, or if there is a continual stitching pain below the floating ribs; but *mercurius* is to be preferred, when there is burning in the region of the liver, with distention from within outwards, accompanied with perspiration, that is excited by the slightest motion.

If a swelling appear to protrude through the intercostal spaces, the pus should be immediately evacuated, by means of the lancet or bistoury, if this be not done, the matter may be discharged in another direction, and give rise to very unfavorable symptoms.

If, after the opening is made, the discharge continue, and become thin, sanious and unhealthy, *ars.*, *carb.-veg.* or *nit.-acid* must be administered; the directions for their use have been already mentioned in a preceding portion of this work. If the opening have a tendency to become fistulous, *calc.*, *silic.*, *sulph.* or *phosph.* should be exhibited.

In all cases the patient should be kept at perfect rest, and if extremely weak, a moderate stimulus should be allowed.

In some instances, when there is a large quantity of pus, it should be evacuated by openings, made at different times, and at longer or shorter intervals; to determine this, however, the general constitutional symptoms of the patient must be taken into consideration. If he be robust and previously healthy, and the inflammation has gone through its stages rapidly though completely, there need be no fear in allowing free vent to the purulent secretion. If, however, the patient has been long suffering from previous disease, the constitution generally weak, temperament nervous, and the signs of a chronic hepatitis have been present, care should be taken, that the removal of a large quantity of matter, does not produce the most alarming symptoms of debility and exhaustion; it is then better to practice the method recommended by Abernethy, already alluded to, in the chapter upon abscess.

Section 4.—*Lumbar Abscess.*

This disease is, in most instances, of a chronic nature; the collection of pus being very gradual; instances, however, may occur, in which the affection is acute, the matter making its appearance in a short time after the premonitory symptoms have been noticed by the patient.

The first manifestations of the disease do not, in many cases, receive sufficient attention, and are allowed to pass unnoticed, until the disorder is far advanced, and the danger too proximate to escape attention. In the incipient stage, the patients are unable to walk with their usual facility, there is a degree of uneasiness experienced about the lumbar region, but there is little very acute pain; rigors are frequently present, the patients also being unable to use any violent exercise. As the disease advances, the testicle of the affected side is drawn up, and there is more or less pain extending along the course of the spermatic cord. Glandular enlargement takes place in the groin, and there is slight protrusion noticed at that part; the swelling then appears on the inner side of the femoral vessels, beneath the pubal portion of the *facia lata*. The precursory symptoms may continue for several months, before rigors, loss of appetite, hectic and other symptoms which denote profuse suppuration, are developed. Mr. Cooper remarks, "the abscess sometimes forms a swelling above Poupart's ligament, sometimes below it, and frequently the matter glides under the fascia of the thigh; occasionally it makes its way through the sacro-ischiatic foramen, and assumes rather the appearance of a fistula in ano. When the matter gravitates into the thigh, beneath the fascia, Mr. Hunter would have termed it a disease *in*, not *of* the part."

The swelling is more prominent in the erect position, and is also increased by exertion of the abdominal muscles; an impulse is also imparted to it when coughing. As the suppuration continues, fluctuation is perceived, generally in some portion of the groin, but large and neglected collections of pus may make their way towards the surface in two or three directions. Lumbar abscess most frequently arises from disease of the vertebræ, but, says a distinguished surgeon, "it must be confessed, that we can hardly ever know the existence of the disorder, before the tumor, by presenting itself externally, leads us to such information."

The pus discharged from a lumbar abscess is generally thin, gleety, and mixed with cheesy flocculi, or with a curd-like substance; in some rare instances, however, the matter has been found to be laudable.

From examinations made *post mortem* of patients, who have died from this affection, we learn, that the purulent secretion is completely enclosed in a cyst, which is often very extensive. If the contents of such abscesses were not circumscribed by such boundaries, the pus would spread rapidly among the cells of the surrounding cellular texture, as does the water in anasarca. The cysts are lined with the pyogenic membrane, that, as has been before mentioned, appears to possess the property of secretion; indeed, during the treatment of lumbar abscess, it is wonderful to observe the immense quantity of pus that is discharged.

This disease, as Mr. Liston remarks, is often attributable to a sprain or wrench of the loins, or is induced by exposure to cold, and over fatigue. Occasionally the mischief is confined entirely to the soft parts; although the vertebræ, a portion of the os innominatum, or the sacrum, may be denuded and of irregular surface, evidently the result of the pressure of the abscess. A strong example of this, and of the extensive destruction of parts, which this affection sometimes produces, may be briefly stated. A very large lumbar abscess formed within a few weeks, in consequence of great and continued fatigue, and exposure to bad weather. At first it had been trifled with. At last it was opened, in the usual situation in the thigh, and a large quantity of matter evacuated. Thirty-six hours afterwards, the patient was suffocated with a flow of purulent matter into and through the air passages. On dissection, the cavity was found to be a large opening, through the diaphragm into the adherent lung, and communicating with the bronchi. The fore part of the lumbar vertebræ were exposed, and in some instances, stript of the theca; but there were no cavities in the bone, and no disease of the interposed cartilages. Such cases are now and then met with, of abscess in the loins, not originating in any vice, either of the bones or of any other part of the apparatus of the spinal column. Most frequently, however, the collections have their foundation in disease of the bodies of the vertebræ.

The causes of this complaint are generally very obscure. It is most prevalent among the lower classes of society, who are scantily clothed and fed, and exposed to vicissitudes of weather, and extreme fatigue and other hardships. Individuals affected with scrofula are most obnoxious to the disease, and it is said to be more prevalent in Europe than on this continent. Dr. Gibson* thus writes: "I have seen only four cases of the disease during the last thirteen years, although professionally connected with extensive hospitals and alms-houses during the greater part of the time."

Dr. Physic also stated, he never met with a case of psoas abscess in America, unconnected with disease of the spine.

In the *treatment* of lumbar abscess, the prognosis is always unfavorable; the radical cure of the affection can scarcely be effected, even when the patient applies for relief at the earlier

* Institutes and Practice of Surgery, vol. i., p. 214.

stages of the disease, which in far the greater majority of instances is not the case, because the pain in the loins, and other premonitory symptoms, are attributed to some other cause.

The following medicines, although they may not effect a cure of the disease, will greatly alleviate the sufferings of the patient; indeed, there have been cases in which, by the careful administration of medicine, the abscess has been partially healed, and there is every reason to believe, that if the diagnosis is formed correctly, at an early period of the affection, a cure may be reasonably anticipated.

The medicines chiefly to be used are, *ars.*, *asaf.*, *aur.*, *calc.-c.*, *hepar*, *lyc.*, *merc.*, *mez.*, *phosph.-ac.*, *silic.*, *sulph.*

Arsenicum is indicated in the first stages, when there is painful stiffness in the small of the back, or bruised sensation, with inability to walk as easily as usual, with burning pain around the sacrum; or if, after the pus has been, or is being evacuated, there is great prostration, shivering, brown tongue, hot dry skin, constant unquenchable thirst, the secreted matter being thin and bloody, or consisting of a fetid ichor.

Asafœtida is called for particularly, when the abscess arises from diseases of the bones, when there is tearing in the lumbar region, or tensive sticking pains, which are aggravated by moving the body; when the pus is transparent and thin, or ichorous and fetid; when the skin is *cold* and dry, and the patients are scrofulous, with disposition to rachitis.

Aurum may be used, when there is pressure and pain in the lumbar region and os innominatum, when the pains in these parts are particularly aggravated at night, and when the patient has been formerly subjected to large doses of mercury; when the pus is thick, yellowish, and contains cheesy flocculi.

Calcarea-carb. should be administered, when the disease arises from curvature or ramollissement of the vertebræ, with constant aching pain in the lumbar region, with stiffness of the whole spinal column, and heaviness of the limbs with inability to move them; when there is profuse discharge of pus, and the cavity shows no disposition to heal.

Hepar-sulph., when the suppuration is profuse, and the skin surrounding the abscess presents an unhealthy appearance; excessive fever at night, at which time the pains are aggravated; tired sensation in the lumbar region, or violent pain in the small of the back, as though it would break or were being cut through.

Lycopodium is indicated by stiffness and aching in the small of the back, the patient being unable to maintain the erect posture, or when there is chilliness in the lumbar region, with large swelling of the psoas muscle and much heaviness and uneasiness of the lower extremities.

Mezereum, when there is dull, pulsative pains in the lumbar region, or drawing and aching extending to the groin, with intolerable burning pains which are aggravated at night; when the periosteum of the vertebræ is affected and the abscess discharges a yellowish pus; excessive failing of strength.

Phosph.-ac., when there is smarting and burning in the abscess, with bruised sensation over the whole person, excessive prostration, with irregular pulse, profuse debilitating night sweats, with intense pain in the lumbar region.

Staphysagria should be employed when there is reason to believe that the disease arises from caries of the bones or curvature of the spine; when there are burning or tearing pains.

If there is unhealthy granulations and disposition in the abscess to spread, *silicea* may prove beneficial. The treatment, in many cases, may be commenced with the administration of *sulph.*, which will prove serviceable as an anti-psoric.

There is frequently some difficulty in diagnosing a lumbar abscess, as it often points very readily at that region where an inguinal hernia would protrude; however, by carefully examining the patient, and inquiring particularly into the history of the case, the error of mistaking the one disease for the other may be avoided. In opening a lumbar abscess, the method recommended by Abernethy* should be resorted to. As the disease is chronic, and the matter has been secreting for some time, it must not be forgotten, that the evacuation of a large quantity of pus at one time, might be productive of serious consequences.

* See chapter on Abscess.

Section 5.—Paronychia—Whitlow.

A whitlow is an inflammation, very much disposed to suppurate, and generally productive of severe pain, commencing in the extremities of the fingers, though the toes are sometimes the seat of the disease.

Writers generally divide whitlows into four varieties. In the first and least severe, the disease commences under the cuticle near the root or side of the nail; the pus not being deep seated and soon evacuated; sometimes, however, the abscess takes place under the nail, in which case the pain is severe, and not unfrequently shoots up as far as the external condyle. The second variety is situated chiefly in the cellular tissue, under the skin, and generally occurs at the very ends of the fingers. In such cases the inflammatory symptoms, especially the pain, is far more violent than in other common inflammations of not greater extent. However, though the pain be severe, it does not generally extend far from the affected part. The intensity of the sufferings and the severity of the inflammatory process are owing to the hard, unyielding nature of the integument covering the fingers; consequently, when the laboring classes are affected by the disease, the pain is much more pungent and deep seated than when those in the higher walks of life are attacked; for the same reason there is often great difficulty in perceiving any fluctuation after the formation of pus.

The third kind of whitlow is distinguished from the others, by the following circumstances. The pain is excruciating, there is very little swelling in the affected finger, but very much in the hand, particularly about the wrist, and sometimes even extending throughout the entire fore-arm; the pain is experienced along the hand and wrist to the elbow, and in the most severe cases to the shoulder; suppuration proceeds slowly, and after the formation of pus, fluctuation can only be perceived in the hand, the affected finger appearing swollen and tense. The patient is deprived of all rest, and suffers for nights and days together; considerable fever also being present, and sometimes delirium.

The disease in this variety, is situated in the tendons, and their sheaths, consequently the power of moving the finger, and often the hand, is entirely lost.

In the fourth variety, the inflammation appears to attack the periosteum. The peculiarity of this form of paronychia appears to be, that however violent the pain, it seldom extends along the fore-arm, nor is there any external swelling of the affected finger. Suppuration is soon established, and unless the disease be checked and the matter evacuated, caries or necrosis of the sub-adjacent bones may be the result.

Whitlow generally arises from local causes, such as splinters, pricks with needles or other sharp instruments, bruises, warmth suddenly applied to parts cold from exposure, &c. Those individuals whose occupation requires frequent immersion of the hands in warm water and other fluids are particularly liable to the disease; however, there are some cases in which it is impossible to assign any cause.

Treatment.—In the first variety of whitlow, when the disease is superficial, *hepar* must be used, it is also suitable for the swelling, allays the stiffness and numbness of the fingers, hastens the formation of pus, and mitigates the pain, itching and throbbing; indeed, in the Materia Medica this medicine is spoken of as being "a specific against panaritia."

Mercurius should be administered when the pains are intolerable at night, with intense aching and burning under the finger nail, when there is hardness of the surrounding skin and the suppurative process is slow.

Arsenicum is a valuable medicine, when the part assumes a bluish-red appearance, with intense burning pain, with stiffness and rigidity of the joints.

The pus in this form of the disease generally soon accumulates, and will evacuate itself without the aid of the knife; it is well, however, if the skin is hard and unyielding, to wrap around the affected finger four or five layers of lint, and keep it constantly moist with tepid water. After the pus evacuates itself, *silic.* or *sulph.* will generally facilitate the cure.

In the second variety, the inflammation being more deeply

seated, when there is tearing and burning in the affected part, and if the surrounding skin have an unhealthy appearance, with brittle and discolored nails, *silic.* is to be administered; or if after the evacuation of the matter unhealthy fungous granulations appear, this medicine is of the utmost importance.

Sulphur is indicated, when there is coldness of the fingers, with stiff red joints, when the patient is of a psoric diathesis, or where the finger appears dead and shriveled, with sticking and darting pains—*hepar* and *mercurius* may also be well adapted to this variety of whitlow, and should be administered if symptoms correspond.

If the affection arise from wounds, a lotion of *calendula* should be applied to the part. *Carbo-veg.*, or *arsen.*, must be given, if there appears a black angry-looking sore, with burnings and tearings, and throbbing pain, and strong disposition to ulceration. There is no doubt that in many cases a free incision with a bistoury should be made, as soon as the surgeon is fully convinced that pus is present, as the non-elasticity of the parts, the slow suppurative process that takes place, together wlth the imperfect formation of matter, all tend to increase the sufferings of the patient, and cause an extension of the disease, until more important parts are involved. If the inflammation arise from a puncture, and the patient complains of coldness and alternations of heat, *ledum* is recommended by M. Teste. Of course in treating any case of panaritia, if there be any extraneous matter present, giving rise to the inflammatory process, it should be removed immediately.

In the third variety of whitlow, when there is violent burning aching under the finger nails, with sensation of ulceration when touching anything, or if the panaris causes a digging burning pain, with tingling, and if there be proud flesh, *causticum* is the medicine. If there be numbness or tearing, *rhus tox.* may be indicated. *Sepia* will be beneficial if there is tearing under the nail, with contraction of the finger with violent beating and stinging. These medicines allay the pains, but often it may be useful to alternate with them either *hepar*, *merc.*, *silic.*, or *sulph.*

It is necessary also in this variety of whitlow to have recourse to the knife; the surgeon must not be content merely to plunge into the sore a lancet, but should lay open with a bistoury the whole sheath, taking care, however, not to sever the tendon; after which, by applying a solution of *calendula* to the part, and inclosing the fingers in lint, the disease may be in a short period cured—if there are unhealthy granulations, (proud flesh,) and the cut surface shows little disposition to unite, *sepia, silic.*, or *calendula* may be administered, and sometimes the unhealthy granulations will have to be slightly sprinkled with *alum-ust.*

In the fourth variety, *merc.*, *mez.*, *phosph-ac. silic.*, are chiefly to be relied on. *Mez.* may be given when there is intense pain. But the matter, as has been before remarked, often forms quickly; here also the knife must be called into requisition. It is useless for homœopathic physicians to decry the knife in all cases, and in every variety of whitlow; in the first, and sometimes in the second form of the disease, the proper manipulation and administration of medicine may produce the desired result, but in the third and fourth, when the pus has formed within the sheaths of tendons, or beneath the periosteum, incision is imperative, and he who neglects it, should be held to a certain degree responsible for the future pain, and perhaps the loss of the finger, to which the patient may have to submit.

In the ordinary progress of abscess the majority of the surrounding textures are pushed aside, and the pus approaches the surface, where a point is destroyed by ulceration, and the matter evacuated. But if nature be balked in her endeavors by resisting textures, as the sheaths of ligaments, periosteum, &c., the pressure is increased to a dangerous degree at various points, areolar tissue is broken up, muscles are detached, bone ulcerates and dies, blood-vessels perforate, joints stiffen, and are rendered useless; therefore, although medicine may relieve pain, hasten suppuration, and after the evacuation of matter exert a controlling influence over the processes of granulation and cicatrization, still the knife must be employed; it must penetrate the periosteum down to the bone.

The toughness of the integuments, and the high grade of inflammation that are present in panaritia, render the incisions very painful; the surgeon therefore must operate quickly, with a very keen-edged knife; but at the same time must do his work thoroughly.

A whitlow may be prevented in almost every case, if, as soon as the pain and the inflammation are perceived, the skin of an egg which has been boiled be wrapt around the affected part. At first the patient will experience aggravation of the symptoms, but if the application be allowed to remain, or perhaps applied at intervals, the affection will often be arrested. Electricity is also said to prevent and cure the disease.

The medicines that have been above stated are those frequently employed in panaritia; however, the following, as they may prove useful in some cases, are subjoined.

For *Panaritia* in general. (1.) *Ars., calc.-carb., caust., hepar, lach., merc., nit.-ac., pet., sep., sil., sulph.* (2.) Alum., amm.-mur., baryta.-c., carb.-veg., con., jod., kali.-c., natr.-m., puls., rhus., sang., mgt.-arc., mgt.-aus.

Under the integument. (1.) *Ars., hep., merc., silic., sulph.* (2.) Calc.-c., graph., nitr.-ac., puls.

In the deeper tissues. (1.) *Carbo-veg., caust., hepar, sep., silic., sulph.* (2.) Graph., merc., nit.-ac., phosph., puls.

Between the tendons. (1.) *Rhus., ledum., caust.* (2.) Hepar, lach., merc., silic., sulph.

Affecting the periosteum. (1.) *Calc.-carb., mez., phosph.-ac., silic.* (2.) Hep., lyc., merc., nitr.-ac., sulph.

CHAPTER X.

ULCERS.

Those sores that are created by the action of the ulcerative process, or in other words, solutions of continuity, effected by ulceration, are termed *ulcers.*

All the textures of animal life are liable to be attacked, although some are more susceptible of invasion than others, but it is more particularly the formation of those sores that appear on the surface of the body, that at present demands attention.

There is no class of diseases in which the truth of the homœopathic law is more fully tested, and the results more satisfactory, both to patient and practitioner, than that now under consideration.

It frequently happens, that those ulcers that have resisted for years all the means to effect their cure, employed by the most skilful physicians of the old school; and that have been successively submitted to the roller, the poultice, adhesive straps, the cautery and the knife with but little benefit, yield to the infinitesimal doses of a medicine exhibited in accordance to the law "*Similia similibus curanter.*"

Although there are some ulcers that are capable of being healed rapidly and permanently, by the internal administration of the appropriate remedy; yet there are many cases, particularly when the sore has assumed an indolent and chronic character, that require the steady and repeated exhibition of medicine for weeks and months together, to produce the desired effect. An ulcer may remain stationary for a length of time after the commencement of the treatment; and the patient perceiving no beneficial change in the nature of the sore, becomes complaining and dissatisfied; when such is the case, it too frequently happens that the practitioner, being weary of treating a disease in which no perceptible improvement is manifested, either becomes neglectful of his duty or entirely relinquishes the case.

Great patience and forbearance on the part of the physician are absolutely requisite, together with the continued exhibition of the remedy, which should not be administered in too low a dilution, (perhaps it is better always to commence with the 30th,) or at too short intervals.

The arrangement into classes of the varied forms of ulcers, simplifies much their description, and to a certain extent their treatment, but the classification differs with different authors. Dr. Gibson mentions three varieties, viz: simple, indolent and irritable ulcers, arranging other ulcerated surfaces under the diseases that cause them. Sir Everard Home forms them into six classes:

1. Ulcers in parts that have sufficient strength to carry on the actions necessary for their recovery.

2. Ulcers in parts that are too weak for that purpose.

3. Ulcers in parts whose actions are too violent to form healthy granulations, whether this arises from the state of the parts or of the constitution.

4. Ulcers in parts whose actions are too indolent, whether this arises from the state of the parts or of the constitution.

5. Ulcers in parts which have acquired some specific action, either from a diseased state of the parts or of the constitution.

6. Ulcers in parts which are prevented from healing from a varicose state of the superficial veins of the upper part of the limb.

Mr. Miller mentions ten varieties, viz: 1. Simple purulent, or healthy sore. 2. The weak. 3. The scrofulous. 4. The cachectic. 5. The indolent. 6. The irritable. 7. The inflamed. 8. The sloughing. 9. The phagedenic. 10. The sloughing phagedæna.

Probably the most simplified method of classifying ulcers, is that of arranging the whole into two divisions; the first comprising the simple, indolent and irritable ulcer; and the second, embracing those sores that have acquired a specific character from the diseases with which they may be associated, scrofulous, syphilitic, cancerous, &c., leaving the more minute consideration of the diseases themselves, to be studied in their appropriate places. This appears, also, the more requisite, because there are many *important symptoms* that may present themselves in any or all the varieties of ulcers, without regard either to name, classification, or the specific disease upon which they may be dependent.

Section 1.—*Simple, or Healthy Ulcer.*

This is, in truth, an example of healthy granulation, following a wound or abscess; or of inflammatory disintegration of a part, previously unbroken in its surface.

The discharge is thick, creamy, easily detached from the granulations, almost inodorous and not profuse; in fact, it is laudable pus. The granulations are numerous, small acuminated, florid, sensitive and vascular; if touched at all rudely they bleed and are pained, the blood is arterial, neither too profuse nor abnormal in quality, and the pain is but the just appreciation of injury done to healthy tissues. The general sensation in the part, when not injured, is slight tenderness, or a feeling of rawness, rather than actual pain; not unfrequently, a sensation of itching is present, to a degree even troublesome. As soon as the granulations arrive at the surface of the skin, cicatrization commences, and proceeds steadily until the part is repaired.*

The *treatment* of such sores is quite simple. The part should be kept at rest, and in a position that may relax those muscles upon which the ulcer is situated, and above all, the strictest cleanliness enjoined. Milk and tepid water commingled in equal parts, should be allowed to dribble over the part, from a sponge or piece of lint saturated in the liquid; this appears to be the best abstersive method, as the frequent passing of a sponge, &c., over the healing parts, may prove a source of irritation, as well as causing a destruction of the

---

* Miller's Principles of Surgery.

delicate granulations, and the healing process thereby be retarded.

The simple ulcer generally heals rapidly, without the exhibition of any medicine. Sometimes, however, after cicatrization has progressed for a time, there appears to be a diminution of action in the healing process ; if this be the case, a few doses of *silicea* 30th, repeated every twelve or twenty-four hours, will overcome the difficulty, and complete the cure.

Section 2.—Irritable Ulcer.

This form of ulcer is generally preceded by an irritable state of the system, or if such be not the case, the constitutional may be produced by the local irritation.

The digestive function is frequently impaired in those persons afflicted with irritable ulcer, and consequently the sore is often found among those in the higher walks of life, who eat and drink to excess ; or among debauchees, &c.

The appearances presented by an irritable ulcer, are as follows: The edges are ragged, undermined and serrated, the bottom appears deeper in some points than in others, and the parts around are red, inflamed, and frequently œdematous; the discharge, which is always considerable, is a thin, greenish or reddish matter, which is frequently so acrid, that it excoriates the surrounding skin, and is sometimes mingled with solid matter. Granulations are wanting, and in their place may be found a grayish film, or a dark-red spongy mass, which is acutely sensible, and bleeds at the slightest touch, the blood being of a dark grumous character.

The medicines that have proved most effectual in removing this form of ulcer, are, *arsen.*, *asaf.*, *carbo-veg.*, *lyc.*, *hepar*, *merc.-sol.*, *nit.-acid*, *silic.*, *mez.*, *con.*, *sulph.*, *thuja*, *staphys.*

Arsenicum.—This is an admirable medicine for irritable ulcer, when it appears in individuals of exhausted, impoverished constitutions, or in those in whom there is a tendency to abdominal plethora, when the serrated edges of the sore are high,

12

and when the pain is burning or tearing; the discharge is greenish, thin, acrid and mingled with blood, the base of the ulcer is covered with a yellowish or whitish film, the pain is severe and is felt at night even while sleeping; and the surrounding parts are bluish, inflamed, and œdematous.

Asafœtida is adapted to nervous individuals or to those of a phlegmatic temperament, with a venous or hemorrhoidal constitution; when the ulcer is extremely sensitive to touch, the margins deeply serrated, and of a bluish color, and elevated above the surrounding textures, the discharge is ichorous, thin and perhaps fetid in character.

Carbo-veg.—This medicine is to be exhibited, when there is pressure and a sensation of tension around the ulcer, which is exceedingly irritable, and bleeds profusely at the slightest touch. The bottom of the sore has a bluish tinge, and there is an areola of the same color, extending to some distance around the part, the discharge is aqueous and corrosive, or may consist of degenerated pus. The remedy is peculiarly adapted to peevish and irritable individuals, or in those in whom there is predominant action of the venous system, as indicated by the bluish tinge of the whole body, particularly around inflamed surfaces.

Hepar-sulph. is indicated, when the pain in the ulcer is corrosive, with burning and throbbing sensations, particularly at night, stitching pains through the sore when laughing, excessive sensitiveness of the surface, which bleeds profusely when lightly touched. There is a disposition in such ulcers to become chronic, and the surrounding tissues present an unhealthy appearance. It is beneficial when the patient is easily irritated, and when the accompanying fever is exacerbated at night.

Lycop., in individuals of mild or melancholy disposition, when the pains in the ulcers are worse at night, with stitching, tearing and itching, or when there are burning and painful stitches in the sore. The pains are aggravated by remaining in a warm room, and ameliorated when in the cool air.

Merc.-sol.—The indications for the employment of this

medicine are, when the pains in the sore become intolerable at night in bed; when, instead of granulations, there is a spongy, bluish mass, which is sensitive and bleeds readily. The ulcers are extremely painful when touched, and discharge an acrid corrosive ichor; the elevations are very irregular at the base, and there is present a sensation as if the part were corroded by insects, together with unequal quick pulse, sleeplessness and dripping night sweats, with great nervousness and excessive irritability.

Nit.-acid must be employed, when the patient is sad and desponding, or impatient, irritable and vehement; when there is coldness of the whole person at night with profuse sweat; when the ulcer at the slightest irritation bleeds copiously. There is a thin, ichorous discharge mingled with blood, that corrodes the surrounding skin, together with shooting, stitching pains in and around the ulcer, with burning as from nettles; or there are itching and prickings in the parts around, or the pains may be so violent, that the patient appears unable to tolerate his condition.

Silicea is useful to complete, after the healing process has commenced, the cicatrization, or when there is a disposition in the sore to become chronic; where there are stinging, burning pains in the surrounding parts, with aching, smarting pains in the sore. It is also indicated, when there is a secretion of thick discolored pus, or of a thin acrid sanies, and when there is frequent formation of large flabby vegetation.

It may be often advantageous to commence the treatment of irritable ulcers with a few doses of *sulphur*, after which, the medicine best adapted to the case may be administered. If the constitutional symptoms presented are such as require treatment, they must be encountered by the proper homœopathic specific. If the above remedies are not sufficient to establish a healthy action in the sore, recourse must be had to some of the following: *phosph.*, *mez.*, *acid-mur.*, *lach.*, *puls.*, *con.*, *sulph.*, *bell.*, *thuja*, *staphys.*

Section 3.—*Indolent Ulcer.*

This variety of ulcer is of much more frequent occurrence than either of those already described. It has received from several authors the appellation "callous," and is the fourth variety in the classification of Sir Everard Home. "Ulcers in parts whose action is too indolent to form healthy granulations, whether this indolence arises from the state of the parts, or of the constitution."

The appearances presented are a complete contrast to those of the irritable sore, although in the first instance it may have assumed the characteristics of that variety of ulcer; indeed, a healthy or simple sore may pass through a variety of stages, and ultimately become indolent, because cicatrization may have been opposed or protracted by its situation, or other adverse circumstances.

From such reasons it is obvious that the ulcer must be most common among individuals belonging to the laboring population, upon whose efforts depend the subsistence of their families, and who therefore are unable to make use of appropriate means (rest, &c.) so necessary to be observed at the first appearance of the sore, that the ulcerated surface may be repaired. As long as the erect posture is practicable, the poor man must strive for the maintenance of his household, and even when the sufferings become aggravated, the cry of his little ones for bread urges him to increased exertions, until finally a simple purulent ulcer becomes inflamed and irritable, and at length assumes those appearances which are the sure characteristics of the indolent sore. But it is not among such alone, that this variety of ulcer is found, nor does it so frequently arise from such continued exertion consequent upon a laudable energy engendered by domestic affection, as from filthy and dissolute habits or long continued intemperance.

An indolent ulcer presents the following appearances:

The edges are elevated, protruded, smooth and rounded, giving to the sore an appearance of deep excavation. The surface is smooth, glossy, pale, and generally void of granulations, although in some instances there is a feeble attempt at such formation; or it is covered partly with a pellicle, or crust, of a whitish or dark gray color, so tenacious that it is inseparable from the ulcer without considerable force. Sometimes the sore is dry, but generally there is a profuse discharge of a thin and serous fluid, nearly destitute of fibrin; the surrounding integument is swollen and discolored.

The most striking characteristic of the indolent sore is the elevation of the margins, which are very callous, and present a whitish appearance, resembling "a dense, high ring of cartilage." The pain is so slight that the patient frequently experiences but trifling annoyance, and is able to perform his usual avocations.

When an irritable ulcer has become indolent, the appearances vary from those described above. The granulations are large, round, pale and flabby, extremely sensitive, and bleed from the slightest scratch, and sometimes rise into a fungous form above the skin. This is what is termed by some writers the "*fungous* ulcer;" by Mr. Home it would be denominated as "an ulcer in parts too weak to carry on the actions necessary for its recovery"—or by others as the "weak sore." "This variety," writes Prof. Gibson, "may, and often does, accompany an ulcer with carious bone, sprouts from the mouth of a sinus, or covers the surface of many specific ulcers. From whatever source it springs, its characters are uniform, and its disposition so truly indolent, that it cannot without impropriety be referred to any other head."

There is another variety of indolent ulcer, which precedes or follows a varicose enlargement of the veins of the leg or thigh, which has been denominated the varicose ulcer; it generally makes its appearance on the inner side of the leg, and is often very difficult to cure. It resembles an indolent ulcer in a somewhat advanced stage; the edges of the skin, however, bounding the sore are not tumid; the sore is seldom deep, usually spreads along the surface, and is oval in shape, The branches and trunk of the *vena saphena* are enlarged, and this varix of the veins prevents the healing of the ulcer. The pain that is present appears to be deep seated, and extends up along the course of the veins, and is exasperated by maintaining the limb in the erect posture.

Treatment.—In the treatment of indolent ulcers, it is necessary that the utmost cleanliness be observed; and if the patient be one whose constitution has been impaired by unwholesome diet, exposure to a foul atmosphere, or by intemperance, these obstacles should be overcome by the substitution of nutritious, easily digested food, proper ventilation and regularity of habits; in fact, as far as possible, every effort should be made to effect the removal of the predisposing cause.

The indolent sore is capable of cure, under homœopathic treatment; indeed, in some instances, without having recourse either to the bandage, straps, or escharotics, and it is not absolutely necessary that the patient be put to bed,* although over-exertion tends to retard recovery.

The restoration of continuity in parts destroyed by the indolent sore is often very gradual, and attended with variations in the healing process. The ulcer may appear to be doing well, when, from some irritation, a retrograde action takes place, but if the practitioner have reason to believe the medicine correctly chosen, it must perseveringly be administered; always endeavoring not to interfere with its action by the too frequent repetition of the dose.

The surgeon, if the sore progresses slowly, is often strongly tempted to administer the medicine at too short intervals, and in a lower potency than that which he is employing, but when allowing himself to be thus led astray, disappointment is invariably the result. So long as there is a perceptible improvement in the appearance of the ulcer, the medicine must be continued, as there is nothing that more retards the progress of cure, than the repeated change of the means employed for the accomplishment of that purpose.

The medicines that are most serviceable in the treatment of

---

* See Whately's Practical Observations on the Cure of Wounds and Ulcers on the Legs, without Rest.

indolent ulcers, are *ars.*, *carb.-veg.*, *lyc.*, *graph.*, *phosph.-ac.*, *sang.*, *sepia*, *silic.*, *sulph.*

The medicines that appear most eminently useful, whose symptoms are most frequently similar to those presenting in indolent ulcers, and that are best adapted to the constitutions of those individuals among whom the sore is most prevalent, are *ars.*, and *carbo-veg.*

Arsenicum is suited to individuals of exhausted constitutions, in whom all eruptions have a disposition to become chronic. There may be a tendency to general plethora of the whole system, or general emaciation. When the sore is consequent upon long continued abuse of spirituous liquors. When the ulcers are of long standing, with burning and lancinating pain, or the sore is covered with a gray scurf, and surrounded by an inflamed margin, or when it is accompanied with shining, hot swelling of the feet. When the ulcer is burning on the surface and in the edges, with tearing pain, particularly when the part becomes cold—also when the edges are raised high above the surrounding skin, and when the areola around is red and shining, the base bluish colored, and having a scurf resembling lard. Further, this medicine is extremely useful, when the discharge consists of thin bloody pus, and the granulations are unhealthy, and the sore has a fetid odor—or the ulcer has slight discharge.

Carb.-veg. is indicated when the constitution has been weakened by excessive losses, or when the sore appears upon cachectic individuals, the tone of whose system has been weakened by gastric affections arising from various excesses, when the margins of the ulcer are elevated, and when they are of a deep blue color, the surrounding skin also assuming the same tinge, and is quite hard and painful to the touch, also when there is a heaviness of the limb, and the pus discharged from the sore emits a cadaverous smell.

These two remedies are indispensable in very many cases of indolent ulcers; indeed, cures have been accomplished by their administration, without the exhibition of any other homœopathic medicine.

But though *ars.* and *carb.-veg.* are adapted not only to many of the local manifestations presented by the indolent sore, but also to the constitutions of those individuals among whom it is most prevalent, the student cannot fall into a greater error than administering them for every case of the kind for which he is called to prescribe, and neglecting other medicines which are of great importance in the treatment of these particular instances.

Graphites is adapted to individuals having a tendency to corpulency, blond hair, unhealthy skin, with disposition to chronic eruptions, when the ulcers appear covered with a scurf, with pain at night, the whole limb is affected when touched or moved, as if the bone would be dashed to pieces, even in those parts distant from the ulcer; itching and pressing in the sore, or there may be tearing or stitching pains; likewise when the scurf upon the ulcer smells like herring pickle, or when there is a fetid odor from the sore.

Phosph.-acid is a remedy for indolent ulcers, particularly when there is much itching, or when there is burning pain; for those that are inveterate or flat, with dirty looking pus and indented base.

Sang. In the pathogenesis of this medicine we find—old indolent ulcers, ill-conditioned ulcers, with callous borders and ichorous discharge.

Sepia, lycop., silex and *sulphur* are other medicines that have been employed with great advantage in the treatment of this variety of ulcer.

Lycopodium is very serviceable in some cases, when the ulcer is old and has a tendency to become fistulous, with hard, red, shining edges and swelling of the affected part.

Silicea is an admirable medicine when the ulcers have become putrid, particularly when they occur in old, psoric, cachectic persons, living in poverty and filth, when there is inflammatory redness extending for some distance around the sore; also for fistulous ulcers, of a dingy appearance, with shaggy, callous edges, extending through to the bone, or when the parts surrounding are hard, swollen, and bluish red.

When proud flesh makes its appearance, or has attained to considerable growth, which frequently is the case in this species of ulcer, the medicines most available are, *ars.*, *petrol.*, *sepia*, *silic.*, *sulph.*

When the ulcer is attended with, or arises from a *varicose* condition of the veins, the following medicines are to be employed: *arn.*, *puls.*, *lach.*, *sulph.*, *sil.*, or in some cases, *ars.*, *carb.-v.*, *acid.-phosph.*

By some homœopathic physicians, the *Hamamelis Virginiana* has been strongly recommended; however, as there has been no regularly instituted proving of the drug, it is impossible to mention to what particular symptom it is applicable, and, therefore, until its pathogenesis is established, it must be considered as unreliable.

The limb affected with varices should always be bandaged, or a laced stocking constantly worn, as it is of great service in supporting the column of blood, which, continually tending to increase in size the already distended vessels, acts as a mechanical obstruction, and tends to retard recovery.

It has been previously remarked, that indolent ulcers can be radically cured by the proper administration of homœopathic medicines, without the necessity of the patient remaining in bed, but there are some individuals in the daily performance of whose duties, the erect posture is required for hours together, and no opportunity offered for any rest being allowed to the part. In such persons, when afflicted with the indolent sore, this excess of exercise may be counterbalanced by proper mechanical support, applied to the limb.

The method best adapted for accomplishing this end, is that advocated by Mr. Critchett, F. R. C. S., and also recommended in the British Journal of Homœopathy,* as an adjunct to the treatment of the variety of ulcer under consideration. It consists in tightly strapping the limb, in the manner presently to be described—the use of straps being considered preferable to the application of the roller, as the bandage is liable to slip, or become loose.

* Vol. vii., pp. 423–425.

Instead of the plaster (*Empl. plumb.*) recommended by Mr. Critchett, the straps should be made from simple wax, or isinglass plaster, as such will not interfere with the medicine administered internally.

The following are the words of Mr. Critchett: "You must seat the patient opposite to you and support his foot upon a small stool about a foot and a half in height, and so constructed as to receive the print of the heel and leave the rest of the foot free. You should be provided with strips of plaster, about two inches in width, and varying in length from twelve to eighteen inches, according to the size of the limb.

"You then take the centre of the first piece, and apply it low down to the back of the heel, and then with the flat part of both hands press the plaster along both sides of the foot. This plan is very preferable to taking hold of the ends and endeavoring to apply them, as it insures a perfectly smooth adaptation of the plaster to the part, and also, because it enables you to regulate that very important point, the amount of tightness you may wish to employ. As you proceed with the remainder, you must always remember the principle is to make one portion fold over another; you must, therefore, alternate them around the foot and ankle. Your second piece should be placed in a similar manner underneath the heel, and then carried upwards at a right angle to the last, so as to cover a portion of each malleolus. The third piece should be again applied to the back of the heel, overlapping the first by about one third. The fourth piece under the foot, and carried upwards, each piece being pushed along, so as to allow it to take its own course; this must be continued until the foot and ankle are covered; the strips must then be carried in a similar manner up the leg, increasing in length as the calf increases, and extending as far as the knee, and in some few cases even above this."

Referring to this method of dressing, the editors of the British Journal, remark, "over this a bandage is to be applied in the usual manner. Small ulcers, situated in the hollow between the malleolus and the os calcis, require more pressure than the rest of the limb, which may be produced by applying small pieces of plaster in a crucial manner over the wound, before putting on the strapping."

Twice a week, in the majority of cases, will be sufficiently often to renew this manipulation. If there be a profuse discharge, a piece of dry lint may be placed upon the sore.

The above concludes the description and a portion of the treatment of those ulcers, that were arranged under the first division. Those sores included in the second division will be mentioned, with their most appropriate medicines, in a different portion of this work. As the symptoms recorded in the next section may be present in any of the different forms of ulcer, without regard to classification, the student should become in some degree acquainted with the corresponding medicines.

Section 4.—Index to the Treatment of Ulcers.

Ulcer with pain as if *bruised*. (1.) *Hepar*. (2.) Sulph. (3.) Ars., con., nux-v.

With biting (smarting.) (1.) *Puls*. (2.) Euphorb., lach., led., lyc., sulph.

Turning *black*. (1.) *Ars., sec.-cor.* (2.) Asaf., plumb. (3.) Silic.

Turning *black* on *bottom*. *Ars.*

Turning *black* on the edges. *Ars.*

Bleeding. (1.) *Ars., lyc.* (2.) Asaf., carb.-veg., hepar, kali-c., lach., merc., nit.-ac., phosph., puls., silic., sulph.

Bleeding on *edges*. (1.) *Ars.* (2.) Lyc., merc., silic.

With *blisters around*. (1.) *Lach.* (2.) Ars.

Bluish. (1.) *Lach.* (2.) Carb.-veg. (3.) Con., hepar.

Boring. (1.) *Silic., sulph.*

Burning. (1.) *Ars., caust., lyc., merc., rhus, silic.* (2.) Carb.-veg., con., hepar, mez., puls., sulph.

Burning in the *edges*. (1.) *Ars., lyc., merc., silic.* (2.) Caust., hepar.

Burning in the *circumference*. (1.) *Puls*. (2.) Ars., asaf., caust., lach., lyc., merc., rhus, silic.

As if burnt. (1.) *Ars*. (2.) Carb.-veg., cyc.

With sensation of *cold*. (1.) *Bry*. (2.) Ars., silic.

With *gnawing pains*. (1.) *Staphys*. (2.) Plat., puls., ranc.-scel.

Crusty. (1.) *Con., lyc., silic., sulph*. (2.) Bell., calc.-c., graph., merc., sep.

With *Cutting*. (1.) *Bell*. (2.) Calc.-c., natr.

Deep ulcers. (1.) *Calc.-c., puls., silic*. (2.) Bell., con., hep., lyc., nit.-ac., sulph.

With *digging* pains. (1.) *Asaf*.

Flat, even ulcers. (1.) *Lach*. (2.) Ars., asaf., lyc., merc., phosph.-ac., selen., sep., silic.

Ulcers *destitute* of *feeling*. (1.) *Ars., con., lyc*. (2.) Calc.-c., carb.-veg., silic., sulph.

Fistulous. (1.) *Calc., lyc., puls., silic*. (2.) Asaf., bell., carb.-veg., caust., nit.-ac., sulphur.

With tendency to *gangrene*. (1.) *Ars., plumb., sec.-cor*. (2.) Asaf., scill.

Hard to the touch. (1.) *Ars., bell., lyc., puls*. (2.) Asaf., bry., calc.-c., chin., clem., hepar, lach., merc., silic., sulph.

Hard on the edges. (1.) *Ars., lyc., merc., silic*. (2.) Asaf., hepar, puls.

Hardness within the circumference. (1.) *Asaf., puls*. (2.) Ars., bell., lyc.

With *high, hard* edges. (1.) *Ars., asaf., silic*. (2.) Lyc., merc., puls.

Difficult to heal. (1.) *Hep., silic*. (2.) Calc.-c., cham., con., graph., lyc., merc., nit.-ac., petro., rhus, sep., staphys., sulph.

With *jerking* pains. (1.) *Caust., puls., silic*. (2.) Asaf., calc.-c., natr.-mur.

With *inflamed* margins. (1.) *Acon., arsen., hepar, merc., silic*. (2.) Bell., bry., lyc., puls., rhus, staphys.

With *itching*. (1.) *Hepar, lyc., silic*. (2.) Ars., caust., chin., graph., phosph.-ac., rhus, sep., staphys., sulph.

With *itching* in *surrounding* parts. (1.) *Hepar, puls., silic.* (2.) Lach., lyc.

With scurf having the appearance of *lard.* (1.) *Hep., merc.* (2.) Ars., nit.-ac.

Painless ulcers. (1.) *Lyc., phos.-ac.* (2.) Ars., bell., cocc., con., phosph., puls.

With *pressure.* (1.) *Silic.* (2.) Graph.

With *pricking.* (1.) *Ars., merc., nitr.-ac., puls., silic., sulph.* (2.) Rhus. (3.) Asaf., hepar, lyc., petro., sep.

With *tingling.* (1.) *Arn., rhus, sep.* (2.) Clem., con.

With *pulsation.* (1.) *Merc., sulph.* (2.) Calc.-c., kali-carb., silic.

With *pustules around.* (1.) *Ars., caust., lach., pulsa., sep.*

Putrid. (1.) *Hepar, mur.-ac., silic.* (2.) Ars., calc.-c., chin., rhus, sulph.

Sensitive ulcers. (1.) *Arn., asaf., hep.* (2.) Ars., bell., caust., lach., lyc., merc., puls., sep., silic.

With soreness. (1.) *Hep., puls.* (2.) Graph., merc., phos.-ac., sepia.

Spongy ulcers. (1.) *Ars., carb.-an., silic.* (2.) Clem., lach., phosph., sep.

With *much swelling.* (1.) *Bell., merc., puls., sep., sulph.* (2.) Bry., hepar, kali.-c., rhus, silic.

With *tearing, drawing* pains. (1.) *Lyc., sulph.* (2.) Ars., calc -c., merc., sep., silic.

With *tension.* (1.) *Con., puls., sulph.* (2.) Asaf., Baryta-c., caust., lach., merc., phosph., rhus, spong.

With pain as of *sub-cutaneous ulceration.* (1.) *Phosph., puls., silic.* (2.) Arn., asaf., bry., con., graph., ranunc-bulb.

Ulcers with *unhealthy pus.*

Pus *serous, aqueous, sanious.* (1.) *Merc., nitr.-ac., sulph.* (2.) Silic. (3.) Ars., carb.-v., lyc.

Pus *albuminous.* (1.) *Ars., sulph.* (2.) Amm., sep., silic.

Pus *brownish.* (1.) *Ars.* (2.) Carb.-veg.

Excessive secretion of pus. (1.) *Sep.* (2.) Chin., lyc., phosph.-ac., puls., silic.

Pus *gelatinous.* (1.) *Arg., merc., sep., silic.*

Pus *gray*. (1.) *Amb.*, *merc.*

Pus *yellow*. (1.) *Ars.*, *lyc.*, *puls.* (2.) Kreos., thuja, silic.

Pus *acrid*. (1.) *Ars.*, *merc.*, *silic.* (2.) Staphys., rhus, sep. (3.) Sulph.

Pus *sanguineous*. (1.) *Ars.*. *asaf.*, *hep.*, *merc.*

Scanty secretion of pus. (1.) *Lach.*, *merc.*, *silic.* (2.) Calc.-c.

Pus fetid. (1.) *Hep.*, *phosph.-ac.*, *sulph.*

CHAPTER XI.

VENEREAL DISEASE.

Section 1.—*History of Syphilis.*

UNDER this head will be classed, not only that specific disease, which has the power of penetrating the organism and producing constitutional syphilis, but also gonorrhœa or blennorrhœa.

The question concerning the origin of syphilis, has given rise to much argument, and to many learned discussions. The three suppositions that appear most worthy of observation, are:

1st. That the disease was brought from America by the Spaniards.

2d. That it originated in Europe.

3d. That it has been noticed from the earliest periods of human existence.

The first of these suppositions was promulgated to a great extent by Oveido, a Spaniard; indeed, he received from writers upon this subject, the entire credit of having traced the source of the disorder. To whatever reputation, however, may attach to such research, Oveido was not entitled, inasmuch as Leonhard Schmauss, Professor at Saltsberg, in the year 1518, had declared the same fact. The opinion of Schmauss was adopted by Chevalier Ulric Van Hutton, (known afterwards for his zeal and attachment to the cause of Luther,) A. D. 1519. The assertion, nevertheless, of its American origin, did not find very many supporters, notwithstanding it was strenuously advocated and enforced by Oveido. Among those, however, whose minds were impressed with its truth, were several individuals of much celebrity. If Oveido was quite sincere in the opinion he expressed, it is certain that feelings of a personal nature, very much contributed to augment the warmth and energy with which he maintained his position.

Among the distinguished opposers of the American origin of the disorder was Van Helmont, who, however believed it to be a new disease, supposed its birth-place to be Europe, and that it was generated in the army of Charles VIII. at the siege of Naples. Howard, at a later period supported the same opinion.

In the year 1680, Samuel Janson, who had resided for some years in the West Indies, not having observed the appearance of syphilis endemically, supposed that it was brought by the slaves from Africa. It is well known that both Sydenham and Boerhaave favored this opinion, and the latter defended it warmly in 1751. But slaves were not carried to America, previous to the year 1503, and at that time the disease was prevailing over all Europe.

An Italian alchemist propagated, also, a very curious *idea*, concerning the origin of this disease. Lord Bacon credited the story, and endeavored by his writings, to render it more plausible. "The length of the siege of Naples," says Leonardo Fioravanti, "having caused a famine among the French and Spanish troops, the merchants who brought food to the soldiers, sold them various articles prepared from human flesh, and all those who made use of the horrible aliment, were soon affected with syphilis, which was disseminated by contagion through Italy, France and Spain." Finally, J. Astruc,* a man of much learning and great natural talent, but whose acquirements, according to Jourdan, have been greatly exaggerated, endeavored, and succeeded in many instances, in convincing the world, that the disease was imported from America. He was

* De Morbus Veneris Libri sex, Paris, 1736.

supported, also, by Christopher Girtanner, a person of many and varied literary and scientific attainments. But Jourdan, taking up the arguments that were brought forward by them, disposes of them one by one in a most satisfactory manner. His pamphlet* bears the impress of deep thought, and of a vast amount of learning, toil and research, and should be perused by every student who is interested in this subject. He says (p. 44,) "the question is generally put, did syphilis appear for the first time, towards the end of the fifteenth century? The terms are not sufficiently explicit, since, as a preliminary matter, it is necessary to explain what is meant by syphilis. Now this definition, which has been neglected by all writers, is the only way of duly appreciating, judging and reconciling the different opinions successively advanced on the subject. By the term *syphilis*, therefore, is to be understood, 1st. A general affection of the system, which presents itself under a most frightful aspect, with many particular modifications, assuming a real epidemical character. In this sense the word designates the disease which broke out towards the end of the fifteenth century. 2d. It may serve to express morbid symptoms arising from an intercourse with a disordered person, communicated in the same way to other individuals, and having with each other a more or less intimate connection. Now, if we use the word syphilis in this last sense, it can be incontestibly proved, that from the remotest antiquity the diseases which it designates were known."

He then proceeds to prove his above statement with a "master hand," and mentions among others who have noted the disease, Guy de Chauliac. Peter Argelata says, that pustules arise on the penis *ex materia "venemosa quæ retinetur et remanet inter præputium et pellem cutis exactione viri cum fœda muliere."* In the thirteenth century, Lanfranc, Salicet, and others, spoke of the same disease, in terms which prove how far they considered it worthy of attention. There has been also, many passages collected by Becket, from manu-

* Historical and Critical Observations on Syphilis.

scripts which make mention of it. What likewise proves that the diseases of that period were considered of a serious and formidable character is, that the authorities in order to prevent their propagation enacted severe laws, the penalties for the violation of which were rigidly exacted. Hence the regulations for the *houses of pleasure* in London, in the years 1162 and 1430. Similar establishments and regulations existed in most of the large cities of Europe, from the time of Charlemagne. Medical and historical writers, make mention of diseases contracted at such houses, called *clapiers.* Jourdan then quotes many authorities in favor of the affection having been noticed and mentioned, by writers at a very early date,* but it is unnecessary that they should be mentioned here.

He is also of opinion, that the terrible epidemic which prevailed about the close of the fifteenth century, originated with the *Marranes*, (hogs.) This term was applied to those Moors and Jews, who had entirely disregarded the teachings of Christianity, and refused to enlist under its banner; for this offence they were expelled from Spain by an edict of King Ferdinand, dated March, 1492. The persecutions were unremitting, and the tortures to which this unfortunate class were subjected, were horrible in the extreme, to avoid which, they concealed their belief, but secretly practised those rules that were prescribed by their religion. They are described as living in the most disgusting and loathsome manner, and leprosy among them was alleged to be common. They were driven from their homes, not allowed to carry with them any of their property, and very many of them retired to the northern coasts of Africa, where they propagated a disease so terribly contagious, that of 170,000 families who crossed to Africa, 30,000 were destroyed. Jourdan says,† "when we compare the testimonies of the most veridical historians and physicians, we think it impossible to doubt its being derived

* See Leviticus, chap. xv., v. 2-27.

† Loc. cit., p. 99.

from the Marranes, who were expelled from Spain before the discovery of America." Fulgosi, among others, tells us that it originated in Ethiopia, "*quæ pestis, ita enim visa est, primo ex Hispania in Italia allatâ, et ad Hispanos ex Ethiopiâ.*" At that time all the parts of Spain occupied by the Moors were called Africa, and afterwards Ethiopia. Infessura, who noticed the first ravages of the epidemic at Rome, calls it *pestis Marranorum : Mortui sunt quam plurimi ex peste et contagione Marranorum.* Beniveni, Benedetti and Trascatorius derive it from Spain. John Trithamius, abbot of Spanheim, likewise informs us, that it originated in that country: *habet suæ infectiones pestiferæ principium in Hispanio.* The period of its appearance exactly corresponds to that of the expulsion of the Marranes. Fulgosi announces its existence in Lombardy, as early as 1492. We find it among the Germans in 1493 and 1494. John Pomarus says it appeared in Saxony in 1493. Henry Bunting affirms the same thing for Brunswick and Lunenburgh. According to John Sciphover, it broke out in 1494 in Westphalia, from whence it soon spread from the coasts of the Baltic Sea to Pomerania and Prussia. And as mentioned by Linturius, it manifested itself in 1494, on the borders of the Rhine, in Suabia, Franconia and Bavaria. Now the expulsion of the Marranes dates from the year 1492. These unfortunate wretches, who left Spain, according to Fabricius, to the number of one hundred and twenty-four thousand families, or of one hundred and seventy thousand, as mentioned by Mariana, lost, according to the same Fabricius and John Nauclerus, thirty thousand families, of a most fatal epidemic, which appeared to be of a peculiar nature. The disease not merely spread to Rome, as mentioned by Infessura, but also infected Naples, according to Zureta and Collenuccio, and even was propagated to the coasts of Barbary. Leo, the African, says, that the disease anterior to the landing of the Marranes, was unknown in Africa. Paul Jovius attributes, also, the extension of the disease to these exiles. Finally some passages from Peter Martyr, Francis de Villaloros and Peter Pinctor, which, owing to their want of clearness, have been refuted by the partisans of the American origin, seem to indicate that the epidemic already existed in Spain, during the last twenty years of the fifteenth century; consequently before 1490. It cannot at all appear surprising, that such considerable collections of people, whom the avarice of Ferdinand had deprived of all the necessaries of life, and consequently thrown into the most disgusting filth, the inseparable attendant on misery, should have spread, wherever they passed, a contagious cutaneous disease, complicated with scorbutic symptoms, which were necessarily produced by the dampness and the excessive heat of the weather. This is the idea we naturally form of the terrible epidemic of the fifteenth century.

The epidemic thus spread over all portions of Europe. In Germany, the propagation of the disease was principally attributed to the Lansquenets,* a military rabble, who were constantly ready to sell their life and blood to the highest bidder. In the latter end of the fifteenth century, the whole of Europe being engaged in war, the disease once propagated among the common soldiers, must readily have been spread over the whole continent. A similar confusion prevailed in regard to the mode in which the disease was propagated. It was believed by many, that the virus could be carried in the atmosphere, or that any article which a person afflicted with the disease had touched, was capable of imparting the disorder. Fallopius supposed that the disease might be propagated by the holy water, into which a syphilitic patient had dipped his finger.

In the year 1556, Fernel proved that the disease originated from a specific cause, emanating from some affected individual, and acting upon one in health; he opposed the idea of the transmission of the virus by the atmosphere, and denied the belief in cosmic, astrological or teleological influences; he also described, with tolerable accuracy, its mode of transmission. After a lapse of three hundred years, Fernel's picture of the syphilitic disease is still true, as is shown by the descriptions of the most enlightened and learned physicians of the present day.

* See Gollmann on Diseases of the Urinary and Sexual Organs, p. 45.

Section 2.—Simple Venereal Disease.—Gonorrhœa.

Gonorrhœa, or a specific morbid secretion from the urethra in males, and from the urethra and vagina in females, is a disease of very ancient date; it arises from impure connection, and presents the following symptoms.

A few days, generally from four to six, or even more,* after copulation, a tickling or slight itching is felt in the urethra, near the frænum; this sensation continues one or two days, when the mouth of the urethra acquires an increased sensibility, becomes red and swollen, and there oozes or is discharged a limpid or yellow matter, which stains the linen. When the running occurs the titillation increases and becomes more painful, especially during the emission of urine, which is followed by a smarting and burning in the affected part. In some persons the first symptom observed is the discharge of thick mucus; in these cases the patient experiences a painful scalding when passing water.

These symptoms usually increase for three or four days; sometimes, however, not sensibly, for eight to twelve days. The glans penis acquires a dark red livid color; the discharge becomes more profuse, the matter becoming of a yellowish green color, the swelling of the glans and sometimes even of the whole penis becomes considerable, the patient experiences a frequent desire to void urine, and suffers, particularly when he has been some time in bed, lying on his back, from involuntary erections, so frequent as to disturb his rest.

In many cases, the inflammation extends to the reticular substance of the corpus spongiosum; the erections, when this is the case, become extremely painful, the frænum being drawn down, while the body of the penis is forced upward, from extreme turgescence; such a condition is termed *chordee*. When in this state the vessels of the urethra are often ruptured,

---

* Gonorrhœa may lie dormant in the system for a considerable time, or it may be retarded in its course, by some other disorder attended with fever. For corroboration of this, see London Lancet, June, 1845, p. 526.

occasioning considerable hemorrhage, while at other times, the discharge is only streaked with blood. The prepuce is also at the same time so inflamed and swollen that it cannot be drawn back, or when retracted it cannot be returned.*

In some instances the urethra discharges small clots or even fluid blood, and there are evident marks of an ulceration of the urethra.

The inflammation may increase to such an extent that there will be no secretion from the glands and the membranes lining the canals. All discharge then ceases, and it is to this form of the disease that some authors have improperly applied the term gonorrhœa sicca, or dry clap.

But the symptoms, their time of appearance, and their violence, vary greatly in different individuals. Mr. Hunter has well remarked† that " the variety of symptoms in a gonorrhœa, and the difference of them in different cases, are almost endless." The discharge often appears without any pain, and the accession of pain is not at any stated time after the appearance of the discharge. There is often no pain at all, though the matter thrown out may be considerable in quantity and of bad appearance. The pain often goes off, while the discharge continues, and will sometimes return again. An itching in some cases is felt for a considerable time, which sometimes is succeeded by pain, though in many cases it continues to the end of the disease. On the other hand, the pain is often troublesome and considerable even when the discharge is trifling or none at all. In general, the inflammation in the urethra does not extend beyond an inch or two from the orifice; sometimes it runs all along the urethra to the bladder, and even to the kidneys; and in some cases spreads in the substance of the urethra, producing a chordee. The glands of the urethra inflame, and often suppurate. The neighboring parts sympathize—as the glands of the groin, the testicle and the pubes—with the upper parts of the thighs and abdominal muscles."

In the worst cases, small indurations may often be felt in the

* See Swediaur on Syphilis, p. 4. † Hunter on the Venereal, p 61.

course of the urethra, and the prostate gland partakes of the inflammation; in which event a sense of heat, weight, and fulness is experienced in the perineum, with pain in the hypogastrium, dysuria, and tensemus, particularly when the disease has spread to the bladder or its cervix. Abscess, fistula, and permanent disease of the prostate, or stricture of the urethra, are the occasional results of such complications. Phimosis, orchitis, and bubo, not unfrequently take place from the extension of the inflammation to the prepuce, testes and glands of the groin, during the course of gonorrhœa.

Gleet, or the existence of a serous or muco-purulent, pale green, or colorless, discharge from the urethra, is not an unfrequent occurrence after an attack of acute inflammation. It is commonly attributed to chronic inflammatory action. The most trifling error in diet, and particularly the use of spirits, wine, and pungent condiments, is generally followed by a frequent inclination to void water, a degree of ardor urinæ, and increased oozing of matter. This state often continues for years, and grows more and more aggravated, until at length a permanent stricture is formed, or thickening of the bladder, disease of the prostate, or even of the kidneys becomes established.

*Treatment.**—Gonorrhœa sometimes proves very intractable, even in homœopathic practice; but if the treatment is commenced sufficiently early, it terminates much less frequently in the secondary form of the malady, and the other serious consequences that have been detailed, than results from allopathic treatment. The medicines which have hitherto been chiefly employed by homœopathic practitioners are, *copaiba*, *petroselinum*, *cannabis*, *aconite*, *sulphur*, *canth.*, *capsicum*, *silicea*, *lycopodium*, *acid-nitric*, *sepia*, &c.

In the milder forms of the affection, or in cases occurring in healthy subjects, the cure is generally easily and speedily accomplished when the patient applies before the second stage

---

* The treatment of gonorrhœa is mostly taken from Laurie's Homœopathic Practice of Physic. The remedies are well selected, and bear the impress of considerable experience in treating this affection.

has set in. The disease has frequently been arrested at its outset (when the orifice of the urethra looks fuller and redder than natural, and a disagreeable itching is felt in the canal, together with frequent desire to urinate, and some pain during micturition) by means of the alternate employment of *aconite* and *cannabis*, at intervals of at first six, and subsequently twelve to twenty-four hours.

So soon, however, as the discharge begins, and ardor urinæ experienced, *copaiba* often proves very serviceable; but should there be a constant desire to make water, *petroselinum* should be used in preference. *Cannabis* is better than either when the inflammation is somewhat of a higher grade, and the pain and difficulty in passing water are constantly more intense. In gonorrhœa with phimosis, or extension of the inflammation to the prepuce, *merc.* is the most important medicine; but it is sometimes necessary to prescribe a dose or two of *aconite* in the first place, when the inflammatory action is excessive, and the gland and prepuce are very much tumefied. *Merc.* is further of considerable efficacy at the commencement of the second stage of the disease, when there remains a muco-purulent discharge, of a white or greenish yellow color, and some degree of pain in passing the last drops of water; or when there is swelling and induration of the lymphatic glands of the penis. *Silic.*, or *hepar*, is sometimes required after *merc.* in the latter case; and *caps.* is often useful in removing any ardor urinæ that may remain. *Sulph.* is still more frequently required than *merc.*, after the inflammatory stage is over, and particularly when the discharge has become serous, and a feeling of uneasiness alone remains in the urethra when voiding urine. In painless gonorrhœa, accompanied with swelling, *merc.*, *sulph.*, or *silic.*, are useful.

In the severer forms of the disease, *acon.*, *cam.* and *canth.* are especially applicable. The curative power of these medicines is frequently very striking, and the rapidity with which they afford relief is highly satisfactory. *Acon.* is more or less useful in cases of gonorrhœa occurring in young and vigorous subjects, and attended with headache, restlessness, and other febrile symptoms; but it is almost indispensable when the inflammation is severe and extensive, the pain during micturition excruciating, the glans, or indeed the entire penis, much swollen, and the sufferings greatly exacerbated by frequent and almost constant erections (*priapismus.*) *Canth.* is generally required after *aconite;* it may be given from six to eight hours after the second or third dose of the latter, when the intensity of the pain and any febrile irritation which may have been present have yielded, but the dysuria, ardor urinæ and chordee still continue distressing; *canth.* may be exhibited without the previous employment of *aconite,* when there is no marked degree of constitutional disturbance; but the scalding during micturition and the chordee are very severe, and the discharge is greenish and tinged with blood. *Cannabis* is sometimes required after *canth.*, especially when the dysuria proves obstinate; and when *cannabis* effects little or no improvement, *petroselinum* may be administered. Sometimes the alternate use of the latter with *cannabis* or *canth.*, is necessary to subdue the urging to urinate, and the pain during micturition. *Merc.*, or *sulph.*, are not unfrequently useful in completing the cure, when the before mentioned medicines have removed the active inflammatory symptoms.

When gonorrhœa has reached the chronic stage before the patient seeks advice, the difficulty in the treatment is greater than during the first or inflammatory stage; the more so, if the patient has previously drugged himself with large and continued doses of cubebs or of balsam of copaiba, or has fruitlessly persisted for some length of time in the employment of astringent injections. In a number of cases, early benefit has been derived from the use of *caps.*, *merc.*, *sulph.*, and *nit.-ac.*

Capsicum is recommended when the discharge is whitish and purulent, and ardor urinæ experienced when making water. *Ferrum, pulsatilla,* and also *nux-vomica,* are also stated to be useful when *capsicum* failed to relieve the symptoms quoted. *Sulph.* and *merc.* are considered the most useful in cases where the patient has previously been under a course of copaiba or cubebs. *Nit.-ac.* is often very serviceable in gonorrhœa as soon as the inflammatory stage is over; but generally requires to be followed by *sulph.*, if the pain has subsided but the discharge continues. When the inflammation has evidently extended far down the urethra, much benefit has been derived from the use of *canth.* and *cann.*, and in some cases from *nux-v.* when the discharge is serous and scanty, the desire to pass water frequent and urgent, the act of urination painful and difficult, the stream of urine broken or forked; in short, when symptoms present the appearance of the formation of stricture or a tendency thereto.

In addition to the above medicines, *nit.-ac.* may be mentioned as useful in gleet; likewise *sep.*, *lyc.*, *cub.*, *silic.*, *calc.*, *thuj.*, *nat.-mur.*, and *dulc.* When, in consequence of errors in diet, the use of wines, spirits, acids, &c., an increased discharge takes place, accompanied with frequent desire to urinate, with scalding pain, *nux-vom.*, or one or more of those medicines enumerated above, must be had recourse to.

Tussilago petasites has been recommended as a most efficacious remedy in recent as well as in chronic gonorrhœa.* If aggravation follows the first dose or two of the medicine, it must be given in a weaker or more dilute form. When there is a complication of gonorrhœa and chancre, or when the discharge from the urethra is found to proceed from chancres within the tube, *merc.* should be prescribed. And when there are condylomata on or in the vicinity of the genital organs, or there is reason to suppose that the discharge from the urethra is of sycotic origin, *thuj.* and *nit.-ac.*, or *cinnabar*, *merc.*, or *sulph.*, are the principal medicines with which the cure is to be accomplished. Against symptomatic buboes *carb.-an.* is considered as one of the most efficacious remedies. *Silic.* and *merc.* may also be named as likely to be useful in some cases.

If cytitis ensue in consequence of the extension of the inflammation to the mucous membrane of the bladder, *canth.* and *cann.* will claim the principal attention.

During the treatment of gonorrhœa, wine, spirits, and malt

---

* British Journal of Homœopathy, vol. iii., p. 125.

liquors should be abstained from. Pure cold water is the best diluent, and may be freely partaken of. Active exercise should be shunned during the inflammatory stage, and when it cannot be wholly avoided, a suspensory bandage should be worn. If the inflammation be extensive, or the parts much swollen, confinement to the recumbent posture becomes requisite.

The more minute indications for the medicines that are serviceable, are as follows:

Agnus-castus is especially adapted to a yellow, purulent discharge from the urethra, after the inflammatory symptoms have subsided; and also to cases of gleet, accompanied by want of erections and deficient sexual desire.

Argen.-nit. is useful when the emission of urine is accompanied with burning, and if a sensation be experienced as though the urethra were closed, not allowing a free passage for the urine; it is also indicated by dragging and cutting pains in the tube, with feeling of soreness after micturition, hemorrhage from the parts, with painful tensive erections.

Balsam-cop. should be exhibited when there is smarting, burning and itching, before and after micturition, with swelling of the orifice of the urethra, and painful soreness of the whole canal, with purulent discharge.

Cannabis presents the following symptoms. Smarting pain, constant urging to urinate, with burning and stingings during micturition, titillation, gluing together of the external orifice of the canal, by a moisture which is forced out on compressing the glans.

In regard to *cannabis*, it may be observed in this place, that it is a medicine which accords in its pathogenesis with very many of the symptoms of gonorrhœa. Its specific suitableness to the complaint is attested by numerous physicians. In further corroboration of its efficacy, the author is assured by a practitioner of this city, who has had much experience in the treatment of gonorrhœa, that he has been not only gratified but surprised at its efficacy in subduing the disorder. The symptoms which point to its use may be present at any period, but exhibit themselves in cases somewhat advanced, and in those more chronic. In the latter especially, is its power apparent; cases that for two, three, or more months had fruitlessly been tampered with by allopaths of high station, were immediately arrested and speedily cured. In truth, the disorder was checked by the first dose, consisting only of a few globules of the medicine; and a few more doses, at intervals regulated by the symptoms, accomplished complete cures. The attenuation, however, of the medicine is an important consideration in the treatment; the exhibition of the lower causing disappointment, while successful result is obtained from the higher potencies only.

The gentleman whose testimony has just been given, commenced with the second and third dilutions, but failed; and it was only by resorting to higher dynamizations that he learned that the sphere of curative action for gonorrhœal disorder, exists in the preparations as highly attenuated as the thirtieth, the latter being the strength of the medicine which he then always administered.

Facts like these, attested by gentlemen of high social position, as well as of acknowledged ability, certainly convert the childlike smile of incredulity into that of imbecility, as expressed upon the countenances of individuals, who with so much pleasant self-sufficiency fancy themselves the sole depositories of all medical science.

Canth. Cutting in the urethra during and after micturition; discharge leaving a yellow stain on the linen, which is increased as the disease becomes chronic. This agent frequently shortens the attack, if administered as soon as the first signs of inflammation become apparent.

Capsicum. Burning at the meatus urinarius externus before, during, and after micturition, with cutting pain and sensitiveness to contact; pricking as with pins in the fore part of the tube, and thick purulent yellow discharge.

Cocc. Tensive, aching pain in the orifice of the urethra, between the acts of micturition, also itching stinging near the fossa navicularis.

Ferrum. Discharge of mucus from the urethra after a cold.

Merc.-sol. Burning pain in the corpus spongiosum when touching the penis. Inflammation and swelling of the fore part of the canal, with suppuration between the glans and prepuce. Redness and heat with painfulness of urethra, when touching the part, or when walking, accompanied by severe pain in the forehead; the urine being voided in a thin stream. Itching and stinging pains accompanied with greenish discharge, especially at night; secretion may not amount to more than a moisture.

Mez. Stinging, titillating, with discharge of a little moisture from the urethra. Tearing and drawing through the whole canal, commencing at the perinæum; also painful soreness of the tube when touching it, partly before and partly during micturition, and discharge of watery mucus during exercise.

Nux-vom. Pressive pain at the meatus urinarius between the acts of micturition, accompanied by shuddering; sharp pressure, as with a cutting instrument, in the fore part of the urethra, also at the bladder perinæum and anus, with contractive pain between the acts of urination, and discharge of mucus.

Petroselinum. Tingling and pressure in the region of Cowper's glands, especially early in the morning in bed, abating when standing or sitting; drawing and pressure in the navicular fossa, with discharge of a yellow glutinous matter.

Puls. Thin stream of urine, occasioned by contraction of the parts, with discharge of blood, swelling of the testes and inflammation of the eyes, caused by suppression of gonorrhœa.

Merc.-cor. Inflammation of the meatus urinarius, with itching, smarting pain during micturition, the discharge being at first thin and watery, but afterwards thick and yellowish.

Sulph. Burning in the forepart of the urethra internally and externally. In the first stages of the disease, the medicine should be employed, when there is redness and inflammation of the meatus urinarius, the urine voided in a thin stream, itching in the middle of the canal, with constant desire to void the urine, with tearing and stinging between the acts of micturition, which is sometimes accompanied with tearing and stinging pain.

Thuja. Burning in the urethra, or piercing stitches near its orifice between the acts of micturition; sensation as though a drop of urine were passing from the canal, with drawing and cutting pains.

During the treatment, the strictest cleanliness must be observed. The penis should be often washed with tepid or cold water, and the rags that are used to prevent the discharge from staining the linen, should be frequently removed, and fresh ones substituted.

Sometimes, a short period after copulation, the glans penis becomes red, hot and sensitive to contact, follicular secretion is much increased, and soon becomes purulent, or of a thick, greenish yellow. This affection has been termed gonorrhœa glandis, or spurious gonorrhœa. As, however, it does not invariably arise from impure coition, the term is not entirely correct, and Dr. Attomyr observes, that the disease should be termed *inflammation of the glans penis.* The best medicines for the complaint are, *acon.*, *cann.*, *corall.-rub.*, *merc.*, *nit.-acid* and *thuj.*

Section 3.—*Syphilis.*

Syphilis is a disease, caused by a morbid principle or poison, which applied, under certain conditions, to any portion of the human body, will determine definite and characteristic phenomena; that this principle being absorbed and carried into the system, will, during the existence of the local or primary symptoms, and for an indefinite period subsequent to their cessation, contaminate the economy; and finally, that this principle is capable of being transmitted hereditarily, and that, too, at a period when its presence in the system is not revealed by any external sign. This capability of quietude for a number of years within the organism, without producing in the mean time any appreciable effect upon it, is a character not peculiar to syphilitic poison.

The existence of a special virus was denied by Broussais, and his school, who believed that chancres were nothing more than simple sores, and treated them accordingly. The existence of a specific morbid poison in syphilis can be demonstrated alone by its effects. The matter of a primary syphilitic sore or chancre, introduced beneath the epidermis, is constant in its results, whoever the individual, or whatever the part of the body inoculated. This is conclusively proved by the numerous experiments of Ricord, Wallace, Mayo, Carmichael, Mairion, Parker, &c. No other secretion, or product of an ulcerated or suppurating surface, will produce the same effects.

It is not necessary here, to enter into the vexed question of the identity or non-identity of the venereal poison; that is, whether the two classes of affections referred to, are due to one virus, or result from the action of several.* It appears, however, from the latest experiments, that gonorrhœal matter applied to a mucous surface, will produce gonorrhœa, but in no instance is it capable of producing *true* chancre; it *may act as an irritant*, but does not produce the *specific sore.* Nor do the phenomena of constitutional syphilis never follow gonorrhœa, although the reverse has been stated, and that, too, by respectable authorities; but in the cases that have been cited to prove the identity of the two viruses, it has been said, that a diseased individual, having had connection with several healthy persons, these latter would be variously affected; some would have chancres, some gonorrhœa, and others both together. Now in these cases, the two diseases coëxisted in the diseased person. Had he or she been properly examined, larvated chancres would have been discovered, either in the urethra, or about the neck of the uterus, or in the cul de sac of the vagina or elsewhere. The speculum should always be used in such cases, for, says Ricord, "all syphilitic cases in

---

* See Hunter on the Venereal, p. 25, and an article on Syphilis in the Med. Chir. Review, July, 1851, p. 182.

women, where the use of the speculum has been neglected, shall be for us as though they never were recorded."*

The classification of venereal diseases proposed by Ricord, is as follows: 1. Primitive or direct, when they occur at the inoculated spot, from the immediate action of the virus. 2. Successive, when they originate in the latter, and are produced elsewhere by absorption, or contiguity of tissue, or accidental contact, as chancrous bubo, and the conversion of neighboring abrasions, or leech bites, into chancres. 3. Secondary, when the skin and mucous membranes are affected after the reception of chancrous matter into the system; and, 4. Tertiary, when the cellular, fibrous and bony structures are the seat of the constitutional symptoms. 5. Diseases unconnected with syphilis.

Concerning this classification, however, it has been remarked, that it is unphilosophical, and wanting in simplicity, and that many of the grounds on which it is founded, are incorrect and untenable. The two first may certainly without violence be included under one head; the second and third divisions are not susceptible of separation, on the grounds given by Dr. Ricord. The so-called tertiary symptoms may arise without the necessary intervention of the secondary. Dr. Ricord asserts, that whilst the former may be transmitted hereditarily, the latter cannot be, except in a degenerated form, as scrofula. This, however, is not well substantiated, and many of the profession, believe both secondary and tertiary syphilis equally liable to propagation by inheritance. With regard to the fifth class, viz: "diseases unconnected with syphilis," it is difficult to understand.

The whole subject may be much simplified by dividing it, 1. Into primary, or local syphilis; and, 2. Into general or constitutional syphilis, which is always strictly the consequence of a chancre.

By chancre is understood, a solution of continuity in the soft parts, produced by the disorganizing action of the syphilitic

---

* Extract from a Lecture on Syphilis.

virus upon the inoculated spot. Chancre, wherever its seat, is the consequence of the application of a specific matter, which a chancre alone secretes, and which produces a chancre, whenever placed in circumstances favorable to contagion. The question of *time*, between the application of the virus and its action, has been productive of much discussion. Ricord has denied that there is a period of incubation, on the ground that, in no instance after his experiments with inoculation, did he observe any.

When the virus is introduced beneath the epidermis, its action may be immediate, but this is far from being the case when the affection is natural. Two friends, after a debauch, had connection with the same woman; three days subsequently, one was attacked with a chancre, but it was not until the twenty-first day that his friend became similarly affected, although he had, in the meanwhile, daily examined the parts, and abstained from all sexual relations.* The period of incubation varies with the degree of susceptibility of the organ, and the manner in which the affection is contracted.

The physical characters of chancres vary with their number and their location. If several of these sores exist at the same spot, the form is irregular, and the edges are jagged and notched; in the natural folds of the skin, and in mucous membranes and in depending parts, where the virus acts in a longitudinal direction, their form is of the same character. The appearance of chancre differs in different tissues. On the lips, which are highly organized, the chancre is granular; on the labia majora, and other cellular parts, the chancre is of a grayish appearance; when situated on the body of the penis, if the ulceration has penetrated to the fibrous envelop of the corpora cavernosa, the ulcer will present that white, shining, brilliant appearance peculiar to fibrous tissue. When on the glans penis, the granulations are generally of a bright red, and bleed when touched lightly. The edges of a chancre are generally

* The above case is reported by Dr. Huguier, one of the physicians to the Female Venereal Hospital, at Paris.

perpendicular, and look as if they had been cut out by a sharp instrument, the primitive venereal virus nearly always acting centripetally. If, however, the virus comes in contact with previous abrasions, the cellular tissue is more rapidly destroyed than the skin or mucous membrane, and the latter are, in some instances, dissected up.

The character of the pus varies with the period that the ulcerations have existed, at first serous, thin, even sanious, and mixed with the disorganizing tissue; then healthier, thicker, and often mixed with blood; and it finally becomes consistent, of a yellowish tinge, of a better character, resembling that on the surface of a blister in full suppuration. It varies too with the nature of the ulcer. There is generally recognized two stages to chancre, one of ulceration, and the other of cicatrization. There is an important difference in these two stages; in the first a specific matter is secreted, which retains its inoculable properties. The specific period has no absolute period of duration. Dr. Ricord, in one instance, saw it last seven years, and inoculate at the end of that time. The usual duration is from one to two months. In the second stage the chancre ceases to be inoculable, granulates and heals. If a chancre is in the second stage, in the progress of cicatrization, connection will not be followed by disease; but if the ulcer is in its first stage, the secreted matter is specifically contagious. Chancres may be divided according as their location is either external or concealed, hence we have *external* and *larvated.* Larvated, or concealed chancres, in the male are situated in the urethra, and in the mucous fold of the prepuce, and at the base of the glans, in which latter situation they are complicated with phimosis; in the female, they are found in the urethra, at the orifice of the vagina, and in or about the neck of the uterus; likewise within the anus, in the rectum, in the fauces, larynx, &c., in both sexes.

It may be well in this place, to describe a chancre induced by artificial inoculation, to which the experiments of Ricord have drawn so much attention. During the first twenty-four hours after the introduction of the virus beneath the epidermis, there is slight inflammation, followed on the second day by tumefaction, and a small ecthymatous papula, surrounded by an areola ; from the third to the fourth day there is a vesicle, filled with a fluid more or less opaque, with a dark point at the apex ; about the fourth or fifth day this becomes purulent, with the centre depressed, resembling a small-pox pustule. The areola, which up to this period had increased, now diminishes, and after the fifth day, the surrounding tissues, hitherto unaffected, become of a cartilaginous hardness. After the sixth day the pustule dries, is covered with a laminated crust, and this, when detached, becomes a characteristic ulcer with a broad base.

Section 4.—*Primary Syphilis.*

Chancres may be divided, according to their characters, into *superficial*, *indurated* or *Hunterian, and phagedenic primary syphilitic ulcers.* Some authors mention two other varieties, viz : the follicular and *furunculous.*

The *superficial chancre* is confined to the upper layer of the skin, destroys only a very small portion of its tissue, and the exudation is trifling.

The *indurated chancre* was first described by John de Vigo. Hunter considered it as the type of the primary venereal ulcer, and from him it receives the name, Hunterian chancre. Ricord has asserted, that a chancre never becomes indurated before the fifth day, and considers the induration as the index of the constitution being affected. This variety of syphilitic sore is certainly the most annoying of all forms of chancre, and the most certain to be followed by constitutional symptoms. The induration is due to the effusion of plastic lymph into the cellular tissue, or, as Ricord believes, into the lymphatic capillaries.

Dr. Fricks, of Hamburg, proved conclusively, that the application of corrosive sublimate to the prepuce, will occasion ulcers with a hard base, and the only means of *true* diagnosis between these and true chancres, is the non-inoculable character of the former. The indurated chancre is usually very indolent, the hardness commencing at the base. It is, in most instances, round when situated in homogeneous tissues, has regular edges, and is of a very dark color. The base may be indurated and not the edges, and the reverse may also, sometimes be found, but usually the whole chancre equally participates in the hardness. Immediately around it, ulcers may exist, which do not present any of these characters.

A *phagedenic chancre* is usually very rapid and destructive in its progress, increasing in *extent*, but not in *depth*, and accompanied with severe pain. Its extension is irregular and serpiginous. It occurs generally in constitutions worn out by intemperance, and follows very often irritating dressings, which have been injudiciously applied to irritated or inflamed chancres, especially mercurial ointment. It is called the black slough in England.

There is a form of phagedenic sore, called the diptheritic or pultaceous, which is exceedingly chronic; (Ricord has seen it last for seven years,) it is covered, either entirely or partially, by a pultaceous diptheritic secretion. The base is œdematous, and the edges are elevated, irregular and serrated; it is surrounded by a dull, purple areola, and it increases by successive ulceration of the depending parts. The constitution becomes seriously implicated, and the patient finally sinks. This form of chancre occurs in ill-fed, badly lodged individuals, in whom there is previous organic disease.

In some cases chancres become gangrenous. In such a case the destruction of the tissue proceeds so rapidly that the whole glans is destroyed in a short period.

The *treatment* of the chancre must be in conformity with its character. Simple chancre is sometimes cured in from two to three weeks, without any signs of constitutional syphilis. The indurated chancre, even under the most careful allopathic treatment, never is eradicated without symptoms of constitutional syphilis supervening after five or six weeks of treatment.

Under homœopathic treatment, which may last from six to eight weeks before the cure is perfected, constitutional disease is in a very large proportion of cases prevented.* The medicine must be continued until every trace of induration is removed, for frequently the sore disappears, leaving induration surrounding the cicatrix; if this hardness be not removed, constitutional syphilis will in all probability develop itself.

In treating chancres, no matter of what description, the external treatment must be accompanied with the utmost cleanliness. The ulcer should be frequently cleansed with tepid water, and the lint that is used as a covering and protection to the sore should be changed several times during a day.

Dr. Attomyr observes, "Syphilitic patients, with very few exceptions, are young unmarried men, who either board at the hotels or sit at table with their relations, or probably superiors. In either case it is unfortunate for the observation of homœopathic diet. To this must be added the fact that patients conceal their disorders, and in order not to excite suspicion, dare not venture on the slightest aberration from their accustomed diet. In consequence of these uncertain dietetic circumstances, I resolved in treating such patients to administer larger doses than usual.

"I am still of opinion that the lower dilutions recall reaction quicker, but that their effects are less extensive and permanent than the higher. Four grains of calomel in the space of a few hours operate violently and excite diarrhœa, while the same four grains, if taken in minute portions, result in an indisposition, which continues several days, and in more intense commotion of the organism. I moreover concluded from these premises, that the larger doses could be repeated more frequently, which would seem essential, on account of the necessarily frequent dietetical errors. Within the period of two years I treated one hundred and fifty-six patients laboring under venereal disease. Every physician knows how it is with office practice, how difficult to learn any thing, or obtain any certain experience in this manner. Generally one half of this class of

* See Gollmann on Diseases of the Urinary and Sexual Organs, p. 110.

patients stay away, so that it is impossible for us to decide with certainty upon the termination of their disorders. The one remains away because the effects of the treatment did not fulfil his anticipations, the other (and among syphilitic patients the majority) because he is approaching convalescence, and is desirous of avoiding the *burdensome thanksgiving* of his cure." Dr. Attomyr also states that out of the one hundred and fifty-six patients, so many did not return to mention the success of the treatment, that only eighty-four can be cited as being perfectly cured.

The medicines that have been found most efficacious in the treatment of syphilis are, *merc.-sol.*, *merc.-corr.*, *acid-nit.*, *hepar-sulph.*, *acid-phosph.*, *lyc.*, *sulph.*, *silic.*, *ars.*, *carbo-veg.*, *thuj.*, and *sepia.*

The selection of the potency should in a measure be guided by the idiosyncrasy of the patient, although perhaps in the generality of cases the lower dilutions are more effectual, and in many instances this may be owing to circumstances mentioned by Dr. Attomyr.

Mercurius-sol. is adapted to those chancres that present an indurated base and margin, (of course this medicine must not be prescribed if the patient have previously been subjected to its action in massive doses,) and covered with a tenacious, thin, offensive matter. Dr. Laurie says, "We should certainly most unwillingly dispense with this valuable remedy in such cases, notwithstanding the bad repute it has acquired from the frightful effects which have so frequently arisen from its abuse in the hands of our allopathic brethren. Such results can never take place in homœopathic practice, assuredly not in the hands of any one at all deserving of the name of a homœopathic practitioner. Where the health of the patient is remarkably good, and the sore neither of long duration, nor has in any way been aggravated by previous treatment, we have repeatedly succeeded in effecting a cure in from ten to fourteen days, by means of *merc. viv.* 6th, a few globules (about a dozen) night and morning for about five or six days. And subsequently, on the ulcer assuming a healing aspect, every second or third day. In other cases, especially, in torpid constitutions, it was found requisite to have recourse to the *third, second,* and *first* of *merc.-corr.*, giving one fourth to half a grain daily, until a copious discharge of healthy pus supervened, or the excavations began to be filled up with healthy granulations. As soon as either the one or the other of these changes took place, a pause of three or four days was made. At the expiration of that period, a few more doses were generally sufficient to effect a cure in the last named instances; but in the former, if no signs of granulation made their appearance, (which, however, was rarely the case,) a dose or two of *sulph.* 6th produced a favorable effect."

Merc.-sol. is also adapted to the following appearances: Red chancre on the prepuce; spreading and deeply penetrating ulcers on the glans and foreskin; pale-red vesicles on the glans and prepuce, forming small ulcers after breaking; readily bleeding chancres; distressingly painful chancres, secreting a quantity of yellowish-white fetid pus; small chancres with a cheesy bottom, and inverted, red edges; inflamed, round chancrous ulcers, with swelling of the vagina; chancres with edges resembling raw flesh; slightly painful ulcers, sensitive to the contact of the linen; vesicles at the fore part and on the sides of the glans, spreading and penetrating rapidly; ulcers of the glans and prepuce, with cheesy, lardaceous bottom, and hard edges; a number of small red vesicles at the tip of the penis, behind the prepuce, breaking after a fortnight, and forming small ulcers, which secrete a strong smelling, yellowish-white matter, which stains the linen; afterwards the large ulcers bleed and are painful when touched; from these latter the whole body was sympathetically affected. These sores were circular, their edges presented a raw appearance, and the bottom of the ulcer was covered with a cheesy secretion.

When granulations appear in the ulcer, but instead of being florid, and firm, are prominent, pale, and flabby, *nit.-ac.* is an excellent medicine.

Merc.-corr. Chancres with ichor adhering to the bottom of the ulcer so firmly that it cannot be removed by washing. Ulcers with thin pus, leaving stains upon the linen, as from melted tallow.

Arsenicum may prove serviceable when, after the administration of mercury, the sore has appeared to improve somewhat; has nevertheless filled up with florid and too elevated granulations, with edges remaining hard, and very irritable, bleeding at the slightest touch, the discharge being thin, acrid and offensive. *Sulph.* and *nit.-acid* may also prove serviceable for such conditions.

Ars. is well adapted likewise to phagedenic, gangrenous ulcers, and accordingly to the indurated chancre of Hunter; its symptoms are, gangrenous ulcers, with bloody edges and corrosive pus; ulcers with copious secretion of watery fetid ichor; painless ulcers with hard edges and lardaceous base; stinging chancres with white places in the middle of the ulcer; gangrenous chancre on the glans penis.

When there is excessive pain, swelling and inflammation, and these symptoms do not yield to the action of *mercurius*, *sulph.* or *aconite*, or, if the sufferings be severe, these in alternation may be prescribed. When the irritation is excessive, and the pain very great, the granulations unhealthy and readily bleeding, *nit.-acid* may relieve. It is suited to chancres of the orifice of the urethra, prepuce and its margin, with bloody, fetid, ichorous pus; small chancres without inflamed borders, flat edges and considerable swelling. Chancrous ulcers, with flat edges, without inflammation, but with violent lancinations, increasing towards evening, preventing sleep, and becoming insufferable in the morning on account of violent erections. Small itching vesicles on the prepuce, bursting in a few days, and becoming covered with a small dry scurf; deep ulcer on the corona glandis, which looks clean, but secretes a strong smelling matter; burning of the inflamed and swollen prepuce, the inside of which is denuded of the epithelium, with small ulcers secreting an ichor that has a pungent, nauseous odor, and stains the linen.

In some cases, when the irritation and pain are excessive, the exposure of the part to the vapor of hot water, together with a spare diet and the recumbent position, greatly relieve the patient. When the ulcer is not very painful the dressing may consist of a small piece of lint. When the chancre is located under the prepuce, and the latter is much swollen and inflamed, an injection of tepid water should be thrown between the parts. This practice is recommended by the most experienced practitioners of our school. "The remedies," says Dr. Laurie, "that we employed against the ulcer with raised edges were, *acid-nit., hepar-sulph., sulph., arsen., silic., carb.-veg., lyc., acid-phosph., sepia, merc.* Most of the cases treated had already existed from six to eight weeks, and upwards, and had been subjected to a smart mercurial course, both outwardly and inwardly. *Acid-nit.* and *hepar-sulph.* were very generally required; to the former the preference was given when the gums were severely affected, and when aching pains were complained of in the bones; the sore itself not painful, yet disposed to bleed easily and profusely, presenting no signs of central granulation, and having the margins elevated and spongy looking. When there was a tendency to the production of condylomata, (sycotic complication,) with secretion of a thin sanious discharge, *sulph.* or *thuj.* was sometimes required after *acid-nit.* had effected all the benefit it seemed capable of. The former when cicatrization proceeded slowly and imperfectly, and the latter (both outwardly and inwardly) when excrescences continued to form and discharge profusely. *Hepar* proved particularly useful when the mouth and gums exhibited unequivocal signs of mercurial action, and when the sore was painful, irritable, and had assumed a disposition to spread rapidly. *Silic.*, and at other times *nit.-ac.*, were sometimes called for, to complete the cure, after *hepar* had subdued the more prominent symptoms of mercurial aggravation, and given a healthy character to the sore. *Sulph.*, as has already been observed, is sometimes of much utility in promoting healthy granulation in the Hunterian chancre, and is also of great service in sores which present a red or bluish margin, and display a tendency to take on a bad character; but it is especially in the treatment of the superficial ulcer with raised margins, that we have derived the most satisfactory results from its employment. When a sore of that character occurred in a strumous habit, or in persons of lymphatic or bilious temperament, or who were subject to hemorrhoidal attacks and obstinate constipation—when, moreover, the edges of the sore were spongy, very sensitive and prone to bleed rather copiously, however gently the prepuce might be drawn back—and, finally, when the secretion from the ulcer was thin and ichorous, or thick, yellow, and rather copious, but the centre of the ulcer flat, and presenting no signs of incarnation, we never failed to derive the most satisfactory results from the employment of *sulph.*"

When the patient has been mercurialized, the breath emitting the peculiar fetor it assumes in those medicated with mercury, and the ulcer presents a blue appearance, *carbo-veg.* may be useful.

When the sore has been retarded in its healing process by intemperance, *nux* or *puls.* should be prescribed, and afterwards the medicines most adapted to the specific disease.

Phosph.-acid and *lycop.* are very serviceable when the sore has been very obstinate and presents the appearance of indolent ulcer.

If the margins of the chancre are elevated, and the sore appear to resist the ordinary administration of mercury, and still there are some symptoms of that mineral present, *merc. præc. rub.* may be employed; and if the middle portion of the chancre should be raised, and appearances indicate the formation of condyloma, *cinnabaris,* first trit. should be administered, or, as has been before mentioned, *thuj.*, providing the symptoms correspond.

In Hunterian chancre, if the sore exhibit a disposition to heal, but still a certain degree of induration remain, the *iodide of mercury,* second or third trituration, at first at short, then at longer intervals, will remove the remaining hardness.

Beside the employment of *arsen.* in phagedenic chancre, *merc. præcip. rub.* is a most efficacious medicine. At a later period of the disease, Hartmann has found more energetic and penetrating mercurial preparations necessary. He says,*

* Chronic Diseases, vol. ii., p. 227.

"Among these *calomel* is excellent, were it not for the ptyalism which it is apt to excite, and for the illusory disappearance of the ulcer under this agent. For these reasons I resort to *merc. corr.*, commencing with one tenth of a grain several times a day, and increasing the dose gradually until the spreading chancre is arrested."

Aur., *caust.*, *china*, *dulc.*, and *staphys.*, may also sometimes be requisite in the treatment of chancre.

In the treatment of chancres the physicians of the old school employ all manner of cauteries; indeed in a late number of the London Lancet there was an article extracted from Ricord's treatment of venereal ulcers, in which searing the whole surface of the sore with a *red hot iron* (actual cautery) is highly recommended. On this subject Hahnemann writes,* "Instances are recorded of small chancres having been burnt away by the repeated vigorous application of nitrate of silver, without being followed by lues venerea; but so rare are such cases that it is highly dangerous to reckon on such a piece of good luck.

"But even let us take for granted that with proper care no evil results ensue. Supposing the chancre to disappear without these bad effects, still (I need only refer adepts in the medical art to their own experience) caustics are cruel remedies in chancres, which, from the torture they occasion in most cases, change the local virus into a general affection, consequently do more harm than good.

"If my enemy remains in front of me, I remain always on my guard, I am convinced I have not yet conquered him; but I cannot be said to overcome him if I drive him into an inaccessible corner.

"There is not a single one of all the so-called corrosive sore cleansing remedies, from calomel to blue vitriol, from lunar caustic to sugar of lead, which does not at the same time possess astringent vessel-contracting properties; that is to say, the power of exciting the lymphatic vessels to absorb, and which does not display all this power in the local treatment of

* Lesser Writings, p. 59.

chancre. Could we find any remedies that would more certainly transform a chancre into lues venera than these?"

Section 5.—Bubo.

Bubo always takes place in those lymphatic glands in the immediate neighborhood of chancre, while the deeper seated and remote glands remain uncontaminated, or at least do not enlarge or suppurate. As chancre generally occupies some part of the penis, the glands of the groin are the ones most commonly affected. Sometimes several glands are enlarged and form a cluster; but according to Mr. Hunter one gland only is usually affected. A bubo does not invariably follow a chancre, and yet the system is not less liable in such cases to contamination. This circumstance, amongst others, has induced some surgeons to believe that bubo does not arise, as is commonly imagined, from the absorption of venereal virus, but from an inflammation in the extremities of the lymphatics excited by chancre.* Bubo seldom arises from a chronic chancre, but usually makes its appearance soon after the sore is established. It is more frequently observed to follow venereal ulcers on the prepuce or frænum, than those situated on the glans penis,† and is late or early in its appearance according to the degree of inflammation existing in the sore. Oftentimes a bubo remains stationary for weeks, neither tending towards resolution nor suppuration; in general, however, it is of a bright scarlet color, exceedingly painful, and suppuration is speedily established. Sometimes erysipelatous inflammation is present.

The ulceration which follows a bubo does not differ from that of common chancre, and the matter from it is equally infectious. The bottom of the ulcer is hard and solid to the touch, and the surface either of a dark red or brownish color, or of a yellowish cast.

---

* See Allan's Surgery, vol. i. p. 200.

† Gibson's Institutes and Practice of Surgery, vol. i., p. 339.

Very extensive ulcerations now and then follow a bubo, and instances are recorded, in which each groin and the greater part of the pubis have been laid bare by the severity of the affection. In certain constitutions buboes degenerate into insensible and very troublesome fistulæ, that are exceedingly perplexing to treat. In some instances the skin covering a bubo entirely closes, but not uniting with the parts beneath, leaves a hollow from which in a short time a thin serum is discharged through small holes or pores formed in the skin. In such cases, the integuments generally assume a leaden or bluish color, and present an unhealthy aspect.

Buboes, or swelling of the inguinal glands, frequently arise from other causes than the absorption of syphilitic virus. For example, from wounds or injuries of the foot, from colds, fevers, and from irritating applications. Such swellings are very difficult to distinguish from the true venereal bubo. The surgeon, therefore, must carefully inquire into the history of each individual case, before he ventures to give a decided opinion respecting its nature.

In the *treatment* of syphilitic bubo there are three objects to be attained.* 1st. To prevent their development (prophylactic treatment.) 2d. To disperse the tumor. 3d. To heal the ulcer after suppuration and discharge of the pus have occurred. The prophylactic treatment implies, 1st. A rapid cure of the primary chancre. 2d. The prevention of a return of the ulcer. 3d. Perfect rest of the diseased part. To accomplish these objects the principal medicines are *merc.-sol.*, *kali-hydriod.*, *silic.*, *calc.-carb.*, *acid-nit.*, *graph.*, and *thuj.*

When the swellings are either small or of considerable size, but neither excessively painful, *merc.* has been of great service, administered in the second or third trituration, a quarter of a grain night and morning until improvement is manifest.

If the bubo be excessively painful, bright red, with intense inflammation, *bell.* will in all probability allay the sufferings.

After suppuration is established *silic.* frequently cures the complaint.

---

* Gollmann on Diseases of the Urinary and Genital Organs, p. 107.

If the patient have been subjected to the previous use of mercury, and the tumor is hard, *hepar* may hasten suppuration, and thus produce relief. If the mouth and gums of the patient are affected by previous drugging, and there is lancinating pain in the hard tumor, *staphys.* will be an excellent medicine, or perhaps *acid-nit.*, *aurum.*, *carb.-veg.*, or *sulph.* may be indicated; *spongia fluviatilis* and *spongia palustris* have proved of striking efficacy in some cases of schirrous glands, either of a scrofulous or venereal origin.

Asaf., *hydriod. pot.*, or *staphys.* may particularly be called for in cases which have evidently been aggravated by the previous use of mercury in massive doses.

Puls. is alleged to be frequently capable of effecting resolution in instances of bubo appearing after the healing of a chancre. Even when suppuration has become established, and the tumor is red, soft, and the bursting of the skin apparently inevitable, this medicine sometimes succeeds in promoting the entire dispersion of the tumor by absorption.

Bell., *hepar*, *silic.*, *sulph.*, *carb.-an*, are important medicines in treating sympathetic bubo; the indications for their administration have already been alluded to.*

Section 6.—*Constitutional Syphilis.*

The secondary or constitutional symptoms of syphilis, present themselves in several forms, which usually appear in regular succession. The parts that appear to be first affected are the skin and throat; probably, in the generality of instances, the latter is earlier attacked. After these, periosteum, bones, fascia, tendons, eyes and ears become involved.

The first development of constitutional symptoms will, in many cases, be noticed by palor of countenance, swelling of

---

* For an excellent description of Inguinal Bubo see Hahnemann's Lesser Writings, p. 76.

the sub-maxillary glands, and shifting pains, apparently of a rheumatic or neuralgic character, in different portions of the body. When the tonsils are examined, they may be found to be the seat of an ulcer, which is coated with an ash colored or brownish matter, that causes the sore to present a foul and unhealthy appearance, while the surrounding edges are slightly inflamed and of a coppery hue. In the more advanced stages the ulcer is excavated, or, as Mr. Hunter has expressed it, "dug out;" if the ulceration still advance, one or both tonsils, the uvulæ, velum palati, membranous portion of the Eustachian tube, and even the epiglottis may be entirely destroyed; giving rise to permanent deafness, incessant cough, and endangering the patient's life from suffocation, by permitting food and drink to enter the larynx. In many instances a communication is established between the nose and mouth, from the ulceration having destroyed the soft parts and bones of the palate. At other times the disease travels along the Schneiderian membrane, undermines the septum and cartilaginous portion of the nose, destroys the periosteum covering the thin and delicate bones, which are soon rendered completely carious, and crumble away, destroying the nose and thereby causing pitiable disfiguration, and reducing the patient to a condition often loathsome, with foul and fetid matter flowing perpetually from the nostrils or into the throat, and a breath so extremely offensive, as to render the sufferer hateful to himself and disgusting to others.

The peculiar eruptive fever generally precedes, with more or less distinctness, the appearance of constitutional affections of the skin aud mucous membranes. In many instances, the whole skin becomes discolored, or mottled or covered by an efflorescence; at other times circular patches appear in distinct spots or different parts of the body, each of which proceeds from an indurated lump of a pale red color. The patch slowly enlarges, and in a little time its centre becomes flat, and encrusted with whitish scales. These gradually desquamate and are succeeded by others of a similar appearance, until finally the skin cracks and discharges a puriform secretion, which, hardening on the surface, is converted into a *copper-colored* scab. This seldom extends beyond half an inch in diameter, and after a time drops off, exposing an ulcerated surface, which gradually spreads and deepens, and becomes covered with a thick, fetid, greenish matter.

The parts of the body most liable to be attacked by venereal eruptions, are the back of the neck, the forehead, breast and groin; sometimes, however, the palms of the hands and the soles of the feet are affected.

It would be trespassing on the limits of a work like the present, to enter into all the varieties of syphilitic erythemata, syphilides, maculæ, tubercles, papulæ, &c.; but the student must refer to works treating on these subjects, if he wishes to become thoroughly versed in the subject.

The *periosteum* and *bones* are often contaminated in secondary and tertiary syphilis.

All the bones do not appear to be equally susceptible of impression from absorption of the virus; those thinly covered by integuments, or situated near the surface of the body, as the cranium, clavicle, sternum, tibia, radius and ulna, are most liable to suffer. The first evidence that the patient experiences, as indicative that the disease has reached the bony structure, is an enlargement, or a tumor called a *node;* this increases slowly, never attains much magnitude, and is seldom painful until it has existed for a considerable time. Finally, however, the integuments covering the tumor become red and inflamed, deep seated and acute pain is felt in the part, and extends from it to a considerable distance, often throughout the limbs; the sufferings are extremely aggravated at night when the patient becomes warm in bed. In a greater or less time the swelling loses its hard and solid consistence, becomes soft and fluctuating, ulceration takes place on the most prominent part and soon opens a communication with the interior, and a discharge ensues of an ill-conditioned glairy matter. The bone may now be felt rough and bare, and it may become completely carious. When the node is seated on the skull, both tables are often perforated with numerous holes, and resemble in some respects a piece of worm-eaten wood. Patients who have suffered from repeated attacks of syphilis, and have taken large quantities of mercury, often have the bones greatly enlarged, and thickened throughout their whole extent. When examined, also, such bones have been found to be much heavier than usual. When a node proceeds from inflammation of the periosteum alone, the swelling may frequently be removed.

Venereal warts, or, probably, "*sycosis Hahnemanni,*" often follow chancres, and usually are found in the same situation. They arise by a narrow neck or pedicle, and are expanded on the surface, resembling a mushroom. They are sometimes exceedingly painful, and bleed profusely upon the slightest touch. Frequently the whole glans penis or vulva are completely covered by these excrescences.

Condylomatous tumors ussually occupy the verge of the anus. They are firm and fleshy, broad at their bases, irregular on the surface, and often ulcerate and become very troublesome.

Alopecia does not invariably follow the secondary symptoms of syphilis, even when the system is thoroughly contaminated. In many cases, however, large quantities of scurfs or scales form about the roots of the hair, which are soon loosened and drop out, leaving the scalp perfectly bare. The eyebrows also, not unfrequently fall off, and are seldem regenerated.

Syphilitic iritis will be alluded to in another chapter.

Treatment.—Syphilitic sore throat, which generally arises from the continued abuse of mercury in the primary disease, is successfully combatted, by *nit.-acid, aurum, carbo-veg.*, or *lycopodium.*

When the patient complains of dryness and scraping in the throat, with swelling and inflammation of the tonsils, *hepar* is an excellent medicine; when, however, there are superficial ulcers of a grayish color situated within the buccal cavity, *nit.-acid* may be employed. After the exhibition of these medicines, when the more violent inflammatory symptoms are mitigated, *silic.* or *sulph.* will often complete the cure.

If, during the first stages of the disease, *mercury* has not been used in massive doses, this medicine is frequently sufficient in itself, to produce the desired effect. *Kali-hydriod.* and *merc.-iod.* are also useful in this affection, as are also *ars.*, *iod.*, *aurum*, *bell.* and *staphys.*

In the treatment of secondary syphilis, *mercury* is the chief medicine, particularly for the syphilitic eruptions. Allopathic physicians, writes Hartmann, "use jodium and sarsaparilla for these eruptions, which homœopathic physicians only use for syphilis complicated with mercurial symptoms. The principal mercurial preparations which are of service in the treatment of these secondary syphilitic diseases, are, *merc.-præ.-rub.*, *merc.-corr.*, *cinnabaris*, *merc.-nitros;* though the other preparations may likewise be useful. Besides mercurials, we have *thuj.*, *nit.-acid*, *hepar*, *clematis*, *staphys.*, *phos.-acid*, *mez.*, etc."

The selection of the remedy does not depend upon the seat of the sore, but upon the nature of the ulcer. A mercurial preparation will have to be used, and the medicine will have to be given in much larger doses than ordinary, otherwise the fauces, mouth, nose, etc., may all be destroyed. The medicine required is sometimes indicated by the attendant syphilitic appearances in other parts of the body; for instance, *merc.-præcip.-rub.*, *cinn.*, *merc.-nitros.*, *nit.-ac.* and *thuja*, are demanded, when out of the secondary exanthematic ulcer, whether it be Hunterian or phagedenic; condylomata have developed themselves. If accompanied with bullæ, (rupia,) *merc.-corr.* is the principal remedy, unless *merc.-præcip.-rub.* or *alb.* is more specifically indicated; if complicated with mercurial ulcers in the mouth and throat, *iod.* and *nit.-ac.* deserve the preference.

If, after the secondary syphilitic ulcer is cured, there should be still a remnant of the secondary syphilitic eruption, some other medicine must be chosen. Lepra and psoriasis syphilitica will frequently yield to *dulc.*, *clem.*, *lyc.*, *mez.* or *calc.* The scurfy eruption to *lyc.* and *calc.*, or to *conium*, *graph.*, *ranunc.*

The medicines for *venereal nodes* are, *asaf.*, *acid-phosph.*, *aur.*, *calc.*, *mez.*, *silic.*, and *sulph.* The intolerable aching pains in the bones are relieved, generally, by *mez.*, *nit.-acid*, *staphys.*, *aurum.* or *sulph.*

15

For alopecia *lyc.* is almost a specific; if its use is not followed by success, *nit.-acid, petrol.*, or *phosph.* may be serviceable.

Condylomata are controlled by *merc.-sol., thuj.*, or *sabina*, and also with *aurum, causticum*, and *phosphoric acid.*

To *onychia* syphilitica, the following medicines are adapted, *ars., graph., hepar, merc., lyc.* and *petrol.*

When the skin appears unhealthy, the slightest cut degenerating into painful rhagades or ulcerated fissures, *merc., sulph., lyc., acid.-nit., hepar*, are very useful medicines.

CHAPTER XII.

CANCER.

Carcinoma, or, as it is most frequently termed, scirrhus, is the occult form of the malignant disease, which, when in a more advanced stage, is denominated cancer. The term scirrhus has been so much employed by practitioners to designate all tumors that possess the qualities of uneven surface and hardness, that the appellation has been sanctioned by custom, as applicable to, or synonymous with all malignant swellings. In this place, however, scirrhus is always used to designate those tumors which, from their peculiarities, are known to be the forerunners of cancer, properly so called. Or, in other words, the ulceration of the scirrhous tumor constitutes cancer.

A true scirrhus is known by certain external marks, and by a peculiar internal structure. Its characteristics are, inequality of surface, hardness, a great heaviness in proportion to its bulk, besides a faint leaden hue and a puckering of skin that covers it; likewise, by the peculiarity of the attending pain, which is acute and lancinating. The growth of the tumor, though more rapid than that of the fibrous tumor, is less than that of the other simple formations, and very much slower than that of the medullary. And it may be stated as a general rule, that the older the patient the slower the growth. In the comparatively young—say those of thirty—months may suffice for its advancement; and in the old—say seventy—years may have passed away, with a tumor yet hard, small, occult, and but little painful. When the swelling appears in the substance of an organ, as in the mamma, the original texture may seem to become smaller, as it grows hard; in other words, the tumor slowly increases, and at the same time the normal texture shrinks by interstitial absorption. As the surface is approached, the intervening textures are involved in the morbid growth, and the skin is ultimately incorporated, becoming dark-colored, dense, depressed and adherent; and this usually happens at comparatively an early stage.* The tumor is at first movable, but afterwards attaches itself to the superficial skin and the muscle beneath, though it may be still capable of as much motion as the elasticity of the surrounding parts will permit.

In all cases of true scirrhus, the matrix or stroma is constituted either by a new formation of fibrous texture, or an induration proceeding from hypertrophy of the areolar tissue. The larger and coarser filaments of this structure, finally become converted into fibrous bands, having the appearance of cartilage, and crossing each other in various directions. In the interstices are found the cancer cells. There has of late been much importance attached to the peculiarity of this variety of cell formation, but it is apparent that there is considerable difficulty in establishing any marked difference in the appearance of the cells that constitute cancer, from those that are found in other malignant growths. Miller is of this opinion, as is also Dr. Bennett, who has paid particular attention to this subject. The cells of all malignant formations are associated with a whitish or yellowish creamy fluid, which can be pressed out in considerable quantities. There is, sometimes, molecular matter discovered in the cancer juice, and, in some instances, even in the cancer cells; when this is the case, the cellules

* See Miller's Principles of Surgery.

present a darkish appearance; and in cancerous formations, there are generally portions of the structure that are more opaque than the surrounding tissues.

In the Monthly Journal of Medical Science,* can be found a description of an instrument for the diagnosis of tumors of different kinds. "It consists in an exploring needle, having at its extremity a small depression with cutting edges. On plunging this instrument into a tumor of any depth, we can extract a minute portion of the tissue of which its various layers are composed. In this manner a microscopic examination of the character of the tumor may be obtained, and its nature ascertained, before having recourse to extirpation. The utility of this method of diagnosis has been verified, and conscientious practitioners have renounced operations previously determined on, when the cancerous nature of the tumor has been thus demonstrated.†"

There is attendant upon cancerous formation, a peculiar diathesis or cachexy; indeed, this may frequently be recognized before the invasion of the local disease. The symptoms are paleness or sallowness of complexion, sometimes irregular attacks of hectic, and emaciation. Youth is not obnoxious to this disease; it belonging more to mature and old age. Females are more disposed to the affection than males, and women who have borne children are not so apt to be affected, as those who have never been pregnant. The mammæ and uterus are most frequently the site of the disease, although there are other organs and tissues that are very liable to suffer, viz: skin, lip, testicles, tongue, &c. When the carcinomatous structure has opened and ulcerated, the term *cancer*—properly so called—expresses the disease.

The scirrhous tumor becomes soft in its interior, its texture is broken down and ulceration and sloughing result; the disease often spreads in different directions, and although there may be sometimes a slight attempt at granulation, such formation is

---

* May, 1847.

† McClellan's Principles and Practice of Surgery.

overcome by the ulcerated process, which continues its onward progress unchecked. Mr. Miller writes, "the characters of the cancerous ulcer are very peculiar, and once seen can scarcely again be mistaken. The edges are hard, serrated and everted, the eversion complete, and the hardness equal to that of cartilage. Sometimes the margin is white, like cartilage; sometimes it is of a red angry hue. The surface discloses the morbid structure, soft and in process of ulceration, studded at some points, more especially near the margin, with the futile granulations already spoken of. The discharge is thin, bloody and profuse; possessed of an intensely fetid odor, so peculiar, as generally to be held of a pathognomonic character. Pain is burning and constant. There is no power of cleaning this sore; under every application it looks foul and loathsome. Sometimes it is covered by a black tawny slough. Not unfrequently a dark bloody oozing takes place from some part of the ulcer, perhaps on separation of such a slough; sometimes there is smart hemorrhage.

"A peculiarity of carcinoma and cancer is, that the disease is especially prone to extend by the lymphatics. Sharp stinging pains are felt in the direction of the main lymphatics, and their ganglia, shadows of the coming event. The hard and tender cords are observed extending from the tumor on the lymphatic aspect; sometimes with small indurations by their side. These cords may stretch unbroken to the ganglia, as in the axilla; and there a second tumor, in all respects like to the first, only of more rapid growth, and more distressful in its symptoms, begins to form."

By most authorities it is allowed that cancer is an hereditary disease. It has been considered by some as contagious, but sufficient evidence has not been adduced to render such supposition fact. The predisposing cause of this disease is probably some constitutional taint; the exciting cause being generally injuries of various kinds, unnatural stimulation of the scirrhus, that tend to advance the ulcerative process. There are also other causes that may hasten ulceration of a carcinomatous tumor—such as bad nourishment, unwholesome atmosphere, neglect of cleanliness, suppression of secretions, &c.

Treatment.—"It is impossible," says Hartmann, "to indicate any general treatment for cancer. In many cases the symptoms are the only guides to the selection of remedies for palliative purposes. It may not however be improper to mention in this place the medicines that have been of service in this most dangerous affection, leaving the more minute characteristics of the drugs to be commented upon, when treating upon particular organs affected with cancer."

Medicines that may be efficacious are *ars.*, *aur.*, *bell.*, *con.*, *carb.-veg.*, *caust.*, *kreos.*, *phosph.*, *petrol.*, and sometimes *lyc.*, *nux-vom.*, *calend.*, *cicuta.*

The iodide of arsenic has been *partially* proved, and from the symptoms it has produced, and from certain cases in which it has been productive of great benefit, it has been highly recommended, as has also the phosphate of iron; the latter is said to have produced "the most happy results; by its administration the pain is lessened, and the ulcer takes on a more healthy appearance."

Arsenicum cured cancerous ulceration on the lip, of the size of a bean, with fatty base, and hard, roll-like margins, surrounded by a dark red areola; at the same time a red spot on the cheek.

In a case where cancerous ulceration had invaded the left half of the upper lip; and the soft parts upwards to the bone, and outwards to the angle of the mouth, *arsenicum* 3d, repeated every eight days, effected a cure.

Bellad. A man, æt. 40 ann., had suffered for three months with a considerable swelling of the upper lip, which was very inconvenient whilst eating or speaking, and considerably disfigured his countenance. In the swelling a hard body could be felt, which was painful on being pressed. In cold, raw weather there were flying stitches through it. Cause of the disease unknown. *Bell.* gtt. 1.12 was given, and in eight days the swelling was considerably diminished. At the end of fourteen days the remedy was repeated in a smaller dose, and in a very short time the swelling entirely disappeared.* The above is reported as a case of scirrhus, but there are not sufficient indications enumerated to prove conclusively that the disease was true carcinoma. However, *bella.* is often a very serviceable medicine, and produces great alleviation of the pain, particularly in cancer of the uterus, when there is severe bearing down, and great weight and pressure, or violent pain in the sacrum.

In a case of scirrhus and prolapsus of the uterus, in which, in the earlier stages of the disease, there was metrorrhagia, in varying quantity and quality; still later the discharge of a fetid whey-like matter, pain in the back, flying stitches in the pubic region, costiveness, the uterus in a state of scirrhus induration: *Bell.* gtt. 1.20 every forty-eight hours, for two weeks, and a dose of *arsen.* every four days, for some time afterwards, together with the local application of a weak infusion of *bell.*, by means of a sponge, effected a perfect cure.

Conium. In the case of a woman æt. 22 ann. Five years before, she had been struck on the left breast, and afterwards a scirrhus had formed in the spot; it had grown until at length it had attained the size of a walnut. It was seldom painful, but immovable. At times there was an itching in the skin over it, which was not discolored. The disease appeared not to affect the general system in the least. With reference to the originating cause of the disease, *con.-mac.* was prescribed. Soon after taking the medicine, the patient felt some additional stitches through the scirrhus. A considerable diminution of the tumor could be perceived the next day, but the improvement soon ceased to advance. *Cham.* gtt. 1.3, was then given, and was followed by peculiar exacerbations and remissions. In the evening the scirrhus would be larger, and somewhat painful, and in the morning smaller and movable. These changes continued to occur for ten days, and during this time the tumor had diminished in size. At the end of fourteen days the improvement ceased. A number of other remedies were

---

* See also Dr. Buchanan Ker's case of Cancer of the Pylorus, treated with arsenicum. British Journal of Homœopathy, vol. vii.

for some time tried, which exhibited no action on the induration. The physician therefore considered it most advisable to employ local applications, and he directed some drops of the tincture of *conium*, prepared from the fresh expressed juice of the plant, to be rubbed in every evening over the induration. Under this treatment, the scirrhus entirely disappeared in the course of eight days.

This remedy has also been found useful in cancer of the lip.

Magnesia-murias removed scirrhus induration of the uterus.

Nux-vom. proved useful in cancerous ulceration of the lips.

A man had a scirrhus of the size of a pea on the middle of the lower lip, which was removed by a surgeon, by means of repeated applications of caustic, but afterwards there appeared at each extremity of the lower lip, adjoining the angles of the mouth, eroding ulcerations, with elevated, uneven margins, of a white color, pale red ground, and discharging a thin fluid, without any perceptible bad odor. The patient had a constant flow of saliva, which every one who trod in it with a bare foot pronounced "very sharp and biting;" his disposition was passionate, but at the present time depressed, and he asserted that his disease and his unfavorable circumstances had taken away from him all desire of life. *Nux.vom.* gtt. 1.13, was given, and was followed by great improvement. On the sixth day, *con.-mac.* gtt. 1.21, was given, and by the tenth day the disease was completely removed.

Phosph. proved very useful in excessively painful and hard indurations in both mammæ, unaccompanied by inflammation.

Sepia has proved beneficial in scirrhous indurations of the cervix uteri. "This remedy removed a cartilaginous and frequently bleeding scirrhus of the lower lip."

Silic. An induration, commencing at the left angle of the mouth, and involving nearly the whole of the left cheek, was removed by *silic.* "This remedy also is said to have cured a cartilaginous induration with a deep fissure, which was seated in the upper lip."

The above cases are recorded from Dr. Jeanes' Practice of Medicine, and serve to illustrate, to a certain extent, the medicines that may be employed in cancer. Other remedial agents will be mentioned in the succeeding sections.

Section 1.—*Cancer of the Face.*

*Cancer of the lip.** It is somewhat extraordinary, that cancer, rarely if ever, attacks the upper lip, while the lower is frequently subject to the disease, which appears under different forms. In the commencement, there is generally observed a small rounded tumor, resembling a shot both in color and size, seated immediately beneath the integument covering the vermilion portion of the lip, and when pressed upon rolling under the finger. The tumor in this state gives no pain, but if frequently handled by the patient, or otherwise irritated, it grows rapidly and soon adheres to the surrounding parts. In other cases, a firm and immovable lump of considerable size is, from the first, deeply imbedded in the substance of the lip. This gradually approaches the surface, finally ulcerates and throws out a prolific fungus of a dark red color, so large, as in some instances to envelop the whole mouth. A third variety of the disease is found in the form of a chocolate-colored, warty excrescence; this never attains a large size, but is constantly casting off scabs, the place of which is speedily supplied by others. These tumors are all capable of contaminating, by extension, the adjoining portions of the face and neck, especially the lymphatic glands, and when this occurs, there is very little hope of the patient's recovery. *Venereal* ulceration of the lip and *lupus* have been mistaken for cancer, and treated accordingly. The surgeon, therefore, should be strictly on his guard, and never without full investigation, pronounce decisively as to the nature of the complaint, or propose an operation, unless well assured of the existence of cancer.

Cancer of the tongue. Tumors of the tongue having all the appearance of scirrhus formation, frequently arise from disorder

---

* See Gibson's Institutes and Practice of Surgery.

of the digestive organs, or from irritation produced by carious and ragged teeth. Sometimes, also, the whole tongue becomes enormously enlarged, fills up the mouth and hangs below the chin. Many cases of this kind are recorded by writers, and in particular two very remarkable ones by Percy. The tongue is likewise studded over, in some instances, with small excrescences, having broad tops and narrow pedicles, resembling mushrooms. At other times deep fissures or irregular cracks occupy the whole surface of the organ. But these are all different from genuine scirrhus, or cancerous ulceration, which is recognized by the hard, rough, broad bottomed, wart-like tumor usually situated about the middle of the tongue towards the tip; or by a ragged, ill-conditioned sore, covered with a fungous growth, and bleeding upon the slightest irritation; either of which is accompanied by a deep-seated lancinating pain, extending to the throat and base of the skull, and terminates, eventually, if its progress be not interrupted, by the total annihilation of the organ. Children are occasionally subject to this disease, but it occurs most frequently in persons beyond the middle age.

Carcinomatous affections of the cheek and nose commence in the same manner, and pass through the same stages as have been already noticed in the other forms of cancer.

Every cancer, including cancer of the tongue, depends (as has been before stated,) upon a peculiar disposition of the organism. The proximate cause may be a blow or contusion; injudicious treatment of ulcers, indurations or excrescences on the face, syphilis, suppression of natural secretions, &c.

The prognosis is very perplexing, although many cases are said to have been cured.* The more extensive the cancer,

---

* Dr. Attomyr relates the following cure of cancer of the lip. "Aloysia Lyde, six years old, lost the left half of the upper lip, and the soft parts extending upwards to the zygoma, and sideways a considerable portion round the angle of the mouth, by a cancerous ulcer. Arsenic (6th dilution) repeated every eight days, brought about the healing of the ulcer in six weeks. As a detergent application, the decoction of marsh mallows was used outwardly." See British Journal of Homœopathy, vol. iv., p. 257.

and the more enfeebled the constitution of the patient, the more unfavorable is the prognosis.

The chief medicine in cancer of the face is *arsenic*, (not Fowler's solution) but pure arsenic. This medicine is the basis of all the "far famed" remedies for this disease; and writes Dr. Wurmb, of Vienna, "there is no affection, except ague, in which it has been, and still is, so often administered. Even among the ancients it was held for a specific against cancer, and at the present day it has the same reputation; it was also known then, as well as now, to be capable of producing cancerous ulcers. The whole difference, therefore, between ancient and modern practice, lies in the fact, that now it is known, or might be known, or ought to be known, that the therapeutic employment of arsenic in cancer, rests on the law of similarity; but that it is no absolute specific against that disease, because there exists no such thing as an absolute specific; further, that we possess certain indications for its exhibition, and understand the method of giving it in suitable doses.

"As regards the criteria for the choice of arsenic in cancer of the lips, it is an easy task for the physician, well acquainted with the positive effects of medicines, to distinguish the cases in which arsenic suits, from those in which other remedies are indicated. Thus, arsenic is to be preferred before *belladonna*, *baryta-carbonica* or *conium*, in very malignant ulcers, which increase on all sides, bleed easily, and have not been caused by any external injury, such as blows or bruises, but from the first show plainly, that they are the outward sign of a deeply seated inward disease, and are, therefore, often met with in cachectic individuals. *Carbo-veg.*, indeed, approaches very near to arsenic in this respect; yet the latter is to be preferred unconditionally, when the tendency to destroy the surrounding parts is distinctly marked in the ulcer."*

The pathogenetic effects of arsenic, which point to cancer, are,† burning swelling in the nose, with pain to contact; tumor

---

* British Journal of Homœopathy, vol. iv., p. 250.

† See Hartmann's Chronic Diseases, vol. ii.

in the nose; ulceration of the nostrils, high up, with discharge of fetid ichor; ulcers in the whole face; wart-shaped ulcer on the cheek; dry, cracked lips, brown streak in the lips, as if burnt; bleeding of the lower lip; ulcerated eruption around the lips; cancer-like eruption on the lower lip, with thick crust, hard, pad-shaped edges, with burning pain, particularly when the parts become cold, and with a lardaceous bottom; spreading ulcer on the lip, painful in the evening, when in bed, with tearing and smarting in the day-time during motion, which is worst when touching the ulcer and in the open air; disturbing the night's rest; corrosion of the edge of the tongue, in front, with smarting; the tongue is blackish, and cracked.

Arsenic may sometimes require to be administered in alternation with some other medicine, but it is, undoubtedly, the most valuable when the cancerous dyscrasia has contaminated the organism; it is a sovereign medicine for cancer of the nose, tongue and alveolæ.

Clematis is asserted to be useful in carcinoma of the lips, arising from syphilitico-mercurial ulcers; when the pains are drawing or jerking, and experienced chiefly in the circumference of the ulcer, particularly when touching the part.

Aurum-met. is also serviceable for cancer complicated with syphilitic or mercurial symptoms; or this medicine may be adapted to scirrhus, appearing in individuals of a scrofulous diathesis. The *muriate of gold* is also recommended for this disease, and may, in aggravated cases, be alternated with arsenic, when the tongue feels heavy, is elongated and its motion much impeded. There may be also great dryness of the mouth and fauces; painful blister on the tongue, accompanied with burning pain; deep ulcer within the buccal cavity, with inverted edges and blackish base.

Mercurius may be of service, if the bones have already become affected; or *nit.-ac.* may be useful if the sore be irritable, bleed profusely, with stinging and burning.

Asafœtida is indicated when the edges of the ulcer are hard, bluish, and sensitive to contact.

Conium has been employed with success in carcinomatous

affections arising from contusions; it is particularly indicated, by a scrofulous diathesis, and when the ulcers on the face and lips spread rapidly, present a blackish appearance, and discharge a bloody and fetid ichor.

Symptoms which may lead to the use of *silic.*, in cancerous affections, are, erysipelatous blotches, lymphatic and suppurating glandular swellings; scirrhous indurations; putrid and rapidly spreading ulcers, particularly when they arise from abuse of mercury, and are attended with boring and stitching pains, also for scurfs and ulcers in the nose, cracked skin and scirrhous indurations of the face and on the upper lip; painful spongy and carcinomatous ulcers on the lower lip.

Sulphur is considered by some as an excellent medicine in cancer of the face. It is generally useful as an intermediate agent, and revives the activity of the organism, when it appears unable to receive the impression of the proper specific.

In cancer of the nose, when the patient complains of violent burning pain in the ulcers, which may be covered with large scurfs, that spread rapidly and become very thick, *sepia* is often the most appropriate medicine; it is also of importance when there exudes from beneath the scab a corrosive ichor, which, by irritating the surrounding parts, essentially favors the extension of the disease. The disposition of the patient should also be remembered, when this medicine is to be prescribed.

Antim.-crud. and *ranunc.-bulb.* have been prescribed with success in cancer of the face. *Nit.-acid* likewise has been employed in carcinomatous ulcers, arising from syphilitico-mercurial disease.

When it is deemed necessary by the surgeon to operate for cancer of the lip,* the diseased growth may be taken away by two eliptical incisions, which include the affected part—the knife being entered in the middle of the prolabial space, and made to pass first on the integumental and then on the mucous aspect of the disease. The morbid structure should then be

* See Miller's Practice of Surgery, p. 190.

carefully dissected out, and the saved integument and mucous membrane brought together by interrupted points of suture.

In some instances it may be preferable to make the including incisions in the form of the letter V, the apex pointing downward, and care being taken not to transgress the general rule, of removing a border of apparently sound texture, together with the truly carcinomatous affection.*

There are two operations† in use for the removal of scirrhus of the tongue—excision and ligature. The former is at present seldom resorted to, on account of the extreme difficulty in arresting the attendant hemorrhage.

The operation by ligature is thus performed. The surgeon takes a curved needle, and having drawn it to the middle of a strong ligature, passes it through the substance of the tongue immediately behind the tumor. The middle being cut and the needle removed, there are left hanging two ligatures, one of which is to be drawn forcibly on the one side of the tumor, and the other tied tightly on the opposite side; these together include a segment of the tongue. A sharp pain is experienced when tightening the threads, but this soon subsides, and the patient experiences little inconvenience, except from salivation, which usually ensues a few hours after the operation. In four or five days the tumor sloughs away, leaving an extensive granulating surface, that fills up with great rapidity.

These are the methods of operating for cancer of the tongue and lip; there are cases on record, in which success is said to have followed the use of the knife. Of course, the medicines before alluded to should be exhibited, and if their administration is followed by amelioration of pain, and diminution of the size of the tumor, even though the latter should lessen very gradually, the practitioner must patiently persist in the use of the remedial agents, and his endeavors may ultimately be crowned with success.

The method of operating by excision was explained, that the student and young practitioner might be able, if the case

---

* Miller's Principles of Surgery, 3d Am. Ed., p. 317.

† Gibson's Institutes and Practice of Surgery, vol. i., p. 277.

required, to understand the use of the knife; although it is to be sincerely hoped, that, as our science progresses, medicines will be discovered and so applied, that in future years surgical diseases will be more frequently removed by the internal exhibition of medicinal agents, according to the law of Hahnemann, than by the mechanical methods now usually employed.

Section 2.—Scirrhus and Cancer of the Mammæ.

This disease frequently arises from small indurations, which are sometimes discovered in the breasts at an early age. If these do not receive timely attention they frequently enlarge and become painful at the critical age.

The usual origin and development of cancer of the mammary gland is as follows:

A hard tumor is discovered in the breast, appearing either spontaneously, or in consequence of pressure, shock, &c. At first the tumor is round and movable; as it increases in dimensions it becomes ragged and uneven; other swellings develop themselves, all of which appear to be united by cords of indurated cellular tissue. These tumors enlarge, combine into one, involve the whole glandular structure, and sometimes spread to the axilla. Lancinating pains at this stage are occasionally experienced, extending to the shoulder and arm, and not aggravated by pressure. The integument, if invaded by the tumor, assumes a streaked, cicatrized appearance, and the follicular glands are frequently filled with a blackish substance. The skin in a short times adheres to the tumor, which becomes elevated and inflamed. These symptoms may disappear, but finally the veins enlarge, the nipple retracts, forming a cavity, the skin breaks and reveals a spreading ulcer, with hard, dark red, shining edges, and an unclean bottom; the discharge is neither very copious nor fetid, and the ulcer resembles rather a deep fissure devoid of excrescences. The axillary, the glands in the clavicular region, and the cervical ganglia, may enlarge, provided swelling have not taken place previously. At this period, when the tumors are seated, immovable, and hard as stone, the patients complain of a troublesome feeling of heaviness, with almost constant stinging, boring, shooting, lancinating pains, the lancinations proceeding to the shoulder, and from the mammæ in various directions; also, of rheumatic pains in various parts, particularly in the loins and thighs. The reproductive process suffers considerably; the face assumes a livid appearance; the arm of the affected side commences to swell, its movement is impeded, and at length excruciating pains and supervening colliquations produce death.

Besides these phenomena, there are a variety of conditions that may occur during the course of carcinoma of the mammæ. Sometimes the scirrhus remains for a long time latent, giving rise to no unpleasant symptoms whatsoever; at others its development is quite sudden, and it extends with rapidity, attended with severe symptoms of constitutional disturbance. Ulceration of the gland is frequently produced by external violence—a blow, a fall, or a bruise, may create suppuration and its consequences, or sometimes the ulcerative process is established immediately after the suppression of the menstrual discharge.

There are some cases on record in which cancerous ulcerations were accompanied with but slight pain; in the generality of instances, however, the suffering is severe, and the peculiar lancinating character of the pains is almost unbearable. The duration of the pain when it is very severe, is said to be less than when it is not so excruciating, and from this circumstance a distinguishing characteristic might be drawn between acute and chronic cancer of the mammæ. The former commences with a hard, deep seated tumor in the breast, which adheres to the integument for a time, the skin then becomes slightly discolored, the whole mammæ gradually partakes of the induration; elevations may be observed in some portions of the gland, while at others there are marked depressions; the surface then becomes soft and presents those appearances that designate the presence of fluid; the pain becomes sharper, and resembles in many respects that experienced by patients suffering from whitlow. The ulcerative process progresses rapidly, the pains increase, the countenance exhibits an expression of anxiety and pain, the skin has a jaundiced appearance, and the patient is much debilitated and very desponding; the edges of the ulcer are raised, and present those characteristics of cancerous ulceration that have already been mentioned.

The chronic scirrhus is dry and of a cartilaginous hardness, and shrinks after having attained a certain degree of development, the contraction and shriveling of the integument forming various indentations; the accompanying pains are not very great, and by proper treatment the disease may remain in this condition for a considerable length of time. This form of the disease is most frequently encountered in old females of a spare habit of body, and of a dry, rigid constitution.

Treatment.—The *scirrhous indurations* in the breasts of young girls, which arise without any assignable cause, yield to several medicines. *Cham.* corresponds to the *drawing rheumatic pains* in the indurated mammary swellings; these are painfully affected by the open air, and are exacerbated at night; or to erysipelatous redness of the indurated mamma,* with drawing and tearing pain, increased by contact. *Arnica* is adapted to the same group of symptoms when the nightly aggravations are absent. *Bell.* is useful when the indurated mammary glands are inflamed, with burning and stinging pains, which are increased by the least motion or contact. *Arsen.* is indicated by a burning pain, with tearing, decreasing by motion, aggravated by external warmth, and rendering it impossible for the patient to lie on the affected side. *Bry.* is suitable for a tensive, burning pain with tearing, aggravated by contact, or by moving the arm of the affected side.

Clematis is an excellent medicine for indurated mammary glands that are painful only when touched; it is likewise useful in open cancer, with burning and throbbing in the ulcer, and stinging pains in the edges when touching them.

---

* For an interesting account of the pathological changes that occur in the mamma to produce an induration of the gland, see Association Medical Journal, July, 1853.

Conium is quite an important medicine in this disease, but it is especially serviceable during the first stages, when the indurated gland is liable to take on inflammatory action from every little cold, and when the lancinating pains are accompanied with burning and stinging, which are especially severe in the evening or at night.

Kreasotum was very serviceable in a case characterized by the following symptoms: The whole breast was indurated, blue-red, and rugged; some of the eminences were covered with a scurf; one of which, situated near the nipple, was of a large size, and fell off frequently, leaving an opening, from which a quantity of thick dark blood was discharged, after which the patient generally fainted. *Kreas.* seemed to arrest the hemorrhage for a long time, but it was impossible to remove the disorganization in spite of *acid-nit.*, *thuja*, *con.* or *hep.;* the patient finally died of hemorrhage. Nevertheless, *kreas.* is a prominent remedy for carcinoma of the mammæ; but should be employed much sooner than in the above mentioned case.

Carbo-anim. is very useful in hard, painful tumors of the breast, though *carbo-veg.* is preferable when the pains are burning, the patient complains of anxiety, want of breath and lowness of spirits, which latter, frequently increases to a whining despondency.

Phosph. may prove suitable to patients with flat chests, tuberculous disposition, great sensitiveness to cool weather; increase of pain; pain in the nape of the neck, stiffness of the arms at every change of weather, &c.

But perhaps the medicines best adapted to cancer, not only when it affects the mammæ, but in any other organ, are, *arsenicum* and *conium;* the former has been used, and with more or less success, from a very remote date; and the famed "cancer curers" of the present day, no doubt following the example of their predecessors, employ the arsenical pastes. *Conium* also is a superior medicine, and should always be remembered in the treatment of this affection, particularly when some contusion or abrasion of surface has hastened forward the carcinoma. The prognosis is always to be formed with the greatest foresight and judgment, but in the generality of cases it has always been found unfavorable.

There has been lately much stress laid by writers upon the treatment of scirrhus of the mammæ, and indeed other forms of carcinoma, by the application of pressure, and there have been several instruments invented for maintaining the requisite amount of compression; by this method it is said that portions of the tumor are gradually absorbed, and that its further growth is much retarded. The application of all stimulating plasters, pastes, friction, &c., are worse than useless; they only tend to hasten the inflammatory process in the tumor, and must therefore always be considered as dangerous in the extreme. It is in these malignant and incurable affections that some practitioners of our school suppose that they may, without dereliction of duty, depart from the law which guides them in the treatment of other diseases, but all deviations invariably fail to produce the desired effect; and finally, in the generality of instances, to ameliorate the distressing accompanying symptoms, the surgeon is obliged to return to those medicines whose symptoms correspond to those which it is the object to remove.

The treatment must always be commenced as early as possible; the medicines must be exhibited steadily and for a length of time, and the patient observe the most rigid dietetic rules. If, after a repeated trial of different medicines, no impression whatever be made either upon the size, color, hardness, or weight of the tumor, the question of amputation of the breast at once arises in the mind of the surgeon, and surely it is one of a perplexing nature. Hartmann in his chronic diseases makes a strong assertion concerning the removal of scirrhus—he says that all operations are useless, or worse than useless, that a cure has *never* been effected, and that all patients that are supposed to have survived an operation were not afflicted with true scirrhus, but only with indurated glands.* Although

---

* Hartmann appears to be partially correct in his statement. See article "Statistics of Cancer," published in Clymer's Medical Examiner, August 5th, 1843, p. 179.

Hartmann was an acute observer, and no doubt a thorough homœopathic physician, yet it can scarcely be allowed that all the most scientific, accomplished, and thoroughly educated physicians and surgeons of the "old school" could possibly be so egregiously mistaken; and although as followers of Hahnemann we cannot agree with them concerning their external applications—mineral acids—arsenic—chloride of zinc, potassa usa—for the removal of scirrhus, still we must respect the extraordinary talent and learning of those who were considered the most accomplished surgeons in the world, and allow freely that they understand as well as ourselves the difference between a true carcinomatous tumor and merely "an indurated gland." This is a question, however, that must be settled in the mind of every conscientious practitioner; but it is necessary in this work to subjoin the prognosis with reference to the operation, and the manner of extirpating the diseased structure.* The following is quoted from a celebrated English surgeon, and bears the stamp of great prudence and skill, as well as experience in the disease; of course the homœopathic practitioner must first use those medicines faithfully that appear to correspond to the disease, and must be guided according to the result of his treatment, with reference to the operation.

"Some, taking an abstract view of the subject, entertain a question as to the expediency of operating at all in carcinoma; inclining to regard the affection as wholly constitutional, and not to be eradicated, or even restrained, by removal of only a local portion of it. This view we do not propose to consider; but, with the majority of the profession, granting that the disease is constitutional as well as local, and that in most cases it shows more of the former than of the latter character; granting that very many cases occur—doubtless the majority—in which operation is inexpedient; and granting that in all cases, looking to the constitutional vice, we can never be certain of

* For a very interesting paper on this subject, see a lecture delivered at St. George's Hospital, by Sir B. Brodie. Huston's Medical Examiner, September 21, 1844, p. 217.

immunity from return, and must invariably issue a guarded prognosis accordingly; still we are of opinion, that there are cases often presenting themselves to the surgeon of extensive practice, in which it is his bounden duty, by operation, to afford his patient the chance either of a definite or radical cure, or at least of a postponement and palliation of the malady. Such cases are those in which the tumor is yet small and comparatively circumscribed; the lymphatics unchanged either in the immediate vicinity or at a distance; the integuments and muscles free from incorporation; the patient not far advanced in years; and the cachexy as yet but little indicated, if at all. On the other hand, affections of the lymphatics *already begun, even though to a trifling extent, contra indicate operation;* for, according to experience, reproduction is sure to follow, even when the surgeon is certain that not only the tumor itself, but the adjoining changed structure as well, lymphatic or not, has been thoroughly taken away. Incorporated skin and muscle can be removed by wide and free incision; yet in such cases it is often difficult, if not impossible, to say that what is left is sound, free from lodgment of the materies morbi already in its texture; and, in these circumstances, experience again speaks loudly in favor of return. In the very aged a carcinoma may exist for years in a latent or indolent condition; still occult and still of small size and circumscribed; the seat of little uneasiness, and attended with but little disorder of the system; indeed, the patient may die ultimately, of disease to all appearances totally unconnected with carcinoma. Under such circumstances, operation is withheld, and the tumor is left undisturbed, and guarded carefully from excitement."

When an operation has been determined upon, if the tumor be small, a single incision through the skin, two or three inches in length, will allow sufficient space for the dissection necessary for the removal of the scirrhus, but, according to Mr. Hunter, as the disease extends further than the eye can detect, the dissection should be carried beyond the immediate limits of the tumor. If, however, the tumor be of large size, the patient should be laid on a table previously prepared with blankets, pillows, &c.,

and the arm of the affected side carried off at right angles from the body, and retained in this position by an assistant.* The surgeon stands on the opposite side, and commencing his incision at the arm-pit, below the edge of the pectoral muscle, extends it along on the lower and outer side of the nipple, two inches beyond the base of the breast. A second incision is commenced at the spot where the first started, and carried downwards, between the nipple and sternum, until the two meet below the breast. An oval space is thus formed between the two curvilinear cuts, which includes the nipple, areola, and perhaps two or three inches, in breadth, of skin. The integuments are next elevated from the outer edges of the breast, until the greater part of it be fairly exposed; then the breast must be separated from the pectoral muscle beneath, by a regular but careful dissection from below upwards as far as the axilla. Should the lymphatic glands be found free from disease, the breast may be removed at once; if, however, the glands are enlarged, or otherwise so contaminated as to require extirpation, then the breast serves as a handle, and by it they are drawn downward, and the whole cluster of diseased mass is removed. During the progress of the dissection the arteries should be taken up the moment they are severed, otherwise they speedily retract among the cellular tissue, and do not afterwards bleed, until the dressings are applied and the patient put to bed. Owing to negligence in this respect, secondary hemorrhage is more frequent after amputation of the breast than any other operation in surgery. Before the edges of the wound are brought together, the whole surface, from which the tumor has been taken, should be accurately examined, and any diseased portions that may have been left carefully removed by the knife or scissors. When the two curvilinear incisions are made in the manner directed, there is no redundant skin, and the edges meet with the utmost nicety; the surgeon has only, therefore, to retain them in contact by a few adhesive straps, supported by lint and a common roller."

* See Gibson's Institutes and Practice of Surgery, vol. i., p. 282.

Section 3.—Cancer of the Uterus.

The uterus is frequently the seat of cancer, but there are so many diseases to which the organ is liable, that the diagnosis is often extremely difficult. Venereal ulcerations, polypus and even prolapsus, have been mistaken for carcinoma, and have been treated accordingly, the error not being discovered until the disease was too far advanced, to admit of successful treatment of any kind. A minute examination and inquiry must, therefore, be instituted, before venturing to offer any decided opinion concerning the character or termination of the affection.

In the scirrhous stage, the cervix and mouth of the uterus become heavier than usual; there is, likewise, some inequality of surface; hardness and softness of structure may be detected by touching; and the organ appears situated lower down in the vagina than natural. There is pain during coitu, and the lancinations which are experienced in cancerous affections, are often exceedingly severe. As ulceration progresses, pain is experienced when touching the part; ulcers appear with spongy bottoms aud callous edges; and frequent fungi sprout from the surface of the womb. In most cases the vagina also participates in the disease, losing its natural rugosity, and becoming much contracted; and finally, as the disease advances, the whole cavity of the matrix becomes filled with one mass of corruption.

Canstatt distinguishes two other conditions of the uterus,* that are very similar in regard to symptoms and termination. The first is the cauliflower or strawberry-shaped excrescence of the os tincæ, seated generally on one of its lips, or in some instances proceeding from the whole circumference. This fungus grows from a broad base, is soft, of a bright flesh color, presents a granular or strawberry-shaped surface, and by the touch conveys somewhat the same sensation as that of the uterine surface of a placenta. This abnormal growth may

* See Hartmann's Chronic Diseases.

spread over the whole vagina, and even involve the external parts.

The second variety is the so-called phagedenic uterine ulcer; this is not preceded by a carcinomatous condition of the parts, but by a pseudo-plastic formation, or infiltration of the surrounding textures. The uterus around the ulcer may be almost in a normal condition, but in the generality of instances, the sore is surrounded by a diseased mass, which is soft and yellow or of a reddish brown color. If the unhealthy action be not arrested, the destruction may extend to the walls of the uterus, to the vagina, rectum and peritoneum.

In the incipient stages of cancer of the uterus, the disease is frequently mistaken for some irregularity of the menstrual function. For leucorrhœa, or chronic metritis; the first symptoms are generally those of menstrual derangement; cessation or too frequent return of the monthly discharge, irregular discharges of blood in place of the catamenia; fluor albus, etc. The menses, after their cessation at the critical age, suddenly reappear, and even increase to a hemorrhagic condition. At first the patient complains of a sensation of heaviness, or drawing within the pelvis, and pressing towards the external organs, these symptoms being aggravated or excited by various circumstances, such as lifting, fatigue, &c. Upon examination, the vaginal portion of the uterus is found to be preternaturally indurated, bleeding readily, of an irregular consistence, swollen, misshaped, tuberculous, and sensitive to pressure; the lips of the os uteri are interstitially distended, indented and elevated, whilst the orifice is more distended than usual. In the course of the disease, the pains become excessively violent, particularly at night, pressing, stitching, shooting and burning, not only in the pelvis, but extending into the lumbar region, and along the thighs, with swelling and tension of the inguinal glands; frequently there is a continual burning pain in the lower part of the pelvis, accompanied with shooting pains in the uterus. A pungent acrid ichor, of a reddish-brown or claret color, and exhaling a deleterious effluvium, is discharged from the vagina, excoriating the surrounding integument, and giving rise to a painful itching of the external organs. Copious discharges of blood, containing coagulated and fibrinous substances, are very frequent, and sometimes cause great exhaustion. The cancer has now changed to an open, irregular ulcer, which is readily recognized by the touch. The neck of the uterus feels rugged, and is studded with the above mentioned soft, readily bleeding excrescences, which are narrow at their base, as though a ligature had been placed around them; these fill up the whole vagina, the walls of which are indurated or disorganized, conveying to the finger the sensation as of a hard, contracted ring.

The symptoms of the cancerous dyscrasia become more and more apparent; the skin becomes of a pale straw-color; the features exhibit an expression of deep suffering; the digestive functions are impaired; sleep is rendered almost impossible, the patient emaciates, and hectic fever supervenes. The disease most frequently occurs between the ages of forty and fifty.

The *prognosis* is very unfavorable.

Treatment. When the disease is completely established, the physician can do little else than palliate the sufferings of the patient, though in the incipient stages it may be cured. In this latter period of the disease, the uterus feels like a hard body lying immediately above the pubic bones, frequently giving rise to the belief that it is impregnated. Pregnancy is really possible in this stage, and occasionally takes place. The real *carcinomatous* condition can be ascertained by a careful external and internal examination. It is characterized by the following symptoms, which correspond to *belladonna.* Pressing and fullness of the inner parts, rendering it difficult for the patient to stand, accompanied with pain in the sacral region. Likewise when a sanguineous ichor is discharged from the uterus, either continually or at intervals. *Platina* is indicated by spasmodic, or pressing colicky pains, accompanied with a discharge of thick, viscous, venous blood, especially if the patient previously suffered with too profuse menstruation. If constipation, nervousness and a long-lasting, though regularly occurring discharge of acrid blood, with burning, smarting and itching be present, a few intermediate doses of *nux-vom.* should be administered. The debility which sometimes supervenes in consequence of the pain and loss of blood, is best relieved by repeated doses of *china.*

Arsenicum is indicated by the following symptoms: Burning sensation in the internal sexual organs and abdomen, exacerbation of the symptoms towards midnight; excessive anguish in the chest, depriving the patient of rest; unquenchable thirst; the uterus is indurated, and there is continual discharge of an acrid, excoriating mucus from the genital organs. *Cocculus* should be given, if, instead of the above mentioned pains, spasmodic contractions occur, attended with discharge of a serous fluid. *Chamomilla* corresponds to labor-like contractile pains, accompanied with a discharge of dark, coagulated blood.

The above mentioned remedies, together with *bryonia, ignatia,* and some others, are more suitable for the incipient stages of cancer. Other important medicines likewise, are—

Kreasotum, which is suitable when the following symptoms are present: Stitches in the vagina, as if proceeding from the abdomen, causing the patient to start as if in affright; voluptuous itching with burning and tumefaction of the external and internal labia; hard tubercles on the neck of the uterus; pain during an embrace, as if from ulceration; the menses appear eight or ten days too soon, and continue for eight days, dark and somewhat coagulated blood being discharged, attended with pains in the back, and succeeded by the discharge of a bloody, pungent, corrosive ichor, with itching and smarting of the contiguous parts; the menses intermit for hours and even days, after which they reappear in a more fluent condition, accompanied with violent colic; the pressing downwards continues after the discharge has ceased; a metrorrhagic condition may be present, or occasionally a continuous, corrosive leucorrhœa, the pains exacerbate during the night, and fainting frequently occurs upon rising in the morning. Slight chills are experienced during the menstrual discharge, accompanied with lowness of spirits, livid complexion, etc.

Jodium is indicated by the following symptoms:—Induration of the lower segment of the uterus; cancerous destruction of the cervix; profuse, long-lasting metrorrhagia, coming on even at every stool, accompanied with cutting in the abdomen, pains in the small of the back and loins, emaciation, atrophy of the breasts, yellowish-brown complexion, languor, with disposition to syncope, and spasms.

Thuja for indurations and rhagades of the neck of the uterus and os tincæ, cauliflower-shaped, readily bleeding excrescences, with a pungent smell; or for dry, wart-shaped excrescences, with severe stitching and burning pains during micturition.

Dr. Wahle, of Rome, Italy, prescribed *graphites*, for the following symptoms:—The vagina hot and painful; swelling of the lymphatic vessels and mucous glands, some of which were of the size of a filbert; the *cervix uteri* hard and swollen, and on its left side three large and painful tubercles of various sizes, each consisting of several smaller ones, which threatened to change to a bleeding excrescence; upon rising a sensation as of great weight is experienced deep in the abdomen, with increase of pain, debility and tremor of the lower extremities; the sufferings are most acute shortly before and during the period of menstruation; the discharged blood is black, coagulated, and emits a disagreeable odor; a sensation of heaviness is experienced in the abdomen, with violent lancinations in the uterus, extending down the thighs, somewhat resembling the passage of an electric current; the pains are burning and lancinating, little appetite, constipation, frequent chilliness, without subsequent heat and sweat; the patient is sad, anxious, and sometimes desperate; complexion livid; pulse frequent and rather hard.

Secale cornutum is indicated rather for putrescence than carcinoma of the uterus; it should not, however, be entirely discarded as a remedy for the latter affection.

Sabina may be administered for the sensation of heaviness, the labor-like contractile pain in the uterus and lumbar region, and for the copious discharge of coagulated blood, which occurs particularly during exercise.

Mercurius and *staphysagria* are suitable intermediate remedies for pains in the pelvic bones and femora. These medicines are particularly indicated, when the disease is complicated with symptoms of mercurial poisoning or syphilis. In the latter cases *acidum nitricum* may be used, particularly when the patient complains of pressure in the abdomen and pain in the small of the back; spasmodic pains as if the abdomen would burst, depriving the patient of rest, pressing even as low down as the vagina, as though the contents of the abdomen would be ejected, attended with pain in the small of the back, and drawing in the hips, down to the thighs, excessive debility, etc., obliging the patient to assume the recumbent posture.

Carbo-veg. is an excellent remedy for an intolerable burning pain, seated deep in the pelvis, coming on at regular periods throughout the course of the day, gradually increasing and then decreasing.

Kali.-carb. may prove availing in this disease, when an acrid, badly smelling menstrual blood is discharged, with chilliness and spasmodic pains in the abdomen.

Conium, which is distinguished by its action on the female glandular organs, is an indispensable medicine in carcinoma of the uterus.

It may be considered necessary, under certain circumstances, to extirpate the cervix uteri, for carcinoma of that portion of the womb. In some instances the patient is entirely relieved from suffering for a length of time, and life may be prolonged. The case recorded by Dr. Croserio and mentioned in this work, (p. 65) may serve for an example.

Professor Osiander, of Gottingen,* was the first to conceive and execute so bold an operation, as excision of the cervix uteri, and his example has been followed by Dupuytren and other European surgeons. The first operation of the kind was performed by Osiander in 1801, on a widow whose vagina was filled by a very vascular fetid fungus, from the orifice of the

* See Gibson's Institutes and Practice of Surgery, vol. i., p. 288.

womb, as large as a child's head. By means of Smellie's forceps the fungus was brought down low in the vagina, but being accidentally broken off, a fearful hemorrhage ensued; undismayed, however, by this event, the operator determined to proceed, and immediately pushed a number of crooked needles, armed with strong ligatures, through the bottom of the vagina and body of the uterus, until they emerged at the inner orifice. These ligatures served to draw down the uterus, and retain it in the vagina near the external orifice. The surgeon then introduced a strong bistoury above the scirrhous portion, and divided the womb completely in a horizontal direction. The hemorrhage for an instant, though profuse, was speedily suppressed, and the patient recovered in three or four weeks. Osiander afterwards performed eight similar operations upon different patients, all of whom recovered without the slightest difficulty.

Dupuytren has also performed the operation eight times; but instead of employing the ligatures and bistoury, recommended by Osiander, he drew down the uterus with forceps, and divided it above the scirrhus, by knives and scissors. This operation is also recommended at the present day.*

Section 4.—Fungus Hæmatodes.—Bleeding Fungus.

This formidable disease, although of not very frequent occurrence, is sufficiently often encountered by the surgeon to demand attention in this place. The profession is indebted to Mr. J. Burns, of Glasgow, for the first detailed account of the affection,† who, however, designated it *spongoid inflammation*, from the spongy, elastic feel, which is peculiarly characteristic, and which continues even after ulceration has far advanced.

---

* See Miller's Practice of Surgery, p. 620.

† Burns' Dissertation on Inflammation, Article Spongoid Inflammation.

Afterwards Hey* and Abernethy† adopted the term Fungus Hæmatodes.

The bleeding fungus may appear in almost any part of the body, but the extremities are particularly liable to it; when it occupies the external parts it is characterized by the following appearances:‡ In the first stages a small tumor may be detected beneath the integument, almost devoid of sensation, smooth on the surface, movable and elastic to the touch. This may remain stationary for years, without causing the patient the slightest uneasiness, until a blow, a strain, or some accidental injury, causes it to inflame, when it increases with wonderful rapidity, the skin losing its natural color, becoming mottled or red in some parts and purple in others. In a few weeks the tumor attains considerable bulk, and in proportion to its growth is rendered protuberant and lobulated; at the same time the veins on its surface are greatly enlarged, and very conspicuous, and at no very distant period, ulceration takes place in one or more spots, from which a fungus sprouts with the utmost luxuriancy. The abnormal growth is of a dark red color, in most instances much contracted at the neck, and thence enlarging, expanding, and presenting an irregular and uneven surface. The disease having advanced thus far, soon contaminates the contiguous lymphatic glands, which are converted into a substance exactly resembling that of the original tumor. In the mean time the patient's health gradually declines, the countenance assumes a yellow, cadaverous hue, the whole constitution is undermined by hectic, and death speedily follows.

In order to constitute a true fungus hæmatodes, three things are essential§—that there shall be a fungous projection of morbid structure—that the fungus be dark and blood-like, and that it bleed more or less profusely. This condition may be of either a primary or secondary character; much more frequently it is the latter. Examples have occurred in which, without other

---

* Practical Observations on Surgery, 3d edition, p. 239.

† Surgical Works, vol. ii., p. 56.

‡ See Gibson's Institutes and Practice of Surgery, vol. i., p. 307.

§ See Miller's Principles of Surgery, p. 334.

morbid formation, a small dark fungus has shown itself, bleeding at intervals so profusely that life has been endangered; but more frequently, there is first a tumor of malignant character, which opens and ultimately throws out the bleeding fungus, and the fungus hæmatodes in this, the most frequent case, is to be regarded as the climax of malignancy in a formation already of an evil nature. The morbid structure on which it most frequently supervenes is the medullary.

In tumors there may be two steps of degeneracy; from the simple structure to the medullary, and from the latter to that of fungus hæmatodes. But usually the medullary formation from which the bleeding fungus springs is of primary origin. All medullary tumors, when open, tend to fungate; but all medullary fungi are not entitled to the appellation of fungi hæmatodes. It is easy to understand, however, how the hæmatoid condition should not unfrequently occur, by softening and breaking down of the medullary texture, whereby one or more of the large vessels found permeating such growths are opened into. A detached portion of the medullary mass, or a fresh protrusion, may temporarily occlude the aperture, but, in its turn, it crumbles away and the bleeding recurs. The part is obviously incapable of adopting the ordinary natural hæmostatics.

The morbid mass, when examined by dissection, exhibits appearances altogether distinct from those met with in any other disease. A very thin and undefined capsule invests the whole tumor, and, within this, lobes separated from each other by membranous partitions of soft pulpy matter, resembling brain in consistence and color, compose the greater portion of the distempered fabric. In the midst of this medullary-like matter, are often found cells filled with clotted blood; at other times small cysts are met with, containing a thin, sanious, fetid serum. So extensively involved are all the textures in the neighborhood of the tumor, that the muscles are often annihilated, or their structure so subverted as to be scarcely recognized, arteries, nerves, veins and cellular tissue all being blended into one confused mass. When the lymphatic glands and those in the course of circulation are examined, they are often found equally diseased throughout the body. The same may frequently be said of the liver, lungs, kidneys and brain, all of which exhibit proofs of universal contamination.

When fungus hæmatodes attacks the eye, the first symptoms are observable in the posterior chamber; an appearance like that of polished iron presenting itself.* The pupil becomes dilated, and is of a dark amber, or sometimes of a greenish color. This change becomes more and more perceptible, and is at length discovered to be occasioned by a solid substance, which proceeds from the bottom of the eye towards the cornea. The surface of this substance is generally rugged and unequal, and ramifications of the central artery of the retina, may sometimes be seen running across it. The anterior surface of the mass at length advances as far forward as the iris. At this stage of the disease the amber or brown appearance of the pupil has been mistaken by surgeons for cataract, and operations have been attempted for the removal of the supposed obstruction of vision. After a time, the disease continuing to increase, the eye-ball loses its natural rotundity, and assumes an irregular and lobulated appearance, and the sclerotica becomes livid or dark blue. Sometimes matter collects between the tumor and the cornea, the latter membrane being destroyed by ulceration, after which the fungus shoots out. In a few instances, it forces a passage through the sclerotica, and is then covered by the conjunctiva. The surface of the excrescence is irregular, often covered with coagulated blood, and bleeds profusely from the slightest irritation. Portions of the fungus—if it be large—often slough off, attended by a fetid sanious discharge.

On dissection the diseased mass is found extending forwards from the entrance of the optic nerve, the vitreous, crystalline, and aqueous humors being absorbed, together with the choroid and the retina.

In the *extremities* the disease commences with a small, colorless tumor, which, when devoid of external covering—as

---

* Scarpa on Diseases of the Eye.

fascia—is soft and elastic; but if the swelling commence beneath a tough and unyielding tissue, there is at first no sensation experienced, but after a time a darting pain occasionally is present; this increases in frequency until at length it becomes incessant.

The tumor during the first stages of the affection is elastic and smooth, but the latter characteristic, when inflammation is about being established, is superceded by a lobulated appearance. As ulceration progresses, the integument immediately above the swelling is much attenuated, and finally gives way in numerous places; from these openings, which are generally at the apex of each cone-like projection, a thin, bloody matter is discharged, and from them fungi protrude, which rapidly increase in size, assuming somewhat a carcinomatous appearance, and bleeding frequently and profusely. The discharge which accompanies the abnormal growth is thin and exceedingly fetid, and the pain becomes smarting in character. The surrounding integument assumes a reddish color, and becomes exceedingly tender. After ulceration has taken place, the neighboring glands enlarge, and in a short time resemble exactly the spongy appearance of the primary tumor. If the patient survive when the disease has reached this advanced stage, growths of a similar nature present themselves in other parts of the body, and finally the patient, rendered disgusting to himself and unbearable to others, expires, emaciated to a skeleton by profuse suppuration and hectic.

The *testicle*, when affected by fungus hæmatodes, sometimes bears such a strong resemblance to hydrocele that the most intelligent and experienced surgeon may be deceived. This illusion cannot continue for any length of time, for after the medullary tumor attains a moderate bulk, the constitutional symptoms are sufficient to lead to a diagnosis, and the lymphatic glands in the thigh and groin sensibly enlarge. This disease has also been mistaken for a scirrhus of the testicle, but by careful examination, and a moderate degree of knowledge, the two affections may be readily distinguished. A testicle affected with fungus hæmatodes is soft, fluctuating, pulpy, and in the

17

generality of instances free from pain, while a carcinomatous affection of the gland is attended with increased weight and firmness of texture.

Other organs have been attacked with this highly malignant affection; the thyroid gland, lungs, liver, mammæ, uterus, ovaries, have exhibited unequivocal marks of the disease.

With regard to the *treatment* of fungus hæmatodes, little can be gleaned from homœopathic works, but that little is worthy of profound attention.

Treatment.—It is not desired either to vaunt homœopathy above her deserving merits, or to cast into disrepute the older method of practice, when it is here stated that fungi have been cured by medicines exhibited according to the law, *similia similibus curanter;* on the contrary, with thankfulness to those master minds who, "in times gone by," have occupied the most elevated position in the allopathic school, and with sincere respect for those who still stand foremost in the ranks of her professors, the statement above made, concerning the curability of this terribly malignant disease, is unhesitatingly announced, and maintained by the following "History of the Cure of Field Marshal the Count Radetskey."* The case is not only one of great interest, but also serves as a guide in the treatment of similar affections.

"His Excellency is now entering the seventieth year of his age, and the fifty-sixth of his military career; notwithstanding his many fatigues, both in war and peace, his mental exertions, his eventful life, with all its excitement and activity, yet, as all Europe knows, his mind has lost none of its former energy.

"For many years he has suffered from a cough depending on no disease of the lungs, but on an excessive irritability of the mucous membrane of the bronchia, and to which he never paid much attention. Latterly he has been subject every autumn to an attack of inflammatory catarrhal fever, which passes off in a few days with slight medical assistance. In the year 1836,

* Being a series of letters which appeared in the Homœopathische Zeitung, July, 1841, written by Dr. Hartung, Staff-Physician in the Lombard Venetian States. See British Journal of Homœopathy, vol. i., p. 147.

his Excellency fell upon the edge of a bed and bruised his ribs, on which accident an inflammation of the lung ensued, which was cured in the course of seven days. It was rather remarkable that, on the seventh day, a great quantity of purulent matter was expectorated, and from this time the inflammatory fever ceased. In the years 1837 and 1838, he enjoyed pretty good health. In the months of July and August of the year 1839, his Excellency was attacked with congestion, which produced such vertigo as to cause him to fall. This affection passed away; but soon afterwards inflammation of the eye-lid of the right eye, along with a sense of pressure of the eye-ball, lachrymation, and occasional protrusion of the eye-ball occurred. By remedies which seemed to correspond to the case, these symptoms were alleviated, but the inferior eye-lid still remained inflamed.

"Thus, with more and less inconvenience, did the spring of 1840 pass away. In the month of May he was once again attacked with severe vertigo. During the months of July, August, and September, he remained well, except the lachrymation of the right eye, which still continued. On the 9th of October, he was exposed for five hours to a burning sun and piercing wind when on horseback. Soon afterwards his face became red: in the evening urgent fever set in, attended with a pain in the right side of the forehead, so severe, that although he before never had uttered a complaint, he said to me, if it lasted much longer it would be quite intolerable. The eye was much inflamed and protruded from its socket; the pulse was full, hard, apoplectic. I administered what seemed to me the proper remedies. At one o'clock in the morning, the headache abated, the eye returned to its place, and the following day his Excellency attended the morning parade, (*kirchen parade,*) reviewed the troops, and was six hours in the saddle. In the evening, except being fatigued, he felt quite well. He rested the following day, and then pursued his journey to Milan; the right eye was still red and full of tears.

"By perseverance in the treatment at Milan, the cure was so far effected, that there remained only redness of the under eyelid, tearfulness, and a swelling above the external canthus, without pain or impairment of vision.

"About the end of October his Excellency travelled to Verona, where he tarried six weeks, and made, during very cold, damp weather, a journey to Modena. Here it was that a swelling the size of a bean, proceeding from the internal canthus, became developed on the lower eye-lid; while the swelling in the orbit at the external canthus, as above described, enlarged, and the eye was considerably protruded from its orbit, with occasional pain in the brow, and violent congestion of the head.

"Eight days after this, his Excellency returned to Milan, when I found him in the condition described above. His situation appeared to be alarming; for I plainly saw that a fungus had formed in the orbit, and that there was danger of its increasing. I gave him emollient cataplasms to remove the inflammation, which embraced the whole cheek. They answered the end. I discontinued them, however, lest their application should injure the eye, and directed my treatment against the growth, attempting, if possible, to check its advance, at the same time striving to maintain the whole frame in its former vigor, and to raise the depression of spirits.

"The medical treatment was directed by the homœopathic principle. The medicines which were administered and repeated as occasion required—for respect had to be had not only to the growth of the tumor, but also to the tendency to apoplexy, and the general tone of the system had to be strengthened—were (1.) *Acon.* (2.) Baryt.-carb. (3.) Zinc. (4.) Anacard. (5.) Calc. (6.) Euphras. (7.) Merc.-sol. (8.) Merc.-cor. (9.) Antimon.-crud. (10.) Digit. These were the chief medicines which were used, along with occasional intervening doses of palliatives.

"The consequence was, that his Excellency, on the whole, enjoyed good health, with the exception of congestion of the head. The growth of the excrescence could not be arrested. Both the tumor at the external canthus, which was now evident from its blue color, as well as the tumor at the internal canthus, were increased in size; and now there protruded between the eye-ball and the lower eye-lid, a spongy, elastic, granular, pale-red, painless tumor; and by this the eye was confined in its movements, the pupil looking upwards and outwards, but the power of vision was not impaired.

"I consulted with Professor Flaser of Pavia, who had recognized the disease which I had before believed it to be. He gave the most unfavorable prognosis, saying that 'there was nothing left for us to do.' This opinion deeply affected the spirits of his Excellency, and it was agreed to give him daily one-fourth of a grain of *merc.-cor.*

"After Dr. Flaser, Professor of Ophthalmic Surgery in Pavia, had seen the case upon the 6th of January, he publicly declared, in the presence of myself and others, that in this case neither by allopathy, homœopathy, hydropathy, nor any other method of treatment, could any good be wrought; that his Excellency must die of extreme exhaustion, (*aus zehrung*,) or of an apopletic stroke, and that he, Professor Flaser, would prescribe nothing, being fully aware of the danger. For the sake of giving his Excellency encouragement, I requested the professor to propose something in my presence. So he recommended *merc. sub. cor.*, one-fourth of a grain daily, firmly believing it could do no good; but, as he said to me, 'he knew no more suitable medicine.' In consequence of his advice, I gave the one-twelfth of a grain; but even this he could not bear, on account of the violent congestion in the head, so that I was obliged to give an antidote to allay the congestion.

"At this state of things I wrote out the history of the case, and gave it to his Excellency to be forwarded to Vienna. Thus the whole matter came to the knowledge of our chief nobility, and even of his majesty. His majesty the emperor hereupon determined to send his staff-physician, Dr. Jäger, Professor of Ophthalmic Surgery in the Joseph's Academy at Vienna, to Milan, to consult with me, and in conjunction with me (*vereint mit mir*) to apply all remedies that might prolong the life of the field-marshal.

"In the mean time I did my best to maintain the general

health, having still respect to the fungus. The enlargement of the fungus I could not arrest; on the contrary, it increased in such a way that at the external canthus, near the lachrymal gland, a grayish, blue, hard, spongy excrescence, of more than eight lines broad, developed itself, which, gradually diminishing in its proportions, extended in a crescentic form to the internal canthus. From this place, under the lower eye-lid, a grayish-blue tumor manifested itself, which presented a perpendicular wall, and lost itself in connection with the bones of the nose. The tumor at the internal canthus had increased threefold, and had become harder, and of a deeper red color. The whole fungous excrescence was affected with various pains, lancinating, burning, tearing, and itching; it bled readily; the eye itself was free from pain, and lay in a depression between these two eminences; it was protruded from its socket, motionless, and directed outwards. The powers of vision were also impaired; for on the outside he saw black-like objects without being able to distinguish what they were. The conjunctiva was injected, and of a dark red color, playing into a blue red. The fissure of the eye-lids was covered in the morning with a white, pus-like, tenacious mucus; in the course of the day there was increased sensibility of light, and copious lachrymation; in the evening increased heat, dryness and pain.

"Such was the state of the disease when Dr. Jäger arrived at Milan. Dr. Flaser was also sent for; and on the 26th we three met together to communicate our respective opinions of the case, and consult on its further treatment.

"Professor Jäger declared the disease of his Excellency to be incurable, because, depending as it did on constitutional derangement, (dyscrasie,) an operation would do no good. He knew of no internal remedy, as this disease never had been cured. (*Da diese krankheit noch nic geheilt worden sei.*)

"Dr. Flaser expressed himself again exactly as he had done before.

"If I had been guided by my experience of forty years in the old Rational School of Medicine, I should have been constrained to agree with my colleagues.

"It was very difficult to communicate this to his Excellency, without agitating his mind, and lessening his confidence in me. The full particulars of the case, however, were told to his Excellency, and it was explained to him that his only chance of recovery lay in implicit reliance in me and my remedies. It was explained that bleeding, pain, &c., would occur; that the tumor would become purulent, and that for this the requisite remedies would be administered.

"Professor Jäger, out of his deep respect for his Excellency the field-marshal, acquainted his Imperial Highness the Viceroy with the whole matter, and then, after a three days' stay, departed for Vienna.

"The viceroy, on visiting the field-marshal, observed—'He hoped that his Excellency would put confidence in me and my remedies alone.' On my next visit his Excellency embraced me and said—'My friend, now they are all gone, do with me what you please; I have perfect confidence, and will have no more physicians.' These words affected me most deeply. Two learned doctors and professors of great experience had, with apodictic certainty, declared the complaint incurable, with which I was constrained to agree. Here, in Milan, the most different rumors were afloat, and I received letters with the strangest contents; in short, I felt my situation to be desperate. Day and night did the image of his Excellency stand before my eyes. At last it occurred to me—it is true Professors Jäger and Flaser are rational and long experienced physicians, but no friends of homœopathy; already have I cured many patients of diseases pronounced by the Rational School to be incurable, by following homœopathic principles; as for rumors, they are but talk, which may not annoy me; so, comforted, and with a quiet conscience, did I pursue the course I had begun.

"The consequence up to this time is favorable, for the hemorrhage, which had already commenced, is abated, as also the threatened cancerous transformation (*übergang*.) The pains are entirely gone; the upper tumor, which appeared in the form of a swollen prominence above the lachrymal gland, has now only an inconsiderable elevation; the superior margin of the orbit is comparatively unaffected; the hard swelling at the internal canthus, as well as the tense swelling or visible fungus between the eye-ball and the under eye-lid, are every way less, so that his Excellency can again look towards the nose, and distinguish objects as formerly. The eye moves freely in its socket, and, along with the surrounding parts, has assumed a more natural color. In other respects his Excellency enjoys good health; his mind and body both retain their former energy and power.

"I shall continue the homœopathic treatment. I cannot say whether I shall be able to improve the condition of his Excellency, inasmuch as the malignity of the disease, especially in so aged a person, is but too well known, and cure never yet has been effected; but even if no cure be effected, I should be well pleased if his Excellency remained in his present condition.

"*Milan*, 19*th Feb.* 1841.—I continued to pursue the homœopathic treatment as mentioned above. The consequence was so favorable, that I have attempted in a drawing to make it manifest.*

"After so favorable a course the hope of ultimate cure might be entertained, after this frightful disease—fungus—which before had extended over a surface of four inches, was now confined to a small fungoid swelling, which could only be perceived by drawing aside the under eye-lid, and the general health of his Excellency was perfect.

"Although all this is true, yet comes the reflection, that a fungoid tumor of so great an extent, in so important a part, and at so advanced an age, has never yet been cured; wherefore I do not venture to speak more of the cure, until this little tumor also be entirely removed.

"The truly homœopathic operation of the medicines was here most striking. Only two remedies were required; and of these, besides their external application, only three globules of

* The drawing is interesting, and gives an excellent idea of the disease and its course. We could not give a copy without risk of injuring the original. (Note to original.)

the decillionth dilution were given alternately, every eighth day in the evening, and on the morning of the ninth. After every dose, his Excellency experienced the sensation of all his previous sufferings, but without pain, and going away like a breath; then did the cure proceed.

"*Milan, 16th March,* 1841.—Since my letter I have been continuing the homœopathic remedies, and I am happy to say, that the tumor of the lower eye-lid is almost gone; there only remains a slight projection of the eye-lid. As this has been for a long time present, and often affects old persons from relaxation of the muscles, perhaps it may remain as it is, without giving further inconvenience—perhaps not.

"The appearance of the eye now shows that the horrible fungus is dissipated, for it has exactly the appearance of the other eye, and the power of vision is restored to it. His Excellency can now drive, and ride, and go through all his business with the eye exposed.

"On the 19th of this month, on the occasion of the emperor's birth-day, his Excellency attended divine service in the immense vaulted cathedral, for an hour and a half, when the temperature was very low, with his eye uncovered. After this duty, his Excellency reviewed the troops, exposing himself for more than an hour to the direct light of the sun (a change of temperature of not less than 15° R.) Neither extreme affected the eye. In the evening he was present at a saloon, where there was upwards of fifty persons present, and above one hundred lighted candles, with his eye uncovered, without experiencing the slightest inconvenience, not to say pain.

"Yesterday and to-day has his Excellency pursued his usual avocations, without the slightest injury to the eye; and this produces the conviction that the disease is cured, and requires no further description.

"*Milan, 22d April,* 1841.—On the 26th of January, in consultation with Professors Jäger and Flaser, at which both declared the disease to be incurable, and declined prescribing, I proposed giving the 30th dilution of *arsenic,* then *psorin, herpetin,* and *carbo animalis;* at the mention of which last, Dr.

Flaser ironically exclaimed, *verbranntes bratl!* (burnt chops.) I heard him, and thought it is not rational, because Dr. Flaser does not know its operation. I shall now give the result of these medicines, which were administered in the order mentioned above. *Arsenic alb.*, 30th dil., 6 globules produced the first day severe pain in the whole of the head, with considerable congestion. He was very restless during the night. The second, no change in the symptoms; the night sleepless. On the third day the headache abated, and diarrhœa set in; the night was quieter. On the fourth day weariness, somnolence, continued diarrhœa. The growth of the fungus advanced; the eye protruded further.

"*Psorin* 30$\frac{1}{6}$, given early on the fifth day, manifested, on the first day, pressure on the right eye; severe pressive headache, extending to the upper jaw; tolerably quiet night. The second day like the first, only the pressure on the eye was less. On the third day the pressure on the eye and the pressive headache, were abated; in other respects no change. On the fourth day no change, only the fungus grew, and hemorrhage was easily produced in it.

"On the following day I gave *herpetin* 30$\frac{1}{6}$. On the first day, pressure, with giddiness of the head, which abated towards evening; a quiet night. On the second day, less pressive headache, attended with slight giddiness, painless borborygmus; a fluid stool in the evening; a quiet night. On the third and fourth days, no pain; in other respects no change for the better, on the contrary, extension of the fungus, and tendency in it to bleed.

"On the following day I gave *carbo animalis* 30$\frac{1}{6}$. The first day, pressure of the right side of the head; itching of the internal canthus of the right eye; increased tearfulness of the eye; the night quiet. The second day as the first; a quiet night. On the third day, pressure on the side of the head diminished; but itching of the canthus and tearfulness increased. On the fourth day, no change in the general symptoms (in Allgemeinen.)

The hemorrhage had abated, and his Excellency felt light

and well; the fungus did not increase any more, but remained unchanged, so I allowed the medicine to work for two days more, but no further change followed. Thus I saw that from the first three remedies no benefit, but rather the contrary, had been derived, while the last seemed to have arrested its growth, but did not cure it. Then I thought that as I had often cured swollen and indurated tonsils with *thuja occident.* alternately with *petroleum;* with *thuja* alternated with *sulph.* and *graph.* I had often cured warty cutaneous excrescences; with *thuja* alternated with *carbo animalis* I twice cured scirrhus of the mammæ; so here I determined to try the effect of *thuja* and *carbo animalis,* and so I prescribed.

"*Thuja occident.* 30; *guttam unam.; aqua distill. com. uncias tres. M. D. S.,* three times a-day a table-spoonful to be taken.

"On the first day, all the affections from which his Excellency had suffered, as headache, night cough, slight diarrhœa, pain in the renal region, with rose-colored deposit in the urine, itching, with red marshy eruption on the inner side of the leg, disappeared, except the cough.

"On the second day, no change, except that the pain was felt at another place, and very slight.

"On the third, no more pain; itching of the internal canthus; excretion of a milky or sweet creamy-like moisture around the whole circumference of the fungus.

"I ordered *tinct. thujæ occid. guttas sex, aquæ distill. com. uncias quatuor M. D. S.* to be applied warm to the eye every two hours. On the fourth day no pain; cream-like excretion increased; the fungus, particularly at the upper margin of the orbit, decidedly lessened. On the fifth, sixth, and seventh days no pain; the excretion diminished; the lower part of the fungus, and that at the internal canthus, diminished to the astonishment of all who had before seen the case. The external application of the *thuja* was continued.

"After ten days' use of *thuja* I gave *carbo animalis* 30⅛ in the evening, and on the following morning, a similar dose of the same. On the first and second day, pains occurred in the right side of the head, as after the *thuja*, only they extended to the left side as far as the ear, and passed away like a breath (*wie ein Hauch vorübergeheand.*) The discharge from the tumor continued; there were no pains in the eye.

"On the third, fourth, fifth, sixth, and seventh days no headache; discharge continued. I now moistened the prominent part of the tumor with the 12th dilution of *carbo animalis*. The *thuja* embrocations were then continued, the fungus decreased most markedly, the eye returned to the orbit.

"The internal and external use of these two remedies, *thuja* and *carbo animalis*, alternately every eight days, was persevered in. The result was, beyond all expectation, so successful, that, in the course of one month and a half, the whole fungus had disappeared, the eye, with its vision restored, moved freely as the other in its orbit; only the lower eye-lid still protruded somewhat, and the eye ran with tears. These two symptoms likewise improved in the course of time.

As his Excellency had long suffered from both watering of the eyes and protrusion of the lower eye-lid, brought on partly from their natural conformation, partly from severe exercise—as also the latter symptom was caused by the failure of the muscular action, the consequence of his advanced age—especially as the fungus had disappeared, and the eye was recovered, further treatment was not considered necessary.

"His Excellency has continued, under all changes of weather, and after various considerable journeys, without the eye having become in the slightest degree morbidly affected; hence, I can say, *this disease, declared incurable, has been permanently, quickly, and harmlessly healed by the homœopathic principle.*

"It is very remarkable, and confirms the permanent nature of the cure, that many trifling complaints which used formerly to annoy his Excellency, such as headache on the right side, with congestion in the head, cough of long standing, without any affection of the lungs, pains in the loins, itching of the arms, and acid eructation from the stomach, all entirely disappeared on the disappearance of the fungus; and his Excellency continues perfectly healthy and well."

The following medicines have been recommended for fungus hæmatodes:* *Ars.*, *carb.-an.*, *carb.-veg.*, *phosph.*, *sep.*, *silic.*, *thuja*, calc., crot., lyc., merc., nit.-ac., sulph.

Phosph. Fungus hæmatodes in the thigh, somewhat painful, accompanied with continued discharge of venous blood.

A small fungus on the finger disappeared after one dose of phosphorus.

Fungus hæmatodes of the cornea, with chronic ophthalmia, complicated with ulcers on the cornea, great photophobia, burning, lancinating and boring pain in the eye, the sight fast decaying; *calc.-c.* as the chief remedy, with *lyc.* 12, *sep.* 30, *silic.* 12.†

An elderly negro man in Surinam, had a bleeding tumor on his knee, which was removed by excision. Sometime afterwards a tumor formed in each hip near the trochanter major. That on the right was much larger than the one on the left hip. Two years and a half after the operation, it had a diameter of four inches, was of a conoidal shape, slightly movable, hard, elastic, of the natural temperature, and without pain or pulsation. After being ruptured by a blow, it bled slowly, but almost incessantly, and became slightly painful and somewhat warm. On wiping, the blood, which was apparently venous, from the opening, "*the structure of fungus hæmatodes could be clearly discerned.* Cinchona 1.12, and shortly afterwards phosph. 1.30, were given. About the same time the patient filled the wound with tinder. The tumor continued to increase in size, as also did a fungus growth from the opening, which had made its appearance previously to the administration of the medicine, and the hemorrhage was considerable till the fourteenth day, when there was a slight fever, which disappeared without medicine. After this period, the tumor began gradually to diminish in size, and the hemorrhage ceased until the thirtieth day, when it occurred suddenly, but soon ceased of itself. After the second or third week, the patient being very much debilitated, was allowed to take a glass of wine occasion-

* Jahr's and Possart's Manual, p. 620.

† See Guide to Practice of Homœopathy, p. 155. London, 1844.

ally. The tinder remained adherent in the opening till after the fiftieth day. On the sixtieth the wound was unclean, of a bad odor, and again bled a little. But the tumor had greatly diminished, as had also that on the left hip. By the eightieth day the improvement had advanced much farther, which advancement was attributed by the patient to a common adhesive plaster, which had been applied to gratify him with the idea of active local treatment. By the ninetieth day, there only remained an indurated cicatrix. The induration gradually diminished, and at the end of four months had entirely disappeared."*

The extirpation of the diseased mass, even in its most incipient stage, cannot be warranted by good surgery. Dr. Gibson writes, "even extirpation of the tumor, and that too in its very incipiency, answers so little purpose, that there is hardly a case on record where the operation has succeeded."† The futility of operation in this affection is well illustrated by a case detailed by Mr. Allan.‡ The patient suffered during thirteen years from a very large tumor which occupied the left hip. When it attained the size of a child's head, it was dissected out by Mr. Newbigging, of Edinburgh, apparantly with success, for the wound healed and the patient felt perfectly well. At the end of nine months, however, it grew again, and in seventeen months from the first operation, a second was performed by Mr. Russel, upon a tumor as large as the two fists. The wound soon closed, but in nine months following the tumor recurred, and soon equalled in size a very large mamma. A third operation was now undertaken by Mr. Allan, and so extensive was the dissection, that the wound was as large as the crown of a hat. In a few weeks it healed perfectly; but the tumor appeared again in seven months. The late Mr. John Bell was then consulted, and performed a fourth operation upon it—the tumor at the time being as large as the head of a child eight years old. Several months after the diseased mass

---

* See Jeanes' Homœopathic Practice of Medicine, p. 236.

† Institutes and Practice of Surgery, vol. i., p. 314.

‡ Allan's Surgery, vol. i., p. 264.

was reproduced, and from the surface a fungus sprouted, in shape and size resembling a large cauliflower. This, Mr. Allan removed by ligature, and the patient for the time was relieved. His constitution, however, was completely ruined, and although he lived for several months afterwards, he died at last from the long continued discharge from the fungus, nearly eight years having elapsed from the time of the first operation. "This case," continues Dr. Gibson, from whose work it is taken, "plainly shows how little we are to expect from extirpation."

Section 5.—Chimney Sweeper's Cancer—Soot Wart.

The disease of the external parts of the male genital organs, commonly called chimney sweeper's cancer, is one of a very formidable and often very intractable nature, but fortunately not often met with.* The scrotum is the part usually attacked. A wart forms, generally at the most depending portion, assumes an irritable appearance and quickly degenerates into open ulceration of a malignant character. The ulcer extends rapidly, consuming the neighboring integument, and involving the testicle and other subjacent parts. The induration frequently extends along the spermatic cord, and the lymphatics participate in the diseased action at an early period. The discharge from the sore is acrid, sanious, and possessed of much fetor; sometimes fungi protrude, but more commonly the surface is excavated and smooth. Not unfrequently the skin surrounding the ulcer is studded, to a considerable extent, with numerous clusters of warts of an unhealthy and angry aspect. The general health is soon undermined, and the disease advances from bad to worse, with the usual certainty and rapidity of malignant action.

"Other people besides chimney sweepers," says Pott,† "have cancers of the same part; and so have others, besides lead

* Liston's Elements of Surgery, p. 413.

† Pott's Works, vol. iii.

workers, the Poictou colic, and the consequent paralysis; but it is, nevertheless, a disease to which they are peculiarly liable, and so are chimney sweepers to the cancer of the scrotum and testicles."

It cannot always be determined why a cancerous growth should arise in one locality rather than in another, but there appears to be conclusive evidence, that the habitual handling of certain substances and direct violence are much concerned in the development of cancer in particular regions. Mr. Lawrence once operated on a chimney sweeper, who presented cancerous formation, anterior to the concha of the left ear. This patient appeared especially obnoxious to the action of soot, for previously a genuine chimney sweeper's cancer had been removed from the scrotum; but it is probable that when the disease reappeared on the ear, it was caused by the same substance, for the patient was in the habit, whilst engaged in his trade, to carry bags of soot on his left shoulder, and it is very likely that the ear on that side was often covered with the substance; thus the growth of the tumor may be accounted for.*

Treatment. *Arsenicum* appears to be very serviceable in the treatment of this affection, when there is inflammation and swelling of the scrotum, and the ulcer is particularly painful in the morning, with burning in the circumference, and uneasiness when the part becomes cold; also when the ulcerative process rapidly consumes the adjoining structures, and the constitution of the patient is in a debilitated and impoverished condition. It would seem that this medicine, together with *carbo-veg.*, were especially indicated by the habits and mode of life of that class of persons who are liable to the affection. The latter medicine should be administered, when the parts surrounding the ulcer are bluish or purple, and when there are pressure and tension around the sore, which emits a corrosive humor.

Thuja may be prescribed in the commencement of the disease, when the warty formation presents itself, and when the surrounding integument appears indurated, also when there is itching and stinging in the tumor.

---

* London Lancet, Nov. 1850, p. 488.

Secale should not be overlooked when the parts assume a blackish hue, become dry, or, in fact, when gangrene threatens.

China may also be suitable if the swelling is large and the gangrene humid.

Rhus-tox. may be useful when the ulcer spreads rapidly, and the skin of the scrotum appears thickened, or becomes thicker and harder, with itching; or when there is tingling and smarting in the sore.

Clem.-erect., *hell.*, *iod.*, *mur.-ac.*, *merc.-corr.-sub.*, may also prove serviceable in this affection.

CHAPTER XIII.

SCROFULA.

The term *scrofula* is supposed to have derived its origin from the circumstance, that swine were said to be subject to the disease, though the correctness of this etymology has been rendered very questionable, by the remarks of Dr. Henning,* and the statement that these animals are really liable to be attacked, appears to be erroneous. The disease received, likewise, the appellation of *struma*, or *king's* evil, from the custom of submitting patients affected, to the royal touch. It is an affection, one of the chief or most palpable symptoms of which, is a chronic swelling of the absorbent glands in various parts of the body, with a gradual tendency to imperfect suppuration. Our ideas of scrofula, however, would be very indefinite, were we to define the disorder as a morbid condition of the lymphatic glandular system; for, as a judicious author observes,† the system of absorbent glands, it is true, seldom or ever fails to become affected in the progress of the disease; but there is reason to believe, that scrofula appears for the first time, in parts that do not partake of a glandular nature. There are, perhaps, but few of the textures or organs

* Critical Inquiry into the Pathology of Scrofula.

† Thompson's Lectures on Inflammation, p. 134.

of the human body that are not liable to attacks of scrofula, even as an original idiopathic affection.

At the present day, the term scrofula is usually applied to a constitutional affection, occurring for the most part in early life, of essentially chronic development, and characterized by a tendency to various destructive diseases of the bones and joints; often accompanied by enlargement of the lymphatic glands, and by disorganizing affections of the skin and mucous membranes, occurring either separately or together, and without obvious or adequate exciting causes.

Under this somewhat comprehensive definition, it is obvious that a great number of different local disorders may, and indeed must, necessarily find a place, and accordingly the term scrofula or scrofulous disease, is applied by many writers to types of local affections, which are only very indistinctly, if at all, connected with a constitutional cachexy.

The cachectic tendency is either hereditary or acquired. In, by far, the greater proportion of cases, it may be traced in descent from parent to child, from generation to generation. But, in some instances, a child may be born in all respects healthy, and of healthy descent, both immediate and ancestral, and yet in the course of years exhibit all the signs of a confirmed strumous diathesis.* The circumstances likely to induce the unhappy change, are those of a peculiarly debilitating tendency; such as exposure to atmospheric vicissitude; to insufficient clothing and shelter; improper and scanty food; lingering and wasting disease; *mercury;* habitual deprivation of healthy excercise. Or again, such circumstances may not be the means of producing this disorder in a frame previously healthy, but only the direct and exciting causes of it, in a system already predisposed by hereditary taint.

The disease is not communicable by contagion or inoculation, as has been proved by direct experiment; and it is found to prevail more in temperate climates than in either the extremely hot or cold, variability seeming to be especially favorable to its acces-

* See Miller's Principles of Surgery, p. 54.

sion. It is also more frequent in towns than in the country; as are all other diseases of debility. Males are more liable to external scrofula, than females;* while in the latter the phthisical diathesis is more frequent.†

The association of scrofula with a peculiar form of morbid product, called tubercle, has been long observed; this formation, however, is not present in all cases, and therefore cannot be relied on as pathognomonic of the disease.

The treatment of the various diseases, which either directly arise from scrofulous cachexy, or are dependent thereon, would comprise more space than can be allowed here; the following medicines, however, may serve as an outline to guide the student in the selection of others, which may prove appropriate to each presenting case. Many of the diseases dependent upon struma will also be mentioned in different portions of this work.

The medicines are in general, *ars.*, *asaf.*, *baryta-c.*, *bell.*, *calc.*, *cina*, *con.*, *hepar*, *iod.*, *lyc.*, *merc.*, *rhus-tox.*, *silic.*, *sulph.;* also aur., bromine, carb.-an., carb.-veg., cist., dulc., graph., kreos., merc.-iod., staphys.

At the commencement of the disease, when children exhibit a tardiness in learning to walk, the principal medicines are *bell.*, *calc.*, *silic.*, *sulph.*, and perhaps ars., china, cina, ferrum, lyc., magnesia-mur., pinus, puls., sep.

In the second stage, when there are glandular affections, the medicines especially indicated are, *bary.-c.*, *bell.*, *bro.*, *calc.*, *cist.*, *con.*, *dulc.*, *hepar*, *lyc.*, *merc.*, *phosph.*, *rhus-t.*, *silic.*, *staphys.*, *sulph.*

Cutaneous affections, *aur.-met.*, *bary.-c.*, *calc.*, *cist.*, *clem.*, *con.*, *dulc.*, *hepar*, *lyc.*, *merc.*, *mur.-ac*, *rhus-t.*, *silic* and *sulph.*

For affections of the osseous system, *aur.-met.*, *calc.*, *lyc.*, *merc.*, *phosph.*, *phosph.-ac.*, *puls.*, *silic.*, *sulph.*

Atrophy—marasmus: *ars.*, *calc.* and *sulph.*, or perhaps baryta-c., lyc., nux., puls., rhus.

---

* "Scrofula and its Nature," by Sir B. Phillips.

† Dr. Walsh's Report on Phthisis. British and Foreign Med. Chir. Rev., Jan. 1849.

The more particular indications are as follows:

Arsenicum. Atrophy, with excessive swelling of the cervical and axillary glands; hard and distended abdomen, puffed face, loose evacuations, excessive debility, with desire to lie down, particularly in leucophlegmatic constitutions; scrofulous cutaneous affections, particularly ulcers, ophthalmia, &c.

Asafœtida. Exostosis, caries, distortion, or curvature of the bones; engorged glands; otorrhœa; ophthalmia and ozœna.

Baryta.-carb. Atrophy; enlargement and induration of the glands of the neck, and nape of the neck; bloatedness of body and face, with distention of the abdomen; physical and intellectual weakness; scald head; ophthalmia; herpes on the face; frequent angina; great liability to take cold.

Belladonna. Hard, swollen or ulcerated glands, muscular weakness of infants; ophthalmia, photophobia and blepharitis; cough with rattling of mucus; otorrhœa; inflammatory swelling of the nose; swelling of the lips; frequent epistaxis; oft-recurring phlegmonous angina; asthmatic sufferings; enlargement and hardness of the abdomen; incontinence of urine; precocity of intellect.

Calcarea-carb. Enlargement of the head with open fontanels; distortion of the spine; incurvation of the bones, and other diseases of the osseous system; various cutaneous affections; engorged, indurated and suppurating glands; ulcers; enlargement and hardness of the abdomen, with swelling and hyperæmia of the mesenteric glands; excessive emaciation with bulimy; wan, wrinkled face, with dull appearance of the eyes; dry, flabby skin; difficulty in learning to walk; difficult dentition; ophthalmia, photophobia and blepharitis; otorrhœa; red swelling of the nose; leuco-phlegmasia; constipation or frequent diarrhœa.

Cina. when there are, besides other symptoms, verminous affections, paleness of the face, emaciation, great voracity and incontinence of urine.

Conium. Engorgement and induration of the glands; ophthalmia; photophobia; frequent bronchial catarrh, asthmatic sufferings, cancerous affections, &c.

Hepar. Leucophlegmasia; induration and suppuration of the glands; atrophy; scald-head; ophthalmia; otorrhœa; swelling of the nose and upper lip; cancerous ulcers; tendency to phlegmonous angina; unhealthy skin.

Iodium is useful when there is excessive emaciation; engorgement and induration of the glands, with affections of the whole lymphatic system; diseases of the bones; ophthalmia; blepharopthalmia; otitis and otorrhœa.

Lycopodium. Inflammation, suppuration, and ulceration of the glands; affections of the mucous membranes; inflammation, distortion, and other affections of the bones; atrophy; herpetic eruptions; ophthalmia, otitis and otorrhœa; frequent angina, &c.

Mercurius. Physical and intellectual weakness; inflammation of the mucous membranes; great liability to take cold; diseases of the glandular system; exostosis, distortion, curvature, caries, and other affections of the bones; cutaneous affections, &c.

Rhus-tox. Engorgement of the glands; scald-head and other cutaneous affections; emaciation; hardness and distention of the abdomen, &c.

Silicea. Diseases of the bones and skin; cancerous affections; tendency to ulceration; swelling of the face.

Sulph. This medicine in many cases is useful when commencing the treatment of scrofulous affections; it has very many symptoms, which it is unnecessary to mention here.

A *scrofulous ulcer* is distinguished from other sores by its inert, pale and torpid appearance, and the peculiar character of the pus, which at first contains many cheesy flocculi, but after a time becomes thin and corrosive. The state of the atmosphere is remarked by some authors to possess influence over the appearance of the ulcer. In fair weather it may appear disposed to heal, but in damp, cloudy and rainy seasons it presents a most unhealthy appearance. The bottom of the sore is uneven, warty, fungous or ash-colored; it is extremely difficult to heal, but sometimes after suppurating for years the sore closes, leaving a disfiguring cicatrix. These ulcers frequently arise in glandular parts, after inflammation and suppuration.

If the gland is merely swollen when the surgeon is called, by the exhibition of *aur.*, *baryt.-c.*, *cistus-can.*, *con.*, *dulc.*, or *rhus-t.*, in accordance to presenting symptoms, suppuration may be prevented.

Hartmann writes—"To judge by the symptoms, the *cistus-canadensis* seems to be a highly important remedy for scrofulous ulcers. It has swelling of the glands, also with suppuration; scrofulous ulcers, and other scrofulous ailments; violent chilliness with shaking, followed by heat, with redness and swelling of the ears, and swelling of the cervical glands; discharge of moisture and badly smelling pus from the ears; inflammation and painful swelling of the nose; caries of the lower jaw; even the swollen, loose, readily bleeding, and sickly looking gums. The frequent nausea, the diarrhœa after eating fruit, and the pains in the larynx, are indications of the anti-scrofulous nature of this drug."*

Dr. Hempel relates a case, in which the ulcerative process had invaded the nose, and one whole side of the face, threatening to totally destroy all the surrounding parts, and to relieve which American and European physicians of the highest standing had exhausted all the resources of their skill without any apparent effect, that was radically healed by using an infusion of *cistus-canadensis* internally, and embrocations of the same plant externally. The patient was an interesting young lady of eighteen years of age.†

The more minute treatment of scrofulous diseases will be detailed in other chapters.

---

* See Hartmann's Diseases of Children, p. 379.

† Loc. cit. p. 380.

CHAPTER XIV.

SPLINTS AND BANDAGES.

A SUCCESSFUL treatment of casualties, as well as other surgical cases, can be accomplished only by a skilful application of splints, bandages, and the other varied apparatus which have been contrived and introduced within the province of surgery. Much practice is required before that degree of neatness, promptness and carefulness are attained, which are essential components in the character of a good surgeon.

In regard to fractures especially, it is absolutely required that a precise knowledge, likewise, be had of the indications to be fulfilled for a satisfactory use of the means. Without the possession of such knowledge treatment should never be attempted. There would be but little practical profit from an acquaintance with all the very numerous kinds of bandages and other contrivances, however ingenious or highly recommended, which from time to time have been introduced to the notice of the profession. By such as are curious in these matters, the older surgical writers may be examined. In the present work it is designed to invite attention to means now in use, selecting those only which by the most talented and experienced in the profession are considered best adapted to accomplish the ends desired.

The term dressings* may be used to denote those portions of different substances applied directly to parts which have been subjected to surgical operations or to injured surfaces, the object of which is to retain parts in proper coaptation; unite them, or prevent their too hasty union; shelter them from the action of the atmosphere or from external injuries; absorb discharges, prevent dessication of surface; and last, though not least, ensure cleanliness.

The different articles employed, and the means for which

* Most of the following chapter is taken from Smith's Minor Surgery.

they are to be applied, are known under the general head of Apparatus of Dressing. These consist of two parts, one containing the *instruments for dressing*, the other the *pieces of dressing* to be applied.

The instruments for dressing must vary according to the nature of the case, but usually they may be limited to such as are generally found in the assemblage furnished by the cutlers, and known under the name of the pocket-case. This, if required for general use, should contain dressing or ring forceps, simple forceps, scissors, both straight and curved, probes, directors, spatulæ, bistouries, abscess-lancets, one male and female catheter, a tenaculum, straight and curved needles, ligatures, and often such others as the taste of the cutler or his interests may lead him to select. Under this head, also, the surgeon should, in serious cases, include razors, basins, sponges, towels, buckets, &c.; in fact, all that is requisite for the preparing of a part for the application of a dressing, or the removal of the previous one.

As the proper use of the instruments just referred to is not always known by those purchasing them, a brief description of the objects and method of handling each may not be out of place.

The *dressing forceps* are employed for removing the different pieces of dressing, not only in order to protect the fingers of the surgeon from discharges that are often very irritating, but also on account of their enabling him to seize them with less risk of injury to surrounding parts, especially by pressure. In cases of fistulæ or sinuses they are also often necessary, in order to cleanse the bottom of the sinus, or remove deep-seated portions of dressing, or other foreign matter. In using them, the thumb and second finger are to be passed through the rings of the handle, and the fore-finger extended towards the joint of the blades, in order to render them more firm.

The *simple* or *dissecting forceps* may be frequently substituted for the dressing forceps, especially where minute portions of dressing, such as ligatures, &c., are to be removed. They are, however, more frequently used for seizing such portions of integument as may require to be cut off by the knife or scissors. As similar forceps are employed by each student in dissection, no information need be here given as to the manner of using them.

The *straight scissors* are employed in dressing, for the ordinary purposes of scissors; but those which are curved, either on the side or front, are mainly required to facilitate the removal of such dressings as adhere closely to the body; as adhesive strips, bandages, &c., especially where it is desirable to remove them without deranging the position of the part. Scissors are also occasionally used for excision of portions of integuments, as in hair-lip; but they do not answer as well as the scalpel for such operations, because they are apt to bruise the edges of the part divided, and thus interfere with its subsequent adhesion. If scissors have a rough edge and cut harshly, light pressure of the thick skin of the thumb along the blades will remove it.

Probes are intended as substitutes for the fingers where the space to be examined is too narrow to admit a larger body. But where it is possible to introduce the finger it should always be preferred, on account of the greater accuracy of the touch. The probe should always be made of silver, or some equally flexible metal, in order that it may be readily bent, to suit the position of the part to be examined.

The *director* is a broad probe with a groove in it, which is generally used to direct the point of a scalpel or bistoury, in the division of deep-seated parts, especially where important organs are in the neighborhood of the incision. Sometimes it is formed with a flat end for a handle, and sometimes it has a ring, or other slight expansion, to enable the operator to hold it firmly. When the director is required to facilitate incisions, it should be held with the thumb on the top of the handle, and the fingers of the same hand beneath its shaft, in order to prevent its slipping out of place. The knife being held in the opposite hand, is then made to pass along the groove as far as may be desired.

The *spatula* requires but little description, and is used chiefly in the preparation of dressings.

Bistouries and *scalpels* are of various shapes, and should be selected mainly with reference to the probable wants of the practitioner. As their use varies much in the different operations to which they are applicable, these uses will be described with the operations in which they are necessary.

The straight and curved needles, tenacula and ligatures, are too well known to require notice.

The articles used for dressing are, lint, charpie, cotton, tow, compresses; adhesive strips, &c., &c.

Lint is a soft, delicate tissue, or mass, prepared in two ways, in one of which the transverse threads of soft old linen are drawn out by a machine, leaving the longitudinal ones covered by a sort of tomentum or cotton-like mass; whilst, in the other, the cotton-like surface is produced by scraping with a sharp knife a similar piece of cloth, previously fastened to some firm substance. The first is known as the patent lint, and may be obtained of any druggist, being now generally manufactured. The second is the domestic lint, and may be made at a moment's notice, when the first is not convenient.

Charpie is a substance much employed by the French surgeons, and now gaining a more general application in the United States. It is made by collecting the threads torn from pieces of linen, four or five inches square, such as is used for patent lint. The process, however, goes a step further than that for making lint, and tears the threads entirely apart instead of preserving the cloth. The linen from which it is made should always be new, and not worn out table-cloths, &c., as sometimes employed; Gerdy having proved that when charpie is made from new linen it absorbs better than when from old. Charpie is usually divided into two kinds, according to the length and fineness of the thread composing it; that which is long and coarse being employed to keep open sinuses, fistulæ, and to act as an outer dressing; while the softer, finer kind is placed in immediate contact with the part, especially where the secretion of pus is abundant.

Various names are given to charpie, according to the way in which its fibres are arranged previously to its application.

Thus, we have the pledget, roll, tent, mesh, bullet, tampon, pellet, &c., each of which has its peculiar advantage.

The pledget is a mass of charpie formed by collecting the threads and laying them parallel to each other, with the ends folded underneath; this being flattened between the palms of the hands, may be moulded into any shape to suit the convenience of the practitioner.

The *roll* is composed of a smaller mass of charpie, rolled into the form of a cylinder, the fibres all running in a longitudinal direction, and then being tied in the middle. The roll is useful for absorbing pus in deep wounds, arresting hemorrhages, &c.

The *tent* is a conical form of charpie, made by doubling the roll, and twisting the free ends to a point; it is generally used as a dilator. It is frequently made by soaking a sponge in melted beeswax, and then cutting it to suit the emergency of the case.

Bullets, tampons, pellets are masses of charpie, generally circular in form, and chiefly used for suppression of hemorrhages, or absorption of pus.

Compresses are pieces of linen of various sizes, used to make pressure, confine dressings, prevent external injuries, and equalize the surface of limbs, in order better to adapt them to the application of the bandage, or the compression of the soft parts. Compresses should be made of some soft substance. The various manner of folding compresses has given rise to the names by which the different forms are designated; thus we have square, oblong, triangular, and cribriform compress. The latter is made by folding a square piece of linen or muslin several times, and nicking it in several points with the scissors.

There is also the perforated, graduated, and pyramidal compresses.

The *perforated* compress is used to relieve affected parts from pressure, and to allow the slough or pus to escape at the same time; it is formed by making a square soft pad, and cutting a circular opening in the centre; it is very useful in bad sores, &c. These pads are now manufactured of India-rubber cloth, and can be inflated in the same manner as the ordinary circular life preservers, indeed they bear great resemblance to the latter.

Graduated compresses are named from their construction, and are of several kinds; the substance of each being folded differently, according to the object in view.

The *common* graduated compress is made by folding a piece of muslin several times on itself, so that each fold may not entirely cover the one that has preceded it. It may be graduated at one end, or from end to end, as would be the case if it had another folded end at its left extremity.

The *pyramidal* compress is one that is most accurately formed by placing square pieces of muslin, gradually decreasing in size, on top of each other, and stitching them together so as to form a pyramid. It may also be made by folding a piece of 2½ inch bandage on itself, so as to form a pyramid graduated from end to end, and then placing a piece of cotton, or other substance, in the centre of the last turns. Thus formed, it is very useful in making pressure upon certain points, as in cases of hemorrhage from the deep-seated vessels of the leg or forearm.

The following excellent rules for dressing are laid down by Dr. Smith, and cannot be too strictly observed by the young practitioner, as they not only promote to a great degree the comfort of the patient, but also facilitate the process of the removal of old, and the application of new dressings:

1st. Let the surgeon make, or see made, everything that is requisite for the new dressing before removing the old one.

2d. Let him have a sufficient number of capable aids, to whom special duties shall be assigned before commencing the dressing, as this prevents confusion. Thus, in dressing a stump, or wound, there should be one assistant to support the limb; another to furnish hot water, and change it as required; heat the adhesive strips, &c., &c., by which means the surgeon can give his attention wholly to his own duty.

3d. Let him arrange the bed, as a general rule, *after* the dressings are changed; or, if in a case of fracture, *before* the patient is placed on it.

4th. Let the position of the patient be such as will cause him no unnecessary fatigue.

5th. Let the surgeon, as a general rule, place himself on the outside of the limb, with his face to the patient, as this will give more freedom to his movements, and prevent accidental jars.

6th. Let all the assistants be especially careful to guard against hasty and inconsiderate movements, in order to prevent unnecessary pain to the patient.

The *roller* is to be prepared from a piece of muslin of the requisite length and width, by tearing it from the piece and then winding it into a cylindrical form, either by a machine constructed for the purpose, or by the hand, that it may form one or two masses, and constitute what is called a single or double-headed roller.

With a machine at hand, there can be no reason why every surgeon should not keep himself supplied with bandages. But as there is frequent necessity for the re-application of the same bandage, both for economy and convenience, and to be able in case of emergency to manufacture one speedily and neatly, the surgeon should accustom himself to the manipulation required in the formation of the roller. In order to accomplish this end, the following directions have been found serviceable. Fold the terminal end of the band five or six times on itself, that it may form a sort of axis, and roll it a few turns on the thigh to give it size, then place the cylinder between the thumb and forefinger of the left hand; allow the body to run over the right forefinger, seizing it firmly between the thumb and finger of that hand so as to make traction, and tighten the cylinder. Having thus arranged it, give a rotary motion to the band, and cause the cylinder to revolve upon its axis by means of the fingers and thumb of the left hand, whilst, at the same time, the right thumb and forefinger

Fig. 15.

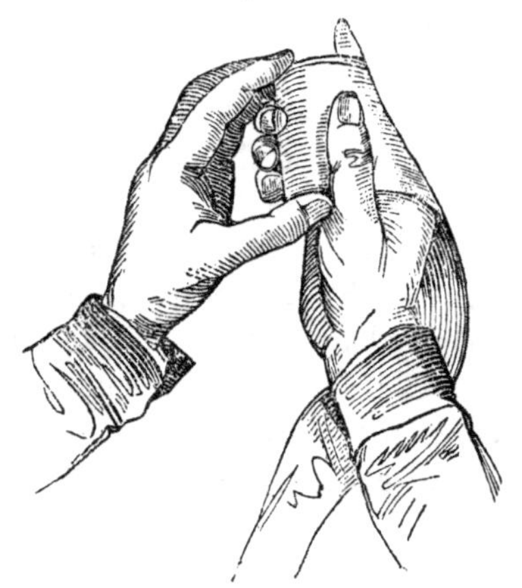

revolve partially around the cylinder itself, which, by this compound movement, is soon formed as required. See fig. 15.

The *single headed roller* consists of two extremities; of an initial and a free end; of a terminal one or that found in the centre of the cylinder; of two surfaces, an external and an internal; and of a body, or portion between the two extremities.

The *double headed roller* has the same portions as the single one, excepting that both ends are wrapped into cylinders. The application of this roller, therefore, always commences with its body.

The *spiral bandage* is that which is most frequently employed in the treatment of all affections, whether of the extremities or trunk.

In applying this bandage, each turn should cover at least one-third of the preceding; and as most parts to which it is applied are conical in shape, especially in the extremities, it is obvious that in ascending from the lower to the upper portion of them, we must follow the direction from the apex to the base, and consequently, that portion of the bandage which is nearer the latter, will press firmly on the limb, while the former will be but loosely covered, on account of the projecting folds, thereby leaving not only openings or gaps, but causing unequal pressure upon the parts. The necessity of obviating such inequality is important, and upon this subject Mr. Fergusson writes, "for whatever object a bandage is applied, it is important to observe, that an equal amount of support or pressure is afforded on all sides." The surgeon, therefore, overcomes the difficulty in making what are termed *reverse* turns.

The following rules for making reverse turns, are taken from Dr. Smith's Minor Surgery; indeed, many portions of this chapter have been compiled from that practical work.

1st. Hold the roller in the position in which it is generally applied, that is, either by its body or its two extremities, the hand being in a state of supination. 2d. Apply the initial extremity to the limb, and continue to make simple spiral turns, until you approach the enlarged portion of the limb.

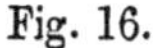

Fig. 16.

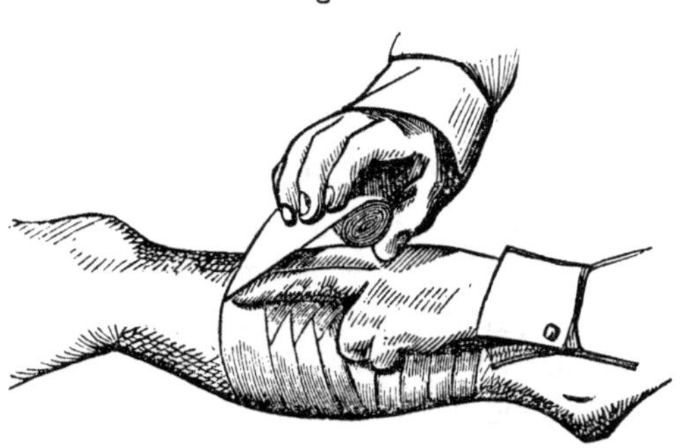

3d. Apply a finger of the free hand to that portion of the bandage, that is already in contact with the limb, not to assist in forming the reverse, or to fold it down, but to prevent the turns already applied from slipping or becoming relaxed while the reverse is being made. 4th. See that no more of the bandage is unrolled, than will enable you to separate the cylinder a short distance, say four or six inches from the limb. 5th. Let that portion of the bandage be loose, which is between the finger fixing the body of the roller, and the cylinder. 6th. Turn the hand holding the roller from supination to a decided pronation, by motion of the wrist alone, without moving the fingers from the cylinder, as shown in (fig. 16,) taking especial care *to make no traction,* nor to sink the cylinder below the level of the limb till the fold or reverse is made, when it may again proceed up the limb, it being recollected that each turn should ascend spirally, and only cover in about one-third of that which preceded it. 7th. Keep each turn and each reverse parallel with its fellow.

CHAPTER XV.

FRACTURES.

Section 1.—*Definition—Symptoms—Mode of Union.*

Fracture, or solution of continuity in bone, is usually the result of external violence;* sometimes it is effected by muscular action alone. And this, too, is not a mere local causality, but apt to be followed by inflammation, suppuration, gangrene or erysipelas, bringing life into the greatest danger.

The parts of the skeleton most liable to fracture, are the long bones, more especially of the extremities; and these may suffer by violence applied either directly or indirectly. The flat bones, with the exception of those of the cranium, are less liable, and seldom give way, except under violence which is both direct and severe.

A bone does not always break at the point struck. A blow on the symphysis menti often occasions fracture of the jaw, near its angle; a concussion applied to the bones of the leg, through the foot, ordinarily produces fracture of the tibia near the ankle, and of the fibula at its upper part. The broken fragments usually become more or less displaced. The force, wherewith the injury was inflicted, may push one or both aside; and the weight of the limb may increase displacement, when the part is raised, or when an attempt is made to use it. But the paramount displacing agent is the action of those muscles which are implicated in the injury. Sometimes there is retraction of the fragments, and elongation of the part; as in transverse fracture of the patella. Most frequently the fragments cross and overlap each other, with consequent shortening of the limb. Sometimes one fragment alone is displaced; as in fracture of the clavicle; the sternal portion remaining nearly in situ, while the lower passes downwards and forwards. In other cases, both suffer displacement, as in fracture of the

* See Miller's Principles of Surgery, 699–708.

humerus below its bicipital groove; the upper fragment passing in toward the chest, the lower being elevated, and displaced outward by the deltoid.

By the displacement, neighboring parts are liable to be compressed, torn or otherwise injured; and hence the most serious consequences may ensue; unless such displacement be detected, understood, and speedily rectified. For example, the displaced fragments of a broken rib may puncture and irritate the pleura and lungs, exciting violent inflammation there; and displaced portions of a broken cranium may cause a like injury to the brain and its membranes, followed by results still more disastrous.

The *symptoms* of fracture are usually very plain; there is obvious deformity of the part; and its muscular power is all but lost. A fractured arm, for example, is swollen, and the patient is unable to move it without the assistance of the corresponding member. Sometimes, as in the case of the patella, the part is elongated; much more frequently it is shortened; the lower extremity, in fracture at the hips, may be abbreviated to the extent of two inches or more. Voluntary motion is much abridged; in many cases the patient of himself, can move the injured limb little, if at all.

Involuntary motion on the other hand, is much extended; that is to say, the surgeon can, though not without inflicting much pain, move the limb in directions and to an extent of which it was previously incapable; and at the site of fracture, the slightest examination usually makes it abundantly plain, that the part is remarkably and preternaturally mobile. Pain is great and constant; and ever and anon liable to sudden exacerbation, from spasmodic twitchings of the muscles implicated in the injury, whereby the bones are displaced anew, and the soft parts irritated and torn. If either fragment come in contact with nervous trunks, compressing, puncturing, or in any way irritating these, the pain is likely to prove extreme. Swelling invariably occurs, and is of three kinds. 1. The displacement and overlapping of the fractured ends, produce a greater or less enlargement of the part immediately after the infliction of the injury. And if muscles be relaxed by the displacement, the bulging into which they are consequently thrown will contribute to the immediate swelling. 2. The first swelling is increased by extravasation of blood; which inevitably follows solution of continuity of the bone, and coëxistent laceration of the soft parts. If any considerable vessel have been injured, this kind of swelling may prove very great; partly by blood accumulating around the fracture, partly by its being infiltrated into the surrounding tissues. The second swelling in its turn, is followed and modified by the 3d, which attends inflammatory action; beginning to form after the lapse of some hours. The tissues then become infiltrated; partly by serum, partly by fibrinous exudation.

But the peculiar and diagnostic sign of fracture, is what is termed *crepitus;* a sensation of rubbing, grating, or crackling, which is imparted to both hand and ear, when the fragments are moved one upon the other, with contact of their broken surfaces. When there is no great displacement, the fractured ends remaining partly in opposition, this crepitus may be felt on the slightest movement of the limb; and often both the patient and his attendant are made very plainly aware of its existence, by the involuntary movements, which spasm of the muscles from time to time occasions. But when the fracture is transverse, the displacement great, and the fragments completely overlapping, crepitus is not so easily found. Reduction must be effected in the first instance; in order that the broken surfaces may be brought into contact with each other; and then by movement, the desired sound will be plainly enough emitted.

Certain fractures termed *impacted* rarely afford crepitus. One fragment is driven into and lodged in the cancellous texture of the other, by the same violence which caused the fracture; and so the bone is scarcely broken, when it again becomes fixed, with its continuity apparently restored.

The manipulations neccessary to ascertain the nature of an accident, and which are specially directed towards detection of crepitus, are to be conducted with all gentleness, that unnecessary pain may not be produced, or the soft parts further endangered by aggravation of subsequent inflammatory action, and yet with determination, sufficient for fully satisfying the examiner as to the diagnosis. It is much better that a thorough examination should be made at once, painful though it be, than that more gentle movements and inquiries should be made with frequent repetitions, delaying the means of cure. Also, let it be borne in mind, that, at whatever cost of suffering to the patient, it is our paramount duty to make such a thorough examination; for two reasons. In the first place, in order that the required repose and treatment of the part may be immediately instituted; in the second place, and mainly, that error of diagnosis may be avoided.

The mode of union or reparative process, is a subject of much importance; on the right understanding of which, the indications of treatment depend. It may be conveniently divided into the following stages; understanding that the fragments have been duly readjusted, and are so retained. 1. Blood is extravasated at the site of fracture; and accumulating, distends the surrounding parts into a kind of pouch, in which the fractured ends are laid; and the cavity of this pouch is occupied by the extravasated blood, partly fluid, partly coagulated. The surrounding parts are condensed; and obeying the stimulus of the injury and displacement, become more energetic in their circulation, prepared for the unusual effort in nutrition which is about to be demanded of them. 2. The extravasated blood is absorbed, and the ends of the fractured bone also undergo alterations, being deprived of their earthy matter to a great extent, and so prepared for higher efforts as a vascular tissue. Liquor sanguinis is exuded from the parietes of the pouch, from the ends of the bones, and from the periosteum which invests them; and this plasma assumes the position which the blood occupied. The pouch, however, has somewhat contracted from its first dimensions, by tumescence of the parietes; favored, or at least permitted, by gradually decreasing extravasation. It has been a source of hot dispute, to determine from what tissue this plasma proceeds. Probably it is the offspring of every tissue implicated; exuded from bone and from periosteum, and also from the textures constituting the parietes of the containing pouch, whether these be muscular, fibrous, fatty, or areolar. Perhaps, it may be held enough for the practical inquirer, that there is the plasma, come whence it may; the plasma having been exuded, consolidates, its serous portion is absorbed; the fibrin remains and becomes organized. And this organizing plasma not only occupies the pouch, but is also situate between the fractured ends of the bone, and in their interior. At the same time, fibrinous exudation is taking place in the soft textures exterior to the pouch, whereby they are still further condensed. A portion of this is imperfectly organized; and remains for a time, sometimes of considerable duration. The rest is absorbed, previous to organization, on subsidence of the excited action by which it was exuded. 3. The period of plastic exudation may be said to have passed, after eight or ten days. Then the process of organization advances. The plasma sometimes passes into the transition state of fibrous tissue; at others into fibro-cartilage, or even true cartilage. 4. The organized and transitional mass contracts, by interstitial absorption; increases in density; and gradually passes into the condition of bone. At the same time, the surrounding parts, that are immediately in contact with the ossifying mass, are more and more condensed, they become continuous with the ruptured and engorged periosteum; and assume the general characters of that texture, as well as its function of investing and administering to bone. 5. Ossification advances from the periphery. The most exterior part of the plasma is the first ossified; and thence ossification gradually approaches the interior; as it advances the mass contracts more and more, ultimately restoring the bone. This ossifying mass, commencing at the circumference and contracting, forms an osseous ferrule, by which the fractured ends are tightly clasped. This new formation is termed provisional callus. 6. The definite callus is that which is formed between the ends of the bone, and which constitutes the final medium of incorporation of the ends. Its organization and ossification are accomplished by a more slow and gradual process, than that of provisional callus. 7. The definite callus is at first preternaturally dense and compact; but is gradually modified by absorption, and ultimately is so changed, as to render continuity of the normal texture of the bone complete. On making a section of a recently united bone, a dense compact mass of new osseous matter is found intersecting the cancellous texture at the site of fracture; but after a few years, section discloses that part of the bone's interior, perhaps a little more dense than elsewhere, yet open and quite of the cancellated character. And thus it would seem, that not even the definite callus can be said to be truly permanent. On the contrary, all callus is temporary; it has a certain duty to perform; and that having been achieved, it is taken away more or less gradually by absorption.

The *exciting causes* of fractures are mechanical violence and muscular action. Mechanical violence may be *direct* or *indirect*. It is direct when the fracture is produced at the point to which the force is applied. It is indirect when the force is applied at one point and the fracture occurs at another.

The *predisposing causes* of fractures are old age, mollities ossium, fragilitas ossium, and original brittleness.

Fractures occur in three directions, viz., *transverse*, *oblique*, and *longitudinal*.

There are several varieties of fractures, viz., *simple*, *compound*, *comminuted*, and *complicated*.

A simple fracture is a solution of continuity in the osseous tissue at one point, without external injury to the soft parts.

A compound fracture is a solution of continuity in the soft parts and osseous tissue, with an external opening.

A comminuted fracture is where the osseous tissue is separated at several points, or crushed, thus producing many fragments of bone. It may either be simple or compound.

A complicated fracture is one in which the fracture is accompanied with luxation of a joint, laceration of large vessels, rupture of ligaments and tendons, or gun-shot wound.

The *danger* from simple fracture is inconsiderable; but from the other varieties it is often extreme, and may terminate fatally in a few hours, from loss of blood and shock to the system, or from inflammation, fever, tetanus, and typhoid fever or hectic, dependent upon excessive suppuration.

The homœopathic treatment of fractures will be mentioned hereafter; it may, however, be well in this place to remark, that immediately after the injury, if the patient appears to suffer from the shock, either *arnica*, *ignat.*, or *cham.* should be prescribed. The former of these medicines deserves the preference in the generality of cases, but there may be occasion for the exhibition of the other two.

Ignatia may be used when the patient is not so much affected by the shock as he is fearful of consequences; when there is trembling and excessive weakness, or vertigo, violent anguish about the pit of the stomach, and cold sweat.

Cham. may be prescribed when the patient faints frequently, with uneasiness about the heart, twitching of the limbs, and oppression of the chest.

After reaction has taken place, the limb should be adjusted, if the parts require it; *arnica* or *calendula* applied, according to the presenting circumstances of each particular case. After the more violent inflammatory symptoms have subsided, to hasten the deposit of ossific matter, either *calc.-carb.*, *calc.-phosph.*, *ruta*, or *symphytum off.*, may be used.

If there are excessive pains in the periosteum and bones, with nightly aggravations, *phosph.-ac. mez.*, or *rhododen.*, relieve.

Section 2.—Fracture of the Cranium.

In fracture of the skull, there may be *simple fissure* of the bone, or fracture *with depression;* or the *outer table* alone may be fractured and driven into the diploe. This can only occur in middle age, since the diploe does not exist in infancy or old age. The inner table alone may be fractured. Generally both tables are broken, and the bones are sometimes split to a very great extent.

Diagnosis.—This is not difficult. These fractures are the result of great violence; and when the seat of fracture is upon the surface it can be felt by the finger, which should be passed into the wound if there be an opening in the scalp. If the patient be not seen until a hard, puffy tumor has formed upon the scalp, the exact nature of the injury cannot be ascertained until this subsides. It should be remembered that, although the fracture generally occurs at the seat of the injury, yet it often takes place at a part of the arch more distant from the application of the force. Thus, a blow or fall upon the top of the head may, and often does, produce fracture of the *base of the skull.* This injury may be recognized by the escape of blood from the ears, nose and mouth, (caused by tearing the sinuses of the dura mater,) with early and severe symptoms of compression of the brain, and, after the lapse of some days, a discharge of watery fluid from the ear, (thought to be due to the escape of serum from the sac of the arachnoid membrane.) In fracture with depression there are symptoms of compression; yet these symptoms accompany fracture without depression of bone, where there is effusion of blood or accumulation of pus upon the brain. Crepitation can be felt when there are detached fragments of bone. Symptoms of concussion are observed in simple fracture, as well as in more serious cases, preceding the more dangerous symptoms of compression.

Prognosis is always doubtful in these cases, and generally unfavorable.

Treatment.—A dose of *arnica* should be immediately administered internally, and afterwards a lotion of the same drug applied to the wounded part; or if there be a tendency to encephalitis erysipelatosa, the meningeal membranes being the seat of the inflammation, which is manifest by sudden violent headache, delirium, etc., *bell.* is one of the most suitable medicines. If effusion should have actually commenced, *arnica* should be at once administered; indeed, from the commencement of those symptoms indicative of inflammation of the brain, and particularly when such arise from fracture, *arnica* appears to be the specific medicine.

"*Arnica*," writes Dr. Henriques,* "is the antivulnerary specific, (if I may be allowed this expression,) which is employed in homœopathic surgery to prevent as well as to cure local pain, swelling, and inflammation, following an injury. In the old system it is by antiphlogistics that these effects are controlled. I allude to these without discussing their effects on the organism, or their ultimate results in inflammation."

In fracture with depression of bone, accompanied with compression of brain, it is necessary to relieve the patient by the use of the trephine; the elevator can scarcely ever operate advantageously until the trephine has made a suitable point for its application. Another great advantage in performing this operation is that of giving egress to the blood escaping from wounded vessels. Even where symptoms of decided compression have not yet supervened upon depression of a fragment of bone, it has been advised to elevate the depressed structure, provided the danger of inflammation and compression appear urgent or very likely to occur from the presence of the foreign body; this is both reasonable and good practice. But the trephine should not always be resorted to when depression and slight symptoms of compression manifest constitutional treatment—application of *arnica* or *calendula* to the head, and perfect rest, should be the means looked to for relief. The instrument above mentioned has also been employed successfully in relieving the brain from compression and effusion of blood.

In the application of the trephine it is generally advisable to avoid the sinuses and the meningeal artery. The most advantageous point near the seat of mischief should be selected for the operation, and great care taken, upon approaching the inner table of the cranium, to avoid wounding the membranes of the brain. If the integuments be not sufficiently divided by the accident, an incision must be made through them, sufficiently extensive to allow the free application of the trephine. Either

* British Journal of Homœopathy, No. XLI., p. 452.

of the following forms of incision may be made for this purpose, and the flap raised by a scalpel.

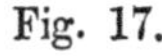

Fig. 17.

In cases of comminuted fracture of the cranium, where fragments of bone are detached, they have become foreign bodies, and should be removed. In fractures of the cranium generally, however, little can be done with the fracture: the main points in the case are compression and inflammation; these must be guarded against, if possible. Non-interference with the seat of injury, with the exception of the local application already alluded to, is the best general rule that can be given.

Section 3.—*Fracture of the Nose.*

Fracture of the nose is ordinarily a very simple accident, but may be dangerous by great violence being applied to the bones of the nose, and through them breaking the cribriform plate of the ethmoid bone, and forcing it in upon the brain. Ordinarily there is mere fracture of the nasal bones, which is easily recognized by the deformity produced.

Treatment.—The bones should be re-adjusted by pressure upon the outside with the fingers, and from within by a director or other convenient means, a solution of *arnica* applied externally, and the same medicine administered internally. By these means the tumefaction is soon subdued and inflammation prevented.

Section 4.—*Fracture of the Lower Jaw.*

Fracture of the inferior maxillary bone is of frequent occurrence, and is always the result of considerable force; it is

Fig 18.

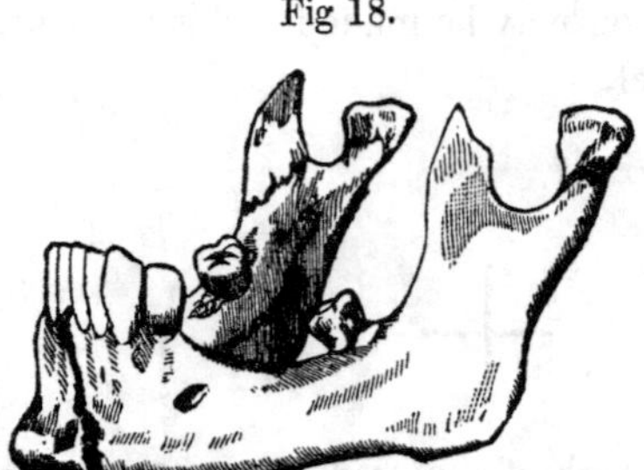

generally broken in the mental region, (Fig. 18,) or the middle of the horizontal ramus. In children it sometimes takes place at the symphysis, but fracture may occur in any part of the lower jaw.

Diagnosis is very easy in this injury: the anterior fragment is drawn downwards; there is pain on moving the jaw, crepitus, and irregularity in the teeth and alveoli.

Prognosis is favorable.

Treatment consists in coaptating the fragments and insuring rest by pressing the teeth (which makes an admirable splint) firmly together, and securing the part by the application of a piece of pasteboard, or a compress of linen applied under the jaw, and secured by one of the following bandages.

The four-tailed bandage is probably the best that can be applied. It is made of a piece of muslin about four inches wide, and one and a half yards long: this is torn longitudinally at both ends, leaving eight inches in the middle entire; in the centre of this a slit is made, to allow the chin to pass through; the two ends of the lower half are carried up the side of the face, and tied on the top of the head; the remaining ends are carried around the neck and fastened behind, the bandage being so arranged as to embrace the chin and keep the jaws firmly applied to each other. This bandage is more firm, and sets better, when long enough to pass several times around the face and neck.

Dr. Gibson's bandage (Fig. 19) consists of a roller an inch and a half wide. This is passed in circular turns under the jaw, up the face, and over the head several times; it is then pinned at the temple and turned at right angles, encircling the back of the head and forehead by several turns; it is pinned again at the temple, and carried down the side of the face and pinned on a line with the chin; carried then, at right angles, several horizontal turns are made, embracing the chin and back of the neck. A strip of roller is then carried over the top of the head and pinned to the several turns, to secure the bandage from slipping.

Fig. 19.

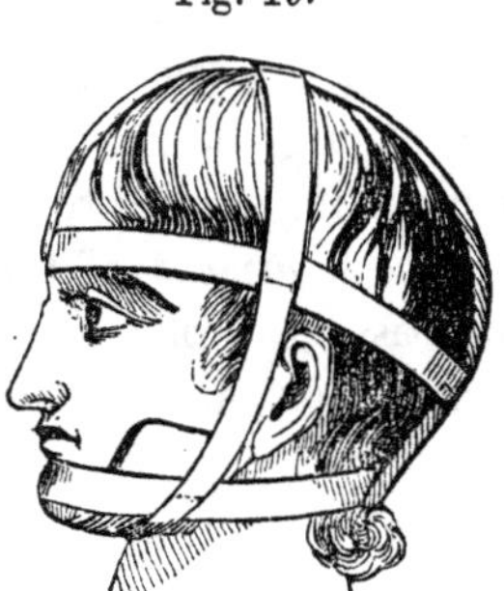

Dr. Rhea Barton's bandage, with the use of a pasteboard splint, (see fig. 20,) is one of the simplest and best that has been recommended. It consists in a narrow roller, the initial end of which is to be placed under the occipital protuberance; the bandage is carried over the right parietal bone, obliquely across the coronal suture to the left temple, down the left side-face, under the jaw, up the right side-face, and obliquely over the coronal suture to the left ear, (above it,) being carried around under the occipital protuberance to the right side, then passing under the ear, is carried around the chin, embracing the neck and chin by a circular turn; it is then carried on under the occipital protuberance, over the right parietal bone, and again obliquely over the coronal suture to the left temple, and continued in these turns until expended.

Fig. 20.

With each of these bandages it is necessary to have the compress or wet pasteboard well adapted to the jaw. The patient must be supported by sucking liquids, the teeth always leaving sufficient space for this purpose. When the position of the fracture makes it practicable, it is a good plan to bind the teeth together at the seat of fracture, by passing a silk ligature around them.

Section 5.—Fracture of the Scapula.

Fracture of the scapula, in its body, occurs from great violence directly applied.

Diagnosis.—In this injury there is but little displacement. Voluntary motion is impaired; the part is swollen and painful. By placing the hand flatly upon the seat of injury, and communicating motion to the scapula, crepitus can be felt.

The *treatment* of this injury consists in restraining motion by passing a roller around the thorax, so as to bind the scapula firmly to it, and placing the hand in a sling.

Fig. 21.

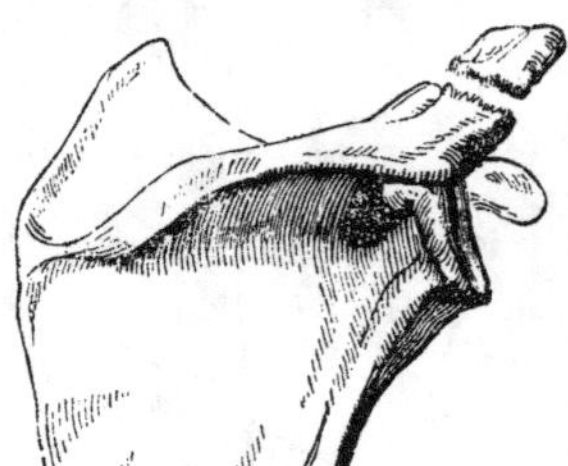

Fracture of the Acromion Process (Fig. 21) is caused by direct violence.

Diagnosis.—It may be recognized by flatness of the shoulder, the fragment being drawn downwards by the deltoid muscle. The clavicle and broken fragment are drawn downwards and forwards by the action of the subclavius, deltoid and pectoralis major muscles. By forcing the head of the humerus upwards against the *acromion process*, crepitus can be felt, whilst rotation of the arm does not cause crepitus.

The *treatment* consists in elevating the humerus, thus making a splint of the head of the bone, which keeps the broken parts in apposition. The arm should be maintained in this position by the application of the apparatus for fractured clavicle, without the wedge-shaped pad, the indication in fracture of the acromion being merely to raise the arm.

Fig. 22.

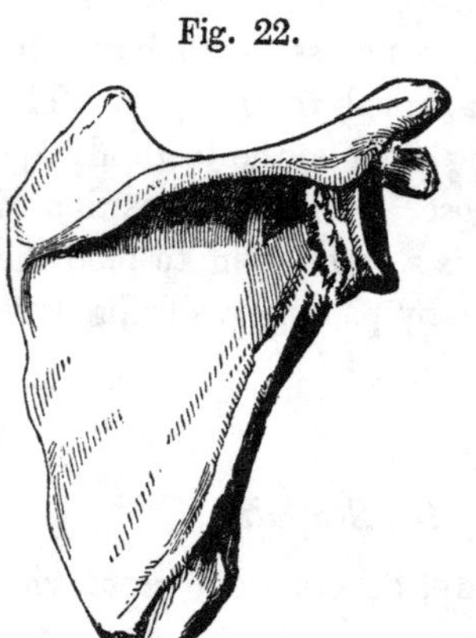

Fracture at the Neck of the Scapula (Fig. 22). In this accident the broken fragment consists of the glenoid cavity and coracoid process.

Diagnosis.—Much care is necessary to distinguish this accident from dislocation. The fractured portion of the scapula is retained in contact with the head of the humerus by the long heads of the biceps and triceps muscles: the head of the humerus, with the detached fragment of the scapula, is drawn downwards and forwards into the axilla by the subscapularis, pectoralis major, and latissimus dorsi muscles. There is flatness of the shoulder, prominence of the acromion, with a vacancy beneath it; the limb is somewhat lengthened, and the head of the humerus lodged in the axilla, as observed in cases of dislocation of the head of the humerus. But, by very gentle effort, the head of the bone may be replaced, and the deformity disappears. When support to the part is withdrawn, the displacement and deformity re-appear, which is not the case in dislocation. Crepitus may also be distinctly felt by placing the thumb on the coracoid process, (which can be readily felt under the outer end of the clavicle,) and pressing the fingers in the axilla; then, by pushing the arm upwards and outwards, signs of fracture, not to be mistaken, are made evident.

Treatment of fracture of the neck of the scapula consists in coaptating the broken fragments, and keeping the parts at rest. For this purpose the apparatus for fractured clavicle is probably the best, and should be applied so as to arrest both the movements of the arm and scapula: here the wedge-shaped pad meets one of the most important indications.

The *coracoid process* and *articular surface* of the scapula are occasionally fractured; but it is not of frequent occurrence. When these accidents are met with, the fore-arm should be placed in a sling, and the part kept at rest. M. Velpeau's bandage for fractured clavicle answers the indications for fracture of the coracoid process of the scapula better than any other.

Section 6.—Fracture of the Clavicle.

Fracture of the clavicle is of very common occurrence. It usually takes place near its middle, (Fig. 23,) and is generally oblique. It is the result of force applied either directly or indirectly.

Fig. 23.

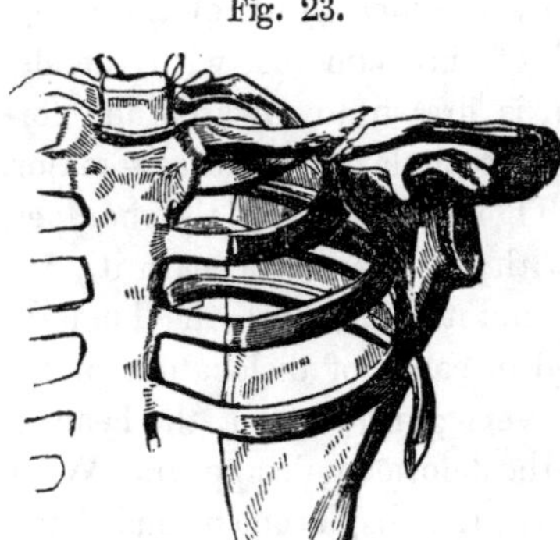

Diagnosis in this case is perfectly easy. By passing the finger along the clavicle, the natural line of the bone is observed to be interrupted, and the broken extremities perceptible: the shoulder falls forwards and inwards; the outer fragment is drawn downwards by the action of the subclavius and deltoid muscles. By pressing the shoulder upwards and outwards crepitus can be felt at the point of separation.

Treatment of fractured clavicle consists in adjusting the broken extremities of the bone, by forcing the shoulder *upwards, outwards*, and *backwards*, and retaining it in this position.

The following apparatus is employed for this object. A padded belt is placed around each shoulder, and drawn together on the back by a strap, and the fore-arm placed in a sling: or a folded towel is placed in the axilla, and a bandage is passed from shoulder to shoulder, forming a figure of 8 (see fig. 24) across the shoulders. This plan is recommended by Mr. Fergusson. Mons. Desault's apparatus consists in a wedge-shaped pad and three rollers: the base of the pad is placed in the axilla (see fig. 25) and secured to the body by passing a roller in circular turns around the chest. (Fig. 26.) The fourth and fifth turns of the bandage are carried over the sound shoulder and under the arm-pit. The arm is now brought down upon the pad, which acts as a fulcrum,

Fig. 24.

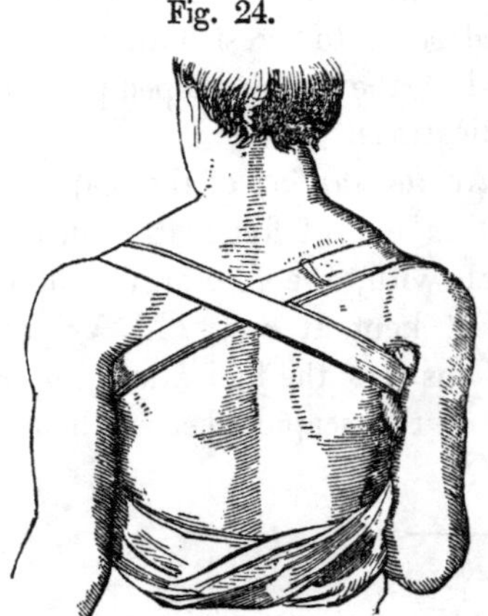

Fig. 25.

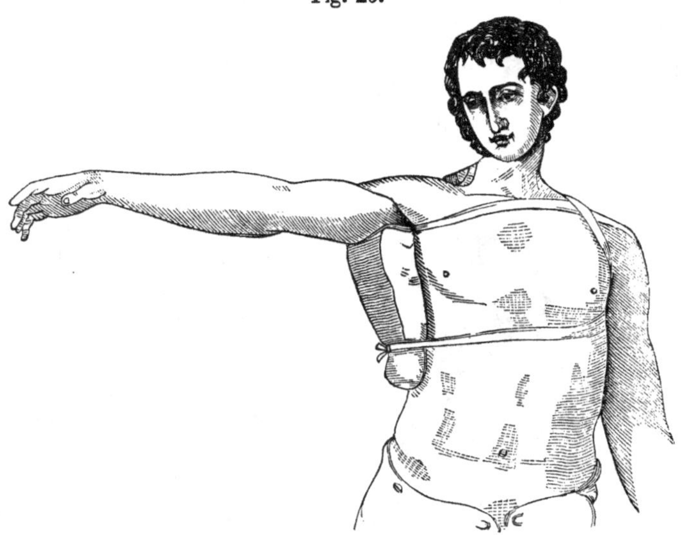

and the fracture being adjusted, the fore-arm is placed across the chest. The second roller is now applied, by placing the

Fig. 26.

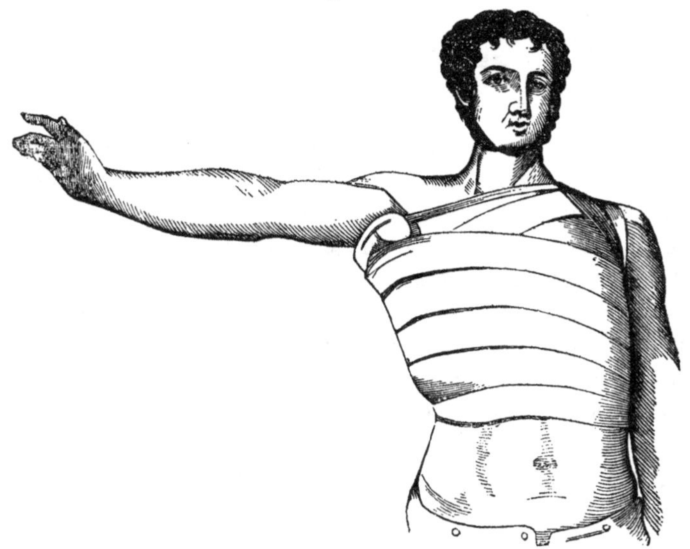

initial end in the axilla of the sound side, and carrying it to the shoulder of the injured side, around the body; then continue, by circular turns, binding the arm to the pad from the shoulder down below the elbow. (Fig. 27.) A compress of muslin is placed upon the injured part, and the third roller is commenced at the arm-pit of the sound side, and carried obliquely over the shoulder of the injured side, down the back of the arm, under the elbow, across the chest, under the arm-pit of the sound side, across the back, over the injured clavicle and down in front of the arm, under the elbow, obliquely across the back to the arm-pit, and continued, forming a triangle in front and behind, until exhausted: the hand is then placed in a sling. (Fig. 28.)

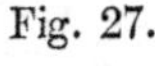
Fig. 27.

The last and best apparatus is that of Dr. Fox, which consists in a sling for the elbow, made of stout linen, or other material; this should be in length about two-thirds of the fore-arm, and deep enough to embrace the fore-arm; it can easily be made out of a piece of stuff, cut into a parallelogram, twice the width of the fore-arm, and two-thirds of its length; this is to be doubled in its shortest diameter, and one end sowed up; at the upper angle, and the corner of each side, a strong loop of tape is attached. A ring of linen, stuffed with carded cotton, is made to embrace the shoulder and axilla; a wedge-shaped pad, which should be three inches thick at the base, six inches long, and four or five wide; strong pieces of tape or bandage complete the apparatus. The application of it is as follows: (Fig. 29.) the base of the pad is placed in the axilla of the injured side, and temporarily secured by being held, or by tapes tied around the neck; the arm of the sound side is passed through the padded ring, which rests in the axilla and over the shoulder: the sling is applied to the fore-arm, the elbow placed firmly in its angle, and the arm is now brought down to the side, the fracture coaptated; tapes having been passed through the loops attached to the sling, are now carried through the ring at the sound shoulder; the tape at the elbow carried behind the chest, and those at the wrist in front; these are firmly drawn so as to place the shoulder and clavicle in proper position, the hand being put in a sling. Raw cotton should be placed under the tapes where they touch the skin, to prevent excoriation. It is necessary to avoid much pressure in young subjects, as well as to exercise great care in protecting the skin from abrasion. This apparatus is easily

Fig. 28.

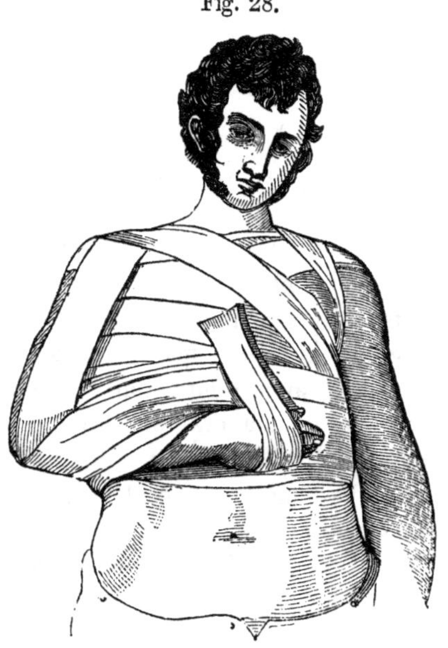

Fig. 29.

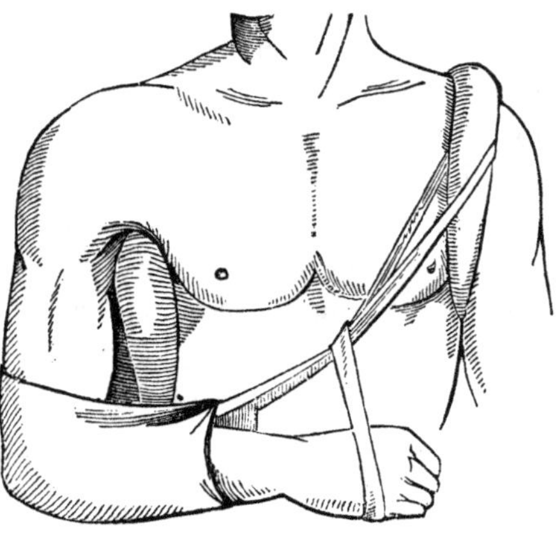

applied, and can be worn without inconvenience, and probably fulfils the indications better than any that has yet been proposed.

Section 7.—Fracture of the Sternum.

Fracture of the sternum is generally transverse, and the result of great violence, so that the injury done to the thoracic contents is often of more moment than the fracture.

Diagnosis is readily made in this case; there is deformity by displacement, and crepitus during respiration.

Prognosis is unfavorable in fracture of the sternum, from the probability of inflammation and suppuration in the thorax, with caries of the bone; this accident often results in death.

Treatment of the fracture consists in passing a roller around the chest, to arrest its motions; compresses, moistened with a solution of the tincture of *arnica,* should be applied to the fractured part, and a dose or two of the medicine administered internally.

If the fever is synochal, the pulse hard, quick, and full, the face red, excessive chilliness or heat; the pains in the chest violent, and the respiration oppressed and accompanied with anxiety, *aconite* should be given in repeated doses.

If the pain in the chest is not exceedingly severe, but there is evident signs of inflammation being established in the lungs; if a loose cough be present, the oppression not excessive, with constant desire to inspire, *bryonia* should be exhibited.

Bella. will be found suitable, when the fracture has occurred in plethoric subjects, when there is a tendency to congestion of blood to the brain, with delirium, when the face is bloated and very red, the lips and tongue cracked and dry. This medicine may, in severe cases, be used in alternation with *aconite.*

When there are evident symptoms of violent pneumonia, with sticking pains in the chest excited by coughing or breathing, (also pleuro-pneumonia,) when the pains are violent and extend over a large surface, when a considerable portion of the lung is inflamed, also dyspnœa, when the cough is dry and the *sputa rust-colored, phosphorus* is indicated, and will probably relieve the patient in eight or twelve hours. This medicine may be given in alternation with *aconite* or *bella.*, agreeably to the presenting symptoms. For further treatment of pneumonia the student is referred to works on the Practice of Medicine.

Carious portions of the bone can be removed by Hey's saw, bone-nippers, and forceps; but aid in this way should not be rendered too officiously, lest harm instead of good result.

The trephine has been successfully used in evacuating collections of pus in the anterior mediastinum.

Section 8.—*Fracture of the Ribs.*

Fracture of the ribs is generally transverse, and may be produced by direct force, or by violence applied at their extremities; in the former instance the displacement is internal; in the latter, external.

Treatment in these cases consists in lessening the respiratory motions of the chest, by passing a roller around the thorax, thus causing the patient to breathe by the action of the diaphragm. If there be internal displacement at the point of fracture, pressure should be made upon the extremity of the rib, by placing a compress upon it, and binding it down firmly by the bandage; if the angular displacement be external, the compress should be placed upon the point of fracture. If the lungs have been wounded, or any of the internal structures implicated, *arnica* or *calendula* lotions should be kept applied to the part, and either administered internally, according to the character of the wound and the symptoms manifested. If inflammation of the pleura supervene, *arnica* is an excellent internal medicine; its characteristic indications are, stinging pain in the affected part, dyspnœa, short, dry cough, general internal heat with coldness of the hands and feet. Other medicines are *sulph.*, *scill.*, *bry.*, *rhus*, *nux-vom.*, *bella.*, &c.

Section 9.—*Fracture of the Spine.*

Fracture of the spine rarely occurs, but when it does, it is always the result of great violence.

Diagnosis in fracture of the spine is not always easy; in some cases paralysis of the lower extremities occurs from violent concussion of the spine, without fracture.

In fracture of the spine above the *fourth cervical vertebra*, death follows almost instantly, from injury to the phrenic nerve.

In cases of fracture *below* the *fourth cervical vertebra*, there is paralysis of the upper extremities, with difficult respiration, and death occurs in four or five days.

When the *dorsal vertebræ* are the seat of fractures, there is paralysis of the lower extremities and torpor of the intestines; the abdomen is frequently enormously distended by air contained in the intestines. Death usually occurs the third or fourth week.

In fracture of the *lumbar vertebræ* the bladder and rectum are paralyzed, and the urine and fæces pass involuntarily; the lower extremities are paralyzed, and insensible to stimulants, but retain their heat and circulation undiminished. Death follows, at latest, in five or six weeks.

Fractures of the *spinous processes* of the vertebræ are not followed by serious consequences, unless accompanied by concussion or some other injury.

Prognosis in all cases of fracture of the vertebræ is unfavorable.

Treatment.—If there be violent fever, with inability to pass urine, *acon.* may be prescribed; at the same time compresses moistened with arnica solution may be applied to the seat of fracture. If there be much urinary tenesmus, *canth.* alone, or in alternation with *arnica*, will probably relieve the patient; if not, *bell.*, *camph.*, *hepar*, *puls.*, or *sulph.*, may produce the desired effect. If these means also fail, the catheter should be used.

If there is a tendency of the spinal cord to take on inflammatory action, *acon.* should be used; it is one of the most highly recommended medicines in the treatment of myelitis.

When the inflammation is seated in the lumbar and sacral regions, when the adjoining abdominal organs are affected, and the alvine evacuations difficult, *bry.* should be administered.

Ars., *bella.*, *cocc.*, *dulc.*, *dig.*, *ignat.*, *nux-vom.*, *puls.*, and *veratrum* may also have to be employed.

Effusion of blood and suppuration sometimes occur in the course of the spinal marrow, and in its sheath, which give rise to very untoward symptoms.

The patient must be kept at perfect rest, in the horizontal posture, and the greatest care be taken to prevent gangrene of the nates. This may be effected by arranging pillows or Macintosh air-cushions in such manner that the parts may be equally supported. If the skin assume a bluish appearance, or, from the constant irritation of the parts, bed-sores are present, a solution of *arnica* applied to the part greatly relieves the sufferings of the patient.

Section 10.—*Fracture of the Pelvis.*

Fracture of the pelvis occurs only from great violence; the displacement is not great, and little can be done to remedy it; the injury sustained by the soft parts within is of more interest than the fracture.

Prognosis in this fracture is always unfavorable, for when the fracture is extensive death usually follows; and when the injury is less severe, inflammation and abscess result; making the case tedious and doubtful.

Treatment consists in placing a broad bandage around the pelvis, and combatting inflammation received by the pelvic viscera. Here again *arnica* would be one of the first medicines employed; and if the intestines have suffered from the *contusion*, this medicine would be peculiarly applicable. Other remedial agents, however, must be employed for the symptoms presenting, and the organ or organs chiefly involved.

In fractures of the *os pubis*, *coccyx*, and *ischium*, by passing the finger into the vagina or rectum the fragments may be adjusted, but low diet, perfect rest, and the usual applications, must likewise be relied on in the treatment of these accidents.

CHAPTER XVI.

FRACTURES OF THE UPPER EXTREMITIES.

Fractures of the bones of the fore-arm and hand are of common occurrence. In all instances where amputation is not requisite, there is little trouble in replacing the fragments, or in keeping them in proper position.

Section 1.—*Fractures of the Fingers.*

In fractures of the phalanges it is occasionally difficult to detect the nature of the case. In such examples the fragments are not displaced, and there is scarcely any necessity for apparatus, as the pain which the patient suffers, on any considerable motion of the part, will induce him to keep it sufficiently steady. When there is displacement, a slight extension will suffice to put the fragments in apposition; and a little slip of pasteboard in front, and another behind, kept on by a bandage, or by a few turns with a narrow strip of adhesive plaster, will constitute all the apparatus required. If the phalanx connected with the metacarpal bone happen to be the one under treatment, it will be most satisfactory to prevent all motion of the joint above; and this may be done by carrying the splint along the palm of the hand, and fixing it by a few turns of a roller, broader than that used for the finger.

Fractures of the Metacarpal Bones.—The metacarpal bones when broken are seldom much displaced, and there can be no difficulty either in detecting such injuries, or in replacing the fragments. There is no need of a splint, (except when the destruction of the soft parts has been considerable,) as the neighboring entire bones will answer the same end. However, should one be deemed necessary, a piece of pasteboard, about the breadth of the hand, should be placed on the palm, and fixed there by means of a bandage. The splint should extend a little above the wrist, and as far down on the fingers as to allow them to rest upon it; by such means the most perfect quietude will be insured.

Fracture of the Carpal Bones.—When the bones of the carpus are broken, the injury is generally of such a nature as to endanger the safety of the hand; for violence sufficient to cause such fractures is likely to have produced great destruction of the soft parts. Should amputation not be deemed necessary, a splint of pasteboard should be applied in front, so as to prevent all movement. As little force as possible should be used in putting or keeping the fragments together.

Section 2.—Fracture of the Fore-arm.

The bones of the fore-arm are often broken, either singly (Figs. 30 and 31) or conjointly, (Fig. 32,) and the radius is most frequently the seat of injury. This bone generally gives way, in consequence of a fall, when the hand is thrown out to support the body; and when fractured near the wrist (see fig. 33,) may be mistaken for dislocation, but can easily be recognized by crepitation, and the deformity returning after having been once reduced. The ulna may be broken whilst the radius is left entire.

The *olecranon* process of the ulna may be fractured, either by the action of the triceps muscle or direct violence.

The *coronoid* process is sometimes fractured, but this is of rare occurrence.

Fig. 30. Fig. 31. Fig. 32.

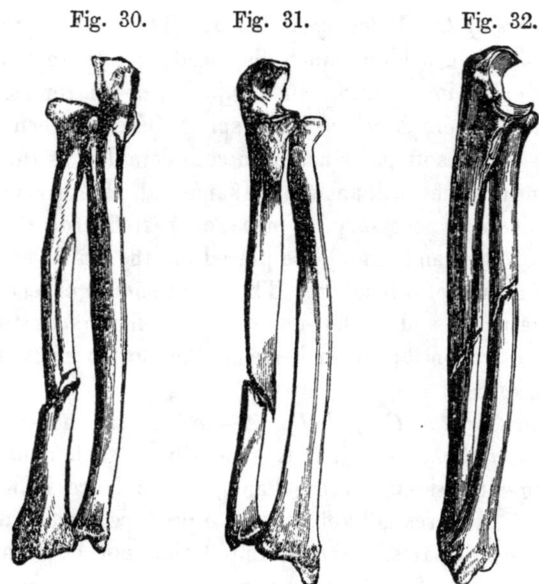

Diagnosis in fracture of both bones is evident from the angular deformity which exists: in fracture of one bone alone crepitation can readily be felt, by taking hold of the hand and making the movements of pronation and supination; the other hand placed upon the seat of injury, will feel the crepitation from the upper fragment of bone not rotating with the other.

Fracture of the *olecranon process* is recognized by the space between the broken points; the upper portion of the olecranon is generally drawn up, by the action of the triceps, some distance above the joint. The joint can be readily bent, but is straightened with difficulty.

In fracture of the *coronoid process* there is dislocation of the ulna backwards, with great projection of the olecranon process, and difficulty in bending the elbow.

Treatment of Fractures of the Fore-arm.—The treatment of fractures of the fore-arm consists in making the soft parts in the interosseous spaces serve as a splint to force the fragments outwards, and to keep the bones in apposition. Two splints, long enough to reach from the elbow beyond the fingers' ends, and wider than the fore-arm, (this is an important point,) so as to avoid lateral pressure, are requisite. These splints should be convexly padded with lint, tow, or cotton, along that part of their length which corresponds to the interosseous spaces, and wrapped with bandage. The fracture should be coaptated by extension, and the fore-arm placed with the thumb uppermost, or intermediate between pronation and supination. The splints must now be applied upon each side of the fore-arm, to press firmly on the interosseous spaces, and should be applied with care, so as not to bear hard upon the condyles of the humerus, else troublesome excoriation is sure to take place. The elbow should be well protected also, by placing cotton under the ends of the splints; the splints being firmly bound to the limb by circular turns of a roller; the fore-arm is then placed in a sling.

Fig. 33.

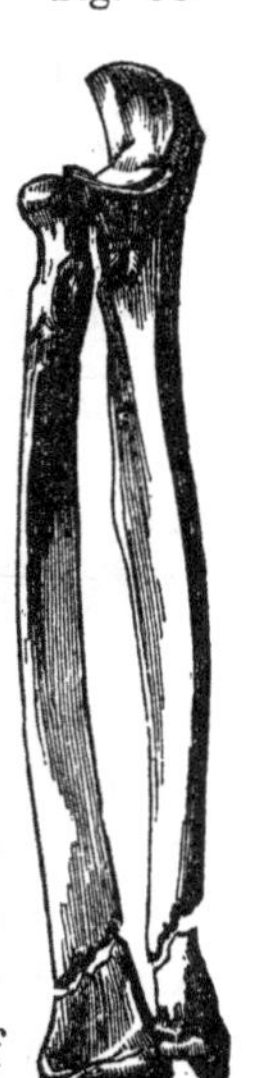

Fig. 34.

The deformity, and consequent loss of pronation and supination of the fore-arm, and great impairment of its utility, by neglect of the foregoing rules, are demonstrated in fig. 34, an error that cannot be too anxiously avoided.

In the treatment of fractures of the fore-arm, it secures more perfect rest to the part, and answers remarkably well, to have the internal splint made like the right-angle splint for fractured condyles of the humerus, binding its upper limb to the arm, thus preventing motion of the elbow joint.

Fracture of the Lower End of the Radius may readily be mistaken for dislocation of the radius at the wrist joint. (Fig. 35.) Great care should therefore be used in making a diagnosis in injuries about this joint. Fracture of the radius at this point may be distinguished from dislocation, by crepitus, and the easy reduction of the deformity, also by the return of the deformity as soon as forcible distension is discontinued.

Fig. 35.

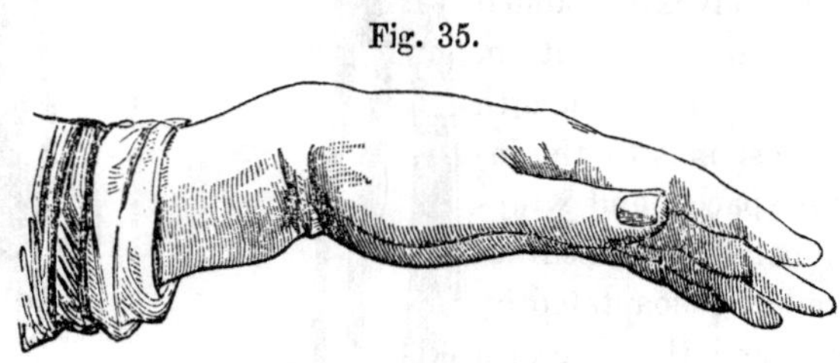

The fracture should be reduced by extension and direct pressure upon the broken fragments, and the padded splints recommended in fractures of the fore-arm, or the apparatus of Dr. Rhea Barton, applied to keep the bones in apposition. This last consists in two wedge-shaped pads, about three inches long, and as wide as the wrist; two splints, as directed for other fractures of the fore-arm, and a roller.

The fracture being reduced, the pads are placed one upon the front and the other upon the back of the wrist, pressing upon the broken ends of the bone in such a manner as to insure and continue their coaptation. The splints are then applied as in the former cases, (without being padded,) and secured by circular turns of a roller; the fore-arm is then placed in a sling.

After the lapse of a couple of weeks, passive motion of the joint should be commenced with care, and continued to the end of the treatment, to prevent anchylosis.

Fig. 36.

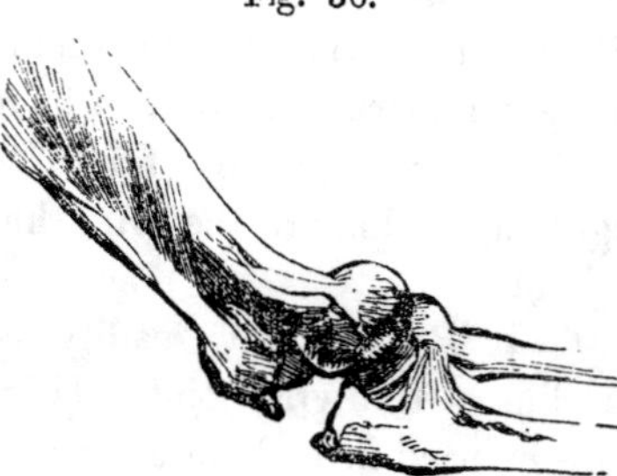

In fracture of the *olecranon process* (Fig. 36) the elbow joint is to be straightened, and bandaged by circular and reversed turns of a roller, from the hand to the injured joint; the fragment should then be brought down and adjusted, the roller passed above it, and around the joint, in the form of a figure 8, until it is firmly fixed; the roller is continued up the arm to the shoulder, to annul the action of the triceps muscle. A splint is now placed in front of the joint, extending some distance along the arm and fore-arm, and the roller passed in circular turns, binding the splint firmly to the limb. In three weeks' time passive motion should be communicated to the joint, and frequently repeated, to prevent anchylosis. The union in this case will be ligamentous.

In fracture of the *coronoid process* the joint must be restored by extension, the limb bent at right angles, bandaged to keep it in this position, and the fore-arm placed in a sling. Union will be ligamentous here also.

In this fracture the coronoid process is drawn upwards by the action of the brachialis anticus; probably, therefore, the best treatment is to flex the fore-arm upon the arm, binding them together by circular turns of a roller. If there should be a disposition to displacement backwards in the ulna, apply an angular splint in such manner as to rest upon the back of the arm and fore-arm, and embrace the elbow joint.

Section 3.—*Fracture of the Humerus.*

Fracture of the humerus may occur in any part of the bone, but its middle is oftener the seat of fracture than any other point.

The *surgical neck* of the bone is sometimes the seat of fracture. (See fig. 37.)

(The surgical neck signifies a point without the capsular ligament, just below the tuberosities of the bone.)

The *condyles* are also liable to be broken off obliquely, by force directly applied; one or both may be fractured at the same time.

Diagnosis in fracture of the *shaft* of the bone, (see fig. 38,) is quite easy. There is pain, and incapability of using the limb, which is the case in all fractures; the line of direction of

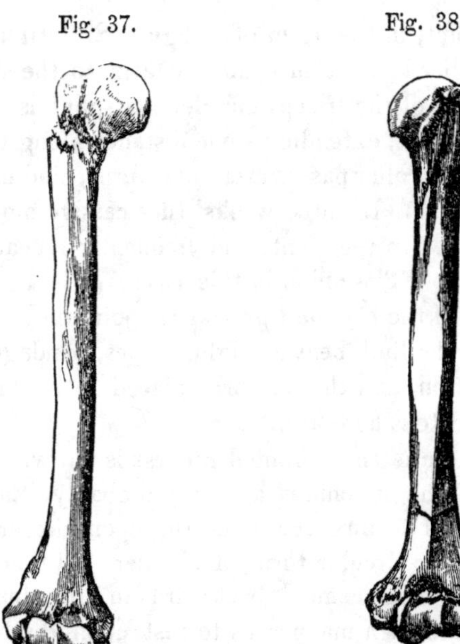

Fig. 37. Fig. 38.

the bone is altered, consequently deformity of the limb exists; by fixing the upper fragment with one hand, and rotating or moving the lower with the other hand, crepitus can be felt.

Fracture of the *neck* of the humerus generally occurs in old subjects; this accident has often been mistaken for luxation, and a little care is necessary to avoid the error. In fracture, the natural form and roundness of the shoulder-joint are unaltered, because the head of the bone remains in the glenoid cavity, and by taking hold of the elbow, and rotating, or moving it, crepitation is distinctly perceptible.

The *condyles* are often fractured, and sometimes have been falsely diagnosed for luxation of the radius and ulna backwards. Fracture may be distinguished by crepitation, induced by moving the fragments one upon the other; also by pressure upon the olecranon and bend of the arm, increasing the width of the elbow, when both condyles are fractured.

The *head* of the humerus is sometimes fractured by direct violence, or by gun-shot wounds.

Prognosis is favorable, except in fractures of the condyles; in these cases inflammation and anchylosis are apt to follow the injury; still, excellent cures are frequently made.

Treatment of Fractures of the Arm.—Treatment of fracture of the shaft consists in coaptating the broken bone, by extension from the wrist or elbow; the application of a roller by circular and reversed turns from the hand to the shoulder; four wooden splints, nearly a quarter of an inch thick, shorter in length and breadth than the humerus, the inner one being the shortest, and placing one upon each side of the arm, and binding them firmly over the fracture with the remainder of the roller; place the fore-arm in a sling across the chest. It sometimes happens that the bandage on the fore-arm causes swelling and pain; where these effects are produced, commence the roller just above the elbow, bandaging the arm only, leaving the fore-arm bare, and slinging it as in the former case.

Fracture of the Neck of the Humerus should be accurately adjusted, and Fox's apparatus for fractured clavicle, or any other suitable apparatus applied; the wedge-shaped pad forming the best possible support to the inner side of the separated bone. If in any case additional support be found necessary, the leather splint of Mr. Liston should be applied, or a roller passed around the arm and thorax, binding the former firmly to the pad; the elbow should not be as forcibly raised in this case as in fractured clavicle. What most contributes to prevent deformity in the management of this injury, is in getting a firm, well fitting padding in the axilla, high up, so as to bear upon and firmly support the fragments.

Desault's apparatus consists in passing a roller from the fingers to the shoulder by circular and reversed turns; arriving at the shoulder, the bandage is carried across the breast, around the shoulder and arm-pit of the sound side, and across the back to the shoulder of the injured side; three splints, two inches wide, and the length of the arm, are now placed on the anterior, posterior, and outer parts of the arm, and the roller passed firmly over them in circular turns to the elbow, placing cotton, tow, or lint, under their extremities, to prevent excoriation; the wedge-shaped pad is fixed in the axilla, the injured arm brought down upon it and secured by passing around the chest and arm his second roller for fractured clavicle; the fore-arm is then placed in a sling.

Mr. Liston recommends the following apparatus for injuries about the shoulder joint and clavicle, (see fig. 39,) he says: "The separate bandaging of the fingers, hand, and fore-arm, for this purpose, the position of the pads, the mode of fixing the shawl which contains the wedge-shaped axillary cushion, and the bandage surrounding the chest, are here exhibited. In bandaging the hand a pad of lint is first placed on the palm to fill up the hollow where the bandage would probably exert no pressure. A sling completes the apparatus for all the injuries of the clavicle and shoulder joint." He also recommends a leather splint in these cases. "If the fracture have occurred in the upper end of the bone, betwixt the insertions of the tendons of the latissimus dorsi, pectoralis major, and deltoid, then a leather splint may with advantage be applied from over the shoulder-joint to the point of the elbow. A piece of skirt-leather, (as it is called by saddlers,) dressed without oil, is cut so as to fit the limb; it is soaked and softened in warm water, and then applied and retained by a roller. It soon becomes a firm mould to the limb; it can then, after its edges are well pared and rounded off, be stuffed with wadding, or lined with wash-leather, and thus forms an excellent support and protection to the injured part."

Fig. 39.

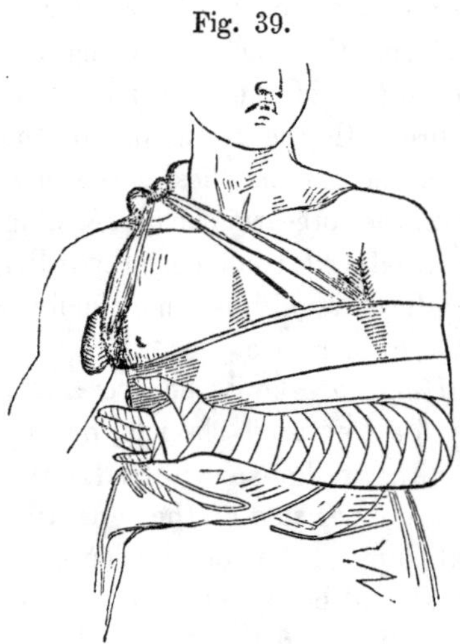

Fracture at the Anatomical Neck of the Bone, (which is above the tubercles,) occurs sometimes in young subjects. The articular head of the bone is also the seat of fracture; but both of these accidents are rare, and do not differ in management from the former case.

Fracture of the Humerus, occurring above the insertion of the deltoid, and below the insertion of the pectoralis major, latissimus dorsi, and teres major, requires some care to prevent deformity; for the lower fragment is drawn forcibly outwards by the action of the deltoid muscle, whilst the upper fragment is drawn strongly inwards by the latissimus dorsi, teres, and pectoralis major.

The *treatment* consists in reducing the fracture by extension of the arm, the application of splints to the fore, outer, and back parts of the arm, and the nice adjustment of a wedge-shaped pad to the axilla, so as to pass high up, and give equal and firm support to both fractured extremities of the bone. The arm is brought down to the side, properly placed upon the pad, and then bound down firmly by a roller passed around the arm and thorax: the fore-arm is placed in a sling.

Fracture of the Lower Extremity of the Humerus, when just above the condyles, (see fig. 40,) so closely resembles dislocation of the radius and ulna backwards, that much care is necessary to distinguish the true nature of the injury.

Fig 40.

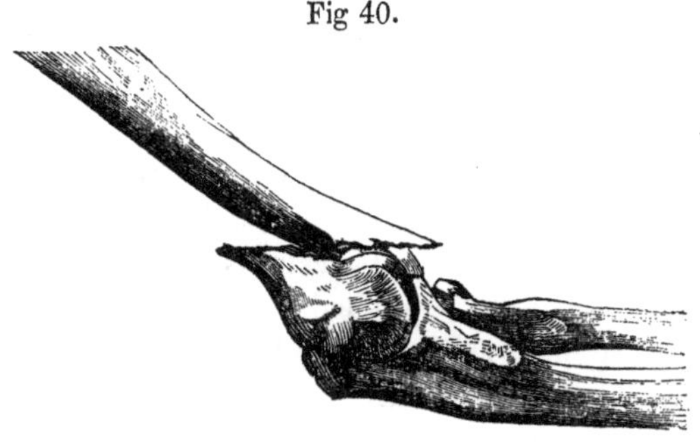

Diagnosis.—In fracture, crepitus can be produced; the deformity can also be readily removed by moderate extension of the arm, but the deformity returns as soon as the extending force is withdrawn; the length of the arm of the injured side, when measured from the acromion process to the fore-arm at the bend of the elbow, is shorter than that on the sound side. None of these conditions are found in dislocation at this joint; they serve, therefore, to distinguish fractures.

Treatment.—Remove the inflammation and tumefaction by rest, and the application of the appropriate homœopathic means; reduce and coaptate the fracture by extension, and apply two angular splints, narrower than the elbow; placing one on the anterior and the other on the posterior surface of the arm, the two horizontal limbs of the splints resting upon the upper and lower surfaces of the fore-arm; pass a roller around the fore-arm and arm, binding the splints firmly to the limb.

Dr. Physick's angular splints for fractured condyles answer very well also for this injury.

In Fracture of the Condyles of the Humerus it is necessary to reduce the fracture, and distortion of the joint, by extension and manipulation about the point of injury, in order to adjust the broken portions of the humerus: retain them in this position by Dr. Physick's apparatus, which consists in four pairs of splints, or one pair with a movable joint, to vary the angle long enough to reach from the shoulder to the elbow, and thence three inches beyond the ends of the fingers, being about two inches broad. The first pair is to be made at a *right angle*, the second *more obtuse*, the third *a more obtuse angle still*, and the fourth *straight;* these, with a roller, complete the apparatus.

The fracture being reduced, and the elbow bent at a right angle, the roller commencing at the hand ascends the fore-arm and arm by circular and reversed turns to the shoulder; the two right angle splints are applied, one upon the outer and the other upon the inner side of the limb. The roller is then brought down by circular turns, binding the splints firmly to the extremity, and the fore-arm is placed in a sling: the ends of the splints must always be padded with cotton or lint, to prevent excoriation of the skin. After two or three weeks the rectangular splints can be taken off, and obtuse splints substituted; removing the dressings, after two or three weeks, every five or six days, passing alternately from a right angle to a straight line, making gentle flexion and extension of the joint, to prevent anchylosis.

CHAPTER XVII.

FRACTURES OF THE LOWER EXTREMITIES.

Fractures of the lower extremities are, generally speaking, more serious in their nature than those of the upper, being accompanied with more danger to life and limb. They likewise cause much more trouble in their treatment.

Section 1.—*Fractures of the Foot.*

Such injuries are of comparatively rare occurrence; and when they do happen, the destruction of the soft parts is usually so extensive that each case must be considered more as a contused and lacerated wound of all the textures around, than as a fracture, whether simple or compound. One or more of the toes may be thus injured by heavy weights, as happens to coal-heavers, quarry-men, stone-masons, and others similarly exposed; and as amputation is the advisable recourse in most of such cases, the question of greatest importance for consideration will be with reference to the seat of operation. Unless the tarsus be involved in the injury, the idea of amputating the foot ought not to be entertained: and as a general rule applicable here, as in most other parts of the body, the smallest possible degree of mutilation ought to be inflicted, consistent with the object of the operation, which is to remove such parts as are irrevocably injured, and, at the same time, leave a properly formed stump. In instances of fracture in the foot where there is no necessity of resorting to the knife, it is scarcely requisite to use any apparatus to keep the fragments in apposition; in the toes the phalanges are so short that, if properly adjusted at first, they will remain so, unless the patient injudiciously bears his weight upon the foot at too early a period: even in the longer metatarsal bones it is not found necessary to employ splints. The application of *arnica*, etc., at first, and complete rest of the foot for about twenty days afterwards, constitute the most important parts of the treatment.

Section 2.—Fractures of the Leg.

Fracture of the Head of the Tibia is the result of direct violence, the fracture extending into the knee-joint.

Treatment.—Inflammation must be reduced by the appropriate means, the fractured bone and joint being kept straight by the application of splints, behind the joint, so that the condyles of the femur may act as splints, and keep the fragments in place. Passive motion should be communicated after five weeks, or as soon as the consolidation has advanced so far as to admit of it.

Fracture of the Tibia or Fibula, or of both bones, by careful examination, can be readily recognized. Both these fractures require the same treatment, except fracture of the fibula near the ankle.

Treatment of fractures of the *tibia* and *fibula* is effected by two different kinds of apparatus: one consists in laying upon a firm mattress four pieces of tape or roller, over these a splint-cloth, upon this a soft pillow, on this sufficient strips of the bandage of Scultetus to cover the leg from the ankle to the knee. The fractured leg is then laid upon this bandage and the centre of the pillow; the fragments are coaptated, and the bandage of Scultetus applied from the ankle up; two splints, three inches wide and a half inch thick, longer than the leg, are rolled, one in each end of the splint-cloth, and brought up so as to cause the pillow to fit the leg snugly; the tapes are tied, and the foot is supported by a sling. Pressure from the bed-clothes is prevented by two halves of a hoop crossed at their centres.

Fig. 41.

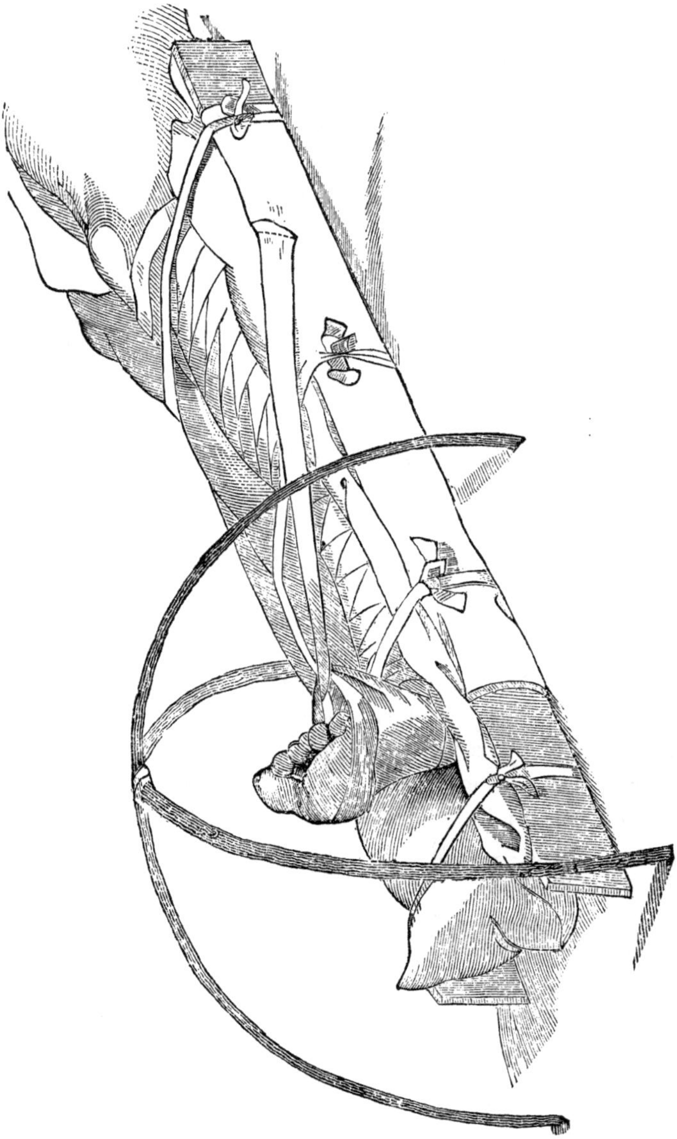

The *fracture-box* is preferable, (see fig. 41); it consists of three splints, or light boards, fastened together by hinges, which may be of leather. The sides and bottom of the box should extend from the knee beyond the foot. Fastened to the lower end of the bottom should be a foot-board, and the upper end of the sides should have mortise-holes in them, to fasten counter-extending bands, when this is necessary. In this simple box a pillow, filled with oat-chaff or feathers, is placed, and the fractured leg put upon it. The fractured extremities are adjusted, and the sides of the box brought together and retained by strips of bandage. Where extension is necessary, a gaiter or bandage of a handkerchief, in the form of a figure 8, is placed around the ankle, and fastened to the foot-board. Counter-extending bands, if needed, are made fast to the upper part of the leg by means of a roller, and tied in the mortise-holes of the side-pieces of the box.

Fracture of the tibia just below the insertion of the ligamentum patellæ is exceedingly difficult to treat, from the tilting forward of the upper fragment by the action of the rectus femoris muscle. In this injury there is no difficulty in the diagnosis.

Treatment.—The best mode of treatment in this case is to reduce the fracture by extension of the leg, and pressure upon the superior fragment. Counteract the action of the extensor muscles of the leg by passing a roller firmly around the thigh; place the base of a wedge-shaped pad upon the upper fragment, over this a splint extending down the front of the leg, and bind them down firmly by a roller extending from the foot to the knee. If it be thought necessary, the limb may then be placed in a fracture-box.

Fracture of the Fibula, about three inches above the ankle-joint, is not uncommon, and is often accompanied by dislocation of the foot. (Fig. 42.)

Diagnosis is very plain. The foot is turned outwards, and the natural line of direction of the fibula is lost. By turning the foot inwards, and placing the thumb on the seat of fracture, crepitus can be felt.

Treatment in this injury is accomplished by the application of Dupuytren's apparatus, which consists in applying the base

Fig. 42. Fig. 43.

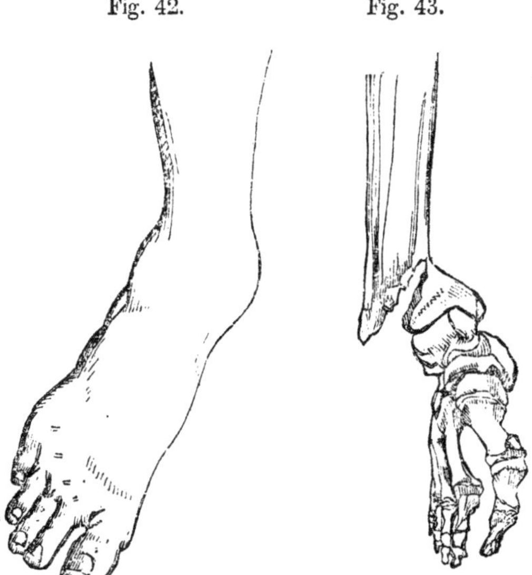

of a thick wedge-shaped pad just above the internal malleolus; a splint, three inches wide, extending from the knee three or four inches beyond the foot, is laid upon the compress, and fastened to the leg by a few turns of a roller passed just below the knee. A roller is then passed in the form of a figure 8 around the heel, external malleolus, and end of the splint: the foot is in this way carried inwards and retained there, and the fractured extremities of bone are thus brought in contact by making a fulcrum of the pad, and converting the lower fragment of the fibula into a lever.

Fracture of the Internal Malleolus (Fig. 43) occurs by violently twisting the foot inwards. Sometimes the fracture includes the whole of the lower end of the tibia.

Diagnosis is not difficult. The foot is turned or dislocated inwards, and crepitus can be readily recognized.

Treatment for this injury is the same as for fracture of the lower part of the fibula—merely applying the apparatus upon the opposite side.

Section 3.—*Fracture of the Femur.*

Fracture of the femur should be made a subject of careful study, from the fact, as Mr. Pott remarks, "they so often lame the patient, and disgrace the surgeon."

Fracture of the *neck of the femur* (Fig. 44) occurs both within the capsular ligament and external to it. Fracture within the ligament is the more common, but it is very rare in persons under fifty years of age, and is mostly met with in old women; in addition to the changes which the bones undergo in advanced life, as deficiency of bone-earth, and sponginess of the cancelli—the neck of the femur is always peculiarly *atrophied*, *shortened*, and *shrunk*, from the *oblique* to the *horizontal* position; changes which necessarily render it more liable to fracture.

Fig. 44.

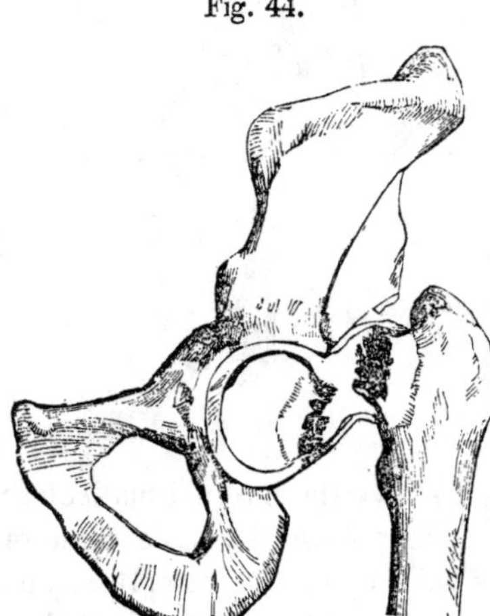

Diagnosis in fracture of the neck of the femur is sufficiently easy, with a little care, to avoid the error of confounding it with luxation. In fracture there is pain in the hip, the limb is shortened half an inch to two inches; the foot is turned outwards, (see fig. 45); crepitus may be felt by placing the hand on the trochanter, and extending the limb to its proper length, then rotating it. The trochanter is less prominent than on the sound side, and the limb may be freely moved, although with pain. In some cases the shortening of the limb does not occur until some days after the accident, and is in some cases inconsiderable. The limb is sometimes turned inwards. But fracture should be suspected, whenever an old person has received an injury about the hip, and complains of pain in it, whether there is shortening of the limb or not.

Prognosis is very unfavorable in these cases; they are always tedious, bony union rarely taking place in the old subject, and sometimes no union at all occurs.

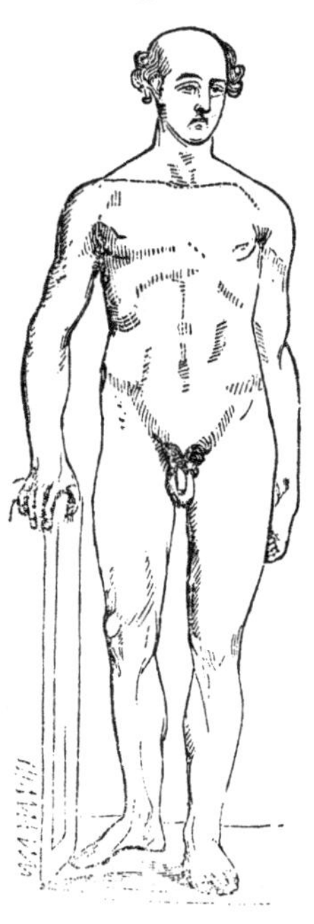
Fig. 45.

Treatment in very old subjects consists merely in placing the patient in bed and keeping the limb quiet, or by a felt splint, or the curved splint of Dr. Physick for coxalgia, for a couple of weeks, or until the shock and contusion occasioned by the accident have passed off, and then allowing the patient to get about as well as possible on crutches. After a time a false joint is formed, the stump of the cervix becomes rounded and covered with a smooth porcellaneous deposit, and plays in a socket formed by the absorption and hollowing out of the head of the bone. But if the patient be young, this fracture may unite by bone; the fractured extremities therefore should be coaptated and kept in apposition by Physick's Desault's apparatus for fracture of the femur, or Liston's long single splint, which acts on the same principle, but is less complete in answering the indications.

Fractures immediately outside the joint, through the trochanter, unite readily enough even in very old persons. It may not always be possible, Mr. Liston observes, "to decide exactly whether the joint is involved or not; but the greater degree of shortening and mobility of the limb, with the more distinct feeling of crepitation, will often enable the surgeon to distinguish the nature of the case, and to decide upon the practice. Mr. Druitt remarks that "fracture of the femur *just below the trochanters*, is liable to be followed by great deformity and non-union; because the upper fragment is tilted up forwards by the psoas and iliacus muscles. The best plan of treatment is to place the patient on a fracture-bed, with the trunk and thighs bent at a very acute angle, in order to relax the counteracting muscles."

Fracture of the Trochanter Major is produced by great violence.

Diagnosis.—The trochanter is displaced upwards, by the lesser glutei muscles, and by placing the hand upon the seat of fracture, and rotating the thigh, crepitus may be felt.

Treatment in this accident consists in recumbency, and a position securing relaxation of the displacing muscles. Union in this case is generally ligamentous.

Diastasis, or separation of the *shaft* of the bone from its epiphysis, may occur in the young subject, by direct violence or twisting of the limb. Reduction in these cases is effected by extending the limb, and fixing it by splints of wood or pasteboard.

Fracture of the Shaft of the Femur may be the result of force directly or indirectly applied.

Diagnosis is very plain in this case; there is deformity of the thigh, which may be angular in transverse fractures, and in oblique fracture considerable shortening; crepitus is perceptible, and the lower fragment is generally drawn backwards, whilst the upper is tilted forwards.

Treatment of this fracture is accomplished by extension, and coaptation of the broken extremities of the bone, and the application of Desault's apparatus, as improved by Dr. Physick, which answers the indications better than any fracture apparatus that has been employed in this injury. This improved apparatus consists of five or six pieces of *broad tape,* or pieces of roller; a *splint cloth* (which is a piece of muslin a yard wide and one and a half long); a *splint* of binder's board, two inches broad and nine long. *Scultetus' bandage: two bags* four inches wide, and long enough to extend from the hip to the foot; these are loosely filled with oat chaff; two silk handkerchiefs folded diagonally, or some other material, for *extending and counter-extending bands; three wooden splints,* one four inches wide, and long enough to reach from near the axilla to some distance beyond the sole of the foot; at the upper and lower extremities of this splint there are mortise-holes to pass the extending and counter-extending bands through; about four inches from the lower extremity, a cleat three inches long, with a notch in it, stands off at right angles to the splint: the second is nearly as wide as the former, and long enough to extend from the perineum to the foot: the third is as long as the thigh.

The application of this apparatus is as follows: a firm mattress with a hole in it for the evacuations, is covered by a sheet. Or what is far better and more convenient, is a frame the size of the mattress (which should always be hard); in this frame strong canvas is set, with a hole in the centre for the nates; it is to be covered by a sheet, and laid upon the mattress. Under each corner of the frame is a leg six or eight inches long, fastened to it by a hinge; when the frame and patient are raised from the mattress, the legs fall and rest upon the bedstead, and thus sustain the patient while he has his passage, with ease and without disturbance of the fracture.

The patient may be raised with greater facility by having an arm attached to each corner of the frame with a strong hinge; these allow the arms to hang by the side of the bed when not in use. This simple fracture-cot should be employed in all cases of fractures, dislocations, or other injuries, wherein the patient cannot rise from the bed to evacuate the bowels.

Upon the sheet is laid the pieces of strong tape or roller; the splint-cloth is laid over them lengthwise across the mattress; near the upper edge of the splint-cloth, midway between its ends, is laid the splint of binder's board; over the splint is laid the bandage of Scultetus, beginning at the top and laying down sufficient to reach from the groin to the knee. The patient, divested of clothing, is now laid upon the dressings with the injured thigh over the strips of Scultetus, the extending band is passed round the foot in the form of a figure 8, and given to an assistant; the counter-extending band is placed in the perineum, between the genitals and the injured thigh, one end in front of the body, the other behind it, and given to an assistant:

by these, extension and counter-extension are made, and the fractured bone coaptated by the surgeon, who then applies the bandage of Scultetus, commencing with the strip nearest the knee: the two long splints are rolled up, one in each end of the splint-cloth, the stuffed bags are applied to fill the spaces between the splints and the limb: the extending and counter-extending bands are passed through the mortise-holes and fastened; the lower one passing over the cleat at the bottom, to make the extension in a line with the axis of the limb; the tapes are now tied to keep the splints applied.

An equally efficient and more easily managed application of this principle is to make a fracture-box, by taking the two long splints of Desault, as the outer and inner sides, making the inside splints long enough to extend beyond the foot; and by applying a back splint of sufficient width, the same length as the inner one, fastening the three splints by hinges, and by attaching a foot-board worked by a screw, the fracture-box is complete. In this should be laid a cushion loosely stuffed with oat-chaff; which should extend from the hip to the heel, embracing the limb. The extending and counter-extending bands having been applied in the same way as before, or a laced gaiter may surround the foot instead of the handkerchief; the limb is placed upon the cushion, and extension and adjustment of the fracture having been made, the sides of the fracture-box are brought together and fastened by strips of bandage.

The plate (Fig. 46) is a representation of Hagerdorn's apparatus modified by Dr. Gibson, late Professor of Surgery in the University of Pennsylvania. The wood-cut describes itself better perhaps than would a labored description.

The apparatus of Mr. Liston (Fig. 47) consists of a single splint, pad, roller, and extending band; the preparation of the splint is shown in the treatment of fracture of the neck of the femur.

The application of this apparatus consists in applying a narrow roller, from the foot to near the site of fracture, to prevent infiltration, the perineal band and splint are then applied, and the roller, carried under the sole of the foot, turned round

Fig. 46.

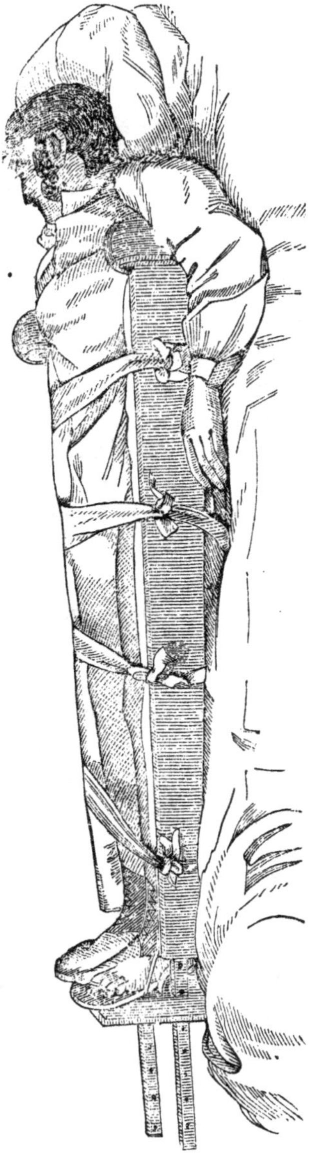

the ankle and heel, being protected by wadding; the roller is carried repeatedly through the notches in the end of the splint, and crossed over the dorsum of the foot, and ultimately turned round the limb near to the groin. This is the only apparatus employed or recommended by Mr. Liston in fractures of the femur.

Oat-chaff is probably softer than any material that can be employed for this purpose; it is the best chaff that can be used.

Extending and counter-extending bands should consist of hose, or tubes, made of cotton, linen, or buckskin, well stuffed with raw or carded cotton, the best material for protecting the skin from painful pressure and excoriation. These bands should always be made as large as the part to which they are to be applied will admit. Shawls and handkerchiefs are objectionable as extending bands, from the hardness of their edges and plaits cutting into the skin.

A *foot-board* fitted with a screw, to an apparatus for the treatment of oblique fracture of the thigh, is of great advantage, by enabling the same amount of extension constantly to be maintained, by turns of the screw counteracting the stretching of the bands; whereas, without such a foot-board, we are obliged to untie the extending band before we can tighten it.

Fig. 47.

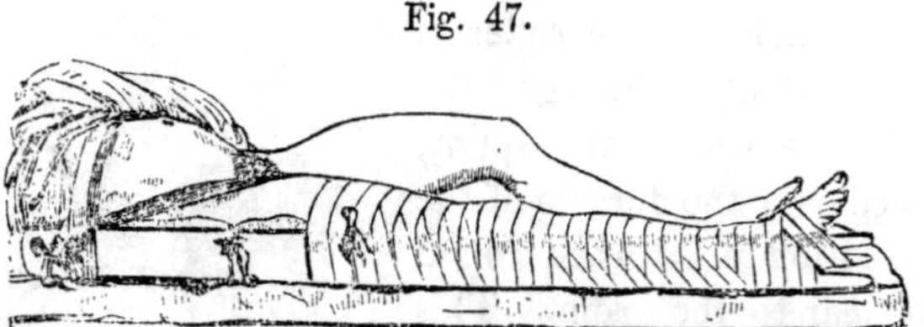

Fracture of the Femur below the Trochanter is exceedingly troublesome to treat, and is liable to be followed by deformity and non-union. The upper fragment is tilted up by the action of the psoas magnus and iliacus internus muscles, whilst the abductor muscles of the thigh draw the lower fragment upwards and inwards.

Treatment.—Probably the best treatment that can be pursued in this case is the double inclined plane, placing the patient as nearly as possible in a sitting posture, to relax the psoas and iliacus muscles; placing the base of a wedge-shaped compress over the upper fragment, and applying over this a splint extending down the front of the thigh near to the knee, and binding down firmly by a roller. The limb is then to be placed over the double inclined plane, the weight of the hips (for they should not press upon the bed) keeping up constant extension upon the limb.

It is rare to see an oblique fracture of the femur cured without more or less shortening.

Fracture of the Condyles of the Femur may extend into the knee-joint. Crepitus in this case is felt upon slight motion of the part; there is also much pain and swelling of the joint.

Treatment.—The knee should be placed in an extended position, and the fragments of bone retained in apposition by splints and bandages. After the first two weeks, if the part be not too painful, passive motion should be frequently communicated to the joint, to prevent anchylosis.

Section 4.—*Fracture of the Patella.*

Fracture of the Patella longitudinally is the result of direct violence.

Treatment.—If motion of the joint be prevented by placing a straight splint behind the knee-joint, and retaining it there by bandage, bony union will readily take place.

Transverse fracture is more common, and is oftener the result of muscular action than direct injury.

Diagnosis is perfectly easy here; for whilst the lower fragment remains in situ, the superior portion is drawn up by the extensor muscles of the leg, and a wide hiatus is perceptible. (See fig. 48.) The patient can flex the leg with facility, but can scarce extend it.

Fig. 48.

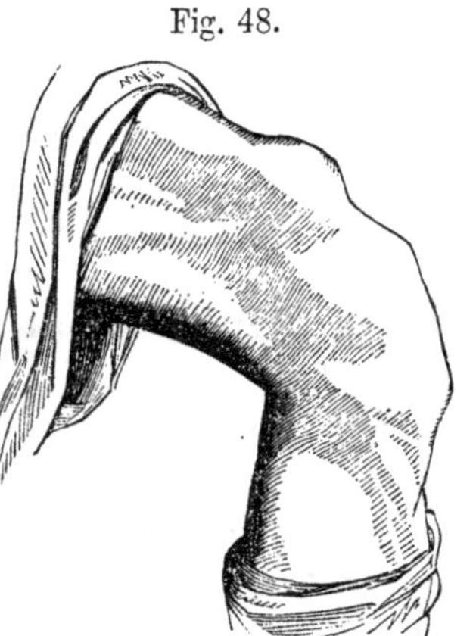

Treatment in this case consists in passing a roller, by circular and reversed turns, from the foot to the lower fragment. The upper fragment is then brought down in contact with the other, and the roller is passed above the patella and around the knee in the form of a figure 8, and with circular turns, in such manner as to retain the fragments in contact. The roller, by circular turns, next confines the muscles of the thigh. A straight splint is now placed behind the joint, fastened by the roller, and the limb kept quiet.

Union is generally ligamentous, but may be bony, if the parts be kept in perfect contact. In six weeks' time, or sooner, passive motion should be communicated to the joint.

Desault's apparatus for fracture of the patella consists in one splint two inches wide, long enough to extend from the tuberosity of the ischium beyond the heel, two rollers, and a compress or strip of bandage the length of the limb. In its application the compress is laid along the front of the leg and thigh;

a roller is applied by circular and reversed turns from the foot to the knee; two longitudinal slits are now cut in the compress at the knee-joint, into which the fingers are passed, the upper fragment is drawn down and coaptated, the bandage passed like a figure 8 around the joint, binding the fragments of the patella together, and then carried up the thigh by circular and reversed turns. The splint is applied to the back part of the limb, and secured by circular turns of the second roller, and the thigh is flexed upon the body, to relax the rectus femoris muscle. Ligamentous union generally results, and the patient is enabled to walk with care in eight or nine weeks, by the aid of a cane.

CHAPTER XVIII.

TREATMENT OF COMPOUND FRACTURE, ETC.

THE treatment in compound fracture differs from that of simple fracture in the following respects:

If the end of a bone protrude, and cannot be returned, it must be sawn off. All detached fragments of bone must be removed at once, and if necessary the wound may be dilated for this purpose. After reduction, the great object is to procure adhesion of the external wound, so as to convert the compound into a simple fracture. In the application of splints and bandages, the wound of the soft parts should be so arranged, if possible, that it may be dressed without disturbing the whole limb. For the accomplishment of this important point, Dr. A. Hays' splint is one of the best that can be employed in compound fracture of the femur, and the same principle may be applied to compound fractures of other bones.

This splint (see fig. 49) is made by taking Physick's Desault's splint, and cutting out a portion of the long splint opposite the wound, sufficiently large to allow free access to it, so as to dress it as often as necessary without disturbing the extension and counter-extension. The two pieces of the splint are united by a strong strip of iron, secured by screws. The iron is made of such shape as to keep the covering of the bed off the wounded part. A thin piece of board should be placed between the portion of the limb dressed and the ends of the splint, so as to give support to the part whence the segment of the splint has been removed.

Fig. 49.

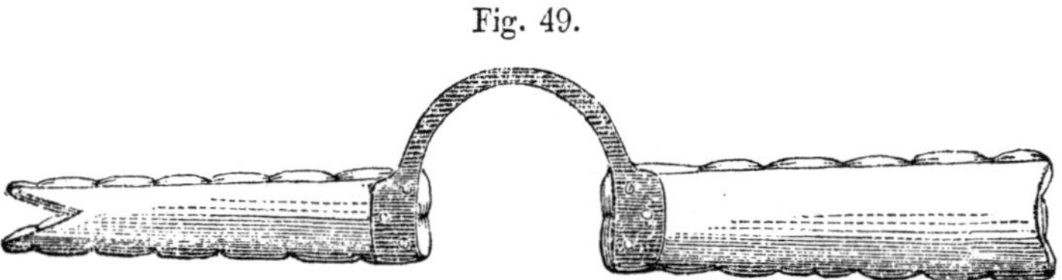

Dr. Hays remarks: "This plan I found to meet my wishes and expectations very fully. The extension and counter-extension being continued, the dressing might be repeated as often as requisite, without in the least disturbing the position of the limb."

If inflammation and swelling supervene, the bandages must be loosened, and a lotion of *arnica* or *calendula* applied to the part; if the pain is very severe and synochal fever be present, *aconite* may be prescribed, or if cerebral symptoms develop themselves, *arnica, bella., cuprum,* or *hyos.* may be indicated; if strangury be present, *acon., nux, cann., canth.,* or some other appropriate medicine must be resorted to—other indications for the treatment have been already alluded to in the chapters upon wounds and abscesses.

The great object in the subsequent treatment is to prevent the lodgment of matter, by sponging and pressing it out carefully at each dressing, and applying compresses to prevent its accumulation, and, if necessary, to make openings for its discharge. In this state of excessive discharge, dry bran, as an absorbent, is one of the best beds the limb can be laid upon. If the patient seem likely to sink under the discharge and irritation, notwithstanding the application of *calendula,* and the administration of *acon.*, *bella.*, *china*, *hepar*, *merc.*, and other medicines that have been mentioned for such conditions, amputation is the last resource.

In all cases where the application of splints and bandages is made, great care should be taken to avoid inordinate pressure. The integuments should be well protected by lint or cotton from the excoriating pressure of splints and bandages. Splints should never be applied over prominent processes of bone, where it can be avoided, as troublesome ulceration is apt to follow.

In fractures of the lower extremities, the use of the limb should be resumed gradually, crutches being employed at first, lest consolidation be not complete, and shortening occur.

The employment of the *starch* or *dextrine* bandage (the immovable apparatus) is very useful in cases of simple fracture and dislocation, after all inflammation and swelling have subsided.

In the application of these bandages a dry roller should first be applied next the skin, the cavities about joints being filled up with cotton or lint, to make the surface as even as possible for the starch or dextrine bandage. Where considerable strength is desirable, pasteboard, soaked in hot water, can be neatly fitted to the part, and the starch or dextrine bandage applied over it.

The *immovable apparatus* possesses the great advantage of never slipping or slackening, and does not require reapplication. In its use, however, care should be employed; as much mischief has sometimes been done by putting it on limbs whilst they were inflamed and still swelling: in these cases gangrene has followed.

Section 1.—*Pseudo Arthrosis, or False Joint.*

False joint may result from fracture of any bone, but it most frequently follows fracture of the shaft of the humerus and neck of the femur. It arises either from premature use of the limb, old age, peculiarities of constitution, disease of the osseous system, or non-contact of the fragments of bone.

In pseudo arthrosis, the fractured extremities of the bone become round, smooth, and generally covered with a cellular or ligamentous substance. In some instances an arthrodial joint is formed, the ends of the bone rolling upon each other.

This unfortunate termination of fracture may in some instances be prevented by the internal administration of *calcarea carb.*, or perhaps the phosphate of lime; the latter has been recommended for such conditions, but there are no indications in the meagre proving of this medicine which would lead the practitioner to have recourse to it. The former, however, is a well known medicine in our school, and in numerous instances has been of essential service in the treatment of fractures and other injuries occurring in individuals of a weak, sickly constitution, and scrofulous diathesis. This medicine improves the tone of all the organs in the body, by giving additional power to the functions of assimilation and sanguification, therefore it is a valuable assistant in the treatment of those cases of fractures in which the reproductive process appears to proceed tardily, from a deficient activity.

Ruta has been employed by homœopathic surgeons to hasten the formation of ossific matter. Dr. Henriques,* in recording the treatment of a case of oblique fracture of the superior third of the femur below the capsule, which occurred spontaneously in an aged patient, of enfeebled and vitiated constitution, who had been liable to periodical attacks of diarrhœa and cerebral congestion, dysuria and cough, remarks concerning the action of *ruta*, that it "appears to possess a decided elective affinity for the periosteum, as well as the osseous system in general; and it was in order to avail myself of the known specific property of *ruta*, that led me to employ it as a means of promoting the process of ossification. I have no doubt in my own mind

* See British Journal of Homœopathy, vol. x. p. 448—a paper entitled Fractures, and their Homœopathic Treatment, by Dr. Henriques.

that it had the desired effect; for if the unfavorable prognosis of the case be compared with the ultimate happy and prompt result obtained, I do not think it possible to deny that the action of this medicine contributed in some degree to the final consolidation of the fracture."

Symphytum has also been recommended for the purpose of inducing ossific deposit.

The general health of the patient should receive attention; if the constitution is worn out by disease, or debilitated either from hereditary taint or more proximate causes, the general tone of the system should be strengthened by the administration of the appropriate medicine; by such means the patient may be restored to perfect health, and the performance of painful operations avoided. However, if, after the patient administration of medicines, the formation of false joint does occur, it may then be advisable to have recourse to friction of the broken surfaces; this in some instances has produced the desired effect.

Dr. Physick's method of treatment has been successful in many instances; it consists in passing a seton between the fractured surfaces. A long, narrow instrument, called "a seton needle," is armed with a skein of silk or other material; the limb is extended, to separate the fragments, and the seton is passed between them, care being taken to avoid all large vessels and nerves. Violent inflammation follows the application of the seton in all cases, and even in ossific structure, the least liable to inflammation of all other textures of the system, this abnormal action occurs, and bony union may take place.

Professor Mütter of this city has performed the following operation to remedy pseudo arthrosis: the fractured extremities of the bones are exposed by incision, and by means of gimblets, perforations are made on each side of the false joint; into these openings ivory pegs are driven, and the wound dressed as usual. Union is said to have followed this operation, and absorption has removed the extraneous matter forced into the bone.

Dr. Smith* of this city objects to all the modes of treating this accident at present in use, as founded on a wrong principle. He objects particularly to the opinion that absolute rest is necessary to the cure, and thinks that this idea is one very fruitful source of failure. His plan is to fix the limb in an iron frame-work, constructed with joints to allow movement of the limbs; by straps and pads to steady the extremities of the broken bones in a proper position. Fixed in this apparatus he allows the patient to use the injured limb, and he asserts that union is effected with much less constitutional and local disturbance, than by means of the various plans of treatment at present used by old school practitioners, viz. violent friction, the seton, resection, Dieffenbach's plan, and others—while at the same time the patient is less exposed to phlebitis and other risks, he escapes the disagreeble monotony of a long confinement.† This method appears to have many advantages over the others, which savor much of the coarse practice of surgeons a century back. If, however, homœopathic medicines are administered, together with the use of the apparatus of Dr. Smith, the results doubtless would be more speedily accomplished than when the apparatus alone is used.‡

Resection has also been practised, but generally it is a last resource, for it should be remembered that cutting down to the extremities of the bone and *scraping* or removing portions of them, at once converts the simple to a compound fracture.

---

* American Quarterly Journal of Medical Sciences, January, 1855.

† See Rankin's Abstract, vol. xi., July, 1855.

‡ Dr. Smith's plan has been tried in several cases with these results:

	Cases.	*Cured.*	*Relieved.*	*Failed, but able to walk.*
False joint in the femur,	4	3	0	1
" " leg bones,	8	7	0	1
" " humerus,	2	0	2	0
	—	—	—	—
Total,	14	10	2	2

Section 2.—Cracked Bones or Incomplete Fracture.

It sometime happens that a bone is cracked when the force applied has not been sufficient to produce an entire separation, but only adequate to break the continuity of some of its fibres, whilst others remain entire. This injury is generally found where there are two bones, as in the leg or fore-arm, when the uninjured bone supports that which is partially broken. It is probable that it occurs occasionally in both bones, although the occurrence is rare.

Diagnosis.—Diagnosis is more difficult when the bone is merely cracked, than when the solution of continuity is complete; still, with care, it may recognized.

The patient is unable to use the limb without considerable pain; he has also a sense of pricking about the seat of injury, and when the bone is closely examined, there may be a slight deviation from the direct line of the bone, but there is no crepitus; yet, when the above signs follow a severe blow or fall upon the part, and the pain and inability to use the limb freely, exist after the effects of the contusion have subsided, it is probable there is a solution of continuity in some of the fibres of the bone. In other words, the bone is cracked, but not entirely broken.

Treatment.—The treatment for the repair of this injury is the same as if the bone were broken into two fragments. It is not necessary, however, to keep the apparatus quite as long applied as in complete fracture.

CHAPTER XIX.

DISLOCATIONS.

The term dislocation, or luxation, is used to indicate the separation of articular surfaces from each other, either by accident or disease. The former cause is the most frequent, but the latter is by no means the least formidable, for in such cases it is not only the displacement that the surgeon must encounter, but the disease of which this displacement is a feature.

The separation of articular surfaces, when caused by external violence, may be partial or complete. In the one instance the cartilages may not be entirely severed, while in the other there may be no contact whatsoever. The luxations of the knee and hip are used by Mr. Fergusson* as illustrative of these different forms of dislocation. He writes—"The articular surfaces of the knee-joint are so extensive that it rarely happens that the tibia is completely parted from the femur, whereas in the hip-joint, the articular cartilages are invariably thrown out of contact, and the luxation is termed complete. The practical value of such a distinction is, that the lesser degree of separation implies a proportionally small amount of injury.

"It is impossible for any displacement of the articular ends of bone to occur, without extension and perhaps laceration of the tissues connected with them; when the separation is very palpable, the synovial membrane must be torn more or less open, and when this tissue is exposed to the air the dislocation is termed *compound;* when the parts are still covered, the luxation is denominated *simple.*

A dislocation is said to be *complicated* when, beside the injury inflicted upon the parts composing the articulation, the neighboring tissues or organs are involved.

Luxations are generally occasioned by great violence, but

* Practical Surgery.

diseases and peculiarities of constitution render some individuals more susceptible to receipt of such injuries; among these may be noticed, peculiar conformation of bone, diseases of the osseous system, and laxity of a joint.

A simple dislocation may be regarded in many respects as a severe contused or lacerated wound, having, however, a strong disposition to heal rapidly; but if the injury be compound, or, in other words, if the injured joint be exposed to the air, then inflammation is almost the inevitable result, and suppuration and ulceration, as consequences thereof, may be expected; but such untoward events need not follow necessarily, for there are occasional dislocations of such joints as the knee and shoulder, in which such unfortunate complications are entirely wanting.

It should always be remembered that so long as the displaced extremity of the bone is allowed to remain in its unnatural condition, that its action is similar to that created by any extraneous matter, and therefore if the luxation be reduced in a short time after the injury has been received, a considerable amount of inflammation will be prevented.

Occasionally dislocation is complicated with fracture: the fibula is generally broken in dislocation of the tibia; in dislocation of the hip the acetabulum may be either chipped or broken through, or in dislocation of the elbow the coronoid process of the ulna may be detached.

The *treatment* of dislocation consists principally in *reduction*, and this cannot be attempted too soon—it consists* by *extension* to move the bone from its abnormal position, and to bring it on a plane with the articulating surface from which it has been forced; *counter-extension*, to steady the latter part, and to admit of extension being satisfactorily effected; and *coaptation*, to replace the surfaces in apposition. If the patient be seen immediately after infliction of the injury, still faint, with his frame prostrate and relaxed, and incapable by effort of throwing any part of his muscular system into strong resisting reaction—reduction may be expected to prove comparatively

---

* See Miller's Principles, p. 132.

easy. But when hours and days have passed, the obstacles to reduction are ever on the increase. The muscles, which at first are spasmodically rigid, by degrees adapt themselves to their new position; the track from the original articulating surface, through the lacerated ligamentous apparatus, is becoming more and more occupied with plastic exudation; and the displaced extremity of the bone is busy accommodating itself to the parts with which it is now in contact. Sometimes the head of the bone merely projects through a narrow fissure of the capsule, and this, tightly embracing the bone's neck, becomes agglutinated thereto by plastic exudation, constituting a most serious obstacle to replacement.

If only a few hours or days have elapsed, the extension may be intrusted to assistants, but when a considerable period of time has passed, mechanical aid must be employed; extension being accomplished by ropes and pulleys, by which means a less degree of force may succeed when applied with steadiness and precision. A sudden pull or jerk may often reduce a recent dislocation, but never can accomplish this end if the injury have been allowed to remain without treatment for a considerable time.

The method of extension by pulley is as follows:

The patient usually being in a recumbent position, a broad belt is passed under the perineum, if the dislocation is of the lower extremities: or over the chest if the superior limbs are the seat of the injury—this belt is fixed to some stationary point. This secures a fixed position to the patient while counter-extension is being exerted; a damp towel is then wrapped round the affected limb, to prevent excoriation from the bandage which is afterwards applied, and secured by what is termed a *clove-hitch*, (see fig. 56,) the advantage of which is, that it cannot be tightened by the force exerted by the pulleys to which it is attached. The points of application of the bands will be mentioned in the succeeding chapters.

There is some risk, however, to be encountered when using the pulleys to reduce luxations; a muscle may be ruptured; an artery or vein may be lacerated, and extremely serious complications ensue. Therefore, there must be great caution observed when attacking an affected limb with mechanical force.

But there are powerful auxiliary means, which, if called to the assistance of the surgeon, will not only render the condition of the patient similar to that which is noticed immediately after the receipt of the injury, when the opportunity is so favorable for reduction; but will relax every voluntary muscle in the system as completely as in death, rendering these tissues more thoroughly inert than by any other agent; and, at the same time exempting the patient from considerable pain, which otherwise would be the necessary attendant of reduction. Such a condition is effected by allowing the patient to inhale an anæsthetic agent until its full effect is produced upon the system; by such means the use of hot baths is dispensed with; antimonials, in repeated doses, that formerly were administered until the already suffering patient was nauseated to a most distressing degree, are not needed; tobacco in fume, by chewing, or in the form of enema, is either forgotten or intentionally thrust aside; and for an expenditure of the precious fluid *ad deliquium animi*, is substituted a simple and effectual means, which, if skilfully and judiciously employed, is destitute of danger.

Two fluids are employed to produce anæsthesia, the oxide of ethyl, or ether, commonly called sulphuric ether; and chloroform, chloroformyle, or the perchloride of formyle.

Mr. Horace Wells, a dentist of Hartford, Connecticut, in 1844, when under the influence of the nitrous oxide, had a tooth extracted without experiencing pain. He was informed that the inhalation of sulphuric ether would induce a similar state of insensibility, the truth of which information he confirmed by trials upon his patients. To this gentleman, therefore, and not to Dr. C. T. Jackson, or Dr. Morton, as is generally supposed, is due the credit of introducing sulphuric ether as an anæsthetic agent to the notice of the public.

The ether used for inhalation should be highly rectified; it should be deprived of its acid and alcoholic properties by washing; and its specific gravity should be about one half more than that of distilled water. The following method for its application is extracted from the work of J. F. B. Flagg, M. D.*

"No apparatus should be used as an *inhaler* which does not amply provide for the admission of atmospheric air, or that would render the breathing difficult. A good sponge, well and frequently saturated with ether, is probably the best and simplest method of administering it.†

"The pulse should always be consulted. Its general tendency is upward, or quickened; when this takes place very rapidly, it is proper to cease giving the ether for a few inspirations, or until reaction takes place, when a repetition of the ether will not unfrequently promote its downward tendency. Under ordinary circumstances, I consider it safe to increase a pulse to 160 (one hundred and sixty) beats in the minute; or to suffer it to decrease to 50 (fifty); but, of course, there must be exceptions to this rule, too obvious to need particularizing.

"The expression of the countenance and temperature of the head should be observed. When the face becomes suddenly turgid, cold water should be applied to the forehead and temples, suffering the patient to breathe ammonia, or concentrated vinegar, allowing at the same time plenty of fresh air, and directing full and rapid inspirations. The variation of the temperature of the head is best detected by the habit of taking the pulse from the temporal artery.

"The ether should always be brought gradually to the mouth of the patient; by so doing all irritation of the larynx and lungs is avoided. Direct to take natural and regular inspirations, to avoid swallowing the vapor, and should the breathing become stertorous, or in any way distressing, desist from its use until the natural breathing is restored.

"Never suffer yourself to be thrown off your guard by any demonstration on the part of the patient. It is not unfrequent

* Ether and Chloroform, their Employment in Surgery, Dentistry, Midwifery, Therapeutics, &c., by J. F. B. Flagg, M. D., Surgeon Dentist. Philadelphia, 1851.

† Before dipping the sponge into the ether, wet it with warm water, then compress it, and leave it slightly damp.

that a loud outcry may be induced, a distressing groan or other manifestations of inconvenience or pain, which invariably pass off, and the strongest assurances are given by the patient, if aware of this fact, that he knows of no particular reason for such conduct.

"It will be found, after inhaling for a minute or two, if no effect is produced, that by allowing the patient to take one breath of atmospheric air, considerable dizziness is felt; as a general thing, a very few inhalations after this are sufficient; and if the patient should resist, it is best not to meet that resistance by any physical force, but by a firm, yet kind treatment.

"If ether should produce much prostration (which it is apt to do when the atmosphere is least charged with oxygen) it is well to recommend self-exertion, as walking about, &c.; but if the desire to sleep is too strong to be resisted, entertain no fear from that indulgence, as the patient will soon awake refreshed.

"After inhaling for a certain period, should any spasmodic action occur to retard breathing, sprinkle suddenly a little cold water upon the face; or a pretty active slap between the shoulders will be sufficient to relieve any obstacle in this respect. The knife should not be used until the patient is brought completely under its influence; and fresh ether and fresh air be alternately inhaled in such proportions as the case may require to keep the patient perfectly passive. For an operation requiring ten minutes as much as six ounces may be necessary."

The other anæsthetic agent, chloroform or perchloride of formyle, although known as a chemical product so far back as 1831, and occasionally used in minute doses as an antispasmodic, was unknown as an anæsthetic agent till the year 1847, when Professor Simpson, of Edinburgh, after experimenting upon himself and some friends, announced its power of producing a state of insensibility to pain.

Chloroform, when pure, emits a pleasant and fragrant odor, has a sweetish taste, evaporates rapidly, and is dense and colorless.

Its mode of exhibition is as follows: Moisten well, but do

not saturate, a piece of lint or sponge, a glove, or what answers better, and is always at hand, a cambric or muslin handkerchief with the fluid; the handkerchief should be made to assume the form of a cone, or cup. Its concavity is then brought gradually to the face of the patient, not too slowly, lest too much of the fluid should evaporate, and the mouth and nostrils be lightly covered, avoiding all compression of the latter, lest a free access of the vapor into the air vessels should be impeded. Its entrance is likewise facilitated by laying the patient on his back; the vapor of chloroform having a specific gravity much heavier than atmospheric air.

The quantity required varies in different individuals; an average may be set down as from one to three drachms. The purer the article used, the more promptly will it produce the desired effect. When it becomes necessary to remove the handkerchief, for the purpose of moistening it again, its reapplication should be quick. Any effort made by the patient to push aside the handkerchief must be resisted; these efforts are made just before the period of insensibility. That the chloroform has acted favorably is known by an increased loudness of respiration. During the application the patient's attention must not be diverted by the conversation or movement of persons around; to prevent vomiting, it should not be used soon after a meal; if excitement or much muscular action be produced, the handkerchief must be more closely applied and the dose renewed.

Its use is contra-indicated in persons who have a tendency to congestion of the brain, or disease of the heart—likewise in operations upon the nose and mouth; in these latter cases the blood readily finds an entrance into the lungs, owing to the patient's entire inability either to swallow or expel by coughing; hence suffocation must certainly take place.

Mr. Syme,* in a lecture upon chloroform, thus writes:

"So far as I can ascertain, from what I have heard and read upon the subject, there are important differences between the mode of administration of chloroform here (Edinburgh) and in

* London Lancet, March, 1855, p. 200.

London. It appears that here it is given according to principle, there according to rule. There great attention is paid to the number of drachms or minims employed; here we are entirely regardless of the amount used, and are guided only by the symptoms of the patient. The points that we consider of the greatest importance in the administration of chloroform are, first, a free admixture of air with the vapor of the chloroform. . . . Secondly, if this is attended to, the more rapidly the chloroform is given the better, till the effect is produced; and hence we do not stint the quantity of the chloroform. Then—and this is a most important point—we are guided as to the effect, not by the circulation, but entirely by the respiration; you never see anybody here with his finger on the pulse while chloroform is given. So soon as breathing becomes stertorous we cease the administration. Attention to the tongue is another point which we find of great consequence. When respiration becomes difficult, or ceases, we open the mouth, seize the tip of the tongue with artery forceps, and pull it well forward; and there can be little doubt but that death would have occurred in some cases if it had not been for the use of this expedient. We also always give chloroform in the horizontal position, and take care that there is no article of clothing constricting the neck."

It is confidently asserted that chloroform does not increase a susceptibility to erysipelas after surgical operations, and although it may in some instances irritate the air passages, it occasions no permanent ill effects; and that no apprehensions need be entertained of its aggravating morbid sensibility in hysterical females.

The surgeons of the United States, however, in their operations, almost universally resort to the inhalation of ether—European surgeons to chloroform.

Although habit, or prejudice, or both, may operate in the selection of one or other of these powerful agents, an impartial review of the whole subject leads to a conclusion favorable to the sulphuric ether. It possesses all the desirable properties of chloroform, without subjecting patients to ill consequences, and danger of death itself, which well attested testimony proves has been produced by the latter.*

As soon as the anæsthesia is complete, the luxation should be reduced, and the part immediately washed with a solution of *arnica,* and the same medicine should be administered internally; or cloths saturated with the solution should be laid on the site of the injury. If the inflammatory symptoms are violent, and there be fever, &c., *aconite* may be alternated with the *arnica,* and administered every one, two, or three hours. If the patient is extremely restless at night, &c., *cham.* should be prescribed. Perfect rest for the first few days must be enjoined, after which, when pain and swelling have subsided, motion may be gradually and gently essayed. To restore the part more speedily to its natural strength and flexibility, *caust.*, *rhus,* or *petrol.* will be demanded, the selection depending upon the group of symptoms which may present.

Section 1.—*Dislocation of the Jaw.*

Dislocation of the jaw is produced by direct violence upon the chin, or by muscular action in yawning, laughing, etc., and can only take place forwards. It may be complete or partial, as one or both condyles are dislocated.

Diagnosis.—The condyles rest in front of the base of the zygomatic process (see fig. 50): the mouth cannot be shut, the chin is depressed, the condyloid space is vacant, and a prominence may be felt beneath the zygomatic process; articulation is indistinct and accompanied with pain.

Treatment.—This consists in placing the thumbs on the molar teeth, and the fingers beneath the chin and base of the jaw; firm pressure is then made downwards by the thumbs,

---

* Vide "Some Account of the First Use of Sulphuric Ether by Inhalation in Surgical Practice." Read before the Boston Society for Medical Improvement, April 12th, 1847, by George Hayward, M. D.

Fig. 50.

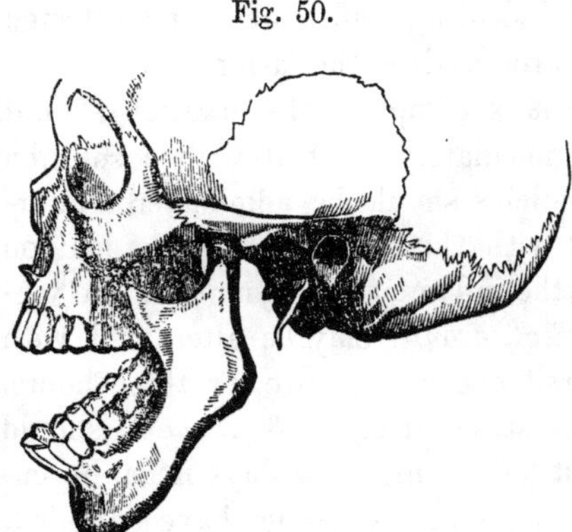

whilst the chin is elevated by the fingers; the moment the bone is slipping into place, the thumbs are slipped off the teeth upon the gums, or they may be protected by a pair of thick gloves. If there be difficulty in reducing both condyles at the same time, one should be reduced before the other is attempted; this plan rarely fails.

In those persons disposed to spontaneous dislocation of the jaw from gaping, &c., the recurrence of the displacement may very probably be prevented by the exhibition of a dose of *staphys.*, a few globules of the 6th attenuation every fourth day for three months. Should this medicine not accomplish the desired object, *rhus-tox.*, from its known specific action upon ligamentous tissue, might be tried, in like manner. A successful preventive treatment of this accident is much to be desired; its frequent repetition in some individuals, especially females, is a source of considerable annoyance as well as pain.

Section 2.—Dislocation of the Clavicle, Ribs and Vertebra.

Dislocation of the clavicle may occur at either extremity. The sternal end may be displaced *forwards* or *backwards:* the former is the more common. The *scapular articulation* may be displaced *upwards*, gliding over the acromion process.

Diagnosis is easy in these cases. In luxation of the sternal end forwards (Fig. 51) the dislodged extremity is plainly seen and felt in front of the sternum, whilst the backward displacement leaves a hollow at the superior edge of the sternum. There is likewise a tumor formed by the end of the bone, which may be felt at the base of the neck.

Fig. 51.

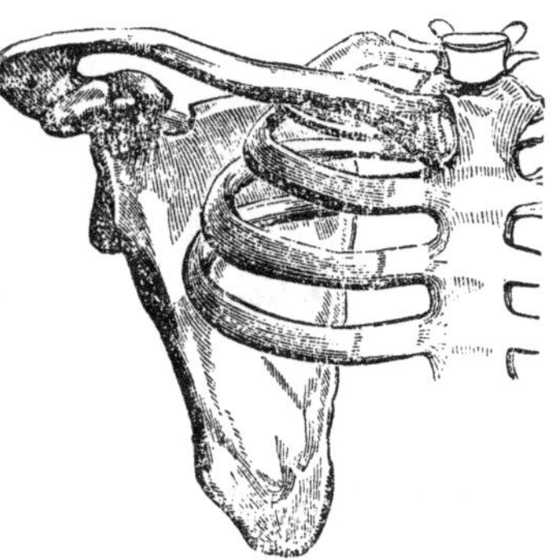

In luxation of the *scapular extremity* (Fig. 52) the shoulder is depressed, and the end of the clavicle may be felt above the acromion process.

In both these varieties the deformity disappears upon elevating and carrying the shoulder outwards and backwards.

The *treatment* of this injury is effected by carrying the shoulder upwards and outwards, pressing, at the same time, the clavicle into its articulation, and retaining it in its proper position by means of the apparatus for fractured clavicle. As the ligaments unite slowly in dislocation of the acromion extremity, it is necessary to keep the limb in the dressings much longer than would be done in fracture.

Fig. 52.

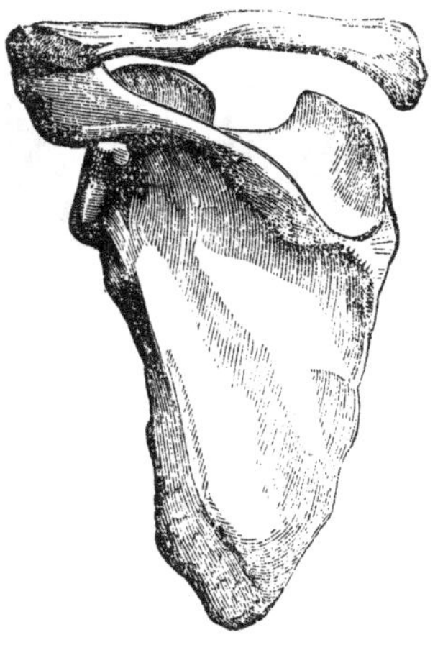

Dislocation of the Sternal Extremities of the Ribs from their cartilages sometimes occurs, and may be recognized by an unnatural protuberance.

Treatment.—These cases are managed by placing a compress upon the extremity of the rib, and passing a roller around the chest, to secure the compress, and control in a measure the action of the muscles.

Dislocation of the Vertebræ can hardly occur without fracture, and is the result of such violence that other symptoms demand our attention. Absolute rest is the most important object of treatment.

CHAPTER XX.

DISLOCATIONS OF THE UPPER EXTREMITIES.

Section 1.—*Dislocations of the Fingers.*

Dislocation of the fingers takes place sometimes at the metacarpal articulation, though generally between the first and second phalanges. The nature of the injury is evident, (Fig. 53,) and may be reduced by extension, made by the hand alone, by a bandage or tape applied by a clove-hitch.

Fig 53.

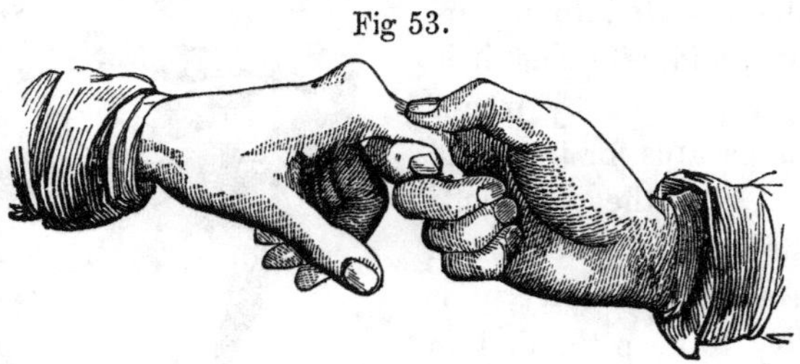

Dislocation of the Thumb backwards on the dorsum of the metacarpal bone (Fig. 54) is of frequent occurrence.

Fig. 54.

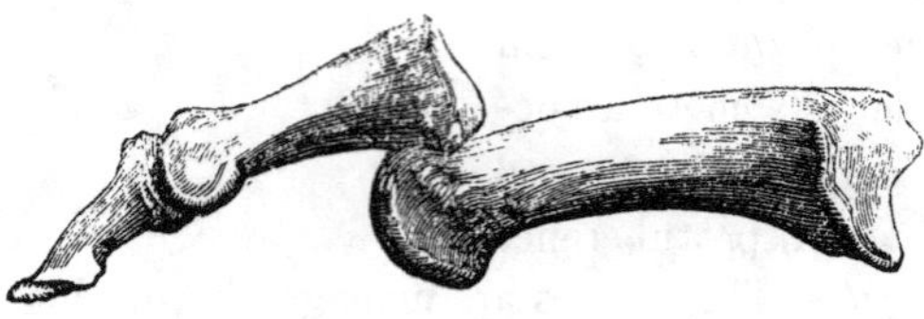

It sometimes takes place in the opposite direction. (Fig. 55.)

Fig. 55.

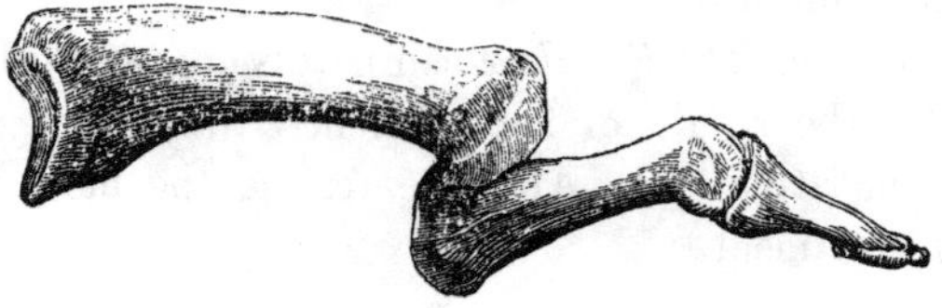

The accident is easily recognized, but with more difficulty remedied.

Treatment.—A clove-hitch (Fig. 56) should be placed upon the first phalanx, and extension employed for some time. Forcible and steady flexion is made towards the palm of the hand, and firm pressure applied by the thumb of the surgeon at the same time upon the head of the bone. By these means the reduction is usually accomplished. This luxation is sometimes so unyielding as to call for the subcutaneous section of one or both lateral ligaments before the deformity can be removed.

Fig. 56.

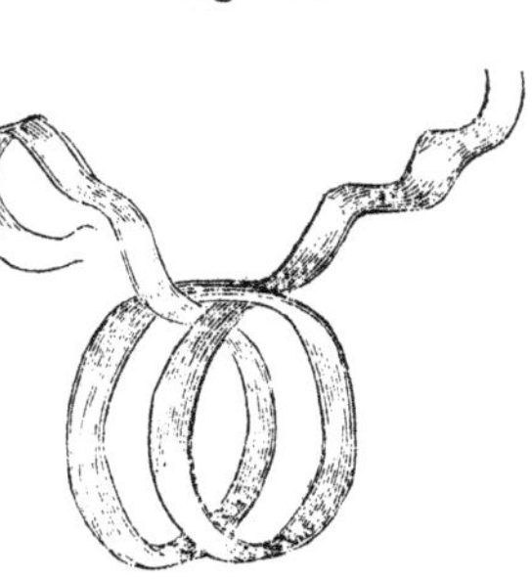

Before division of the ligaments is made, the following mode of action should be resorted to in difficult cases, and it will generally succeed; for one of the greatest obstructions to the reduction is the lapping of the extremities of the bones, which from their form become completely locked. Soak the hand in warm water; apply a piece of wet leather around the thumb, and over this a clove-hitch of strong tape. In dislocation upwards, a loop of tape embraces the upper end of the phalanx, and is drawn with great force, by an assistant, perpendicularly upwards. Another loop of tape embraces the lower end of the metacarpal bone, and is drawn downwards by another assistant. Whilst the extremities of the bones are by these means unlocked, the surgeon draws the thumb, by the clove-hitch, towards the palm of the hand, and the bone usually slips into its normal position.

The *metacarpal bones* are, perhaps, never luxated, except by a gun-shot wound or some similar violence, the effects of which are generally more serious than the dislocation.

The *carpal bones* are so firmly connected to each other by short ligaments, and by a ball and socket joint, as to be scarcely susceptible of luxation. Instances, however, are now and then met with of displacement of the os magnum and os cuneiforme, either from violence or from extreme relaxation of their ligaments.

To restore a displaced os magnum or cuneiforme will often be found very difficult, and to retain it fixed in its natural situation still more so, especially when the luxation is occasioned by relaxation of the ligaments. Well directed pressure, and an appropriate bandage, are the only remedies.

Section 2.—Dislocation of the Fore-arm.

Dislocation of the Elbow Joint may occur in five directions, although from an examination of the structure of the joint it might be supposed that luxation could scarcely happen in any direction. Both bones may be dislocated backwards; both dislocated laterally; the ulna dislocated backwards, the radius dislocated forwards; and, lastly, the *radius* may be dislocated *backwards*. Luxation of *both bones backwards*, however, is the most frequent.

Diagnosis.—In displacement of *both bones backwards*, there is a projection at the posterior part of the joint; on each side of the olecranon process there is a depression; the lower extremity of the humerus is felt at the fore part of the elbow joint, as a hard tumor, the hand and fore-arm are fixed in supination, (see fig. 57,) and cannot be entirely pronated, whilst flexion of the joint can scarcely be accomplished.

Treatment for this injury is as follows: Seating the patient in a chair, the surgeon places his knee in the bend of the arm, taking hold of the wrist, bends the limb, at the same time pressing on the radius and ulna with his knee, so as to separate them from the humerus, and throw the coronoid process from the posterior fossa of this bone. Whilst the pressure is kept up by the knee, the fore-arm is slowly and forcibly bent upon the arm, and the bones slip into their sockets.

Fig. 57.

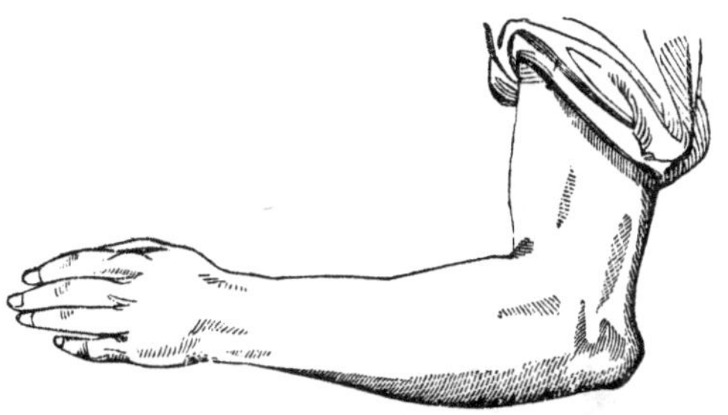

This reduction may be accomplished also by bending the arm forcibly, yet gradually, around a bed-post, or whilst the patient is seated in an arm-chair, passing the arm through the opening in the back or side, thus fixing the body and limb, and reducing the luxation by forcibly bending the fore-arm, with one hand placed upon the olecranon process to lift the bones into their places. The reduction having been accomplished, the fore-arm must be placed in a sling, the elbow bent at an obtuse angle, and supported with a splint.

Diagnosis in lateral dislocation of both bones, backwards and outwards, (Fig. 58,) is arrived at by the greater projection of the ulna backwards than in the former case, and the coronoid process rests upon the back of the external condyle of the humerus. The radius forms a tumor on the outer side and behind the external condyle, and a depression is seen above the head of the bone. If the hand be rotated, the head of the radius is distinctly felt to move.

In dislocation of both bones, *backwards* and *inwards,* (Fig. 59,) the same posterior projection of the elbow exists. The ulna rests behind the internal condyle, whilst the head of the radius occupies the posterior fossa of the humerus, the external condyle of the humerus forming a large tumor on the outer side of the elbow.

Treatment is the same as in the former case.

Dislocation of the ulna backwards is recognized by the contortion of the hand and fore-arm inwards. The olecranon process can be felt, as it projects behind the humerus. The

Fig. 58. Fig. 59.

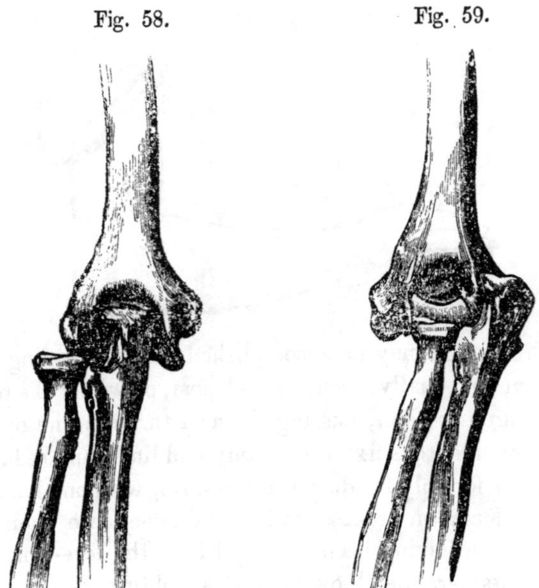

fore-arm cannot be extended, nor even flexed to more than a right angle.

Diagnosis in this accident is sometimes difficult, but its distinguishing features are the contortion of the hand and fore-arm, and the projection of the olecranon process backwards.

Treatment in this case is more easily effected than where both bones are dislocated. Bend the arm over the knee, grasp the wrist, draw the fore-arm downwards, and the bone slips into its socket.

Dislocation of the radius forwards.—(See Fig. 60.)—In this accident the head of the radius occupies the hollow above the external condyle of the humerus.

Diagnosis.—The fore-arm is slightly bent, but cannot be flexed to a right angle, nor completely extended. When the fore-arm is quickly flexed, there is a sudden check, and one bone is distinctly felt to strike against the other. The hand is pronated. If the thumb of the surgeon be pressed in front of and just inside the external condyle of the os humerus, the head of the radius may be felt; and by rotating the hand the head of the bone rolls also. This last sign, and the sudden check in bending the elbow, distinguish this accident from any other.

Treatment of this accident is effected by extension from the wrist, supinating the hand at the same time, and with the thumb pressing down the head of the radius, which slips into its place. The fore-arm is placed in a sling.

Dislocation of the radius backwards (Fig. 61) may be recognized by feeling the head of the bone, (which makes a

Fig. 60. Fig. 61.

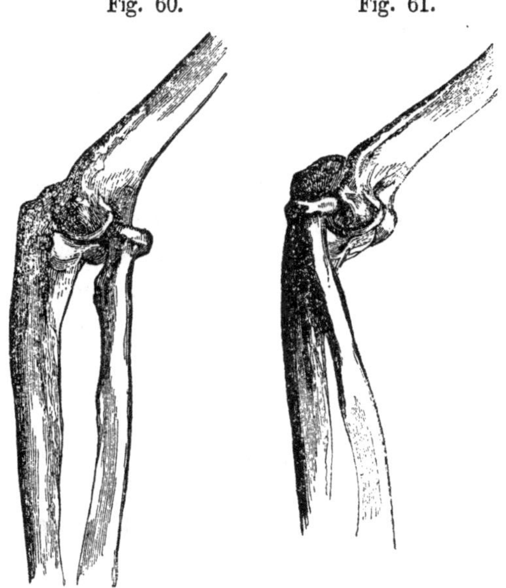

prominence on the back of the external condyle,) and the partial loss of the movement of the joint.

Its *reduction* and *treatment* are the same as in the former case.

Dislocation of the radius and ulna at the wrist may take place *backwards* and *forwards*.

Diagnosis.—In luxation of both bones backwards, there is a tumor upon the fore and back part of the wrist (Fig. 62); the hand is bent back. The extremities of the radius and ulna can

Fig. 62.

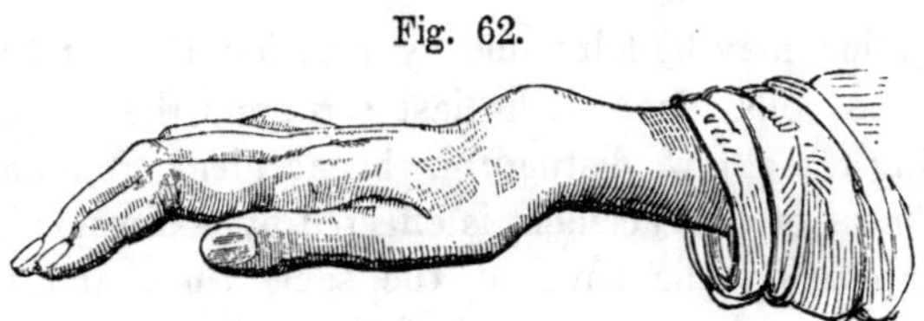

be felt one one side, and the carpus on the other, if the injured part be examined soon after the accident has occurred. In dislocation forwards, the relation of the bones to each other is altered. Sprains about the wrist, from severe falls, sometimes assume the appearance of dislocation of the bones, but may be distinguished from it by there being but one swelling in sprain, and that having come on gradually; also the relative position of the styloid processes of the radius and ulna with the carpus is unaltered in sprains.

Treatment.—Reduction is effected with facility in these cases, by making extension upon the injured hand whilst the fore-arm is fixed; the bones are then easily forced into place. The wrist and fore-arm are to be placed in splints and slung.

Dislocation of the radius at the wrist may take place *anteriorly*, *posteriorly*, and *laterally*. The signs and treatment of these are so like the former case, that the same rules are applicable.

Dislocation of the ulna from the radius at the wrist occurs oftener than the last mentioned. It is easily recognized by the altered position of the styloid process, the projection of the ulna above the level of the os cuneiforme, and the twisting of the hand.

Treatment in this case consists in replacing the end of the ulna by extension and direct pressure on the end of the bone, confining it there by means of splints on the back and fore part of the wrist and fore-arm, and placing a compress upon the end of the bone, (which has a tendency to displacement, on account of the rupture of the ligament.) A roller is then applied to retain the compress and splints.

Section 3.—Dislocation of the Humerus.

Dislocation of the humerus from the glenoid cavity is usually the result of indirect force. The head of the humerus may be dislocated in three directions; *downwards,* into the axilla, which is the most frequent; *forwards,* beneath the pectoral muscle; *backwards,* on the dorsum of the scapula. *Subluxation* inwards on the coracoid process is sometimes met with.

Fig. 63.

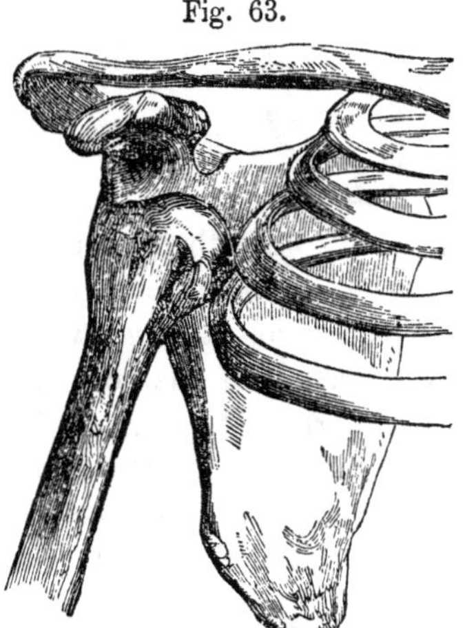

Diagnosis.—In dislocation *downwards* (Fig. 63,) there is a hollow beneath the acromion; the roundness of the shoulder is lost; the arm is somewhat lengthened; the elbow stands off from the side; the patient usually supports the fore-arm of the injured limb with the other hand, to prevent its head pressing painfully upon the axillary nerves. By carrying the elbow from the body the head of the humerus can be distinctly felt in the axilla; the patient cannot raise the arm to his head; the power of rotation is lost, but the motion of the limb backwards and forwards, as it hangs by the side, is still retained. On moving the limb, a slight crepitus will sometimes be felt. From the effusion of synovia and serum into the cellular tissues, this crepitation is not like the grating that fracture produces, and even disappears by continuance of the motion. Added to these signs is a change in the axis of the arm; a straight line, drawn from the elbow to the head of the bone, leads to the axilla, instead of the glenoid cavity of the scapula.

In dislocation *forwards* (Fig. 64) the nature of the accident is evident. There is depression beneath the acromion; the head of the humerus forms a tumor below the clavicle,

Fig. 64. Fig. 65.

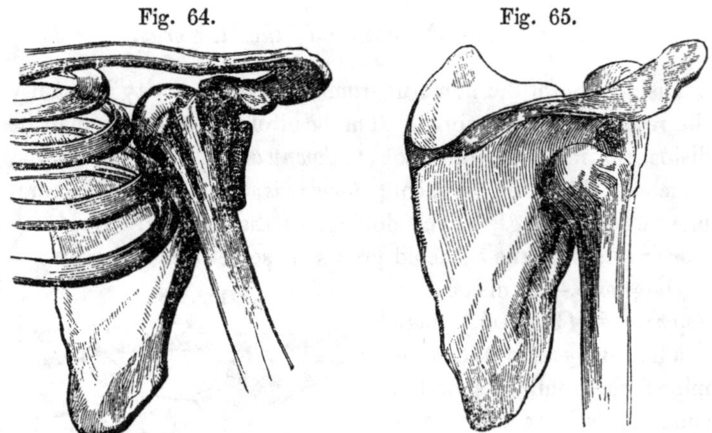

which rolls beneath the touch as the arm is rotated; the limb is shortened, and carried backwards and outwards.

In dislocation *backwards* (Fig. 65) there is a protuberance on the dorsum of the scapula, below the spine, which rotates with the arm; the arm and fore-arm are approximated to, and carried across the chest. To these are added the other signs common to luxation of this joint.

Treatment of these dislocations is various. The reduction of dislocation *downwards* is effected by putting the patient on his back. A ball is placed in the axilla between the pectoralis major and latissimus dorsi muscles; the surgeon's heel is placed upon the ball, (Fig. 66,) whilst he takes hold of the wrist,

Fig. 66.

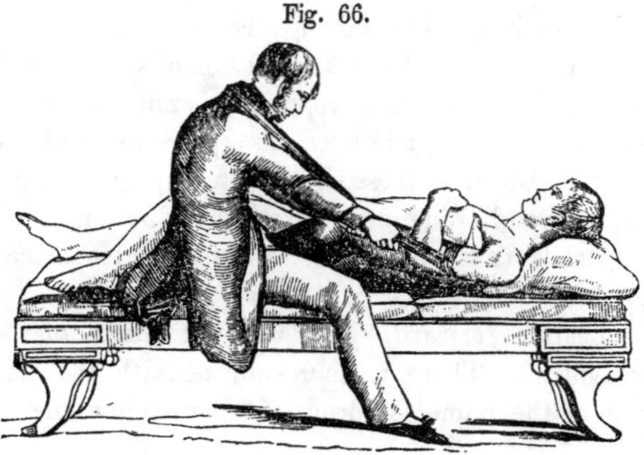

and, by gradual and steady force, pushes the head of the bone into the glenoid cavity. If this power do not prove sufficient, a wet roller should be passed round the arm, above the elbow, and an extending band tied over it, this the surgeon either passes around his own shoulders, or allows several men to draw steadily upon it until the deformity is removed. If the foregoing means fail, the patient must be seated in a chair, and the scapula fixed by a bandage, which allows the arm to pass through it, setting firmly against the axilla and the acromion process, two men taking hold of this band, and two hold of the one already applied to the elbow, steady strain is brought upon the limb for some minutes, the surgeon places his foot upon the chair (see fig. 67) and his knee in the axilla of the patient; he should now raise the knee by raising the foot, at the

Fig. 67.

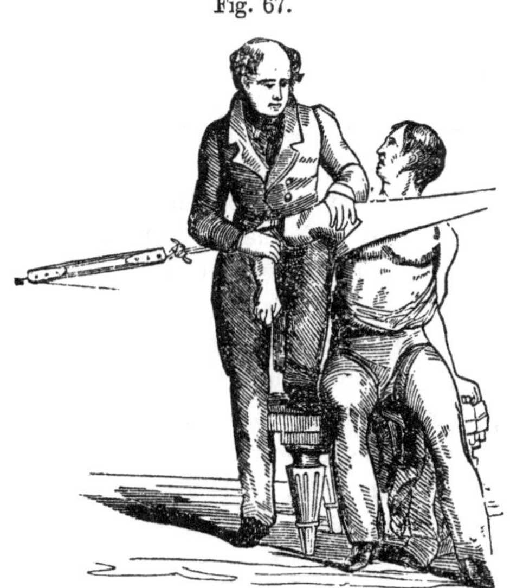

same time he presses the acromion downwards and inwards with his hand. The head of the bone usually slips into the glenoid cavity with a snapping noise. Sometimes these means fail for want of power, and then pulleys must be applied to the bands, instead of men. (Fig. 68.) When the pulleys are employed,

Fig. 68.

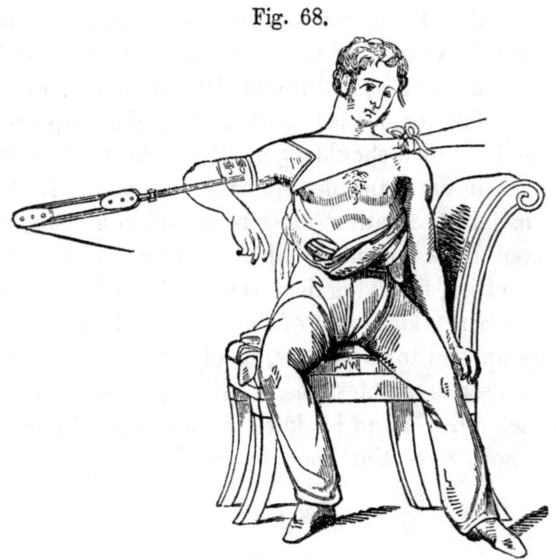

advantage may be derived from rotating the arm by using the fore-arm as a lever; the head of the bone usually slipping into the socket without noise.

An easy method of reducing luxations in old subjects, delicate females, and those of relaxed habits, is by seating the patient upon a chair, the surgeon placing his knee in the axilla and his foot upon the chair; taking hold of the elbow of the injured arm, he presses with his hand upon the acromion, and thus converts the arm into a lever and the knee into a fulcrum. By engaging the patient in conversation, to attract his mind from the injury, he bears down upon the elbow, fixing the scapula, and raising the knee at the same time, the head of the bone slips into the glenoid cavity, and the luxation is reduced. Sometimes, even in muscular subjects, this plan succeeds. The fore-arm should then be placed in a sling and the joint kept quiet.

Sir Astley Cooper advises, as a general rule, that the reduction of dislocations of this joint ought not to be attempted after they have existed twelve weeks.

Mr. White's mode of reducing this dislocation, and practised by M. Malgaigne, is as follows: Lay the patient upon his back, and raising the arm perpendicularly by the side of his head, so as to relax the supra-spinatus muscle, the surgeon seizes the elbow with one hand, whilst with the other he presses upon the acromion process, to fix the scapula; and the head of the humerus is drawn directly upwards into the glenoid cavity.

Dislocation *forwards* and *backwards* is reduced by the same means and management as dislocation *downwards*.

CHAPTER XXI.

DISLOCATIONS OF THE LOWER EXTREMITIES.

Section 1.—*Dislocation of the Pelvis.*

Dislocation of the pelvis is the result of great violence.

The *os innominatum* has been displaced upwards, separated from the sacrum at the sacro-iliac junction.

Diagnosis.—In this case the limb of the affected side is shortened and powerless, but the signs of dislocation and fracture of the thigh-bone are absent, and the limbs, when measured from the anterior superior spinous processes of the ilia, are found to be of the same length. The anterior superior spinous process, and the crest of the ilium of the injured side, are on a higher level than those of the opposite side, and some difficulty may be experienced in evacuating the bladder.

Separation of the symphysis pubis occurs occasionally from a direct blow, or from difficult labor.

Treatment.—Efforts may be made, in both cases, to adjust the displaced bones, and the pelvis should be kept quiet by a broad bandage or belt. The bladder must be relieved by a catheter, and the effects of internal injury and inflammation combated.

Section 2.—Dislocation of the Toes.

Dislocation of the toes and foot from the metatarsal bones, as well as their phalanges, one from another, occur occasionally, and are with facility recognized, and easily reduced by extension and counter-extension.

Dislocation of the astragalus, though rare, sometimes occurs, and is always a serious accident. The nature of the injury is evident; the bone is generally dislocated forwards, and is readily felt.

Treatment for the correction of this accident consists in extension of the foot, with the leg flexed, and direct pressure applied to the astragalus, and the bone usually slips into its natural position. The tension of the integument may be so great that sloughing is inevitable, unless the displaced bone be restored, which is not always possible; therefore the dislocation may become compound secondarily, and calls for the same treatment as if it were originally compound.

When the displaced bone cannot be replaced, three modes of treatment present themselves, viz. to retain the parts as they are, and risk suppuration; to amputate at the ankle joint, or to excise the displaced bone in the attempt to save the limb and joint. This last method is preferable.

Dislocation of the os calcis and astragalus from the other bones of the tarsus may take place. The foot will then be turned inwards, as in talipes varus.

Reduction is easily effected by extension and direct pressure. The limb should then be supported by splints and bandages.

Section 3.—Dislocation of the Knee Joint.

Dislocation of the Patella.—Dislocation of the patella or knee-cap may occur in *three directions: outwards,* (see fig. 69,) *inwards,* (Fig. 70,) and *upwards.*

Fig. 69.

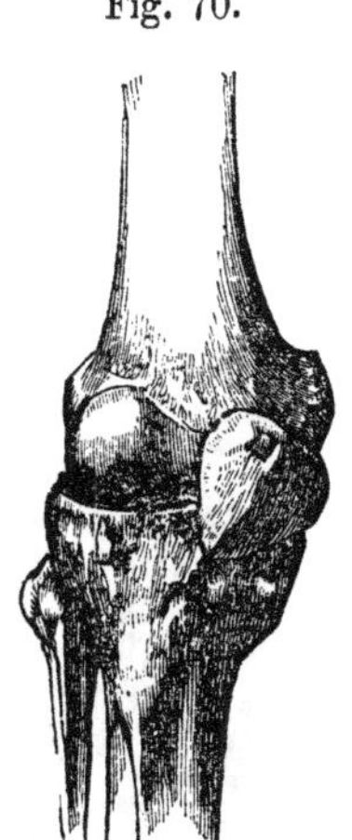
Fig. 70.

A partial dislocation of the patella outwards is not uncommon, and is attended with faintness and a sickening pain.

Luxation outwards is the most common.

Diagnosis.—The nature of the accident is self-evident.

Treatment.—The patient is placed in the recumbent position, the leg is raised by the heel, which relaxes the muscles of the thigh; the surgeon now presses down the edges of the patella farthest from the joint, and the bone glides over the condyle of the femur into its natural position.

Dislocation of the patella *upwards* is caused by the rupture of the ligamentum patellæ, whilst the bone is drawn upwards by the action of the rectus femoris muscle.

Treatment.—The same apparatus is to be applied as recommended for *fracture* of the patella, and continued for one month, before passive motion is communicated to the joint.

Section 4.—*Dislocation of the Leg.*

Dislocation of the Tibia.—This accident may occur at the knee joint in *four directions;* viz. *backwards, forwards, inwards,* and *outwards;* though the two latter are both rare and incomplete.

Diagnosis is very plain in these dislocations. In luxation *inwards* the tibia projects on the inner side of the joint. (Fig. 71.) Dislocation *outwards* is recognized by the tumor being on the outer side of the knee-joint. (Fig. 72.)

Fig. 71. Fig. 72.

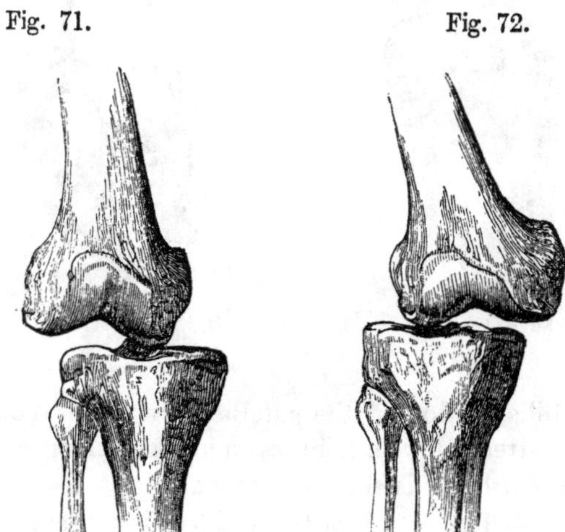

In dislocation *forwards* the tibia is felt above and in front of the thigh bone, (Fig. 73,) whilst the latter may be felt in the popliteal space. Dislocation *backwards* may be readily

Fig. 73. Fig. 74.

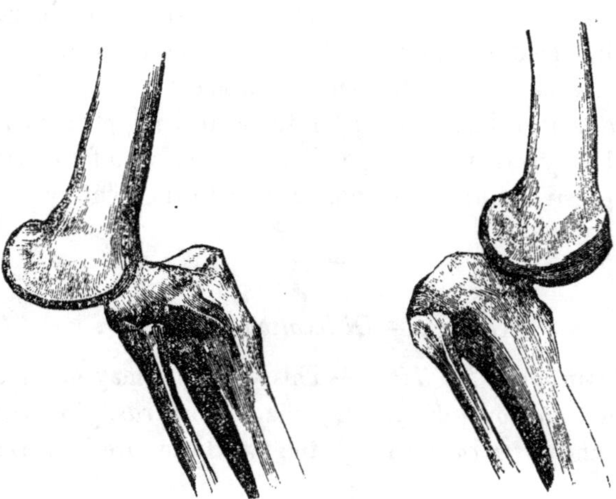

known by the shortening of the limb, projection of the condyles, of the femur, (Fig. 74,) depression of the ligament of the patella, and by the leg being bent forwards.

Treatment.—In these four varieties of luxations, reduction is accomplished by extension of the leg, and direct pressure to the ends of the dislocated bones. Inflammation is combated, and the joint confined for two or four weeks, (or longer, according to the nature of the case,) by splints and bandages.

Compound dislocation of the knee joint is a very rare accident, and generally requires immediate amputation.

Dislocation of the head of the fibula from the tibia may occur. The head of the bone is thrown *backwards;* it can be readily felt and reduced, but slips from its position directly.

The patient suffers fatigue in walking and taking exercise; much weakness is also experienced.

Treatment.—After having reduced the dislocation, a solution of *arnica* should be applied to the part; this may have the effect of producing absorption of the superabundant synovia; or *ledum* may be used, as this medicine acts powerfully upon the knee joint, and also upon the absorbent vessels generally; after this a compress should be placed behind the head of the line, which should be bound tightly to the tibia, either by a bandage or a strap buckled round the upper part of the leg.

Dislocation of the tibia at the ankle joint may occur in *four directions: inwards, forwards, outwards,* and *backwards.* This last variety is rarely met with: dislocation *inwards* is of most frequent occurrence.

Diagnosis.—In luxation of the tibia *inwards,* the internal malleolus forms a tumor which threatens to burst the skin. The foot is thrown outwards; it rotates easily on its axis; there is a depression above the outer ankle; the foot can be moved laterally, and crepitus is felt about three inches above the end of the fibula, at which point that bone is almost invariably fractured in this dislocation.

Treatment.—The patient should be placed upon his back, and the leg bent at a right angle to the thigh; extension should then be made upon the foot, whilst the thigh is fixed by an assistant, and direct pressure applied to the end of the tibia, and thus the deformity is removed. Dupuytren's apparatus for fracture of the lower part of the fibula is now to be applied, or splints and bandages, to keep the foot at rest and at a right angle to the leg, and the patient kept in bed five or six weeks. Ten or twelve weeks will have elapsed before the use of the foot is restored. After the eighth, passive motion will be required to restore the mobility of the joint. *Causticum, lycopodium,* or *rhus,* will very much facilitate this latter object. First, however, the inflammation of the joint must be attended to, as in all other cases of dislocation.

Diagnosis in dislocation of the tibia forwards.—The foot is fixed, and appears much shortened, the heel projects backwards, and is firmly fixed; whilst the toes are pointed downwards. The end of the tibia is felt as a hard tumor upon the tarsus.

Treatment.—The reduction and management of this case is the same as for luxation inwards, with the exception that Dupuytren's apparatus is not applicable. Side splints, and bandages to keep the foot at right angles to the leg, with the heel on a pillow, are preferable.

Partial dislocation of the tibia forwards sometimes occurs. In this case the tibia rests half on the os scaphoides, and half on the astragalus. The fibula is broken in this accident.

Diagnosis.—The foot appears shorter, is pointed downwards, and cannot be placed flat upon the ground without difficulty. The heel is drawn up and slightly projects; the foot is almost immovable.

Treatment.—This luxation is reduced by extension and direct pressure upon the tibia and heel, and retained by means of Dupuytren's apparatus for fractured tibia. Dilute tincture of arnica should be applied to the joint.

Dislocation of the tibia outwards is attended with more injury to the joint, and is more dangerous than either of the other varieties. The malleolus internus is separated from the shaft of the bone, and sometimes the fracture passes obliquely through the articular surface of the tibia. The astragalus is sometimes fractured, and the lower extremity of the fibula is broken into several pieces.

Diagnosis.—The foot is turned inwards, the tibia thrown forwards and outwards upon the astragalus, and can be readily felt. There is great deformity of the joint, and the nature of the accident is evident.

Treatment.—The reduction of the dislocation is effected by the same means as in the other cases. A pad is placed upon the fibula above the ankle, extending up a few inches; two splints, with a foot-board, are applied to the sides of the leg and ankle; the foot is bandaged and fixed in the splints, so as to prevent the slippling of the tibia and fibula from the astragalus, and the limb laid upon its outer side. The local and general treatment is the same as in other cases. Some time will generally elapse before the patient can leave his bed, and even then crutches may be necessary. Passive motion and friction are then to be employed, and in ten or twelve weeks the cure is complete.

Compound Dislocation of the Ankle Joint is always a serious injury; of it Sir Astley Cooper says, "The first question which arises upon this subject is the following—*Is amputation generally necessary in compound dislocation of the ankle?* My answer is, certainly not."

The nature of this accident is evident at the first glance.

Treatment.—The treatment of compound dislocation of the ankle must depend in a great measure upon the extent of the injury and the constitution of the patient. The displacement is reduced as in simple dislocation, and the principles before given for the management of compound fractures and simple luxations must be combined in these instances. There are many cases that require immediate amputation; but if this be not imperative, an attempt to save the limb should always be made, whenever there is the least ray of hope. A proper rule of action in such accidents is to keep the part quiet, and to meet symptoms as they arise.

Partial or complete anchylosis is almost an unavoidable result from these injuries. Under the most favorable circumstances, three months generally elapse before the patient can walk even with crutches, and many cases far exceed this time.

Section 5.—Dislocation of the Hip Joint.

Dislocation of the hip joint takes place in four directions: *upwards*, upon the dorsum of the ilium (Fig. 75); *downwards*, into the foramen ovale (Fig. 76); *backwards* and *upwards* into

Fig. 75. Fig. 76.

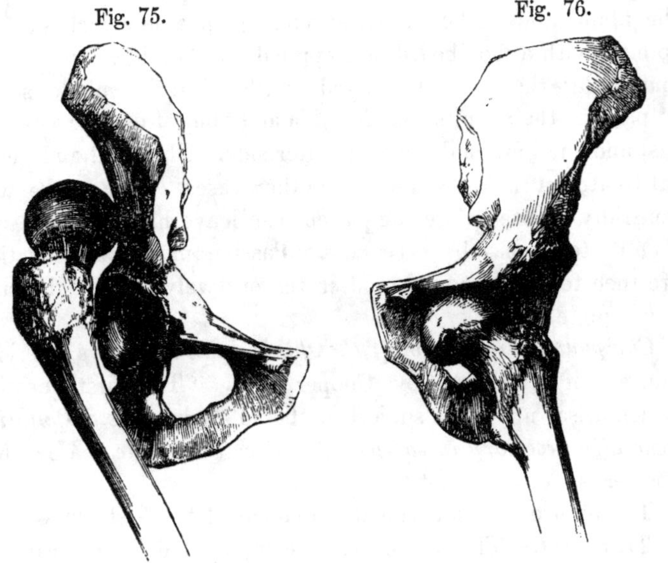

the ischiatic notch (Fig. 77); and *forwards* and *upwards* upon the body of the pubes (Fig. 78).

Diagnosis.—In dislocation of the head of the femur *upwards upon the dorsum of the ilium,* the limb of the injured side is from one to two inches and a half shorter than the opposite limb. The toe rests upon the top of the other foot, and the knee and foot are turned inwards (Fig. 79); the knee is a little advanced upon the other, and the thigh cannot be turned outwards, but may be carried slightly across the other. In the absence of swelling, the head of the femur may be felt moving, upon the dorsum ilii, when the knee is rotated. The trochanter major is much nearer the anterior superior spinous process of the ilium than is natural; though less prominent than on the

Fig. 77.

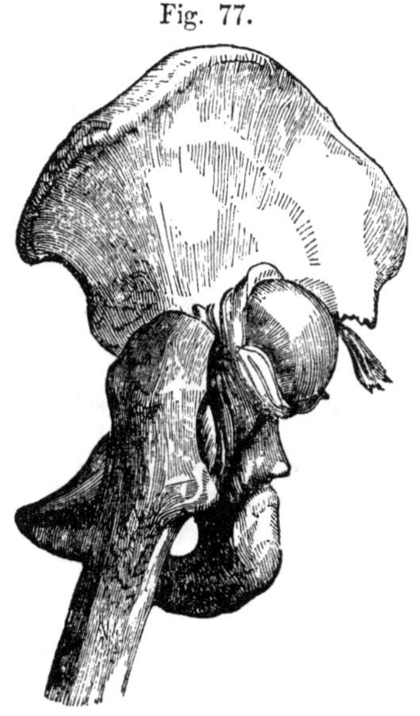

Fig. 78.

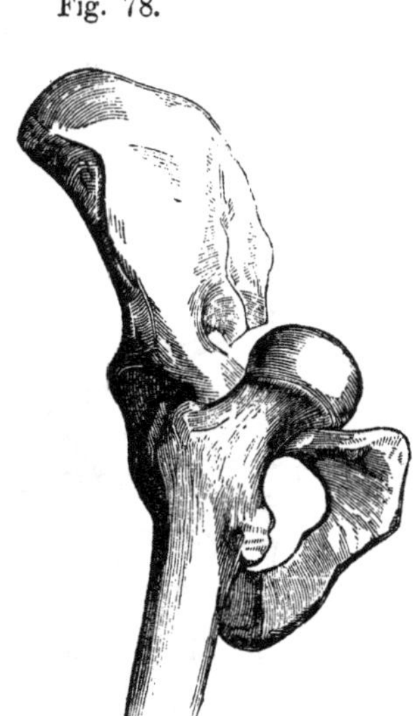

other side: the roundness of the hip on the injured side is lost.

This dislocation differs from fracture of the neck of the femur (for which it has been mistaken) in the following points, viz.: In fracture, the knee and foot are generally turned outwards; the thigh can readily be bent towards the abdomen; and what makes the nature of the accident still more clear, is that the limb, by moderate extension, is made the length of the other, but returns again to its previous position as soon as the extensive force is removed; and there is also crepitation at the seat of injury.

Fig. 79.

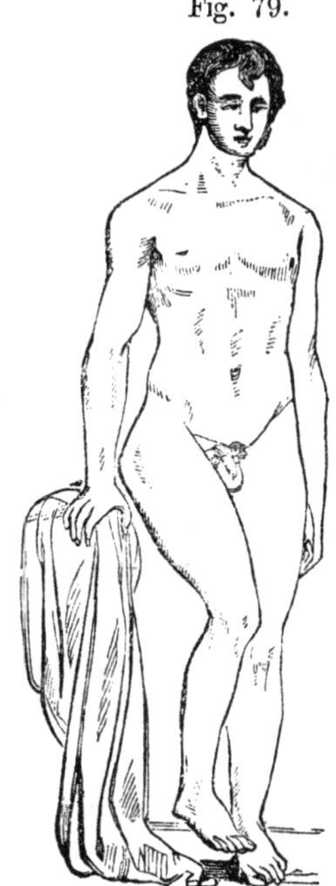

Treatment.—In all dislocations of the hip joint the constitutional means recommended are necessary. The muscles being relaxed, the patient should be laid upon his back, and a strong band placed in the perineum, made fast to a fixed point (Fig. 80): above the knee is passed a wet roller, over this is fixed a band or towel by a clove-hitch, and hooked to a pulley at a point in a direct line to the perineal band.

Fig. 80.

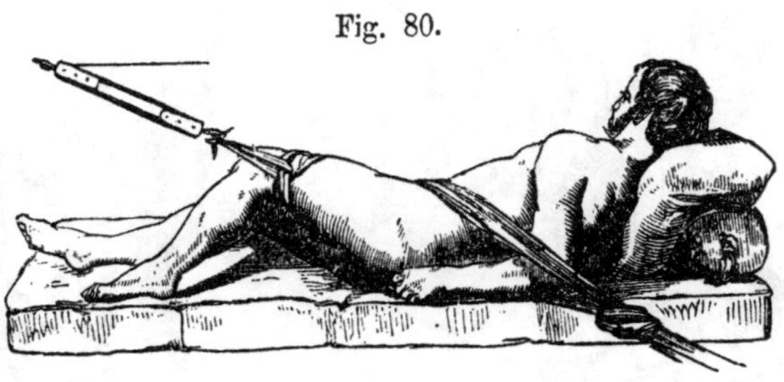

The knee is bent at a right angle: a strain is brought upon the limb by the pulley, which must be steady, continuous, and without violence; stopping occasionally when much pain is experienced. As the head of the bone approaches the acetabulum, the surgeon rotates the limb inwards, and the bone slips into its socket.

As the head of the femur often catches against the edge of the acetabulum, it is good practice, when the bone is yielding to the traction of the pulley, to pass a towel or band under the thigh, near to the groin, and by this lift the head of the bone over the acetabulum.

The injured limb should then be kept parallel with the sound one by means of a bandage embracing both limbs, and the patient placed quietly in bed for two weeks or more. Subsequent inflammation must always be looked to in cases of dislocation, and be treated by *acon.*, *arn.*, &c.

Dislocation downwards into the foramen ovale.—Diagnosis. The injured limb is two inches longer than the other. In thin subjects the head of the bone can be felt towards the perineum; the trochanter is less prominent; the body bent forward; the knee is advanced and separated from the other: the foot is generally straight. (Fig. 81.)

The position of the head of the bone is below, and a little

anterior to the axis of the acetabulum, and there is a depression below Poupart's ligament.

Fig. 81.

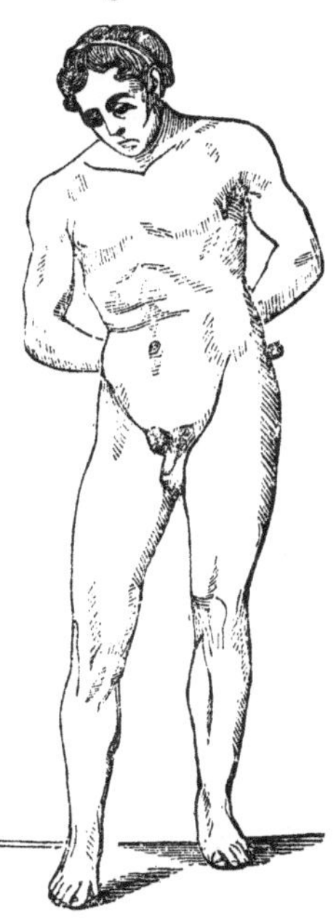

Treatment.—The patient is to be placed upon his back; a band or girth is passed in the perineum, around the injured thigh, and hooked to a pulley, made fast to a point obliquely above the hip.

A counter-extending band or girth surrounds the ilia; this is made fast to a point opposite the injured hip. Traction is gradually made by the pulley, and when the head of the bone is moving from the foramen ovale, the surgeon should grasp the ankle, and draw it towards the middle line of the patient's body, (see fig. 82,) when the head of the bone readily passes into the acetabulum.

Fig. 82.

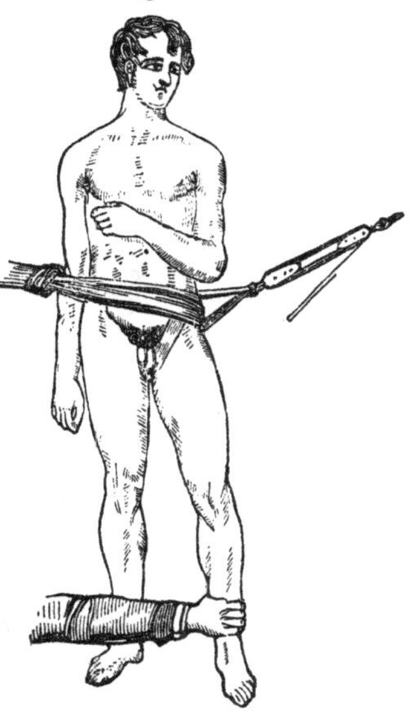

Dislocation backwards into the ischiatic notch is the most difficult to detect and to reduce.

Diagnosis.—The limb is half an inch, sometimes one inch, shortened; the trochanter is behind its natural position; the knee and foot are turned inwards, but less than in dislocation upwards, upon the dorsum of the ilium; the toe rests against the side of the other foot (see fig. 83); the heel does not reach the ground; the knee is a little in advance of the other, and slightly bent; the limb is fixed, so that rotation and flexion is scarcely possible.

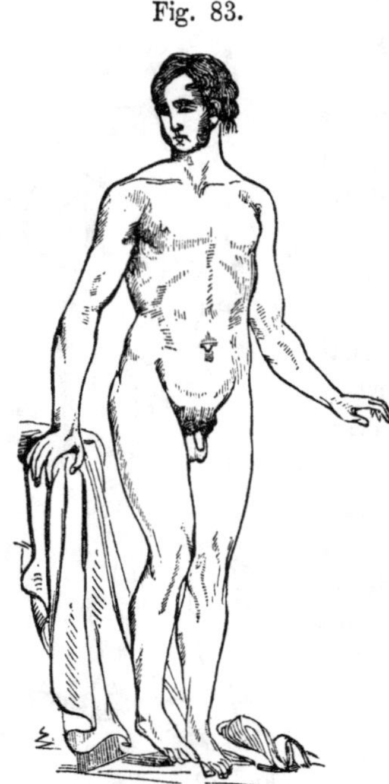
Fig. 83.

Treatment.—The reduction of this dislocation is extremely difficult. The patient is laid upon his side (Fig. 84); the bands and mode of reduction are the same as in the former case; but in this injury the band, or towel, to lift the head of the femur, is indispensable; the trochanter should also be thrust forward by the hand of the surgeon at the same time.

Dislocation on the pubes is the most easy of detection of all the dislocations of the hip joint.

Diagnosis.—The limb is an inch shorter than the other; the knee and foot are turned outwards, and cannot be rotated inwards (Fig. 85); the head of the bone can be distinctly felt upon the pubes, at the outer side of the femoral artery and vein, and above the level of Poupart's ligament; upon moving or rotating the thigh, the head of the bone is felt to move with it.

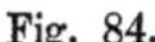
Fig. 84.

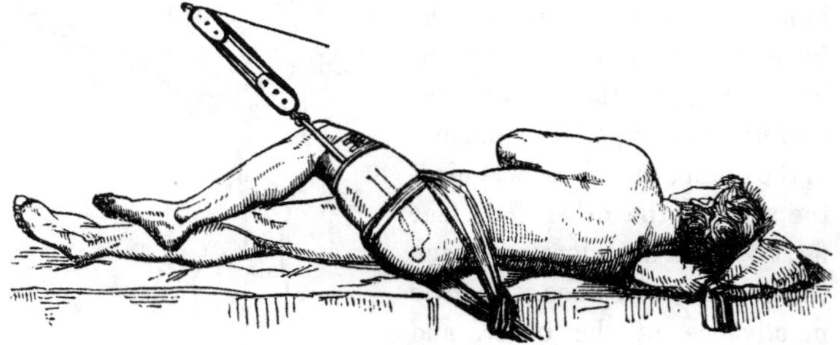

This dislocation has been mistaken for fracture of the neck of the femur. It should be remembered that *shortening* and

Fig. 85.

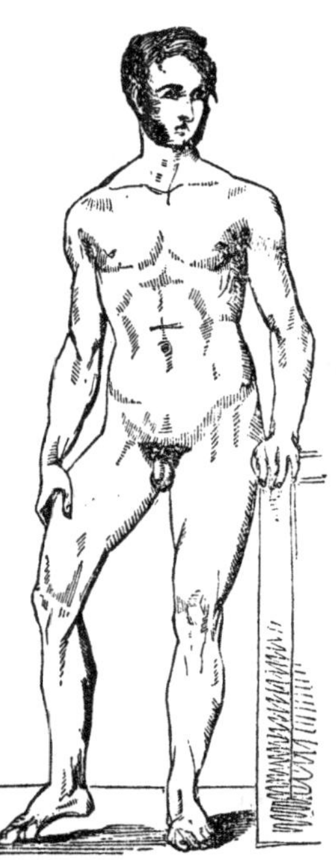

eversion are common to both; therefore, care is necessary in the diagnosis.

Treatment.—The patient is placed upon the sound side; a girth is passed in the perineum and fixed to a point in front of the line of the body. The pulley is hooked to the band above the knee, (Fig. 86,) and made fast to a point behind the axis of the body, so as to draw the bone backwards. The head of the bone is lifted over the pubes and edge of the acetabulum by means of a band or towel, and drops into its place. The subsequent treatment is the same as in the other cases.

A much more extensive description, and many minutiæ, might have been introduced into the preceding chapters on fractures and dislocations, but it is presumed that sufficient detail has been entered upon, to instruct the student and young practitioner in the management of most injuries of this description.

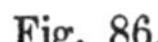

Fig. 86.

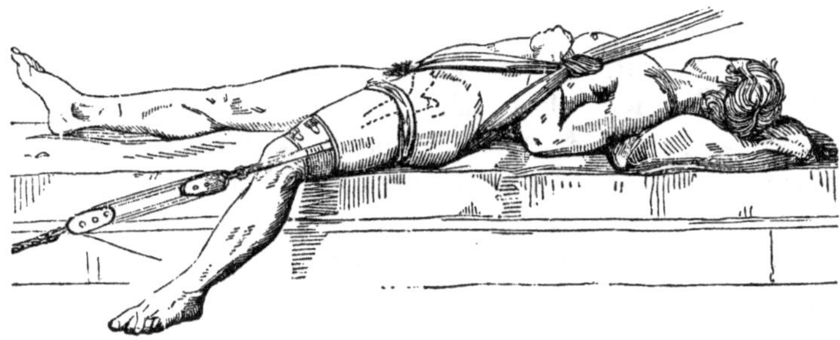

CHAPTER XXII.

SUBLUXATION, SPRAINS, ETC.

THESE injuries are sometimes very painful. They arise often from momentary displacement of bones, which strain or partially tear the ligamentous apparatus of the joints. They are accompanied frequently with some constitutional disturbance; the affected part swells, and the synovial membrane may be involved.

The *treatment* of such injuries, consists in restoring the bones to their normal position by extension and direct pressure, and applying a solution of *arnica* to the part, which must also be bandaged to support the limb, and prevent recurrence of the accident, and a few globules of the same medicine of the 12th dilution administered internally.

When an individual muscle has been injured by the effect of a violent strain, Dr. Goullon remarks that *rhus* will more readily restore its tone, and remove the pain, than any other medicine. This is a truthful observation, as most practitioners of our school can testify. *Rhus* is particularly adapted to sprains occurring in tendinous parts with swelling and great pain. It may be used both externally and internally; the solution that is used as a lotion should be adapted to the sensitiveness of the skin of the patient. There are some individuals who are particularly susceptible to the action of the poison oak; and the surgeon should therefore exercise caution and discretion when prescribing this medicine: it possesses considerable power over the tendons of the lower extremities and the submaxillary bone, it is also recommended for the bad consequences of strains, and prevents liability to such accidents. This medicine has been alternated with *arnica* in some cases, but the indications for its use are generally sufficiently well marked to render entirely unnecessary any such alternation.

If the patient should have injured himself by lifting heavy

weights, *rhus* is also an important medicine, particularly when the dorsal and cervical muscles and the vertebral column are affected, and there is headache, accompanied with general bruised sensation of the whole body, pains in the back or gastric ailments. *Bryonia* should be exhibited if the pains are occasioned by the same cause, but are aggravated by motion, and the muscular system is chiefly involved.

If pain is experienced immediately after raising a heavy weight, *calc.* will prove serviceable, and may also remove the existing predisposition to such accident; it should also be remembered, when, after the injury, there is congestion of blood to the head, or there are pains, as from bruises, in the joints and small of the back, the parts being sensitive to touch.

Amm. carb. has been mentioned by some authors as useful in the variety of injury under consideration, but there have been no particular indications given. In its pathogenesis we find sensation as if bruised in the whole body, with fatigue and weakness of the limbs; pains, as if sprained in the joints; drawing and tension in the joints, as though the tendons were too short: Sprains.*

Lycop., *petrol.*, or *ruta* may be applicable in some cases. *Sepia* is recommended by Dr. Goullon for many troublesome constitutional symptoms that may supervene upon a sprain.

If an inguinal hernia should have been caused by lifting or straining the part, or if an old protrusion becomes painful, *nux-vom.*, *sulph.-ac.*, *cocc.*, or *sulph.* should be administered. If a prolapsus of the womb has been occasioned by such causes *nux* has proved almost a specific medicine; after its exhibition *bell.* or *sepia* may be required.

If the accident occasion nausea and vomiting, *veratrum* or *sulph.* may be required, either of which may be used in alternation with *arnica.*

For the ill effects of making a mis-step, or pressing the foot to the floor with too much violence, *arn.* and *bry.* are often sufficient; sometimes, however, *con.*, *puls.* and *rhus* may be indicated.

---

* See Mat. Med., vol. i. p. 80.

Section 1.—Rupture of Muscles und Tendons.

Laceration of muscular fibres often occurs from violent muscular action. It is characterized by immediate lameness. The patient falls and is unable to resume the erect position; much pain is experienced at the seat of injury. There is generally consciousness of something having given way, accompanied with a sensation of a blow upon the part. There are seldom more than a few fibres of a muscle separated. This accident usually occurs in the gastrocnemius, and is generally situated at that part of the muscle at which the tendon commences. In rupture of tendons the same symptoms are observed as in the former case, accompanied often with an audible snapping noise, and the gap between the ends can be detected by the touch. The tendo achilles is more frequently ruptured than any other.

Treatment.—A great portion of the management of these cases consists in position and rest. *Arnica* may be applied in some instances, particularly when muscular fibres have been torn. *Rhus* and *ruta* are preferable when the tendons are involved. *Acon.* and *bella.* may also be used if the constitutional symptoms call for their administration. If the seat of the injury be the gastrocnemius muscle or tendo achilles, a slipper should be placed upon the foot; a belt or band secured around the waist or loins, and to the heel of the slipper a stout cord or tape attached; the leg is flexed on the thigh, the foot is extended, and the tape made fast to the belt or tape around the body. This position is maintained until the divided parts unite. Reparation is slow, especially in rupture of tendons. The application of the apparatus must be continued for some time, indeed, even longer than necessary when treating fractures. When the patient commences to walk he should use a stick or crutch, and wear a high-heeled shoe.

CHAPTER XXIII.

DISEASES OF THE PERIOSTEUM AND BONES.

It appears proper in this place, after having mentioned the injuries to which the bones are liable, to record the diseases or morbid conditions which affect the osseous system, the chief of which are *periostitis*, *caries*, *necrosis*, *exostosis*, *rachitis*, *mollities ossium*, *fragilitas ossium*, *spina ventosa*, *osteo sarcoma*, &c.

To effect a cure of diseases of the bones, the causes upon which such affections depend must be removed; a want of such knowledge induces the most distinguished surgeons to employ severe methods of treatment, which, in the generality of instances, rather aggravate these affections than produce upon them a beneficial effect. But by the administration of the proper homœopathic medicines, the constitution of the patient can be improved, and the disease more successfully treated; the dilution of the medicine, and the repetition of the dose, are of paramount importance. Experience teaches that the exhibition of medium dynamizations, from the 12th to the 30th, (better to commence with the latter,) is more speedily followed by beneficial effects than when the lower potencies are employed; the system by the latter being excited to a reaction prejudicial to favorable results, whilst the frequent repetition of medicines often disturbs their curative action, and thereby retards recovery.

"We are often at a loss to determine," writes Dr. Jeanes,* "which of the remedies that are indicated by the morbid condition, or its particular development, as caries, hyperostosis, &c., is the appropriate remedy for the individual case. The circumstances which can guide in the choice of the remedy, are the temperament, the disposition, the character of antecedent diseases, and the treatment to which they have been subjected,

* Homœopathic Practice of Medicine.

and the nature of the exciting cause of the existing disease of the bone. The symptoms which indicate the remedies are those of the disease of the bone: viz., the appearances, the pains and other molestations which accompany it, and the symptoms which affect the whole system, or particular parts of it, other than those immediately implicated by the disease of the bone. But most of the latter, which may be termed the general symptoms, namely, hectic, loss of appetite, emaciation, debility, &c., are often merely the result of the local irritation."

It is also of some importance for the practitioner to become acquainted with the manner in which any antecedent disease may have been treated, as all such circumstances tend to aid in the selection of appropriate remedial agents.

Section 1.—*Periostitis.*

Periosteum is the name given to the strong white fibrous membrane that closely envelops bones, excepting such of them as are covered with cartilage. This membrane is connected externally to adjacent cellular substance, and therefore indirectly with muscular tissue; the inner surface adheres closely to the bone, by means of short strong fibres, which enter the numberless foramina that are noticed on the surface of ossific structure.

Although fibrous tissues are not as liable to be attacked by inflammation as other textures of the body, still, when such abnormal action is found, the sufferings of the patient are often exceedingly severe; and if the inflammatory process be considerable or acute, it is seldom limited to the tissue originally affected, but extends to all the surrounding parts.

Great pain is the usual attendant upon this disease, whether acute or chronic, and when in the former variety, if the inflammation has extended to the bone, the sufferings of the patient are excruciating. This increase of suffering may be readily accounted for, if we remember that the inflammatory process progresses with greater rapidity in tissues which are secondarily involved, consequently there is a greater amount of exudation, which, being confined by the external membrane, tends greatly to increase the pain.

The swelling in periostitis is small, compared to the violence of the inflammatory action; this may also be explained in the same manner alluded to when speaking of the unusual degree of pain that is present in the disease, viz. the confinement of the exudation. All the symptoms are aggravated at night.

The constitutional symptoms are well marked in periostitis. If the disease be acute there is a high degree of inflammatory fever; if chronic, the system is gradually undermined by the continued loss of sleep, caused by the severe nocturnal sufferings. Emaciation, loss of appetite and spirits, and hectic, often supervene, rendering the patient extremely miserable.

In the acute form of the affection the membrane is softer, and loosened from its connection with the subjacent bone; in the chronic variety it becomes more dense, and adheres with unnatural firmness.

When inflammation does not become fully established, or, in other words, if active congestion be only present, fibrin is exuded, and the swelling is termed a *node*, which, when arising from syphilis, is denominated the *venereal*, when complicated with the results of large doses of mercury, the *mercurial*, or the two causes may be combined, giving rise to the mercurio-syphilitic node.

If inflammation proceeds a step further, and the bone becomes involved, a purulent formation (abscess in the bone) is the result, which not being able to approach the surface, from the strength and non ulcerative property of the periosteum extends laterally, denuding the bone of its membrane.

The same process may be present in ossific structure as has been heretofore related concerning inflammation occurring in other textures; the inflammatory process having established suppuration, gradual "molecular disintegration" (ulceration) of the bone may ensue, and if this be not restrained necrosis may take place.

Sometimes, in the acute form of this disease, these terminations may become apparent in a short time after inflammation has developed itself; if chronic, weeks and months may elapse before caries or necrosis is established, but the patient will exhibit unmistakable signs of severe constitutional irritation.

Treatment.—The medicines that are of service in periostitis are *aur.*, *calc.*, *carb -an.*, *caust.*, *kali.-c.*, *lyc.*, *merc.*, *mez.*, *nit.-ac.*, *ruta*, *rhododen.*, *staphys.* and *sulph.*, or croc., fluor-ac., magnes.-c., natr.-mur., petrol., pulsat., silic.

Aurum should be prescribed when the periostitis has arisen from or is complicated with a mercurio-syphilitic dyscrasia; it is suitable for the nightly aggravation of the pains, and also to nodes. This medicine possesses considerable power over inflammations of the membrane covering the bones of the nose and palate, and may, if timely exhibited, prevent caries, necrosis, or exostosis; it may likewise be used when the right nasal bone and the superior maxillary are sensitive to touch, when there is cramp-like tearing in the metacarpal bones, with swelling of the same; when there are nodes on the inferior extremities, with stinging and burning. Also, when the patient is of a scrofulous diathesis.

Calcarea carb. is adapted to a scrofulous habit, and is especially suited to children, who, though they appear tolerably healthy, are extremely weak, with bloated, distended abdomen, uneasiness of the whole body, with trembling, languor, and emaciation.

Kali-carb. is curative when there are aching and tearing pains; if the parts around the knee joint are affected, or when there is stiffness and tension of the part, with throbbing and beating, tearing on the inner side of the foot and sole, tearing in the tarsal joints, &c.; when the patient dreads the open air, easily takes cold, loses his appetite, is affected with feverish chills, diarrhœa, &c.

Lycopodium possesses a special influence on the periosteum and bones; it is recommended for periostitis and ostitis with nightly pains, even when occasioned by the abuse of mercury. It may also be used when there are drawing pains in the bones of the arms as far as the fingers, nightly bone pain in the elbow, pains in the tibia when touching the part; all the limbs are painful when touched or pressed. The pains are mostly drawing, tearing and pricking. Sensation in the bones as though they contained no marrow.

Mercurius.—This medicine should always be remembered in periostitis, and in nodes, as it exercises considerable influence on the periosteum and bones. It should, however, never be administered when the patient has been previously subjected to the action of the drug in massive doses. The diseases of the bones and periosteum that so frequently are encountered by the homœopathic practitioner, when treating secondary syphilis, in very many instances result from the injudicious administration of mercurial preparations by old school physicians when treating the primary disorder. It is recommended for nightly bone pains, inflammation of the periosteum, characterized by stinging, boring and gnawing pains, becoming intolerable at night; redness and swelling of the soft parts covering the bones; sticking, cramp-like pains in the muscles or periosteum; boring pains along the tibia, and aching in the bones.

Manganum aceticum has been highly extolled for periostitis.

Mezereum.—This is a highly serviceable medicine, and should be administered when there are nightly pains in the bones; periostitis of the tibia consequent upon ulcers of the leg, the parts being covered with a brown dry skin and surrounded by reddish-blue spots, with violent burning pains caused by the slightest pressure; swollen periosteum; the pain is so violent that it is impossible to place the foot on the ground; nightly aggravation of the pains, with cramp in the calves; violent tearing in the left ulna, or in the fore-arm and elbow; pain in the periosteum of the right olecranon, which is much aggravated by pressure; violent pain in the tibia after midnight, as if bruised, or as if the periosteum would be torn off, with chilliness passing rapidly through the whole body, and continual violent thirst; dull darting in the middle of the tibia or in the periosteum covering that bone.

Nit.-acid has been used with success in periostitis and diseases of the bones, and especially when the inflammation is chronic; when there is tearing in the bones of the limbs, pain in the periosteum of the os calcis, drawing pain in the periosteum of all the bones, pain in all the limbs, apparently in the bones.

Ruta should be employed when the pain resembles that caused by a bruise, aggravated by the slightest touch; it is also recommended for contusions and injuries of the bones and periosteum; bone pains with burning and gnawing in the periosteum, which increase during rest, relieved by motion, and are worse in damp and cold weather.

Rhododendron.—Tearing pain in the right tibia; sharp pains in the left tibia, commencing in the knee, as if in the periosteum; boring, beating pain in the right tibia; tearing, as if in the periosteum, in the right arm, only when at rest. Almost all the sufferings reappear, or are aggravated, at the approach of rough weather.

Staphysagria and *sulph.* have also symptoms that may be present in periostitis, but for the precise indications of these, as well as the other medicines before mentioned, the student must refer to the repertory and symptomen codex.

By the administration of some of these medicines the disease may be arrested before the inflammatory process has reached the suppurative stage; at all events, many of the most distressing symptoms of the patient certainly will be alleviated, thus rendering him comparatively comfortable.

But when pus has formed and collected beneath the periosteum, the matter must be evacuated, and that as speedily as possible, or caries and necrosis may be the result of delay. If the operation of dividing the periosteum be performed, as soon as the surgeon has satisfactory reason to believe that matter is present, simple ulceration only may have taken place, and as soon as the pressure occasioned by the pus is removed, the reproductive process will in all probability complete the cure in a short time. But although this practice is eminently beneficial in acute abscess of the bone, it must never be employed unless the signs of suppuration are sufficiently obvious to render it certain that pus is accumulating rapidly and in quantity, between bone and periosteum. Cod liver oil, (*ol. jec. asc.*) has been employed by practitioners of our school for this disease, when it arises from a scrofulous taint.

Section 2.—Caries.

Ulceration of bone.

The term caries is used to denote a peculiar ulceration of bone, in which reparation is scarcely effected by nature, and is with difficulty obtained by the most skilfully applied artificial means.* Or, according to Mr. Miller,† a breach of continuity of bone of altogether a peculiar kind; of itself very difficult to cure, yet not in any degree partaking of truly malignant action.

Every portion of the osseous system is liable to be attacked with caries; but it has been observed that those bones that partake most of the cancellated structure are more frequently the seat of the disease than those of a more firm and compact conformation; thus the vertebræ, the bones of the carpus and tarsus, the sternum and the extremities of the long bones are the most frequent seat of this disease. For a similar reason the ossific structure in young persons is more subject to it than those of advanced years.

Surgeons of the olden time confounded caries with necrosis, the latter being termed by them dry caries; others have considered it the same as necrosis. These suppositions appear the more strange, when we consider that the *caries* was described by Galen as being somewhat analogous to ulceration of the soft parts.‡

It has been previously remarked that ossific matter, when attacked by inflammation, becomes acutely sensible, hence, in the commencement of this disease, in which the inflammatory process is always present, the patient often suffers considerable

---

* See Liston's Elements of Surgery, p. 70.

† Principles of Surgery, p. 435.

‡ See Cooper's Surgical Dictionary, vol. i., p. 320.

pain; so great in the generality of instances as to prevent the enjoyment of repose for weeks and months together. The affected part is considerably swollen, but the enlargement is seldom so general or so great as is present in the diseased condition of the ligaments and other apparatus of the joints, although affections of the bursæ, ligaments or synovial membrane may in time extend to the adjacent bones, and breach of continuity be the consequence.

In caries, the affected portion appears neither to possess vital action enough to enable it to repair the solution of continuity, nor is the diseased mass sufficiently deprived of vitality to be thrown off by the surrounding tissues. When the affected parts have remained a considerable time in this inactive state, the surrounding vessels become somewhat excited, and the surface of the bone in the vicinity is studded with small points of new osseous formation; these new deposits, however, are not limited to the affected bone, but may be traced to those with which it is articulated. The soft parts surrounding the diseased mass are commonly more or less thickened, and rendered exceedingly dense by effusion of lymph into the cellular tissue, which sometimes becomes of a cartilaginous hardness. As the ulceration proceeds, a cavity forms in the bone, with soft spongy margins with an unequal bottom, deep at one portion and comparatively shallow in another; the substance of the bone may crumble easily, or the part may be covered with pale and unhealthy granulations; often a loose, fungous growth sprouts from the interstices formed on the surface of the diseased bone, bleeding readily at the slightest touch; from the decaying structure also a thin, fetid and corrosive ichor is discharged, in many instances through a sinus which has been formed in the soft parts; these symptoms, however, as well as the tendency in the accompanying ulcer or sinus to produce large fungous granulations, are more constantly met with in necrosis than caries, for the latter disease has been known to exist for a considerable length of time unattended with any outward sore, abscess or sinus.

A superficial caries may be ascertained without much difficulty, and when the affected bone is deep-seated it may be discovered by the use of the probe; for if the disease exist, the surgeon can often readily detect the inequalities of surface, and, owing to the spongy character of the diseased part, the instrument can readily be made to penetrate the substance of the bone; in some instances, however, when there exists the unhealthy granulations already mentioned, a moderate degree of force is required; the latter fact, if remembered, may prevent in some instances an incorrect diagnosis.

There are some bones which may be diseased, and which, from their situation, do not admit of the use of a probe; in such cases the diagnosis may be more difficult; however, if a fistula, from which a fetid, corrosive and dark-colored matter is discharged, be found leading directly from the surface of a bone, and if the surrounding part be at the same turgid and indurated, there is every reason to suppose the existence of caries.

"If a person," writes Boyer,* "affected with certain constitutional disease, feel deep-seated or acute pains in any of his bones, and if the pained part swell and become the seat of an abscess, from which a purulent matter of a bad quality flows, there is reason to believe that the bone affected with pain is carious. Inert abscesses are attended with nearly the same symptoms, with this difference, that they are not preceded by pain. Caries occasioned by syphilis affects most commonly the tibia, os frontis, ossa nasi, ossa palati, and sternum. Whenever, therefore, any of these bones become carious, whilst the person labors under syphilis, there is just ground for concluding that the caries is a symptom of the venereal affection.

Caries may be divided into three varieties, *simple*, *scrofulous* and *tubercular*. The simple form is such as has been described; the scrofulous variety is dependent on a constitution affected with scrofula; and in tubercular the disease is accompanied by deposit of tubercle in the loose texture of the bone.

* See "The Lectures of Boyer upon Diseases of the Bones, Arranged by Richerand, Translated by Farrell, and Edited by Joseph Hartshorne, M. D.," p. 167.

The causes of caries are various. It may arise from disease of the soft parts—ulcers, &c., having extended to the bone, or constitutional taint may be the remote, and recent injury the proximate cause, but probably the disease most frequently arises from scrofula, syphilis, or abuse of mercury.

Treatment.—Much vigilance should be exercised, with a view to prevent the occurrence of this morbid condition; therefore, if there be ulcers, abscess, &c., in the soft parts, which appear to have a tendency to involve the bones, they must be carefully watched and judiciously treated.* If simple suppuration occur, as a consequence of diseased periosteum, the medicines before mentioned for periostitis should be administered, in accordance with the presenting symptoms.

By careful watching, the formation of matter may be averted; but to accomplish such desirable result, the treatment must be commenced early. When there is merely an *inflammation of the bone*, with slight swelling, redness of the integument, and extreme sensibility to touch, *bryonia* and *pulsatilla* are recommended. The latter being more adapted to the disease when it occurs in persons of a phlegmatic temperament, with mild disposition, apathy, &c.; the former deserving preference if the patient be of a dry, meagre habit, with bilious or nervous temperament. *Mercurius* is an important medicine for *ostitis* as well as periostitis, and by its administration the inflammatory action occurring in the bone may be checked before other untoward symptoms present themselves. The indications for the administration of this medicine, as well as others, have been mentioned in the previous section. If inflammation of the bone is chronic, the following medicines may be resorted to, according to the correspondence of symptoms in each individual case, *asaf.*, *calc.*, *phosph.*, *phosph.-ac.*, *silic.*, *staphys.*, and *sulph.* When the affection has arisen from the abuse of mercury, and the disease is accompanied with mercurial, or mercurio-syphilitic symptoms, *aurum*, *hepar*, or *nitric-acid* may be used. If from a blow or bruise ostitis threaten, *arn.*, *calen.*, *ruta*, or *symphy-*

* See Abscess Chap. IX.—Ulcers, Chap. X.

tum, may be employed; but when there is considerable erysipelatous redness around the wounded part, *bella.* may be used, and in some cases in alternation with *arnica.*

Other medicines that have been serviceable in the treatment of bones are, *baryta., carb.-veg., dulc., fluor.-ac., lyc., mang., mez., staphys.*, &c.

If a patient affected with *caries* apply for relief, the first duty of the physician must be, if possible, to remove the causes which have either proximately, remotely, or both, given rise to the disease.

The paucity of symptoms *recorded* in our Materia Medica, belonging to caries, makes it difficult to select appropriate medicine for each case. The medicines mentioned, however, have proved beneficial, *ex usu morbis*, in the treatment of this disease. The following cases were cured while subjected to the use of the medicines which are appended :*

Caries of the right fore-arm and right leg, with much swelling, ichorous discharge and slow fever. *china, asaf., phosph., sulph., silic., acid-nit., carb.-an.*

Caries of the fore-arm after a fall, *arn.* 24, *silic.* 30, *calc.* 30, *sulph.* 30.

Caries of the leg, *sulph* , *silic.*

Caries of the elbow joints with fistulous ulcers of the bone, *calc., silic., lycop.*, and *sulph.*

Caries of the thigh in a scrofulous boy, *sep.* 30, and *nit.-ac.*

Caries of the lower jaw with fistula of the parotid gland, *silic.*

Caries of the bones and face, *calc.* and *silic.*

Caries of the phalanges of the third middle finger, *silic.* 30.

Caries of the foot, with hectic fever, *arn., lyc., silic.*

Caries of the radius, with bluish red swelling of the fore-arm, with hectic fever, *puls., mez., sabin., silic., calc., lyc.*

Caries, syphilitic, of the palate and nasal bones, *aur.*

Caries, syphilitic, of the alveolar processes with ozœna, *aur.-mur.*

---

* See A Guide to the Practice of Homœopathy, by Edward Hamilton, M. D., p. 44. London, 1844.

Caries of the tibia, with swelling of the whole foot. The slightest touch cannot be borne, fetid ichorous discharge, *silic.*, *asaf.* 18, *calc -carb.* 30, *mez.* 18, *sulph.* 30, *acid-nit.*

Caries, recent of the tibia, *silic.* 30.

Caries, tibiæ, in the inner side of the left leg, a very painful, bluish ulcer, with hard edge; a fetid, dark colored pus exuding; at the inner side of the left ankle a cold tumor, *asaf.* 18, *gutt.* 1.

Caries of the tibia and left fore-arm, with many fistulous ulcers; sinking of the vital powers, and debilitating diarrhœa, *sulph.*, *asaf.*, *acid-nit.*, and *acid-phosph.*

Asaf. In a caries of the leg with exfoliation of a piece of dead bone.

Aurum. Caries of the palate and nasal bones from abuse of mercury.

Nit.-ac., with the assistance of *silic.*, *asaf.*. *calc.*, *mez.*, and *sulph.*, in caries of the tibia, with great pain in the bone, and a bad colored, fetid ichor discharged from the ulcers; in a boy eight years of age.

Angustura is said to have cured caries, when given daily in doses of the 1st to 6th. The use of coffee being avoided.

Sepia. Caries femoris, with fistulous openings on the outside of the thigh, discharging a watery ichor. A probe introduced into this after a long progress towards the knee, touched a rough carious spot upon the bone. At the lower extremity of the radius there was an enlargement of bone, which was painful when touched, *sepia*, and after six weeks *acid-nit.*, effected a cure in little short of two months.*

In caries ossium digitorum, *silic.* has proved very serviceable.

Fluoric acid is said to possess a powerful action upon the osseous system, and from recorded cases appears to be especially adapted to caries.†

---

* See Jeanes' Practice of Medicine.

† See Laurie's Homœopathic Practice.

Section 3.—Necrosis.

The term Necrosis, which literally means only destruction, is by surgeons applied to bone deprived of its vitality. It was first used in this particular sense by M. Louis, who restricted its appellation, however, to cases in which the whole thickness of a bone was destroyed. The ancients termed the disease "*dry* caries."

Between caries and necrosis, says Weedmann, there is all that difference which exists between ulcers and gangrene, or sphacelus of the soft parts. In caries, the nutrition of the bone is impaired, and an irregular action disunites the elements of bony structure, which consequently sustains a loss of substance. In necrosis, on the contrary, the vitality and nutritive function cease altogether in certain portions of the bone, the separation of which then becomes indispensable.

Bones are not as extensively supplied with blood vessels as other textures of the body, and their natural powers are inferior to those of the softer parts; and this circumstance may serve to explain the frequent occurrence of the disease under consideration.

Necrosis may appear at various periods of life, but is most commonly met with in young subjects, in whom the inflammatory action is allowed to make some progress before it is noticed or attended to. It may affect the external or internal structure of a bone, or nearly its whole thickness. An entire bone seldom dies in consequence of increased action; and it is in rare instances that the whole thickness of any portion of it is found necrosed,* although a large proportion may be involved.

Mr. Miller divides the process of necrosis into several stages. 1st. The bone or portion of bone inflames. 2d. The bone dies. 3d. The dead portion is separated from the living. 4th. Separation of the dead portion is complete. 5th. The dead portion is extruded.

The following symptoms characterize the whole process.—

---

* Liston's Elements of Surgery, p. 75.

Intense pain is experienced in the part; and as there is no very prominent swelling in the commencement of the disease, the sufferings are generally attributed by the patient to rheumatism or neuralgia. The pain which was first felt about the middle of the bone, extends towards its extremities—that is, if one of the long bones be affected. The part then becomes somewhat swollen; the surrounding integument is inflamed; and the tumor, which was at first hard, becomes soft and fluctuating, and gives evidence of the formation of abscesses: these are either allowed to open spontaneously, or the pus is evacuated by incision; in either case, however, fistulæ form, through which there is a frequent discharge of a thin, fetid, and often corrosive ichor. The surface of the bone, if not deep seated (as the tibia), is often visible through the fistulous orifices, in which case the nature of the disease may be readily ascertained: if the bone is well covered by other textures, the surgeon must have recourse to gentle probing.

When the disease has not far advanced, there is a copious discharge of purulent matter,* and the external openings, through which the pus finds exit, are found to lead to *cloacæ*, or apertures in the new bone which encases the old; through these the dead portions can be discovered by the probe. Sequestra are also sometimes cast off, the hue of which resembles that of ossific matter which has been for some time buried in the earth. When a sequestrum is discharged, the disease may be considered at its height; for nature is throwing off the dead structure, which can no longer be of any service to the economy. Often at this period, by introducing a probe, several pieces of detached bone may be readily felt. These symptoms of necrosis, thus evident in affections of those bones that are covered with thick muscular fibre, are still more so in cases of flat superficial bones, and those of the skull: in disease of the latter, the skin at first becomes thick, hard, and reddish; but

* "Formation of matter is occasionally the cause of necrosis. I have seen several instances in which it occurred from neglected erysipelas of the leg." Liston's Elements, p. 76.

soon ulcerates, and discharges matter of the character before mentioned.

The prognosis varies according to the situation of the bone affected, and the circumstances with which the disease may be complicated. If necrosis occurs, and is confined to a small surface of a bone, it is not very difficult to cure; but when large portions of the osseous system are involved, and if the introduction of instruments be required to separate the exfoliated portions (sequestra), the prognosis is extremely unfavorable.

In cases of necrosis, in which the dead bone is entirely inclosed in that newly formed, the prognosis may vary, according to the state of the surrounding soft parts, the age and strength of the patient, and the form of the new osseous substance. The tumefaction of the limb may be excessive; the fistulæ numerous; the suppuration abundant; and the patient reduced by colliquative diarrhœa and hectic: under such circumstances the danger is much greater than if the suppuration were trifling, the patient young and healthy; and favorable termination of the disease may be anticipated, if, together with these latter conditions, the newly formed bone is perforated by nature, that the dead portion may be readily withdrawn.

The causes of necrosis may be divided into internal and external:* among the latter may be classed—contusion, excessive pressure, imprudent application of caustic,† &c.; and of the former, syphilis, scrofula, or mercury. In persons thus constitutionally affected, a blow, or other external accident, may prove an exciting cause of the disease.

Concerning the death of bone, and the reproduction of new ossific matter, Dr. Gibson writes:‡ "So far as opportunities have been afforded me of ascertaining this point, I have no hesitation to express the belief, that the *periosteum* is the chief agent in both processes. If from any cause the periosteum in-

---

* See Boyer on the Bones, p. 159.

† As happened in the case of a woman, who had caustic potash applied to an exostosis on the internal side of the tibia.

‡ Institutes and Practice of Surgery, vol. ii., p. 55.

flame, and matter is poured out between it and the bone, so as to separate one from the other, all vascular intercourse must cease—or, at least, the bone then depends exclusively for its support upon the internal periosteum and marrow; but these being inadequate to furnish the requisite supply, a part or the whole of the bone will necessarily perish."

Violent inflammatory fever attends the excited action of the bone and periosteum, which precedes necrosis. But, after the matter has accumulated, and been discharged, most of the painful symptoms subside.

Frequently fresh collections of pus are generated, as each portion of the dead bone approaches the surface. When the effusion of new ossific material has extended to the neighboring joint, its motion may be very much impeded, and if the limb is kept at perfect rest, anchylosis may occur.

Treatment.—In the treatment of this disease,* as in caries, the great object is prevention; by the successful treatment of ostitis, periostitis, caries, and of the constitutional affection (if any be present), upon which death of the bone may follow as a consequence.

One of the principal indications is the evacuation of the purulent formation, which frequently bathes the inflamed bone and detaches from it the periosteum.

Separation of the sequestrum may be hastened by the administration of medicines, which, acting beneficially upon the surrounding osseous structure, tend to increase the action by which exfoliations are cast off. The affected part must be allowed to remain at rest, and all stimulating applications avoided. In the first stage of the disease, if there should be severe or extensive inflammation of the soft parts, *acon.*, *bell.*, *bry.*, *hepar.*, *merc.*, or *sulph.*, are indicated.

Asaf., *calc.*, *phosph.*, *silic.*, *sulph.*, and, according to some

---

* For an interesting paper on this subject, see Quarterly Homœpathic Journal, vol. i., p. 86—an article entitled, "Case of Necrosis of the Posterior Portion of the Superior Maxillary Bone, and Gangrene of the Gums and Cheek." By J. Lloyd, Martin, Md.

authorities, *symphytum*, when properly prescribed, materially lessen the tendency of parts to renewed inflammatory action, and also exert a specific action upon the osseous system; either of them may be administered, according to the presenting symptoms, to hasten the separation of the dead from the living bone. After this is accomplished, it is the duty of the surgeon to interfere, and, by the requisite incisions and proper mode of extraction, liberate the necrosed portions of bone—which, if allowed to remain, acting as extraneous matter, irritate the parts and give rise to increased inflammation, and profuse suppuration. But the surgeon must ascertain that the sequestrum is entirely detached before attempting its removal. On this point Mr. Miller writes: "A common error in practical surgery is, interference with the sequestrum before it has become loose. To lay hold of it, and use violence, after exposure by incision, is certainly to induce a combination of evils. The evulsive effort fails, and consequently the patient has been put to a grave amount of pain, unnecessarily and fruitlessly. By the violence, inflammatory reaccession is certainly induced in and around the part originally implicated. In other words, a fresh ostitis—probably, both acute and extensive—is induced; and aggravation of the necrosis is most likely to follow. Also the loss of blood which attends on such attempts, whether successful or not, is invariably considerable; coming from a wound of soft parts, which are not only unusually vascular, but besides unfavorable to natural hemostatics. And the patient's state of system is generally such, in the advanced stages of necrosis, as to be altogether intolerant of a repetition of such hemorrhages. Therefore, on this last ground alone, it is plain that the operation for removal of a sequestrum should never be undertaken, unless the surgeon be tolerably certain that his efforts will then prove successful.

"In probing, the simultaneous use of two instruments is sometimes advantageous. One probe resting on the end of the sequestrum, a second is introduced through another cloaca; and by pressing with each alternately, looseness of the sequestrum may be made plain in circumstances otherwise extremely doubtful."

If the disease arise from syphilis, or scrofula, or if from scorbutic symptoms complications arise, the medicines must be selected with the view of meeting, if possible, both the constitutional vice and the local affection; although in many cases by removing the former, the latter will also be remedied. If the disease originate from injury, the application of *arnica* externally, and the administration of a few globules of the same medicine, greatly relieves pain.

Asaf., in alternation with *phosp.-acid*, have cured necrosis; and these two medicines with *nit.-ac.*, after an improved secretion of pus had been induced by *sulph.*, cured the disease, which was situated in the shaft of the tibia.

Calc. carb. effected a great improvement in a necrosis of the tarsal bones, in the case of a boy. Shortly after the administration of the medicine, there was a separation and painless discharge of a large spiculum of bone.

Nit.-ac., preceded by a dose of *sepia*, proved very efficacious in an osseous swelling above the knee on the external part of the thigh, from which portions of dead bone were discharged.

Silic. In a case of diseased phalanges, occurring in a female of sixty-two years of age, who had for a whole year covered the part affected with all kinds of ointments; from the part a necrosed portion of bone had been extruded; relieved the pain in eight days; after the discharge of another sequestrum, a cure followed.

A man, æt. 28, ann., fell from a tree, and seriously injured his arm by striking it against a stump: for the space of four months all motion was prevented; after which, though mobility in a degree returned, the limb was somewhat painful, and at times quite rigid. Two years subsequent, several fistulous openings were formed, through which fragments of bone frequently were discharged. *Arnica* relieved the pain. *Silic.*, *calc*,, and *sulph.* effected a cure. A remaining stiffness of the joints was removed by *colocynth.**

* See Jeanes' Homœpathic Practice, pp. 55–57.

The forceps are the best adapted instrument for the removal of sequestrum: in many instances, when the dead portion of the bone is large, the ordinary forceps of the pocket case are too small, and not possessed of sufficient strength; therefore, in their stead, strong, blunt pliers, somewhat resembling those used by locksmiths for twisting wire, should be substituted—with this difference, however, that the blades and handles should be somewhat larger. By means of these the dead portion is firmly grasped, and moved to and fro to ascertain the complete freedom of the bone from surrounding structures, and then by steady traction the sequestrum may be brought to the surface—leverage being used, if necessary.

Section 4.—*Exostosis.*

Exostosis is a preternatural growth of ossific matter, generally producing a circumscribed swelling on the bone upon which it originates.*

The formation of exostosis is similar to that of new bones; a plasma is exuded and becomes organized; then it passes into transitional cartilage, and thence the osseous structure is gradually completed. At one time the term was made to include all growths — fleshy, osseous and cartiliganous — but with propriety it is limited to growth of bone from bone.†

Sir Astley Cooper writes, "Exostosis has two different seats; it is either *periosteal* or *medullary*. By the *periosteal* exostosis I mean a deposition seated between the external surface of the bone and the internal surface of the periosteum, adhering with firmness to both surfaces; and by the *medullary* is to be understood a formation of a similar kind, originating in the medullary membrane and cancellated structure of bone."

With regard to the nature of this disease, it is found to con-

---

* Cooper and Travers' Surgical Essays. Exostosis, by Mr. Astley Cooper. See p. 123.

† Miller's Principles, p. 475.

sist of two varieties. The first is the eburneous, or *dense ivory-like exostosis*, and the other is the common cancellated exostosis. The first is smooth, shining, and presents a polished appearance, resembling ivory or pearl, is solid throughout, and appears almost destitute of those vessels by which an internal circulation is carried on. It usually appears on the flat bones, especially on the cranium, but the most frequent site of this form of the disease is the supercilliary ridges.* The growth of this tumor is slow, and it is often unattended with pain.

Cancellated exostoses appear to be mere enlargement of processes of the parent bone, the cancellated tissue extending itself and forming the interior of the new bony formation, while the exterior resembles a proportionate extension of the outer lamina.† This kind of exostosis seldom occurs but in the long bones of the extremities, and is most frequent in the femur at its lower part. The cancellated texture usually predominates; the external laminæ being thin and delicate.

Exostosis, according to Boyer,‡ rarely proceeds from an external cause, such as contusion. In most cases it is produced by an internal disease, and principally by lues venerea, or scrofula.

The effects of exostosis may be divided into general and special; thus the swelling is accompanied by a sense of weight, pain is produced by the morbid action, and the affected part is necessarily deformed. Its particular or special effects arise from its situation; thus, if an exostosis forms in the orbit, the eye is expelled from its cavity, and the patient deprived of sight; if a tumor of this nature arise from the clavicle or sternum internally, death might result by compression of the principal blood vessels.

The *prognosis* differs according to the nature of the primary disease from which the exostosis originates, and according to the particular change in the texture of the bone. The ivory

---

* See M'Clellan's Principles and Practice of Surgery, p. 343.
† Liston's Elements, p. 114.
‡ See Boyer on the Bones, p. 177.

exostosis if so situated that it does not impede the action of any organ, is said to be the least dangerous of all.

Treatment.—The medicines that are best adapted to exostosis are *arn., asaf., calc.-c., dulc., led., lyc., merc., mez., phosph., rhus, sep., silic., sulph.* The primary ostitis must be treated as before recommended, and if the disease still progress, any of the above mentioned medicines may be selected in accordance to the presenting symptoms. For exostosis syphilitica *aur., bell., nit.-ac.*, and *phosph.* are recommended.

Arnica administered in a case of exostosis femoris, arising from injury of the thigh by a blow, produced immediate relief of the pain, and subsequent abatement of the swelling and suppuration.

Aurum. Syphilitic exostosis and caries; nodes on the head, fore-arm and tibia; extensive caries of the palate bones; discharge of fetid ichor from the nose; ulceration of the throat, syphilitic rheumatism; excessive emaciation and debility; night sweats. Ten grains of the first (1st trit.) of aurum. were triturated with two drachms of sugar. This was divided into eight powders, of which the patient took one twice every day. The medicine was thus taken for ten days, with evident improvement. Again, two grains of aurum. of the same trituration as before, were mixed with two drachms of sugar. This was divided into six powders, of which the patient was directed to take one every six days. In three weeks he was perfectly well, and remained so at the end of three years. *Aurum.* also cured entirely, in fifteen days, a swelling of the frontal, nasal and superior maxillary bones, complicated with syphilitic ozœna and rheumatism.

For exostosis after abuse of mercury, *bella.* has proved effectual. It also was useful in a case of exostosis on the forehead, with intolerable pain; the palate being covered with deep gray painful ulcers, arising from the abuse of mercury.

Lycop. 30th, *silex* 24th, three doses, then *mez.* 24th, and finally *ledum.*, cured exostosis in the foot of a scrofulous boy, eight years of age.

Merc. has proved very serviceable in exostosis of the tarsal bones.

Mez. Exostosis of the radius of the left fore-arm. *Asaf.* had previously been administered in large doses. To counteract this, *puls.* 12 was given on the sixth day; *mez.*, one drop of the 6th, on the fourteenth day. On the thirty-first day, *silic.* 18. On the sixty-second day, *cacl. carb.* 30. The improvement both in the local disease and the general health, which had been progressive under previous medicines, continued also to advance after the administration of *calc.*, until the joint recovered perfect mobility, the bone had regained its natural size, and a fistulous orifice which existed at the commencement of the treatment, had become completely cicatrized. The cicatrix was covered by a scurf, which, after the employment of *lyc.* 30, speedily disappeared.

Phosph. has cured exotosis on the frontal, the parietal, and occipital bones, from the size of a bean to that of a hazel-nut; it has also, in the 30th dilution, proved effectual in the treatment of large exotosis of the clavicle, where the pain was intense, aggravated by the slightest touch, of a tearing or boring character, with nocturnal exacerbations.

Sepia. At the lower extremity of the radius, enlargement of the bone for a length of four inches; painful when touched; *sepia* 30, and after six weeks *nit.-ac.* 30 effected a cure.

Silex. Exostosis femoris, in a man æt. 28 ann. The disease commenced two years before, apparently from a blow on the thigh. Sticking, boring, and tearing pain in the anterior surface of the thigh, so severe that sleep was impossible. The thigh was very much swollen from the knee to the groin. The femur much enlarged. From the fistulous openings nearly a pint of pus, mixed with blood, was discharged every morning and evening, upon the removal of the dressings. The patient was excessively emaciated, and suffered from "phthisis pituitosa" and constant sweat. As the pain in this case appeared to be an important symptom—since it had commenced with the disease, and apparently originated from the effects of mechanical injury—and, as it had not diminished through the whole course of the disease, *arnica* was prescribed. Immediately after the administration of this medicine the patient slept for eight hours, and when he awoke the pain had in a great degree abated. From this time there was improvement, as evinced by increase of appetite, and abatement of the swelling and suppuration. The improvement continued progressive until the tenth day; and on the eleventh, as there appeared to be a cessation of favorable symptoms, *lycop.* 28 was administered. Improvement again commenced, and in its course the phthisis pituitosa gradually disappeared.*

If the bony tumor is large, and medicines do not appear to produce any beneficial effect, the surgeon may think proper to remove it by mechanical means. This may conveniently be done by the knife, Hey's saw, and trephine. Sometimes a spring saw will be found to answer a better purpose than any other instrument.

Section 5.—Spina Ventosa—Osteo Cystoma.

By this term is understood an expansion of a bone from a collection of matter, which is not purulent but serous, or of a glairy or gelatinous character. The cyst is not a pyogenic membrane, but is composed of a structure resembling that which is found in some encysted tumors. Its growth is slow, but the bulk acquired may be enormous.† The disease may be produced by external injury exciting inflammation, and consequently suppuration in the cancellated tissue; or the inflammatory action may be of a less acute kind, particularly in weakened and unhealthy constitutions. As the disease progresses, the fluid accumulates, the cancelli are broken down, and the much attenuated parietes of the bone are pressed outward. Occasionally the inflammatory action may be excited on the external surface, from the pressure of the contained fluid; and, when this is the case, minute nodules of osseous matter are effused, as if nature endeavored to strengthen the parietes,

* The above cases are taken mostly from Jeanes' Homœopathic Practice.

† Liston's Elements, p. 117.

which from diseased action daily become thinner and more incapable of affording support. Sir Astley Cooper describes this disease as a species of *exostosis*;* Boyer† mentions it under osteo sarcoma; but the difference between the latter and the affection now under consideration appears to be, that in spina ventosa the discharge is uniformly fluid and of a serous character, though sometimes mixed with a cheesy matter, there is no fungus protruding after a portion of the attenuated bone has given way, and the tumor is not of a malignant character.

There is considerable pain while suppuration is being established; but after the formation of matter the more acute sufferings subside, and in some instances there is but slight inconvenience, and the tumor remains stationary. In other cases the enlargement is enormous, and the constitution of the patient is very materially affected.‡

Treatment.—Previous to the development of the disease, if the patient complain of weariness, heaviness, and aching in the limbs, *arnica* or *phosph.-acid* may be prescribed. These medicines are also suitable, if, upon careful examination, slight swelling of the bone be detected, which is sensitive to pressure. By the exhibition of those medicines, together with *mezereum*, this disease may be arrested in its incipient stage.

Merc.-sol., according to Hartmann, appears suitable when the bone is swollen, but not much inflamed. He further says, "It seems to me, however, that inflammation was rather promoted, than arrested by *mercurius;* and I now never give it until I feel perfectly convinced that it is adapted to this particular disease."

Mez. is a valuable medicine in the treatment of spina ventosa, particularly when psora, syphilis, or scrofula exist in combination, or the patient has been poisoned by large doses of

---

* See Gibson's Institutes and Practice of Surgery, vol. ii., p. 62.

† On the Bones, p. 182.

‡ For a very interesting case of Spina Ventosa of the Cranium, which was skilfully and effectually removed by the late Dr. Geo. McClellan, see McClellan's Principles and Practice of Surgery, pp. 348–352.

mercury. Although the proving of this remedial agent is not as complete as it might be, still its general physiological character is sufficient to convince the student who examines the symptoms that have been produced by this drug, that it must be an admirable remedy for diseases of the osseous system, particularly when there is swelling of the part and burning pains, which are aggravated at night.

Asaf., *phosph.*, *sulph.*, and *silic.*, the two last never lower than the thirtieth potency, have also been recommended for this disease.

Other medicines are: *Calc.*, *phosph.*, *staphys.*, *hepar*, *sepia*, &c.

Together with this treatment, a moderate degree of long continued pressure upon the part may also be resorted to. This method alone is said to have effected the cure of the disease.

Should any of the large cylindrical bones be the seat of spina ventosa, and after a thorough trial of remedial agents, the disease appears to be steadily advancing, amputation may be resorted to.*

Section 6.—*Osteo Sarcoma.*

An osteo sarcoma—as its name implies—is a tumor consisting partly of osseous matter, and partly of a fleshy substance. This morbid change appears to be the consequence of inflammation, and its origin is frequently attributed to some mechanical injury or local irritation. In the commencement of the disease the bone is slightly enlarged, perhaps somewhat thickened in its outer laminæ; and if a section of it be made, it is found to contain a brown fleshy substance instead of the usual cancellated structure.† The osseous portions of the tumor are

* See Question of Amputation,

† Liston's Elements of Surgery, p. 115.

in the form of spiculæ, radiating outward, leaving interstices which are occupied by the sarcomatous tissue; partly cartilaginous, or fibrous, resembling ordinary fleshy substance, or cystic. Most frequently it is composed of sarcomatous substance, containing portions of cartilage.* If the structure is composed of cysts, these are lined by a secreting membrane, and it is thought by some that on the perverted action of this formation that the increase as well as peculiar structure of the disease depends. By the pressure of the new formation, the parietes of bone are forced outwards; in some cases attenuated, in others thickened by deposition of new osseous matter, inflammatory action having been induced by the pressure. As the disease advances, the bone becomes more attenuated, becoming in some places extremely thin, diaphanous, and somewhat flexible and elastic. From the latter condition it would appear that the part of the osseous system affected had lost its proportion of earthy matter.

The pains experienced by the patient are at first dull and deep seated, but in a short time they become more intense, the volume of the bone increases, though the soft parts appear yet in their natural state. The latter, however, soon become red and inflamed; the pain becomes severe, and is lancinating in character; the system is deranged, the tumor softens, often presents a sense of distinct fluctuation, and on being freely handled, is found to crepitate in consequence of loose spicula of bone being pressed against each other. Ultimately the integuments become livid, or dark red, ulcerate, and allow a portion of the softened tumor to protrude, in the form of a frightful fungus. There is profuse discharge, thin and sometimes bloody; and as may be supposed, much constitutional irritation and exhaustion. Not unfrequently during the progress of the disease, especially if it be situate in the cylindrical bones, fractures occur either from muscular contraction or external injury. This accident gives rise to serious complication, as the process of reproduction in the diseased bone is very slow, if indeed, it is not altogether suspended, consequently the fracture does not unite,

---

* Miller's Principles, p. 482.

suppuration is increased, and the disease is therefore much hastened.

Although after the protrusion of the fungus, the soft parts are not readily involved, the tumor may properly be pronounced malignant. At an earlier stage of progress it is confined to the tissue in which it originated by laminæ of bone, but after this barrier has given way, it projects further through the aperture, and contaminates all the surrounding structures until again held in check by bony formation.

In the commencement of this affection, several medicines may be indicated in accordance with symptoms which present themselves, among which are *bell.*, *merc.*, *mez.*, *phosph.*, *phosph.-ac.*, *nit.-ac.*, *sulph.*

If the constitution of the patient suffers severely from the exhausting suppuration, *china* or *hepar* should be administered. If the disease has been occasioned by a blow, *arnica*, *ruta.*, *rhus* or *symphytum* may be called for.

From the action of *thuja* upon fungous formation, this medicine must be remembered, and should be prescribed if the sarcomatous formations are red and fleshy, pouring out blood profusely at the slightest touch, if the patient is debilitated both in body and mind, and the symptoms are all aggravated towards evening or at night.

Calc.-carb. must be prescribed when the constitution presents evident marks of scrofulous cachexy, and when the parts around are red, swollen and indurated, with several fistulous openings.

Causticum and *silicea* may also be called for. And *arsenicum* or *carbo-veg.* may be indicated by the prostration, excessive thirst, dryness of the skin, and frequent shudderings.

In allopathic therapeutics the *mercurial* preparations are often used. Sir Astley Cooper highly recommended the oxymuriate of mercury, and, according to other authors, the treatment has proved quite efficacious. The latter treatment is noticed in this place with the hope that some may be incited to experiment with the mercurial preparation just mentioned.

If medical treatment fail, surgeons of the present day have recourse to amputation or extirpation; the result, however, is seldom favorable, the disease returning with renewed vigor either in the stump or in some other portion of the body.

There is another malignant disease of the osseous system, to which the term *medullary sarcoma* is applied; it arises in the cancellous structure, the pain being very intense, because the affection progresses rapidly and the bone is mechanically forced open, from the continued and increasing pressure of the diseased mass in its interior.

The characteristics which distinguish malignant from non-malignant tumors in bone, are that the former increase with greater rapidity; are accompanied with more severe suffering; are softer, and have a tendency to involve the subadjacent textures.

The chief indication in the treatment of these tumors is to commence early the medicinal treatment. Frequently, if the primary affection can be subdued, or the constitutional symptoms successfully combated, the disease may be eradicated; these ends may be accomplished by the treatment that has previously been mentioned for disease of the periosteum and bones.

The medicines that are best adapted to the medullary sarcoma are *asaf.*, *bell.*, *calc.*, *mez.*, *merc.*, *phosph.*, *phosph.-ac.*, *silic.*, or *sulph.*

Section 7.—Mollities Ossium and Rachitis.

Both of these affections are occasioned by a deficiency of the requisite proportion of earthy material in the bony structure, and differ only in this, that in the latter the cretaceous matter is not deposited originally, while in the former it is absorbed after having been deposited.

Softening of the bones, according to Liston,* "is met with at all ages and in different degrees. It often follows dentition, measles, hooping-cough, or other infantile diseases which in-

* Liston's Elements of Surgery, p. 80.

duce general debility; and in females it appears to be produced by the weakening effects of leucorrhœa, miscarriages," &c. Mercury, administered in inordinate quantities, also produces the disease; but by far the greater proportion of cases are said to depend on scrofulosis. As all other chronic dyscrasiæ, the development of the affection is gradual; the first symptoms that are noticed being generally those of derangement of the digestive functions, alteration of secretion, &c.; by degrees, a material change in the solids of the body takes place, particularly in the osseous system, and the alterations of composition in the latter, give birth to many functional derangements.

The gastric symptoms that are noticed, as precursors of the disease, especially when children are affected, are: flatulence, acidity of the stomach, distention of the abdomen, sour eructations, and vomiting. The appetite is impaired, the patient usually desiring those articles of food which are particularly indigestible, the countenance is pale and cadaverous, the urine becomes turbid and cloudy, and if subjected to chemical analysis, is found to contain a superabundance of phosphate of lime, and probably benzoic and oxalic acids.

In children* there is much emaciation; the skin and muscles become flaccid, the face is wrinkled, distorted, and resembles that of the aged. The growth of the child is arrested, walking is difficult, and in the more advanced stages altogether impracticable; the teeth become yellow, brown, or streaked transversely, are at length attacked by caries, and soon fall out.

During the progress of the disease the bones flatten and bend, are soft, cellular, and of a brown color, contain a dark fluid, and are very deficient in earthy matter. In many instances, this latter component of ossific structure is almost entirely removed—the bones consisting of an extremely thin external osseous shell, covered by thickened periosteum, and containing a pulpy substance resembling fatty matter. Although this disease has been said by Mr. Liston to attack individuals of all ages, by far the greater proportion of those affected are young children.

* Hartmann's Diseases of Children, p. 397.

Certain rare cases, however, have been recorded, in which all the bones of the adult were softened to a very great degree.

The vertebral column is particularly liable to be affected with rachitis, and the disease may be in certain instances confined to it alone. When the cervical vertebræ are attacked, the anterior part of the neck projects, the head falls backwards, and appears sunken between the shoulders. When the affection is general, the vertebral column becomes shorter, and is curved in various directions; the breast becomes deformed, not only in consequence of the curvature of the spine, but by the depression of the ribs and projection of the sternum; the bones of the pelvis fall inwards, and generally the pubis approaches the sacrum.*

According to the observations of Mr. Stanley, when the tibia and fibula become affected they acquire increased breadth in the direction of the curve, losing a proportional degree of thickness in the opposite direction.†

The proximate cause of softening of the bones is involved in much obscurity; various authors have endeavored to explain the origin of the affection, in accordance with their own peculiar views. These conflicting suppositions, although possessed of much interest to the curious, are of no practical value, and therefore need no comment in this place.

Treatment.—In this disease great advantage is to be derived from the general treatment; the patient, if residing in a city, should if possible be removed to the country, where an elevated and dry situation should be chosen, nourishing diet, with a moderate quantity of wine may be allowed, and the strictest cleanliness, with regularity of habits, should be observed. But as the poor, among whom the disease is most frequently observed, are not enabled to procure change of residence, the patient should be placed in a room that is well ventilated and clean, and in temperate weather be allowed to walk or sit in the sunlight. A straw or wheaten chaff mattress should be

* See Boyer on the Bones, p. 190.

† Med. Chir. Trans., vol. vii., p. 402.

used, as it is dry and does not yield to the weight of the body; the clothing should be sufficient to prevent uncomfortableness from extremes of heat and cold, and should be changed to suit the variations of temperature. In the first stages of the disease, when gastric derangements predominate, *ipecac.*, *bry.*, *nux* and *verat.* are indicated, and their administration is frequently followed by beneficial results.

In children, when the abdomen is hard and distended, the gait unsteady and staggering, and the complexion pale, with occasional flushes of heat, *bell.* is particularly indicated.

Sulph., *calc.*, *hepar* and *silic.* are also powerful agents in the treatment of rachitis; by their exhibition the general health improves, and the disease has been known to be arrested in a short period of time. The attenuation of these medicines, however, is an important consideration; the practitioner will fail in his endeavors if recourse be had to the lower, inasmuch as the most beneficial results are more certainly attained by the administration of the thirtieth dilution and upwards.

Hartmann writes,* "I have employed with great success *brucea antidysenterica*, particularly when the feet were turned outwards and the children walked on the inner ankles."

In another work,† he further says, "According to my experience, it is in the preliminary stage that cod-liver oil will do the most good, and actually effect a cure, and remove the danger of a relapse, provided a proper dietetic and hygienic regimen is observed. The oil may be used internally, and at the same time rubbed on the abdomen. If no improvement should set in after using the oil a fortnight, or if the child should evince an insurmountable repugnance to taking the medicine, it is a matter of course that some other remedy will have to be used."

Acid-phosph., *ruta.*, *staphys.*, *mez.*, *lyco.*, *calc.*, and *asaf.* may be indicated in the treatment of this disease.

According to Dr. Patzack, *pinus-sylvestris* is often of great benefit in the treatment of rickets. The medicine may be used internally and externally.

* Chronic Diseases, vol. i., p. 63.

† Diseases of Children, p. 401.

Curvature of the bones are either congenital malformations, or constitute the most aggravated form of rachitis. The same medicines will therefore be indicated.* But it must be clearly understood, that together with the internal medicinal treatment appropriate mechanical apparatus must be employed to retain the parts in situ. These consist of stays, belts and straps, which must be selected by the surgeon as best adapted to each particular case. The mechanical means employed by Mr. Thomas Engall,† with so much success, in connection with homœopathic treatment, is here mentioned:

"A couch is provided, twenty-six inches wide, the same in height, and a foot longer than the patient, with head and foot-posts above the mattress; into the former a board is fitted, and into the latter a winch, formed of a bar of iron, with a rack wheel at one end, into which a catch turning on a centre in the footpost, falls, and prevents its return when extension is made by it; the floor of the couch is made throughout of wood, and twenty-six inches from the foot an iron bar is placed across it, on which the floor turns, so that it may become an inclined plane; on the under surface of the upper part a frame is placed on hinges, which, falling into teeth formed on the side rail keeps the floor elevated to any inclination desired; a footboard is provided, fitting, by means of two pins, into the end of the inclined plane. On the floor of the couch is placed a horse-hair mattress, made perfectly firm and smooth, divided into three compartments. The extension is performed by the winch, from which two straps pass, which are attached to others coming from a belt fastened round the patient's pelvis, the head or arms being fixed; when the former is the case, a well-stuffed band is placed round the occiput, another round the chin, these are laced together and secured to the headboard, when the latter two stuffed bands are passed under the axilla, and fastened

---

* For an interesting paper on the "Mechanical and Homœopathic Treatment of Spinal Curvature," vide British Journal of Homœopathy, vol. v., pp. 63—165.

† British Journal of Homœopathy, vol. v., p. 193.

like the former. Extension is not employed upon young children, nor upon cases in which the parts can be replaced without it; hence it is inadmissible in cases of distortion from ligamentous lengthening, as it would only increase the malady. The patient wears a common dress, all the garments made to open behind, the stays to open in front also. In a case of *posterior distortion* a pad is made the length of the spine, and nearly the breadth of the back, so arranged as to cause at first very little pressure upon the prominent parts; this is placed upon the back, the stays laced over it, and the patient laid supine. Every morning the stays are opened in front, and the chest well rubbed, Florence oil being used to prevent abrasion of the skin and to relax the parts; the oil is then washed off, the stays laced, the garments drawn on at the feet first, and the patient turned prone in a sheet held tight at the side; the stays are then unlaced behind, the pad removed, and the back treated as the chest, during which time the spine is elongated; after this process the pad and stays are replaced, the garments fastened, and the patient again turned supine, which position is constantly maintained. In the evening the dress is unfastened and drawn off at the feet, everything being removed in this way except the stays and shields; ordinary night habiliments are worn, bed-clothes are drawn under, and placed over the patient, who thus passes the night on the couch. As the patient can bear it, the pressure is increased by placing a splint behind the pad, which is then termed a shield, and raising the centre of it so that the ribs shall not be pressed upon; and, by lessening the support of the parts above and below the protrusion, the pressure is also aided by the manipulation of the medical attendant. For this purpose various instruments have been used; but I prefer that formed by the Divine Artificer, the hand, which possesses a sensibility so acute, as to inform the mind of what is passing under it. Every procedure in the treatment should be gentle; if pain is felt by the patient, something in the arrangement is certainly wrong. The object of the manipulation and pressure being to reinstate the parts, this end must be attained by causing them to retrace their steps; hence the parts last protruded should be the first replaced; all the means adverted to are aids; the recumbency suspends all muscular action; the extension destroys the form of the arch by weakening the ends on which its strength depends; manipulation and friction assist these means. In *semi-lunar distortion*, a back splint is applied to keep the parts in their natural positions; the lateral curve is reduced by means of a side shield, which consists of a piece of wood half an inch thick, three inches wide, as long as necessary, with pads at each end to keep the centre hollow, in this case extending beyond the extreme ends of the arch, and applied on the concave side, over the centre of which and round the convex side of the body a broad band passes, which, aided by extension and pressure, will generally succeed. A modification of this plan must be adopted in *double lateral distortion.* In *lateral distortion, with a projecting shoulder* from rotation, the posterior and lateral treatment must be combined. In this case it is of importance to ascertain if the projection preceded or followed the lateral distortion; if you cannot obtain this information from friends, you will by observing the direction in which the spine most readily yields. If the spine rotated before the curvature took place, the curvature must be first reduced, and the projection after; if the contrary, the projection must be first reduced; if both originate at the same time, pressure must be applied in the opposite direction to that in which it came out, by means of a tilting-board sufficiently wide to press on the projection, having another piece rising at right angles to it at one end, and formed internally so as to press equally on the side and back of the projection, which is covered by a properly adjusted shield. On this the patient lies; by means of a block placed under the opposite end, the inclination can be adapted to the requirements of the case; a band fixed to the horizontal and buckled to the vertical piece will increase the pressure as needed, and aid in depressing the prominent parts of the chest. A modification of this plan is also very useful in lateral curvature, where the ends of the arch extend beyond the axilla, in which case the shield on the concave side will be inefficient; here pressure on the convex side, with the prolongation of the splint above the shoulder and to the ilium, without touching either, with a band from each end extending over the opposite extremities of the arch, will effect the desired intention. For simple lateral and semi-lunar distortions, the pressure of the medical attendant must be directed against the spinous processes, for which purpose an instrument made of either wood or metal, with a rounded edge four inches long, and a handle attached to it, will be found useful; in distortion from rotation, where the object is to untwist the spine, this pressure, for the reasons already given, must be made on the concave side."

Section 8.—*Fragilitas Ossium.*

This disease occurs chiefly in old people whose osseous system contains an undue quantity of earthy material. Boyer* states, that a certain degree of fragilitas ossium necessarily occurs in old age, because the proportion of lime in the bones increases with age, while the organic matter decreases in the same ratio; but Mr. Wilson† observes, that they are never found so friable and fragile as to crumble like calcined bone, but on the contrary contain a large quantity of oil. The latter fact is also noticed by Mr. Liston,‡ who gives as a definition of the disease, that the bones become brittle on account of an undue proportion of earthy matter, are endowed with little vascularity, and are full of an *oleaginous* fluid.

In persons who have been long afflicted with cancerous diseases, the bones are said to become as brittle as if they had been calcined. In inveterate syphilis, deprivation of organic material in the osseous system has been noticed, and in those individuals who have been frequently afflicted with severe

---

* On Diseases of the Bones, p. 197.

† On the Skeleton and Diseases of the Bones, p. 258.

‡ Elements of Surgery, p. 80.

attacks of scurvy, the bones become so brittle that they are fractured from the slightest causes.

Treatment.—This disease, particularly when occurring in the aged, is very difficult to cure, the patient should be allowed a generous diet, and prohibited from much muscular exertion; indeed all circumstances that would be likely to produce sudden action of any particular combination of muscles, should be studiously avoided.

The medicines that are best adapted to this affection are—*ruta*, *phosph.-ac.*, *nit.-ac.*, and from the effects that have been produced by *symphytum*, this medicinal agent should exercise much influence in this peculiar disorder. If the fragility of bone depend upon constitutional affections, *syphilis*, *scrofula*, &c., great advantage may be derived from the internal treatment of these diseases.

CHAPTER XXIV.

DISEASES OF THE JOINTS.

Section 1.—Synovitis.

This disease may be either acute or chronic. It generally commences with severe aching in the joints, together with shooting pain, sometimes extending into the surrounding parts. After a short period of time the joint enlarges, becomes of a reddish hue, is extremely sensitive to pressure, and symptoms of severe constitutional disturbance develop themselves. The fever is intense, with redness of the cheeks, glistening eyes, coated tongue, high-colored urine, and, in some instances, derangement of the digestive functions. The swelling often advances rapidly, and is caused by rapid effusion into the synovial cavity. If the joint be superficial, fluctuation is distinct; the inflammation may terminate in suppuration, and the formation of purulent secretion within the cavity, to which the term *arthropyosis* is applied.

In *chronic synovitis*, the pain is not so severe and is of a dull aching character, the part is but little sensitive to pressure, and there is experienced a sensation of weakness and relaxation of the limb. The swelling appears a few days after the pain, which in cases of an indolent character may be of trifling moment. To such, the term *hydrops articuli* is applied.

The disease may follow local injuries, or be dependent on constitutional causes; as rheumatism, gout, syphilis, scrofula, abuse of mercury, &c. Children are seldom attacked; and the knee joint is most generally the site of the affection. In such instances the patella is protruded, and there is fulness at each side of it, and also at the lower and anterior portion of the thigh. At the elbow, the swelling is most marked above the olecranon: at the hip and shoulder articulations, there is general swelling of the surrounding muscles.

The disease is considered of a serious nature when it arises from penetrating wounds of the joint, as in such instances the constitutional disturbance is so severe, that life is brought into imminent danger.

Delirium and typhoid symptoms are very unfavorable. In severe cases suppuration within the cavity may ensue, or ulceration of cartilage and complete anchylosis may result.

Treatment.—The limb should be kept at rest until the violent inflammatory symptoms have been subdued—which may be accomplished in the first stages by the employment of *aconite.* This medicine is especially indicated by the severity of the fever, and when there are drawing and sticking pains in the affected joint, with tension, aching and gnawing; when the patient complains of frequent chilliness and thirst, together with prostration and trembling of the limbs.

Bella. should be employed in acute synovitis, when there is congestion to head, with flushed cheeks, &c.; when the pain is excessive, with sensation as if the surrounding ligaments were contracted; or when there is bubbling, as from drops of water in the fore part of the knee, with cutting and drawing pains.

Calc.-carb. is more suitable to this disease when it assumes a chronic character; when the patient is pale, debilitated, or of a scrofulous habit; with drawing pressure in the joints; or when the disease is accompanied with other affections of the osseous system.

Caust. may be employed when there is stiffness of the joints; bruised, tearing, and sticking pain; profuse sweat; numbness of the parts, and the sufferings aggravated in the evening.

Ledum is especially adapted to disease of the joints, but particularly to affections of the knee. It possesses a powerful action on the absorbent vessels, and should be used in both acute and chronic synovitis when there is effusion, with sensitiveness of the parts to pressure; aching, tearing pains; great coldness, or constant chilliness.

Iodium is an important medicine where there is much swelling of the parts, with erratic, tearing pains.

Merc. should be prescribed when the disease is accompanied with syphilitic complication; when there are drawing pains, with aching in the bones, and rigidity of the parts; particularly when the symptoms are exacerbated at evening and at night, with profuse sweat.

Lycop. may be used if there is stiffness of the joints, when the pains are relieved by warmth, and aggravated in cold rainy weather.

Kali-carb. may in some instances prove valuable, when there is aching in the joint, dread of the open air, and liability to take cold.

Rhus-tox. is indicated, when, beside the ordinary pain, there are stitchings in the tendons surrounding the joints, accompanied with tingling and burning, with rigidity of the joints; or when there are sticking pains with stiffness, and especially if the constitutional symptoms tend to a typhoid condition.

Sepia should be remembered when the patient is delicate; or, if females are affected, when there are jerking, sticking pains; or when the disease has been occasioned by violent strains of muscles or tendons.

Silicea is also highly recommended for diseases of the synovial membrane, particularly that of the knee joint.

Aur., calc., lyc., nit.-ac., phosph.-ac., sulph., together with *silic.*, have been found useful in inflammation of the synovial membrane, in consequence of effects of *mercury;* and *bry., china, lyc., nux-vom., rhus,* and *sulph.*, when the disease occurs in gouty or rheumatic individuals.

Calc.-carb. and *sulph.* have been chiefly recommended in lymphatic or scrofulous enlargements of the knee. If suppuration ensue, *silic., merc.*, and *hepar;* and in that of serous infiltration, *silic.* and *sulph.*, or *calc., merc* , and *iodium.*

Other medicines are: *hell.* (particularly in hydrops articuli), *ign., petr., phosph., rhod., ruta, stront.*, and *sulph.*

Section 2.—Morbus Coxarius.

The hip joint is exceedingly liable to disease: persons of all ages may be affected, but children of a scrofulous habit are particularly obnoxious to it. The disease has been supposed by many to commence in the cartilages. It appears, however, according to Mr. Liston, to originate indiscriminately in the cartilage and the bone, as well as in the capsule and investing membrane of the joint; but it is of little import what particular structure the diseased action invades.

The first manifestation that is experienced, is awkwardness in moving the limb of the affected side, or slight lameness. No severe pain is experienced; and, if there is any uneasiness, it is generally referred to other parts, and particularly to the knee. This circumstance should lead the practitioner to close investigation—for frequently other diseases than the true one are diagnosed; and the patient may thus be led to believe, that the affection under which he is laboring is slight and easily curable, until the true nature of the affection is detected, when considerable censure, with charges of dishonesty or insincerity, may be cast upon the surgeon.

The pain in the knee joint is generally the prominent symptom in this affection, but occasionally it is referred to the ankle or sole of the foot. As the disease advances, severe suffering is occasioned by moving the hip joint, or by suddenly forcing the head of the femur against the acetabulum. The limb of the affected side is apparently lengthened; the patient moves with the hand grasped round the thigh, and otherwise contrives to prevent the affected limb from supporting the body; the spinal column becomes curved, and other deformity of the trunk occurs.

The nates are much altered—they become flattened; and those parts which are naturally the most prominent, are reduced to the level of the surrounding parts. The inguinal glands enlarge, are painful, and emaciation of the limb is more and more visible. If the disease still progresses, the leg is considerably *shortened;* large collections of matter, occasioning much swelling, are found behind the trochanter major, and the part assumes various accidental positions. Sometimes it is turned inward, as in dislocation of the dorsum ilii; or outwards, as in fractures of the neck of the femur.

Treatment.—In the first stages of morbus coxarius, when the patient complains of pain in the knee, *bella.* is a medicine, by the administration of which, in some instances, in alternation with *mercurius,* the disease may be entirely subdued. *Aconite* may also be used with great advantage in the commencement of the affection. If there is tension of the part, with severe pain, *colocynth* should be employed; and, if there are evening exacerbations, *puls.* is indicated. The chief medicine, however, is *bella.,* which, according to Hartmann, is characteristic to the pain in the knee, though this symptom is only symptomatic of the disease of the hip. He has never used it below the 24th dilution, and speaks in the most unqualified manner regarding its action.

Rhus-tox. should be employed when there are darting, or dragging, tearing pains in the hip joint, increased by pressing the head of the femur into the acetabulum, accompanied with tension or stiffness of the muscles; painful while at rest, but increased when arising from a sitting posture.

Colocynth is particularly indicated when the pain extends into the knee, and the patient experiences a sensation as though the part were clasped with an iron band.

Cacl.-carb. removed the disease from a scrofulous child, who without previous injury commenced to limp; in walking dragged one foot along the ground; complained of little or no pain, except when pressing the femur into the acetabulum. The diseased limb was longer than the other, and the foot always turned outward. In another case, *tinctura acris* cured the affection.

Sulph., *lyc.*, *hepar*, *silic.*, *zinc.*, *mez.*, *phosph.*, *phosph.-ac.*, *bry.*, *cham.*, *puls.*, *staphys.*, and *sepia*, should also be remembered in the treatment of this disease.

Absolute rest must be enjoined; and the starch or dextrine bandage,* leather or felt splint be applied. When shortening of the limb has commenced, great comfort and advantage may be derived by maintaining constant extension of the limb, by a weight attached to the thigh above the knee by means of a cord passing over a pulley at the foot of the bed. During the suppurative stage, the patient's strength must be sustained by nourishing diet, and *hepar*, *merc.*, *silic.*, *sulph.*, or *calendula*, be internally administered, and other means resorted to which have been recommended in the treatment of abscess.

Dr. Physick's *mechanical treatment* was as follows: —

After placing the patient upon a hair mattress, he then applied a curved splint, which was constructed in such a manner as to fit the limb perfectly, extending from the middle of the side of the thorax to the internal malleolus. This splint should be wide enough to extend nearly half way round the limb to

---

* Dextrine is a substance obtained by the continued action of diluted sulphuric acid upon starch at the boiling point. The bandages are soaked in a solution of the dextrine in water, having been previously moistened thoroughly with tincture of camphor, to prevent it from leaking when the water is added. The solution should be of the consistence of molasses.

which it is applied; and, to prevent excoriation, the inside of it is carefully wadded, and retained in its position by rollers. After a time, when inflammation and swelling have been relieved, a straighter splint may be substituted.*

Section 3.—Fungus Articulorum.

In fungus of the joints the synovial membrane becomes inflamed, ulcerates, and is finally converted into a thick pulpy substance, intersected by white membranous lines. There is not much pain, but there is stiffness together with considerable swelling of the joint, which is elastic, but there is no fluctuation. The tumefaction presents an irregular appearance, being more protruberant in one part than in another, from the accumulation of fluid or solid matter in the directions where least resistance is afforded by the surrounding tissues. Pus often accumulates within the cavity of the joint, and the suppuration is accompanied with much constitutional disturbance; or the matter may be effused into the bursæ, into the surrounding cellular tissue, or into that beneath the tendinous sheaths of the muscles in the neighborhood. After a time the capsular ligament ulcerates, the pus is evacuated, and caries of the bone is added to the already alarming disease.

It has been a matter of some difference of opinion, whether in this affection there is enlargement of the articulating extremities of bone. It is probable, that, in the first stages of the disease, they are seldom or ever affected; but, as abnormal action increases, inflammation and ulceration of the osseous parts ensue. Frequently the knee is the seat of the disease; and when this articulation is affected, the lymphatic glands in the groin become sympathetically enlarged. The same fact may be noticed when the swelling occurs in the elbow joint, in which instance the axillary glands participate.

---

* For an interesting cure of Morbus Coxarius, see Jeanes' Practice of Medicine, p. 58.

When the patient has suffered for a considerable time, hectic supervenes, with its alarming train of symptoms, which are always aggravated after the opening of the abscess. Emaciation, excessive debility, loss of appetite, night sweats, and diarrhœa are also present. In some cases health is restored, and the disease abates spontaneously; in others, complete cures are effected by careful and judicious treatment. A method of resolution resorted to by nature is anchylosis, which may be either ligamentous or osseous. New bone is deposited, whereby the ulcers become as it were cicatrized, and the articulating extremities are joined by firm bony union. The process of ossification is assisted by the effusion of lymph, and consequent thickening and induration of the ligamentous substance exterior to the joint. By such means the parts are retained in exact apposition, and the calcareous matter is regularly deposited, as in fractures retained in situ by the application of splints.

This disease, however, may again recur, and both ligamentous and osseous formation be destroyed by the ulcerative process. In many cases, however, the anchylosis remains permanent.

Treatment.—According to Hartmann, *silic.* is the principal medicine in the treatment of fungus articulorum. He recommends it to be repeated every eight days If it should not effect a cure, the following should be employed (one dose every week): *Ant.-crud*, *petrol.*, *iod.*, *clem.*, or *sulph.*

In the first stages of the disease, when there is inflammation of the synovial membrane, *acon.*, *bell.*, *mez.*, *nit.-ac.*, *phosph.-ac.*, *lyc.*, *sulph.*, or *calcarea*, should be employed. When the pulpy fungus makes its appearance, *phosph.*, *thuja*, *caust.*, or *sepia* may be indicated. In the event of suppuration, *silic.*, *hepar*, *merc.*, or *calend.* should be remembered.

If the swelling is shining, white, soft, and doughy, *puls.* is to be prescribed. In many cases *iodine* is useful, and may be employed in alternation with *puls.* When the swelling is red and very painful, *bryonia* would perhaps be more appropriate; when there is serous infiltrations, *ledum*, *calc.*, *iodium*, *merc.*, or *sulph.* may be required.

Of the imperfectness of the above treatment the author is fully aware; but it should not create surprise, when the present unscientific arrangement of our Materia Medica is remembered. So long as catalogues of disjointed symptoms, recorded with total neglect of the order of occurrence, and with entire disregard of all pathological inquiry, have to be examined; and when, together with these circumstances, the void in our literature, occasioned by the absence of recorded surgical diseases, treated in accordance with the law of Hahnemann, is recollected, any result less defective could not be anticipated. We are happy, however, to remark in this place, that such impediments to the advancement of true science will, in a short period of time, be removed in a great measure, by the publication of a complete Materia Medica by our English brethren, in which symptoms will be arranged in connection with those diseases with which they are most frequently associated.

Section 4.—*Anchylosis.*

By the term anchylosis is understood, an intimate union of two or more bones, which were naturally connected by means of a joint. All articulations originally designed for motion, may become anchylosed. Conner describes a remarkable case of this disease, in which there was general anchylosis of all the bones in the body; and a still more curious case is recorded of a child, only twenty-three months old, whose articulations were universally affected.

Anchylosis may be *spurious, ligamentous,* or *bony.* In the first case, when the joint is diseased, the extensor muscles become emaciated; the flexors are rigid, and may also be atrophied; and there is thickening of the synovial membrane, together with contraction of ligaments. This variety often follows acute synovitis, and should be considered as rather a favorable termination of that disease. In ligamentous anchylosis, the union is effected by means of the union of the articular surface by ligaments, and follows often upon disease of the cartilage and compound dislocation. Bony anchylosis is produced by the formation of ossific matter within the cavity of a joint, uniting the extremities of the bones. The symptoms that accompany the disease have been already adverted to in the chapter upon Morbus Coxarius.

Treatment.—In the first two varieties of anchylosis, much service may be rendered by passive movement of the joint, together with friction of the joint, and the internal administration of *graph.*, *rhod.*, *rhus-tox.*, *sepia*, or *sulph.*, and, in some instances, *cham.*, *bry.*, *lyc.*, and *staphys.*; and probably by the early use of these remedial agents, together with passive movement of the joint, the disease may be cured. When we have reason to believe that bony union is about to occur, *phosph.*, *phosph.-ac.*, *mez.*, *nit.-ac.*, *silic.*, *staphys.*, and *sulph.* may be employed with advantage. When rigidity of muscles and ligaments produce immobility of the joint, *bry.*, *rhus-tox.*, *ruta*, *lyc.*, *sulph.* should be employed. The patient may also be placed in an anæsthetic condition, from the inhalation of ether, and the limb flexed and extended, even if considerable effort is required. If these means fail, they may be of the utmost service after subcutaneous division of ligaments, which operation has been performed with considerable success. In bony anchylosis excision of the joint may be resorted to; and from the testimony recorded in favor of such mechanical aid, we are led to infer that the operation may be as successful as the generality of such as are now practised among modern surgeons.

Excision or resection of joints is not only practised in anchylosis, but also in *articular caries*, and may be resorted to in either of these diseases, provided all other remedial measures have failed. The operation is one of modern times, although it was practised first in France, and with considerable success by Moreau (father and son); but, either from prejudice, or tenacious adherence to established routine, it was some time before it became known among surgeons in England. Sir Philip Crampton practised it once in Ireland, but his example was not followed by others of the profession.

In 1828, Mr. Syme, of Edinburgh, was bold enough to perform the operation on his own responsibility; and, in 1831, he published a treatise upon the subject. However, the surgical faculty did not appear to follow Mr. Syme's method, and mainly on account (according to the latter gentleman's own words*) "of the principles of its performance being overlooked." These consist mainly in the mode of making the incision, and cutting off the extremities of the bone.

The division of the integument should be free, and in the form of the letter H, the same as that originally practised by Moreau. When the flaps are raised and dissected back, the articulating extremities of the bone are sufficiently exposed, and should be cut off in portions, in order to avoid the risk which would be incurred by severing a nerve; which, if any are exposed, should be pushed aside, before proceeding with the operation. After the removal of a sufficient portion of the articulation, the wound closes neatly by the aid of sutures and adhesive straps.

It may be well to observe here, that these remarks are especially applicable to excision of the elbow joint; but there can be no doubt that similar methods may be resorted to in other cases, although operations on the coxo femoral articulation are attended with great difficulty and danger.

Section 5.—Ecphyma Cartilagineum; or Movable Cartilage.

Foreign bodies, resembling pieces of cartilage, are occasionally met with, in the various articulations of the body. They vary in number—from one to twenty-seven have been found in the same joint; and in size, from that of a lentil to that of a large kidney-bean. Their shape is quite as variable as their bulk—sometimes they are round or oval, or they may be

---

* Vide London Lancet, May, 1855, p. 393. "Mr. Syme on Clinical Surgery."

smooth or irregular. Those resembling in appearance ordinary cartilage, consist chiefly of albumen; while those that are of a firmer construction contain a considerable proportion of phosphate of lime. The knee joint is their most frequent location.

The etiology of this affection is very obscure; and, although many opinions have been advanced, as yet little positive information concerning the origin and growth of these extraneous bodies has been ascertained. However, certain it is that they commence as pendulous growths upon the synovial membrane; that the capsular ligament is distended with increased accumulation of synovia; that they increase in size; and, that they more or less impede motion. They appear after swelling of a joint, occasioned by a blow or fall; or they may arise without any assignable cause. In either case, their presence is known by the pain which is experienced by the patient, and by the tumefaction of the part, which increases during rest, but subsides during moderate exercise. Authors formerly supposed that these foreign substances were portions of articular cartilage, which from time to time had been torn away by external injury. This, however, was disproved by Morgagni; who, from frequent experiment, found the cartilage of the joint entire and perfectly healthy in those subjects in whose articulations these movable bodies were met with in the greatest number.

It often happens that, after a time, the pedicle, which connects these abnormal formations to the synovial membrane, is ruptured; and, in such cases, they pass from one part of the joint to the other, and sometimes cause excruciating pain, by becoming impacted between the articular extremities of the bones. In the knee joint, they are very liable to fix themselves between the posterior face of the patella and the pulley-like surface of the femur. In some situations, the foreign substance can readily be detected beneath the integument; and Dessault mentions a case, in which they could be seized and twisted with the fingers.

Treatment.—We know of no medicine that is homœopathic to this affection. Indeed, from the position they occupy as foreign bodies, and their formation, as it were, *sui generis*, it would seem that they were rather without the sphere of medicinal or vital action. Strictly surgical means are the only resort. Surgeons have advised to force the cartilaginous formation to a part of the capsule, where it will not interfere with the motion of the joint, and there to retain it by bandages, straps, &c., to endeavor to excite adhesive inflammation; however, such result can scarcely ever be attained, and therefore operation must be had recourse to. The patient, however, before proceeding with any such means, should be candidly informed of the danger incurred in opening the cavity of the joint; should be told of the ratio of successful performances of operation; and should be allowed to determine what course to be pursued. If he consents to the operation, it should be performed in the following manner: —

The patient having been placed on a mattress, or table, with the leg extended in such a manner that the integuments of the joint may be relaxed, the surgeon should search for the foreign body, and having found it, should bring it to the inner side of the patella, and retain it in that position. The integument immediately over it should then be drawn as tense as possible with the finger and thumb (this may be accomplished with the left hand of the surgeon, or by an assistant), and with a single incision the skin should be divided. The foreign body can then readily be pressed through the opening, and the wound immediately closed, to prevent the admission of air. If there is any connection with the surrounding parts, they may be divided with scissors or a sharp-pointed knife. Forceps, fingers, or any instrument likely to bruise the joint, should never be used.

The pain of this operation is trifling, unless a branch of the internal saphena nerve happen to be divided. The wound may be closed with isinglass plaster, and compresses moistened with solution of *arnica* or *calendula* applied. It is after the operation that medicinal treatment is most important. To prevent inflammation of the synovial membrane, it would be well to immediately administer a dose of *aconite;* or, if other symptoms are present, those medicines already mentioned in the treatment of synovitis must be employed. After the wound has healed, spurious anchylosis may follow, which may be relieved by the administration of *arn.*, *rhus*, *bry.*, or *caust.*, together with moderate motion, which should be daily increased. If the patient recover with partial stiffness of a joint, the operation may be considered as successful.

Fleshy and *gristly tumors* may produce the symptoms as related of movable cartilage—the treatment is the same.

Wounds of the joints may generally be known by the escape of the synovial fluid, which commonly appears as small, oily globules. The desideratum in the treatment is to prevent inflammation of the synovial membrane (see synovitis). Immediately after the receipt of the injury, the parts should be brought in apposition; the joint placed in a splint and perfect rest enjoined. If the cavity of the joint is exposed, and cannot be covered by integument; if the general health of the patient is bad; the question of amputation must be seriously considered.

Section 6.—Diseases of the Bursæ.

The bursæ are lined by a membrane, resembling the synovial in function, appearance, and disease; they are frequently the seat of inflammatory action, which in the generality of instances is of short duration, and terminates in an increased accumulation of the secreted fluid. The abnormal action may be either acute or chronic, and may take place in those bursæ situated over the patella, olecranon, inner side of the head of the tibia, the angle of the scapula, or about the carpal articulations.

When the inflammation is acute the pain is severe, and there is much swelling and fever. The affection may be distinguished from inflammation of the synovial membrane by the superficiality and regularity of the tumefaction. Occasionally the action terminates in suppuration; pus being effused to a greater or less amount within the cavity. The affection is frequently encountered among servants; and inflammation of the bursæ of the knee joint is found particularly among females, who, from resting upon their knees while performing household duties, irritate the bursæ; hence the term *house-maid's knee.* However, those in the higher walks of life are not exempt from the disease. Chronic enlargement of the bursæ on the metatarsal joint of the great toe is also frequently met with, especially among those advanced in years, causing some deformity, and at times considerable pain; to this affection the term *bunion* is applied.

Treatment.—The medicines for inflamed bursæ are, *acon.*, *bell.*, *graph.*, *hepar*, *iod.*, *led.*, *merc.*, *rhus*, *sulph.*

Acon. and *bell.* are particularly adapted to the affection termed house-maid's knee, when the pain is excessive, and the fever considerable. When there is swelling of the part, and lancinating pains, these frequently arrest the affection, without the employment of other medicines. After the more violent inflammatory symptoms have been subdued, *iod.*, *ledum.*, or *arnica*, will in many instances remove the remaining swelling; a bandage should also be tightly bound around the joint. *Arnica* is particularly useful when the swelling and pain result either from a blow or constant friction of the part; *ledum.* also is recommended for such a condition, when there is considerable fever, with preponderance of the chilly stage; *graph.* may be employed when there is chronic enlargement of the bursæ, with redness of the surrounding parts, with swelling of the toes, with itching; *agaricus* is very serviceable to allay the latter symptom.

Hepar and *merc.*, or *silic.*, should be used when there is tendency to suppuration; when there are shooting pains *bry.* or *lyc.* may prove serviceable.

The bursæ may also be punctured, and the effused fluid pressed out. The instrument should be finely pointed, of good material, and should contain a groove, the sides of which should have cutting edges. Sometimes considerable pressure is required to force the instrument through the walls of the bursæ; and to prevent the instrument from snapping, steady pressure should be used.

Section 7.—Deformity of the Joints.

All the joints of the body are more or less liable to deformity, or derangement of their articular surfaces. Distortion of the neck, torticollis, wry neck,* arises from a variety of causes. The head may be retained in an unnatural position for a long time by glandular swellings; or by rigidity, or spasmodic action, or both, of the sterno-mastoid muscle; the head in such instances is much displaced, and the neck is twisted. The head may be either bent forward or turned to one side; usually, however, the chin looks towards the shoulder of the side opposite to the offending muscle. Induration of muscular fibre and tendons of the cervical region, curvature and other diseases of the osseous system, and rheumatism and other inflammatory affections may also produce torticollis. In like manner, the shoulders may be either preternaturally elevated or depressed. *Round* shoulders, as they are termed, are exceedingly common, and arise from the habit acquired by children of throwing their arms forward and supporting them on the front of the chest. Curvatures of the spine are frequent among boys and girls who are growing, and proceed from indulgence in unnatural positions. The bones or joints of the lower extremities are frequently deformed, and may be inclined either inwards or outwards; in the former case the patient is said to be knock-kneed, in the latter bow-legged.

But the most important deformity is that which is denominated *talipes* or *club-foot,* the description and treatment of which, however, will be treated of in the following section.

Treatment.—If torticollis arise from improper positions assumed by the patient, braces or other mechanical means to prevent the indulgence in the pernicious habit must be employed. If the inclination of the head is caused by glandular swellings, the medicines that are suitable for such indurations will probably rectify the evil. Among these may be *rhus, carbo-an.,* or *conium.*

---

* See Liston's Elements of Surgery, p. 314.

If wry-neck is occasioned by rheumatic or other inflammatory affections, it may be advantageously treated with *bry.*, *puls.*, *bell.*, *acon.*, &c. For pains as if the cervical vertebræ were dislocated, which often are felt in the affected part, *bry.*, *nux-vom.* and *cinnabar* may be suitable. For the contraction of single tendons of the cervical muscles, *natrum-muriat.*, *rhus-tox.*, *stram.*, *hyos.*, *dulc.*, *zincum*, *selen.*, or *arsenicum*, appear to be appropriate medicines.

For permanent spastic rigidity of the muscles, tenotomy will sooner or later have to be employed;* and that not merely on account of the deformity, but to avoid a more serious evil—curvature of the spine—which often supervenes, and which may, if unchecked, become both extensive and confirmed. The tenotomy needle is inserted obliquely, at the origin of the muscle from the sternum and clavicle; the division is effected by cutting either from without inwards, or in the opposite direction, as circumstances may seem to require; great care being of course taken not to injure the important parts which lie immediately behind the muscle. To insure safety in this respect, it may be well, in some cases, to puncture with the ordinary tenotomy needle, or knife, and then, withdrawing this, to substitute an instrument with a probe point, wherewith to effect the muscle's section. Sometimes it may be sufficient to cut one origin only; but, usually, division of both heads is essential. By resilience of the extremities, restoration of the normal state is at once produced; and this is maintained by suitable bandaging, if need be, until consolidation of the divided parts occur, with the due amount of elongation.

If sufficient force and steadiness cannot be gained by simple bandaging, Jörg's apparatus may be used. This consists of a pair of leather stays, and of a band fillet, which encircles the head; on the centre of the fore part of the stays, is a kind of pulley, or grooved wheel, which can be turned round with a

---

* The following description of the operation is taken from Miller's Practice of Surgery, p. 253, to which is added the method of application of Jörg's apparatus for torticollis, from Samuel Cooper's First Lines.

key in one direction, but not in the other, in consequence of becoming fixed by means of a spring. From this pulley or wheel proceeds a band up the neck to the fillet on the patient's head, to which it is fastened directly behind the ear, close to the mastoid process. The band lies in the same direction as the sterno-cleido-mastoideus muscle, and when drawn towards the breast, by means of the wheel, produces the same effect as would arise from an increase in the action of that muscle. In short, it pulls the mastoid process downwards and forwards towards the sternum, counteracts the opposite muscle of the same name, and rectifies the position of the head. Professor Jörg makes his patient wear this apparatus day and night.

Section 8.—*Talipes.**

By this term is understood the deformity of *club-foot;* generally congenital, yet not unfrequently acquired. The original development of the bones is not faulty; but their displacement is gradually effected, by a predominance of action in certain muscles; such predominance being dependent, either on spasm of those which so act, or in want of action in those which ought to be their antagonists. There is no actual dislocation of the tarsal bones; there is merely gradual change in their relative positions.

There are several varieties of this deformity.

I. *Talipes Equinus.*—The muscles of the calf are contracted; the tendo achillis is rigid; the patient steps on the toes without bringing the heel to the ground; the foot is, in other respects, well-formed; but the extensor tendons being on the stretch, there is a turning up of the toes, independently of that which is caused by pressure in progression.

II. *Talipes Varus.*—This is the most common variety; consisting of extension, adduction, and rotation of the foot—the

* The following section is taken mostly from Miller's Practice of Surgery, pp. 675-678.

rotation being analogous to supination of the hand. The muscles of the calf and the adductors of the foot are contracted; the heel is drawn up; the toes turn inward; the outer edge of the foot rests on the ground; and, in progression weight is borne on the outside of the foot and on the outer ankle, where adventitious bursæ usually form of some size. The toes are extended as in the former case.

III. *Talipes Valgus* is the reverse of the preceding. There are abduction, rotation, and partial flexion of the foot; the rotation being analogous to pronation of the hand. The front of the foot is raised from the ground; and the patient rests on the inside of the instep, and on the inner ankle. The tendons of the peronei muscles are chiefly to blame.

IV. *Talipes Calcaneus.* The muscles in front of the leg are contracted; the foot is extremely flexed; and, in progression, the heel alone touches the ground.

One foot, or both, may be affected by Talipes. In the former case, the affected limb is found thinner, and more flabby than the other; and, sometimes, by arrest of development, it is shortened as well as weak. The mode of progression is painful and imperfect, and, not unfrequently, contraction takes place at the knee, to a greater or less extent.

Spurious Talipes is said to occur, when displacement of the foot takes place by muscular change or integumental contraction, following on burns, extensive suppurations, ulcers, &c.

Treatment.—In the minor cases, which occur in children, mechanical means — early employed, skilfully adapted, and duly persevered with—are alone sufficient to effect a normal relation of parts. Many such cases occur; and it is quite unnecessary to subject the little patients to the pain of tenotomy.

Natr.-muriat., *rhus-tox.*, *ruta*, *con.*, and *caust.* are servicable medicines, when the deformity is occasioned by contraction of the tendons. *Nit.-ac.* and *silic.* may be employed, when cicatrices give rise to the deformity—they are particularly indicated when there is pain in the contracted integument during damp weather. *Carbo.-veg.* should also be remembered for such symptoms.

Nux., *graph.*, *dulc.*, *colch.*, may also in many cases, be indicated.

The selection of the dilution of the medicine employed must rest with the practitioner. The age of the patient, the constitution, the duration and intensity of the affection require to be carefully considered, and the potency accordingly chosen—either from among the triturations and lower dilutions, or from the higher dynamizations.

Tenotomy is had recourse to, when structural shortening of muscle, of tendon, or of both, has occurred; and when the obstacles to replacement cannot otherwise be overcome. A large number of cases are so circumstanced. The operations, however, are but part of the remedial means; and will certainly fail, unless suitable apparatus be afterwards employed, skilfully and sedulously. Instead of waiting for reunion of the tendons, and then extending their new bond of union, painfully and slowly, it is better to effect the required change of relative position immediately after section, leaving the interspace to be filled up by new matter. In the congenital form, the operation may be had recourse to about the twelfth or fourteenth month, when the patient is just beginning to walk; the mechanical and general remedial means having been in use previously. Extreme cases in the elderly should be regarded as irremediable. Tenotomy will fail to effect a cure; and may do harm, for a time at least, by impairing very seriously the acquired usefulness of the limbs.

In talipes equinus, division of the tendo achillis is usually sufficient. In talipes varus, division of this tendon may suffice, along with the use of mechanical aid. But, very frequently, it is also necessary to divide the tibialus posticus and flexor longus pollicis. In confirmed cases, the tibialis anticus and extensor proprius pollicis must be added to the list. In talipes vulgus, the peronei are divided along with the tendo achillis. In talipes calcaneus, the tibialis anticus is cut, along with the extensors of the toes.

The tendo achillis is divided a little above its insertion into the calcaneum. The patient having been placed in a prone position, the limb steadied, and the foot bent, a tenotomy knife or needle is introduced obliquely; and, by bringing its edge or point on the rigid tendon, the fibres are cut from without inwards; an assistant flexing the foot forcibly, so as to assist in the disruption.

This having been completed, the instrument is withdrawn, and a compress is applied to the aperture. Or division may be reversed—from within outwards; but there is thus a risk of accidentally wounding the integument. The tibialis posticus may be divided, either above the ankle, or near its insertion into the navicular bone. The tibialis anticus is divided in front of the ankle, from below outwards, so as to save the joint. The flexor longus pollicis is divided, where it is felt tense, in the sole of the foot. Sometimes it is expedient to divide the plantar fascia also, from below outwards, to save the important textures beneath. The peroneus longus and peroneus brevis may be divided above the external malleolus, or near their points of insertion; the rest, at such points as circumstances may render apparently most suitable. As a general rule, in such operations the knife is moved away from, not towards, arteries and nerves.

It is not improbable that, occasionally, reunion of the divided tendon does not take place, but that a new attachment is formed. Obviously, section of tendon should be avoided within thecæ; as, in such a locality, there is but little capability of the expected plastic exudation.

The mechanical apparatus need not be described. Many varieties are in use, the simplest usually the best. For the talipes equinus and the talipes varus—the two most common varieties—the indications are simple, and may be easily followed: flexion of the foot, by acting on the ankle; and restoration of the normal position of the foot, as regards rotation and abduction, by acting on the foot itself.

CHAPTER XXV.

INJURIES AND DISEASES OF THE BLOOD VESSELS.

Section 1.—*Diseases of the Arteries.*

The arteries are liable to inflammation, suppuration, and ulceration; their texture also may be altered by the formation of calcareous concretion. The internal coat is more subject to inflammation than either the middle or external, as is evinced by the effusion of lymph, which is often poured out in large quantity upon the inner surface of an artery, in consequence of inflammation of contiguous parts from the application of ligatures, from wounds, and from the pressure of tumors. Chronic inflammation often precedes or follows calcareous deposition; although arterial integument resists for a long time the ulcerative process, it is liable eventually to be destroyed, though this generally takes place on account of improper ligation.

But the most frequent disease of the arteries which is encountered, is the degeneration of tissue and the deposition of calcareous matter. To a greater or less extent this disease is present in the arterial system of those advanced in age, and for the same reason that fragilitas ossium is more common among those at the same period of life.

Treatment.—In the treatment of inflammation of the arteries, the medicines exhibited will frequently arrest the disease in its first stages, and thus the sequelæ will be prevented. The principal medicines are *aconite*, *bell.*, *cham.;* also in some cases *arnica*, *ars.*, *carb.-veg.*, *lyc.*, *puls.*, and *sepia.* Perhaps the best medicines for the deposition of calcareous matter within the arterial coats, are *lyc.*, *calc.*, *graph.*, *silicea*, and *sulphur.* In the treatment of these affections, the practitioner should regard with particular attention the predisposing and exciting causes of the disease, whether these be constitutional or local.

Section 2.—Aneurism.

Sir Charles Bell* defines aneurism as a pulsating tumor, formed of arterial blood; but Mr. Miller, with his usual preciseness, writes, that by the term aneurism is understood a pulsating tumor, composed of a cyst, which is filled with blood, partly fluid and partly coagulated, and whose cavity communicates with the arterial canal.†

Aneurisms have been variously divided, viz.: external, internal, spontaneous, traumatic, true, false, circumscribed, diffused, dissecting, aneurismal varix, and aneurism by anastomosis. According to Sir Astley Cooper, there are three forms.

Aneurism situated upon the surface of the body (*external aneurism*).

This latter presents itself as a small tumor, pulsating very strongly, containing only fluid blood, of which it can be readily emptied if pressure be made near the distended artery on the cardiac side. Little pain is experienced at this time, excepting cramps, which may occur in the limb below the situation of the aneurism. In a more advanced stage, the tumor is larger, more solid, and cannot be completely emptied as in the former case, the blood being partly coagulated in the interior of the sac, which is much thickened. The circulation in the surrounding parts is retarded, and pain is experienced when pressure is made upon the tumor; the pulsation is distinct, but not so well marked as in the first period of the affection. In the third stage, the tumor is larger and more solid, pulsation is indistinct, and the sac is filled with layers of fibrinous matter, and contains but little fluid blood. There is pain and inconvenience when moving the limb, which becomes œdematous and deprived of sensation from pressure upon the nerves.

Internal aneurism occupies the cavity of the abdomen, chest, and cranium, and the diagnosis is frequently difficult.‡

---

* C. Bell's Operative Surgery.

† Miller's Principles of Surgery, p. 551.

‡ Hasting's Practice of Surgery, p. 351.

True aneurism, or when the sac is composed of all the arterial coats, may occur by *dilatation*, by *dilatation and rupture*, and by *rupture*.

Aneurism by dilatation is most frequent in the aorta. The coats of the vessel do not give way, but are gradually and evenly distended; the integrity and the continuity of the tunics remaining entire, which can be distinctly traced, particularly after maceration.

The dilatation may be *cylindroid*, *fusiform*, or *sacciform*.

In the first instance, the expansion is abrupt and uniform; in the second—as the derivation of the word would lead us to suppose—the enlargement is spindle-shaped; and in the third, the dilatation is partial, and the hollow swelling that results is said to be sacciform.

Dilatation and *rupture* of the arterial tunics do not occur at the same time. In the first instance, the abnormal cavity is formed by dilatation, and after a time the internal and middle coats are ruptured, either by muscular exertion or ulceration. The external coat expands, and receives strength from organized fibrinous deposit, afforded by effused blood.

Aneurism by *rupture* generally arises from sudden muscular exertion, the internal and middle coats give way by laceration, and aneurismal formation speedily follows.

When blood passes between the tunics of an artery, separating or dissecting the one from the other, the aneurism is termed *dissecting*. In this instance, the inner coat may remain entire, or both the inner and external tunic preserve their continuity.

An aneurism is said to be *pedunculated*, when the sac is connected with the artery by means of a narrow neck. A *limited* aneurism is one in which it is bound within the limits of a proper cyst; and *diffuse* aneurism is formed by the blood escaping from a wound in an artery into the surrounding celluar texture.

In *false* aneurism the cyst is not composed of any of the arterial coats, but consists entirely of tissues exterior or adjoining the vessel. It may result from wounds, lacerations, ulceration external to the vessel, &c. According to Mr. Liston, "*false aneurism* is the most common form of disease following accidental wounds of the artery at the bend of the arm; the vein is stretched over the fore part of the sac, compressed, and perhaps obliterated. The cicatrix appears stretched and thin on the surface of the tumor, and there is sometimes a degree of blue discoloration around it. The progress of the tumor is steady and uninterrupted, until operative procedure is resorted to."

A *varicose* aneurism is where a vein and artery have been punctured at the same time and place, and a false aneurism formed between them, communicating with both vessels.

Aneurism by anastomosis was first particularly noticed by Mr. John Bell,* who writes:

"The tumor is a congeries of active vessels, and the cellular substance through which these vessels are expanded resembles the cellular part of the penis, the gills of a turkey-cock, or the substance of the placenta, spleen, or womb." In the early stage of the disease, the skin assumes a mottled appearance, apparently arising from small sacs of blood distributed throughout the tumor. Frequently this affection is closely allied to vascular spots, termed *nævi materni*, that are quite often met with on the head and other parts of new-born children.

In the incipient stage of aneurism, the tumor is small and free from pain, by pressure readily disappears, but returns immediately after compression is removed. The skin for a considerable period of time retains its normal color, but as the swelling augments, it becomes pale and œdematous. The pulsation in the tumor is greater during the early than in the advanced stage, which circumstance is explained by the formation of coagula in the sac. If the tumor acquires a large bulk, the integument covering it becomes livid and painful, cracks, and through the fissures a bloody serum exudes, ulceration follows, which extending to the sac opens a communication with its cavity, from which issues in a stream fluid blood, mixed with

---

* Principles of Surgery, vol. i., p. 456.

coagula. As the ulcerative process extends, the opening increases in size, and the hemorrhage becomes more and more frequent, and if not arrested, destroys the patient.

Aneurisms are more frequent among males than among females, and seldom occur before the period of puberty. The predisposing causes of the disease are principally degeneration of the arterial coats, which may be either steatomatous or earthy. The exciting causes, are muscular exertion or mental emotion, besides certain occupations that favor the disease. In some instances, there is steatomatous degeneration of the whole arterial system. Patients so affected, are said to labor under the *aneurismal diathesis.*

The *diagnosis* of aneurism is a very important point to be understood; a subject that has already been alluded to when treating of abscess.*

Treatment.—In simple *nævi,* or small aneurisms by anastomosis, it will be well to have recourse to medicinal agents before subjecting the patient to an operation. The medicines mentioned are more or less empirical, and the practitioner therefore has only the very vague index of clinical experience to point to a choice. In one case, in which an infant was afflicted with several nævi-materni, after the exhibition of *caust.,* suppuration was observed to be going on in one of the tumors. However, the child was removed from the city, and no further information has as yet been received. Should beneficial results accrue from the further administration of the medicine, the profession will be acquainted with the same through the medium of some homœopathic periodical.

Hartmann writes,† "if the arterial capillaries are involved, we may have recourse to *sulph., bell., lyc.,* if the venous, the principal medicines are, *sulph., phosph., nux-vom., puls.,* and *carbo-veg.,* the latter particularly is indicated when there are bright-red, round, flat aneurisms, by anastomoses, bleeding profusely from the slightest injury. *Calc.-carb., hepar, petro., silic.,* and *sulph.-ac.,* may in some cases be called for." He also

---

* See page 147–148.

† Diseases of Children, p. 61.

writes—"There seems to be some resemblance between the nævus vasculosus and acne rosacea, and it may therefore be advisable to try, if otherwise proper, such medicines as *rhus-tox.*, *kreas.*, *carb.-an.*, *ars.*, *ruta*, *led.*, *aur.-mur.*, *sep.*, &c."

If medicinal means do not remove the nævus, recourse may be had to vaccination; the virus to be inserted on the top of the tumor, precisely in the same manner as in ordinary vaccination; or several needles armed with ligatures may be passed through the aneurism, the threads then divided close to the eyes of the needles, and the free ends tightly secured, the result of which, of course, will be the destruction and sloughing away in a few days of the morbid formation.

A more certain arrest of the diseased action is oftentimes accomplished by *moistening* the threads with nitric acid. The application likewise of nitric acid to the surface of the tumor, and repeated occasionally, has likewise effected a cure.

The cure of aneurism may be *spontaneous*,* occasioned by pressure on the cardiac side of the tumor; by occlusion of the aperture of communication; by inflammation and gangrene of the cyst; by the aneurism becoming diffuse, or by obliteration of the artery on the distal aspect. These occurrences are, however, comparatively rare, and in the majority of cases surgical treatment is indispensable to cure the disease. There are several methods of treatment. *Ligatures* may be used and may be applied at the cardiac side of the tumor, as practised by Mr. Hunter, or as it is designated the Hunterian site; or the reverse of this operation, that of *Brasdor*, ligating the artery at the distal aspect. Further directions for the ligation of arteries have already been considered.†

Pressure is also a means of cure, and there are two methods for its employment; first,‡ by retarding the aneurismal flow, and favoring consolidation, or else aiding the textures which

---

* Dr. Gibson writes that he has never known but one spontaneous cure of aneurism by anastomosis. Institutes and Practice of Surgery, vol. ii., p. 150.

† See page 137—146.

‡ See Miller's Principles of Surgery, p. 581.

overlay the aneurism, and which are as it were continually striving to keep it down and repress its growth. The one method diminishes the expansive power from within, the other increases the repressive power from without. In former times the pressure exerted was continuous and severe; lately, however, it has been found that by using compression, at intervals, and not severe, a stimulus as it were is given, whereby an action is established in the part which may result in an arrest of the disease. The pressure is made at the Hunterian site by the instrument of Signoroni,* at a point where the coats of the vessel may be expected to be sound, and therefore not liable to ulcerate from slight causes. The pressure is maintained until it becomes inconvenient to the patient, when it should be lessened for a time and afterwards increased. It is preferable to employ two instruments, so that while one is slackened the other can be tightened, and vice versa. Throughout the whole period of treatment, not only by pressure but by ligature, absolute rest is necessary, while the limb below the compressed point should be equally supported, lest œdema and congestion supervene. The application of galvanism by acupuncture; or galvano-puncture, has been productive of good results in certain cases. This method of cure was proposed by Mr. B. Phillips in 1832, and is performed by introducing acupuncture needles, partly coated with gum-lac varnish,† to protect the ordinary textures which they have to traverse, and having inserted them within the tumor, and retarded temporarily the aneurismal circulation by means of pressure, the galvanic current is set on, of such strength as the patient is able to bear, anæsthesia being employed or not, as circumstances may require. By such means coagulation has been effected and aneurisms cured.

The treatment of aneurism by *injections of the perchloride of iron* has lately excited much interest among surgeons. Dr. Pravaz‡ first introduced the practice, and it has been since used

---

* See page 125. † Miller's Principles of Surgery, p. 587.
‡ London Lancet, 1854.

by many surgeons with varied success. Its failure in some instances has been attributed to the fact, that either too much or too little of the perchloride was injected; the quantity of fluid to be used not having been specified. The effect is generally the immediate formation of a clot in the sac—arrest of pulsations and finally obliteration of the trunk of the vessel.

The dangers attendant upon this practice should receive serious consideration. Fever results, and formation of pus in the artery has taken place.

Excessive injection excites acute inflammation of the sac, followed by ulceration and expulsion of the clot; the essential part of the operation consists in so managing that there should be slow resorption of the foreign matter introduced within the tumor.

Pravaz remarked that in the case of an aneurism the size of a pigeon's egg, he would not inject more than four or five drops of the perchloride, and that he would repeat the operation, should the pulsations in the tumor not cease after a certain time.

The danger, however, in all the cases related is perhaps greater than that attendant upon the old method of ligature.

Section 3.—*Injuries and Diseases of the Veins.*

Wounds of the Veins.—The veins are frequently wounded during the performance of operations, but the hemorrhage can generally be arrested by properly applied pressure; in some instances, however—though the proceeding, if possible, should be avoided—cases may occur in which ligatures become absolutely necessary.

Inflammation of the Veins.—*Phlebitis* may be either acute or chronic, the former may terminate fatally if not arrested; the latter is not dangerous, and generally affects varicose veins of the lower extremities. In *acute phlebitis* the countenance of the patient expresses anxiety and depression of spirits, there are repeated rigors, dry, brown, or blackish tongue, cadaverous skin, great prostration, pulse rapid and weak, muttering delirium, and vomiting of bile.

Consecutive abscess is said to be a characteristic termination of acute phlebitis; excessive pain may be experienced in any of the joints, which is rapidly succeeded by a copious formation of pus; purulent formation may, after this, speedily collect in other parts of the body.

Treatment.—The treatment of acute phlebitis is somewhat difficult, which in many instancess is owing to the disjointed character of the homœopathic Materia Medica. However, from the presenting symptoms, particularly in the first stages of the affection, when the fever is high, with a quick, full pulse, dry, furred tongue, &c., *aconite* should be employed.

If after a time the brain appears to participate in the disease, *belladonna* is indicated; but the medicine that is best adapted to inflammation of the veins is *pulsatilla,* which may be alternated with *aconite* or *belladonna* in the first stages of the inflammatory process; but when the tongue becomes dry, brown, and cracked, when the patient is much prostrated, with burning thirst, and hot, dry skin, *arsenicum* is distinctly required. *Carbo-veg.* may be prescribed for a somewhat similar group of symptoms, and perhaps would be a preferable medicine, when the action of the arterial system has been almost entirely overpowered, and venous congestion is indicated by a blue tinge of the skin over the whole surface of the body, attended with fearful anguish about the heart, and icy coldness of the surface.

If suppuration threaten, or if it has actually occurred, and the amount of purulent secretion is considerable, *silicea* should be administered, or the case may strongly call for *hepar, merc.-sol.,* or *sulphur.*

For *chronic phlebitis,* besides the medicines just mentioned, *arn., cham., lyc., nux-vom., spig.,* or *zincum,* may be demanded.

Varix.—The term varix designates a hypertrophied condition of the veins, in which they are divided into irregular pouches, the valves not being able to sustain the reflux column of blood. Deep-seated, as well as superficial veins, are frequently rendered varicose by undue muscular action, by interruption of the circulation from ligatures, by the pressure of tumors, and by the gravid uterus. The veins of the upper extremities are rarely affected by hypertrophy, while those of the lower, especially the saphenæ and their branches, are very liable to the disease. In the commencement, numerous small circumscribed swellings are observed, but after a time, the venous trunks and branches appear enlarged throughout their whole extent; sometimes they are knotted or doubled upon each other, and these gyrations are particularly conspicuous in the neighborhood of the valves.*

Treatment.—Great advantage may be derived from allowing the patient to encase the limb in an elastic stocking, which is constructed especially for the treatment of varicose veins;† this should be constantly worn, and at the same time medicines should be internally administered, which are chiefly *agaric.*, *ars.*, particularly when the veins are of a livid color, and attended with severe burning pains; *bell.*, when erisypelatous inflammation surrounds the varices; *carbo-veg.*, *graph.*, *lyc.*, *puls.;* the latter is perhaps the most efficacious medicine when there is considerable inflammation, excessive pain, and swelling, and when the limb assumes a livid hue; *arnica* is a valuable medicine in the treatment of this affection; it is particularly useful when the patient is obliged to maintain an erect posture for a length of time, or when the veins have become diseased in consequence of wounds, blows, &c.; very beneficial results have been obtained by the exhibition of *arnica* and *pulsatilla* in alternation, a dose every night. *Hamamelis virginiana* has been highly recommended by Dr. Okie of Providence, in the treatment of this affection. It has been used with beneficial effect both as an external application and as an internal medicine.

If this treatment fail to produce the desired effect, the surgeon may have recourse to an operation, although we believe

* Gibson's Institutes and Practice of Surgery, vol. ii., p. 166.

† Vide page 185. Treatment of Varicose Ulcers.

that as the science of true medicine progresses a resort to the knife for the treatment of varicose veins will be abandoned. From the amount of successful experience which we possess in the treatment of this disease, this assertion is very confidently advanced.

Sir Benjamin Brodie thus writes—"For this operation I have generally employed a narrow, sharp-pointed bistoury, slightly curved, with its cutting edge on the convex side. Having then ascertained the precise situation of the veins, or cluster of veins, from which the distress of the patient appears principally to arise, I introduce the point of the bistoury through the skin on one side of the varix, and pass it on between the skin and the vein with one of the flat surfaces turned forwards, and the other backwards, until it reaches the opposite side. I then turn the cutting edge of the bistoury backwards, and, in withdrawing the instrument, the division of the varix is effected. The patient experiences pain, which is occasionally severe, but which subsides in the course of a short time. There is always hemorrhage, which will be often profuse if neglected, but which is readily stopped by moderate pressure, made by means of a compress and bandage correctly applied."

CHAPTER XXVI.

INJURIES AND DISEASES OF THE HEAD

Section. 1.—*Wounds of the Scalp.*

Mr. Pott has observed that though the scalp be called the common integument of the head, yet from its structure, connections, and uses, injuries inflicted upon it by external violence, become of much more consequence than those of other parts of the body. It is a well known fact that wounds, however slight, when inflicted on the head, are very liable to be followed by inflammation and suppuration either within or without the cranium. In some instances the lips of the wound will unite readily, and little inconvenience result; in others, however, adhesion will take place only at certain points, while suppuration will occur at others; this is particularly noticed in contused wounds, in which the integument has immediately been destroyed by the violence of the injury, or in cases in which the scalp has suffered considerable laceration.

Small wounds, that is, such as are caused by instruments or bodies which pierce or puncture, rather than cut, are in general more liable to become inflamed, and are known to be productive of greater constitutional disturbance than those which are of a greater extent.

If the wound affect the cellular membrane only, and has not reached the aponeurosis or pericranium, the inflammation and tumefaction involve the whole head and face; the latter frequently assuming a jaundiced hue, and being covered with small bullæ containing a yellow serum.

Treatment.—If a blow on the head has caused extravasation of blood beneath the scalp, and if there be visible increase of the accumulation of fluid, the surgeon may suspect that an artery has been divided; in this case the course of the vessel, if possible, should be ascertained, and pressure made in order to arrest the hemorrhage; after which, compresses saturated with a solution of *arnica* should be applied to the contused part. If the scalp be nearly or quite detached, it should be carefully washed and replaced as nearly *in situ* as possible, and the *aqua calendula* be used as a lotion; the parts should then be brought together with adhesive straps, and a bandage lightly placed around the cranium; sutures in the generality of instances should be dispensed with, as the punctures that are made by the needle are liable to become the seat of inflammatory action. If erysipelatous inflammation supervene, *bell.* may be administered internally, or *rhus radicans;* the latter exerts a powerfully beneficial action over erysipelas of the scalp. If the fever be high, *aconite* and *bell.* may be administered, in accordance with symptoms that have already been mentioned in various places in this work.

Should symptoms of effusion within the cavity of the cranium be present, *arn.*, *bell.*, *hell.*, *cup.*, or *zincum* are the most appropriate medicines. If suppuration ensue beneath the scalp or occipito-frontalis muscle, the pus should be evacuated by early incision, and *calend.*, *hepar*, *merc.*, or *silicea* should be exhibited. If extravasated blood be noticed beneath the scalp, there is no need of incision, for by enjoining perfect rest, with the employment of *arnica* externally and internally, absorption of the clot will in all probability take place.

Section 2.—Concussion of the Brain.

According to Mr. Abernethy,* concussion of the brain may be divided into three stages. The first is that of insensibility and derangement of the bodily powers, which immediately succeed the accident. While in this condition the patient is insensible to injury, pulse intermitting, extremities cold, and breathing difficult, but in the generality of instances without stertor. This stage has but a short duration, and is succeeded by the second, in which the symptoms gradually disappearing, the pulse and respiration become more natural, and though not entirely normal, are sufficient to diffuse warmth throughout the extreme parts of the body, and to maintain life. As the effects of the concussion still diminish, the capability of exerting the mind becomes increased, the patient can reply to questions, and refers the chief cause of his sufferings to the head. As long as stupor remains, inflammatory action appears to be moderate, and as the former abates, the latter increases; and this constitutes the third and most important stage of concussion. Death, however, sometimes instantaneously supervenes, from cessation of the heart's action.

Treatment.—The medicine that is most essentially serviceable in the treatment of concussion, is *arnica;* and its early

* Essay on Diseases of the Head.

administration, if the injury be not extremely severe, will not only prevent many of the evil consequences that may result, but by its influence upon the vessels may limit extravasation of blood within the cavity of the cranium. If the injury be severe, and there is extreme restlessness and jactitation of the muscles, quick, small pulse, rigors, and delirium, *bell.* must be employed. If there is jerking of the tendons of the extremities or clenched hands, foam at the mouth, *stram.* will be of service. If the patient rolls the head from side to side, and there is much oppression, stertorous breathing, hiccup, etc., *hyos.* is indicated. The medicines that are homœopathic to irritation, and which should be employed at the commencement of the third stage, are *ignatia* and *cicuta virosa.** It would perhaps be the better practice, when the cause of the affection is considered, to alternate *arnica* with other medicines which the symptoms may render most applicable. *Aconite* should not be forgotten, when after the injury the mental faculties of the patient appear considerably impaired, as inability to think, weakness of memory, vertigo on raising the head, blackness before the eyes, nausea, and sometimes vomiting; when the latter symptom is prominent, and the matter ejected is blackish or brownish, with prostration of the vital powers, *ars.* should be employed.

Section 3.—*Compression of the Brain.*

Mr. Pott remarks, "The shock which the head sometimes receives by falls from on high, or by strokes from ponderous bodies, does not unfrequently cause a breach in some of the vessels, either of the brain or its meninges; and thereby occasions extravasation of the circulating fluids. This extravasation may be the only complaint produced by the accident; or it may be joined with, or added to, a fracture of the skull. But this is not all, for it may be produced, not only when the cra-

* For more particular indications for the employment of Cicuta, vide p. 117.

nium is unhurt by the blow, but even when no violence of any kind has been offered to or received by the head."

It seldom happens that mere depression of the bones of the cranium, unconnected with other injury, produces such aggravated symptoms as those which characterize compression of the brain, for according to Dr. Gibson,* the records of surgery furnish numerous examples of perfect recovery after the most extensive depressions, from which the patients sustained but little inconvenience, and for the relief of which no operations were performed. On the other hand cases have occasionally occurred in which from depression of both tables of the skull, or from extensive fracture of the inner table, the most urgent symptoms have resulted, but have been speedily relieved upon elevating the bone to its natural level.

The symptoms of compression resemble those of apoplexy. If the cerebral functions cease totally or partially in consequence of the pressure of extravasated blood upon the brain, the symptoms of nervous apoplexy or paralysis are present, which in many respects closely resemble those produced by violent concussion. The patient is extremely pale, with pulse feeble and irregular, and the whole body appears totally paralyzed; vomiting sometimes occurs. In some instances, after such a condition has existed for a time, the pulse becomes fuller, the face assumes a more natural color, or becomes very red, and all other symptoms of hyperæmia make their appearance, precisely as after concussion.

In other cases the patient is deprived of consciousness or sensation, is totally or partially paralyzed, feces and urine pass off involuntarily, or the latter may be retained: the breathing is stertorous, the pulse is hard, full and slow, the eyelids droop as if paralyzed, the mouth is drawn to the side, and the eyes are staring and protruded, with insensible and often dilated pupils. In many cases the patient vomits, and the face looks livid and turgescent. Pus, as coagula formed by extravasated blood, may also produce compression. Suppuration, however,

* Institutes and Practice of Surgery, vol. ii. p. 183.

does not immediately follow an injury of the skull, and often proceeds from irritation occasioned by the shattered fragments of the internal table.

Treatment.—The first act of the surgeon, when called to a patient suffering from compression of the brain, is to administer a dose of *arnica.* This medicine is now employed by many of the most distinguished surgeons in the treatment of this particular variety of injury, but none of them (we refer to allopaths) acknowledge their indebtedness to Hahnemann for the introduction of this important remedial agent. If symptoms are present that in a measure call for the exhibition of other medicines, they may be administered in alternation with *arnica.*

Veratrum should be employed when there is coldness of the whole person, with distorted and protruded eyes, disfigured countenance, flabby muscles, trismus, and imperceptible breathing. *Coffea* by the mouth and anus has frequently succeeded in relieving such symptoms.

Aconite is an important medicine in the treatment of compression, and *belladonna* has frequently produced the most desirable results.

Coffea is an excellent *palliative,* but must always be succeeded by other more appropriate medicines. *Opium* also, restores the reactive power of the organism, and is indicated when there is stupor, with coma, stertorous breathing, red, bloated face, constant motion of the lips, full slow pulse, and frequent profuse sweat.

Lauroc., hyos., stràm., merc., plumb., and *iodine,* are useful medicines; the latter, especially when there are violent pulsations of the whole body, with anguish and dyspnœa. Other remedial agents may also be called for, but want of space will not permit their insertion in this place. Full details may be learned from the various works upon the Materia Medica. When this treatment does not relieve the patient, and there is reason to believe that the brain is still oppressed by a coagulum, the trephine must be resorted to, and the coagulum removed.

If after injury inflicted upon the skull, a depression is observed, and there are but slight symptoms of compression, the surgeon must remember that fragments of bone, though at first producing little irritation, may after a time create the inflammatory process, which may terminate in suppuration, and thus the most disastrous consequences may ensue. The question of operation in this, as in all other cases, requires serious consideration.

The *trephine* is a circular saw, moved by a light and rapid movement of the hand, whereby a portion of the skull is separated, and may be removed.* Dr. Gibson† says, that the object of the surgeon in applying the trephine, is either to make an opening for the removal of coagulated blood, or for the introduction of the elevator beneath a depressed bone. Very frequently it happens that there is a sufficient space between the edges of the fragments of a bone to insinuate the elevator, and with it restore the depressed portion to its natural level. When the operation is undertaken for the elevation of depressed bone it is seldom necessary to remove an entire circle, as all that is required is sufficient space for raising the depressed portion and removing fragments, if need be. This can in many cases be accomplished by fixing the centre pin of the trephine on the brink of the sound bone, and so removing by the saw only a segment of a circle.

The *spinal cord* is also subject to *compression* and *concussion* from blows or other injuries. In compression and concussion the symptoms are similar to those of compression of the brain, paralysis being most prominent. If dislocation or fracture give rise to the compression, the proper treatment will be found in that portion of this work which is devoted to those subjects. If inflammation produce the disease, the student may refer to any work on the practice of medicine. The prognosis in such cases is generally unfavorable.

---

* Miller's Practice of Surgery, p. 66.

† Institutes and Practice of Surgery, vol. ii., p. 188.

CHAPTER XXVII.

DISEASES OF THE EYE.

THE class of diseases which is the subject of the following chapter is too often superficially noticed by the student, indeed the study of affections of the eye is frequently altogether omitted. This is to be the more regretted in consequence of the very great importance which attaches to the subject, as well as the frequency with which the organ of vision is attacked with some one or other variety of the diseases to which its exposed situation, as well as its complex anatomical structure, render it liable.

A distinguished physician recommends all students to inquire particularly into diseases of the eye, as many affections in miniature may thus be observed. The stages of inflammation can readily be noticed; suppuration is manifested by the formation of a yellowish, or in some instances a milk-white fluid in the chambers of the eye.

A dark red color of the parts with swelling affords an instance of extravasation, as is witnessed after injuries, or in scurvy or fevers of a typhoid character. The yellow appearance of the conjunctiva in jaundice, exhibits the same pathological condition as is noticed in the skin of patients suffering with that affection. The peculiar inflammation, which is supposed to constitute rheumatism, is seen in a slight injection of the minute vessels beneath the conjunctiva. Erysipelas, a variety of inflammation, frequently attacks the eyelids.

Tumors of various formation, the result of the inflammatory process, are also frequently met with in the organ of vision. Medullary sarcoma in its first stages produces a red, gray or turbid appearance in the posterior chamber of the eye which advances with the progress of the disease.

Morbid structures behind the ball, occasion its protrusion, thereby altering its position. Encysted tumors of the lachrymal glands, fatty and other degenerations, osteo sarcoma, aneurism and exostosis, which may arise in the maxillary nasal and cerebral cavities, also cause increased convexity of the organ.

A moderate protrusion which arises quickly, exhibits hyperæmia of all or part of the structures within the orbit.

Inflammation of the *iris* is known by exudations of lymph, on it and within the pupil, sometimes accompanied with yellow specks.

If the iris presents a dirty grayish appearance, and is covered with small red or yellowish-gray elevations, syphilis may be suspected.

When the iris is attacked with arthritic inflammation, it presents an ashen gray, leaden hue, having lost its distinctive appearance.

Besides these morbid conditions, there are deviations from the normal functions of the eye, which are often important indices to the physician. If the eye gradually becomes sunken or hollow, the surgeon may suspect atrophy of the parts posterior to the eyeball: such occurs in phthisis, and may be considered as an unfavorable sign; long fasting may also engender retraction of the ball, or it may be owing to the smaller amount of fluids contained in the vessels, as is the case in cholera, violent diarrhœa, or after repeated venesection.

In these instances if both eyes are affected, the prognosis cannot be regarded as otherwise than unfavorable.

When extravasation is the result of injury, or of great bodily exertion, the symptom is not very unfavorable, but if such appearance is noticed during severe internal inflammation, the most unfortunate results may be anticipated.

In diseases of the brain the size and form of the pupil afford important indications.

A dilated pupil, if not the effect of cataract, or of obstructed entrance to the rays of light, denotes cerebral irritation, which latter may be symptomatic of gastric disturbance.

Dilatation of the aperture is likewise noticed, when pressure on the brain is occasioned by extravasation of blood, inflammation, effusion of serum, and by narcotic poisons.

When soporose conditions are present with the dilatation, the prognosis may be considered as unfavorable.

Permanent expansion of the pupil may be congenital, or occasioned by iritis.

In syphilis the iris may be dislocated, upwards and inwards.

At the commencement of violent diseases, such as affections of the heart, &c., the lustre of the eye is impaired. In gangrene, typhus fever, and Asiatic cholera, the eyes appear to be covered with a fine powder, and are of a dull dirty color.

In paralysis of the muscles of the organ of vision, the eyeball is immovable, which may also be present in effusion on the brain, or in apoplexy.

Turning up of the eyes, except in sleep and in amaurosis, is an evidence of great debility.

Extremely frequent movements is a sign of clonic spasm, or occurs when the mind is vigorously employed, or it may be present in acute affections of the brain, when it indicates apoplexy, or it is noticed in general spasm, delirium, variola, and at the crisis of diseases.

Squinting or strabismus indicates encephalitis, apoplexy, or hydrocephalus. If it occurs in hydrophobia and typhoid fevers, it may be regarded as an unfavorable symptom, unless crisis is about being established, when the unnatural appearance is of less import: if it be connected with epilepsy, hysteria, or verminous affections, it is not important.

By a single *look* or *glance*, the attentive observer may derive much information. A wild or rolling eye denotes irritation or inflammation of the brain; an anxious expression may indicate disease of the heart; a timid look is often connected with hysteria and hypochondriasis, and is also observed at the commencement of many acute diseases.

Despair, when exhibited by the eye, is indicative of violent inflammation of the abdomen, or of softening of the stomach, and is likewise frequently seen in Asiatic cholera.

Temporary stop of vision may be occasioned by diseases of

the brain and optic nerves, by tumors of the encephalon, exostoses, inflammation of the investing membrane of the optic nerve, and in some acute diseases; deprivation of sight may also be occasioned by irritation of the intestinal canal, by morbid alterations in the liver and spleen, and by intermittent fevers.

Permanent dimness of vision may arise from inflammation of the retina, from extravasations in the chambers of the eye, paralysis or alteration of the structure of the parts, or from pressure on the optic nerves.

In diseases of the retina optical illusions are frequent, objects are seen in unnatural positions, and colors cannot be distinguished; lights, sparks, or fiery balls seeming to appear before the eyes, are indications of irritation of the retina, congestion of the eye, or of internal ophthalmitis; such optical deceptions are also present in inflammation of the brain and its membranes, in amaurosis, apoplexy, and epistaxis.

If the cornea or crystalline lens is diseased, or there is irritation or inflammation of the retina and surrounding parts, congestion of the brain or irritability of the nerves, the patient complains of dark specks or moats, of a larger or smaller size, floating in the surrounding air.

This subject might still be extended, but to pursue it more in detail, would somewhat encroach upon the limited space generally allowed for the consideration of such minutiæ in works of this description; but a knowledge of the few facts and illustrations that have been selected, may in a measure exemplify to the student the importance of minute observation in the establishment of both diagnosis and prognosis.

In a few preliminary remarks to an excellent treatise, "On the Homœopathic Treatment of Diseases of the Eye," Dr. Dudgeon writes: "The eye symptoms recorded in our Materia Medica are sadly defective in clearness of description. The particular seat of the objective and subjective symptoms is very seldom noted. 'Inflammation of the eye,' is often the vague term used to denote the appearance observed; or if with greater pretensions to accuracy, we have sometimes 'inflammation of the white of the eye,' whether that be of the conjunctiva or sclerotic, we are left to guess. An equal vagueness is observable in the details of most of the subjective symptoms. Again the clinical records in many cases are as ill described as the pathogenetic symptoms of the remedies; and it would be often hard to say what was the real disease the practitioner treated."* With the hope that some of the obstacles to the successful homœopathic treatment of ophthalmic surgery, may be overcome, the medicines that are best adapted to each particular affection of the eye will be mentioned, in connection with the description of the disease; and to enable the student to select the appropriate remedial agent with less labor and greater precision, the symptoms of those medicines that possess the most powerful action on the organ of vision, will be appended to the end of the chapter.

Section 1.—*Ophthalmitis and Catarrhal Ophthalmia.*

Ophthalmia is a generic term—particular names being given to the different parts of the eye which may be affected. When all the tissues are involved at the same time, the term *ophthalmitis* is given, to which belong the usual symptoms of inflammation; heat, pain, redness, swelling (diminished or increased), secretion of tears, to which is superadded great sensibility to light (or photophobia). The commencement of the attack is indicated by a stiffness in the movements of the eyeball, with dryness and heat, together with redness, which may sometimes be observed in the sclerotic coat.

There is also an itching in the eyelids, or a sensation as if sand or small particles of some foreign substance had accidentally lodged under the eyelids. As the disease advances, the lachrymal glands secrete very freely, the tears being often extremely acrid. These, in consequence of the swollen condition of the puncta lachrymalia, cannot escape through their natural

* British Journal of Homœopathy, vol. vi. p. 191.

channels, and running over the cheeks occasion much smarting and inflammation. The conjunctiva of the lids is of a deep red color, and where it passes over the eye itself, sometimes projects like a wall around the cornea, and in very aggravated cases presses apart the eyelids, presenting the appearance of a fungous mass. (To express great turgescence of the conjunctiva, the term chemosis is used. German writers, however, understand by this appellation not only turgescence, but a very highly colored redness, with *intense* pain.)

The conjunctiva scleroticæ is so covered with red vessels, that the white color of the eye is lost. By pressing upon the conjunctiva, if the inflamed vessels be movable, the diagnosis of conjunctival inflammation is made. As the disease advances the pain increases, becomes burning, throbbing, and lancinating, darting through the eyeball into the head; the eye also feeling so much increased in size, that it seems as though it would burst or be protruded from its socket. There is likewise intolerance of light, and usually all the symptoms are aggravated towards evening.

In the last stage of ophthalmia, the conjunctiva secretes mucus, and often in such large quantities, that the disease resembles a genuine blenorrhœa, the secretion being purulent in appearance. This mucus, together with the exudation from the meibomian glands, often collects, and hardens about the eyelashes, occasioning nocturnal agglutination.

Should the abnormal action advance still onward, and exhibit its worst possible phase, the other tissues then participate in the disease, suppuration ensues, the humors of the eye are evacuated through an ulcerated opening, and blindness results.

Sometimes phlyctenæ make their appearance, for the most part on the edge of the cornea—these become small ulcers. In other cases, a large portion of the conjunctiva becomes thickened or ulcerated.

If the ophthalmitis be violent in degree, or progresses to an advanced stage, the symptoms continuing severe, the constitution participates in the derangement, and febrile symptoms more or less violent are developed; the pulse becoming frequent and hard, the tongue coated, and the appetite destroyed.

The causes of ophthalmitis are such as produce inflammation in other parts of the body. Sudden changes of temperature acting either upon the eye itself, or the body generally; exposure to cold after the body has been very much heated (hence individuals exposed to such sudden withdrawals of heat, are often attacked with it—workmen in glass foundries, cooks, bakers, and smiths); acrid vapors coming in contact with the eye, from mercury, lead, sulphur, arsenic, mineral acids, and such like; too long-continued exertion of the eye, reading small type, microscopic examinations, reflection from snow in the bright sunlight, foreign bodies lodged in the eye or under the eyelids.* A vitiated state of the atmosphere also produces ophthalmia, being occasioned by such a cause in overcrowded places of public resort, as well as from the glare of light usual in such places.

Ophthalmitis is also occasionally produced by the presence of insects, especially of the pediculus ferox pubis, attaching itself to the roots of the hair of the eyebrows and eyelashes, instances of which are mentioned by Scarpa and Beer. Injuries also produce the disease, as blows, wounds, &c. Inflammation of the brain likewise causes it; the morbid action being propagated along the tunics which envelop the optic nerve. The reverse also happens; the inflammation extending itself from the eye to the brain.

Itching is indicative of conjunctivitis. *Burning* is also another symptom, as likewise *smarting*, which perhaps depends on the conjunctiva being deprived of its epithelial covering. The sensation as of sand and dust in the eye is often experienced, and also belongs to conjunctival inflammation. There are likewise *raw*, *corrosive*, *gnawing*, and *burning* pains, which may be caused by an altered state of the lachrymal secretion, or the conversion into a fatty acid of the fat globules which are found in tears.

* Such bodies may remain for a long time within the eye, without occasioning any inconvenience, after the irritation occasioned by their introduction subsides. Pieces of iron are often seen imbedded in the eyes of smiths, and minute portions of wood in those of carpenters, &c.

In the more acute forms of ophthalmia, *aconite* is very decidedly indicated. The symptoms which solicit it are, dryness, especially of the upper lids, with pressure on the eyeball; smarting, itching, and burning—the latter sometimes being experienced in one, then in the other eye; sensitiveness to the open air; redness of the conjunctiva; photophobia; lachrymation; chemosis. In the inflammation induced by the application of acrid substances, by burns and wounds, this medicine has proved very efficient.

A few globules of the 6th attenuation, dissolved in eight tablespoonsful of water, of which solution a tablespoonful may be administered every six, eight, or twelve hours, until the symptoms are alleviated; it may be then altogether omitted, or given at longer intervals, should the progress of improvement again appear arrested.

Catarrhal ophthalmia may be diagnosed, if, together with the itching, burning, smarting, and lachrymation, the palpebral conjunctiva is found covered with fine striæ of a vermillion red, somewhat relaxed and enlarged in volume; or the redness of the conjunctiva may present a dingy hue, inflammation may commence at the canthi, the cornea be less transparent, with burning and sensation of pressure in the eyes, as from sand. To these symptoms may be added, considerable secretion of mucus, with phlyctenæ, and particularly a *white space* of about two lines in diameter, which completely circumscribes the cornea. The latter appearance may be thus accounted for: There is a regular distribution of blood vessels, which, converging from the circumference of the orbit towards the centre of the eye, bifurcate and terminate in fine points about a line or a line and a half from the cornea, thus leaving the space alluded to destitute of any visible anastomosing branches.

Catarrhal ophthalmia, in some instances, has been known to be contagious, and is generally occasioned by damp and cold weather; it is often epidemic, and of more frequent occurrence in Europe than in this country. The tears are very acrid, and excoriate the parts over which they pass, and the carunculæ are the seat of very severe pain.

In the early stages, when there is no lachrymation, and a sensation of pressure is experienced when moving the lids, together with agglutination and catarrhal fever, *cham.* should be prescribed.

If dryness occur, with a high stage of inflammation of the conjunctiva, with congestion to the head, together with acrid, thin coryza, dry, hacking cough, and ordinary catarrhal symptoms, *belladonna* is indicated. It is also called for if the conjunctiva is swollen, and also the eyelids; if there is great sensibility to light, and dimness of vision. Also if the coryza produces excoriation and pimples under the nose, from its acridity, a few globules of the 6th dilution, dissolved in six tablespoonsful of water, is sometimes sufficient to effect a cure. At the expiration of twelve hours, should not a favorable effect have been produced, the dose may be repeated.

Euphrasia is indicated, if there is much pressure and redness, with *profuse* discharge of *acrid* tears, with *excessive coryza* and cephalalgia. The sensation of sand under the eyelids is also experienced, which sensation is owing either to distension of the vessels, a vesicle or phlyctana, or an ulcer. It is also serviceable, if both eyelids are agglutinated and much swollen, with a bloody viscid discharge; if the margins of the eyelids are moist and ulcerated; frequent blinking and great sensitiveness to light. A solution of a few globules of one of the lower dilutions, repeated at several hours' interval, may be directed.

Hempel alleges that, for catarrhal ophthalmia, *aconite* is a most valuable medicine, and says that even in mismanaged cases, with ulceration of the conjunctiva, deep-seated aching and sore pain in the eyeball, boring or sharp aching in the frontal sinuses, even if fever be not present, this medicine is of great service. If the inflammation is less marked, but there is severe pain in the eyes, much lachrymation, photophobia, with fluent coryza, *ignatia* is indicated.

Arsenic, besides exercising a powerful action upon the sclerotic and choroid coats, is very beneficial in inflammation of the conjunctiva. The symptoms which require its use, are violent and intense redness of the membrane, with congestion of the vessels; swelling of the eyelids; a profuse flow of acrid tears; nightly agglutination; great photophobia; aggravation of pain from exposure to light, and a feeling as though sand were lodged in the eyes.

According to Dr. Dudgeon, when the affection is recent, in the first stage, and the chief symptoms are dryness; itching or smarting sensation in the eyes and lids; sensation as though a foreign body were lodged in the eye; frequent winking and occasional discharge of tears, but little secretion of mucus; *sulphur*, in almost any dilution, suffices to effect a rapid cure.

When the inflammation is intense, the mucous secretion excessive, the redness of the eye considerable, and the caruncula particularly inflamed, *argent-nit.* will prove specific.

When the meibomian glands are much affected, and the edges of the lids are red and swollen, the secretions forming deep yellow crusts upon the eyelashes at night, *mercurius* and *hepar* may be administered. When the symptoms are exacerbated towards evening, *puls.* may be found useful. *Dulcamara* has been recommended when the symptoms are slight, and the attack has been produced by exposure to cold and wet.

Knorre found *digitalis* useful, when the affection of the eye occurred after the sudden suppression of coryza. *Kali-bichrom.* should also be remembered, when the disease has become chronic, and there is profuse yellowish secretion. *Merc.*, *hepar*, *euphr.*, *arsen.*, *puls.*, *sulph.*, are frequently indicated. When the caruncula and general conjunctiva are the seat of the chronic mucous affection, *argent-nit.*, *lyc.*, *zinc.*, *rhus-tox.*, or *bry.*, should be employed. When there is a tendency to the formation of pustules, vesicles, and indolent ulceration, *euph.*, *ars.*, *sulph.*, *coloc.*, *merc.*, or *silic.*, may be exhibited.

The sensitiveness to light (photophobia) accompanying pure catarrhal ophthalmia is seldom important, but when it exists to any degree, and fails to yield to other remedial agents, *con.* or *bell.* will almost certainly procure relief.*

There are other medicines which may in some cases be called

* See Peters' Diseases of the Eye, p. 49.

for, among which are *caust.*, *digit.*, *phosph.*, *nux-vom.*, *sepia*, *silic.*, *zinc.*, the selection of which will depend upon the group of symptoms which the individual cases exhibit.

Section 2.—Purulent Ophthalmia.

Purulent Ophthalmia.—This variety of ophthalmia has received various names, in accordance with the nature of the secretion which accompanies it. As the disease most frequently is met with in infants, the term ophthalmia neonatorum has likewise been given it; and, as its characters are strikingly defined and developed in them, the best description of the disease can be given from its progress in such cases.

Sometimes it appears immediately at birth—sometimes three, six, or ten days after; at others, when the child is three or four months old. For one person affected above three months, twenty at least are subject to it under that age.

It commences with some redness of the palpebral conjunctiva, accompanied with a slight discharge of puriform-looking secretion, and intolerance of light. At this period of the disease, the conjunctiva covering the eyeball is not inflamed: an adult will complain of itching, or the sensation as if a grain of sand were within the eye. As the disease advances, these symptoms become aggravated, there is great difficulty in separating the lids; the discharge, which was thin, whitish, and small in quantity, becomes viscid and of a yellowish or grayish color, resembling pus. The palpebral conjunctiva is much swollen and reddened; and this swelling increases to such a degree as to prevent the raising of the upper lid, and is so protruded as to cover entirely the lower palpebra. The surgeon, in examining the eye when in this condition, must be cautious lest during the struggles of the child the upper lid be everted, to reduce which is very difficult, and sometimes impossible.

The *external* surface of the palpebra reddens and swells, which redness and swelling spread to the cheeks and face, sometimes assuming a livid hue—accompanying these local symptoms there is pain, which extends into the head, temples, or deep within the brain, with the sensation of the eye being too large for the orbit. Sometimes hemorrhage takes place from the eye before the muco-purulent secretion occurs; when such takes place, an amelioration of all the symptoms ensues. In consequence of the swelling of the conjunctiva the cornea appears imbedded in the eye, and very often only its centre can be distinguished, and if an incrustation of dried matter attaches to it, suppuration of the *cornea appears* to have taken place. If the disease advances the corneal conjunctiva becomes affected, and the cornea itself becomes opaque, either impairing or destroying vision; further progress results in suppuration and bursting of the coat with an escape of the humors of the eye. Before this rupture of the cornea takes place, ulcers more or less deep are to be seen, which working entirely through, occasion that variety of *staphyloma* called mulberry, from its granulated structure and peculiar color. The cornea now either cicatrizes, losing its convexity and transparency, or the whole eye suppurates. This description applies to the disease in its most aggravated form; fortunately, however, the result is not often so disastrous—the symptoms, under judicious treatment, are arrested, and the disease is entirely subdued. This disease, with the results just described, accords in many respects with that of the celebrated Egyptian ophthalmy—though differing from the latter in attacking weak cachectic individuals.

Children, as before observed, are most liable to be attacked with purulent ophthalmia, especially those badly fed and clothed. The disease frequently prevails in lying-in and foundling hospitals. The chief cause has been supposed to be morbid vaginal secretions. Authorities however of weight, imagine it owing to the sudden exposure of the eyes at birth to light; the former supposition is much more probable.

Treatment.—If the affection is slight, frequent washing with a clean sponge dipped in warm water will be sufficient. If the symptoms increase, *aconite* every four hours may be given, to be followed up by *euphrasia.* The symptoms calling for the administration of the latter, being a copious secretion of tears and mucus, and when the conjunctival and sclerotic coats are both much inflamed with small ulcers around the circumference of the cornea, together with cephalalgia, profuse coryza, and evening exacerbations.

Ignatia is to be had recourse to when there is less inflammation than demands *euphrasia* but severe aching in the eyes, lachrymation, dimness of vision, and fluent coryza.

Belladonna should be directed when there is *dryness* of the eyes with a high degree of conjunctival and sclerotic inflammation, with determination of blood to the head, and more urgently if there is profuse excoriating coryza, with a dry, hacking, short or spasmodic cough.

Arsenic is advantageously used in some stages of purulent ophthalmia, especially when the pains are very violent and *burning*, and there is a secretion of an acrid serous nature—an intermittent character will also recommend its use.

After the disease is subdued there often remains a soreness and redness of the margins of the eyelids, increased or renewed by changes of weather, for which *nux-vomica* is the proper medicine; a dose should be administered at bed-time, and repeated every night, until relief is afforded; and as individuals accustomed to indulge in alcoholic or vinous drinks are liable to such sequelæ, which are generally accompanied with headache, eight or ten ordinary sized globules of the medicine in a tablespoonful of water may be prescribed.

If diarrhœa, intertrigo-miliary eruption, flaccidity of the muscles, and restlessness attend, *chamomilla* is the proper remedy, which may be succeeded by *belladonna*. If the infant is at the breast, the diet of the nurse requires attention, and it will generally be found that either *bry.*, *nux-vom.*, or *puls.*, are indicated. Constitutional symptoms are most frequently met by *merc.-sol.* or *sulph.* *Euphorbium* may be used when there is severe ulceration of both lids, with violent itching and irritation, but with rather pale swelling and profuse secretion of pus.

We know of a case of a most aggravated nature cured by repeated and steadily continued doses of *calcarea carbonica.*

There may in some instances local applications be required. Among old school practitioners solutions of alum, sulphate of copper, nitrate of silver, and oil of turpentine, have been recommended. These, according to Peters, are quite homœopathic enough, "but," says he, "a weak solution of tartar-emetic is still more so, and in a few cases I have found it the most useful one; it is decidedly homœopathic to pustular, purulent, and suppurative inflammation; has a well-earned old and new school reputation against inflammation in general, and is certainly not more irritating than turpentine and nitrate of silver, which have been found very useful. Still, I prefer, as a general rule, a solution of *kali-chlor.*, *kali-carb.*, or *kali-hydriod.*, to be used several times a day for three days; these, although they will not decidedly check the profuse purulent discharge, will alter its character, render it less noxious, thick and purulent." Dr. Peters then mentions, that out of over forty cases of purulent ophthalmia in children, treated by himself and colleague, Dr. W. S. Stewart, at the Home for the Friendless, not a single eye was lost, though in some instances the disease was obstinate, and the progress of cure protracted.

There are other medicines homœopathic to this disease, among which are *rhus.*, *clem.*, *mez.*, *cann.*, *hepar*, &c.

The sequelæ of purulent ophthalmia have been arranged in the following manner:

1st. Sloughing of the cornea, especially when the swelling of the conjunctiva of the ball and the chemosis are very great. 2d. Bursting of the *cornea.* In some instances there is no perceptible change in the cornea previous to the rupture; but in others, a small line across the coat is observed, which gradually increases until the cornea not only becomes opaque, but projects in an irregular cone, finally a paroxysm of excruciating pain is suddenly terminated by a sensation of something giving way; a little hot fluid runs down the cheek, and great relief is experienced. 3d. Suppuration of the cornea. 4th. Ulceration of the cornea. 5th. Interstitial deposits, forming opacities in every degree, from the thinnest film to the most dense leucoma. 6th. Opacity of the cornea from cicatrization of ulcers. 7th.

30

Prolapsus of the iris. 8th. Adhesion of the iris to the cornea. 9th. Loosening, sponginess, vascularity, and thickening of the mucous membrane covering the cornea, with enlargement of its blood-vessels, and more or less diminution of its transparency. This change occurs in various degrees, from slight vascularity to pannus. 10th. Staphyloma, general or partial; and dropsical enlargement of the ball of the eye or collapse of its tunics.*

Section 3.—*Gonorrhœal Ophthalmia.*

Gonorrhœal ophthalmia somewhat resembles the purulent variety, and is occasioned either by the direct application of gonorrhœal matter, or by metastasis. The mucous membrane of the eyeball and lids is the seat of violent inflammation, and there is a profuse discharge of purulent matter, resembling that which issues from the urethra in gonorrhœa. This variety of ophthalmia is said to be the most violent and destructive to which the eye is subject. It often destroys the sight in a short period of time, and frequently when the patient applies for relief the disease is so far advanced that the organ is irreparably injured.

In this affection there is a great degree of vascular congestion, chemosis, excessive tumefaction of the conjunctiva, and palpebræ. In the first stage, which is generally short, the inflammation is confined to the conjunctiva, and the usual symptoms of such pathological condition are present—soreness, stiffness, photophobia, &c. After a time, however, the disease extends to the cornea, and the patient experiences severe, often excruciating pain in the orbit and head, which is aggravated by exposure to light; there are also constitutional symptoms present—shivering, fever, delirium, &c. If the disease still advance, the inflammation extends from the mucous membrane to the cornea and globe of the eye; the tumefaction of the orbicular conjunctiva is often so great that it laps

* Quoted by Peters from Lawrence on Diseases of the Eye.

the cornea, effusion takes place in the lids, and the swelling may be so great that it is impossible to obtain a view of the cornea; this tumefaction declines after a time, and both eyelids may become everted, the convex edge of the tarsal cartilage being pushed forwards by the swollen conjunctiva. The effects of gonorrhœal ophthalmia are as follows—suppuration, ulceration, and sloughing of the cornea, interstitial deposit, escape of the humors, obliteration of the anterior chamber, staphyloma, prolapsus iridis, corneal opacity, and obliteration of the pupil.

Three distinct forms of ophthalmic inflammation occur in conjunction with, or dependent on, gonorrhœa, viz., acute inflammation of the conjuctiva; mild inflammation of that membrane; inflammation of the sclerotic coat, sometimes extending to the iris.*

Treatment.—As the same tissues are affected in the first stages of gonorrhœal ophthalmia, as are primarily involved in ophthalmia neonatorum, the medicines that are adapted to the one disease are in a measure suited to the other. The great activity of the inflammation, and the more intense febrile disturbance accompanying it, render the employment† of *aconite* indispensable at the commencement of the disease, and the most striking beneficial results are said to have followed its administration.

Arg.-nit., *sulph.*, *merc.*, *cham.*, *puls.*, *rhus*, and, perhaps, *ignat.* or *bry.* may be indicated.

When the tissues that are more deeply seated become involved, when the pains are pressive, and there is throbbing in the eye, *bell.* should be employed. This medicine may also be used in alternation with *aconite.*

Arsenicum is indicated when the pains are severe, occurring in paroxysms, when there are violent stabbings in the eye; the eyeball feeling like a coal of fire. Dr. Dudgeon recommends

* See Hastings' Practice of Surgery, p. 442.

† Dudgeon on Diseases of the Eye. British Journal of Homœopathy, vol. vii., p. 4.

highly a solution of nitrate of silver as homœopathic to gonorrhœal ophthalmia, as well as to the severe forms of ophthalmiæ catarrhales. The solution he recommends is composed of from two to four grains of *arg.-nit.* to an ounce of distilled water; a small quantity of this solution is carefully introduced beneath the eyelids with a camel's hair brush once a day, every two, three, or four days, according to the severity of the symptoms.

Although we have mentioned the treatment by local application of a solution of nitrate of silver, as recommended by Dr. Dudgeon, we by no means agree with that gentleman as to its necessity or superior efficacy. On the contrary, we believe, and the conviction is the result of much personal knowledge, that by the internal exhibition of the appropriate medicines cures are more prompt and certain. The attenuations likewise being high rather than low. The same remark we would apply to nearly every instance of external application, with a view to medicinal action, mentioned throughout this volume.

Besides this topical application, he has derived advantage from the local use of weak solutions of *euphrasia*, *arsenicum*, *rhus* and *mercurius*. On this subject Dr. Dudgeon writes that, judging by analogy, equal advantage might be derived from the local use of the other medicines in these local diseases. He says, further—"The mode in which I usually employ the remedies locally, is to mix a drop or two of the mother tincture, or of the 1st, 2d, 3d, or 4th dilution, or of the dilution taken by the patient internally, with a teacupful of water, to be applied one, two, or three times a-day to the eye with a soft rag.

Tussilago petasites is said by Dr. Rosenberg to have proved effectual in gonorrhœal ophthalmia; but Dr. Dudgeon remarks that the case given by the former in illustration of the virtues of *tussilago*, was not a genuine ophthalmia gonorrhoica, but a species of blephar-ophthalmia, with scrofulous or other dyscrasic complication.

Acid-nit. is useful when the anterior chamber looks as though filled with a dirty looking pus, and the whole eye appears to threaten disorganization. If symptoms of iritis develop themselves, *aconite* in alternation with *merc.-corr.-sub.* are said to be invaluable agents.*

Section 4.—*Syphilitic Ophthalmia.*

This affection is intermediate between secondary and tertiary syphilis. By Ricord it is supposed to belong to the former, and Gollmann coincides in this opinion.

The *iris* is the primary seat of the disease, although, if the symptoms are violent, the other tissues of the eye may be involved; in most cases but one eye is affected, and the organ affected presents many of the properties and appearances of common iritis. When syphilitic ophthalmia is accompanied with sclerotical injection, the latter is said to depend upon an accidental rheumatic complication; however, sometimes among the anatomical signs of ophthalmia syphilitica is noticed a zone of violet red, from a line to a line and a half in width, of uniform tint, and in which cannot be observed any distinct vessels. This zone is called the *dyscrasic circle.* In the commencement of the disease the iris becomes duller, and presents a grayish appearance, the radii being more or less effaced; the small circle of this membrane is livid or copper-colored; its tissue is tumefied, and forms an elevated ring composed of thick, downy flakes. The pupil is more or less contracted, and assumes an irregular, or angular shape; the cornea is somewhat dimmed, and on its inner surface careful examination detects small fasiculi of congested vessels; the tunica albuginea is of a rose-color, which at its juncture with the cornea is converted into a dark-red hue. As the disease advances the iris becomes more discolored, its surface is covered with exudation, its free margin is tumefied, and upon its anterior surface there are elevations of a yellowish or gray tinge. The pupil at length becomes perfectly immovable; pedunculated excrescences, termed *condylo-*

---

* See Gollmann's Diseases of the Urinary and Sexual Organs, p. 77.

mata of the iris, sprout from the membrane, and adhesion takes place between the iris and the lenticular capsule. In such cases the pupil still remains open, and presents a gray instead of its usual black appearance. At the bottom of the anterior chamber, through the dim cornea, a more or less elevated layer of pus, sometimes mixed with extravasated blood, can be perceived. The patient experiences in the suborbital region of the affected side violent constrictive, boring pains, which radiate sometimes to the neighboring regions of the head, are increased towards evening, most violent at midnight, and abate towards morning. The visual faculty is more or less altered, by reason of the intensity of the inflammation, and of the plastic exudations formed in the pupillary opening. Photophobia is never present in true syphilitic ophthalmia, and when the symptom is noticed, other complications are the cause of its appearance.

The terminations of the disease are, resolution, condyloma of the iris, exudation within the pupil, or obliteration of this aperture.

This variety of ophthalmia, although it is sometimes met with alone, is generally accompanied with other symptoms of secondary syphilis; such as eruptions of the skin, ulceration of the fauces, pains in the periosteum, &c.

In the treatment of this specific disease,* the desideratum to be attained is to arrest the further progress of the syphilitic process, and to prevent the permanent or temporary loss of vision that may be occasioned by the closure of the pupil or adhesion of the iris from an effusion of lymph. The medicine which the experience of our allopathic brethren has shown to possess specific virtues in this opthalmia, is, as is well known, *mercurius;* and this is the only substance with which we are acquainted, that possesses the power of producing iritis and inflammation of the membrane of Descemet. But it so happens that the disease is usually encountered, when the violence of the inflammatory process within the iris threatens a closure or obliteration of the pupil—an evil which may be prevented by producing

* See British Journal of Homœopathy, vol. vii., p. 23.

artificial dilatation of that orifice, by *bell.* or *hyos.* But these medicines have not, according to experience, proved useful in checking the syphilitic process, and therefore the main reliance must still be placed in *mercurius.*

A resort to the external application of belladonna or hyoscyamus in a concentrated form to dilate the pupil, is equivalent to a mechanical force, the object being to irritate muscular fibre into unnatural contraction—very different from exhibiting an infinitesimal dose to produce *curative* action.

In the more chronic stages of the disease, advantage will be derived from the use of *sulph., hepar, puls.,* and perhaps *nit.-ac.* When condylomata appear in the iris, *thuja, nit.-acid,* and in some cases *caust.* and *sepia* may be employed.

When *abscess* forms in the iris, *hepar, merc., silic.,* and *sulph.* are valuable medicines.

For the chancrous ulceration that sometimes attacks the cornea; besides *mercurius, arsen.* and *calc.* should not be forgotten.

In those cases in which mercury has been abused, *nit.-ac., hepar, sulph., mez.,* and *dulc.* will prove useful.

Colchicum will be of service when there is an exudation of lymph, or the inflammation is of a very chronic character.

Section 5.—Rheumatic Ophthalmia, or Sclerotitis.

Rheumatic ophthalmia is seated in the serous and fibrous membranes of the eye, and although generally complicated with other rheumatic affections, may exist independently of such diathesis. This disease commences with a violent stitch in the eye, and with a sensation as though some extraneous matter had suddenly and accidentally been introduced between the lids; red vessels can be observed in the sclerotic, which are either in converging patches, situated near the tendon of a muscle, or in the form of radii, which extend more or less perfectly around the cornea, terminating at its edge, or in some instances, running a short distance into it.

There may be some conjunctival inflammation; and, when such is the case, a net-work of larger vessels anastomosing over the immovable pinkish-colored fine injection of the sclerotica can be perceived.

The palpebral conjunctiva generally escapes implication. The pains are tearing, shooting, aching, throbbing, and deep seated; extending round the orbit, over the brow, in the temple, cheek, and side of the nose; the eye feels stiff, immovable, and painful, if motion is essayed; there is also photophobia. Cold and wet increase the symptoms, which are most severe from sunset till midnight. Phlyctenæ, ulcers, and abscesses may form; and, if the inflammation extends to the anterior capsule of the lens, the latter becomes dim, and resembles the appearances presented in cataract. The inflammation, though rarely, extends to the retina. If the membrane of the aqueous humor is affected, there may be a fine circle of vessels on the inside of the cornea; and if the secretion of the aqueous humor is increased, the cornea bulges outwards.

When the latter is the chief seat of the inflammatory process, the red vessels may be seen to extend to its centre; white or bluish spots are formed by exudation, which are to be distinguished from other affections of the corneal conjunctiva, by examining the eye from the side. The entire cornea may become opaque, and maculæ may form. This state of things is accompanied with almost intolerable pain.

The disease may continue from two to six weeks; or, becoming chronic, may last for years, with intermissions of longer or shorter duration.

If the inflammation is slight at the commencement, *pulsatilla* will relieve the *pain*. For the inflammation itself *bryonia* should be given.

If the inflammation and pain are excessive, *acon.* should be prescribed, especially at the beginning of the attack, if the sclerotica is red, with a burning pressure, protruded eyes, and cutting pains.

Clematis erecta is indicated, if the eyelids are glued together in the morning, with burning and lachrymation increased in the open air; and if the iris should likewise be inflamed.

If there be sudden dartings through the ball of the eye, and rending, boring pains in the orbit and frontal sinuses, and adjacent parts, with a *bright* red *weblike* arrangement of the red vessels of the *sclerotica*, with copious secretion of tears and dim-sightedness, *mercurius-sol.* is the remedy.

If the photophobia lessens, but the pains, especially of the head and face, increase, *euphrasia* has proved very effectual. *Caust.*, *calc.-carb.*, or *sulph.* will generally be required for the remaining symptoms.

For the stiffness of the eye and great pain during movement, *spig.*, *bry.*, and *rhus* may be employed. If the pain extends into the head, *spig.*, *bell.*, *merc.*, *coloc.* should be remembered. When the morbid process has extended to the iris, *bell.*, *merc.*, or *sulph.* will be found useful. When the rheumatic is complicated with catarrhal ophthalmia, those medicines should be selected which possess a marked action upon the conjunctiva, as well as on the more deeply seated structures—among which are *ars.*, *bry.*, *calc.*, *hepar*, *merc.*, *puls.*, and *sulph.*

Section 6.—*Arthritic Ophthalmia.*

Arthritic ophthalmia, or the venous or varicose ophthalmia of some authors, is often seen in persons who, so far from having indulged luxuriously, are poor, and badly nourished; the distinctive term gouty ophthalmia is not well chosen.

The disease commences with a prickling sensation in the eye; a feeling as if a hair were drawn over it, with formication in the orbital region, together with a sensation of coldness in the parts; pains then follow of a boring, digging kind, in the orbit or bones of the cranium; there is likewise numbness in the forehead, eyelids, surface of the eye, and corresponding side of the head. Photophobia though present, does not exist in as aggravated degree as is noticed in rheumatic sclerotitis. The vision is not much impaired so long as the inflammation occupies the conjunctiva, but as the zone of congested vessels forms around the cornea, the bottom of the eye becomes greenish, the sight becomes dim, and total blindness may ensue. The terminations of the disease are resolution, deep ulceration of the cornea, glaucoma, exudation in the pupil and obliteration of its opening.

The *conjunctival* injection is composed of large, distinct, and nearly varicose vessels, which pass under the conjunctiva of the lids, and ramify by bifurcation. When arthritic ophthalmia is the sequence of ophthalmia catarrhalis, the injection of the conjunctiva presents often only the characteristics of the latter, with this difference, however, that the vessels are of a deeper color, intermixed and larger. In the *sclerotica* there exists a deeper colored circle of vessels than is noticed in the rheumatic variety, but the appearance which chiefly characterizes the venous injection, is the presence of a *whitish blue ring*, surrounding the cornea, which latter may become the seat of effusion or of circumscribed ulceration in more advanced stages of the disease; the ulcer is of irregular form, with abrupt uneven edges, and covered with a grayish matter. As the iris becomes involved it changes color and appears to be deprived of its pigment, assuming a marbled aspect, and is spotted with patches, more or less large, of a bluish gray or pearly hue. The membrane loses its fibrinous structure, the pupil is dilated, immovable, and perpendicularly or transversely oval; or it may become irregular and contracted on account of adhesions which are formed between its margin and the anterior crystalline membrane. Arthritic ophthalmia is constantly accompanied with inflammation or congestion of the *choroid*, which is manifested by the injection of the external membranes of the eye. The secretion is often of an acrid and corrosive nature, the mucus sometimes resembling a whitish foam, (arthritic foam,) which collects in the angles or in the folds of the conjunctiva.

Acon. and *bell.* are prominent medicines in the commencement of the attack, when inflammatory symptoms are strongly marked, with lachrymation and considerable pain.

Colocynth should be directed if the pains are of a burning, cutting kind, and there is also pressing and tearing pain, directing itself to the forehead, and extending also to the root of the nose: these symptoms compelling the patient, from their intensity, to a constant change of position.

For the *internal* inflammation and that of the retina which frequently accompanies the disease, *belladonna* is the remedy, especially when the eyeballs feel as if they would be torn from the sockets, or pressed into the head; with aching pain *above* the eyes; with muscæ volitantes, with bright fiery borders and flashes and sparks before the eyes—and this medicine should be continued should the coroid, iris and scleorotica be inflamed and the pupil indented and dilated

Spigelia is adapted when the deeper-seated tissues are affected; when the pain is digging, boring, and sticking, with a direction to the inner angle of the eye: the eyeballs feeling enlarged, with a wreath of red vessels around the cornea, with a narrow white band between; (an important diagnostic sign to which allusion has already been made when giving the detail of symptoms). This medicine is also indicated when the eyeball is covered with enlarged blood-vessels, and if the eyes for an instant are opened the pain becomes almost insufferable; flashes of light before the eyes.

Sulphur, a remedy so efficient in all cases of arthritis may be prescribed very advantageously in arthritic ophthalmia, more especially *immediately after aconite.*

Digitalis, when there is *horrible* pain in the eyeball if touched, acrid tears, the lachrymation being greater in a room than in the open air, sensation of weakness in the eyes with agglutination in the morning—together with the objective symptoms already stated as characterizing the disease.

Hepar-sulph., *rhus-tox.*, *phosph.*, *caust.*, *natr.*, *mur.*, *china*, *sepia*, *puls*, and other medicines are sometimes required.

Section 7.—Erysipelatous Ophthalmia.

Erysipelatous ophthalmia frequently accompanies, or is the result of an extensive erysipelas of the face; the pain is sometimes considerable, and is occasioned by the pressure of the ocular conjunctiva against the palpebræ, there may also be experienced a sensation of tension, or there is itching and prickling in the eye. There is neither photophobia nor alteration of vision. The disease is principally seated in the ocular conjunctiva, or sometimes may extend to surrounding cellular tissue, particularly that of the eyelids, causing considerable tumefaction.

The injection of the vessels of the conjunctiva is confluent, the membrane swells, assumes a pale-yellow color, becomes relaxed, and presents somewhat the appearance of infiltration; the sclerotica is often entirely concealed by the swelling of the subconjunctival cellular tissue, and the choroid and iris preserve their integrity. The mucous secretion is scarcely augmented, and there is no epiphora.

Treatment.—This disease is generally subdued by the exhibition of *bell.*, or *rhus ;* in other cases, when the affection has assumed a more chronic type, *sulph.*, *graph.*, or *hepar*, may prove serviceable.

Section 8.—Variolous Ophthalmia.

The integument of the eyelids, and portions of the conjunctiva, are the seat of this variety of ophthalmia. The variolous pustules may be numerous on the external surface of the eyelids, and there may be inflammation and swelling of the surrounding parts. A sensation of tension or of the presence of gravel or sand, with lancinating pain, generally announces the appearance of the exanthema, and the sufferings are proportionate to the extent of tissues involved, as is also the trouble of vision, and obscuration of the cornea; photophobia is very great, and the tears are burning. If the disease be not arrested, suppuration of the cornea may ensue, terminating in the total destruction of the latter; or chronic conjunctivitis and blepharitis may supervene. Falling of the eyelashes, trichiasis, ectropion, ertropion, obliteration of the lachrymal sac, and blenorrhœa, may also be mentioned as sequents of this variety of ophthalmia.

The pustules that are developed upon the conjunctiva are small, yellowish, and elevated above the level of the membrane. The sclerotica is the seat of vivid injection, and if the cornea is also affected, this membrane becomes the seat of suppurative points which are at first whitish, afterwards yellow, finally extend, and destruction of the part may result. The iris and choroid may be secondarily affected.

Treatment.—The danger attendant upon variolous ophthalmia, is not great when the affection is treated according to the homœopathic law, as the primary disease is generally so much modified, that the danger of the attendant ophthalmia is also diminished in proportion. The medicines that are best adapted are *acon.*, *bell.*, *hepar.*, *puls.*, *stram.*, *sulph.*, and *variolin.*

Dr. Dudgeon records a case* in which the latter medicine effected a permanent cure, after a diminution of the inflammation, and photophobia had been effected by other remedial agents mentioned.

Section 9.—*Scrofulous Ophthalmia.*

Ophthalmia scrofulosa, or scrofulous ophthalmia, is generally a conjunctivitis. It has been called by some phlyctenular ophthalmia, from vesicles or phlyctenæ being associated with it. The redness is not very intense. A bundle of enlarged vessels runs from an angle of the eye *to* the *cornea;* or it may be scattered pretty generally over the conjunctiva, its course being *directed to* the cornea. The intolerance of light being, in some instances, very great, though unaccompanied with pain;

* British Journal of Homœopathy, vol. vii., p. 27.

the patient is compelled to keep the lids almost closed, and to remain in a darkened room.

As the disease advances the sclerotic may participate, and red vessels pass over the circumference of the cornea, and at their terminations a small vesicle may be perceived, which at first contains a transparent, then a milky fluid. These vesicles are often seen *on* the cornea, but generally they are not found beyond its border. These after a time burst, and become ulcers of a whitish appearance, which have a strong bias to extend towards the centre of the eye, by involving the parts in that direction; they are also accompanied with much pain. Though the vesicles which form on the sclerotica are larger, they are of less import than those of the cornea. These phlyctenæ may be resolved without ulceration, and when such termination is accomplished, there remains a slight speck, which designates the spot they occupied; the cicatrix, however, which remains, should ulceration have ensued, is more reluctant in its departure, or may remain during life. The phlyctenæ produce the sensation of a foreign body under the lid.

The pain that accompanies scrofulous ophthalmia is severe, and the patient is sometimes awakened at midnight with acute stabbing pain in the ulcer, or in the surrounding parts. There is either a secretion of clear, acrid tears, or of a white, thin mucus, which corrodes the cheeks. The pains in the eyeball are shooting and burning. All the symptoms are worse during the day, but diminish in such a remarkable manner towards evening, that the patient can frequently open the eyes without inconvenience, and no signs of inflammation can be perceived.

In this disease the palpebral conjunctiva is inflamed, as are also the meibomian glands; the edges of the eyelids swell and become red, and the eyelashes fall out. The lachrymal sac is also frequently implicated.

Vision is not much affected; there being sometimes, however, the appearance of mist before the eyes. When the cornea and deeper seated tissues become involved, the imperfection of sight is increased.

Scrofulous ophthalmia is generally accompanied with other

manifestations of a strumous habit, such as cutaneous eruptions, lymphatic ulcers, glandular engorgements, or affections of the osseous system. In children relapses are apt to occur, the disease varying in activity at different periods.

Treatment.—In the commencement of the attack, when there are aching, stinging pains in the eyes, with redness, intolerance of light, corroding tears, and secretion of much mucus, *puls.* is indicated. With such symptoms, and the disease decidedly aggravated in the morning, *nux-vom.* has been productive of much benefit. For symptoms somewhat similar, *euphras.* is likewise called for.

Arsen. is indicated, when the eyelids are swollen, their edges reddened, and there is profuse secretion from the *meibomian* glands; when the cornea is dim, with opaque spots on its outer edge, with deep ulcers about its circumference; when the puncta lachrymalia are swollen and inflamed; when there is copious lachrymation, and piercing, burning pains, with violent stitches in the eyes.

Hepar is among the best remedies for the disease—it is advantageous at any period. Hartmann recommends two or three grains of the 2d or 3d trituration as a dose, two or three times a day.

The alternate use of *calc.-carb.* and *sulph.* has been followed by the happiest results. *Calc.-carb.* one day, and *sulph.* the next: the 2d or 3d trituration, two or three grains of either, to be administered morning and evening at a dose. It is alleged, that the disease, though of years continuance, has been cured by these means in one or two weeks.

When the bundles of red vessels are numerous, extending themselves into the cornea, and the phlyctenæ or ulcers are present, *bell.* may be given with great benefit. Also when a painful pressure is experienced when turning up the eyes, and when the symptoms are increased by cold and damp.

Calc.-carb. is to be selected, if there be a sensation as though a foreign body had got into the eye; pressure inward, especially in the evening; acrid tears, and secretion of mucus.

When there is present at the same time with the *ophthalmia scrofulosa* herpetic eruptions on the face, *rhus-tox.* should be directed.

Conium is a powerful agent in the treatment of scrofulous ophthalmia, particularly when there is great photophobia, dimness of the cornea, redness of the eyelids, with profuse discharge of mucus and tears; sensation as though the eyes would be pressed from their sockets.

Merc-sol. and *merc.-corr.-sub.*, are both useful preparations in the treatment of this disease; the latter is particularly indicated when there is spasmodic closure and swelling of the lids, discharge of thick pus and mucus from the eyes, the cornea covered with red vessels, also with ulcers, which threaten perforation, &c. The alternation of *arsenicum* and *euphrasia* has effected a cure of ophthalmia scrofulosa. *Cann.*, *caust.*, *dig.*, *nit.-acid.*, *puls.*, *sep.*, *silic.* or *sulphur* may in some cases be required. The disease, however, not being local, will often resist all efforts for a considerable period; though it may be relieved or even be made to disappear, it will from time to time recur, until by appropriate treatment it has been eradicated from the system.

Section 10.—*Iritis.*—*Iritic Ophthalmia.*

The iris is capable of taking on inflammatory action of itself. It is distinguished by a severe lancinating pain extending from the eyebrow to the orbit, from thence backward to the optic nerve, and into the cranium; there is also great intolerance of light, and many red vessels are apparent on the sclerotic coat, especially near the cornea, the conjunctiva not being inflamed. The iris loses its lustre and becomes of a reddish or greenish hue; upon its surface, also, red vessels may be perceived; the pupil contracts, becomes irregular, and is turned backwards. The inflammation generally terminates in effusion, and spots of coagulable lymph may be deposited upon the iris, on one side of the pupil, the remainder of the opening being left unaltered;

this condition is termed by surgeons "imperfect closure of the pupil," (*atresia iridis imperfecta,*) and is always attended by more or less impairment of vision.

When considerable effusion has taken place into the posterior chamber, the plastic material becomes organized into a dense opaque substance, to which the entire circumference of pupil is closely fixed, the opening itself being greatly contracted, or entirely closed. By this complete "obliteration of the pupil" (*atresia iridis perfecta*) the communication between the two chambers is destroyed, while the passage of light into the eye is almost wholly intercepted, being accompanied with a corresponding loss of sight.

The usual causes of inflammation occasion the disease; also wounds produced by operations for cataract; exposure to a bright light; syphilis or abuse of mercury.

In the early stage *aconite* should be employed to reduce the inflammation. The medicine is to be prescribed in a tolerably low dilution, and frequently repeated; if, however, there is much pain in the forehead and occiput, *bell.* is clearly indicated. These medicines, however, may be given in alternation; the latter to be used in cases, even should the pupil be contracted or less dilatable than natural. When there is *aching* pain in the head, with great dryness and pressure, with immovable contraction of the pupil and frequent scintillations, *cina.* has great influence upon the disease.

If the vision is very much impaired *mer.-corr.-sub.* is to be directed. *Plumbum* rapidly absorbs the effused lymph.

In iritis produced by the abuse of mercury *clematis* has been used with advantage—also in scrofulous individuals.

In arthritic iritis, with inflamed cornea and sclerotica, intolerance of light, lancinating pains, and contracted pupil, *cocculus* should be selected.

If there is lancinating pains in the orbit also, *cocculus* is still further indicated. *Staphys.*, *bry.*, *lyc.*, *calc.-carb.*, and *conium,* are also suited to this kind of iritis. For iritis from abuse of mercury, *hepar-sulph.* stands foremost in the list of medicines.

If the above treatment fail and the pupil is completely obliterated, the surgeon can have recourse to an operation which may restore sight to the patient, by means of an artificial pupil. The considerations which should influence the operator, before the knife is called into requisition, are of importance, and demand some notice in this place, although the minutiæ cannot be entered into as fully as would be quite satisfactory were sufficient space allowed.

Concerning the admissibility of making an artificial pupil, when one eye is free from disease, many discussions have arisen, and different conclusions arrived at. On this subject Mr. Walton writes*—"My own opinion is against operating, as a rule, so long as one eye is efficient, for in all probability the vision that may be restored to the faulty eye will not be equal to that of the other, which will continue to be used alone. A more forcible objection, however, is that as a new pupil cannot be made to correspond to the natural one, there will most probably be confusion of sight, double vision or squint.

"When the true tissue of the cornea has been lost, and its place supplied by a cicatrix, an operation is contra-indicated, although there may be a part of the cicatrix nearly transparent; for the iris is necessarily incorporated with the new material. An operation is also contra-indicated when the iris is adherent to the corneal tissue. An iris that has lost its characteristic fibrous appearance and lustre, and bulges forward, affords but a doubtful prospect of success, from the tendency there is for the breach that is made in it to close by adhesive inflammation."

A long interval should be allowed to elapse after the cessation of the disease that has caused the obliteration before attempting an operation. "If the original disease has long passed away, and a fair trial has been given to means calculated to subdue inflammation, if the health is good, and the eye is free from irritability, and there is much encouragement from the soundness of the retina, I do not hesitate to operate.

"An eye that has seemed to be in an almost hopeless condition directly after the subsidence of the disease that has rendered

* Vide Walton's Operative Ophthalmic Surgery, p. 549.

its pupil useless, may, on the restoration of the general health, improve considerably, and be brought into a proper state for successful operation." There are additional considerations which the practitioner, before attempting the formation of artificial pupil, would certainly consider, as well as the size and construction of instruments employed, together with other minutiæ of the operation.

The method of operating is a revival of Chesselden's, by Sir William Adams—Chesselden being the first surgeon who suggested and performed the operation. The directions of Sir William Adams are viz.: "The patient being seated as in the operation for cataract, and the eye rendered steady by a gentle pressure with the concave speculum placed under the upper eyelid, the artificial pupil knife should be introduced through the coats of the eye, about a line behind the iris, with its cutting edge turned *backwards* instead of *downwards*. The point is next brought forward through the iris, somewhat more than a line from its temporal ciliary attachment, and *cautiously* carried through the anterior chamber until it has nearly reached the inner edge of that membrane, when it should be almost withdrawn out of the eye, making a *gentle* pressure with the *curved* part of the cutting edge of the instrument against the iris in the line of its transverse diameter. If in the first attempt the division of the fibres of the iris is not sufficiently extensive, the point of the knife is to be again carried forward and similarly withdrawn, until the incision is of a proper length, when the radiated fibres will immediately contract, and an opening of a large sore will be formed. After the operation is thus completed, the eye should be covered over with a plaster of simple ointment, spread on lint, and the patient put to bed with his head raised high.

If the obliterated pupil should be combined with an opaque lens or capsule—which can be seen behind the pupil, of a whitish or bluish appearance—the surgeon when dividing the iris should cut or tear up the lens, capsule, or both, and push them forward through the pupil, which they will contribute to keep expanded.

By Wenzel, Guerin, Azalini, Beer, Reissinger, and others, modifications have been made in the method of operating, and with much success; but to detail the method of procedure in each would occupy more time and space than can be here allowed.

The iris may also be prolapsed (*procidentia iridis*) through a wound or ulcer of the cornea. The pain of this disease is excessive, and there is much photophobia; the pupil becomes irregular in shape, though generally of an oval figure. Sometimes there are several projections of the iris, each through a separate orifice in the cornea. After a time adhesions take place between the cornea and iris, and the part of the iris beyond the cornea may become dry or hard, or it may slough away.

If the occurrence follows a wound of the cornea the surgeon must immediately replace the iris; if it passes through an ulcer of the cornea, the ulcer must first be healed before the iris can be retained in its natural position. The application of a solution of nitrate of silver upon a fine camel's hair brush, or a solid piece of the nitrate shaved down to a very fine point, and the edges of the ulcer gently touched, has been found to be a successful mode of treatment. The morbid sensibility of the iris is also allayed by the caustic, and the projecting and superfluous portion of the membrane may also be destroyed by its application.

It may be well to remark here that the nitrate of silver is much more preferable than the vegetable caustic or potassa, the former confining its action to the parts to which it is applied, the latter diffusing itself to adjacent parts and rapidly destroying animal fibre.

Section 11.—*Psorophthalmia.*

The above term is used to designate an inflammation or ulceration of the eyelids. Other names have been applied to the disease, such as ophthalmia tarsi, lippitudo, tinea ciliaris, &c.

The inflammation first appears on the margin of the lids, the tarsal cartilages and glands—the adjoining mucous membrane of the parts being often involved, the disease extends along the conjunctiva to the globe of the eye, attended with pruritus, redness, and sometimes severe pain. The roots of the eyelashes at first become stiff and dry, but as the disease advances they are moistened by increased secretion. The meibomian glands always participate more or less in the affection, and no longer pour out the mild and unctuous fluid which is destined to lubricate the lids, but their secretion is suspended, so that during the night the eyelids are glued together by the increased conjunctival discharge.* The inflammatory action may terminate in suppuration, followed by ulceration of the tarsi, which sometimes creates considerable deformity.

When pustules form on the margin of the lids, especially about the roots of the eyelashes, the term *tinea ciliaris* designates the affection. These ulcers break and discharge a yellowish matter, which concretes in the form of yellowish brown scabs. As this disease is seated along the roots of the ciliæ, their growth is affected and their direction altered.

Treatment.—Dr. Peters, in writing on this affection, remarks, that a large portion of the treatment falls to the share of the patient or his attendants. The lids if possible should always be prevented from becoming agglutinated at night, and if this cannot be effected, they never should be separated in the morning, until the matter by which they are glued together has been completely softened. By forcing the lids roughly asunder, the irritation is constantly enhanced, and the discharge daily aggravated; tepid milk or water should be used, or the agglutinated lashes should be anointed with olive oil, or some other simple unguent (simple cerate or fresh lard is better). The margins of the lids should be carefully examined with a magnifying glass, and all inverted lashes carefully extracted; by such means a great degree of inflammation may be prevented, and the cure be more readily accomplished.

---

* See Peters on Diseases of the Eye, p. 10.

Borax is homœopathically indicated when the eyes become agglutinated at night with hard, dry gum. *Alumina* may also be employed for such condition, and may be rendered preferable by the presence of other symptoms.

Arg.-nit., *amm.-mur.*, *carb.-an.*, may also be called for.

One of the chief remedies for psorophthalmia, and one which has been productive of most beneficial results, is *euphrasia*. In many cases its exhibition is sufficient to effect a cure without the administration of any other remedial agent. Abundant experience in relation to its action when there is "inflammation and ulceration of the margins of the eyelids," was furnished to the author, while physician to the Philadelphia Homœopathic Dispensary.

Kreas. is recommended for chronic swelling of the margin of the lids.

Eupat., *spig.*, *merc.*, and *clematis* may also be required, and in obstinate cases *calc.* or *sulph.* may be productive of beneficial results.

Section 12.—*Hydrophthalmia.*

This affection has been described under different names, as *hydrops oculi*, *hydrophthalmus*, *dropsy of the eye.* It is a partial or general enlargement of the globe of the eye, caused by increase in the quantity of the humors, or by the effusion of an aqueous fluid. The water may be effused either into the anterior or posterior chamber of the eye, and if much protrusion take place from an increased accumulation of water, there is much pain both in the eye and head; vision is impaired; the iris trembles when the patient moves the head, and the aqueous humor becomes turbid. This condition is attended with the same inconveniences as are experienced in staphyloma, and is accompanied with equal or greater deformity. By the enlargement and irregular figure of the globe, which continually presses upon the lids, and irritation of the latter is frequently the result.

Of this disease Scarpa says—"The generality of surgeons teach that the immediate cause of the dropsy of the eye is sometimes the increase of the vitreous, at other times of the aqueous humor. In all the cases of dropsy of the eye which I have operated upon, or have examined in the dead body, in different stages of the disease, I have constantly found the vitreous humor, accordingly as the disease was inveterate or recent, more or less disorganized, and in a state of dissolution; nor have I been able in any instance to distinguish, on account of the increased quantity, which of these two humors, vitreous or aqueous, had the greater share in the formation of the disease."*

Treatment.—When vision is almost or entirely destroyed, and the eye projects beyond the lids, it is proper to evacuate the water, which may be done with a common lancet or couching needle. When the water collects, the operation may be again repeated. The evacuation of the effused fluid is resorted to to prevent irritation and suppuration.

Before, however, having recourse to the mechanical treatment, there are many articles of the Materia Medica, the administration of which offer a more than reasonable hope of removing the water by absorption. Should the disease occur after debilitating losses *china*, *ferrum*, *merc.*, and *sulph.*, might correspond to the presenting symptoms; if from a repercussion of an eruption, *dig.*, *hell.*, *rhus-tox.*, and *sulph.*, should be remembered.

Ars., *bry.*, *kali-carb.*, *phosph.*, and *samb.*, would also offer themselves for consideration.

If these medicines do not succeed in removing the disease, the operation for the radical cure of staphyloma must be performed; the after deformity being remedied by an artificial eye.

---

* Hastings' Practice of Surgery, p. 451.

Section 13.—*Pterygium, or Eye Wing.*

This affection derives its name from the supposed resemblance of the abnormal growth to the wing of an insect. Authors have divided it into four varieties, viz. cellular, vascular, fatty, and fleshy; but, according to Walton,* pathology warrants no such arrangement, while distinction for the sake of description is useless. The disease is not uncommon, and consists in a thin, triangular, membranous expansion of the conjunctiva, and of the subconjunctival cellular tissue, increased in vascularity, and presenting various appearances in regard to thickness and color.

The disease generally commences at the inner canthus, with the base of the abnormal growth connected with the semilunar fold and caruncle from which it appears to grow. In very rare instances the base may be at the cornea. A bifurcated pterygium has been described by Weller.

The affection is more common in some localities than in others; warm climates being said to be more favorable to the propagation of the disorder than those of a colder temperature.

It is a singular fact that pterygium scarcely ever passes beyond the centre of the cornea.

Treatment.—The only medicine that is mentioned as suitable to this affection is *arg-nit.* Probably *thuj.*, *caust.*, or *sep.*, might be of some service. Excision is frequently resorted to by surgeons of the present day, and the operation is said to be quite successful; however, it should never be attempted, unless the abnormal structure encroach upon the cornea, and threatens to obscure vision.

There are two modes of operating for pterygium. One consists (the lids in both cases being separated by the fingers or speculum) in elevating the thickened tissue by means of small forceps, then dissecting it all or in part away by scissors or knife. The second operation consists in elevating the ptery-

---

* Vide A Treatise on Operative Ophthalmic Surgery, by H. Haynes Walton, p. 288.

gium, as in the former case, and passing a knife or scissors perpendicularly through it, thus dividing it into two parts; then by introducing the sharp point of a pencil of nitrate of silver and cauterizing the cut surfaces, reunion is prevented; the thickened membrane is then absorbed, or at least the advance of its growth over the cornea is arrested.*

Section 14.—*Diseases of the Cornea.*

The cornea is variously affected by diseased action; when inflammation attacks it, the term *ceratitis* indicates the affection. In this latter there is not much redness, and the cornea being possessed of little sensibility the pain is not severe, but an increased secretion of tears and intolerance of light are always present. The cornea assumes a dingy, faint, and dim appearance, which dimness varies in degree and extent of surface, giving rise to several morbid appearances, to which different names have been assigned; the translucency itself being occasioned by a deposit of lymph between the lamellæ of the cornea. If the inflammation is severe the effusion is greater, and a pseudo membrane is formed; or the cellular structure between the corneal layers may entirely be absorbed, and a direct union of the parts be the result. Should this take place, the whole texture of the membrane is entirely altered.

In simple opacity the dimness is diffused, and is gradually lost in the more transparent portions of the cornea; it is generally directly beneath the conjunctiva, its situation being readily detected by examination of the eye laterally with a magnifying glass. The iris and pupil may both be perceived through the opacity, and vision is but slightly impaired.

Albugo, according to its cause, varies both in color and form. It is always the consequence of a wound or ulcer, hence its name *cicatrix*. The pupil may be very much distorted in consequence of

---

* Vide Hastings' Practice of Surgery, p. 447.

being attached to the cornea at the albugo; or the former may be covered with cicatrices, having its color and form both destroyed thereby.

Leucoma is a circumscribed opacity, of a white or pearl color. If situated beneath the conjunctiva, it will present a dull or leaden aspect; if deeper seated within the cornea, its appearance is polished or shining; and if directly in front of the pupil, vision may be either entirely or partially destroyed, in proportion as the opacity obstructs the admission of a portion, or of all the rays of light. In some instances, before the disease has reached an advanced stage, the patient possesses the faculty of seeing during the evening and night, although deprived of sight during the day—this is in consequence of the pupil dilating, and permitting the passage of a greater number of visual rays.

Pannus is an opaque and vascular condition of the anterior membrane of the cornea. The appearance presented by an eye affected with this disease, resembles that of a piece of cloth or rag covering the cornea; hence the name.

Corneal opacities are caused by the application of corrosive or acrid substances to the eye, wounds, &c.; and are likewise owing to constitutional affections, such as rheumatism, gout, scrofula, &c.

Treatment.—If the inflammation has been induced by mechanical injury, the use of *arnica*, internally and externally, should immediately be had recourse to. A few drops of the tinctæ. arnicæ, diluted with a fluid ounce of water, should be applied upon linen cloths to the injury, and the 6th attenuation—fifteen or twenty globules dissolved in f℥vj of water—of which solution a tablespoonful should be given every four hours. The tincture for internal exhibition being made from the root only, is a different preparation from that which is obtained from the stems, leaves and flowers of the plant, used for external application. This is a difference which should be carefully borne in mind in practice. *Calendula officinalis*, which has been found so beneficial in lacerated wounds, may prove very advantageous.

The steady and long-continued use of *iodine* will often remove opacities of the cornea. One drop of the tincture in a tumbler of water (f℥viij), a dessertspoonful every evening; or a grain of *hydriodate of potassa* in f℥vj of water (dose the same) may be given. These medicines will be found efficacious, especially in persons of a scrofulous habit.

The tincture, diluted with water, may likewise be applied by means of a camel's hair pencil to the opacity, to facilitate absorption—one drop diluted is the proper strength when thus applied.

Among the medicines to be administered, *hepar* is highly recommended—a dose of the 2d or 3d trituration to be used at bedtime.

Cannabis is also held in high estimation by some homœopathic physicians. It may be used both as an external application and as an internal medicine. It is said to have proved of great benefit in *pannus*.

Euphrasia may be employed, when there is opacity or cloudiness of the cornea. *Spig.*, *bell.*, *puls.*, and *calcarea* are also medicines which may be used in this affection—the latter is especially serviceable in children, and has proved effectual without the exhibition of other remedial agents. A few globules dissolved in a teaspoonful of water, and administered every third or fourth night, may lessen the opacity in a short time; after which, the interval between the doses should be of much longer duration.

Mag.-mur. and *nitric-acid* are efficacious medicines, when the corneal opacity presents a decidedly whitish hue, arising from traumatic or arthritic ophthalmia; when there is itching and burning in the eyes and eyelids, dilated pupils and photophobia.

Sep., *ol. jec. asc.*, and some other medicines, have also been used and recommended.

The *cornea* is also liable to *ulceration:* it may be superficial, directly under the conjunctiva, deeper seated, or in the cellular structure between the lamellæ. It is frequently met with; it often follows ophthalmia, or arises from the application of corrosive substances to the eye. The ulceration may be confined to the conjunctiva only, where it covers the cornea, and may be seen by viewing the eye laterally. Opacity in these cases does not always follow, in consequence of a thin, shining crust forming upon the exposed surface, which arrests the disease. If, however, the ulceration follows purulent ophthalmia, it commences externally, and often extends itself into the anterior chamber.

If the centre of the sclerotica be the site of the ulcerative process, it will resemble a collection of matter in the substance of the cornea, whence it either advances to form an external solution of continuity, or penetrates the anterior chamber, causing *hypopion*. This latter disease will hereafter be alluded to.

In ulceration of the cornea the pain is less than that of the inflammation which generally precedes it. Sometimes, however, it is complained of as being as sharp as though a needle were thrust through the eye; movement of the eyelids and light increase the sufferings. Around the ulcer there is usually a slight cloudiness, and in certain cases vessels may be seen coming from the conjunctiva (vascular ulcer of the cornea). When the ulcer heals these vessels disappear, the cicatrix being *always partially* absorbed.

If the ulcerative process is accompanied with inflammation of the sclerotica and conjunctiva, those medicines must be used which have already been mentioned in the treatment of inflammation of those tunics. In obstinate ulcerations the most successful allopathic treatment has been, and is, to apply a solution of the the *nitras. argenti* (lunar caustic), of the strength of four or six grains to an ounce of distilled water, with a camel-hair pencil—this is to be used, should the ulcer remain transparent, or show no disposition to cicatrize. When a deposition of new matter is perceived undergoing a vascular organization, and the ulcer cleans, its application should either be less frequent or omitted. Dr. Gibson advises the caustic to be lightly applied till an eschar forms, and when this drops off, which it does in twelve or eighteen hours, to reapply the solution, taking care to wash away any superfluous caustic from the eye or eyelids.

If the stitches are very violent, and the pain much increased by moving the lids, or there be a sensation as if red-hot needles were passed into the eye, the pains very much aggravated by light, or a sensation of sand being lodged in the eye, *arsenicum* is the proper remedy. It is also indicated by throbbing accompanying the stitches, together with dark redness of the vessels, with œdematous swelling of the lids, and especially should these symptoms arise in gouty or rheumatic individuals.

Calcarea carbonica is indicated, if with the photophobia there is a desire to press in the eyes for relief; also itching, especially in the evening, and burning when the lids are closed; also lachrymation, sometimes of a smarting fluid, particularly in scrofulous individuals, and in those who are of frail constitution with an impoverished nutrition; and *especially* in *very young children*, of a *scrofulous diathesis*, with *muscular* and nervous weakness, disposed to inordinate discharges from the mucous surfaces.

Belladonna, if the ulceration commence in the cellular structure connecting the lamellæ; when, in closing the eyes, a deep aching pain is experienced; dryness and burning; likewise with pain in the orbits.

Sepia is a very effectual medicine in the treatment of those ulcers which are vascular: *merc.*, *hepar*, *euphra.*, *puls.*, *silic.*, have likewise been employed. *Thuja* especially, in the 30th dilution, together with *cann.*, in the same potency, are recorded as having been productive of most happy results.*

Section 15.—*Hypopion.*

Violent and deeply seated ophthalmia may terminate in the formation of pus within the anterior or posterior chambers of the eye, constituting the disease called hypopion. The matter

* See a paper on Vascular Tumor of the Cornea, by J. J. Drysdale, M. D. British Journal of Homœopathy, vol. vii., p. 244.

secreted being heavier than the aqueous humor, sinks to the bottom of the anterior chamber, where it can be observed, and frequently presents the appearance of a yellow crescent-shaped spot, which gradually increases until the whole cavity may be filled; there is much photophobia and other symptoms of ophthalmia experienced, which, however, in some instances may gradually subside, and the pus be absorbed; or the matter may remain for many weeks mixed with the aqueous humor, which it renders turbid. The affection generally terminates unfortunately, in consequence of the humors of the eye being discharged through an ulcerated opening or slough.

Treatment.—The object will be to subdue the inflammation which accompanies the disease, the reduction of which will either lessen the quantity of pus or promote its absorption. The medicines to accomplish which will be among those already detailed for the different forms of ophthalmia, some one or other of which will accord with the symptoms which present themselves in connection with hypopion.

The custom formerly resorted to by surgeons of perforating the cornea, to allow the exit of pus, is at the present era entirely exploded—for matter is rapidly absorbed, so soon as the inflammatory process is arrested. The distinguished oculist Beer, when appealing to his *former* experience with regard to the evacuation of the purulent secretion by means of openings, thus wrote:

"Any one who has successfully and completely cured by incisions so many cases as I have, will not think it worth while to hear, or read, and much less to refute such objections." Subsequent experience entirely changed his opinion, and in another work he writes: "That when matter shows itself in the anterior chamber, the surgeon must on no account think of opening the cornea, for the eye will certainly be much injured."*

The medicines that have proved *remedies* for hypopion, are *arsen.*, *euphra.*, *hepar*, *merc.-sol.*, *merc.-corr.-sub.*, and *sulph.*

* Peters on Diseases of the Eye, p. 107.

Arsenicum, 4, every four hours, cured entirely in fourteen days a violent inflammation of the eye, with effusion of pus into the anterior chamber. Several cases have been cured by *hepar*, *merc.*, and *merc.-corr.-sub.* The two latter, when the formation of pus followed upon rheumatic and scrofulous ophthalmia. *Sulph.*, according to Rummel, accomplishes extraordinary results in hypopion, even when it arises from gonorrhœal ophthalmia.*

Section 16.—*Staphyloma.*

Staphyloma is an affection of the cornea, in which the latter is destroyed either partially or *in toto*, and its place supplied by a projecting opaque substance.

Mr. Jones' explanation of the pathology of this disease,† appears to be correct according to Walton. The former gentleman affirms, that staphyloma is not a bulging of the cornea, as is generally taught; and he explains its formation by pointing out the fact, that when the iris is exposed by the loss of the cornea, it becomes covered by an opaque firm tissue, resembling that of a cicatrix, which is incorporated at the base of the tumor with the cornea, constituting a partial staphyloma, which consists of protruded iris, covered by new tissue, intended to supply the loss of corneal substance; and he remarks, that the formation of a total staphyloma is precisely the same, the degree only differing, and the form of the tumor depending on the extent to which the cornea has been destroyed. This has been confirmed in a dissection by Mr. Bowman, the results of which are briefly given in his lectures on the parts concerned in the operations on the eye.

Accompanying the staphylomatous state, there are occasionally changes in the crystalline lens, whereby it is ossified or rendered cretaceous; and although it is not possible to know when it is so changed, or to be able to refer with precision

---

* Loc. cit.

† London Medical Gazette, vol. xxi., p. 847.

to any set of symptoms indicative of those alterations, proof is not wanting that a calcareous lens is prejudicial, acting as a foreign body within the eye.

There may be greater opacity in some portions of the cornea than in others, the sight being either partially impaired or completely destroyed.

Treatment.—In the commencement of the disease, when inflammatory symptoms are present, with their usual concomitant sensations, the exhibition of *acon.*, *bell.*, *euphra.*, *hepar*, *merc.*, or *sulph.* may not only subdue the inflammation, but prevent the appearance of *staphyloma.*

Many other symptoms in staphyloma are found in connection with affections of the eye already treated, to which reference must be made for detailed treatment.

When the affection has reached its acme, and the opaque firm tissue has been formed, operations have been resorted to with success.

The most convenient method of removing complete staphyloma is thus mentioned by Mr. Walton:*

The operator should stand behind the patient, and raise the upper lid; "and, after an assistant has transfixed the staphyloma with a curved needle, or seized it with a hook, the required portion is cut away with a scalpel. It may look neater for the operator to entrust the lids to an assistant, while he pierces the staphyloma; but then the assistant would most likely press too much on the globe, and squeeze out its contents. Care should be taken, in case the lens is in its place and healthy, to avoid injuring the capsule with the instrument that transfixes the staphyloma. I recommend this, because I am in the habit of leaving the lens; some surgeons, however, always remove it, under any condition, lest it should become the seat of calcareous matter, and if examples of such occurrence can be adduced, the rule for the removal should be absolute.

"After the operation the lids should be closed directly, and

* Operative Ophthalmic Surgery, p. 353.

cold water" (or solution of *arnica*) "applied by means of bits of rag, for some time after, as a safeguard against bleeding, and the patient should be watched for several hours, that such occurrence may be promptly met, for it is prone to occur; and from neglect I have known a child nearly bleed to death. The operation is very painful, far exceeding what would be expected; and the collection of blood within the remaining tunics of the globe, over which we have no control, may cause prolonged suffering."

For many distressing symptoms which take place after operations upon the eye, the *Asarum Europæum* has not only a close correspondence, but is asserted to possess a strong elective medicinal affinity for the organ. In a dilute form it may be applied externally, while at the same time it must be internally administered.

Section 17.—*Cataract.*

By the term cataract is understood a *partial* or *general opacity* of the *crystalline lens*, of its *capsule*, or of the *morganian fluid*, either separately or conjointly, with a corresponding diminution of sight. The opacity may be within the lens or capsule, or without the lens and its investing membrane; when in the latter location it is owing to the presence of blood, pus, or some other foreign matter within the pupil, and is denominated a *spurious cataract;* when in the former, (within the lens or capsule,) it is called a true cataract, *cataracta vera,* of which there are four varieties, viz., *lenticular*, *capsular*, *capsulo-lenticular* and *morganian.*

The formation of a cataract is generally slow, requiring weeks, months, or years for its complete development. It may appear in one eye, or in both; but when the former is the case, the other eye is generally affected either sooner or later. The diagnosis between cataract and amaurosis is very necessary, and is correctly reached by the due appreciation of the appearances presented by each of these affections. In cataract, all objects

32

appear to be encompassed with a cloud or mist, especially those that are white. When looking into the eye through the pupil, an opacity may be seen in the centre of the opening, and as the dimness of vision increases, a blackish ring, which is the shadow of the iris reflected upon the lens, is perceived around the pupilary aperture: this appearance is more perceptible in light than in dark colored eyes. In the commencement of the disease, the opacity being seated in the centre of the lens, objects directly in front of the individual cannot be observed, while those laterally situated are capable of being seen. Early in the morning, or in the evening, in consequence of the lesser degree of light, the pupil dilates, and the rays passing into the interior chamber of the eye, around and beyond the part which is opaque, vision is considerably improved. The flame of a lamp appears as though surrounded with a white circle, which widens as the distance from the light is increased. In a more advanced stage of the disease, the idea of the distance of the flame can only be conjectured, it being very indistinctly seen. The movements of the iris are not affected by incipient cataract.

In *amaurosis*, the cloudiness is perceived at a greater distance behind the pupil, is of a *reddish* or greenish hue, and appears *concave;* the pupil is angular or dilated, and the cornea is less bright and clear than in a healthy state; the dimness of vision is not varied by the degree of light. Violent mental emotion, stimulating drinks or food, will improve for a short time the visual function; while it will be impaired by depressing passions, watching, or fatigue. The flame of a lamp or candle, instead of being encompassed with a white halo as in cataract, is surrounded with a circle of variegated colors. In cataract, convex glasses assist; in amaurosis, their use does not facilitate vision.

On examining the eye, if a cataract is present, the pupil—which naturally is black—appears gray or white, except in the instance of black cataract. The *catoptric examination* affords unerring diagnostic signs of cataract.

The late Professor Sanson began to observe in 1836, and pointed out to his clinical class, in 1837, that when a candle is placed before the eye of an amaurotic patient, whose pupil is dilated, three images of the flame can always be distinguished, succeeding one another from before, backwards. The first, or anterior one, which is the brightest, is erect; the second, or middle one, which is less bright, is reversed; and the third, or posterior one, is much fainter than the other two, and is erect like the first one. M. Sanson and his pupils arrived at the same results, and ascertained that the anterior erect image is produced by the cornea; that the middle reversed one is owing to the posterior segment of the crystalline capsule; while the posterior erect image arises from the anterior segment of the same capsule. Opacity of the cornea destroys all three images. Opacity of the anterior capsule destroys the two posterior images. Opacity of the posterior capsule prevents the production of the reversed image.

In other words, when there is a posterior capsular cataract, we cannot see the middle or reversed image; in anterior capsular cataract, the anterior erect image is alone visible; and so it is in capsulo-lenticular cataract. The experiments of M. Pasquet, combined with these, have confirmed the conclusion, that a cataract, even at its commencement, can always be distinguished from amaurosis and glaucoma. For since in glaucoma and amaurosis, the alteration does not affect the crystalline apparatus, the three images of the flame still remain.*

The causes of cataract are often very obscure. Persons exposed to the glare of fires—as men working in furnaces, glass-houses, &c.—are often its subjects. It is supposed sometimes to have an hereditary origin. External violence may also produce it, or it may arise from metastasis of scabies (itch), suppressed hemorrhoids, syphilis, or gout. Intense heat frequently and constantly applied to the eye, or the very constant use of the visual organ, may produce the disease; hence students, artizans, &c., are frequently affected. Statistics of three hundred cases show, that three-fourths of that number had been persons long exposed to the sun, in a stooping posture; the

* Clymer's Medical Examiner, July 15, 1845, p. 142.

eyes being thus subjected to the sun's reflections from the soil.

The proximate cause of cataract has been considered to be an inflammation of the lens, or of its capsule; in proof of which oculists have asserted, that by microscopic examination red vessels can be distinctly seen in the substance of the lens. Dr. Jacobs,* however, in his work on "Inflammation of the Eye-ball," remarks, that he could not detect them in the lens, but has seen them in the cornea. There has been considerable discussion among oculists regarding the preëxistence of inflammation being necessary to the formation of cataract, which it is unnecessary to detail here.

Cataract occurring in aged individuals has been reasonably ascribed to a rigidity and consequent obstruction of circulation; and it is asserted that, from the same cause, the cornea in old persons is affected with what is denominated *arcus senilis.*

Many varieties of cataract are mentioned by surgical writers, a few of which may be pointed out, viz.:

Lenticular cataract is generally hard and firm, though it has been classified into hard and soft. The darker the color, the harder is the cataract; the grayer its appearance, the softer its consistence. Lenticular cataract is sometimes radiated, the opacity appearing in streaks or radii, with comparatively transparent interstices; the radii generally beginning in the circumference of the lens, the reverse of the ordinary form of opacity, which commences in the centre.

The milky or fluid cataract presents the appearance of the conversion of the lens into a whitish or other kind of fluid. When the substance is a medium between hard and fluid, the term caseous, or *soft cataract,* is used—the lens in this latter variety is much enlarged.

In *morganian cataract* there is an opacity of the fluid situated between the lens and its capsule. Its existence without a further extension of morbid change, is denied by many authors. It is hardly possible for it to exist alone for any length of time.

---

* Walton's Operative Ophthalmic Surgery, p. 385.

Cataracta capsularis, or opacity of the capsule of the lens, has been divided into anterior capsular, posterior capsular, and complete capsular cataract.

In *anterior capsular cataract*, the opacity, which is whitish and glistening, is noticed on a level with the pupillary margin of the iris. The capsule cannot become extensively involved, without the lens also being affected.

Posterior capsular cataract can be recognized, by the opacity being seen at a distance behind the pupil, the anterior portion of membrane retaining its transparency. The opacity has not the white or glistening color which distinguishes the anterior variety, and is concave.

When the capsular cataract is complete the whole membrane is involved. If the anterior part of the capsule have become opaque, it will prevent the diagnosis being easily arrived at; which can only be certainly ascertained in the early stages of the disease, when the anterior capsule is but slightly affected. It often happens, that the lens participates in the disease, constituting *capsulo lenticular cataract*, which is frequently met with. In the latter form a variety of appearances are present, to which the older writers gave different appellations, in accordance with the fancied resemblance of the opacity to some object—as cataracta stellata, pyramidal, or disseminated cataract.* Another variety is the arborescens of Richter, which is always the result of violence, which has separated and lodged upon the capsule a portion of the tapetum of the uvea. At first this can scarcely be perceived; but inflammation coming on, the uvea is united to the capsule, the iris is sluggish, and the lens finally becomes opaque.

It is impossible to explain, in the present state of our knowledge, the causes of these varieties; but, that they are occasioned by essentially different morbid actions, will not be questioned. They cannot be supposed the result of the same kind of inflammation or morbid processes.

---

* For an interesting account of peculiar appearances presented in Cataract, see Medical Examiner, April 1843, p. 72.

Treatment.—Before proceeding to the considerations connected with the operation, and the different methods of relieving the patient by means of the knife, mention will be made of those remedial agents that have been found instrumental in *curing* the disease. Allopathic medicine repudiates the idea of curing a *fully developed* cataract. Quite an authoritative author observes: "That cataract has often been checked in its progress by the administration of remedies adapted to correct that peculiar diathesis of the system from which it has originated; but there is no single instance on record where the disease can be said to have been cured, or, in other words, where the opaque lens has again become transparent by such means."

At one time certain medicines were much in vogue, among which were *puls.*, *bell.*, *merc.*, &c.; and that they obtained considerable reputation, could only have been from cures having been effected by their use; and their failure since must be attributed to a want of knowledge in their selection, or their imperfect administration as to dose and repetition even when adapted to the cases.

The passing of galvanism through the opaque lens has instantaneously caused the disappearance of cataract; and its transmission through a transparent one has produced the affection—a beautiful illustration of the law, "*similia similibus curanter.*"

In selecting a medicine for the relief of this disease, the first consideration must have reference to the diathesis of the individual, and the endeavor should be made to ascertain, if possible, the connection which may exist between it and the local affection. Should scrofula be detected, *sulphur* immediately suggests itself, and we find upon inquiry that this mineral substance has materially contributed to cure the disease.

Puls. presents much claim to attention; and, as noticed already, old school practitioners have employed it. We know of an instance in which cataract was cured by its continued exhibition for eight months, at intervals first of forty-eight hours, and afterwards, when the action of the medicine was decidedly established, every four or five days. A few globules of the 6th or 7th attenuation, dissolved in a small quantity of water, was the prescription employed.

Another case is recorded to have been cured by *pulsatilla*, the cause of the disease being supposed to have been suppressed scabies. *Cann.* was also used after the *puls.*, to complete the cure.

The capsulo lenticular variety has been cured with the decillionth of *carbonate of magnesia*, followed by *cann.* A cure likewise of lenticular cataract by *puls.*, and *cann.*; *opium* also having been used. *Sulph.* and *caust.* also are asserted to have cured.

For cataract produced by a wound, *cann.* has successfully been administered.

For traumatic cataract, *conium* is much extolled.

The other medicines recommended are, *con.*, *phosph.*, *silic.*, *euphra.*, *ruta*, *nit.-ac.*, *digit.*, *hyos.*, *chelid.*, *carb.-baryt.*, and *ammonia murias.*

In the treatment of disease of this kind much patience is required on the part of both physician and patient, as a favorable change in by far the greater number of cases can only be anticipated by a regular and long continued use of the means prescribed.

The administration of medicines failing in the removal of the opacity, the last resource is a surgical operation; the propriety of which must be determined by the consideration of a variety of circumstances. Among those which either forbid its performance or render the result doubtful are; when a violent pain in the head has preceded the formation of the cataract; under which circumstance the disease is said almost invariably to have returned after an operation. (Would not the cure of the headache by homœopathic treatment have prevented the formation of the cataract?) If the patient is much affected with rheumatism of the joints, or of the eye, and especially if the arthritic affection is not present in the spring or autumn, at which period the individual had usually suffered.

When the patient has suffered from severe ophthalmia—or when a particular diathesis, as scrofula, is present; when there is a disposition to erysipelas of the face; when the patient has suffered from frequent convulsions—epileptic or others, especially in early life—and when different degrees of light cannot be appreciated.

If the cataract appears in hysterical and hypochondriacal individuals, or if complications exist—as glaucoma, amaurosis, &c. From these various considerations, therefore, it is apparent that an operation should not be resorted to, without much reflection.

The several conditions of lenticular cataract require different operations.* The hard cataract should be extracted, that is, removed from the eye, or displaced by being pressed into the vitreous humor, though considerable time may elapse before absorption takes place. Soft cataract, though allowed to remain in its position, should be sufficiently lacerated or broken, in order that absorption may remove it, the softer textures readily yielding to the process. Capsular cataract must be removed from the eye, although there are exceptions, in which laceration or division may suffice.

Cataract is not a disease of emergency, for which operative surgery must be immediately resorted to; therefore, all circumstances connected with the use of the knife in order to restore sight to the afflicted individual, should be carefully considered.

A successful result, according to the justly distinguished Scarpa, may be anticipated when the cataract is simple or unconnected with any other disease of the eyeball. In subjects not unhealthy or decrepid, and in whom the opacity has been gradually formed, *not* from external violence or frequent ophthalmia, and where there has not been oft repeated cephalalgia, an operation may be performed. When the pupil dilates and contracts freely and has preserved its circular figure; when the patient can distinguish between light and darkness, and when the pupil dilates to that degree which it generally does in a moderate light.

---

* Vide Walton's Operative Ophthalmic Surgery, p. 408.

Before operating, the patient should be in a perfectly healthy condition, and should have for some time lived moderately, in order to prevent all tendency to an excited state of the system. For the purpose of dilating the pupil, the extract of *belladonna* mixed with a sufficient quantity of lard to the consistency of an ointment, must be rubbed upon the forehead, over the eye, upon the temples, and under the eye, a half or three quarters of an hour before the operation. *Stramonium* and *hyosciamus* have also been used for the same purpose, and in like manner.

If both eyes are affected, and concomitant circumstances are favorable, the operation may be performed upon both at the same time.

Several different operations may be performed for the relief of cataract—*extraction,* which was introduced by Davel, a French surgeon; *couching* or *depression,* which method was employed and described by Celsus; *reclination,* which is a modern variety of depression, and *solution* or *absorption;* by the latter is understood the breaking up of the substance of the lens, and bringing it into the anterior chamber of the eye, there to be absorbed by the aqueous humor; the term *keratonyxis* has also been applied to this operation, which may be either *anterior* or *posterior,* according as the needle passes into the eye, through the cornea or sclerotica.

In operating for *extraction,* the patient should be seated on a low chair or stool, and the upper eyelid raised by the fingers of an assistant, whilst the operator depresses the lower; or the lids may be separated by a speculum. The surgeon then directs the patient to roll the eye to the internal canthus, and having taken the cataract knife, enters it at the external side, about a quarter or half a line anterior to the junction of the cornea with the sclerotica, above the middle of the cornea, and pushes the instrument forwards until it emerges at the inner margin of the cornea, (see fig. 87,) and by being carried forwards, cuts itself out, thus making a section of the cornea, the aqueous humor discharges itself through the opening, after which the lids should be closed for a few moments. The next step in the operation is to separate the lids, raise the corneal flap, and

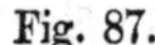

Fig. 87.

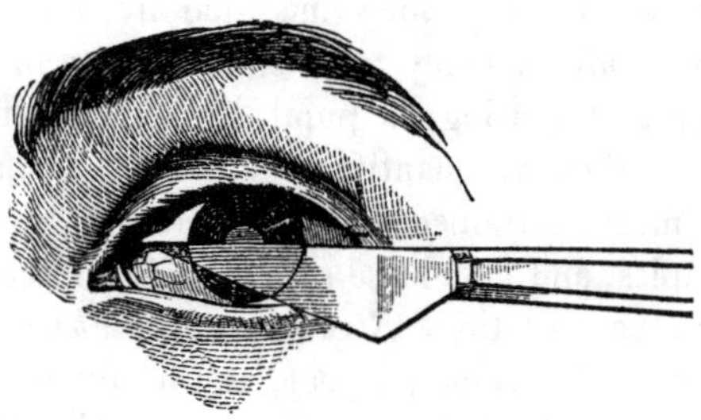

divide the capsule of the lens in its centre with the point of a needle; the lens then gradually approaches the surface, and passes out through the corneal opening; if, however, it remain in situ, gentle pressure on the ball of the eye will suffice to dislodge it; the cornea is then adjusted and the lids closed by a loose bandage.

Should inflammation occur after the operation, the remedies should be selected that correspond with the symptoms which present themselves. These symptoms and the medicines for their removal will be found by referring to the chapter on ophthalmia.

The only medicine omitted at that time, and which especially demands notice here, is the *Asarum Europæum*, which relieves the darting pains so apt to occur in irritable temperaments after operations upon the eye.

The operation of *couching* or *depression* is performed in the following manner: The patient should be seated as before mentioned, and the surgeon, holding the couching needle as a pen, passes it through the sclerotica, at the external angle of the eye, about two lines posterior to the iris, (see fig. 88.) The needle must then be pushed forwards until its point is distinctly seen in the pupil, anterior to the lens; the anterior capsule should then be carefully but freely opened with the point of the instrument, and the lens pressed downwards and backwards, until it is lodged in the bottom of the vitreous humor; the needle is then carefully withdrawn and the eye closed. The operation of *reclination* is performed in a similar manner, ex-

Fig. 88.

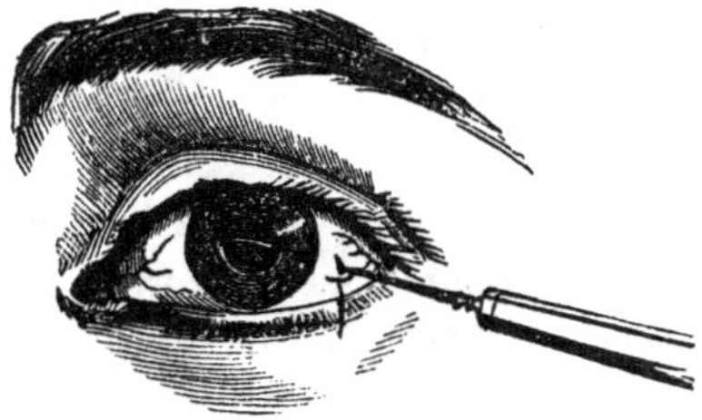

cept that the lens is merely reclined, by pressing upon its upper edge, and forcing it below the axis of vision.

Absorption or *solution* is performed with an instrument similar to that used in couching; the anterior operation is performed, after having placed the patient in the position already mentioned, by inserting the needle about a line anterior to the union of the cornea with the sclerotica, and pushing it forward through the pupil; the capsule and crystalline lens are thus broken up, and the fragments deposited in the aqueous humor, from which they are afterwards removed by absorption. The *posterior* operation is distinguished from the anterior by the surgeon entering the needle through the sclerotica in the same manner as directed for couching. The latter is the method generally preferred. Several weeks may elapse before the lens and capsule are entirely removed by the process of absorption, and in some instances the operation may have to be repeated several times before a cure is effected.

Section 18.—*Glaucoma.*

Among the older pathologists, this word was used synonymously with cataract, but it is now ordinarily applied to an opacity of the vitreous humor. It first appears as a slight opacity far within the eye, which increases and approaches nearer and nearer the pupil, which no longer exhibits its black shining lustre, but displays a sea-green color, and becomes oval, its longest diameter being the transverse. The vision from being impaired is finally lost, and there is pain in and around the eye, in the side of the face, in the orbit, and extending into the brain; the pain is increased by the warmth of the bed, and relieved if the patient rises and breathes a more moderate atmosphere. The pain lessens as the glaucoma increases, and the crystalline lens after a time assumes the same green color as the vitreous humor. As the lens enlarges, the anterior chamber is destroyed, the iris is either thrown forward on the cornea or is seen forming a narrow ring around its circumference.

This disease is often connected with a gouty diathesis; also with morbid conditions of the liver or some of the abdominal viscera. It has been known to succeed the rapid healing of a chronic ulceration of the extremities.

If the eye presents a similar appearance to that sometimes observed in persons advanced in years, or from a diminished secretion of the pigmentum nigrum, it may be distinguished in such instances from glaucoma by the fact of vision not being impaired.

Pathologists have not been able to ascertain positively whether the seat of the disease be the septa of the hyaloidea, or the fluid within their cells, or both.

Treatment.—The disease when fully formed is considered incurable. To arrest it, allopathic practice consists in local and general bleeding, purgatives, epispastics to the temples or behind the ears, and warm aromatic applications to the eyes.

Phosphorus is the only homœopathic medicine which appears to be recommended for this disease. It is stated to have cured it. If *phosphorus* has cured it, the belief cannot but be entertained that were opportunities afforded for the exhibition of those agents which we know produce powerful action upon the eye, this affection might be removed from the catalogue of incurable diseases.

Section 19.—*Amaurosis—Gutta Serena.*

The above terms are applied to an insensible condition of either the retina or optic nerve. The disease may be either primary or secondary, and its first symptoms are defects of vision, as seeing only portions of objects which are presented to view; words, syllables, or whole lines, are wanting when reading, and the individual is compelled to move the head before the vision can recover the lost portions. Sometimes an object is seen in one position, and if removed it is lost to the view; at others, everything appears surrounded by a circle of variegated colors, or covered with gauze or network; or black spots, or moats, muscæ volitantes, visus muscarium, appear flitting before the eyes.

The patient cannot bear a bright light—and to some amaurotics all colors appear a shade darker, or they are crooked and distorted, or all objects may appear of the same hue. Double vision also sometimes exists. The disease may come on slowly or suddenly, and may be owing to the *gastric irritation* of worms, to other irritating matters in the stomach or bowels, or to repressed cutaneous disease. It sometimes exhibits an intermittent character, appearing every second, third or fourth day, or at intervals of months. The dimness of vision it occasions may be experienced either during the day or night; the former being designated hemeralopia, the latter nyctalopia. When amaurosis exists as a purely local affection it may be complicated with other diseases of the eye, or it may be associated with organic diseases of the abdomen, brain and cranium; it sometimes occurs during pregnancy.

When the disease is present the pupil generally remains permanently dilated, or in some instances very much contracted,—or it may be irregular, or angular in shape, and of a grayish or dark green hue, resembling the humors of the eye of a horse. Often when looking into the eye a splendid disc of a white or greenish yellow tint a little to the side of the visual axis may be perceived. The pupil likewise generally is drawn to the internal and upper portion of the eye. The iris is sluggish, or very irritable, and there is pain in the supercilia and temples, shooting into the orbit, or the sufferings may be intermittent; as the disorder progresses these pains lessen, the eye feeling swollen and dry. If the affection is connected with a paralytic condition, there is ringing in the ears, pulsation in the brain, tottering gait, difficulty in moving, vertigo, and flushed face—complication exists which renders the prognosis unfavorable. The disease attacks for the most part persons of middle age, although it is often met with in youth; persons with dark eyes are supposed to be most liable to the affection.

The causes of amaurosis are steady application of the eye upon minute objects—hence in tailors, clerks, and students it is frequently encountered; looking upon the sun and moon; reflected light from snow and sand, likewise produce it: hence in northern regions, as well as in very warm climates, it is not unfrequent. Long confinement in dark chambers or cells, depressing passions—typhoid fevers, excessive venery, onanism, suppuration from extensive ulcers, profuse salivation—hemorrhagia, cholera, dysentery—narcotics, as belladonna, hyosciamus, opium, stramonium—mineral substances, as arsenic, lead, &c., are also causes. The absence of the pigmentum nigrum, and blows upon the eyebrow, are also enumerated as causing the affection; in the latter case the injury done to the frontal nerve is supposed by sympathy to affect the retina; and from the latter cause the amaurosis is long in its development.

If the disease has suddenly occurred, a more favorable prognosis may be made, than when it is of gradual development. If the figure and structure of the eye are altered, the affection has been considered incurable. If it appear in one eye and no cause can be assigned for it, it will in all probability attack the other organ of vision. The condition of the pupil will not enable us to form a satisfactory opinion, for it may possess the power of contraction and dilatation in incurable cases, and be very slugglish and immovable in others, that are capable of permanent relief. When amaurosis does not exist to any considerable degree it may disappear after an eruption has invaded some part of the body, or upon the formation of abscesses, or the recurrence of menstrual or hemorrhoidal discharges.

When dependent upon gastric irritation the prognosis is most favorable.

Very many of the medicines in the Homœopathic Materia Medica are recommended.

For the incipient stage a case is related to have been cured, in which there was no sight in the left eye; dimness of vision of the right eye; eyelids red and swollen, and a discharge of pus from the right eye, with the following medicines: *calc. carb.* 12, *silic.* 18, *acid-nit.*, *phosph.*, *petrol.*, *caust.*, *silic.* again, and ending with *causticum.*

Bella. with the aid of *puls.*, when there is frequent double sight with muscæ volitantes, also when there is mistiness befor the sight, dilated pupils, and an ability to see duiing the day only. *Bella.* also is indicated when gastralgia is present, and when a sense of pressure and sensibility to light is experienced, and when the patient sees all objects as through a mist,

Cinchona cured the disease in the case of an intemperate man, who at a short distance from an object could but perceive its outlines; a printed page appeared as a black surface with white borders; pupils dilated; interior of the eye appearing smoky.

Merc. Incipient amaurosis, muscæ volitantes, photophobia, temporary blindness, and lachrymation; the latter symptom was cured by *euphras.*

Phosph. Almost perfect inability to read, and as little ability to distinguish objects.

Ruta. Incipient amaurosis, diminished power of vision, objects near encompassed with mist, those remote undistinguishable.

In a case of hemeralopia, *bell.*, *hyos.*, *puls.* and *verat.* *Puls.* was very serviceable in a case when there was deficient menstruation, and the hemeralopia accompanied by a sensation as if the eyes were firmly bound by a handkerchief.

Verat. was of much use when the hemeralopia was complicated with diarrhœa, which was aggravated at night.*

Sulph. When, with other symptoms, there was a sensation of a little piece of feather below the upper eyelid.†

Section 20.—*Fistula Lachrymalis.*

Permanent obstruction of the nasal duct may be occasioned either by acute or chronic inflammation, by extension of disease from the nose, either syphilitic or other, by caries or exostosis of the surrounding bone, or from morbid formations originating in the nose or antrum. In persons of a scrofulous diathesis, affected with inflammation of the Shneiderian membrane, the disease is frequently met with, and is occasioned by the abnormal process extending itself to the lining of the lachrymal sac. In the first stages of the disease, there may be considerable pain, extending down to the nasal bones, but after a time, more acute sufferings abate, but the patient is greatly troubled by the passage of the tears over the cheek, the discharge of the lachrymal secretion through the nose being either totally or partially obstructed.

Treatment.—Under allopathic treatment, according to the best authority, fistula lachrymalis cannot be relieved by the internal action of remedial agents; by homœopathic treatment, however, the affection has been entirely cured. The medicines that are most serviceable in the treatment are *calc., carb., caust., nit-ac., natr., stann., silic., sulph.* In such diseases as the one now under consideration, it is necessary that the medicine be well selected, persevered in, and administered in the correct dynamization.

Calc. carb. effected three complete cures, two of which were

---

* For the above, vide Jeanes' Homœopathic Practice, p. 197.

† Vide Guide to the Practice of Homœopathy, by Edward Hamilton, M. D., p. 3. London, 1844.

accomplished by the 30th dilution, one by the 200th potency; we know of others in which the result was similar from the 7th attenuation. *Natrum* was successful in one case, as was also *stann.*, *silic.* and *sulph.**

The operation for removal of obstruction of the nasal duct, consists in passing a narrow bistoury into the canal, introducing the point of the instrument just below the orbicularis palpebrarum muscle; then by pressing it downwards, backwards and inwards, it will enter the duct, the remaining obstruction of which must be cleared by a probe; a silver, or as some prefer, a catgut style, with an expanded head, and of sufficient length to reach from the internal canthus to the termination of the duct, must then be inserted in the wound and allowed to remain for a considerable time, in some instances it is recommended to be worn permanently.

Section 21.—*Tumors of the Eyelids.*

Tumors, varying in size from a pea to that of a large bean, are frequently seated beneath the conjunctiva, or in the substance of the eyelid. They are generally soft, devoid of pain and roll under the finger. When the tumor has attained a considerable growth it is liable to interfere with vision, or produce eversion or other diseases of the eyelids. These abnormal growths may be either horny, resembling warts, glandiform, steatomatous, vesicular, &c.

Treatment.—*Horny excrescences* on the lids are said to consist of inspissated sebaceous matter. The medicines for their removal are *antim.-crud.*, *calc.*, *caust.*, *sab.*, *thuj.*

For *glandiform tumors* the medicines recommended are chiefly *calc.*, *thuj.* and *merc.*

Steatomatous tumors have been cured by *carb.-an.*, *calc.* and particularly *thuj.*

---

* See Peters on Diseases of the Eye.

33

The medicines that should be employed in *vesicular* tumors are *canth.*, *euphorb.*, *mez.*, or *rhus.*

For encysted tumors on the eyelids, *baryta*, *sepia* or *silex.*

For scirrhoid indurations, *con.*, *baryta-mur.*, *iod.-pot.*, *iod.-hydrarg.*, and *thuja*, deserve attention.

If these medicines fail, operations should be performed. If the tumor is situated immediately beneath the conjunctiva it must be removed by incision from the inner side of the lid, but when it is deeply seated in the substance of the orbicular muscle, or lies exterior to it, the incision should be made through the lid from its outer side, parallel with the edge of the eyelid; the tumor may then readily be seized with a hook, and removed with a few touches of the scalpel. The lips of the wound if external, must be brought together and retained in situ with strips of plaster, but if the incision has been made upon the conjunctival surface, no dressing is required. Should inflammation supervene, *asarum*, *arn.*, *acon.*, or *bell.* may be called for.

Section 22.—*Strabismus.*

By strabismus is understood an affection of the eye, in which the ball is drawn from the centre of the orbit towards the internal canthus, accompanied sometimes with defective vision.

Treatment.—If strabismus be the result of irritation of the brain or optic nerve, it may be removed by *coff.*, *ign.*, *bell.*, *hyos.*, *stram.*, *zinc.*, or other medicines. If, however, the deformity be owing, which is generally the case, to a permanent contraction of the internal rectus, an operation must be resorted to, which is simple, easily performed, and generally succeeds, both in correcting the deformity and improving the vision. The patient should look outwards, and have the eyelids separated by the fingers of an assistant, or by a speculum; the best instrument for this purpose is the spring-wire speculum, although Pellier's elevator answers very well. Then with the double hook catch the eye about midway between the edge of the cornea and canthus; raise the conjunctiva at the canthus by a pair of forceps, and with the curved scissors divide it as well as the cellular tissue beneath; take then the blunt hook and pass it under the tendon of the muscle, raise this on the hook and divide it with the scissors; the moment the blunt hook is passed under the tendon of the muscle, the double hook may be taken away. The tendon being divided, the operation is finished; yet sometimes the eye has still an inclination inwards, even after the tendon has been divided—this is owing to the *intermuscular fascia.* The blunt hook must be placed under this fascia, which is to be divided to the requisite extent; care being taken not to cut through too much, else there will be reversion of the eye.

The operation finished, which occupies but two or three minutes, the eye should be dressed with a piece of lint and bandage, to keep out light and place the eye at rest. If inflammation threaten, it must be combated by appropriate means; but this seldom occurs. There is sometimes, after the operation, a small tumor or exuberant granulations, which spring forth from the incision, occupying the corner of the eye; these are removed by the exhibition of *silex.*, *ars.*, *petrol.*, and *graph.* There is also, after the operation, a certain degree of double vision, which is owing to objects being presented to eyes of different powers and adjustments; this passes off after a time. It often happens that the eye looks a little goggled, from the bulging out of the inner side of the ball. The operation for deformity or false direction, in every other case, is performed in like manner with the one already described, and needs, therefore, no especial notice.

Section 23.—*Ectropium.*

The term ectropium signifies a turning out or eversion of the eyelid; it is the reverse of entropium, and, according to Walton, is not only of more rare occurrence, but also is less severe in its effects. In ordinary cases but one lid is affected, and the patient is much inconvenienced by the flow of the lachrymal secretion over the cheek; when both lids are everted, there is considerable danger of inflammation attacking the globe of the eye from the absence of the necessary secretion. Ectropium may be either *temporary* or *permanent*. In the former variety it is occasioned by inflammation of the eye, particularly purulent ophthalmia; the latter may also arise from the same cause, or may be the result of wounds, burns, or other injury inflicted upon the eyelids. The constant exposure of the mucous membrane of the eye, when the disease is permanent, often causes inflammation and thickening of the external tunic, which may finally degenerate into a smooth cuticular enlargement near the margin of the lid—to such affection the term fleshy ectropium (ectropium sarcomatosum) is applied.

Treatment.—When ectropium threatens from severe ophthalmia, the medicine must be carefully selected in accordance with the existing symptoms.

When the eversion arises from excoriation and contraction of the skin of the eyelid, together with a sarcomatous state of the conjunctiva (ectropium sarcomatosum), *caust.*, *thuj.*, *silic.*, *phosph.*, or *calc.* should be employed.

If the disease follow suppuration, *ars.*, *merc.*, *hepar*, *silic.* must be remembered.

If inflammation and swelling of the lids are present, together with the eversion, *bell.*, *puls.*, *euphra.*, *bary.-mur.*, &c., should be exhibited.

The debility of the orbicular muscle, occasioned by chronic inflammation, may be remedied by the administration of *ang.*, *nux.*, *rhus*, *caust.*, or *arn.* If disease and contraction of the cartilage have given rise to the deformity, *ars.*, *mez.*, *merc.*, *ruta*, *silic.*, or *sulph.* are applicable.

If remedial measures are not sufficient, recourse must be had to mechanical means; by which the lid may, in a measure at least, be restored to its natural position. When the eversion is considerable, and has been present for a length of time, the tarsus having become elongated and changed in figure, that it can no longer accommodate itself to the convexity of the globe, a portion of the lid should be removed by an incision like the letter V. The operation may be performed with scissors or knife, and the lips of the wound having been carefully brought together, should be retained by the twisted or interrupted suture.

Dieffenbach's operation is performed as follows: An incision is made through the skin and orbicularis muscle, beginning two or three lines from one angle, and ending at the same distance from the other. Each end of the incision should be about a line from the margin of the lid, and the middle of the division two or three lines—the small flap of skin thus made is turned up. The incision should then be continued to the conjunctiva, which should be divided to the extent of the external wound. The external edge of the divided conjunctiva should next, with forceps, be drawn to the wound of the integuments, which must now be united by sutures passing through the conjunctiva as well as the skin. Considerable traction is thus applied to the ciliary margin of the everted lid, which is drawn into its natural position.

Dr. Jaeger's operation consists in passing a sharp-pointed double-edged knife through the conjunctival surface near the inner angle of the eye, and bringing it out through the skin on the cheek; it must then be carried on transversely through the outer angle. The detached lid must now be fixed accurately and firmly in contact with the globe, while the integuments of the cheek must be drawn up towards the eye, and retained in that position by adhesive straps, compresses, and bandages. This operation can be performed on either eyelid.

Section 24.—*Entropium.*

This is an affection in which not only the eyelashes, but also the margin of the eyelid are turned inwards towards the ball of the eye, and is attended with the unpleasant consequences of trichiasis in an aggravated form. It may be either temporary or permanent. In the former instance, it is the result of inflammatory œdema of the eyelid; the tumefied conjunctiva, according to Littell,* pressing on the orbital edge of the tarsus, whilst its ciliary margin is turned inwards by the action of the orbicularis. This variety seldom lasts over twelve or twenty-four hours. Permanent entropium is most frequently met with in the upper lid, and is generally the result of protracted ophthalmia tarsi, psorophthalmia, or other chronic diseases of the eye; or it may depend on excessive development and spasmodic action of the orbicularis and tensor tarsi muscles.

Treatment.—Dr. Dudgeon has the credit of being the first to propose homœopathic treatment for the cure of entropium. He suggests *borax* as applicable to some forms of catarrhal and senile ophthalmia, particularly when accompanied with entropium. The indications for this medicine are chiefly itching and burning in the eye, with agglutination of the lids at night and derangement of the eyelashes, which have a tendency to *turn in.*†

In the temporary form of the affection inversion should be opposed by means of a strip of adhesive plaster, fastened at one end to the inverted lid, whilst the other is attached to some part of the face, so that sufficient traction may be exerted to remedy the deformity, until its cause has been removed by medicines principally directed towards the removal of the inflammation and tumefaction.

Permanent entropium is not so readily remedied; and it is generally found that operative interference is required. If, however, the affection appears to depend on a vitiated action of the tensor tarsi and orbicularis muscles, beneficial effect may be derived from the administration of *nux.*, *ignat.*, or *ang.;* or, in other instances, by the external and internal use of *bell.*, *stram.*, or *conium.*

Several operations have been practiced for the removal of

---

* Littell on Diseases of the Eye, p. 95.

† Peters on Diseases of the Eye, p. 39.

this deformity. The most common method consists in the removal of an elliptical piece of the integument of the eyelid. A careful examination is necessary, in the first instance, to determine how much is to be removed in order to rectify the position of the lid, and yet avoid taking away an unnecessary amount, and thus perhaps produce an opposite condition of the parts or ectropium. When this has been determined, a fold of the skin should be taken up between the blades of suitable forceps, and removed by means of a knife or scissors; the edges of the wound should then be united with sutures, and adhesion follows.

Mr. Tyrrell recommends that the lid should be merely divided at its centre, by a single perpendicular incision. The pressure caused by the contracted cartilage is thus relieved; and as the wound, shaped like an inverted V, becomes filled with granulations, little deformity results. This operation, however, is only applicable when the disease arises from a contracted state of the tarsal cartilage.

The operation of Professor Jaeger, of Vienna, is a very effectual method of removing the deformity. A smooth, slightly concave piece of horn, adapted to the lid, is introduced under it as a means of extension and support, though the part to be removed may be drawn outwards by forceps; a horizontal incision is then made through the skin and orbicularis muscle, a line and a half from the ciliary margin, and carried to each extremity of the inverted portion. The part thus marked out is to be carefully dissected off by repeated short strokes of the knife, carried obliquely, so as to include the bulbs of the inverted lashes and leave the mucous surface entire.

Section 25.—Hordeolum—Stye.

By the term hordeolum is understood a red, painful, and inflamed tumor, involving one or more of the meibomian glands. It bears, in many respects, a strong similarity to the common furuncle, and is usually seated near the inner angle of the lower eyelid. The affection is one of very common occurrence, and is attributed by some to a deranged condition of the gastric functions. In many individuals, especially young females, there appears to exist a predisposition to the formation of styes.

Treatment.—Puls. is not only a specific for this affection, but also is a prophylactic.

In several cases where styes frequently occurred, they shortly disappeared after this medicine was prescribed; and by persisting in its use—about two doses of the 6th dilution —the return of the affection was prevented.

Ferrum should be given when there is redness and swelling of the lids, with burning in the eyes and agglutination of the lids.

Phosph. is said to be best adapted when the hordeola appear upon the lower lids; when there is photophobia, discharge of acrid tears, with ulceration of the internal angles of the eye.

Rhus may be employed when the eyes secrete much mucus, and the styes are large.

Sepia is an excellent medicine, and is of great service when suppuration progresses slowly—for the latter condition *hepar* and *merc.;* and when the hordeola frequently return, the 30th dilution is recommended. *Staphys.* and *sulph.* may also be applicable in some cases.

Section 26.—*Ptosis, &c.*

Lapsus palpebræ superioris, or *blepharo-ptosis,* are terms, together with *ptosis,* which are used by surgeons to designate a falling of the upper eyelid, with partial or complete want of power to elevate it. In this affection, if the eyelid be lifted, it slowly falls again over the eye. It may arise from wounds or disease involving the muscles or nerves.

Treatment.—Dr. Peters recommends for this disease *ars.*, *plumb.*, *nux.*, *ign.*, *ang.* Other medicines are *bell.*, *cham.*, *crocus*, *hepar*, *hyos.*, *viol.-odor.*

Trichiasis denotes an unnatural direction of the eyelashes, in which they turn inwards and press against the eyeball. By the term *distichiasis* is understood an affection in which the misdirected eyelashes are in a separate row from others, which remain properly directed.

Treatment.—The medicines best adapted to the treatment of trichiasis are *bor.* and *puls.* In many instances it is necessary to extract the offending eyelashes with small forceps, and after their removal to administer the appropriate medicine to prevent the return of the affection.

Foreign bodies in the Eye.—Various substances may become lodged between the eyelids, or may pass into or through the cornea. Pieces of wood, steel, or hot iron often penetrate the surface of the cornea, producing considerable inflammation. Lime, also, is sometimes accidentally projected into the eye; and, if the substance is pure, it is very destructive to the cornea, destroying its transparency and creating violent inflammation of the conjunctiva.

Treatment.—The first desideratum in the treatment is the removal of the extraneous matter from the eye, which may be effected by the forceps, by paper rolled with a pointed extremity, or by the point of an ordinary quill toothpick.

When glass or other substances have deeply penetrated the cornea, it may be necessary to make a section of that membrane with the cataract knife, in order to remove the foreign body, after which a weak lotion of *arnica* may be applied externally, and the same medicine internally administered.

Angustura has been recommended, to be employed in like manner; *conium* may also be useful. If inflammation of the conjunctiva supervene, those medicines must be employed which have already been mentioned when recording the different varieties of ophthalmia.

CHAPTER XXVIII.

INJURIES AND DISEASES OF THE EAR.

Section 1.—*Otitis.*

The mucous membrane and other textures of the ear may be attacked by acute inflammation, and to such the term *otitis* is applied. *External otitis* generally occurs in children, from exposure to cold; while the *internal variety* may arise from some constitutional vice, or may be caused by severe injury to the part. The inflammatory process extends from the external ear, or from the nares and fauces, along the Eustachian tube to the tympanum. The disease generally commences with ringing and buzzing in the ear, which in some instances is very troublesome, and impairs the hearing. In most cases the pain is of a lancinating character, extending to the more internal structure of the parts, and sometimes even to the alveolar sockets. There is slight fever, unless the inflammatory process has reached a high point and is about to terminate in suppuration, and infiltration of the surrounding textures; when together with much fever, there is excruciating pain, restlessness and delirium. Sometimes a number of purulent vesicles are seen in the meatus auditorius.

If the inflammation should penetrate to the tympanum or inner ear, (internal otitis,) there is deep-seated intolerable pain, throbbing, well marked inflammatory fever, which is generally followed by suppuration (*abscess of the ear*); this is an event which, from its consequences, may be considered as extremely dangerous, and when it is about to occur, the lancinations become less, and the pain, though intense, is duller in character. After a time the tympanum ulcerates, and a copious purulent secretion is suddenly discharged. Suppuration in the organ of hearing often follows eruptive diseases, and either one or both ears may continue to discharge for a long time; if this be the case, and if it is accompanied by inflammatory symptoms, openings may form over the mastoid process, communicating with the cells, and these are often connected with abscess betwixt the dura mater and pars petrosa of the temporal bone. Formations of pus in the middle lobe of the cerebrum, or in the cerebellum, are sometimes evacuated through the meatus auditorius. In all cases, but in the last more particularly, the patient suffers extremely when the discharge is suppressed, and is again relieved immediately by its reappearance.

Treatment.—The chief medicines for otitis are *bell.*, *merc.*, *nux-vom.*, *puls.*, and *sulphur ;* or in other cases, *borax*, *bry.*, *calc.-carb.*, *cham.*, &c.

Pulsatilla is a specific remedy in most cases of otitis; its effects in some instances are truly surprising, as exhibited by almost immediate amelioration of the violent symptoms, after the administration of a few globules of the medicine. It is particularly indicated when there is heat, redness, and painful swelling of the outer and inner ear, with buzzing and tingling, with discharge of pus.

Belladonna is indicated when the inflammatory symptoms are of the higher grade, when there are lancinating pains extending from the upper jaw to the internal ear, with stitches in the parotid gland, tingling, roaring, and tearing in the external parts, from above downwards; deafness and inflammatory swelling of the parotid gland.

Mercurius should be employed when there are tearing and sticking pains in the ear, with sensation of extreme coldness, or as if ice had lodged in the part, together with buzzing, ringing, and pulsative pains, with discharge of pus. This medicine is also recommended for abscess of the mastoid cells.

Nux-vomica corresponds when the inflammation has even extended to the parotid gland; when there is tingling and hissing in the ears, with lancinations from within outward, particularly in the evening, and when the patient is of a dyspeptic habit.

Many other medicines for the treatment of this affection can readily be found in the Repertory and Materia Medica, to which the student is directed for further information upon the subject. It may be well, however, to remark in this place, that when the mastoid process has become involved, and suppuration has occurred within its cells, that besides the medicines already specified, *hepar*, *silicea*, *mez.*, *nit.-ac.*, and *sepia*, are appropriate.

Section 2.—*Otorrhœa.*

By this term is understood a puriform discharge from the ear, generally preceded by symptoms of acute or chronic otitis, or dependent upon sub-acute inflammation resulting from exanthemata.

Scrofulous children are mostly subject to this disease. The ear should be examined carefully with a speculum, and if the continuity of the tympanum be found unbroken, the affection may be considered as comparatively simple; but if the membrane has lost its integrity, or has been partially destroyed by abnormal action, the prognosis is decidedly unfavorable.

Treatment.—For catarrhal or mucous otorrhœa, the medicines best adapted are *bell.*, *calc.*, *carb.-veg.*, *hepar*, *merc* , *nat.-mur.*, *puls.*, *silicea*, and *sulphur.* It may be well here to recommend to the notice of the profession a medicine which appears to have been little employed in the treatment of purulent otorrhœa. In the majority of instances we have found that *bovista* more speedily and more radically cured the affection than other remedial agents. Cases of this description, that had resisted for years all efforts directed to suppress the discharge, yielded to one or two doses of the sixth attenuation of this medicine.

Otorrhœa resulting from exanthemata is best combated by *bell.*, *carb.-veg.*, *colch.*, *hep.*, and *lycopod.* If the disease arise in consequence of abuse of mercury, *aurum*, *asa.*, *hep.*, *nit.-ac.*, *sil.*, and *sulph.;* and if accompanied by caries of the ossicula auditoria, *aurum*, *mez.*, *phos.*, *nat.-mur.*, *silicea*, and *sulphur.* For scrofulous otorrhœa, with ulceration of the concha, *hepar*, *lyc.*, *merc.*, *puls.*, *sulph.*, and *rhus.* When there is *hemor-*

rhage from the ear, the medicines recommended are *bry.*, *cicuta*, *graph* , *merc.*, *petrol.*, *puls.*, and *rhus.*

Section 3.—*Otalgia.*

This is a neuralgic affection of the ear, constituting true ear-ache. It may be connected with an irritation of the fauces and mouth, but in the generality of instances, the affection cannot be traced to any other disease. It is frequently occasioned by exposure to cold, wounds, &c.

Treatment.—The chief medicines for the relief of this affection are *bell.*, *cham.*, *merc.*, *spig.*, *puls.*, *sulph.*, and in some instances *arn.*, *china*, *dulc.*, *hepar*, *nux-vom.*, *platina.*

Belladonna is indicated when there is tearing and shooting pains extending into the throat, with twitting, roaring, or humming in the ear; when there is excessive sensibility to the least noise, accompanied with painful affection of the eyes and face, with congestion of blood to the head.

Chamomilla should be employed when there is cutting as from knives, extending into the lobes of the ear, dryness of the parts, with sensation of stoppage; the least noise renders the pain insupportable; the patient is also restless, ill-humored, and disposed to be offended at trifles.

Mercurius is indicated when there is a sensation of cold in the ears, with aggravation of the pains in the warmth of the bed; inflammatory redness of the ear, discharge of cerumen, and profuse perspiration, from which no relief is experienced.

Pulsatilla is a very important medicine in the treatment of otalgia, and is indicated when there is redness and swelling of the lobes of the ear, with sensation as if something were endeavoring to pass out through the ear, with tearing pains on the whole side of the head; it is especially suited to persons of a mild disposition, females and children.

Spigelia when there are drawing and shooting pains extending to the bones of the face, or when there is a sensation as if something were lodged in the ear.

Sulphur is homœopathic when there is drawing and tearing, particularly if the left ear be affected with humming, whizzing, or cracking, or with tearing pains that extend into the head.

Arnica is the proper medicine when the disease arises from external injury, or when there is a return of the sufferings from the slightest cause, with internal heat and great sensitiveness to noise.

China when the pains are aggravated by contact, and manifest themselves rather externally than internally, accompanied with shooting and tinkling in the parts.

Nux-vomica may be employed when there are tearing or shooting pains, particularly aggravated in the morning, which extend into the forehead and temples, with tearing in the bones of the face.

Platina is appropriate when there are violent spasmodic shocks, with roaring or thundering in the ears, which feel cold.

Section 4.—*Deafness.*

Deafness may proceed from affections already named, as well as from a variety of other causes. The first care of the surgeon, when called to attend to such cases, should be to examine carefully the external and internal ear by means of a speculum. Accumulation of cerumen, which has become inspissated within the meatus, is a frequent cause of deafness; or the defect in hearing may be produced by deficient secretion of cerumen. Disease of the mucous membrane lining the ear, causing induration and thickness, may also give rise to the affection. Diseases of the membrana tympani, the Eustachian tube, of the brain, of the auditory nerve, repercussion of eruptions, or congestion to the head, also occasion the disease.

Treatment.—When the surgeon has reason to believe that the dysecoia proceeds from congestion, or determination of blood to the head, the medicines required are *bell.*, *aurum*, *graph.*, *mer.-sol.*, *phosph.*, and *silicea.* If the defect in hearing originate from nervous diseases, *caust.*, *petrol.*, *phosph.*, *phosph.-*

ac., and *spigelia*, may be indicated, and in some cases, *anacard.*, *mur.-ac.*, *verat.*, &c. When caused by suppression of discharge, *bell.*, *hepar*, *ledum.*, *mer.-sol.*, and *puls.* If the deafness arise from deficiency of ceruminous secretion, *carbo-veg.* and *graph.* are the principal medicines. If accumulation of inspissated cerumen has given rise to dysecoia, *conium*, *selen.*, *sil.*, and *zinc.*, should be employed; in very many cases, the patient can be relieved, by moistening the indurated secretion several times during the day, and particularly at night when the patient retires, with a few drops of *glycerine*, which, softening the hardened cerumen, allows it to be readily removed by means of a simple probe, or the handle of a director.

The more precise indications for the administration of medicines are as follows: *Calcarea*, when there is constant dryness of the ear, or else purulent discharge, pressive pain in the forehead, with humming, roaring, and tinkling in the ears, with throbbing and heat.

Causticum when there is a sensation of obstruction in the ears, with humming and roaring in the head, loud vibration of all sounds, and even of the patient's voice, with oterrhœa; it is also applicable when there are rheumatic pains in the ears and limbs, with extraordinary sensitiveness to cold winds, &c.

Graphites is indicated by great dryness in the ears; the difficulty of hearing is somewhat alleviated by motion in a carriage; humming or a noise as of thunder in the ears, especially at night, or a sensation as if air penetrated to the Eustachian tube; this medicine should also be remembered when there are herpes or scabs around the ears, or the patient suffers from other cutaneous affections.

Ledum is especially useful after a suppression of otorrhœa from a cold, when there is a sensation of stoppage and humming in the ears, confusion and giddiness of the head, with sensation of torpor of the integument.

Mercurius-sol. is a very important medicine in the treatment of deafness, and is indicated when every sound reverberates in the ear, with tinkling, roaring, or humming, which is worse in the evening, when there is sensation of coldness in the ear, discharge of cerumen, or purulent otorrhœa, with ulceration of the parts.

Nitric-acid must be employed when there is great dryness in the ear, with cracking, and particularly when the affection is accompanied with scorbutic symptoms.

Petroleum is an excellent medicine when there is troublesome dryness of the internal ear, or discharge of blood and pus; when there is a sound of tinkling or rolling in the ear; when the patient is affected with herpes or other eruptive diseases.

Phosphorus should be employed when there is difficulty in hearing sounds, especially that of the human voice, with excessive reverberation of all sounds, and especially of words; congestion of blood to the ears, with throbbing and pulsation.

Pulsatilla is homœopathic when the deafness is occasioned by the presence of hard and black cerumen, or when the secretion is too profuse and liquid, and there is humming, tinkling, and roaring in the ears. This medicine is especially suitable to persons of a mild disposition, or women disposed to leucorrhœa or other uterine disorders.

Silicea is the medicine when there is obstruction of the ears, which is dissipated by blowing the nose, or when the deafness alternates with excessive acuteness of hearing.

Sulphur when there is difficulty of hearing, especially the human voice, aggravated when eating or blowing the nose; when there is a sense of gurgling or fluctuation in the ears, as if caused by water; when there is disposition to catarrh and mucous discharges. Space will not permit further detail in the treatment of deafness; for more particular information on this subject, however, the student should consult the Repertory and Materia Medica.

Section 5.—Congenital Occlusion of the Meatus and other Affections.

The ear though fully developed at birth may be covered by integument, causing either partial or total deafness. In such cases a simple incision relieves the patient; care, however, should be observed in dressing the wound after operating; and lint or other extraneous matter be inserted between the lips of the wound, to prevent adhesion; if this be neglected, the defect will not be removed, indeed, from the contraction of the parts, it may be more permanent than previous to the operation. If the covering of the meatus is thick, fleshy or cartilaginous, the obstruction should be removed by careful dissection. Some individuals, though born without the external ear, have been known to possess the sense of hearing. In such cases it is presumed that sound is conducted along the bones of the cranium to the internal ear, which is perfectly constructed.

Hypertrophy of the Auricle.—Hypertrophy of the whole auricle, though of rare occurrence, is occasionally encountered by the surgeon; partial hypertrophy, affecting one lobe only, is frequently met with,* and chiefly in women. If excessive and irksome to the patient, from its unseemliness, the redundancy should be removed by the knife.

Polypus of the Ear.—The sense of hearing is sometimes obstructed by the presence of polypi, which may be either soft and pulpy, resembling the mucous polypus that affects the nose, or firm and fleshy,† like the solid polypus of the vagina; both varieties are simple in structure and tendency.

Treatment.—The medicines that have been chiefly recommended for polypus in the ear are *calcarea*, *carbo-an.*, and *staphysagria*. The polypus may be removed by mechanical means, in the following manner: The tumor should be grasped as close to its pedicle as possible, with delicate forceps; when the pain and bleeding have subsided, if any portions of the tumor remain, either of the above medicines may be administered, or others which may be called for by existing symptoms. If otitis supervene, the treatment already has been mentioned.

---

* Miller's Practice of Surgery, p. 243.

† Hastings' Practice of Surgery, p. 419.

34

Section 6.—*Perforation of the Membrana Tympani.*

Perforation of the membrana tympani is not frequently required; it is deemed advisable when atmospheric air is prevented entering the cavity of the tympanum, from obstruction of the Eustachian tube.

The performance likewise of the operation is rendered necessary when the cavity of the tympanum is obstructed by extravasated blood from wounds, &c.

The object to be accomplished is not only to make an aperture in the membrane, but also to render it permanently pervious, and thus afford entrance to the accustomed supply of atmospheric air in the middle ear. The best instrument for accomplishing such an end, is that of Fabricci. "It consists of a canula, into which slides a spiral wire, somewhat resembling that of a corkscrew. It is to be used in the following manner: Pass the canula with the spiral wire down upon the inferior part of the membrana tympani (so as not to interfere with the manubrium of the malleus), retain it there with the left hand, being careful not to press too firmly on the membrane; then, with the right hand, take hold of the small handle which revolves the spiral wire, and turn it from right to left, being what is usually called turning the *wrong way.* The instant the membrane is perforated, a peculiar sensation is imparted to the operator. The wire is now no longer to be turned, though by its handle the instrument is to be retained in its situation; then gently revolve the canula, which has a cutting edge, from left to right, when a circular portion of the membrana tympani, corresponding to the diameter of the canula, will be cut out, and at the same time drawn into the canula and held fast by the spiral wire."* Or, instead of this instrument, a trocar, with volute and sharpened sides, may be used. The punctured portion may be excised, by rapidly turning the instrument upon the membrane.

* Williams on the Ear, p. 204.

CHAPTER XXIX.

DISEASES OF THE NOSE.

Section 1.—*Ozœna.*

This affection consists in a troublesome ulceration of the lining membrane of the nostrils, attended with fetid purulent discharge. Occasionally it is followed by destruction of the nasal cartilages, and by caries of the nasal bones. In some instances the senses of smell and taste are entirely destroyed.

Though the origin of the disease is somewhat obscure, yet there is reason to believe that, in most instances, it is connected with the primary or secondary forms of syphilis; and in others with the purely scrofulous diathesis. The most disagreeable feature of the affection is the accumulation of inspissated mucus, or incrustations, within the nasal cavities, which sometimes form in such considerable quantity as to entirely close the passages. After ulceration is fairly established, not only is the cartilaginous septum affected, but the ethmoid, the spongy, and other bones of the nose; and, in the worst cases—particularly when there is complication with syphilitic or mercurial disease—even the palate and superior maxillary bones exfoliate, and in consequence of such ravages the contour of the nose is destroyed, and an otherwise frightful deformity of the face results.

Treatment.—The remedies which have chiefly been employed in this affection are: *alumina, teucrium, puls., sulph., calc.,* or *magnes.-mur., bryonia, bell., lycopod., nat.-mur.,* and *causticum* in the first stage, whilst there is yet merely mucous obstruction. In the second stage, when the secretion has been transformed into pus and the nasal bones are affected, with fetid odor from the nose and loss of smell, *mercurius* and *aurum* are to be administered. These may be followed, if required, in ozœna scrofulosa by *sulph., sil., acid-nit., phosph., conium,* or *kali-bich.* In *syphilitic ozœna, mercurius* constitutes the principal remedy;

if, however, the patient has previously been subjected to an injurious course of treatment with this medicine, *aurum* is to be preferred, and succeeded, if it be found requisite, by *acid-nit.*, *hepar*, *asafœtida*, *conium*, or *thuja*.

The following are the more particular indications for the administration of the medicines.

Alumina. Constant discharge from the nose of a thick, yellow, fetid matter, especially in the morning; at the same time anorexia, with obstinate obstruction of the nose.

Aurum. A thick, yellow, half-watery, half-dry discharge is blown from the nose; fetid odor from the nose; loss of smell, especially in ozœna syphilitica, with discharge of bloody pus; yellow, ichorous crust over the alæ nasi; the nose, forehead, and upper part of the face red and swollen.

Magnes.-mur. Ozœna benigna; soreness in the inner part of the nose; yellow crust on the nose; discharge of a yellow ichorous matter; redness and soreness of the upper lip, and swelling of the lower part of the nose.

Mercurius is indicated, especially in syphilitic ozœna; swelling of whole nose, the nasal bones themselves being enlarged; dryness of nose, with yellow discharge and fetid smell. This medicine is also suited to ozœna scrofulosa.

Pulsatilla must be employed when there is discharge of yellowish, green, ichorous matter, with fetid odor; the nose swollen. This medicine is also serviceable when the disease attacks females, with retarded menstrual discharge or leucorrhœa.

Section 2.—Polypus Nasi.

A polypus of the nose may arise from any portion of the Schneiderian membrane, but it originates most frequently from either the superior or inferior spongy bones. Occasionally the seat of the tumor is so high, that instead of falling towards the anterior nares, it takes a backward direction, hanging behind the palate, and sometimes even reaching the pharynx. It is most commonly pyriform, narrow at its base and expanding below, though this depends much upon the natural form of the cavity in which it is situated; sometimes the base of the tumor is exceedingly large. Either one or both nostrils may be affected, and when the latter is the case, the patient breathes with much difficulty and with a peculiar rattling noise; and in damp weather the tumors often project beyond the exterior of the nostrils, but assume their former position upon the reappearance of dry weather.

The consistence of nasal polypi is not less variable than their form. In some instances they are solid, fleshy, and firm; whilst in others they are extremely soft and tender, liable to be torn upon the slightest touch—most of them are extremely vascular, and if not handled with care, bleed profusely. No age or sex is exempt from the affection; which sometimes assumes a malignant form, and at others destroys life, producing by its pressure caries of the ethmoid and spongy bones, inflammation of the brain, &c.

Treatment.—The medicines which have proved most efficacious in this disease, are *calc.-carb.*, *teucrium*, *sulphur*, and *phosph.*;* *puls.*, *silicea*, *staph.*, *carbo-an.*, and *sepia* may also be called for in some cases. Sometimes it is necessary, when medicines cannot effect a cure, to remove the polypus by mechanical means: this may be done in a variety of ways, but in most cases the use of the forceps is preferable. These should be stronger than the ordinary dressing forceps, well serrated and slightly curved. The patient is seated on a low chair, before a powerful light, with the head moderately thrown back and firmly supported; the surgeon then carefully introduces the instrument with its blades expanded, grasps the tumor firmly at its root, and then by twisting rather than pulling removes it. A copious flow of blood generally follows, but the

---

* For several interesting cases of polypi nasi, cured by the three former of these medicines, see British Journal of Homœopathy, vol. viii., p. 283; and vol. x., p. 484.

forceps should again be introduced, until not a vestige of the polypus remains; the best criterion of the operation being complete is, that the patient can breathe freely through the nostrils. Care must be taken not to use unnecessary violence, as in some instances the ethmoid bone has been broken up, and other serious mischief resulted.

Excision and the ligature have also been recommended by some writers, for the removal of these troublesome tumors—the former when it is of large size, and arises from a broad base; the latter when it arises by a narrow neck, and hangs beyond the posterior nares. The hemorrhage which results may be arrested by the administration of one or more of the medicines mentioned under epistaxis; or, if these should fail, a plug of lint may be introduced into the nasal cavity.

CHAPTER XXX.

DISEASES OF THE MOUTH.

Section 1.—*Hare-Lip—Labium Leporinum.*

By the term hare-lip is understood a congenital malformation of the upper lip, the deformed part being supposed to bear a resemblance to the natural development of the hare. The deformity may exist either singly or doubly, and is frequently complicated with deformity of the alveoli, causing irregularity and projection of the teeth, or with cleft or fissure of the hard and soft palates.

Simple hare-lip consists of a fissure extending through the whole thickness of the labium, situate on either side of the mesial line, and partially or totally dividing the lip. The deformity is great, even when the affection occurs simply and singly, and the functions of the parts are necessarily much interfered with.

Treatment.—An operation must be resorted to, the object of which is to approximate the edges of the fissure accurately at every point, and secure union by adhesion. Although this operation has been repeatedly performed a few days after birth, yet probably the most preferable period is after the child has passed its second year; for at this time the process of dentition has generally been accomplished, and there is greater tolerance of pain and less loss of blood.

Operation.—The arms and legs having been completely confined by means of bandages or cloths, the child is held on the lap of a nurse or assistant, with its head secured between the knees of the surgeon, who is seated on a chair in front of the patient and nurse. The free margin of the lip, on one side of the fissure, is first taken hold of and put on the stretch, when a straight and narrow sharp-pointed bistoury is inserted at the upper or nasal angle of the deficiency, and carried down its whole length, removing a strip sufficiently wide to leave a smooth, flat surface for union. The opposite margin of the fissure is then treated in the same manner. Hemorrhage from the superior coronary arteries sometimes is very profuse; but a ligature is never required, the flow of blood being readily arrested by pinching or twisting the bleeding vessels with forceps. The lips of the wound should then be carefully brought together, and accurately adjusted in every particular; a hare-lip pin, or an ordinary sewing needle, is then passed through both sides of the lip, penetrating at least two-thirds of its thickness, and entering and emerging about a quarter of an inch from its cut edges. The first pin should be placed near the margin of the lip, to hold it in accurate adjustment, when the twisted suture of unwaxed silk-ligature should be passed several times around this pin, in the form of a figure 8. A second pin should then be passed above the first, and the suture applied in a similar manner; and the ligature may be carried from one pin to the other, care being taken not to pucker the lip. Two pins generally suffice, although if the length of the wound should require it, more may be inserted.

Mr. Fergusson* recommends very highly an instrument which he almost invariably employs, for assisting the action of the sutures in maintaining close approximation. It consists of a semicircular spring, padded at both extremities; the latter are applied to the cheeks in such a manner, as to relieve the needles of the strain which would otherwise be imposed on them. The instrument is maintained in its proper position by means of straps or bandages passed over the cranium.

When *double hare-lip* exists, there is a fissure extending from each nostril, with an intermediate structure, which is either fully or partially developed; the cleft in these cases is usually complete.

Treatment.—The operation for *double hare-lip* does not differ in principle from that in the preceding variety, the ordinary incisions being made to each fissure. The pin should be passed through the three flaps, piercing the central portion of each, and emerging a quarter of an inch beyond the farthest incision.

Complication exists more frequently in the double than in the single form. Fissure may exist in the hard and soft palates, or the gum and teeth may project between the clefts. The abnormal condition of the palate does not interfere with the operation on the lip; but the traction which is necessary to bring the parts together may have a beneficial effect in diminishing the palatine chasm. In cases in which the alveoli and teeth protrude, these must be removed.

Section 2.—Malformation of the Frænum Linguæ.

It sometimes happens, though by no means so frequently as is imagined, that children are born with the frænum of the tongue so short, that they are unable to raise the organ to the palate, and consequently sucking is materially impeded. This

* Practical Surgery, 1853.

condition is made apparent by raising the point of the tongue with a spatula. If the surgeon should fail in this attempt, and the tongue appear, upon examining it laterally, to be unnaturally confined, little doubt can remain of the frænum being defective.

Treatment.—This complaint is readily removed by means of an operation, which, however, trifling though it may be considered, is one which should not be lightly performed, nor upon every ordinary occasion. Petit relates two instances, in which death followed from the frænum being so much loosened as to permit the tongue to fall backwards into the pharynx, thereby occasioning suffocation; and other cases are recorded of fatal hemorrhage following the operation, from wounds of the ranine arteries and veins.

A pair of probe-pointed scissors are used for the operation. The tongue should be pressed upwards, by means of the index and middle fingers of the left hand, and the frænum should then be divided in its transparent portion as far as may be deemed absolutely necessary; at the same time taking care to direct the points of the instrument downwards, keeping as close to the lower jaw as possible, that the arteries and veins may be avoided. If carefully performed, there is scarely any hemorrhage attending the operation; but, if hemorrhage should result, it may be arrested by applying small pieces of sponge, a solution of alum, gun-cotton, or some other styptic.

Section 3.—*Ranula.*

By the term ranula is understood an obstruction of one or more of the ducts of the sublingual glands, giving rise to the formation of a semi-pellucid tumor, supposed by the older anatomists to resemble the belly of a frog, hence the name. The swelling may attain a considerable size, interfere with deglutition, or even displace the teeth; the tumor is cystic, and is generally filled with saliva, though sometimes it contains a fluid resembling albumen. It arises from a natural imperfection, or adhesion of the duct, or from the lodgment of calculous concretion within its passage. This disease chiefly affects children.

Treatment.—The medicines which have been found most successful in relieving this affection, are *merc.-sol.*, *calc.*, and *thuja*. *Mercurius* should be employed when there is an excessive secretion of saliva, with soreness of the surrounding gums, and there is disposition to profuse sweat, the sufferings being aggravated at night.

Calcarea-carb. is an excellent medicine, and is particularly adapted to children affected with scrofulosis; when there is violent burning in the buccal cavity, with difficulty of speech.

Thuja should be employed, when the tumor is transparent, jelly-like, blue-red, or gray; and when the disease is accompanied with soreness of the whole palate, and with swelling of the salivary glands.

Other medicines are *petrol.*, *puls.*, *silicea*, *stram.*, *staph.*, and *sulphur*.

Section 4.—*Tonsillitis, or Cynanche Tonsillaris.*

This term denotes an inflammatory affection of the fauces, chiefly resident in and around the tonsils. It is ordinarily the result of atmospheric exposure, and is characterized by swelling and redness of the back part of the throat, accompanied with difficulty of swallowing, impeded respiration, difficult articulation, marked alteration of the voice, fever, and other ordinary constitutional accompaniments, according to the intensity of the inflammatory action. As the local affection progresses, the foregoing symptoms become aggravated, and suppuration ensues, constituting *abscess of the tonsils*. The affection occasionally, though rarely, is dangerous, if not properly treated. In its simple form it becomes of moment should it assume a putrid type, as in such instances the attendant fever is of a typhoid character; from which circumstance a peculiar constitutional tendency may be inferred.

In scrofulous constitutions, *chronic enlargement*, or *hypertrophy of the gland*, frequently follows inflammation; in such a condition there is considerable dryness in the throat, which is worse in the morning on waking, together with a sensation of scraping in the parts, and the patients often are obliged to sleep with the mouth open; the vocal cords are frequently involved, causing alteration of the voice. Suffocation has occurred in inveterate cases of the disease.

Treatment.—The principal medicines for cynanche tonsillaris are *acon.*, *bell.*, *merc.-sol.*, *merc.-subl.*, *hepar-sulph.*, *cham.*, *ars.*, *ignatia*, *nit.-ac.*, *nux-vom.*, *baryta*, *silicea*, and *sulphur*.

In the first stages of the disease, when the patient is troubled with an undue secretion of saliva, inducing constant and painful deglutition, and when the inflammation is accompanied by synochal fever, *aconite* should be prescribed. After the fever has been subdued, *bell.* is particularly efficacious, and frequently in alternation with *aconite* rapidly cures the affection. It is especially indicated by the following symptoms: Phlegmonous redness of the tonsil, with shooting pains during deglutition, sensation as if the fauces were spasmodically constricted, with slimy white mucus on the throat and tongue.

Mercurius-sol., or *viv.*, is required when there is much swelling of the glands, profuse secretion of saliva, deglutition much impeded; or should suppuration unfortunately have ensued, when there is throbbing and shooting in the gland, and small ulcers appear, which are isolated and round, with a tendency to become indolent in character.

Cham. may prove useful in mild cases of cynanche, when there are stinging pains in the part, with great restlessness at night.

Ignatia is called for when there is soreness during deglutition, with a sensation of a lump in the throat, shootings into the ears when not swallowing, and greater difficulty experienced in swallowing liquids than solids.

When the disease appears in persons who are affected with

dyspepsia, *nux-vom.* should be employed, particularly when there exists a feeling of excoriation in the throat, and there is a sensation of constriction during deglutition.

Hepar may be employed together with *sulph.* *Silic.* or *sulph.* promote granulation and cicatrization after the discharge of pus.

In chronic enlargement and induration of the amygdalæ, the medicines are chiefly *bell.*, *baryta-c.*, *merc.*, *silic.*, *sulph.*, or *sep.*, *puls.*, *ars.*, *nit.-ac.*, &c. Chronic enlargement of the tonsils is a disease which for successful treatment requires the utmost patience and unwearying perseverance, not only of the practitioner but also of the patient. The medicines must be well selected, administered in not too low a potency, and at considerable intervals; at the same time it is of great importance that the patient should strictly observe the proper dietetic rules, and avoid exposure to a damp and cloudy atmosphere. It may confidently be asserted that from the negligence of patients, and the want of perseverance of practitioners, many cases quite curable are abandoned as hopeless.

In some instances, however, it may be advisable to excise one or both tonsils. The instrument usually employed for this purpose is that of Fahnestock; although some practitioners prefer merely a tenaculum and scissors or scalpel. In the annexed plate is a representation of an instrument invented by Dr. Francis Sims—late Professor of Surgery in the Homœopathic Medical College—which, from the simplicity of its mechanism, its strength, and its easy application, is preferable to any other. It meets every indication for the complete excision of the offending part. It was first made by direction of Dr. Sims by Mr. Jacob H. Gemrig, surgical instrument maker, No. 43 South Eighth Street, Philadelphia.

The following is the description of the tonsil and uvula scissors (see fig. 89). The instrument is eight inches in length, with the cutting edges of the blades concave, in order to prevent the escape of the part to be excised, thereby avoiding the necessity of a second cut. The length from the pivot to the point is two inches (see fig. 90). Three inches from the points,

Fig. 89.

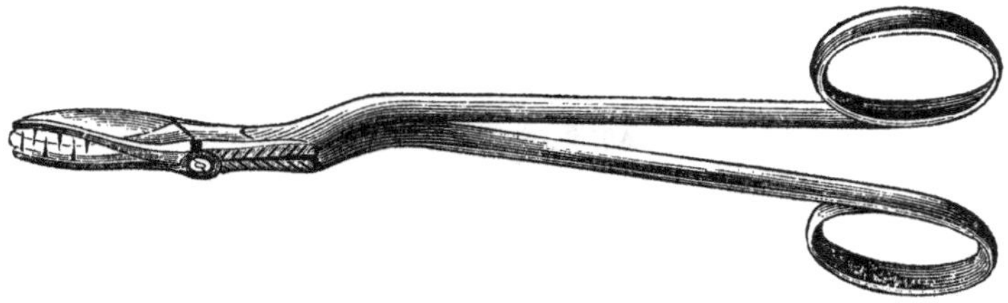

or one inch below the pivot, the instrument is curved at an angle of about twenty degrees, in order to throw the hand of

Fig. 90.*

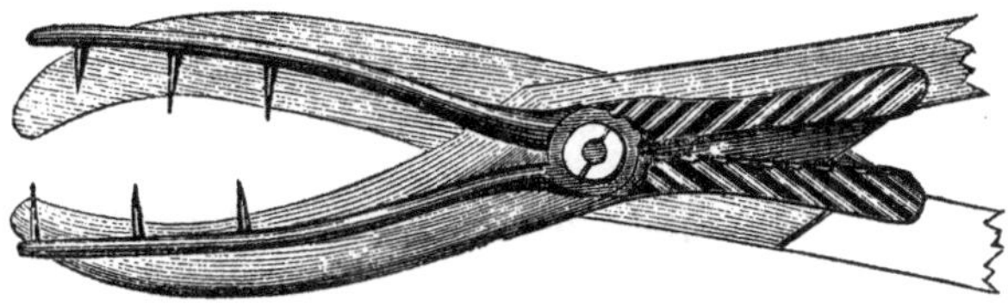

the operator aside, and prevent its obstructing a view of the part to be removed. On the outer side of the blades is placed a pair of jaws armed with six teeth, three in either jaw; these fit in corresponding holes drilled in either jaw; thus effectually preventing the excised part falling into the patient's throat; the blades and their jaws work on the same pivot, so that their relative position to each other remains always the same.

* Fig. 90 is a full sized representation of a portion of the instrument.

CHAPTER XXXI.

DISEASES OF THE NECK.

Section 1.—*Stricture of the Œsophagus.*

Spasm of the œsophagus, or *spasmodic stricture*, is an affection which occurs at intervals; the patient suddenly finding himself incapable of swallowing, and at the same time experiencing a sensation of choking in the throat. In *organic* or permanent stricture, the obstruction to deglutition is always the same, and the bougie meets with resistance when it is passed into the throat, differing in this respect from spasmodic stricture, in which the instrument can be passed through the contracted parts with slight pressure. The affection is said to be dependent upon a prostrated condition of the body, or from disease. There are cases on record, which disappeared upon the removal of hemorrhoids.

Treatment of spasmodic stricture. This affection, if not depending upon incurable disease, can be totally removed, indeed it can be palliated in every instance, as has been already mentioned when speaking of hydrophobia. The chief medicines are *bell.*, *hyos.*, *stram.*, or *verat.*, or in certain cases *con.*, *lyc.*, *merc.*, *nux-vom.*, &c. For the indications of these medicines the student must refer to the Materia Medica.

Permanent stricture of the œsophagus consists of a thickening of the mucous or sub-mucous coats of the tube, the result of inflammation or other cause. Females are said to be more liable to the affection than males. The constriction is generally situated near the termination of the pharynx. The advance of the disease is very gradual, and the patient for years may complain of some difficulty in swallowing, which from some exciting cause increases, is attended by considerable pain, and occasionally aggravated by spasm. There may be pain in the throat, which extends to the head, or there may be stitches from the chest to the shoulders. When a bougie is introduced, considerable pain is experienced, and when the instrument is withdrawn, upon its surface can be found the marks of stricture. This affection may terminate fatally from starvation, by irritation causing inflammation or ulceration of the lungs.

Treatment.—The medicines that appear to be best adapted to the treatment of this disease are *bell.*, *hyos.*, and *conium.* These remedial agents, judging from their pathogeneses, would be the most appropriate, indeed the latter two (*hyos.*, *con.*) are highly recommended even by allopathic authority; others, however, may be required, among which are *lyc.*, *nux.*, *stram.*, *acid-sulph.*, *verat.*, &c. Should the administration of these alone fail to relieve the patient, they may be employed together with the use of the bougie, which instrument should be curved to correspond to the passage. The patient should be directed to throw his head well back, and to swallow while the surgeon introduces the bougie, which should be warmed, and passed steadily and gradually from the posterior part of the pharynx to the seat of stricture. The instrument is to remain a short time within the œsophagus, and the operation repeated once or twice a day, or at longer or shorter intervals, according to the judgment of the surgeon.

The best method of treating stricture of the œsophagus is that introduced by Jameson, who used eight or ten separate probangs, each consisting of a stick of whalebone, having affixed to one of its extremities a spindle-shaped piece of ivory. The instrument first introduced is small, but, after the stricture has been removed sufficiently to readily admit the passage of the probang, a larger size must be selected. The operation must be frequently repeated, each time using a larger sized probang than formerly, until the obstruction is removed.*

---

* The following is a case of stricture of the œsophagus cured by Dr. Jameson's probangs, by the late C. B. Matthews, M. D., Professor of Materia Medica and Therapeutics in the Homœopathic Medical College of Pennsylvania. It is quoted from a letter of the above named gentleman to Dr. Sims, late Professor of Surgery in the same Institution.

"Miss ———, aged about 18, applied to me about the year 1829. She was unable to swallow anything except fluids, and those in small amount.

Section 2.—Foreign Bodies in the Œsophagus.

Extraneous matter frequently lodges in the œsophagus; particularly articles of food, portions of which, from hurry or voraciousness in swallowing, are impacted generally in the superior portion of the tube; such articles, in most instances, are beef, gristle, tripe, cheese, &c. On other occasions the patient is choked from having accidentally swallowed articles carelessly placed in the mouth, as coins, pins, needles, &c. Death has ensued from such accidents.

Treatment.—The foreign substance in many instances is lodged between the thyroid cartilage and the cornua of the os hyoides; in this situation, if the body be large, it may be reached and extracted with the finger; if small, as a fish bone, pin or needle, forceps should be employed. Sometimes by tickling the fauces with a feather, or by exciting vomiting by emetics, the irritating substance can be expelled. Curved and other forceps have been employed, but when the surgeon is suddenly called to a patient, who is in imminent danger of suffocation, these instruments may not be at hand, and the delay occasioned in procuring them may prove fatal to the sufferer. In such instances, the handle of a spoon, the finger, or other convenient article, should be selected, and the foreign substance either dislodged, withdrawn, or, if the article be digestible, forced into the stomach. The ordinary *probang*—a whale-bone rod,

---

She had been treated by Dr. George M'Clellan by means of a flexible sound of block tin, without benefit. I began using the smallest sized probang and Bell's sound, which passed with difficulty, but continuing it several days, it passed easily several times backwards and forwards, through the stricture. I followed with the next size in the same manner, using each four or five days, or until it passed easily, thus continuing up to the fifth, or largest size. This occupied four weeks, or more, at the end of which period I was convinced the stricture was subdued, but the patient was afraid to swallow solids; I obtained a piece of meat of ordinary size, say seven-eighths of an inch cube, and made her swallow it in my presence—this broke the charm, and she could swallow well ever after. I have seen this woman this autumn, (1850,) and she remains perfectly free from her stricture."

with a round piece of sponge attached to one end, and a blunt hook to the other—is the instrument used by surgeons for this purpose. After the extraneous matter has been dislodged, the patient should gargle the throat frequently with a weak solution of *tinct. arnicæ*, and the same medicine should be administered internally.

Section 3.—Extraneous Bodies in the Larynx and Trachea.

During the act of deglutition, articles of food instead of passing into the œsophagus are diverted from their natural course and thrown into the glottis; producing instantaneous violent cough, and labored respiration, and if the substance remain in the glottis, death, from suffocation, speedily follows. In the majority of instances, however, the body passes into the trachea, or else is forced into the laryngeal pouches, in which situation it has been known to remain for a considerable time—in some instances for years—without producing any very serious consequences; in many cases, however, the presence of the foreign body excites constant irritation, and if not removed death may supervene.

Treatment.—The surgeon seldom succeeds in extracting by forceps, &c., extraneous bodies, which have become impacted within the larynx, the operation of *laryngotomy* or *tracheotomy* being required for their removal. The former is thus performed:* The patient being laid on a table, with his head supported by a pillow, and thrown moderately backward, the surgeon after having found the membranous space situated between the thyroid and cricoid cartilages, makes a perpendicular incision, about an inch in length, through the integuments, platysma myoides, and between the sterno-thyroidei and sterno-hyodei muscles. Vessels that may be divided are next carefully secured, and the bleeding having entirely ceased, it only remains

* See Gibson's Institutes and Practice of Surgery, vol. ii., p. 335.

to push the knife through the crico-thyroid membrane, when the extraneous substance will be immediately thrown out, or be visible at the wound, if the body be too large for spontaneous expulsion, in which case the incision should be prolonged upwards, by separating from each other the two lateral parts of the thyroid cartilage. After the substance has been removed, the wound may be drawn together with adhesive straps, and permitted to heal.

When *tracheotomy* is necessary, the surgeon makes an incision from below the cricoid cartilage, and extends it through the skin and platysma-myoides nearly as far as the sternum. The sterno-hyoidei and sterno-thyroidei muscles are next carefully pushed aside, until the surface of the trachea is cleared, and when all hemorrhage has ceased two or three of the rings of the trachea may be divided by a perpendicular incision.

Section 4.—*Bronchocele—Gôitre.*

An enlargement of one or both lobes of the thyroid gland, constitutes the disease known by the name of gôitre. The affection usually occupies one lobe of the thyroid gland; but as the tumor increases the other lobe becomes involved. The swelling may continue stationary for a length of time, and indeed never attain considerable size; but in other instances its magnitude is enormous. Other tumors of the neck may be mistaken for gôitre, but the latter may readily be diagnosed, by directing the patient to imitate the action of swallowing, and if the tumor follows the motions of the larynx and trachea, and at the same time occupies the natural situation of the thyroid gland, there can be very little doubt of its nature. The causes of the disease have not been as yet satisfactorily explained. By many it is supposed, though erroneously, to be of a scrofulous nature. Unwholesome diet, intermittent fevers, and the drinking of snow water, have been imagined by others to give rise to it; but all these causes are extremely hypothetical.

Treatment.—The principal medicine in the treatment of this disease is *iodine*, which has been used by allopathic practitioners from a remote date, but with inconsiderable success from its improper administration; indeed, in many instances, the drug, instead of ameliorating, aggravated the affection. The *iod.* should be used in the 30*th potency*, and, according to Mr. Cameron,* repeated every second day.

Natr.-carb., repeated a few times, has relieved a globular and somewhat indurated enlargement of the upper part of the thyroid gland. In another case *calc.-carb.* afforded speedy relief. *Staphys.* together with *lyc.* has also been of great service. *Spongia* is also a medicine of great power in effecting relief, if it does not cure the disease.

CHAPTER XXXII.

DISEASES OF THE THORAX.

Section 1.—Hydrothorax—Emphysema—and Empyema.

By the term hydrothorax is understood an accumulation of fluid in the cavity of the chest; empyema may also be included in this definition; but generally by the latter term surgeons understand a collection of pus within the thorax. In this place hydrothorax is applied to an accumulation of serous fluid in one or both plural cavities. In the incipient stage the symptoms are very uncertain, and may be mistaken for those of affections of the lungs, heart, &c. There is transitory oppression of the chest, after exercise, talking or ascending an eminence, with increased dyspnœa in the evening. This condition

* Vide a very interesting and highly important paper on Bronchocele, by H. Cameron, Esq., M. R. C. S. E. British Journal of Homœopathy, vol. iii., p. 469.

may pass away with expectoration or profuse sweat; but it is very liable to return, particularly in the warm season. The difficulty of breathing increases, the patient is unable to lie down on account of the gravitation of the fluid within the chest; there is palpitation of the heart, livid countenance, disturbed sleep, and dullness on percussion. If the effusion is on one side only, the patient lies most comfortably on that which is affected. The above symptoms are paroxysmal, in time sopor and insensibility supervene. There is often cough, with extreme irritation of the chest. Where the percussion sound is faint the respiratory murmur disappears; and when there is much effusion bronchial respiration is sometimes heard. The vibrations of the thorax when talking are feeble or entirely absent.

It is important that the practitioner should remember, that the diaphragm, liver and spleen, are often forced downward into the abdominal cavity, presenting appearances very analogous to those observed in ascites.

Persons of advanced age, with weak lungs, occasioned by frequently returning catarrhs, are peculiarly liable to this affection. Malformations of the thorax, curvatures of the vertebral column, and deformities of the ribs and sternum, also engender the disease.

Treatment.—*Ars.-alb.* is one of the principal medicines; it corresponds to many of the symptoms, particularly the dyspnœa, and torturing feeling of suffocation. Other indications which call for its exhibition are the complete prostration of the patient and burning thirst, together with nocturnal exacerbations.

Ipecac., *pulsatilla*, and *ignatia*, may also, in some cases, be called for. *Scilla* is an efficient medicine when there is constant cough, with expectoration and dyspnœa. When there are rheumatic and constrictive pains in the chest, palpitation of the heart, restlessness and excessive anxiety, *carbo-veg.* is indicated, particularly when the disease arises from excessive loss of animal fluids.

Lycopodium should be prescribed when together with the

dyspnœa there is excessive palpitation of the heart, occurring principally after a meal, with cold feet. Hartmann* states that he has cured hydrothorax with *am.-carb.*, one dose every four days.

Other medicines are *bry.*, *china*, *colch.*, *dig.*, *hell.*, *kali-carb.*, *spigelia*, and sometimes *stannum* and *dulcamara.*

Frequently by the exhibition of these medicines the disease is arrested.

To evacuate the fluid the operation of *paracentesis thoracis* is had recourse to, and which is thus performed: An incision into the chest is made, with a knife, and a canula passed into the opening; or a trocar may be thrust directly into the cavity, the stilet withdrawn, and the canula allowed to remain. In this operation care should be taken while passing the instrument within the cavity, that the lung be not irritated, else troublesome cough will be the consequence; the part selected for the operation should be as dependent as possible, and the patient placed with the face up, and the head and shoulders thrown back. Whichever method of operation is resorted to, the instrument should be made to pass in close proximity with the superior edge of the sixth or seventh rib, to avoid wounding the intercostal artery which courses along the inferior margin of the bone. The opening should be valvular, in order to prevent the passage of air into the cavity; this can readily be effected by drawing tense the integument over the place of entrance, and it will be found that when the instrument is withdrawn the skin will roll over the aperture, thus forming an integumental valve.

Empyema.—Empyema is a collection of pus within the cavity of the thorax; it may be the result of acute inflammation, whether traumatic or idiopathic. The symptoms are similar to those of hydrothorax.

In the *treatment* of this affection the operation described above (paracentesis thoracis) may be performed. But the formation of pus may be prevented, in some instances, by the

* Chronic Diseases, vol. i., p. 194.

administration of medicine, by which the inflammation will be subdued, and consequently suppuration prevented.

Emphysema, or a collection of air within the pleura, may be caused by wounds of the lungs, fractures of the ribs, and penetrating wounds of the chest. According to Hastings,* "There is absence of respiratory murmur upon the affected side, where it is caused by wound of the lungs, with an exceedingly clear sound on percussion, with immobility of the ribs; in the sound side there is *puerile respiration*. Where the injury is dependent upon the bursting of an abscess, a *metallic tinkling* is audible, and upon directing the patient to cough, a drop of fluid falls from the orifice in the lung and drops to the bottom of the chest with this peculiar sound; or if the chest be shaken, the fluid can be heard to splash."

If from the collection of air suffocation is threatened, and medicinal treatment prove of no avail, the same operation as is recommended for empyema and hydrothorax may be performed.

Section 2.—Injuries of the Chest.

In wounds of the lungs great danger is to be apprehended from inflammation, suppuration, or hemorrhage. The patient generally experiences, when afflicted with such injury, great dyspnœa, with a sense of suffocation. Arterial blood, mixed occasionally with clots, is expectorated, or if the wound be extensive, there may be profuse hemorrhage from the mouth. Inflammation always supervenes, and unless the abnormal process be prevented, profuse suppuration, hectic, and debility result.

Treatment.—If the external opening be large, and the lung protrude, it should be returned by gentle pressure, and retained within the cavity by means of bandages and compresses. It is

---

* Practice of Surgery, p. 248.

very important that the latter be moistened with a solution of *arnica*, as by such application bleeding may be restrained, inflammation prevented, and the healing process advanced; the internal administration of the same medicine, perhaps in alternation with *aconite*, if the fever be intense, would materially assist in accomplishing the same favorable result.

If the intercostal artery has been wounded, it must be ligated, even though extension of incision be necessary. If extraneous matter have lodged within the lung or surrounding textures, it should be gently removed, otherwise profuse suppuration may follow, and the patient be destroyed. Secondary hemorrhage may be arrested by means of the internal administration of *aconite, arnica, crocus, diadema, phosphorus*, and in some instances *bryonia;* the latter particularly is applicable, when, together with the cough, there is expectoration of blood-streaked mucus, with stitching or sticking pains, especially when the pleura is also attacked by the inflammatory process. *Phosphorus* is an important medicine, when, after granulation has commenced, there is threatened inflammation of the parenchyma of the lung, with prostration, and dullness on percussion.

The external wound should be closed with lint, plaster, and bandage, the patient kept perfectly quiet in a well ventilated apartment, and all causes of excitement studiously avoided.

In *simple contusion* a bandage should be placed around the chest, *arnica* administered internally and externally, and inflammation of the contents of the thorax combated by those means already adverted to.

CHAPTER XXXIII.

INJURIES AND DISEASES OF THE ABDOMEN.

Section 1.—*Wounds of the Abdominal Viscera.*

Wounds *of the abdominal viscera* have generally been considered as perilous as those of other parts of the body; the danger, however, must obviously depend on the organ that is wounded, and the extent of the injury inflicted. Superficial wounds of the abdominal muscles, or their integuments, are seldom of much consequence, and should be treated according to common principles. When the wound is penetrating and extends deeply into the cavity, the peritoneum is involved. Inflammation of this membrane constitutes the chief source of danger in all wounds of the abdomen. But though this membrane is so liable to inflammatory action, cases have occurred in which balls, swords, or bayonets have passed entirely through the abdomen, transfixing the peritoneum, and several convolutions of intestine, without proving fatal, and giving rise to but few untoward symptoms.

The most certain sign that an intestine is wounded, is a discharge of blood from the anus, or of fæces, bile, or food from the wound; the absence of such signs, however, is no proof that the viscera are intact.

Wounds of the duodenum are much more dangerous than those of the larger intestines, as there is greater difficulty in nourishing the patient, and more risk of effusion.

Wounds of the stomach may be known by the seat of injury, great depression, vomiting of blood, and by the matter that escapes. In wounds of the intestines, fæces sometimes are extravasated into the peritoneal sac, giving rise to excruciating pain. In these wounds, the danger always is imminent.

Wounds of the substance of the liver are almost certainly fatal, from the great vascularity of the organ. From slight injury of this viscus, patients, however, often recover.

Wounds of the kidneys may be suspected from the position

and direction of the injury, and a discharge of bloody urine; this accident is dangerous from three causes—hemorrhage, inflammation, and profuse and continued suppuration.

Treatment of wounds of the abdomen.—When the surgeon is called upon to treat a wound of the abdomen, probing should be dispensed with as much as possible—such examinations made thoughtlessly, are productive of great mischief. If an intestine protrude, it should be replaced; or, if this is impracticable on account of the distension of the gut with flatus, etc., a dose of *nux-vomica* should be prescribed; or, if there is considerable vomiting, and cold, clammy skin, and great prostration, a dose or two of *veratrum* in alternation with the *nux.* When the distension abates, and vomiting and other symptoms are relieved, the intestine should be returned, and the lips of the wound brought together and retained by adhesive straps. If, from the extent of the injury, straps are not sufficient, a suture may be required, although it is better, if possible, to avoid its use.

If there is no solution of continuity of the external parietes, and the peritoneum has sustained injury from external violence, *arnica* should be prescribed internally, and at the same time a diluted tincture of the medicine should be externally applied. If either from blows or from wounds the symptoms of peritoneal inflammation arise—which are, painful tension and tumefaction of the abdomen, with excessive sensibility to touch, and frequently ischuria and constipation—*aconite, bell., bry.* should be employed, in accordance with the presenting symptoms. *Nux-vom.* is the proper medicine when there is painful sensibility and distension of the abdomen, with vomiting and other symptoms of gastric derangement, together with ischuria.

Mercurius should be employed when there is quick, weak pulse, nocturnal sweats, and prostration.

When the features are collapsed, and there is rapid sinking of the vital energies, and if the inflammation appear to have extended to the upper portion of the alimentary canal, with vomiting of blackish matter, *arsenicum* is plainly indicated; in other instances, *carbo.-veg.* is equally demanded.

If the kidney is the seat of injury, the wound should be treated in accordance with principles already laid down; and the inflammation of the gland combated with the means employed in the treatment of nephritis.

If the intestine or part of the stomach that protrudes from the wound is divided, it is recommended by surgeons to sew up the wound with a fine needle and silk; in the performance of which, care should be taken to bring the edges together in such a manner, that the two surfaces of the outer or serous membrane be opposed to each other, as adhesion does not take place between mucous surfaces.

An *artificial anus* not unfrequently follows gunshot wounds of the intestines; or it may be the sequence of a penetrating wound, an abscess, or ulceration. "In all examples of this description I have seen," writes Dr. Gibson,* "spontaneous cures have taken place, after the contents of the bowels have been discharged, for several weeks, through the fistulous opening."

The consequences of artificial anus are both dangerous and revolting—dangerous, since the patient may suffer from inanition; revolting, from the constant escape of fecal matter and flatus.

The principal medicines in this affection are, *calcarea, causticum, phosph., silic.*, and *sulph.*

When, as a consequence of wound or contusion, *abscess of the abdominal parietes* takes place, the location of the secreted matter is generally between the layers of tissues constituting the walls of the abdomen. In the first stages of this affection a hard and painful tumor is observed, which increases in size, becomes softer, and, in some instances, fluctuation may be distinctly felt.

Treatment.—If the surgeon is aware that suppuration may ensue in the abdominal parietes, by properly directed treatment, as previously mentioned,† the tumor may be discussed; if, how-

---

* Institutes and Practice of Surgery, vol. i., p. 185.

† Chapter ix., p. 146.

ever, suppuration is the result of a wound, a free incision should be made as soon as possible; indeed, some surgeons recommend that an opening be made with a knife in the most prominent part of the tumor, before the inflammatory process terminates in suppuration, and thus avoid the great danger of the contents of the abscess being emptied into the cavity of the abdomen, and often as a further result, ulceration of the intestines.

Section 2.—Tumors of the Abdomen.

Tumors of the abdominal parietes demand great attention, lest by their enlargement they extend to the deeper layers and involve the peritoneum. Tumors composed of adipose tissue are more frequently found in this locality than in any other, and in the generality of instances are easily removed by the knife.

Ovarian tumors are more frequently met with than any other within the cavity of the abdomen, and though generally cystic, may be of compact structure. In the commencement of the disease there is a sensation of pressure and heaviness experienced at the junction of the horizontal ramus of the pubic bone and the crest of the ilium, with a sensation of numbness in the affected side; a tumor is then observed, which gradually increases, and the patient experiences a sensation as if a globular or cold body were falling from one side of the abdomen to the other. By an examination, per vaginam, fluctuation can be perceived, and the uterus is felt pushed to the opposite side.

Treatment.—If the inflammation of the ovaries is attended with a high degree of fever, *aconite* is necessary. When there is induration of the ovaries, with ulceration, *bell.*, *china*, *canth.*, *calc.-carb.*, and *platina* have been found more or less successful. When the ovaries are swollen from inflammation, which has been caused by excessive venery or onanism, *china*, *nux-vom.*, or *staphys.* should be employed. Platina is an excellent medicine when there is considerable pain, which is of a bruised character, and when there is a continual irritation of the internal genitals, accompanied with nymphomania.

Ambra., *canth.*, *puls.*, and *antim.-crud.* are also recommended for the treatment of ovarian induration and inflammation. There is a medicine that has lately been proved, which exercises a powerful influence upon the ovaries, particularly when the tumor formed is of a cystic character; this is *apis mellifica.* Under its use, we have known an ovarian tumor, of years' standing, to have entirely *disappeared;* and appended to the proving of the medicine can be found several interesting cases of ovarian disease successfully treated. The doses of this medicine should not be too frequently repeated, aggravation instead of amelioration thereby being produced.

Other medicines for ovarian dropsy are *ars.*, *prunus*, *iod.*, *sulph.*, *hell.*, *graph.*, *hepar*, *silex.*, &c.

In many instances, however, these medicines only produce a palliation of the symptoms, and the operation of tapping must be resorted to. It is performed in the same manner and with the same instruments as will be mentioned when treating of ascites.

Section 3.—*Ascites.*

By ascites is understood a dropsical effusion in the cavity of the peritoneum; it may be complicated with hydrothorax, or general anasarca. Dypsnœa, cough, dryness of the skin, diminished secretion of urine, loss of appetite, constipation of the bowels, and prostration of strength, are symptoms which are generally present in the commencement of the affection; these are succeeded by general fullness of the abdomen, and by a sense of fluctuation easily recognized by percussion, which should be performed by pressing one hand on the side of the abdomen, and striking it with the other.

The causes of ascites generally are disease of the viscera of the abdomen, particularly of the liver, pancreas, spleen, &c. In some instances, a very large amount of fluid collects in the cavity of the peritoneum.

The prognosis in this affection depends upon the nature of

the case, and the age and temperament of the patient. When combined with organic disease of the abdominal viscera, or when occurring in individuals of a sickly constitution, or in persons of advanced age, apprehensions may be entertained of an unfavorable termination.

Treatment.—The principal medicines in the treatment of ascites, are *ars.*, *bry.*, *china*, *hell.*, *ledum*, *lyc.*, *merc.-sol.*, *sulph.*

In some instances, in the first stages of the disease, *aconite* is useful to allay vascular excitement; after which *hellebore* should be prescribed, if there is a tendency to torpor, prostration, extremely scanty secretion of urine, with shooting pains in the extremities.

Arsenicum is indicated when there is extreme debility, and in cases connected with organic affection of the abdominal or thoracic organs; when the patient emaciates, and there is stiffness and immobility of the limbs, with aggravation of the sufferings at night.

China should be employed when the disease can be traced to losses of the animal fluids; when there is paleness of the skin, short cough, with expectoration.

If there is excessive nausea, palpitation of the heart, &c., *digitalis* should be employed. A dingy and livid complexion points to *ferr.-acet.*

Mercurius is the appropriate medicine, when there is disorganization of the abdominal glandular system, with occasional paroxysms of pain, &c.

Other medicines are *euphorb.*, *solanum*, *kali-carb.*, *conium*, *sulph.*, *iod.*, *zincum*, *apocy-cann.*, *ol. tereb.*

The operation of *paracentesis abdominis* is frequently called for in the advanced stages of the disease, to palliate the sufferings of the patient. It is performed in the following manner:

The patient is seated on the side of the bed, or on a chair—the bladder having been previously evacuated—and a broad bandage placed around the abdomen in the following manner: its middle should be on the anterior wall of the abdomen, and its ends should be of sufficient length to be brought around the body and firmly held by an assistant. In the centre of this band, in the lower part of the abdomen, and directly opposite the linea alba, an opening should be made, sufficiently large to admit of the introduction of the trocar, which with its canula should be thrust through the abdominal parietes at the point aforesaid, in an oblique direction; and, after it has pierced through the integuments, the trocar should be withdrawn, allowing the canula to remain, through which the fluid generally passes in a continued stream. If the intestine or omentum obstructs the passage of the fluid, it should be gently removed by the introduction of a probe through the canula; and if, after a considerable portion of the water has been withdrawn, the stream lessens, the bandage may be tightened by traction made upon its extremities, which compressing the abdominal parietes, forces out the remaining fluid.

Care, however, is necessary in the performance of this operation, that the evacuation of the abnormal secretion be not too speedily effected, lest the patient, already somewhat debilitated by the evacuation of so large an amount of fluid, incur great risk from extreme prostration; indeed, in most instances, when the water has been withdrawn slowly, towards the end of the operation a feeling of faintness is experienced, to relieve which, a small quantity of brandy and water is required, after which *china* and *arsenicum* may be administered.

CHAPTER XXIV.

HERNIA—RUPTURE.

By the term hernia is understood a protrusion from within an internal cavity, of part of the contents of that cavity. But the term is usually limited to the most frequent form of such protrusion, namely, that from the cavity of the abdomen; and of this hernia there are varieties, according to the site of protrusion.

They are designated as inguinal and ventro-inguinal, femoral, umbilical, phrenic, perineal, vaginal, labial, obturatorial, ischiatic.

They vary according to the anatomical relation of their parts, as, for example, congenital, infantile; and again, according to the parts protruded, as enterocele, if the intestine alone be displaced; if the omentum, epiplocele; and if both, entero-epiplocele; and further, other varieties depend on the pathological condition of parts—reducible, irreducible, incarcerated, and strangulated.*

The causes of hernia are predisposing and exciting: among these may be mentioned, severe exercise on foot or on horseback, lifting heavy weights, playing on wind instruments, long continued exertion of the abdominal muscles, natural want of closeness of development of the abdominal parietes, costiveness, strictures of the urethra, hooping cough, parturition, &c.

In consequence of laceration, or separation of fibres, the disease may occur suddenly; or the protrusion may appear and gradually increase, where the tendons are naturally weak or deficient.

Hernia, ordinarily, is a soft tumor,† situated at one of the abdominal openings, which enlarges upon coughing and exertion of the abdominal muscles; if the protrusion be intestine, it may be returned to the abdominal cavity by pressure, retiring with a gurgling sound. But hernia may be mistaken for other diseases; it is necessary, therefore, to use much care in diagnosis. *Hydrocele* simulates hernia, but differs from it in being more or less translucent. Hernia is almost invariably opaque; the only exception being in case of descent of a large fold of intestine, distended alone by gas, and covered by thin integument. In hydrocele the tumor is constant, and undiminished by pressure; hernia is always varying more or less in size, and can generally be made to disappear by pressure. In hydrocele, a part of the cord can be felt distinct from the tumor, at its

* Miller's Practice of Surgery, p. 386.

† Hastings' Practice of Surgery, p. 263.

apex; in hernia, the cord is never distinctly felt in any part. Hydrocele, unless congenital, does not enlarge upon or feel the impulse of coughing, or exertion of the muscles of the abdomen. In hydrocele, the testicle can scarcely be felt, if at all; in hernia, it can be felt distinct and separate from the tumor, at the lower part of the scrotum. The history of the two diseases differs also: the hernial tumor appears suddenly, is developed above, and descends; hydrocele forms gradually, and is developed from below upwards. But these two diseases sometimes coëxist. In *hydrocele of the cord*, the tumor is circumscribed, leaving a portion of the cord clearly to be felt above and below the tumor, and has most of the other distinguishing signs of hydrocele. But when that portion of the cord within the inguinal canal is the site of such serous effusion, the difficulty of diagnosis is great, for the tumor may be made to disappear upon pressure. *Cirsocele* may be distinguished from hernia by the non-reducibility of the swelling, and its characteristic form, which is like a bunch of earth-worms. Yet it is like hernia, in diminishing during recumbency and under pressure; the tumor returns upon assuming the erect posture, even though the abdominal ring may be closed by pressure of the thumb. But when the enlarged veins occupy the upper part of the cord and inguinal canal, with an accumulation of serum, the diagnosis is extremely difficult.

The enlargement of the veins of the cord often facilitate hernial protrusion. *Bubo*, from its history, from the sensation detected by the fingers, and progress of development, differs essentially from hernia; but there may be enlargement of the inguinal glands occurring at the same time, with either femoral or inguinal protrusion.

Descent of the testicle, in some cases, being unusually late, may be arrested in the inguinal canal, thus causing a painful swelling, presenting appearances somewhat similar to those of hernia; but a distinction may be drawn by the absence of the testicle from the scrotum, and by the characteristic pain produced by pressure. From *sarcocele* hernia may be ascertained by the history of the disease, its negative signs when coughing, and freedom of the cord, except in some cases of malignant disease. *Psoas abscess*, though simulating femoral hernia, may be known by the history of the case, by evidences of spinal disease, by the distinct fluctuation in the swelling, and by the site of the abscess, which is generally exterior to that of hernial protrusion. *Varix of the femoral vein*, when projecting through the saphenic opening, may be mistaken for femoral hernia, but correct diagnosis may be arrived at by placing the patient in the recumbent posture, and having reduced the tumor by pressure, allow him to rise: If the case be one of hernia, the pressure prevents a return of the tumor, but if it be varix the swelling quickly reappears.

*Reducible** hernia may be distinguished from other varieties of the disease by the following symptoms: The tumor descends in the erect, and retires within the abdomen during the recumbent position, or when pressure is made upon it. If the sac should contain intestine, a peculiar rumbling or gurgling noise will be heard, both by the surgeon and patient, at the moment the gut slips into the abdomen. The tumor also of hernia possesses a tense, elastic feel. Omentum, on the contrary, communicates to the finger a doughy sensation, and is with greater difficulty restored to the abdomen. Besides these indications, a reducible hernia may be recognized from other diseases by the circumstance of its being larger after a meal than when the stomach and intestines are empty, and by an impulse being communicated from the tumor to the surgeon's finger when the patient is directed to cough. If suffered to increase, a reducible hernia may in time become enormously large, and the patient not only experiences great disorder of the digestive organs, but he is always liable to a strangulation of the gut.

By an *irreducible* hernia is understood a protrusion of the gut which cannot be reduced, and is permanently fixed in the extra-abdominal position. This state of things may be caused† 1. By adhesion of the sac, on its external aspect, to the parts

* Vide Gibson's Institutes and Practice of Surgery, vol. ii., p. 369.

† Miller's Practice of Surgery, p. 361.

into which it has been protruded; and by adhesion of its internal surface to the hernial contents. 2. By the nature of the protrusion, which may become too large to repass the orifice through which it has emerged, and by displacement of the subadjacent areolar tissue. 3. By contraction of the abdominal cavity.

Irreducible herniæ are of course exposed to all the consequences of external injury and violence;* hence various cases are recorded,† in which the protruded bowel has been ruptured by blows, falls, &c.

The symptoms of *strangulated* hernia are, in the majority of instances, so well expressed as to allow of easy recognition; yet it occasionally happens that the disease is confounded with *ileus* and other intestinal affections. According to Pott,‡ the swelling in the groin or scrotum resists the impression of the fingers; if the hernia be of the intestinal variety, it is generally painful to the touch, and the pain is increased by coughing, sneezing, or standing upright. These are the very first symptoms, which, if not relieved, are soon followed by others, viz.: sickness of the stomach, frequent retching, stoppage of alvine discharges per rectum, frequent, hard pulse, fever, &c. After a time the tumor becomes harder and more tender to the touch, the pulse more frequent, the peritoneum inflames, and the abdomen becomes extremely tender to pressure. If the strangulation be not relieved, vomiting of bile, mixed sometimes with fæces, occurs, the tumor inflames upon its surface, hiccup sets in, and the patient is covered with a cold perspiration. As the last stage approaches, pain ceases, and in some instances the spirits of the patient are heightened, and he entertains hopes of recovery; however, ulceration and gangrene of the protruded intestine take place, and death soon follows.

An *incarcerated hernia* is one in which the protruded portions of the abdominal contents are retained in their abnormal situation, without strangulation or the occurrence of the inflam-

* Lawrence on Ruptures.

† Vide Sir A. Cooper on Hernia, Part II. Scarpa on Ruptures, p. 310.

‡ Pott on Ruptures.

matory process. Generation of gases, accumulation of fluid and solid contents, &c., &c., may prevent reduction.

General Treatment of Hernia.—For reducible hernia an appropriate truss should, as soon as possible, be applied. The best method of fitting a patient with a truss, according to Dr. Gibson,* is to try a number of instruments, and select the one that most readily adapts itself to the abdominal and pelvic inequalities; of course such an one will be worn with the least inconvenience. Many of the great variety of trusses that are at present offered to the public, by those who have made the subject a particular study, are well adapted to retain the protruded intestines within the parietes of the abdomen. A well-contrived truss should, as has been already observed, fit accurately to those parts of the body to which it is applied, should cause no inconvenience by unequal pressure, and in addition should, by its lightness, no way impede the motions of the wearer.

It is in the treatment of strangulated and incarcerated hernia that homœopathy has been found to possess powerful remedial action. By the judicious employment of a few of its medicines, the knife may be in many instances dispensed with, and the peril which in all instances attaches to the operation need not be encountered. Mr. Yeldham writes†—"But although the superiority of the homœopathic treatment of hernia, as distinguishing it from that of the old school, will be found to reside chiefly in its power of preventing those accessory symptoms on which the danger of the displacement depends, its influence will not stop here. A careful survey of the allopathic mode of treating strangulated hernia, together with the results of homœopathic experience, limited though it be, warrant us in asserting that many cases, now submitted to the knife, would yield to a more rational and scientific management. In contemplating the teachings of the allopathic school on this subject, one is struck with the want of precision in their rules of pro-

---

* Gibson's Institutes and Practice of Surgery, vol. ii., p. 374.

† British Journal of Homœopathy, vol. viii., p. 309.

cedure. They appear to be constantly wavering between the fear, on the one hand, of operating too early, and therefore unnecessarily, and on the other, the danger of a too protracted and often fatal delay."

Mr. Yeldham further remarks*—"Putting out of the question division of the stricture by the bistoury, I cannot but consider the allopathic mode of treating strangulated hernia in other respects as highly unscientific and objectionable. In order to overcome the tension of the stricture, and relieve the swelling and congestion of the strictured part, it is customary to bleed the patient in the arm, put him into a warm bath, give anodynes, &c. . . . . If they succeed, all well and good; but supposing, as too frequently happens, that the result is not so fortunate, and that after all the knife is the only alternative, in what a condition does it find the patient! what front can he oppose to the dangers of a hazardous operation? Previous to those operations that admit of delay, it is customary to place the patient under a preparatory course of medical and dietetic treatment, in order to bring the system into as favorable a state as possible, to bear the shock of the operation, to meet successfully any untoward accident that may attend upon or result from it, and to carry on afterwards the process of reparation. The urgent nature of strangulated hernia precludes the possibility of this salutary preparation; but that, surely, is no reason why the unhappy condition of the patient should be rendered still more hopeless by the adoption of such measures as may effectually rob him of his best and only prospect of safety! This is the rock on which the allopathist splits—his weak point in the treatment of hernia.

The medicines that are best adapted to the treatment of hernia are, *aconite*, *nux-vom.*, *sulph.-ac.*, *opium*, and *lycopod.*; and in some instances *ars.*, *rhus.*, *sulph.*, and *veratrum*.

Aconite should be employed when there is inflammation of the affected part, with excessive sensibility to the touch, accompanied by considerable fever, and quick, hard, full pulse; it is also indicated when there is bilious vomiting, cold and

* Loc. cit.

clammy sweat, and violent burning pain in the abdomen; the dose should be repeated every half hour until symptoms of amelioration present themselves, after which the intervals of repetition should be considerably lengthened.

Nux-vomica, for its specific action, is however the most important medicine in the treatment of this morbid condition, and is to be preferred when respiration is laborious and oppressed, when the tumor is sensitive to pressure, but not in so great a degree as when *aconite* is called for; when there is bitter vomiting, and when the strangulation has been occasioned from errors in diet, or exposure to cold.

Perhaps the safer method of treatment in the generality of instances—unless the particular indications for the administration of a single medicine are very prominent—would be to exhibit *aconite* and *nux* in alternation.

According to Hartmann *sulph.-ac.* is a specific not only for certain cases of hernia, but also for the chronic diathesis which leads to intestinal protrusion.

If the above medicines do not produce the desired effect, and there is cold, moist skin, coldness of the extremities and profuse vomiting, *veratrum* should be administered; and if after a few doses of this medicine relief is not procured, and there is vomiting even of fæcal matter, with hard distended abdomen, and a somewhat comatose condition, *opium* may be exhibited.

Dr. Laurie, in his Homœopathic Practice of Physic,* has inserted some very practical remarks of M. Traub, on the homœopathic treatment of incarcerated hernia. The latter gentleman from his own experience, recommends most highly *nux-vom.*, *sulph.-ac.*, *lyc.*, *bell.*; and moreover remarks concerning *aconite*, that although it does not offer in the series of symptoms that it is capable of producing, those which accompany the formation and incarceration of a hernia, yet it cannot be dispensed with as an appropriate or intermediate auxiliary remedy, in certain forms of incarcerated ruptures, on account of the unlimited influence which it exercises upon the vascular, and chiefly upon

* Page 503.

the capillary system; and accordingly not only comprises among its symptoms the type of inflammatory fever, but also the type of acute local inflammation. Further, on account of its effects upon the mind, which manifest themselves particularly in the form of inconsolable anguish, forebodings of death, and great disposition to be frighted—states of mind which we not unfrequently meet with in persons affected with incarcerated hernia. M. Traub also mentions *three* varieties of incarceration.

In the *first*, the rupture is of recent occurrence; or one that had formerly existed, has suddenly become incarcerated; in which case the rupture is small, and the symptoms appear suddenly and with great intensity. They consist in a pinching or squeezing and pressive sensation in the region of the rupture; violent dragging pain with periodical tearing, and spasmodic constriction in the abdomen; nausea, inclination to vomit, and actual vomiting of an acrid mucus; obstruction, with frequent inclination for stool. Most of these symptoms are increased by the slightest pressure on the rupture, as also by movement. *Nux-vom.* corresponds with the symptoms of this form of incarceration, and according to the above authority, a dose consisting of ten or fifteen globules of one of the higher potencies, frequently ameliorates the symptoms; if, at the same time that relief is afforded, a sensation of movement takes place in the rupture, or if a gurgling noise be heard, a remission of the incarcerating muscular contraction, and a speedy replacement, without external treatment, may be expected. Should this not be the case, but, on the contrary, the sufferings return again with unabated vigor; or if an oppressive soreness or pain, as if from a wound, and a violent burning prevail in the region of the rupture, and the superincumbent integuments become very sensitive to the slightest touch; or if the heat in the affected parts increase, and thus betoken an increased determination of blood to those parts; or should the incarceration have been preceded by a fright, or some other mental affection, and the patient be in a state of general irritation or excitement, *aconite* should be administered; and an hour afterwards, *nux-vom.* (in a lower dilution than in the first instance) should be had recourse to.

The *second* variety of incarceration generally appears somewhat suddenly, and the rupture is small; there is a tearing, dragging pain, which is often the most prominent symptom, and is experienced both in the rupture itself and in the whole abdomen; there are also fugitive stitches in the region of the hernia, and the symptoms return periodically—disappearing almost entirely for a time. The patient is much exhausted during the remissions, he complains of a general sensation of cold; the abdomen is much distended by flatus; and after a continued desire to vomit, the patient eventually throws off an acrid tasting fluid. There is also a very urgent inclination for stool, but no evacuation takes place.

In this form of incarceration, likewise, *nux-vom.* is an excellent medicine; but *lyc.* vies with it in efficacy. According to Traub, these may be administered in alternation. If, however, the symptoms appear in a crural rupture; if the patient is a female; and if, moreover, the individual is of a mild, yielding disposition, *lyc.* is to preferred. If throbbing, burning, and other symptoms, indicating *acon.*, become predominant, of course that medicine should be administered.

The *third* form of incarceration occurs chiefly in aged persons, and in ruptures of long standing, and generally appears insiduously. It betrays itself at first by a distressing, pinching, and constrictive sensation in the region of the rupture, by uneasiness and fullness in the abdomen, and by periodical sickness and constipation. The hernia is not very painful to the touch, and the incarcerated part is not so tense and hard as in the two preceding forms, but feels more doughy. This strangulation may exist for days, without any perceptible increase in the concomitant symptoms; gradually, however, twitchings and pinchings, combined with periodic, transitory, tearing pains, supervene in the abdomen and groin. The sickness then becomes more lasting; a sweetish, saline, or bitter fluid is sometimes eructated; and is not unfrequently followed by vomiting of a watery fluid, and subsequently of ingesta.

With this form also two medicines concur, and the one is again *nux-vom.*, which competes here with *sulph.-acid* for the rank of preëminence. If the patient is of a sanguineo-choleric temperament, which, however, is but seldom the case, *nux*, in a low dilution, may be administered; and, should the removal of the incarceration not be effected in twelve hours, *sulph.-ac.* must be exhibited.

The operations for the different varieties of hernia will be mentioned in the following sections:

Among the means, however, to remedy strangulated or incarcerated hernia which present themselves, the taxis stands prominently forward as so natural a mechanical means for overcoming a mechanical difficulty, that it should at once be attempted.

By taxis is understood the endeavor to reduce a hernia by the hands.* The operation consists in varied endeavors to return the protruded intestine to its natural position within the abdomen. The patient is generally placed in a recumbent posture. When the case is an inguinal or femoral hernia, the pelvis should be placed higher than the shoulders, and, if possible, the patient should avoid straining, coughing, and every exertion of the abdominal muscles.

Mr. Lawrence, concerning the treatment of ruptures, has written some applicable remarks, which are here inserted at length.

"The position of the patient must also be regulated with a view to the opening, through which the parts have descended. Hence, in inguinal and crural hernia, the thigh should be bent and rolled inwards, in order to relax the tendon of the external oblique muscle. It is also recommended to elevate the shoulders slightly, as well as the pelvis. This brings the trunk into a curved state, and completely relaxes the abdominal muscles. Since the position now described is the most favorable to the return of the protruded parts, it should be continued, as nearly as circumstances will admit, until the rupture is replaced. When things are thus prepared, the surgeon begins his attempt by a gentle pressure on the tumor, which may be gradually in-

* Vide Dorsey's Elements of Surgery, vol. ii., p. 57.

creased, but should not be carried to such an extent as to cause pain. Violence cannot indeed be beneficial, as it is more likely to press the parts in a mass against the ring, and thereby bruise and injure them, than to urge them through the opening. Numerous instances are recorded, in which this unscientific roughness has produced the most injurious consequences. Suppuration of the omentum, and gangrene or rupture of the intestine, have been its more immediate or remote consequences; and the danger of the subsequent operation must be greatly increased, if the attempts at reduction are ineffectual.

"We usually grasp the tumor with one hand, while the other is placed at the aperture, where it may be employed in facilitating the entrance of the parts, and in keeping up those which have already been returned. Success will often be obtained by exerting a general pressure on the whole surface of the swelling; in which method both hands must be employed, in order to subject the entire tumor to the action of the force. This method is strongly recommended by Petit.

"The pressure should be exerted according to the course in which the parts have been protruded. Thus the contents of a bubonocele pass obliquely downwards and inwards; those of a femoral rupture downwards, and then forwards; yet we should not confine ourselves entirely to such a kind of pressure as the course of the hernia would suggest, but in failure of those attempts, make other trials in different directions. The following manœuvre will sometimes succeed in a bubonocele or scrotal hernia, after the more ordinary methods have failed, particularly in cases where the strangulation seems to have been caused by an accumulation of fæcal matter. Let the surgeon embrace the neck of the swelling, close to the tendon, with the finger and thumb of one hand, and carry them down with a moderate pressure, so as to remove the contents from the portion next to the ring; this will reduce the size of that part, which he may then attempt to pass into the ring with the other hand. Indeed, since the obstacle exists at the mouth of the sac, reduction will in general be more easily effected by pressing the upper part of the tumor towards the ring, than by exerting a general pressure over the whole swelling.

"The return of a piece of intestine is generally preceded by a peculiar noise, caused by the passage of air through the strictured part. It recedes at first gradually, and then slips up suddenly. The omentum goes up slowly to the very last portion, which must be actually pushed through the opening."

If the taxis should not succeed at first, it may often be successfully repeated after the exhibition of *nux-vom.*

Section 1.—*Varieties of Hernia.*

By *inguinal hernia* is understood that variety of protrusion of intestine, which passes through one or both abdominal rings. There are six investing tunics to an inguinal hernia. 1st. The integument. 2d. Superficial fascia, composed of several layers. 3d. The intercolumnar fascia. 4th. Cremaster muscle. 5th. Fascia propria. 6th. The hernial sac.

There are several varieties of inguinal hernia, viz.: *oblique, direct, congenital,* and *encysted;* of these, the *oblique* is of most frequent occurrence. It follows the course of the spermatic cord, and commences at the internal abdominal ring, passes into the inguinal canal, where it receives the name of *bubonocele;* and, continuing its course, passes through the external abdominal ring, and descends to the *labium* in the female, constituting *labial hernia;* and into the scrotum of the male (see fig. 91), when it is termed *oscheocele,* or *scrotal hernia.*

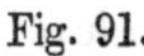
Fig. 91.

Direct or *ventro-inguinal* hernia is not covered by the cremaster muscle, because the protrusion does not follow the course of the spermatic cord, but passes through the tendons of the internal oblique and transversalis muscles, opposite the external abdominal ring. Sometimes the tendon is not ruptured, but merely distended and pushed along in front of the gut, thus becoming one of the investing fasciæ of the hernia. In this variety of rupture, the epigastric artery is upon the outer side of the neck of the sac.

Congenital hernia occurs soon after birth. At this time the intestine or omentum passes out of the abdomen, accompanies the testicle in its descent, and becomes lodged in the pouch of peritoneum which forms the tunica vaginalis testis, before its communication with the general peritoneal cavity has become obliterated. The sac of this hernia is therefore formed by the tunica vaginalis, having all the other coverings of the oblique variety.

Encysted, or *hernia infantilis*, is a variety of the congenital, but is more complicated than the latter, because it has as it were two sacs. The communication between the cavity of the tunica vaginalis and that of the abdomen is closed at its upper part; but the former is unusually large, and continues high on the cord, containing more or less serous fluid. Behind this a hernia descends, invested by the ordinary peritoneal sac.

Femoral or crural hernia.—At the point where the femoral vessels emerge from the abdomen, the mouth of their sheath is wide and loose, and a space is left between them and the os pubis; this is the *femoral ring;* and through this aperture the intestine protrudes in crural hernia. (See Fig. 92.)

It has the os pubis behind, Gimbernat's ligament on the inner side, the femoral vein exteriorly, and Poupart's ligament in front. To prevent the ready descent of the intestine into the femoral ring, the latter is filled with loose fibrous tissue enclosing lymphatic glands. When, therefore, the protrusion takes place, this fibrous lamina is forced before the intestine along the crural canal, forming one of the coverings of the hernial sac, and has received the name of *septum crurale.*

The crural canal, therefore, is merely the sheath of the femoral vessels, derived from the fasciæ lining the anterior and posterior parietes of the lower abdomen. When, therefore, the hernial tumor reaches the termination of the crural canal, in the fossa ovalis, its further descent is prevented; and the dis-

Fig. 92.

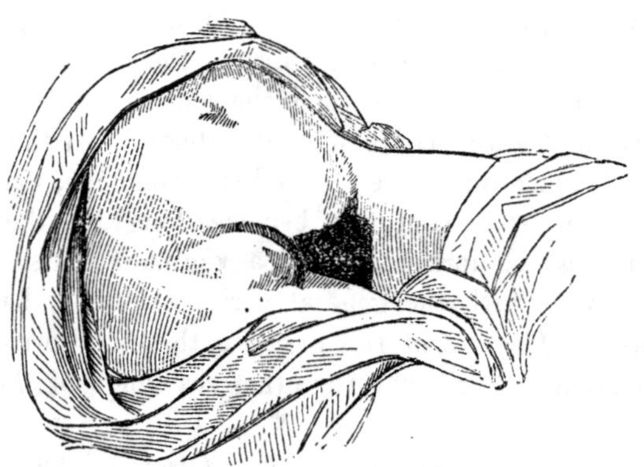

tended sac is found to consist of the following layers: 1. The skin. 2. The superficial fascia. 3. The cribriform fascia. 4. The sheath of the vessels. 5. The septum crurale; and 6. The peritoneal sac.

Crural hernia may be distinguished from psoas abscess by the latter being generally more external, by its yielding a sensation of fluctuation, not being tympanitic, and generally accompanied by disease of the spine. Bubo, and other tumors of the groin, sometimes simulate crural hernia, but they may be recognized by not being accompanied with general disturbance of the abdomen. If, however, with swelling, &c. symptoms of strangulation are present, the tumor may be cut down upon, and its true character ascertained.

Umbilical hernia is a protrusion of the intestine at or near the umbilicus, and generally occurs in infants, and females who have borne children.

In *obturator hernia* the gut passes through the obturator foramen. *Ischiatic hernia* protrudes through the ischiatic notch.

By *ventral hernia* is understood the passage of the intestine through the parietes of the abdomen, at other points than those already mentioned.

Perineal, vaginal, labial or *pudendal hernia,* are of comparatively rare occurrence. Their names designate the parts into which the intestine protrudes.

When there is a separation or rupture of the fibres of the diaphragm, occasioned by a fall, or blow upon the abdomen, through the fissure a hernia may protrude into the cavity of the thorax. The term *diaphragmatic hernia* designates such condition.

Section 2.—Operations for Hernia.

In strangulated oblique inguinal hernia,* the most frequent form of the disease, the operation consists in placing the patient on his back, upon a convenient bed or table, with his thighs separated and flexed, his feet resting upon chairs. The surgeon places himself between the thighs of the patient; then picking up the skin over the hernial tumor between his fingers, making a fold of it, he passes a scalpel through the base of this fold and cuts upwards, managing the integuments and knife in such a way, that by this means he will have made an incision about three inches, or at most, four inches, long. No case of hernia, however large, requires a longer incision. This incision should have its upper edge at the neck of the tumor, and extend down on the body of the hernia. (See dotted line in fig. 93.) This is an excellent rule for division of the integuments in most operations, and should always be adopted where there is not good reason for omitting it, since it divides in an instant the skin and subcutaneous cellular tissue. This being done, we come to the superficial fascia, which should be pinched up by the forceps, and a small transverse cut made through it by the scalpel, into which the grooved director must be passed and carried along in the direction of the first incision; the point of the scalpel then carried along the director divides the fascia; the cremaster muscle and fascia propria are to be treated in the same way; the sac then appears, and this is to be managed the same as the fascia, using great caution not to take up the omen-

---

* The above methods of operating for strangulated inguinal and femoral hernia are taken from Hastings' Practice of Surgery.

Fig. 93.

tum or intestine in the forceps along with it. When the sac is divided, a quantity of fluid sometimes escapes. At this stage of the operation, we have the intestine, or the omentum, or both before us. The intestine should be examined well to see that it is sound, before being returned to the abdomen; if mortified points or spots be found upon its surface, or if it have been wounded by the knife, these spots should be included in a ligature, both ends of which must be cut short off, and the intestine returned in this way to the abdomen. These ligatures are soon enclosed by deposit of fibrin, and they gradually ulcerate through into the canal, and are discharged per anum in the form of loops, whilst the intestine is repaired from without by the organized fibrin deposit. If the intestine be completely mortified, (which is the case when the operation has been too long delayed,) then it cannot be returned, and it is necessary to form an *artificial anus*. For this purpose it will be necessary to relieve the stricture and retain the intestines at the groin, at the same time administering *hepar.*, *merc.*, or *silic.* to favor separation of the mortified part. This may afterwards be cured either by Dupuytren's or Dr. Physick's operation. The former consists in the application of the *enterotome*, a peculiar forcep, constructed for the occasion. With this the two sides of the intestine, which lie together, are pinched, and the instrument left until by ulceration it comes away, or sufficient irritation has been excited by it. Dr. Physick's plan has been considered preferable. This consists in passing a ligature, by means of an armed needle, through the contiguous sides of the intestines as they lie side by side. The ligature should be passed at least an inch from the extremities of the intestines, and then tied rather loosely, otherwise great pain will be occasioned; after about three weeks, the ligature has ulcerated out, the sides of the intestines are fast glued by adhesion, and the fæces pass per anum. A compress and truss are applied to the opening in the groin, and *caust.*, *calc.*, *phosph.* or *silic.* exhibited to promote the healing process, which however, in the generality of cases, is somewhat protracted.

If, however, upon examination the gut be found healthy, (which will be known by its color being natural, or darkened but slightly,) then the forefinger must be carried up between the sac and the intestine to discover the seat of the stricture; which will be in one of three spots: these are the neck of the *hernial sac*, the *external abdominal ring*, or the *internal ring*. The same exploration serves to discover whether it is an *oblique* or *direct* inguinal hernia, by finding the situation of the epigastric artery, which in the former lies inside of the neck of the sac, in the latter it is on the outside of it, and can readily be felt pulsating. In old inguinal hernias, this is often the only means we have of telling which of the two forms it is.

Having ascertained the point of stricture, all is ready for the insertion of the knife. This should be a probe-pointed bistoury, (Fig. 94,) or scalpel, having only about half an inch of cutting edge, commencing near the point. The ordinary probe, or

Fig. 94.

blunt-pointed knife, may be covered by a bandage from the heel down, leaving only half an inch of cutting edge exposed.

While the nail of the forefinger of the left hand is kept under the point of stricture, (Fig. 95,) push the knife, with its side

Fig. 95.

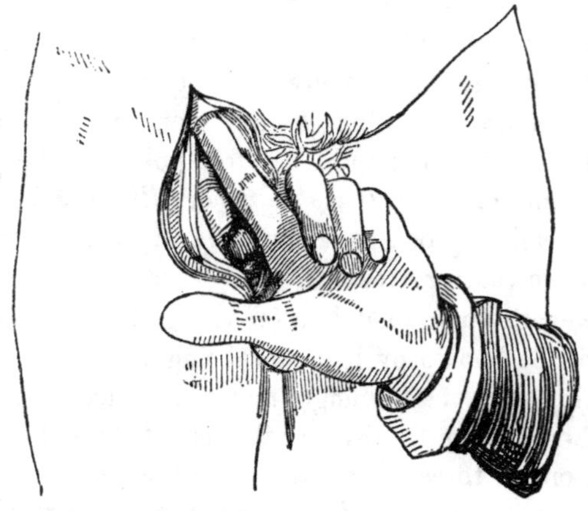

lying on the finger, (Fig. 96,) along it, until it is introduced into the neck of the sac under the stricture. When the edge is

Fig. 96.

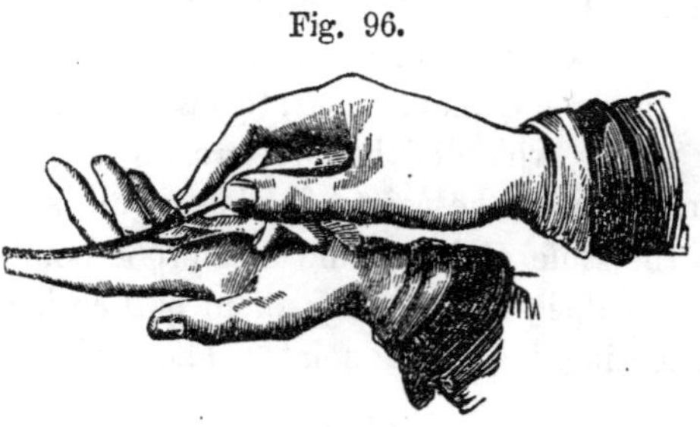

under this point, it should be turned directly upwards, and a slight incision made; it rarely ever requires more than a slight touch of the edge of the knife, against the tightened band which strangles the intestine, to suffice for its liberation. The stricture removed, the intestine and omentum must be carefully returned to the cavity of the abdomen, the wound brought together by adhesive straps, and *dil. tinctæ arnicæ* applied during the cure. Absolute rest is demanded, and the administration of a tepid water enema must prevent constipation. After the part has healed, a proper truss must be applied.

In the operation for *direct inguinal hernia*, the only difference is in the number of tunics covering the hernial sac; this variety being deficient in the coating of the cremaster muscle. But any numerical arrangement of tunics in these operations must always lead to disappointment and perplexity, if they be expected and looked for. In old hernia, for instance, the fasciæ are all thickened and increased, so that no certain number of coverings can be found shutting in a hernial tumor; therefore, the only good rule for operation in this disease is to proceed carefully, dividing everything that intervenes between the operator and the hernial sac (which can always be recognized from the superincumbent tissues); this gained, all uncertainty is at an end.

In *femoral hernia*, Sir Astley Cooper operates by making an incision in the form of an inverted ⊥. Mr. Liston makes an incision parallel to and directly over Poupart's ligament; from the centre of this an incision is carried down over the tumor; the length and manner of incision being the same as in the former case.

Other surgeons employ, with equal propriety, a perpendicular incision directly over the tumor, beginning at Poupart's ligament: this makes a smaller external wound, and as the only object is to approach the strictured point, the smaller the opening necessary to accomplish this object, the better.

The integuments being divided by either of these incisions, the superficial fascia must then be raised and divided as already described; we next come to the fascia propria, which must be raised in like manner, and the hernial sac is brought into view. This, as well as its contents, must be treated in the manner directed for inguinal hernia.

The point of stricture in femoral hernia may either be the *neck of the sac*, the *cribriform fascia*, the *falciform process of the fascia femoris*, the *femoral ring*, or *Hey's* or *Gimbermat's ligament*. The latter is most frequently the seat of stricture. After the place of stricture has been correctly ascertained, the forefinger of the left hand is thrust into the neck of the sac and the stricture, and the same operation performed as has been mentioned for inguinal hernia.

The mechanical treatment of *umbilical hernia* of children is as follows:* The protrusion is returned within the abdomen, and compression is made by means of a conical pad—such as a piece of cork, covered with wadding or soft leather—which is made to occupy the space usually filled by the protrusion, and is retained in its place by strips of adhesive plaster; the integument is closed over it in a fold; and the whole may be secured by a circular bandage. This simple contrivance is more effectual than any truss or belt, being much less likely to slip; and it has the equally important advantage of not acting as an excitant of protrusion elsewhere. In the adult the case is not so easily managed. The tumor is larger and less repressible. A corresponding compress is necessary, secured either by a belt or by the spring of a truss; its use is merely palliative. When strangulation occurs relief is obtained in the ordinary manner, either by recourse to medicine, the taxis, or operation.

The other varieties of hernia that have been mentioned are of very rare occurrence, but the principles of treatment are the same.

CHAPTER XXXV.

DISEASES OF THE RECTUM.

Section 1.—*Prolapsus Ani.*

A PROTRUSION of a portion of the rectum, or of its internal coat, from the anus, is denominated a prolapsus, or procidentia ani. In some cases a considerable portion of the rectum protrudes.

---

* Miller's Practice of Surgery, p. 409.

The causes of the complaint are such as tend to weaken the action of the muscles which support the intestine, and violent exertions of the rectum in consequence of certain irritations. The frequent use of cathartics, especially those which contain aloes—the presence of ascarides in the lower portion of the alimentary canal—habitual costiveness, and hæmorrhoids, all occasionally produce prolapsus ani. Cases are on record in which the affection was engendered by the tenesmus attending dysentery.

In some instances the intestine remains a considerable length of time unreduced without any ill consequences, but more commonly it swells and inflames very speedily.

Treatment.—When called to a person suffering from a prolapsed rectum, the surgeon should immediately attempt reduction. This is readily accomplished by grasping the displaced gut, having first smeared the protruded part with fresh lard or simple cerate, and pressing upon it inwards and upwards. It will slowly, or in some instances quickly, return to its natural position. If a larger portion have escaped, as sometimes happens, especially in females rather advanced in life, a smooth towel folded cone-like, and well greased, must be placed against the central and most dependent part, and pressure then made firmly and steadily upwards—from time to time it may be necessary also to press inwards and upwards upon the circumference of the intestine. If, however, the surgeon be not called until the protruded intestine is swollen and painful, an immediate attempt at reduction may prove abortive; therefore a dose of *ignatia* or *nux-vomica* should be administered, and the patient placed at perfect rest. These medicines, possessing a powerful influence over the intestinal canal, will probably relieve the patient in a short time, when the part may be returned to its normal condition, in the manner above mentioned. The vapor of hot water retards rather than facilitates reduction. This complaint is, unfortunately, very apt to recur; to prevent which the proper means should be used—among which are, that the patient be strictly prohibited overloading his stomach, and that his diet should consist of the plainest aliment. Dr.

Physick succeeded in completely curing some cases of prolapsus ani, by confining his patients exclusively to a diet of rye mush and sugar; and the same means have proved equally beneficial in the hands of other practitioners.

There have been many bandages and contrivances invented to prevent the recurrence of prolapsus ani, but they generally fail in accomplishing the desired end, which latter is much more certainly attained by the administration of appropriate medicines, and rigid dietetic observances.

The principal medicaments are, *ign.*, *nux-vom.*, *merc.*, *sulph.*, or *ars.*, *calc.*, *lyc.*, *rut.*, *sepia.*

For the particular symptoms indicating a choice of the above, the Materia Medica must be consulted.

Section 2.—Hæmorrhoids.

Hæmorrhoids, or piles, according to Druitt,* are small tumors situated near the anus. They commence as varicose enlargements of some of the hæmorrhoidal veins, the irritation of which causes various morbid changes in the mucous membrane and cellular tissue adjoining. The general division of hæmorrhoids is into internal and external; the former are firm tumors, varying in size, of a reddish-brown color when indolent, but dark or bright red when inflamed; great inconvenience is occasioned by their protrusion, which slight movement is liable to induce, and they are exceedingly liable to bleed. The external are hard tumors at the margin of the anus, covered with skin and mucous membrane, or are formed of oblong ridges of skin external to the sphincter; these do not bleed, and from this circumstance are termed mariscæ, or blind piles.

Piles when indolent produce no great inconvenience, except that resulting from their bulk and situation; when inflamed, however, they occasion pain, heat, itching, fullness and tension

* Modern Surgery, p. 447.

about the anus, with sensation as if a foreign body were in the rectum, with more or less bleeding. In violent cases irritation of the bladder, frequent micturition, pain in the back, and aching in the loins, are also experienced.

Treatment.—The medicines that are best adapted to the treatment of this affection are as follows:

Aconite, though not a specific, is exceedingly useful when the hæmorrhoidal tumors are highly congested or inflamed, giving rise to symptoms of general vascular excitement; after which the most appropriate medicine should be administered. The most efficient medicine in the treatment of either variety of piles is *nux-vomica*, particularly in individuals leading a sedentary life, when there is shooting, burning, and itching in the tumors, bruised pain in the loins, difficult urination, constipation, colic, and other symptoms of gastric disturbance.

Arsenicum should be employed when there is itching and burning in the tumors, with stinging pain in the day time, particularly when walking.

Belladonna when there are sudden lancinations in the rectum, pain in the back, and difficulty in voiding urine.

Lycopodium when the hæmorrhoidal affection is chronic, attended with congestion to the head, constipation, painful protrusion, and acrid discharge; palpitation of the heart during digestion.

Pulsatilla when there are discharges of blood and mucus, accompanied with smarting and sense of excoriation.

Causticum when there are large and painful tumors, with stinging and burning and excessive itching of the anus day and night.

Platina when there is frequent inclination to go to stool, creeping, itching and piercing in the anus, succeeded by general shuddering, and a feeling of weakness in the abdomen.

Antim.-crud. discharge of blood and mucus at every stool, followed by severe colic, burning at the anus, and acrid discharge, particularly at night.

If the hæmorrhoids are attended with excessive colic, *colocynth* is an excellent medicine. *Sulphur* may follow the administration of *nux; hepar,* and *belladonna* symptoms often present; *rhus* is useful after the latter, to relieve the severe aching in the back.

Other very important remedial agents are, *cap., calc.-carb., chin., merc., ipecac.,* &c.

Section 3.—*Fistula in Ano.*

When an abscess forms in the cellular membrane surrounding the rectum, or about the verge of the anus, and leaves, after its contents are discharged, one or more small openings communicating with its cavity, the disease is denominated fistula in ano. Other appellations have also been employed, expressive of the particular situation of the fistulous orifice and the extent of the disease.

If the fistula opens upon the surface of the integument, it is called an *external* fistula; if it communicates with the rectum, and not with the integuments, an *internal* fistula; and if the sinus open internally through the rectum and externally through the skin, a *complete* fistula.

The formation of a fistula in ano is often denoted by rigors, painful swelling about the ischium or perinæum, difficulty of passing urine, and by irritation in the rectum and neck of the bladder. During the progress of the disease, the patient in many instances suffers extremely; at other times, however, the abscess forms and breaks almost without his being aware of its existence. Generally the abscess communicates with the integuments by a single opening, but occasionally there are three or four.

In healthy constitutions the abscess does not differ from that met with in other parts of the cellular tissue, but in consumptive and scrofulous subjects the disease often assumes a different character. The surface of the integuments is covered with an erysipelatous inflammation, the constitutional symptoms are considerable, the matter is discharged in small quantity, and from a sloughy, ill-conditioned opening, or from a ragged, unhealthy surface.

The cause of fistula in ano cannot be always satisfactorily ascertained. Sometimes it arises from irritation about the rectum; from local injury; from the lodgment of undissolved articles of food taken into the stomach, and passed through the intestine as far as the rectum (for example, small bones of fish or fowls); severe and long-continued exercise, particularly on horseback; hæmorrhoids, &c.

Treatment.—When the inflammation is erysipelatous, and spreads rapidly, *bell.* or *rhus* may be prescribed. *Silic.* is a very important medicine, not only in the commencement of the affection, but also when the fistula is fully established. In the former case, if the abscess has not discharged, and the cellular membrane be found in the sloughy state, a free incision should be made, to permit the escape of the purulent secretion. If healthy action does not display itself, *ars.* and *china* must be prescribed.

Merc., *sulph.*, *silic.*, *hepar*, or *calc.-carb.* must be exhibited, if incarnation proceed imperfectly. If the constitution of the patient is impaired before operation is thought of, appropriate medicines must be administered, to eradicate any disease that may be present. In cases where the fistula has not been subjected to homœopathic treatment from the commencement, *merc.* or *silic.* may be given. *Hepar* may be required after *merc.*, when the fistula is extensive; and *phosph.* after *silic.*, where there is complication with disease of the lungs. When the digestive apparatus is impaired, *calc.*, *nux*, *merc.*, and *silic.* will prove valuable medicines.

Caust. is very important in cases of long standing, and in alternation with *silic.* we have known a fistula in ano to be healed.

If, however, after a patient trial of the means above mentioned, the disease remain unchanged, recourse must be had to the knife, as a last resort. The operation must be performed in the following manner: The patient being placed upon his face and knees, the pelvis elevated, with the thighs separated — or upon his back, with the thighs separated and flexed upon the abdomen—the surgeon, oiling the forefinger of the left hand, passes it up the rectum; a narrow probe-pointed scalpel or bistoury (see fig. 97) is passed up the fistula,

Fig. 97.

until it comes in contact with the finger. If the intestine be not perforated by the disease, the surgeon must make an opening into it by the edge of the knife, and pass it into the cavity of the intestine; the end of the finger is then firmly fixed upon the probe point of the knife, and by drawing both outwards, the sphincter muscle and all the intervening tissues are divided.

A better and easier mode of performing the operation, is by passing a grooved director through the fistula, against or into the intestine. Then pass into the rectum a smooth, round stick, resembling a rectum bougie, the size of the thumb; the stick having a groove on one side as wide as the finger. This being passed up and held firmly by an assistant, the surgeon takes the director, already introduced, and impinges its extremity firmly against the groove in the stick. He now takes a sharp-pointed knife, and runs it forcibly down the groove in the director, and when it comes in contact with the rectum stick, cuts outwardly against this, and thus divides the fistula at one sweep. This operation is performed in a shorter time than the one previously mentioned, with much less pain to the patient, and greater convenience to the surgeon.

Many of the French surgeons, after dividing the fistula, dissect out its walls—thus cutting out a tube of the indurated soft parts.

In whatever way the operation is performed, after the fistula is divided, lint is to be pushed into the wound, to insure its closing from the bottom by granulations; which, as the healing process progresses, push the lint before them. The patient must be kept at rest; and, if there be any constitutional excitement, it may be allayed by *aconite* and *bella.* in alternation, after which *silicea* and *sulphur* may be exhibited, to hasten granulation.

There is one point that should not be overlooked in this operation. When passing a probe into the fistula, the instrument should be carefully used, lest it perforate the walls of the sinus, and pass into the cellular texture of the perineum. Deep cutting in this region may be productive of the most serious results; and, as the cure of the disease does not call for any such risk, it should never be encountered. The service required of the knife, is the division of the sphincter muscle; and, to accomplish this object, an incision an inch, or an inch and a half, in depth, is all-sufficient, and should never be exceeded.

Section 4.—Tumors within the Rectum—Stricture of the Rectum—Fissures of the Anus—Pruritus Ani.

Tumors within the Rectum.—Various abnormal growths have been found within the rectum, and according to their bulk, or specific character, excite more or less irritation, inflammation, diarrhœa, &c. There are cases on record* of enormous tumors of the lower intestine, involving the whole circle of the anus, and extending beyond it many inches.

Treatment.—The best medicines for such tumors are *caust.*, *conium*, *calc.-carb.*, *lyc.*, *phos.*, *sepia*, *sulph.* and *thuja*; others, however, may be employed according to the presenting symptoms; when these fail, resort may be had to an operation.

If the tumor originate by a narrow pedicle, and admits of motion, it may be pulled down by the forceps, and a ligature applied to its neck. If, however, the abnormal formation is large, it should be drawn down as low as possible with the for-

* Vide Mr. John Bell's Principles of Surgery, vol. iii., p. 188.

ceps, and several needles armed with ligatures must be passed through its base, and their ends firmly tied; circulation thus being arrested, sloughing will result.

Stricture of the Rectum.—The rectum is sometimes the seat of stricture, which may be either spasmodic or permanent; the former is caused, in many instances, by improper or unwholesome articles of food taken into the stomach, which passing undigested through the alimentary canal, excite irritation, which gives rise to the spasm. Permanent stricture generally originates from chronic inflammation of the lining membrane of the intestine, causing thickening and contraction of the part or deposit of sub-mucous cellular tissue. In these diseases there is great pain and difficulty in voiding the fæces, which are passed in narrow flattened fragments, or if fluid, are ejected with considerable force. The stricture may be felt in some instances per anum, by the finger; in others, however, when the stricture is higher up, an instrument must be used. The digestive organs become impaired, dilatation takes place above the seat of stricture, which may result in ulceration of the intestine; in such cases prognosis is exceedingly unfavorable.

Treatment.—In spasmodic stricture *nux vom.* is the principal remedy, and will often relieve the affection if the patient observe the strictest dietetic rules. *Arsenicum*, *bell.*, *hyos.*, *sulph.-ac.*, and *verat.*, may also be called for.

In permanent stricture *ars.*, *bell.*, *canth.*, *colch.*, *ignatia*, *nux-vom.*, *lyc.*, *merc.*, *sulph.* may be indicated, and together with the administration of the most appropriate, the bougie must be employed. The instrument should be soft and at first introduced once in three or four days, and allowed to remain as long as the patient is able to bear it. After a time a larger sized bougie should be used, and introduced more frequently; in some instances, where there is great constriction and the smaller sized bougies cannot be introduced with facility, it is necessary to divide the stricture with a probe-pointed bistoury, passed into the intestine upon the forefinger.

Fissures and Ulcers of the Anus.—The verge of the anus and the mucous coat of the bowel are often the seat of fissures which are exceedingly troublesome, and arise from a chap or other trivial cause. Persons afflicted with dyspepsia are often subject to this troublesome disorder.

Treatment.—The medicines that relieve the patient most speedily, are *graphites* and *nitric acid;* indeed, we have known fissures that have resisted other treatment for a considerable time, yield readily to the action of these remedial agents, especially the latter.

Dr. Perry* has written a valuable article on this subject, and the following are the results of his experience: The chief medicines for this painful affection are *nit.-ac.* and *ignatia;* next in order are *plumb.*, *sulph.*, *ars.*, *nat.-mur.*, *phos.*, and *sepia;* lastly, *caust.*, *sil.*, *nux-vom.*, *thuja.*, *tabac gratio.*, and *mez.; petrol.* is also an important medicine.

Itching of the anus is a very troublesome and inconvenient affection. Frequently it is an attendant upon verminous diseases, or in other cases it may be purely idiopathic. In most instances it is attended with other symptoms, as burning, tingling, &c.

Treatment.—All stimulating ointments, plasters, &c., should positively be prohibited, as in the generality of cases they aggravate rather than ameliorate the pruritus, or convert a simple into a troublesome and sometimes painful affection.

Where there is excessive itching of the anus, a few doses of *causticum* may entirely subdue this unpleasant symptom. If there is burning pain, *alumina* and *capsicum* frequently relieve it. When it occurs during the night, *iod.;* during stool, *terebinth*; after evacuation, *antim-tart.* or *strontia.* Burning, itching and smarting in the anus, is cured by *antim-crud.;* burning, itching, and tingling, by *colchicum;* and itching, smarting, soreness and burning, with sensation as if tumors would form, by *nit.-ac.* *Platina* is homœopathic when there is frequent creeping, with tenesmus, as if diarrhœa would set-in, particularly in the evening before going to sleep.

---

* Journal de la Société Gallicane, quoted by British Journal of Homœopathy, vol. viii., p. 541.

Kali-carb. relieves a stinging, tearing, and cutting, also an itching and burning in the anus. When there is itching, with sensation of contraction of the anus, *plumb.* For the itching dependent upon verminous affections the medicines adapted to those diseases of course should be employed.

CHAPTER XXXVI.

DISEASES OF THE TESTICLE AND PENIS.

Section 1.—*Hydrocele.*

The tunica vaginalis testis secretes, in its natural state, a limpid fluid, which lubricates its internal surface and that of the tunica albuginea ; and whenever this fluid, from any cause, is secreted in an undue proportion, it distends the tunica vaginalis, giving rise to a tumor of the scrotum, which is termed *hydrocele.*

Hydrocele is a disease of not infrequent occurrence ; it is incidental to the young as well as to the old ; though most commonly a local disorder, it is at times combined with a hydropic condition of the system. The causes which give rise to this disease are not well known.* It is probable that the accumulation is the result of excited action in the parts, for its origin is most frequently attributable to external injury—blows or bruises, followed by rapid swelling, which, after a time, subsides, leaving, perhaps, some enlargement of the testicle, or of the more superficial tissues, and succeeded by the gradual appearance of the disease in question. It is also owing sometimes to inflammation of the testis, and is frequently combined with stricture of the urethra, or local irritation along its course. Dr. Physick succeeded in curing a case of this disease by dilating

* See Liston's Elements of Surgery, p. 415.

the stricture with a bougie. When the communication between the cavity of the abdomen and the tunica vaginalis is not closed as it should be at the usual period of time, the fluid descends from the cavity of the abdomen into the cavity of the tunic, forming what is denominated a congenital hydrocele.

This affection is sometimes conjoined with sarcocele, or chronic enlargement; in which case it is termed hydro-sarcocele. It is very important to distinguish between these two diseases; and this distinction may be readily made, by attending to the following circumstances: In sarcocele, the tumor is oval and flattened; it may attain a considerable size, without, however, ascending so near to the external abdominal ring as does a large hydrocele. In sarcocele there is a space between the tumor and the abdominal ring, whereas, generally, there is none in a large hydrocele. The tumor may also be known by its weight and opacity. In hydrocele the swelling commences at the bottom and is generally confined to one side. At first the tumor is flaccid, and the testicle may readily be distinguished; but as it increases in size it becomes firm and incompressible, and the testicle can scarcely be felt. The swelling assumes a pyriform shape, the corrugations of the scrotum disappear, and the raphe is displaced to the opposite side; generally there is little or no pain or inflammation, and no alteration of color. When inflammation, however, precedes this disease, there is pain, swelling, and hardness. The swelling is translucent, and on placing a lighted candle on one side of the scrotum, the light can be discerned through it. In some cases, however, the tunica vaginalis becomes thicker and harder, the fluid is opaque and dark colored, thereby obstructing the passage of the rays of light. Under these circumstances there would be no transparency.

Sometimes an accumulation of fluid takes place in the tunica vaginalis of the spermatic cord, forming an *encysted hydrocele of the cord.* This variety occurs more frequently in children than in adults. The fluid is thin and clear, and contained in a distinct cyst, of a smooth, shining, serous appearance internally; this cyst may be either an unobliterated portion of the congenital spermatic structure, or composed of thickened and condensed cellular tissue, strengthened exteriorly by the expansion of the cremaster muscle. This variety of the disease may be confounded with hernia, from which it is very necessary to distinguish it. In hydrocele of the cord the accumulation takes place gradually, unattended with pain, and is always below the external abdominal ring. When the patient coughs there is no impetus communicated to the finger, and the tumor is not capable of being returned into the cavity of the abdomen; whilst in hernia, the swelling takes place suddenly, after some violent effort, attended with pain; and the peculiar impetus is communicated from the tumor when the patient coughs, and it may generally be returned by pressure into the abdomen. It sometimes happens, however, that both these affections coëxist in the same individual, and in such cases the diagnosis is very difficult.

Of itself, hydrocele is not a dangerous disease. Persons may have it for years, and yet be free from pain; but, if the swelling increase to a great size, pains in the spermatic cord and renal region may be experienced. On account of the enormous size of the effusion, the penis becomes much retracted, and sexual intercourse is rendered impossible. The discharge of urine may be interfered with, and the emission of semen is likewise impeded.

Treatment.—Hydrocele, especially that of children, is an affection very amenable to homœopathic remedies; and a full trial should be given to them, before resorting to an operation. The medicines which have proved most effectual in the treatment of this affection, are as follows: *calc.-carb., conium, dig., dulc., graph., iodium, merc.-sol., puls., rhod., sil., sulph.*

Of these, *calcarea* should chiefly be relied upon, where there is a scrofulous taint pervading the constitution, and the reproductive system is depressed, as indicated by loss of appetite, debility, emaciation, dryness of the skin.

Conium is particularly suitable, when the affection can be traced to mechanical injuries, contusions, &c.

Digitalis is useful, if there is a constant desire to pass water, and is particularly suitable when children are the subjects of the affection.

Dulcamara, when it arises from a cold, suppression of tetters, suppression of a momentary or habitual sweat by exposure to a draught of air, dampness, &c.

Iodium is a valuable remedy in hydrocele, and is particularly adapted to a general scrofulous taint, characterized by glandular swellings and emaciation.

Rhododendron has been highly recommended in this affection. In a case of several years' standing, where there was no disease of the testes or spermatic cord, it effected a permanent cure in a few months.

Graphites and *pulsatilla* are of the highest importance, and have the most marked symptoms of hydrocele in their pathogenesis.*

Should this treatment prove unavailing after a fair trial, an operation must be resorted to; which consists in withdrawing the serum, and injecting a stimulant fluid instead, whereby an acute congestion may be established, whose resolution, when complete, shall have the effect of restoring the normal balance between exhalation and absorption.

When this is contemplated, a round trocar and canula are to be used. The patient is placed in the erect posture, with the thighs separated; the surgeon then takes the scrotum and posterior part of the tumor in his left hand, rendering it tense and prominent in front; the instrument is then entered at the lower and anterior part of the tumor, passing obliquely upwards and backwards (see fig. 98), so as to avoid wounding the testicle, yet at the same time taking care that the obliquity is not such as endangers separation of the coverings of the sac, and non-entrance into the sac itself.

The stilet being withdrawn, the canula remains; this should

---

* For a very interesting account of hydrocele successfully treated by homœopathic medicines, and particularly concerning the action of *graphites* in this affection, see a paper by Dr. Black, in the British Journal of Homœopathy, vol. vii., p. 525.

be pushed well into the cavity. The serum having then been withdrawn, a caoutchouc bottle, with stop-cock and nozzle, is adapted to the canula—or a syringe may be employed, and the cavity partially filled with some stimulant fluid. Port wine undiluted, or two parts of wine to one of water, used to be much employed. Now, the favorite injection is iodine, in solution—one part of the tincture to three of water. Or, a small quantity of pure tincture of iodine having been thrown in, may be permitted to remain permanently in the sac, disappearing ultimately by absorption. If the dilute injection be used, three or four ounces are injected, and temporarily retained.

Fig. 98.

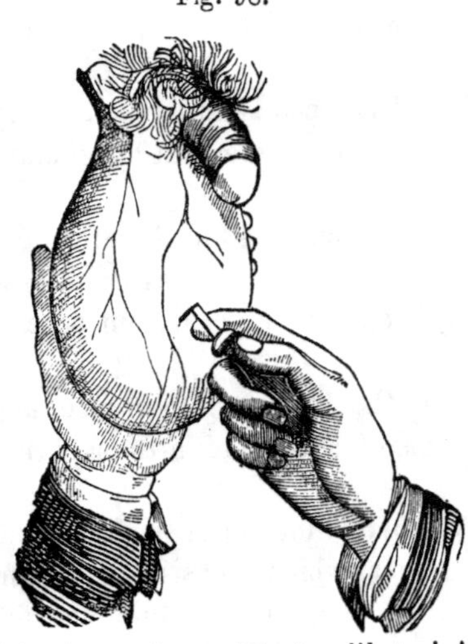

After waiting a few minutes, the patient will experience pain in the testicle, shooting up the cord into the loins, and a sensation of faintness will probably ensue. Then the fluid is allowed to drain away, and the patient is put to bed with the scrotum supported. In a few hours after the parts become much swollen, when *aconite* and *arnica* have to be administered; the swelling usually subsides in two or three days, when a cure may be anticipated.

Before injecting any stimulant, it is necessary that the surgeon satisfy himself that the point of the canula is fully within the cavity of the tunica vaginalis; otherwise the injection would pass into the areolar tissue of the scrotum, which would be followed by ulceration, sloughing, and severe constitutional disturbance.

Section 2.—Hæmatocele.

By this term is understood an accumulation of blood in one of three localities—the areolar tissue of the scrotum, the areolar tissue of the cord, and the tunica vaginalis. It may be either of spontaneous occurrence, or the consequence of external injury.

When it attacks the scrotum it is the result of a bruise or oblique wound; the scrotum becomes swollen, and assumes a blackish hue, like that of urinous infiltration; the swelling has a doughy feel, and at one or more points where the cells are broken down and much blood has collected, fluctuation is perceived more or less distinctly. Hæmatocele of the cord arises from the giving way of a spermatic vein, from external injury, or great bodily exertion, when extravasation into the areolar tissue will result, forming a tense, discolored tumor. Hæmatocele of the tunica vaginalis is the most common variety; and to it, in strict accuracy, the term may be limited. The blood is extravasated into the cavity of the tunica, and may be associated with hydrocele, from a wound of the testicle in tapping, or by a blow or other external injury, or by the spontaneous giving way of a blood vessel—a hydrocele may at any time be converted into hæmatocele, the diagnostic marks of hydrocele thereby being lost. The tumor suddenly increases in size, and is the seat of pain; and when handled is found heavier and less fluctuating than before. The blood, if in small quantity, becomes diffused in the serous fluid; when copious, a portion coagulates, and assumes the fibrinous arrangement. This, acting as a foreign substance, may excite inflammatory action; and suppuration may take place, with much increase of swelling and pain.

Treatment.—The treatment of this affection, when unconnected with hydrocele, is as follows: When the accompanying inflammation assumes a high grade, a few doses of *aconite* should be administered in the first instance; and when it results from a contusion, or any other mechanical injury, *arnica* or *conium* should be given internally, and applied to the affected parts as a lotion; *pulsatilla* also may prove availing in such cases; and *nux-vom.*, *rhus*, *sulph.*, or *zinc.*, may also be found efficient. The use of the knife is not necessary unless suppuration has unfortunately occurred. When the extravasation supervenes on hydrocele, and the medicines mentioned for that affection prove unavailing, simple tapping is in the first instance to be had recourse to. To inject then, however, would be productive of evil rather than good result. The fluid is allowed to collect again, and tapping is repeated, and when, after several withdrawals, the fluid is found once more to be of the same character as in simple hydrocele, then injection may be resorted to with safety, and with much probability of success—provided the testicle be sound. In confirmed cases, however, and more especially when suppuration is already threatened, the only means of obtaining a radical cure, is by free incision; laying the cavity fully open, turning out the coagula, and obtaining closure of the wound by granulation; care being taken during the performance of the operation, to avoid wounding the testicle.

Section 3.—Sarcocele.

Chronic inflammation of the testicle, or, as it is termed, *sarcocele*, may result from acute orchitis imperfectly resolved, or the action may be chronic from the commencement of the disease. It may be either primary or secondary, that is, it may occur as an independent affection, or as a concomitant result of gonorrhœa; it not unfrequently results from disease of the urethra, and in some instances the affection may be traced to syphilis. The tumefaction extends from the epididymis, which is usually the primary seat of the disorder, and gradually involves the whole testicle, which presents the appearance of an inelastic, uniform tumor, which is usually of an oval form, and seldom exceeds two or three times the bulk of the healthy gland. The accompanying uneasiness is slight, is more severe at night than during the day, and, as the disease advances, the characteristic sensibility of the organ to pressure is lost. Occasionally the disease, in its latter stages, is accompanied with a degree of effusion within the tunica vaginalis, constituting what is termed *hydro-sarcocele.* Upon examination more or less yellow solid lymph is found interspersed throughout the substance of the testicle, extending into the vas deferens, and, according to Mr. Curling, deposited in the tubuli semeniferi. By the smoothness and uniformity of the swelling, its gradual progress, and the absence of glandular enlargement, the affection may be distinguished from malignant disease of the testicle.

Treatment.—Rest and a recumbent posture are necessary in the first instance; and in a mild form of the disease, or at its commencement, resolution may be effected by means of the following medicines: *aurum, clematis, lycopodium, agnus castus, graphites, rhododendron,* and *sulphur.*

When the disease has a syphilitic origin, a careful investigation, and an accurate knowledge of the character of the syphilitic affection from its commencement, are required. *Calc.-carb., carbo-veg., aurum, kali-carb., lycopodium, spongia, merc.-sol., acid-nit., clematis, mezereum,* &c., are indicated in this form of the disease; but other medicines may be required. *Graphites, lycopodium, oleander,* and *belladonna,* are recommended if the disease is complicated with a general scrofulous condition, chronic eruptions, glandular enlargements, &c.

Where the tumor, in an advanced stage, gives evidence of the supervention of a malignant condition, *arsenicum, clematis, diadema, carbo-veg.,* and *thuja,* may possibly arrest the progress of the disorder, though in the majority of such instances, the use of the knife can scarcely be avoided.

Section 4.—*Varicocele.*

Varicocele, circocele, or spermatocele, express a varicose condition of the veins of the scrotum, or spermatic cord. Usually the latter is affected. It commonly commences close to the testis, and extends upwards towards the abdominal ring. It is caused by obstruction to the return of blood, the dependent nature of the part predisposing to the affection. Laborious and constant exercise in the upright position, constipation, corpulence, the wearing of tight belts, or trusses, tumors, or whatever affects the upward flow of blood, gives rise to the disease. It is much more frequently observed on the left than on the right side, in consequence of the spermatic vein of that side having a longer and more tortuous course, and consequently having to support a greater column of blood than that of the right, and its being much more liable to compression, by accumulation of fæcal matter in the sigmoid flexure of the colon. The affection is chiefly met with amongst young, vigorous, unmarried men, who have led exemplary lives. The whole of the cord appears to consist of knotty and tortuous veins, which feel like a bundle or congeries of earth-worms twisted upon each other; it is sensitive to the touch, creates a feeling of weight in the scrotum and loins, and often a degree of numbness in the thighs. It may be distinguished from hernia in the following manner: After the patient has been placed in a recumbent posture, and the swelling reduced by compression of the scrotum, the fingers are then pressed on the upper part of the abdominal ring, and the patient is directed to rise; if it be circocele, the swelling will reappear in increased size, from the obstruction offered by the pressure, to the return of blood; but if hernia be present, the recurrence of the tumor cannot take place so long as the pressure is continued.

Treatment.—The radical cure of this affection by means of homœopathic medicines is attended with much difficulty, and in many instances palliative relief is all that can be obtained. *Pulsatilla* and *arnica* are the most useful medicines; the treatment may be commenced with *puls.*, and the testes should be supported by means of a suspensory bandage, or bag truss, made of silk net-work. When the affection has been occasioned by a blow, or other external injury, or by pressure from the pad of a truss, *arnica* should be applied in the form of a lotion. *Nux-vom.* is suitable when constipation exists, and *puls.* is found inadequate; *sulphur* will sometimes prove useful after *nux;* and *arsenic* and *carbo-veg.* may be selected when burning pains are experienced in the tumor: *graph.*, *lyc.*, and *sepia* may also be found useful in some cases. But when the symptoms do not yield to these medicines, and the tumor is large and painful, and there is danger of the testicle becoming atrophied in consequence of the pressure, the varicose veins should be removed. These may be compressed by suture applied by needles passed beneath them, as in ordinary varix, care being taken to exclude the vas deferens and the spermatic artery. Obstruction of the duct is tantamount to castration, and obliteration of the artery can hardly fail to be followed by atrophy of the testicle. Professor Pancoast's operation consists in passing an armed needle behind the veins, excluding always the nerves and vas deferens; the needle is removed, leaving the ligature behind the veins; it is then passed, unarmed, through the same orifices in the scrotum, but in front of the spermatic veins; the loop of the ligature is then passed over one end of the needle, and over the other end the ligature is tied as tightly as possible, so as to completely strangulate the veins. The ligature may be removed in eleven days. Inflammation, consequent upon the performance of these operations, is to be combated by the appropriate medicines mentioned under the treatment of wounds.

Section 5.—Phimosis.

Phimosis signifies a preternatural constriction of the edge of the prepuce in front of the orifice of the urethra. The prepuce occupies its natural relative situation, but great difficulty is experienced in uncovering the glans, and frequently this is impossible.

There are two varieties of this affection, the *natural* or *congenital*, and the preternatural or acquired. The former exists at birth; but the latter may occur at any period of life, and is most frequently the result of an acute inflammatory process following external injury; or of the cicatrization of an ulcer or wound; or is sympathetic with gonorrhœa, balanitis, or venereal sores.

Congenital phimosis is by no means an uncommon affection, and will be met with in two or three varieties. Sometimes, though rarely, the prepuce is imperforate, and consequently the urine, not being emitted, collects between the glans and prepuce, forming a large bag or tumor.

Another variety is that in which an opening exists at the extremity of the prepuce, which, however, is not sufficiently large to allow the urine to escape with the same rapidity as it issues from the urethra; consequently it collects under the prepuce, and distending the latter to a great size, is then forced off gradually, in a fine stream and to a great distance. If the disease continues in this state for several years, pus, and even calculi, may collect within the cavity of the distended prepuce, keeping up a constant irritation.

In the majority of instances, however, there is no impediment to the flow of urine, and no extraordinary elongation of the prepuce, yet it is so closely contracted at its orifice as to prevent the exposure of the glans. This gives rise to many inconveniences. A whitish, sebaceous matter collects in large quantity between the glans and prepuce, exciting great irritation; and inflammation sometimes ensuing, adhesion takes place between the glans and prepuce, only to be relieved by painful dissection.

In after life, the præputial contraction may have the same effect as a tight stricture of the urethra; causing first irritability of the genito-urinary system, afterwards organic change, stricture of the urethra, alteration of the coats of the bladder, dilatation of the ureters, and finally renal disease. Should the patient, at an advanced age, have escaped these dangers, ulceration is apt to take place at the contracted part; or a cancerous condition may ensue, which, involving the glans and body of the penis, demands amputation; for in nine cases out of twelve in which Mr. Hey* had occasion to amputate the penis for cancerous disease, the patients were affected with natural phimosis. It is expedient, therefore, on many accounts, to remove this source of evil as early as possible.

Preternatural or acquired phimosis may be either acute or chronic. In the acute variety, the areolar tissue becomes infiltrated with serum; the swelling thus caused, prevents the glans from being uncovered in the usual way; and discharge accumulating, aggravates the disorder. The chronic form may result from gradual increase of original malformation, or, as before stated, may be occasioned by the cicatrization of a wound or ulcer.

Treatment.—In the acute variety of acquired phimosis the difficulty may be relieved by a well-directed homœopathic treatment; thus obviating the necessity of an operation.

The remedies most appropriate for this affection are as follows: *Acon.*, *arn.*, *bell.*, *bry.*, *calc.*, *camph.*, *cann.*, *canth.*, *caps.*, *cinnab.*, *hepar*, *merc.*, *rhus-t.*, *thuja*, *sepia*, *sulph.*, and *viola-tric.*

When the inflammation has been produced by constant friction, or any other mechanical cause, *arnica* should be employed both internally and in the form of a lotion. If, however, the inflammatory action should be very violent, a dose or two of *aconite* is advisable, to be followed by *arn.* If no beneficial effect appears to result from the use of the latter remedy, *calend.*, *rhus*, or *puls.*, may be administered. When the disease has been caused by uncleanliness, *aconite* should be employed, if there is a high degree of inflammatory action, to be followed by *merc.* or *sulph.* When the affection is accompanied with suppuration, *merc.*, *caps.*, or *hepar*, may effect a cure; and when induration of the affected part, and surrounding integument, supervenes, *sepia* and *sulphur* are the most appropriate medicines. When gangrene threatens, or when it has actually commenced, particularly if the disease is associated

* Practical Observations in Surgery.

with gonorrhœa, *ars.* is highly recommended.* When young children are the subjects of this affection, *acon.*, *merc.*, *calc.*, and *sulph.*, are most suitable. When this difficulty arises from syphilitic causes, the homœopathic remedies with which it should be treated are, *merc.-sol.*, *rhus-t.*, *thuja*, *cann.*, *cinnab.*, *sulph.*, and *viola-tric.* Balanorrhœa generally accompanies this variety of phimosis; indeed, some authors state this to be always the case; and when the above-mentioned remedies are insufficient to effect a cure, it may be necessary to make slight incisions into the prepuce, for the purpose of allowing the secreted pus to escape.†

The congenital and chronic variety of acquired phimosis, however, can seldom be relieved without recourse being had to an operation; which may be performed by several different methods.

When natural phimosis, existing at birth is complete, an immediate operation is required to save the patient's life; generally puncture with an ordinary lancet in the most prominent portion of the tumor, will be sufficient, as the stream of urine will afterwards prevent the closure of the wound.

When the orifice of the prepuce is not entirely closed, but merely contracted, a simple and very suitable method of operating is that recommended by Mr. Liston;‡ which consists in passing a grooved director, open at the end and well oiled, under the prepuce, alongside of the frænum, taking care that it is not passed into the urethra. A sharp-pointed knife is passed along the groove, and emerges at its extremity; then with one sweep the prepuce is divided. If the edge of the prepuce is thickened, it should be seized between the blades of the forceps, and be shaved off. Several fine sutures will now be necessary to prevent the separation of the integument and mucous membrane, in order that they may unite by adhesion.

In phimosis the stricture is caused by contraction and rigidity

---

* For an interesting account of several cases of this nature, effectually treated by *arsenicum*, vide British Journal of Homœopathy, vol. iv., p. 265.

† Gollmann's Diseases of the Urinary and Sexual Organs, p. 64.

‡ Elements of Surgery, p. 410.

of the internal membrane of the prepuce, the external portion consisting of cellular tissue and skin, remaining generally sufficiently loose and yielding. Hence the constriction may be relieved by dividing merely the internal lamina. This operation may be effected, in cases in which the phimosis is not very complete and rigid, by drawing back the external portion of the prepuce as far as practicable, until the tense ring of the inner prepuce, which forms the stricture, is exposed, and then dividing the latter with a bistoury or pair of scissors, at one or more points, sufficiently to permit of the free motion of the prepuce over the glans.*

Another very neat operation is that of Cullerier. It is applicable to those cases of phimosis, in which the integuments appear to be not much condensed or indurated; but in which the stricture is due chiefly to the more unyielding mucous membrane. The instrument employed is a pair of small straight scissors, of which one of the blades is terminated by a little button, like a probe-pointed bistoury. This blade is passed between the glans and prepuce, while the sharp-pointed blade is thrust into the substance of the prepuce, being separated from the other blade by the mucous membrane; the latter is then divided a sufficient length to allow the prepuce to be drawn back.† This operation has frequently been performed by Dr. Peace of this city.‡

Section 6.—*Paraphimosis.*

Paraphimosis is the reverse of phimosis—the prepuce becoming retracted behind the corona glandis, leaving the glans uncovered; the body of the organ is constricted by the tight præputial orifice, and gives rise to unpleasant and sometimes dangerous consequences. The superficial areolar tissue becomes greatly swollen on either side of the stricture, the glans

---

* South's Chelius, vol. 2. † Miller's Practice of Surgery, p. 587.

‡ For an interesting article on the Operation of Phimosis, vide Med. Chir. Rev., April 1851, p. 445.

also being involved in the tumefaction; and an acute inflammatory process is established under adverse circumstances, the strangulated parts being obviously ill provided with the power of resistance or control.

The disease may be either congenital or acquired, though the latter variety is by far the most common. It may be the result of a successful retraction of the prepuce, when the patient had previously been affected with phimosis; but it generally proceeds from inflammation, induced by a syphilitic or gonorrhœal disease. In some instances the swelling and constriction are so great, that mortification ensues, and the glans, or even the whole penis, may be lost; this, however, must be considered a comparatively rare termination. In neglected cases ulceration of the body of the penis may take place, perforating the urethra and producing urinary fistula.

Treatment.—In recent cases, before the swelling has attained any considerable size, reduction is generally practicable. The patient having been placed in a suitable position, and the parts well oiled, the surgeon grasps the glans with the fingers of the right hand, and makes steady pressure thereon, at the same time pushing it steadily from him; then, with the fingers of the left hand, he draws forward the constricting portion—the object being to push the glans, when diminished by pressure, through the narrow præputial orifice. If this should fail, and there is still no marked urgency, the penis should be placed in an erect position, and a stream of cold water poured on the glans for some time. This may have a happy effect in diminishing the bulk of the formerly turgid part, and it may be replaced within the prepuce without much difficulty.

For many of the symptoms connected with paraphimosis, *aconite*, *cannabis*, *sabina*, and *mercurius* are the most appropriate medicines; but, should these, together with the above mentioned means, fail, resort must be had to an operation, which may be performed by either of the following methods:

The tumefied parts are to be separated by the fingers, and the strictured band cut through with the sharp point of a knife, when the prepuce should immediately be drawn forward, so as to occupy its normal position; this operation is recommended by Mr. Hunter. That of Richter consists in raising a fold of the skin and cutting through it; a director is then pushed beneath the stricture, and the latter is divided by a sharp bistoury.

Section 7.—Cancer of the Penis.

Cancer of the penis is generally of the scirrhus, and very rarely of the encephaloid variety. The disease generally commences with the appearance of a small warty excrescence or pimple on the prepuce or glans. It almost always occurs in old persons, and may often be traced to the irritation consequent upon phimosis; commencing by ulceration at the præputial orifice, and from thence extending to the body of the penis. The glans becomes hardened and enlarged, ulcers of an irritable appearance penetrate it here and there, the lymphatics on the dorsum of the penis become swollen and indurated, the glands of the groin are generally involved, and the discharge from the sore is fetid and irritating. The disease follows the ordinary course of cancer, and, if not arrested, the patient dies—his end hastened probably by hemorrhage from the ulcer.

Treatment.—The medicines which have been mentioned for cancer in other parts of the body, may be used in this case; in a great majority of instances, however, amputation is the only resort, and this unfortunately is not always successful, as the disease reappears in the stump, or exhibits itself in the inguinal glands.

Ricord's method of amputating is preferable, being well calculated to obviate the difficulty generally attendant upon the operation—namely, tendency to contraction in the orifice of the urethra.

The procedure is conducted in the following manner:

The penis is put upon the stretch by the left hand, and lopped off at one cut, care being taken to leave integument sufficient to cover the corpora cavernosa; the surgeon then seizing the mucous membrane of the urethra by means of forceps, with a pair of scissors makes four slight incisions, so as to form four equal flaps; then using a fine needle armed with a silk ligature, he unites each flap of membrane to the skin by a suture. The wound heals by the first intention, adhesions form between the skin and mucous membrane (these textures becoming continuous), and the cicatrix, then contracting, tends to open the urethra. When micturition is difficult of accomplishment, in consequence of the shortness of the penis, the inconvenience may be obviated by allowing the patient to urinate through a funnel-shaped canula of sufficient length, placed against the pubes.

Section 8.—*Castration.*

This severe and painful mutilation is occasionally demanded, and may be performed in the following manner:

The scrotum and groin having been carefully shaved, and the patient placed in a recumbent position, the surgeon grasps the tumor behind, in order to render the skin tense. An incision is then made from the external abdominal ring, reaching to the bottom of the scrotum; or the scrotum may be gathered into a fold by the fingers, and transfixed at its base, when a suitable incision will be made by cutting directly outwards. The cord having been exposed, is separated from the surrounding textures, and entrusted to the firm grasp of an assistant, to prevent retraction within the abdominal aperture when divided; the bistoury is carried behind the cord, which is then cut across, and the operator seizing its lower portion draws it forward, and proceeds to dissect out the testicle—a dissection rendered comparatively painless and bloodless, by early section of the cord. The arteries should then be tied, and the wound kept open until all bleeding has ceased; the lower portion seldom healing otherwise than by granulation, need not be closely approximated. Care should be taken, during the operation, not to wound the septum, and thus expose the sound testicle.

The operation may be performed by first separating the testicle from its integuments, before dividing the cord; all fear of irrepressible hemorrhage by retraction of the vessels may be avoided, by dissecting up their cremaster envelope for a considerable distance towards the abdominal ring, and passing a ligature around them before severing the cord.

CHAPTER XXXVII.

DISEASES OF THE URETHRA AND BLADDER.

Section 1.—*Stricture of the Urethra.*

Stricture of the urethra is a complaint more frequently existing than is generally imagined. There are three varieties of the affection. 1. *Permanent* or *organic stricture*, in which the urethra is contracted and condensed from chronic inflammation. 2. *Spasmodic stricture*, arising from spasm of the muscular fibres which surround the membranous portion; and this is, in some instances, combined with a degree of true inflammation, constituting, 3. The *inflammatory stricture*.*

The symptoms of stricture are generally so well defined, that the diagnosis of the disease is as near as may be positive. In its commencement there is a slight uneasiness experienced along the canal, which is increased by urination, which leaves a tingling sensation; the water is not passed in a perfectly round or steady stream, but is more or less broken, diverging, or twisted. The inflammation sometimes extends to the bladder, when, of course, the symptoms of cystitis are present, as pain in the lumbar region, &c. These progress slowly but steadily, till micturition is extremely painful, the urine only emitted by drops, attended frequently with ardor urinæ.

---

* Druitt's Modern Surgery, p. 457.

Treatment.—For the above symptoms, or others which may be present, an appropriate medicine must be selected; which, although it may not be sufficient to cure the disease, will allay the more violent inflammatory symptoms, which would render hazardous the application of instruments.

One method of curing stricture is by dilatation; before commencing which, it is necessary to ascertain the seat of the obstruction. To accomplish this, some employ a silver catheter; others, a graduated bougie. Sir C. Bell recommends a ball-headed probe. Sir B. Brodie uses a full sized plastic bougie, which is to be softened by rubbing it in the hand, and well oiled and bent into the form of the urethra. There are also instruments made in a conical form, which are objectionable, for the reason, that when introduced to a certain extent, you are unable certainly to ascertain whether the pressure conveyed to the finger is caused by the stricture itself, or the larger portion of the instrument at the mouth of the urethra. The most general form of instrument now used by the best surgeons, is the gutta percha bougie; but, whatever be the instrument, as the obstacles to overcome are the same, the greatest caution should be used in its introduction.

The best method of ascertaining the seat of the stricture, after having selected a proper instrument, is to place the patient in a standing position, grasp the glans penis with the ring and little finger of the left hand, and by gentle traction place the penis in a horizontal position; then, having smeared well with oil, and holding the bougie as you would a pen, gently introduce it, by a slight rotary motion, until it reaches the prostate. When it reaches the stricture a sensation will be communicated to the hand, which should be a warning to proceed with increased gentleness.

There are several obstacles which may impede the course of the bougie, which it is necessary to mention. It may become entangled in one of the lacunæ, or in some accidental fold of the urethra. A small and soft instrument may bend, when pressed against the lower portion of the urethra; or its onward course may be arrested by a spasmodic contraction of the canal.

It is always the better plan to commence with small and soft bougies; for the stricture may be an old one, narrow and tortuous; and much additional suffering and danger thereby may be avoided.

Some surgeons recommend a fine catgut bougie—others, a gum catheter, curved and without the wire.

There is some disadvantage in using these pliable instruments, because, on pressure being exerted, they yield very easily; but a skillful hand can readily distinguish between the giving of the bougie or the narrowing of the canal. If a soft instrument cannot be introduced, recourse must be had to a metallic one.

Frequently the obstacle preventing the passage of the bougie arises from the vital action of the part; this may be overcome by steady pressure on the instrument, and care, as it passes down the urethra, that nothing is lacerated.

We can generally tell whether the bougie has entered the stricture, by endeavoring to withdraw the instrument. If it has passed into the contraction, there will be a resisting force.

There has been, by many surgeons, fault found with the term "dilatation" in reference to strictnres. It is argued, and justly too, if a stricture were merely a muscular contraction, then the term would be correct; but, as has been before shown, this is not the case—for there are organic changes which take place. The passage of the instrument modifies the vital properties of the part; while the pressure which it exercises on the newly organized parts induces a tendency to absorption, and gives a stimulus which enables nature to complete the cure.

The effects of the bougie, or, as it has been well termed, the "vital action," are visible from the commencement of the treatment. Hemorrhage is often experienced, and there is almost always a slight discharge.

But whatever be the kind of instrument employed, long experience has demonstrated, that, with certain exceptions, dilatation is the most safe and effectual method for relieving the distressing incidents which attend stricture of the urethra.

The mode of dilatation is not by any means to be disregarded. It may be conducted on different principles; it may be temporary or permanent; or these may be had recourse to in a gradual or rapid manner.

The size of the instrument, whether it be a plastic bougie or metallic sound, must be regulated by the presumed diameter of the contraction; and after having been selected, and introduced in the manner described, it must be allowed to remain for a certain time, and withdrawn at stated intervals. The object is to effect a regular and progressive dilatation of the strictured part, without inflicting any injury on the tissues, or exciting any severe irritation in the urethra. On the first introduction of the instrument it ought not to remain more than a few minutes in the urethra; if it has been borne well, it may be introduced on the following day, and so on, but the best practice is to introduce the bougie every third day at first, and then gradually shortening the intervals, increase the size of the instrument. All this, however, must be regulated by the effect produced upon the stream of urine, which indicates the progress of improvement.

Though dilatation is the safest and most certain, it is nevertheless a tedious method, and hence many surgeons have attempted to effect dilatation in a more speedy manner. This is done by first introducing a bougie of small calibre, quickly withdrawing it, and then passing others of larger size, until the patient complains of uneasiness or pain. The same operation is repeated every day or two. Larger instruments being gradually employed. By the adoption of this method obstinate strictures have been cured in five or six days.

Permanent dilatation, as its name implies, is effected by leaving the instrument permanently in the bladder. The treatment should commence by using a metallic bougie, which should be allowed to remain in the urethra, from twenty-four to forty-eight hours, and then withdrawn.

Temporary dilatation is the method most frequently employed, because it is generally the safest and best. Rapid dilatation may be attempted when the stricture yields readily, or when it is a matter of great moment to the patient to be speedily relieved.

In the treatment of permanent stricture, any disorder of the general health or of the genital organs must be corrected by the administration of appropriate medicines, after which the treatment by dilatation must be resorted to.

Puncturation, or division of the stricture by means of lanceted stilettes, has proved successful in some cases of long standing in which the stricture was in the anterior part of the urethra. If the stricture is situated far back the operation is dangerous and should not, unless under urgent circumstances, be attempted.

In cases of rupture of the urethra and extravasation of urine, the operation of *opening the urethra from the perineum* is necessary. The patient should be placed in a position similar to that directed for the operation of lithotomy—a director passed into the stricture, the left forefinger introduced into the rectum in order to feel for the urethra, and serve as a guide to the incisions. The straight bistoury is then to be plunged into the perineum the depth of an inch, and carried backward until the stricture is divided.

Section 2.—Fistula in Perineo.

By this term is understood an abnormal communication between an external opening in the perineum and the urethra, by means of an orifice in the latter.

It is frequently caused by strictures of the urethra, blows, and other injuries. In proportion as a stricture increases, the urethra at the diseased part is diminished, while that portion of the canal immediately behind the obstruction is enlarged by the continued propulsion of the urine against it. The irritation thereby induced engenders the inflammatory process, which terminates in ulceration; an opening is formed through the urethra, and communicates with the cellular membranes surrounding it; the presence of the urine excites additional irritation; suppuration results, the pus is discharged, and there remains a fistulous opening, through which the urine constantly dribbles.

Fistula in the perineum may also sometimes proceed from *rupture of the urethra,** and the urine is instantly diffused into the loose cellular membrane of the perineum and scrotum, where it occasions much distension, and excites inflammation so intense, that in a few hours gangrene and sloughing of the scrotum may take place, leaving, in many instances, the testicles and urethra bare, and endangering the patient's life.

There is seldom more than one fistulous opening communicating immediately with the urethra, but from it numerous sinuses generally extend in various directions; and in cases of long standing it is not unusual to find the cellular membrane of the scrotum, and all the other parts through which the urine meanders, greatly condensed and converted into indurated tumors, upon the surface of which may be found innumerable small holes that discharge offensive urine and matter—rendering the patient disagreeable to himself and pitiable to his neighbors.

Treatment.—When a fistula in perineo depends upon a stricture of the urethra, the first care of the surgeon must be to get rid of the obstruction by means already adverted to; after which the most appropriate medicines should be administered, among these are, *ars.*, *calc.*, *carb.-an.*, *silic.*, and *sulph.* By such means it will generally be found, that as soon as a natural outlet is established for the passage of the urine, the sinuses will heal.

Section 3.—*Retention of Urine—Ischuria Vesicalis.*

This affection differs materially from suppression of urine. In the latter, the kidneys do not perform their usual functions, while in ischuria, the urine is secreted and passes into the blad-

---

* Gibson's Institutes and Practice of Surgery, vol. ii., p. 465.

der, but cannot be ejected from that viscus. There is always more or less pain in the bladder, which, from distension, is perceptible above the pubes; there is urgent desire to void the urine, with pain and sickness, and but few drops are emitted. The disease is generally easily amenable to treatment, but in some cases it is of a very intractable character.

Treatment.—The chief medicines for this complaint are, *acon.*, *cann.*, *canth.*, *dulc.*, *merc.*, *nux-vom.*, *op.*, *puls.*, *stram.* Others than the above may be required in particular cases. An empirically applied medicine, but one which relieves *spasmodic* retention of urine frequently in a short time, is *buchu.* The powerful action that this plant is known to exercise upon the urinary apparatus, should lead to its proving upon the healthy individual, and there can be but little doubt that it would be a valuable acquisition to our Materia Medica.

The method of preparing it for administration is as follows: Place in a large sized tumbler, or other vessel, a small handful of the leaves of the plant, and pour thereon scalding water; allow this to remain until it becomes cold—of this infusion administer a dessert spoonful every quarter or half-hour, until the patient is relieved. The above is an empirical use of the medicine; but a knowledge of the fact may be useful to the practioner in urgent and peculiar cases, when other means have failed. When the surgeon is called to a case, in which the patient is suffering intense pain from distension of the bladder, the catheter should be immediately used. To accomplish its introduction the patient is first laid on a low bed, couch, or on the floor, with his shoulders and knees slightly raised; the surgeon then standing on the patient's left side, holds the glans with the forefinger and thumb of the left hand, and presses it gently from before backwards, so as to cause the orifice of the urethra to gape, into which he introduces the catheter. Holding the instrument (previously warmed and dipped in oil) in his right hand, he carries it onwards with a gentle pressure—taking care to stretch the penis sufficiently to prevent the movable part of the urethra from remaining bent, or being thrown into folds—until it reaches the angle of the pubes, where the urethra perforates the triangular ligament; the surgeon's right hand being brought by the course of the instrument nearly over the anterior part of the crest of the ilium. At this stage of progress the hold with the left hand is given up, and the right should move into the mesial line; in other words, the instrument should be brought parallel with the linea alba; next, it should be raised and made to describe a portion of a circle, of which the catheter is, as it were, the radius, and then a force little more than the weight of the instrument will cause the point to glide into the bladder. In all instances, whether of a simple nature or attended with difficulty, it is a good general rule to cause the point to move along the upper surface of the urethra.*

The following is the method of passing the female catheter:

The forefinger of the left hand should be introduced between the nymphæ and passed down to the urethral orifice, which is known by a depression, with an elevation on its vaginal aspect. The catheter should be taken in the right hand, and introduced along the finger which is at the urethral orifice, into which it should be inserted, and thence it easily passes within the bladder.

Section 4.—*Urinary Calculi.*

Urinary calculi are formed originally in the kidney, from whence they find their way along the ureters into the bladder, where, if too large to be passed off through the urethra, they remain, and serve as nuclei for other depositions.†

Urinary calculi vary considerably in size, form, character, and chemical composition. They may be composed of lithic acid, lithate of ammonia, phosphate of magnesia and ammonia,

---

* Vide Fergusson's Practical Surgery, p. 589.

† For the different Urinary Deposits, and the Diathesis that give rise to them, see Miller's Practice of Surgery, pp. 436–458; and for the Chemical Constituents of Calculi, and their Tests, vide Gardiner's Medical Chemistry.

phosphate of lime, oxylate of lime, triple phosphate of magnesia and ammonia, and carbonate of lime. Of these, the lithic acid calculi are by far the most numerous.

Urinary calculi may be contained in the kidney, ureters, bladder, prostate gland, or urethra; but the bladder is their most common receptacle, in which they may be loose, or may be contained in cysts formed between the coats of the bladder, the termination of the ureters, or between the folds of a contracted bladder; there may be a single calculus, or great numbers—upwards of a hundred having been found.

During the passage of a calculus along the ureter, the patient suffers, in most instances, excruciating pain, has frequent desire to pass water—a few drops only being emitted at a time, and that high-colored and sometimes mixed with blood. Fever, eructation, nausea, vomiting, and spasmodic retraction of the testicle, are the common accompaniments of the disease.

An encysted stone seldom gives rise to severe symptoms; but one that lies loose in the bladder, and is liable to move about, must always excite more or less uneasiness.*

Stone in the bladder is not generally difficult to diagnosticate. There is irritability of the bladder; frequent and irresistible desire to make water; occasional sudden stoppage of the stream during micturition, by the stone falling upon the orifice of the urethra, the urine probably flowing again if the patient throw himself upon his hands and knees, or change his position; occasional pain in the neck of the bladder, increased after micturition; pain in the glans penis, and if the patient be young, he attempts to alleviate it by pulling at the prepuce, which becomes extremely elongated: but the only sign to be fully relied upon, is actual contact with the stone, by means of a sound passed into the bladder; by this medium, both the senses of touch and hearing may be convinced of the presence of stone.†

The symptoms of stone vary in severity according to its size

* Gibson's Institutes and Practice of Surgery, vol. ii., p. 487.

† See Hastings' Practice of Surgery.

and roughness, the state of the urine, and the condition of the bladder, whether healthy or inflamed. These symptoms may be slight for years; indeed, a little pain and bloody urine, on micturating after riding, may be the only inconveniences experienced. But after a certain time the bladder suffers just as it does from any other cause of irritation; the urine deposits a slight cloud of mucus; the bladder becomes more irritable, and finally inflames; the urine becomes alkaline, loaded with viscid mucus and with the triple phosphate and phosphate of lime; the strength fails, and, after years of suffering, the patient finally sinks under the irritation. Sir B. Brodie remarks, "that if the prostate become enlarged, the sufferings from stone are mitigated; because it is prevented from falling on the neck of the bladder."

Treatment.—The general diagnostic signs for ascertaining the presence of stone in the bladder have been given above, but the positive means for assuring the surgeon that there is present a calculus in the bladder is by *sounding*, by which term is understood the introduction of a solid steel instrument, resembling a catheter in figure, into the bladder, and moving it about in that viscus until it comes in contact with the stone, when a peculiar impulse is communicated along the instrument, or a metallic sound is appreciable to the ear. Sometimes the stone cannot be detected; in such cases, by introducing a finger into the rectum, and pressing the lower part of the bladder upwards, the calculus may be made to touch the sound. When these means proved unsuccessful, Dr. Physick, of this city, whose experience in lithotomy was very extensive, was in the habit of placing the patient nearly upon his head, by which position the stone was dislodged from the fundus of the bladder and thrown against the sound.

In sounding for stone, care must be taken lest the student mistake a stone in the urethra or prostate gland for a calculus within the bladder.

Extraction by the Urethra.—When a stone is known to have recently escaped from the urethra into the bladder, the irritability of that organ must be allayed by the administration of *acon.*, *canth.*, *scill.*, or *calc.-carb.*, *nux-vom.*, *opium*, *puls.*, *kali-carb.*

The patient* should also drink plentifully, in order that the bladder may be quite filled. As soon as a desire to pass urine is experienced, he should be directed to lie on his face, and to grasp the penis, that the urethra may become distended with urine; by these means the sudden gush of fluid which will escape when the grasp is abruptly relinquished will force out the stone. In some cases the urethra may be dilated by passing bougies. But if this plan succeeds not, Weiss's urethral forceps should be tried. The patient being placed on his back, with his pelvis raised, the urine must be drawn off by a catheter, and afterwards five or six ounces of tepid water must be injected into the bladder. The forceps must then be carefully introduced and with them the surgeon must feel for the stone, which, when found, if its size permit, must be gently extracted. If too large to be removed in this manner, other operations must be performed; if of a medium size it may perhaps be brought to the membranous portion of the urethra, where it can be extracted by incision. Some calculi, of particular chemical construction, can be removed by injection. Sir B. Brodie has satisfactorily shown that *phosphatic calculi* may sometimes be dissolved by means of injections of very dilute nitric acid through a double gold catheter.

Section 5.—Lithotomy.

This operation, which has been greatly modified and improved since its first introduction to the notice of the profession, may be performed in several different modes, denominated the *lateral*, *high*, and *bilateral*. The first is most commonly employed, and is conducted in the following manner: The bowels having been previously evacuated, and the urine retained within

* See Druitt's Modern Surgery, p. 485.

the bladder, the patient is placed upon a table of convenient height, his hands and feet are approximated and firmly bandaged together, with the knees elevated; a staff, deeply grooved on its convex and left side, and of sufficient calibre to fill the urethra, should then be introduced. The knees should be separated by an assistant on either side, in order that the perineum, which should be cleanly shaved, may be exposed. The patient having been brought to the edge of the table, the surgeon seats himself in front, with his instruments in a convenient place, and the staff, being in contact with the stone, is brought up under the symphysis pubis, and not pressed downwards upon the rectum, and is then given into the hands of an assistant, who is directed to hold it vertically, and, at the same time, guard the scrotum against injury.

An incision of about three inches in length should then be made, commencing at about an inch behind the scrotum, and extending downwards and outwards to a point between the tuber ischii and anus, and even extending further than this. Various measurements have been given by different surgeons, regarding the point at which this incision should be commenced, but, on account of the diversity in size and depth of the perineum in different patients, the surgeon should not depend on absolute measurement, but rather be guided by circumstances; he should ascertain the probable size of the prostate gland, by means of an examination per anum, and then make his incision, in view of exposing the membranous portion of the urethra, taking care, at the same time, not to cut the bulb of the corpus spongiosum lying in front, nor the rectum behind.

The incision having extended through the skin and superficial fascia of the perineum, the transversus perinei muscle and artery, the lower edge of the triangular ligament, and a few fibres of the levator ani muscle, will then have to be divided. By an examination with the finger, the staff may now be felt in the urethra, which should be opened by a bistoury, when a flow of urine will immediately result.

The gorget or scalpel should now be introduced into the wound, and, if the former, its beak must be firmly fixed in the groove of the staff, pushed in the direction of the bladder, cutting through its cervix and the prostate gland. The handle of the instrument, whilst making this thrust, must be depressed, in order that the rectum may not be wounded. When the bladder is penetrated, urine gushes out, and the instrument should be removed carefully, to avoid wounding the pudic artery; the finger should then be employed for ascertaining the position and size of the stone, and afterwards a strong pair of forceps should be introduced into the bladder, and the stone grasped in such a manner that its short diameter may be presented to the opening, through which it should be removed carefully and gradually.

If, from the size of the calculus, it be found impossible to remove it through the first opening, this may be enlarged on the same, or, if necessary, the other side. After the removal of the stone, the finger should again be introduced, in order to ascertain that no more calculi remain.

The bladder having been freed from the presence of all calculi by means of the forceps or syringe, a tube, by which the urine is to escape, should be passed into the bladder through the wound. The patient should then be placed in bed with his knees together, and a small cup or saucer placed in a convenient position for receiving the urine as it escapes from the tube. In case of wound of the bulb of the corpus spongiosum, or of the urethra-bulbar artery, severe hemorrhage may result; in such cases a ligature should be applied, or, if this is impracticable, the flow of blood may be stopped by compression.

If there be subsequent venous or arterial oozing, the tube should be removed and the wound stuffed with lint, a catheter having been passed through the urethra. In cases in which its removal is not necessitated by hemorrhage, the tube should be allowed to remain until the wound has granulated around it, and the urine has recommenced to flow through the urethra.

The *high operation* is performed by making an incision through the linea alba, and opening the bladder where it is not covered by peritoneum. This method is only necessary when the stone is of enormous size, the prostate gland diseased, or the space between the tuberosities of the ischia less than usual.

The *recto-vesical* operation consists in cutting into the bladder, through the walls of the rectum.

Stone in women is of much less frequent occurrence than in men, mainly in consequence of the renal calculus being more readily passed through the urethra. When, however, the calculus is retained in the bladder, and increases in size, it may be removed either by dilatation of the urethra, or the performance of the lateral operation; in the latter case, the incision should be made from the orifice of the urethra, and through the neck of the bladder.

Lithotrity.—The term lithotrity signifies the boring or drilling of the stone, and was most successfully accomplished by Civiale. His instrument consisted of a straight canula, containing a drill and three claws, which can be protruded after the instrument has been introduced into the bladder. These claws, however, are liable to catch in the coats of the bladder, and the operation has fallen into disuse.

Section 6.—*Lithotripsy.*

By this is understood the crushing of the stone within the bladder, and it is preferable to all other methods of disintegration. It can be most successfully employed in cases in which the patient is an adult, the urethra free from stricture, the bladder void of irritability, and the prostate gland not enlarged. The mulberry calculus, on account of its hardness, is the most unfavorable for the performance of lithotripsy.

The instrument most frequently employed is that of Heurteloup, or a modification of it. It consists of two blades, which are made to slide one upon the other. The instrument is introduced into the bladder as a simple sound or catheter, and the blades are afterwards expanded, for grasping the stone. In the original form of the instrument, the male blade was struck with a hammer; now, however, the crushing force is exerted by means of a peculiarly adapted screw. The extremities of the instrument are fitted with teeth, for the retention of the stone after it has been grasped, and fenestræ, or perforations, to allow the escape of the powdered stone or sand.

It is advisable that, previous to the operation, the urethra be dilated, and the urine should be retained in order that the bladder may not be in a collapsed condition, and thus endanger its coats being caught by the instrument.

The patient should lie on a convenient bed or table, with the pelvis elevated in such a manner as to throw the stone into the fundus of the bladder. The instrument, having been oiled and warmed, is then introduced, and, after encountering the stone and fairly grasping it—an operation which requires skilful manipulation—the calculus is crushed by slowly and gradually turning the screw. The instrument should then be withdrawn, and after the irritation consequent on its presence has somewhat subsided, may again be introduced to crush the fragments; thus many introductions of the instrument may be necessary, before the stone has been broken to sufficiently small particles to allow of their passage through the urethra.

CHAPTER XXXVIII.

QUESTION OF AMPUTATION.

So long as the destructive effects of injuries and diseases of the extremities cannot, in every instance, be prevented by the employment of other means, a necessity for amputation must continue to exist, and the sacrificing of a branch, as it were, thereby making use of the only rational means for maintaining the integrity of the trunk, frequently becomes indispensably proper. It is, however, the imperative duty of the surgeon never to have recourse to this terrible, and sometimes fatal, operation, without a perfectly clear and fully substantiated conviction of its necessity; it should always be regarded as the last expedient to which the surgeon should resort, justifiable only when farther attempt to save the injured or diseased part, would be fraught with danger to the life of the patient. With this conviction, it is evident that a *precise* knowledge of such cases as demand amputation, as also those in which it should be dispensed with, and the exact periods at which its performance is most conducive to the welfare of the patient, are considerations demanding the most marked attention.

The various conditions demanding a performance of this operation are as follows: Compound fractures, extensive contused and lacerated wounds, gangrene and mortification, gun-shot injuries, diseases of the joints, exostosis, and necrosis.

Compound Fractures.—The necessity for amputation in injuries of this nature, does not depend entirely upon the seriousness of the accident, but also, in a measure, upon other circumstances, as the condition of the patient, his mode of life, the facilities for ventilation, &c. If, however, a compound fracture occur in which the soft parts have been extensively involved, and the bones have been so seriously injured that perfect quietude and constant attention are required to afford any chance of recovery, amputation should, in the generality of instances, be performed. On the contrary, when the soft parts have been less extensively injured, and the bones have been broken in such a manner that they can readily be readjusted, and maintained in their proper position; or if but one bone be involved in the injury, amputation is deemed both unnecessary and inhuman: accompanying circumstances, however, are to be considered in concluding for or against amputation.*

---

* The circumstances adverse to a favorable prognosis, in cases of compound fracture, are thus detailed by Professor Miller: "Comminution of the bone, or fracture at several points; extension of the fracture into an important articulation; an open state of the joints; much bruising and laceration of the soft parts, rendering extensive sloughing inevitable, with a risk of gangrene involving the whole limb, and with a certainty of exten-

In compound fractures, as Mr. Pott has pointed out,* there are three distinct periods when it is deemed proper to perform amputation.

The first of these is, immediately, or as soon as practicable after the receipt of the injury. The second, when the bones continue for a great length of time without manifesting any disposition to unite; and the discharge from the wound has continued so long, and is so excessive, that the patient's strength fails, together with general symptoms foreboding dissolution supervene. And third, when mortification has so completely involved the soft parts of the inferior portion of the limb, quite down to the bone, that upon separation of the diseased portions the bone or bones are left bare in the interspace. The first and second of these are matters requiring serious consideration. The last demands scarcely any.

A disposition to mortification is often evinced when fracture occurs in the middle of a bone; but much more frequently when any of the large joints are involved; and in many of the above-mentioned instances, a decision favorable or adverse to amputation, is really a determination for or against the patient's life.

If, after judicious treatment, throughout every stage, by the united efforts of medicine and surgery, the sore, instead of granulating kindly, and contracting daily, does not diminish in size, has a tawny, spongy surface, discharges a large quantity of thin sanies; the fractured ends of the bones, instead of tending to exfoliate, or unite, remain as perfectly loose and ununited as at first, whilst the patient is deprived of sleep and appetite, becomes greatly weakened; hectic fever, with a quick, small, hard pulse, and profuse sweat, contributing at the same time to bring him to the brink of the grave, notwithstanding all efforts

---

sive and tedious suppuration following separation of the sloughs; laceration of a large artery, as evinced either by hemorrhage or by rapid formation of a large, bloody swelling; old age; and enfeeblement of the frame by disease, by privation, by intemperate habits," &c. Principles of Surgery, p. 717.

* Remarks on the Necessity, &c., of Amputation in certain cases. Surgical Works, vol. iii. London, 1808.

to the contrary: under these circumstances, if amputation be not performed, what else can rescue the patient from destruction.

Extensive contused and lacerated Wounds.—These form the second class of general cases requiring amputation; though, when not in conjunction with fracture, they seldom render the operation necessary. But, if a limb is extensively lacerated and contused, and its principal blood-vessels are injured to so great an extent, that a continuance of the circulation cannot reasonably be expected, an immediate removal of the affected limb is recommended, even though no bone is involved in the injury; and as all efforts of the surgeon to preserve a limb so seriously injured generally prove unavailing, and such wounds are more disposed to assume a gangrenous condition than any other, the sooner the operation is performed the more favorable will be the prognosis.

In the preceding varieties of injuries, although amputation may not always be necessary in the first instance, yet it may become so subsequently. Sometimes mortification rapidly takes place, either in consequence of the extreme violence of the injury, or consecutively, from greatly excited action going on in parts whose powers of resistance have been much impaired—or profuse suppuration, with its consequences and accompanying conditions, ensue, which the system is unable to resist; in these instances amputation should be resorted to.

When the surgeon has fully resolved upon operating, it is advisable to wait until reaction has come on, lest the additional injury should increase the collapse which always follows severe injuries, and thus increase the danger.* In particular, says Professor Gibson,† amputation should be avoided so long as the extremities are cold, the pulse weak and fluttering, the wound dry, and the powers of life nearly exhausted.

When patients die from a premature operation, it is owing to the shock communicated to the nervous system before the vital

* Fergusson's Practical Surgery, p. 50.
† Institutes and Practice of Surgery, vol. i., p. 96.

energy has rallied sufficiently to encounter so severe a stimulus. When they die after the full restoration of the circulating system and the establishment of febrile action, then life is assaulted through the medium of inflammation and high action, and the operation is almost sure to be followed by gangrene. Each state, then, it will be seen, is precarious; and it is only by observing a happy medium, that success can be expected to follow.*

Gangrene and Mortification.—Gangrene is another cause, which, when advanced in a certain degree, renders amputation indispensable.

It sometimes happens, that gangrene appears so extensive in either the upper or lower extremities, or that mortification has committed such ravages, as to preclude the hope of saving the limb or even the life of the patient, if such a source of irritation is allowed to remain. The surgeon will seldom be performing his duty, if, in this instance, he leaves the case to the efforts of nature so entirely as in partial slough; for although experience proves that a portion of the hand, foot, fore-arm, or leg, may drop off, or that either member may be separated at its articulation with the trunk, by the process of disjunctive absorption, it is equally certain that the work is done in a tedious, painful, and unsatisfactory manner—months sometimes elapsing ere the parts are entirely separated; and when, at length, this has been accomplished, months more may pass ere cicatrization takes place. There cannot be a doubt that the surgeon is justified in many of these cases, in performing amputation; and the only difficulty is to determine the proper period for such a procedure.†

Practitioners have entertained very opposite opinions concerning the time when the operation should be performed. Some declare, that whenever the disorder presents itself, especially if it be the result of external violence, amputation should immediately be had recourse to, as soon as the disease has began to form, and while it is in the spreading state. Mr. Pott

* Loc. cit.

† Fergusson's System of Practical Surgery, p. 108.

says, that he has often seen the experiment of amputating a limb, in which gangrene had began to show itself, tried, but never saw success follow, and it invariably hastened the patient's death.*

The operation, however, may be postponed too long, and it is sometimes advisable to amputate to prevent gangrene: thus, when the limb has been much injured by mechanical or chemical means—in the case of severe compound fracture or burn, for example—and it is apparent that mortification must ensue, involving the whole thickness of the limb, of an acute character, tending to spread, and from the first accompanied with the most formidable constitutional symptoms—amputation is to be performed above the injured point, as soon as the primary shock has passed away, and the system rallied so far as to afford sufficient tolerance of the operation.

In injuries of this nature, when gangrene has set in, delay, with the object of waiting for the spontaneous line of separation, will be in vain. The gangrene spreads upwards and upwards, with a diffused and streaky margin; typhoid symptoms grow more and more intense; the trunk is reached, rendering operative interference hopeless; or, long ere this, the system has sunk and the patient perished. The only hope of escape is by early amputation: it is a slender chance, but it is the only one, and to it the sufferer is entitled.†

When gangrene is acute and humid, dependent on an external cause, and unconnected with a *previously existing* failure of system, or organic change in the general limb, amputation is performed, if at all, during the progress of the disease, without waiting for a line of demarcation. When it is chronic and dry, dependent on an internal cause only, or on internal more than on external cause, and connected with failure of both general and local power, the line of demarcation is to be awaited, and the progress of separation cautiously watched; and when de-

---

* Surgical Works, vol. iii.

† Miller's Principles of Surgery, p. 289. Lectures by Tyrrell, vol. i., p. 132.

tachment is far advanced, the surgeon interfering merely for facilitating and modifying its completion, amputates in the line of separation.*

When gangrene is an attendant upon one particular cause, as cold, the line of disjunction is to be awaited; and, as soon as it has become evident that this is fairly formed, the surgeon should resort to amputation, which may be performed either at the point of separation of the dead from the living textures, or at a distance above, according as the circumstances of the case may demand.†

Diseases of the Joints.—Scrofulous diseases of the joints, involving the bones, with morbid alteration of the structure of the adjacent ligaments and cartilages, is another condition in which amputation may become an absolute necessity. An unpleasant circumstance attending these affections is, that the majority of subjects are young children, incapable of determining for themselves. All efforts at cure sometimes prove unavailing, and operation is the only resort.

It is a highly important fact, that amputation, in these instances, is attended with a greater degree of success when the disease has considerably advanced, than when undertaken at an earlier period. This is particularly fortunate, as it affords ample opportunity for the administration of those medicines that have been mentioned; and thus, perhaps, all necessity for the operation may be obviated.

Exostoses, under certain circumstances, sometimes occasion a necessity for amputation; but when they merely produce deformity, without pain or inconvenience from the pressure which they exert on neighboring parts, the performance of an operation for their removal is not advisable; for, as Boyer has observed,‡ in a great number of instances, the local affection is much less to be dreaded than the means used for its removal. When, however, the tumor becomes hurtful to the health, and

* See Miller's Principles, p. 290.

† For Question of Amputation in Gunshot Wounds, vide p. 101.

‡ Treatise on Surgical Diseases, vol. ii.

its situation permits of a ready removal, this may be done without an entire division of the part on which it is situated; but frequently its base is so extensive and deeply seated, as to preclude the possibility of a removal by this method. If, in this case, it is situated on the extremities, and has become insupportable on account of its weight, amputation should be performed in preference to any operation having in view the saving of the limb.

Another affection of the osseous system which sometimes demands the performance of amputation, is *necrosis*—or the death of the whole, or a very considerable portion of the bones of the extremities.

The performance of this operation in these cases, however, is the exception, not the rule. It may happen, that in acute necrosis, in the young subject, violent inflammatory action is followed by severe irritative fever, which latter is quickly succeeded by a formidable hectic, that must evidently be relieved at all hazards, by a removal of its cause; or, in more chronic cases, a like summary procedure may be required at a more distant date, after weeks and even months have elapsed, when the separation of the sequestrum is far advanced, but not yet complete, after the system has long resisted the exhausting burden of irritation and discharge, but when, nevertheless, it has evidently become unequal to a prolongation of the contest. On the one hand, the surgeon must beware of sacrificing life in endeavoring to save a limb; and, on the other, must be equally careful not to sacrifice a limb in endeavoring to succor life not yet actually endangered; and, in connection with this subject, it is important to remember, that necrosis is not always so extensive as outward appearances would lead one to suppose.

CHAPTER XXXIX.

AMPUTATION.

Section 1.—*Amputation of Lower Extremities.*

Amputation of the Thigh.—This amputation being probably the most important, and one that is frequently performed, it will be convenient to describe it first; and to embody in the description of it such general precepts as are applicable to other amputations.

In the first place, the surgeon should have his tourniquets, amputating knives, saws, forceps and tenacula, ligatures, bone-nippers, sponges, and curved needles threaded, close at hand on a tray, arranged in due order; and he should, by personal examination, be satisfied that everything that can possibly be required is at hand before he commences.

The next point is, to place the patient in a convenient posture. For amputation of the thigh the patient may be placed on a bed, or on a table covered with a folded blanket; the affected leg should project sufficiently over the edge, and should be supported at the knee by an assistant, who sits on a low stool in front, and the sound limb should be secured to one of the legs of the table with a handkerchief.

Measures then must be adopted for compressing the main artery, and preventing too great loss of blood. This may be done, either by pressure with the hand or with the tourniquet. Pressure with the hand on the main arterial trunk, if effected by an assistant whose steadiness can be trusted, is sufficient in most cases; and, if the limb is amputated so high up, that the tourniquet cannot be applied, there is, of course, no choice—the femoral artery must be compressed against the ramus of the pubes.

This amputation, like others, may be performed in two ways: either by the *circular incision*—that is, by cutting round the limb from without towards the bone; or by the *flap operation*—that is, by transfixing the limb, and then cutting outwards. The flap operation is, in most instances, chosen by surgeons of the present day. It certainly can be performed with much more facility; and it enables the surgeon to select a flap where he pleases, so that when the flesh on one side of the limb be destroyed by disease or injury, the end of the stump may be covered with a flap taken almost entirely from the sound side, and a greater length of limb may be preserved. It affords, too, a greater certainty of preserving a sufficiency of flesh to cover the bone; and it enables the muscles to be more easily retracted, and the bone exposed for the application of the saw. It entirely avoids the difficulty, also, which sometimes occurs in the circular operation, of retracting the skin, when it has become adherent to the parts beneath. But, as Sir C. Bell observes, the cardinal rule in all cases is, to save integument enough to cover the muscle, and muscle enough to cover the bone, and not to scrape off the periosteum. And, if these things are done, it requires ingenuity to make a bad stump.

Circular method.—The surgeon stands on the outer side for the left leg, and on the inner for the right; so that he may use his left hand to grasp and steady the part which he is to amputate. The artery must be compressed by one of the methods before described, and an assistant must grasp the limb with both hands, so as to draw up the skin as high as possible. Then the surgeon commences by putting his arm under the thigh, and makes an incision, at one sweep, completely round the limb, through the skin and adipose structure to the fascia. The assistant is now to draw the skin further up, the retraction being aided with a few touches of the knife; and then the knife, being put close to the edge of the retracted skin, is to divide everything down to the bone, by another clean circular sweep. The next thing is, to separate the muscles from the bone for another inch or two with the point of the knife, especially those connected with the *linea aspera;* and then, the periosteum having been divided by one more sweep, the *retractor*—a piece of linen, with a longitudinal slit in it—is put over the face of the stump, and the muscles are to be drawn up with it. The bone must now be sawn through.

The heel of the saw should first be put on the bone, and it should be drawn up, so as to make a groove, before working it downwards. It should be used very lightly; and the last few strokes should be extremely short and gentle, that the bone may not be splintered; if it is, the irregular parts must be removed by nippers.

The femoral artery must now be tied, its orifice being seized and slightly drawn out by forceps, and afterwards any large branches that appear in the muscular interstices. Then all compression should be *suddenly withdrawn*, that any arteries liable to bleed may do so, and immediately be tied. Hemorrhage from large veins may be restrained by elevating the stump, and making compression for a short time with the finger. If, however, nothing else will do, they must be tied. Obstinate oozing from small vessels should be restrained by sponging with cold water. Then a light bandage may be passed round the limb above the stump, and the edges of the wound should be approximated with a few strips of plaster, with or without sutures. The edges are to be brought together in a straight line, which may be made either perpendicular or horizontal; the latter, however, being probably the better plan. The ligatures should be left hanging out in the interstices of the adhesive straps. The patient should then be removed to bed, and the stump be supported on a pillow covered with oil-cloth. No other application will be needed save a cloth well saturated with a mixture, viz.:

Arnicæ Tincturæ: f ʒj.
Aquæ fluvialis: Oj.
M.

It may be well to state here, that the above prescription is sufficiently strong. The use of the pure tincture produces at times an inflammatory condition, closely resembling erysipelas; a result which has, in many instances, given rise to very serious symptoms. The specific action, which is all that is desired, is fully obtained from the above dilution.

The stump may remain without being disturbed for some days, the discharge being merely wiped occasionally from its surface. But after from four to six days, sooner or later, according to the quantity of the discharge and the feelings of the patient, the dressings should be changed, the straps taken off and replaced one by one, with care not to disturb the ligatures; the hands of an assistant being employed to support the edges, and prevent their falling asunder. At the subsequent dressings the points to be attended to are, to renew the light bandage occasionally, which was passed round the stump soon after the operation, in order to support the muscles and prevent their retraction; to bring together the edges of the wound with adhesive straps; to remove the ligatures when loose (that on the femoral artery should not be disturbed for a fortnight); and to accelerate cicatrization if the granulations appear languid.

There are a few varieties in the manner of performing this circular operation, that require a brief notice. Some surgeons, after having cut through the skin, dissect it from the fascia and turn it back—a proceeding necessary enough if the operation is performed (which it never should be) when the cellular tissue is condensed and adherent. Again, if the patient is *very emaciated*, the circular incision may be carried down to the bone at once, without hesitation, because in such patients the muscles always retract greatly. Sir C. Bell recommends the skin not to be divided quite circularly, but the knife to be inclined a little, first to one side, then to the other, so as to make two oval flaps. The same may be done also in dividing the muscles. He further recommends that the limb should be raised perpendicularly whilst the bone is being sawn, so that the saw may be worked horizontally; by which means, he says, the bone may be divided more evenly and much shorter, so that its end will be no more seen when the stump is depressed.

Flap Operation.—The flaps may be made either from the inner and outer, or from the anterior and posterior aspect of the limb. The latter method is the most convenient if the amputation is low down, but the former if it be in the middle or upper third; because the end of the bone is liable to be tilted forwards by the iliacus and psoas muscles, and to project between the lips of the wound. In performing this operation, the surgeon, standing as before,* grasps the flesh on the anterior surface of the limb with his left hand, and lifts it from the bone (Fig. 99); then passes his knife horizontally through it, carries the point over the bone, and pushes it through the other

Fig. 99.

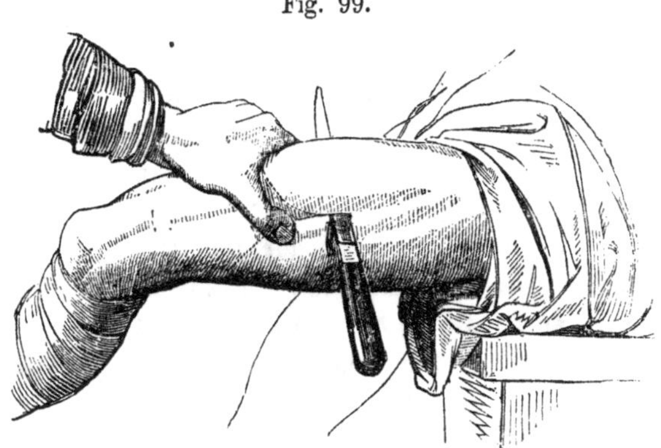

side of the limb as low as possible; then makes it cut its way out upwards and forwards, so as to make the anterior flap.

In amputating the right leg, the knife should be passed in behind the saphena vein. It is again entered on the inner side a little below the top of the first incision, passed behind the bone, brought out at the wound on the outside, and directed so as to make a posterior flap in the direction of the dotted line. This should be a very little longer than the anterior, because the flexor muscles retract more than the extensors, which are adherent to the bone. Both flaps are now drawn back; the knife is swept round the bone to divide any remaining muscular fibres, and the bone is sawn through. In the same manner flaps may be made from the inner and outer sides of the limb, the

* Mr. Fergusson thinks it more convenient that the surgeon should stand on the outer side in amputating the right thigh, as it is awkward to stoop over the sound limb; which, moreover, is in the way of the surgeon's hand.

surgeon first grasping the flesh, and transfixing it, and cutting a flap on one side of the bone, then passing the knife close to the bone on the other side, (without again piercing the skin,) and making another flap.

Amputation at the Hip-joint is performed by Mr. Liston precisely in the same manner in which he amputates the thigh. The femoral artery being compressed, the knife is entered about midway between the anterior superior spinous process of the ilium and the trochanter, and is carried across the front of the articulation, so as to form the anterior flap. Then the anterior part of the capsular ligament being cut into, and the *ligamentum teres* and posterior part of the capsular ligament being divided, the blade of the knife is put behind the neck and trochanters of the femur, and the posterior flap is formed. The vessels on the posterior flap are tied fast. But this method can hardly be preferable to that of making two lateral flaps; first, passing the knife completely through the limb, on the inner side of the joint, and carrying it forwards and inwards, so as to form a flap of the abductor muscles; then cutting into the joint, and severing the *ligamentum teres*, and the muscles attached to the digital fossa, with a short, strong, curved knife; and, lastly, putting in the knife over the trochanter, and cutting downwards and outwards, so as to make the external flap. In this manner Mr. Mayo performed this operation in less than half a minute. He previously tied the femoral artery below Poupart's ligament; but most authorities prefer compressing it during the operation, and tying its cut orifice afterwards.

Amputation of the Leg.—The rule generally given is, that this operation should be performed as near the knee as possible, unless the patient can afford an artificial foot; because a laboring man would find it very inconvenient to have a long stump trailing after him, as it would if he rested on the bent knee with the ordinary wooden leg. But a wooden leg may be procured, which is light and of moderate cost, and which enables the patient to rest on the stump, and to have the use of the knee; and therefore it is better not to sacrifice more of the limb than can be avoided.

Circular Method.—The artery being under command, as in amputations of the thigh, and the leg being placed horizontally, one assistant supporting it at the ankle, and another holding it at the knee and drawing up the skin, the surgeon (standing on the inner side for the right leg, and *vice versâ,*) makes a circular incision through the skin, four inches below the tuberosity of the tibia. The integuments are next to be dissected up for two inches, and turned back, and the muscles are to be divided down to the bone by a second circular incision. Then a long, slender, double-edged knife, called a catling, is passed between the bones, to divide the interosseous ligament and muscles, and both bones are sawn through together, the flesh being protected by a retractor, which should have three tails. The spine of the tibia if it projects much, may be removed with a fine saw or bone nippers, and care should be taken not to leave the fibula longer than the tibia, or it will give much trouble. The anterior and posterior tibial and peronæal arteries, and any others requiring it being tied, the stump is to be treated as directed after amputation of the thigh. The integuments should be put together so as to make a perpendicular line of junction.

All surgeons, however, are agreed that the flap operation is by far the best for this situation, and the easiest way of performing it is as follows: The surgeon passes his knife horizontally behind both bones, at the level of an inch below the head of the fibula, and cuts downwards and forwards, (Fig. 100,) so as to make a flap of the posterior muscle about four or five inches long. A semi-lunar incision with the convexity downwards, is then made across the front of the limb, the skin is slightly turned back, the parts between the bones are divided, and the bones are sawn as before. But the manner in which Mr. Fergusson performs this amputation renders it far more neat and expeditious. He first places the heel of the knife on the side of the limb farthest from him, and draws it across the front of the limb, cutting a semi-lunar flap of skin; when its point has arrived at the opposite side, it is at once made to transfix the limb—this stage of the operation is represented in the following cut—and then the flap is cut as above directed.

Fig. 100.

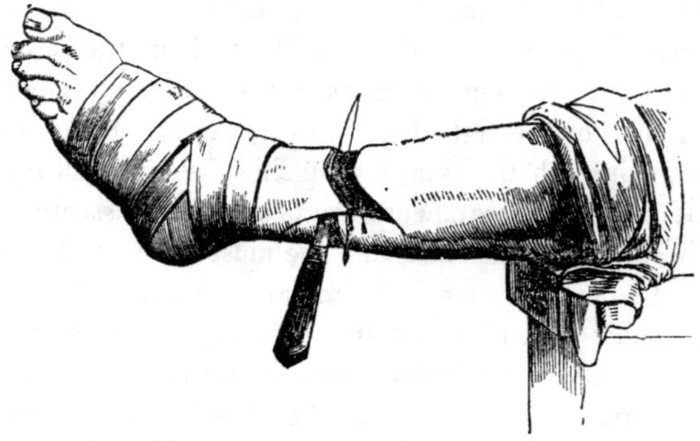

When transfixing the right limb, the surgeon must take great care not to get his knife between the two bones. When the operation is performed high up, the popliteal artery will be divided, instead of the two tibials. The tibia, however, should never be sawn higher than its tuberosity, or the joint will be laid open. The amputation may be performed near the ankle in the same manner. If low down, the *tendo achillis* will require to be shortened after the flap is made. The flap is to be brought forwards, and confined by a stitch or two, the line of junction being of course horizontal.

Amputations of the Foot.—Amputation of the *toes* at any of their joints is performed in precisely the same manner as amputation of the fingers. In removing a single toe from its metatarsal bone, the surgeon should take care first of all to ascertain the exact situation of the joint, which lies rather deeply. Moreover he should not remove the head of the metatarsal bone, as he may of the metacarpal, because it is important to preserve the entire breadth of the foot.

Amputation of all the *toes at their metatarsal joints*—an operation which may be requisite in case of frost-bite—is performed by first making a transverse incision along the dorsal aspect of the metatarsal bones; dividing the tendons and lateral ligaments of each joint in succession; then the phalanges being dislocated upwards, the knife is placed beneath their metatarsal extremities, and made to cut out a flap from the skin on the plantar surface, sufficient to cover the heads of the metatarsal bones. The arteries are to be tied, and the foot laid on its outer side, so that the discharge may escape more readily.

Amputation of the *metatarsal bone of the great toe* is performed precisely like the operation for the removal of the metacarpal bone of the little finger. It is better, if circumstances permit, to cut through the bone, than to disarticulate it from the internal cuneiform bone, and it may be observed that, in dividing the metatarsal bones of the great or little toes, or the metacarpal bones of the fore or little finger, the forceps should be held obliquely, so as not to leave any prominent angle.

Amputation of *all the metatarsal bones* is performed in the following manner: The exact situation of the articulation of the great toe to the inner cuneiform bone (to which the tendon of the tibialis anticus may serve as a guide) being ascertained, a semi-lunar incision, with the convexity forwards, is made down to the bone, across the instep, from a point just in front of it, to the outside of the tuberosity of the fifth metatarsal bone. The flap of skin thus formed being turned back, the bistoury is to be passed round behind the projection of the fifth metatarsal bone, so as to divide the external ligaments which connect it with the cuboid. The dorsal ligaments are next to be cut through, and then the remaining ones, the bone being depressed. The fourth and third metatarsal bones are to be disarticulated in a similar manner, dividing their ligaments with the point of the knife, and taking care not to let the instrument become locked between the bones. The first metatarsal is next to be attacked, and, lastly, the second, the extremity of which, being locked in between the three cuneiform, will be more difficult to dislodge. Perhaps it may be convenient to saw it across. When all the five bones are detached, the surgeon completes the division of their plantar ligaments, and slightly separates the textures which adhere to their under surface, with the point of the knife, and then, the foot being placed horizontally, he puts the blade under the five bones, and carries it forwards along their inferior surface, so as to form a flap from the sole of the foot sufficient to cover the denuded tarsal bones. The flap should be about two inches wide on the inner side, and one on the outer.

Amputation may be performed *through the tarsus*, so as to remove the navicular and cuboid bones, with all the parts in front of them. This is commonly called *Chopart's operation.* In the first place, the articulation of the cuboid with the os calcis, (which lies about midway between the external malleolus and the tuberosity of the fifth metatarsal bone,) and that of the navicular with the astragalus, (which will be found just behind the prominence of the navicular bone in front of the inner ankle,) must be sought for, and a semi-lunar incision be made from one to the other, as in the last described operation. The flap of skin being turned back, the internal and dorsal ligaments that connect the navicular to the astragalus are to be divided with the point of the bistoury—recollecting the convex shape of the head of the latter bone. The ligaments connecting the os calcis and cuboid are next divided; and, lastly, a flap is to be procured from the sole of the foot, as in the last operation.

Amputation at the Ankle-joint—Syme's Operation.—This operation is proposed by Mr. Syme to be substituted for amputation above the ankle, in cases where disease or injury of the tarsal bones implicates the astragalus and os calcis, and for which, therefore, Chopart's operation is inadmissible. The principle of the operation is, that the whole of the bones of the foot are taken away; and the articular surface of the tibia, with both malleoli, are cut off smoothly; but the skin of the heel is preserved, as the best and most natural cushion for the stump to rest upon. Mr. Syme makes one curved incision across the instep, from one malleolus to the other, and carries a second across the sole of the foot. The flaps are dissected from the subjacent parts, which is easily effected, except just at the heel; the astragalus and os calcis, with the rest of the foot, are removed, and the projections of the malleolar processes cut off with forceps. If the ankle-joint itself is diseased, a thin slice of the lower extremities of the tibia and fibula may be removed with a saw. The thick skin of the heel is then brought up to cover the ends of the bones, and is retained by sutures. It appears useful sometimes to make a puncture through the integuments of the heel, to let the discharge escape freely. This operation has been performed very many times in Edinburgh by Mr. Syme, and once in London by Mr. Fergusson, with very good results.*

Section 2.—Amputation of Upper Extremities.

Amputation of the Arm.—In amputating the upper extremity, the flow of blood may be sufficiently commanded by compressing the artery above the clavicle, or in the arm. If it is thought proper, however, the tourniquet may be applied so as to compress the artery against the humerus.

Circular.—The arm being held out, and an assistant drawing up the skin, one circular incision is made through the skin, which being forcibly retracted, another is made down to the bone. These incisions should be made with two slight divergences, so as to cut the skin and muscles rather longer in front and behind than at the sides. The subsequent steps are precisely similar to those in amputating the thigh.

Flap.—The knife is entered at one side, carried down to the bone, turned over it, brought out at a point opposite (Fig. 101) (the vessels being left behind for a second flap), and then made to cut a neat rounded anterior flap two or three inches long. It is next carried behind the bone, to make a posterior one of equal length; and is lastly swept round the bone, to divide any remaining fibres. The division of the bone, ligature of the arteries, and treatment of the stump as before.

Amputation at the shoulder may be performed in several manners. (1.) The patient being seated in a chair and well

---

* Vide London and Edinburgh Journ. Med. Science, Feb. and April, 1843; and several papers in the same ably conducted periodical for 1846.

Fig. 101.

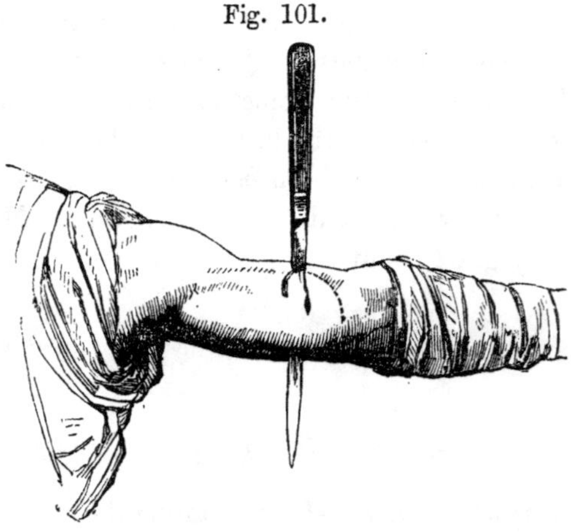

supported,—or, which is better, being placed on a firm table, with the shoulder elevated, and projecting beyond its edge,—and the subclavian artery being compressed, the surgeon enters a long straight knife at the anterior margin of the deltoid muscle, an inch below the acromion. From this point, he thrusts it through the muscle, across the outside of the joint, and brings out the knife at the posterior margin of the axilla. If the left side is operated on, the knife must be entered at the posterior margin of the axilla, and be brought out at the anterior margin of the deltoid muscle. Then, by cutting downwards and outwards, the external flap is made. The origins of the biceps and triceps, and insertions of the infra and supra spinati, are next cut through, and the joint is laid open.

Finally, the blade of the knife, being placed on the inner side of the head of the bone, must be made to cut the inner flap.

(2.) The covering for the exposed part of the scapula, in the preceding operation, was obtained from the deltoid. But it may also be obtained from the muscles in front or behind, supposing the deltoid to be implicated in the disease or injury which demands the operation. One elliptical incision may be carried from beneath the middle of the acromion to the posterior border of the axilla, and another to the anterior border.

These flaps being dissected up, the head of the bone may be turned out of the socket, and the remaining soft parts be divided; or the bone may be sawn through just beneath its neck. An assistant should be directed to grasp the flap which contains the axillary artery as soon as it is divided; because the pressure above the clavicle is generally not sufficient to stop the circulation.

Amputation at the elbow is performed by passing the knife through the muscles in front of the joint, and cutting upwards and forwards, so as to make a flap of them. Then the operator, (who stands on the inner side of the right arm, or *vice versâ*) makes a transverse incision behind the joint. He next cuts through the external lateral ligament, and enters the joint between the head of the radius and external condyle, then divides the internal lateral ligament, and, lastly, saws through the olecranon, the apex of which, with the triceps attached to it, is of course left in the stump.

Amputation of the fore-arm should always be performed as near the wrist as possible.

Circular.—The limb being supported with the thumb uppermost, and an assistant drawing up the skin, a circular incision is made through it down to the fascia. When the skin has again been retracted as much as possible, the muscles are divided by a second circular incision; the interosseous parts and the remaining fibres are next cut through with a catling; the flesh is drawn up with a three-tailed retractor, one tail of which is put between the bones, and the bones are then to be sawn through together, the saw being worked perpendicularly. The radial, ulnar, and two interosseous arteries require ligature.

Flap.—The limb being placed in a state of pronation, the surgeon makes a flap from the extensor side, just as is represented in (Fig. 102;) and he then transfixes the flexor side, and makes the other flap; taking care not to pass the knife between the bones, whilst performing either transfixion. The interosseous parts are next divided, the flesh drawn upwards, and the bones sawn through. If the tendons project, they must be shortened.

Fig. 102.

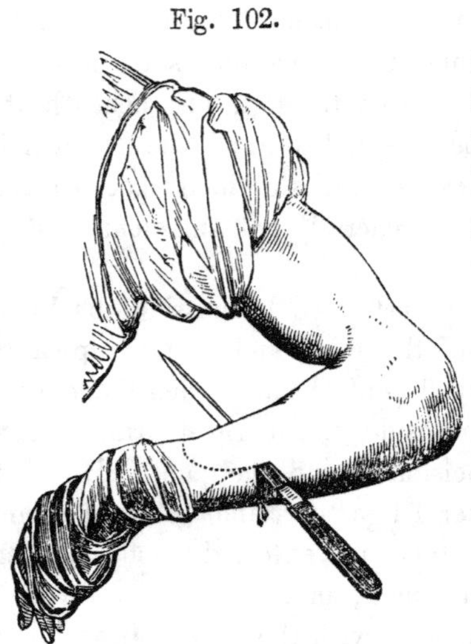

Amputation of the Wrist. (*Circular.*)—The skin being pulled back, a circular incision is made a little below the level of the line that separates the fore-arm from the palm of the hand. The external lateral ligament is then cut through, and the knife carried across the joint, to divide the remaining attachments.

Flap.—A semi-lunar incision is made across the back of the wrist, its extremities being at the styloid processes, and its centre reaching down as far as the second row of carpal bones. This flap being dissected up, the joint is opened behind, the lateral ligaments are cut through, and the knife, being placed between the carpus and bones of the fore-arm, is made to cut out a flap from the anterior surface of the palm.

This operation is scarcely to be preferred to amputation of the fore-arm low down, as the flaps with their numerous tendons may not readily unite, and there may be a difficulty in preserving flesh enough to cover the ends of the bones.

Amputation of the Hand.—Amputation of the *fingers or thumb at their last joint* may be performed thus: The surgeon holds the phalanx firmly between his finger and thumb, and bends it, (Fig. 103,) so as to give prominence to the head of the middle phalanx. He then makes a straight incision across the head of the middle phalanx, so as to cut into the joint, and takes care to carry it deeply enough at the sides to divide the lateral ligaments. The joint being then thoroughly opened, the bistoury is carried through it, and made to cut a flap from the palmer surface of the last phalanx, sufficient to cover the head of the bone; and it is better to leave too much than too little.

Fig. 103.

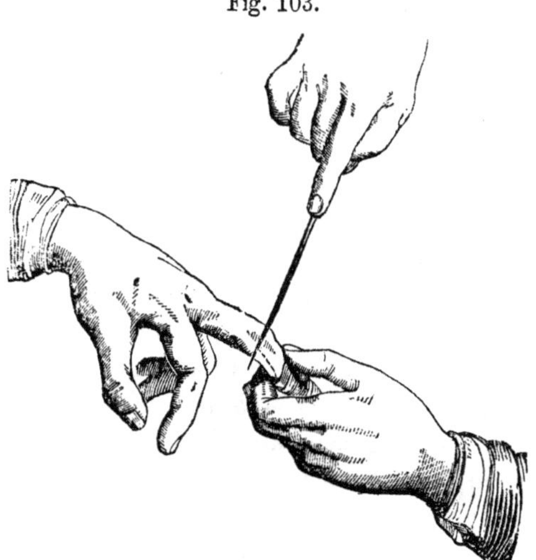

If, however, the joint cannot be bent, this operation may be performed thus: the surgeon holding the phalanx firmly, with its palmar surface upwards, first passes his knife horizontally across the front of the joint, the flat surface towards it, and cuts out the anterior flap; then divides the lateral ligaments and remaining attachments with one sweep of the knife.

Amputation at the *second joint* of the fingers or thumb may be performed in the same manner.

It is always expedient to save as much as possible of the forefinger and thumb; consequently, in cases admitting of it, a flap may be made from the soft parts in front; those behind may be divided by a semi-lunar incision, and then the bone may be sawn through, or be cut with bone nippers.

Amputation of a *finger at the metacarpal joint* may be effected by making a semi-lunar incision on one side of the prominence of the knuckle, from a quarter of an inch beyond the joint, to the middle of the digital commissure on the other side of it. The finger being then drawn to the other side, the extensor tendon is cut through, and the point of the bistoury is passed into the joint, and made to divide its ligaments. This will allow the head of the bone to be turned out, so that the bistoury being placed behind it, may cut through the remaining attachments, and make another flap. This operation may also be performed by making an incision on one side of the joint, (as in the method just described), and then bringing it across the palmar surface, and round the other side, to terminate where it began. The tendons and ligaments are now to be divided, and the head of the bone turned out. The digital arteries must be tied, and, after bleeding has ceased, the wound may be closed by confining the adjoining fingers together. It must be recollected, that the situation of this joint is full half an inch above the line that divides the finger from the palm.

Amputation of the *metacarpal bone of the thumb* is performed thus: The thumb being separated from the fingers, an incision must be carried from the centre of the commissure, between it and the forefinger, down to the articulation with the trapezium. The incision should be inclined rather towards the metacarpal bone of the thumb. The thumb being then forcibly abducted, the blade of the bistoury is to be carried through the joint (which, it must be recollected, lies obliquely in a line extending to the root of the little finger); the head of the bone is to be forcibly dislocated towards the palm, the knife is then made to cut its way out, so as to form a flap of the skin and muscles which constitute the ball of the thumb.

When the metacarpal bone of the thumb alone is diseased, it should, as Mr. Fergusson advises, be extirpated alone, and its phalanges should be preserved. The bone should be exposed by means of an incision along its radial margin; then its articulation with the phalanges should be divided; and lastly, it may be turned out and separated from the trapezium—taking care not to wound the radial artery where it passes between the first and second metacarpal bones.

Amputation of the *metacarpal bone of the little finger*, at the joint between it and the unciform, is performed thus: The flesh and the integuments being grasped, and drawn away from the ulnar side of the bone, a bistoury is passed perpendicularly through them close to the joint, and made to cut its way downwards to a little beyond the articulation with the first phalanx.

The skin of the hand being next strongly drawn towards the thumb side, the bistoury is placed on the other side of the bone (without again piercing the skin), and carried along so as to divide everything down to the digital commissure. Then the ligaments of the joint are to be divided—first, on the inner, and next on the dorsal aspect. It is, however, a much better plan, if it can be effected, to cut through the bone by means of the saw or bone-nippers, than to remove it at the articulation.

Amputation of the *head of a metacarpal bone* is effected by making an incision on each side of it (as in amputation of the fingers at the joint, but extending higher up), and then cutting through the bone with the cutting forceps. Mr. Fergusson recommends the head of the metacarpal bone to be removed, in almost every instance, where the entire finger is abstracted, because the deformity is much less. But the part need not be removed high enough up to divide the transverse ligament. Care must be taken during the cure to keep the fingers parallel, and prevent their crossing at their tips.

If a part or the whole of the shaft of one of these bones is to be removed also, an incision should be made along its dorsum to the point where the two former ones meet; and then the flesh being dissected away on either side, the bone may be cut through or disarticulated, according to circumstances.

Protrusion of the bone after amputation is a very awkward circumstance. It not only greatly retards the healing of the stump, but the cicatrix, when formed, is thin, red, constantly liable to ulcerate, and unable to bear the least pressure or friction. The cause of the *conical stump*, as it is technically called, is generally a want of skin and muscle sufficient to cover the end of the bone. Sometimes, however, it arises from spasmodic retraction of the muscles—especially if they have not been properly supported by bandages during the cure. The remedy is simple, the bone must be shortened. This may be done in slight cases by making a longitudinal incision over the bone on the side opposite the vessels, and sawing off a sufficient portion of it—removing at the same time any diseased portion of the cicatrix; but, if the projection is considerable, a second amputation is necessary.

Neuralgia of the stump is another very untoward event. It sometimes arises because the truncated extremities of the nerves (which, after amputation, always swell and become bulbous) adhere to the cicatrix, so as to be subject to constant compression and tension. Sometimes, however, it is entirely independent of any morbid state of the extremities of the nerves, but arises from some irritation in their course, or from some irritation, centric or excentric, of the spinal cord. Sometimes, again, no local cause whatever can be detected; and the pain is evidently connected with an hysterical state of the system. In any case the symptoms are extreme irritability and tenderness, paroxysms of violent neuralgia, and spasms and twitchings of the muscles, which not unfrequently retract, and cause the bone to protrude and the stump to become conical.

In neuralgia produced by this cause, as well as neuralgia from other causes, the sensations vary in different individuals, and at different times in the same individual. A successful treatment depends upon an exact correspondence between the symptoms of the medicine, and the sensations experienced. Such similarity may be found in the Homœopathic Materia Medica, which contains ample means wherewith to mitigate or entirely subdue the sufferings of the patient.

To this storehouse the surgeon must resort, and with patience and precision select his weapon.

Perhaps among the primary influential impulses which homœopathy received, was the successful treatment, by Hahnemann, of the distinguished cavalry chief, at the Battle of Waterloo, the Marquis of Anglesea, who underwent amputation of the leg in consequence of a wound inflicted by a cannon-shot. Neuralgia of a torturing kind followed, and the fruitless efforts of allopathic physicians induced this renowned nobleman to solicit the advice of Hahnemann, then practising in Paris. The private physician of the marquis, Doctor Dunsford, became a convert to the homœopathic doctrine, after having witnessed the salutary effects of the medicines which Hahnemann administered.

INDEX.

L.

M.

N.

O.

P.

ERRATA.

Page 10. Line 7 from bottom, read *empiricism* for *empyricism.*
" 13. " 16 " " read *lyc.* for *lye.*
" 13. " 10 " " read *natr.* for *nati.*
" 13. " 3 " " read *erethism* for *erythism.*
" 13. " 2 " " read *Trinks* for *Trenks.*
" 16. " 7 " " read *baryta-c.* for *baryta-e.*
" 23. Note.—For *Chapter VII.* read *Chapter IX.*
" 26. Line 12 from bottom, read *its* for *their.*
" 28. Last Note.—For *Chapter VIII.* read *Chapter X.*
" 45. Line 6 from bottom, read *sanious* for *saneous.*
" 206. " 22 " top, read *ever* for *never.*
" 211. " 19, and 22 from top, read *diphtheritic* for *diptheritic.*
" 558. For *Chapter XXIV.* read *Chapter XXXIV.*

HAHNEMANN, LESSER WRITINGS	$4 00
MATERIA MEDICA, PURA.	9 00
CHRONIC DISEASES, 5 vols	10 00
ORGANON.	1 50
HARTMANN, DISEASES OF CHILDREN	3 00
CHIEF REMEDIES, second series	1 00
HELMUTH, ON SURGERY	3 50
HEMPEL, C. J., Domestic, in German	75
French.	75
ORGANON	1 00
HOMŒOPATHY	1 00
LARGE REPERTORY	9 00
MATERIA MEDICA, 2 vols	12 00
HEMPEL AND BEAKLEY, Theory and Practice	3 50
HENDERSON, HOMŒOPATHIC PRACTICE	50
HERING, C., DOMESTIC PHYSICIAN.	2 50
HITCHMANN, CONSUMPTION	75
HOLCOMBE, W. H., Yellow Fever	38
HOMŒOPATHIC COOKERY	50
HUGHES, PHARMACODYNAMICS	2 00
THERAPEUTICS	2 00
HULL, HOMŒOPATHIC EXAMINER, few copies only remain of this very valuable periodical, three vols., handsomely bound	15 00
HULLS, JAHR SYMPTOMATOLOGY	7 00
REPERTORY	4 00
HUMPHREY, ON DYSENTERY	50
CHOLERA	38
HYDRIATICS, MANUAL OF THE WATER CURE	50
JAHR, G. H. G., FORTY YEARS' PRACTICE	3 50
CLINICAL GUIDE OR POCKET REPERTORY, second American from the third German edition, with the addition of the new remedies by Lilienthal	3 00
DISEASES OF FEMALES	2 50
THE SKIN	1 50
NEW MANUAL, with additions, by POSSART, and Clinical REPERTORY	4 50
VENEREAL DISEASES	4 00
JAHR AND GRUNER, PHARMACOPŒIA	3 00
JOSLIN, PRINCIPLES OF HOMŒOPATHY	75
HOMŒOPATHIC TREATMENT OF CHOLERA	1 00
KREUSSLER, ACUTE AND CHRONIC DISEASES	75
LAURIE, HOMŒOPATHIC, DOMESTIC	60
APPENDIX TO DOMESTIC PRACTICE	1 25
PARENT'S GUIDE	1 00
LIPPE, TEXT-BOOK OF MATERIA MEDICA	6 00
Interleaved with writing paper, and bound in two volumes, half morocco.	10 00
LUTZE, THEORY AND PRACTICE.	2 50
MADDEN, UTERINE DISEASES	50

MALAN, FAMILY GUIDE	$0 30
in Spanish	75
MARCY, HOMŒOPATHY AND ALLOPATHY	50
MARCY AND HUNT, THEORY AND PRACTICE, 2 vols.	12 00
MATERIA MEDICA OF AMERICAN PROVINGS	1 00
METCALFE, HOMŒOPATHIC PROVINGS	1 50
MILLARD, CONSUMPTION	75
GUIDE FOR EMERGENCIES	50
MORGAN, INDIGESTION, CONSTIPATION, &c	75
MUNDE, SCARLET FEVER	50
MURE, MATERIA MEDICA	1 00
NEIDHARD, CROTALUS HORRIDUS IN YELLOW FEVER	1 00
DIPHTHERIA	1 75
NEW PROVINGS, CISTUS CAN, COBALTUM ZINGIBERIS, &c.	75
NORTH AMERICAN JOURNAL OF HOMŒOPATHY, per vol.	4 00
whole set, 18 volumes, bound.	50 00
PETERS, HEADACHE AND DISEASES OF THE HEAD	3 00
APOPLEXY	1 00
DISEASES OF FEMALES AND MARRIED WOMEN	1 50
DISEASES OF MARRIED FEMALES	1 00
PRINCIPAL DISEASES OF THE EYE	1 50
INTERNAL DISEASES OF THE EYE	1 00
DISEASES OF THE BRAIN	1 00
NERVOUS DERANGEMENT	1 00
PRINCIPLES AND PRACTICE OF MEDICINE	3 50
PHILADELPHIA JOURNAL OF HOMŒOPATHY, 4 vols., bound	8 00
RAPOU, ON TYPHOID FEVER	50
RAUE, C. G., PATHOLOGY AND THERAPEUTICS	5 00
Interleaved with writing paper	8 00
RAU, Organon	1 25
REIL, ON ACONITE	75
ROKITANSKY, PATHOLOGICAL ANATOMY	75
RUECKERT'S THERAPEUTICS	4 00
RUOFF'S REPERTORY	1 50
RUSH, VETERINARY	50
SCHAEFER, VETERINARY HOMŒOPATHY	2 00
SHARP'S TRACTS, 12 numbers	75
SMALL, HOMŒOPATHIC PRACTICE	3 00
POCKET MANUAL	40
DISEASES OF THE NERVOUS SYSTEM	1 00
STAPF, ADDITIONS TO MATERIA MEDICA	1 50
TESSIER, ASIATIC CHOLERA	75
PNEUMONIA	75
THERAPEUTIC GUIDE, FORTY YEARS' PRACTICE, G. H. G. JAHR	3 50
THERAPEUTICS, THE SCIENCE AND ART OF, B. BAEHR, 2 vols.	10 00
WILLIAMSON, DISEASES OF FEMALES AND CHILDREN	1 00
WOLFF, APIS MELLIFICA	25

www.ingramcontent.com/pod-product-compliance
Lightning Source LLC
LaVergne TN
LVHW010740120826
845150LV00009B/60

* 9 7 8 1 4 2 5 5 6 7 6 5 1 *